Antietam:
The Soldiers' Battle

Antietam:
The Soldiers' Battle

JOHN M. PRIEST

OXFORD UNIVERSITY PRESS
New York   Oxford

To My Family With Love

Oxford University Press

Oxford   New York   Toronto
Delhi   Bombay   Calcutta   Madras   Karachi
Kuala Lumpur   Singapore   Hong Kong   Tokyo
Nairobi   Dar es Salaam   Cape Town
Melbourne   Auckland   Madrid

and associated companies in
Berlin   Ibadan

Copyright © 1989 by John M. Priest

First published in 1989 by White Mane Publishing Company, Inc.
P.O. Box 152, Shippensburg, Pennsylvania 17257

First issued as an Oxford University Press paperback, 1993

Oxford is a registered trademark of Oxford University Press

Library of Congress Cataloging-in-Publication Data
Priest, John M., 1949–
Antietam : the soldiers' battle /
by John M. Priest.
p.   cm.
Originally published: Shippensburg, Pa. : White Mane Pub. Co., c1989.
Includes bibliographical references and index.
ISBN 0-19-508466-7
1. Antietam, Battle of, Md., 1862.
I. Title.   E474.65.P9   1993   973.7′336—dc20   92-46293

2 4 6 8 10 9 7 5 3 1

Printed in the United States of America

Acknowledgements

I feel very much like the high school student who walked out of his history class and blurted, "We coulda gotten through the Civil War quicker if we'd o' lived it." For eight years I have researched the Battle of Antietam, the end product of which is before you now. I claim authorship only because of the assistance from some very special institutions, their staffs, and, as the psychologists would add, some very significant others. They are listed below, not in order of importance, but as they come to mind.

My special thanks to the staffs of the Manuscript Departments and Divisions of the Library of Congress, Duke University Library, the University of North Carolina Library (Chapel Hill), the University of Virginia Library, the Virginia Historical Society, and the Museum of the Confederacy for their tremendous help and cooperation. In particular, I want to commend the staff at Perkins Library at Duke who so kindly showed my wife and two teenagers how to look up and cross reference material in their Manuscript Department. It was a "first" experience that my family will long remember.

I cannot fail to mention Dr. Richard Sommers and his excellent staff of the Manuscript Division, USAMHI, Carlisle Barracks, Pennsylvania. Dr. Sommers treated me with the greatest warmth and he taught me how to work in an archives. It was my first archival experience.

The staff at Antietam National Battlefield, in particular, Betty Otto, who has since retired, Paul Chiles, and Ted Alexander opened their files and their resource center without reservation. They have steadfastly encouraged me in this work. Betty possesses a wealth of knowledge about local history. Paul clarified my misstatements about artillery and the different types of projectiles. Ted, who refers to himself, quite rightfully, as the "Devil's Advocate", kept goading me to resurrect obscure documents from every repository I could reach. I am indebted to him for his persistence.

John and Dennis Frye, who operate the Western Maryland Room at the Washington County Free Library, Hagerstown, Maryland, assisted me greatly. They answered questions I had about local history. Dennis made the David Lilley file available to me and John introduced me to the Southern Historical Society Papers.

Mrs. Phyllis Hill at the Internal Resource Center, Board of Education of Washington County, continually advised me of the new Civil War literature in the Board's library. She also showed me the Benjamin Franklin Clarkson Memoirs, which became my first published work.

Without Tom Renner's help, and the permission from the Parks and History Association to use the map (which they sell at Antietam for $1.00), I could never have gotten the many small unit maps done on time. Tom's timely assistance and professional expertise with the map preparation will insure the value of the book as an historical reference. He is an irreplaceable asset to the Washington County school system.

Bill Hilton, my friend and colleague, never ceased to encourage me. His prodding to make the book readable and thorough guided me throughout the many years of study. He started me on the research by loaning me copies of published recollections and reminiscences from his personal library. They formed the nucleus around which this book was started. He is an avid reader and a very good critic. If he did not like what I wrote, he told me and gave me a reason.

My deepest appreciation goes to Tom Hicks, a former colleague. He opened his collection of family letters to me and loaned me a couple of very interesting stories which were published during the 125th Anniversary of the battle. Tom also read and critiqued the first copy of the manuscript. His friendly support acted like a catalyst to help me refine my writing skills.

A final and, admittedly, inadequate "Thank you" goes to my family. Rhonda, my wife, Douglas, my eldest, Jennifer, and Kimberly have tolerated my obsession with this project with Biblical patience. They have sacrificed their time for years while I dragged them from one library to another, or spent entire weekends typing text or drawing maps.

They volunteered to finish my research at Duke while I worked at the University of North Carolina. Rhonda insisted that I regiment myself to a work schedule with long and short term goals. She helped me balance my rabid drive to do research with our precious family life. To them all, my love. "Their warfare is accomplished."

Table Of Contents

A Note About The Chapter Titles

The opposing armies fought their battle upon land owned by a Christian pacifist sect, the German Baptist Brethren, who were derisively known as "Dunkers", "Tunkers", and "Dunkards". I pulled verses from the 22nd Psalm, which according to many Christian theologians predicted the death of Christ upon the cross. The lines are filled with vivid poetic parallels between Christ's lonely death and the feelings of isolation and abandonment which so many of the soldiers experienced during their three agonizing days at Antietam. Like the pacifists, whose land they died on, the men longed for the war to end and for peace. Their voices were the voices of desperation and pain amid circumstances over which they had little, or no, control.

The time cited at the beginning of each chapter are based upon the times cited in the Cope Maps [1904]. I organized the book to correlate with the maps to give the reader a perspective of how complex and confusing this battle actually was for the participants. Subtitles indicating locations upon the battlefield along with brief summaries of the events, which immediately preceded each time phase, are included in the text to assist the reader in becoming more familiar with the terrain and the flow of the fighting. As a further caution, remember that our generation is much more time conscious than during the Civil War. Synchronization of watches became a phenomenon of the 20th Century warrior. Standard time, in 1862, proved to be whatever time a person had upon his watch when he glanced at it. I chose to use Cope's time phases because they are the result of intense research. They are intended to impart to the reader why the men, particularly the Confederates, thought the sun would never set that day. The times are at best very good approximations.

List of Maps

For the sake of clarity, only troops essential to the understanding of the tactical situation depicted are shown on the maps. The scale appears in (100) one hundred yard increments to the left, top or the lower left of the map number, which is circled in the lower right hand corner of each map. The caption is on the southern end of each map.

List of Illustrations

Introduction
Jay Luvaas

   This is a book about battle. More especially, it is a book about the human dimension in a battle, before generals could rationalize actions, historians could impose order upon chaos, the army could build a tower and lay out the battle lines — and the National Park Service could transform the whole into something approaching a pastoral setting. As a modern English historian who has written a similar study of Waterloo has observed, "The more thoroughly you analyse a battle, in the light of after-knowledge, the harder it becomes to remember what it felt like to the people who were in it."[1]

   Perhaps it is true, as David Howarth has claimed, that the Napoleonic Wars "were the first in which it is still possible to see a battle from the soldier's ground-level, smoke shrouded point of view" because a number of junior officers, sergeants and a few privates wrote reminiscences or letters, but another English historian who analysed Waterloo from the vantage point of the common soldier contends that not until the First World War can we hear the voice of the common man, even though "infant murmurs can be detected during the American Civil War."[2] It is unfortunate that John Keegan did not include a chapter on Antietam in his pioneer work *The Face of Battle*, for in fact the Civil War was the first conflict fought by armies that contained large numbers who could read and write. During the Napoleonic Wars most of the rank and file were illiterate. A few stirring memoirs came out of these campaigns, but in Napoleonic France the primary schools could accommodate no more than one child in eight, while in England, even after the Education Act of 1870, there remained many soldiers whose attainments did not extend much further "than a moderate power of reading and the ability to sign their names."[3]

   Nor is it a coincidence that the Civil War was the first to produce monuments in public squares and on the battlefields to the common soldier and his regiment.[4] Monuments from earlier wars nearly all portray officers who had commanded troops in some military encounter, but at Antietam — to cite a relevant example — all statues feature the common soldier: the only monuments to general officers are some half a dozen upright cannon barrels indicating where a particular brigade or division commander became a fatal casualty. This emphasis upon the common soldier was uniquely American at the time, for in Europe soldiers were still regarded pretty much as the dregs of society — except in Prussia, where conscription had produced a Nation in Arms — and officers — with some exceptions in the technical branches of engineers and artillery — continued to come almost exclusively from the aristocracy.

*   *

   Foreign officers who spent time with the American armies were almost universally of the opinion that these volunteer armies contained good soldier material, but were critical of the dearth of trained officers and the absence of any replacement system. A few weeks before Antietam an English Member of Parliament with an interest in military affairs visited the Union army and described a regiment of New York Volunteers:

> a very fine-looking lot of men indeed, mostly farmers and country people from Western New York. . . . They seemed very jolly and in good spirits, but they had had no drill whatever, and I don't see who is to give it to them. The sentry at the Colonel's tent was sitting on a camp-stool and reading the newspaper. I believe a few of the officers have been in other volunteer regiments, but I could not make out that they had a single regular officer among them. It seems a great pity that such fine material should be thrown away, as they very likely may be, by having utterly incompetent officers.[5]

And yet such regiments fought well at Antietam: one of them — the 132d Pennsylvania Infantry — which had been organized for less than a month, lost 364 out of 750 men before the Bloody Lane and yet held its position. How did they do it?

Even veteran regiments, in the eyes of foreign military observers, displayed serious shortcomings when compared to European regulars. A British officer who spent some time with McClellan's army a few weeks after the battle commented:

> Neither side can be manoeuvred under fire. . . . The men on either side can be brought under fire, and when there will stand well: but they are not good enough either in morale or field movements to advance, change position, or retire. — The moment they have to manoeuvre, they get into confusion and break, this their own officers admit and also that the charges either of Cavalry or Infantry are purely imaginary; they . . . have occasionally made a rush; but never get within 300 yards of one another; but normally wavered, halted, and fired irregularly and when one side or the other get tired first bolts, led by their officers almost invariably on the Northern side.

What was needed, this Royal Engineer captain decided, was competent leadership.[6]

A Swiss Colonel recorded in his official report of his visit that the Army of the Potomac suffered leadership problems because the officers had been elected by the rank and file, often for no better reason than "having known how to entice a few recruits to inns or clubs," and because of the influence of politics in the selection of higher officers.

> For two good officers taken thus from the ranks of the orators, or from the magistracy, there are five or six of them completely incapable in the face of the enemy. . . . The ties of relationship,

of friendship, of party, considerations of speculation even, cause to be named for very important positions men totally incapable of filling them. . . . Owing to the intrigues of parties, and the compliance of the press, it is often difficult . . . for the Government and the superior officers to ascertain whether such an officer is a pretender, an adroit actor, or a man of merit.[7]

This was less true of the Confederate army at Antietam, and of course there were many conspicuous exceptions in the Union Army as well; in any case this particular observer, who had been attached to McClellan's staff as a voluntary aide-de-camp, had returned to Europe soon after the fall of Yorktown that spring, and many unfit officers had since left the service while others had acquired practical experience. There remains, however, the bizarre case of Colonel William A. Christian, who went to pieces in the East Wood, shouted a lot of irrelevant commands, and then rapidly disappeared to the rear.[8]

General William T. Sherman put his finger on the problem. "The greatest mistake made in our civil war," he contended,

> was in the mode of recruitment and promotion. When a regiment became reduced by the necessary wear and tear of service, instead of being filled up at the bottom, and the vacancies among the officers filled from the best non commissioned officers and men, the habit was to raise new regiments, with new colonels, captains, and men, leaving the old and experienced battalions to dwindle away into mere skeleton organizations.[9]

At Antietam there were many regiments so depleted that they could scarcely function as such, while new and essentially untrained regiments, especially in the Union army, were thrown into their first battle largely unprepared.

*   *   *

Scarcely one hundred years before Antietam Frederick the Great had written that soldiers could be governed only with sternness and severity and "can be held in check only through fear." So long as the Prussian soldier feared his officers more than the enemy, Frederick contended, he would move forward. The Duke of Wellington, victor at Waterloo, saw discipline as the key to controlling his men, whom he once described as "the scum of the earth."[10]

But during the nineteenth century professional soldiers began to demonstrate an interest in the human dimension in combat. The Prussian General von Clausewitz, who had first experienced war as a thirteen year old infantry ensign and served throughout the Napoleonic wars as a commander and staff officer, was perhaps the first to address the problem of danger in war.

Let us accompany the novice to the battlefield. As we approach, the thunder of the cannon becoming plainer is soon accompanied by the howling of shot, which now attracts the attention of the inexperienced. Balls begin to strike the ground close to us. . . . We hasten to the hill where stands the general and his numerous Staff. Here the close striking of the cannon balls and the bursting of shells are so frequent that the seriousness of life forces itself through the youthful picture of imagination. Suddenly someone we know falls. A shell strikes amongst the crowd and causes some involuntary movements; we begin to feel that we are no longer perfectly at ease and collected, and even the bravest is at least to some degree distracted. Now, a step farther into the battle . . . to the nearest general of division. Here . . . the noise of our own guns increases the confusion. From the general of division to the brigadier. He, a man of acknowledged bravery, keeps carefully behind a hill, a house, or some trees — a sure sign of increasing danger. Grape rattles on the roofs of the houses and in the fields; cannon balls roar in all directions over us, and already there is a frequent whistling of musket balls. A step farther toward the troops, to that sturdy infantry which has been for hours holding its ground under fire with indescribable steadiness. Here the air is filled with the hissing of balls which announce their proximity by a short sharp noise as they pass within an inch of the ear. . . .

To add to all this, compassion strikes the beating heart with pity at the sight of the maimed and fallen. . . . He must, indeed, be a very extraordinary man who, under the stress of these first impressions, does not lose the capacity of making a prompt decision. . . . Habit soon blunts these impressions; in half an hour we begin to be more indifferent in greater or less degree to everything that is going on around us: but the ordinary never attains complete coolness and the natural elasticity of mind. . . . Ordinary qualities will not suffice. . . .[11]

At Antietam, as this book makes clear, the picture changes only in detail. If brigade and division commanders were not farther forward — as the death of one corps commander, three division commanders, and three brigade commanders might suggest — the increased ranges and accuracy of weapons since the Napoleonic Wars had significantly widened the killing zone. Napoleonic formations had been modified somewhat, but basically the armies deployed and maneuvered in battle in much the same way at Antietam as Napoleon's *Grand Armee* had at Austerlitz fifty-seven years previously. Indeed, many of the illustrations of particular maneuvers in Civil War drill manuals are identical with plates in the 1791 edition of the *Reglement* that prescribed the evolutions of Napoleon's battalions.

Antietam was the last battle fought in the east without one side or the other resorting to field fortifications, although the famed Sunken Road and the quarry holes above the Burnside Bridge functioned — and in Union after-action reports were so described — as rifle pits. At Fredericksburg several of Longstreet's divisions fought behind breastworks and at Chancellorsville both armies constructed hasty fortifications at every opportunity.

In his classic analysis of men in modern combat Colonel Ardant du Picq, a French officer killed in battle five years after the Civil War, contributes to our understanding of battles like Antietam. "The Americans," he declared,

> have shown us what happens in modern battle to large armies without cohesion. With them the lack of discipline and organization has had the inevitable result.... In this American War, the melees of Agincourt are said to have reappeared, which merely means a melee of fugitives. But less than ever has there been close combat. . . . The less mobile the troops, the deadlier are battles. . . . Modern arms require open order.... Modern weapons have a terrible effect and are almost unbearable by the nervous system. . . . Discipline in battle becomes the more necessary as the ranks become more open, and the material cohesion of the ranks not giving confidence, it must spring from a knowledge of comrades, and a trust in officers. . . . Today the artillery is effective at great distance. [du Picq was killed by a Prussian shell before Metz in 1870]. . . . The apparent liaison between arms is lessened. This has its influence on morale.

> This moral effect must be a terrible thing. A body advances to meet another. The defender has only to remain calm, ready to aim, each man pitted against a man before him. The attacking body comes within deadly range. Whether or not it halts to fire, it will be a target for the other body which awaits it, clam, ready, sure of its effect. The whole first rank of the assailant falls, smashed. The remainder, little encouraged by their reception, disperse automatically or before the least indication of an advance on them.

The smallest detail taken from an incident in war was more instructive to du Picq than the most celebrated campaign histories. There are numerous questions that he would have asked of this book.

What were the dispositions taken to meet the enemy?

What becomes of it upon arriving within the range of the guns?

How did the fight start? How about the firing? How did the men adapt themselves?

At what distance did the charge fall back before the fire of the enemy?

The behavior, i.e., the order, the disorder, the shouts, the silence, the confusion, the calmness of the officers and men . . . before, during, and after the combat?

How has the soldier been controlled and directed during the action?

At what instant has he had a tendency to quit the line in order to remain behind or to rush ahead?

At what moment, if the control were escaping from the leader's hands, has it no longer been possible to exercise it? At what instant has this control escaped from the battalion commander . . . the captain . . . the squad leader?

At what time . . . was there but a disordered impulse, whether to the front or to the rear carrying along pell-mell with it both the leaders and men?

Where and when did the halt take place . . . [and] were the leaders able to resume control of the men?[13]

From answers to these and a dozen kindred questions, du Picq hoped to utilize experience — and history — to better equip men for modern combat, for despite all industrial and scientific progress, "one thing does not change — the heart of man."[14]

It was answers to questions like these, asked of men who had just staggered out of combat in World War II, Korea, and Vietnam, that likewise enabled the late General S.L.A. Marshall to arrive at his conclusions — some of them startling in their implications — about men in modern battle. Marshall's task as he described it was "to analyze our infantry line and its methods under pressure, to estimate whether troops are good or bad, to see what is wrong or right in our tactics and to recommend such corrects as are indicated."[15]

*   *   *   *

Modern officers who visit Antietam and other Civil War battlefields are concerned about similar kinds of questions, but perhaps for somewhat different reasons. "How did they get men to stand in line like that?" "How did the officers exercise command and control?" "Why were there no night attacks?" I remember particularly one major, recently returned from Vietnam, who stood silently on the ridge overlooking the Sunken Road where French's Union division lost 40% in about three hours and wondered aloud "who wrote the family when there was a death in the ranks?" And what soldier has ever stood on Burnside's Bridge and failed to imagine the feelings of men ordered to capture the heights beyond it? "A guy would have to be crazy to attempt a thing like that!" Of course, to a modern soldier it would be unnecessary.

Modern tourists see a different battle, for it is as true of battlefields as it is of history itself — answers come only in response to specific questions.

This book asks the participants primarily one question: what was it like? The answers, like the sources, tend to be uneven in perception and accuracy, for as Gerald E. Linderman's recent *Embattled Courage* reminds us, the memory of the veterans quickly became selective because of a "strong psychological propensity to suppress the painful."[16] One has only to compare Henry Kyd Douglas' somber description of what it looked like in the West Woods the night of the battle, written immediately after the end of the war from diaries and notes and when his memory was "fresh and youthful," and John B. Gordon's filtered recollections of what happened in the Bloody Lane, composed forty years after the event, to appreciate how battle is filtered through the minds of participants.[17]

If one were to consult the cache of letters in the National Archives written by participants to the U.S. Commissioners responsible for laying out and marking the battlefield in the 1890's, this would quickly become apparent. Some of the old soldiers could not read a modern map. Others were uncertain whether their battery stood 40 — or 400 — yards from the Dunkard Church. Some could not reconcile what they had witnessed with the official reports of their commanding officers. All tended to be vague about the time a specific event had occurred. Some of McLaws' men described how difficult it was to get over the fences that lined the Hagerstown turn pike: others never so much as mentioned these formidable obstacles. One South Carolina artilleryman wrote a detailed letter to his battery commander hoping that the facts might freshen his memory. "You were a mature man at the time," he explained, "I was a boy. My mind I guess was plastic and retained these things better, or perhaps I was worse scared than you and they were firmly fixed by fright."[18]

The purpose of this book is not to analyze and interpret the battle, but to weave a tapestry of individual experiences. The colors may not always be consistent or true, but in their separate detail the experiences of the participants come alive. One should read this book not so much to understand the movements on the battlefield as to enhance our understanding of the Civil War soldier. It has been forty years since Bruce Catton squeezed the human interest material out of shelves of neglected regimental histories to portray the Army of the Potomac and its campaigns and Bell Irvin Wiley reconstructed the wartime lives of Johnny Reb and Billy Yank. Here is a book that reaches deep into scattered manuscript sources to provide a similar service for the men who fought at Antietam, the bloodiest single day in American history.

Footnotes to Introduction

1. David Howarth, *Day of Battle* (New York: Atheneum, 1968), p. vi.

2. John Keegan, *The Face of Battle* (New York: The Viking Press, 1976), pp. 32-33.

3. Lieut. General W. H. Goodenough and Lieut. Colonel J. C. Dalton, *The Army Book of the British Empire* (London: Her Majesty's Stationery Office, 1893), p. 421.

4. Wayne Craven, *The Sculptures at Gettysburg* (n. p., Eastern Acorn Press, 1982), p. 61.

5. Bernhard Holland, *The Life of Spencer Compton, Eighth Duke of Devonshire* (2 vol., London: Longmans, Green and Co., 1911), I, p. 44.

6. R. A. Preston, "A Letter from a British Military Observer of the American Civil War," *Military Affairs* XVI (Summer, 1952), p. 56.

7. Ferdinand Lecomte, *The War in the United States. Report to the Swiss Military Department* (New York, D. Van Nostrand, 1863), pp. 93-94.

8. Stephen W. Sears, *Landscape Turned Red* (New Haven: Ticknor and Fields, 1983), pp. 187-88.

9. *Memoirs of Gen. W. T. Sherman* (2 vols., New York, Charles L. Webster and Co., 1891), II, pp. 387-88.

10. *Frederick the Great on the Art of War*, translated and edited by Jay Luvaas (New York: The Free Press, 1966), pp. 77-78; Gopdfrey Davis, *Wellington and His Army* (Oxford: Basil Blackwell, 1954), pp. 17-18.

11. General Carl von Clausewitz, translated from the German by O. J. Matthijs Jolles, *On War* (Washington: Infantry Journal Press, 1943), pp. 47-48.

12. Colonel Ardant du Picq, *Battle Studies Ancient and Modern* (Harrisburg, The Military Service Publishing Company, 1947), pp. 111-12, 114-15, 128.

13. *Ibid.*, pp. 5-7.

14. *Ibid.*, p. 109.

15. S.L.A. Marshall, *Pork Chop Hill: The American Fighting Man in Action* (New York: William Morrow and Company, 1956), p. 13.

16. Gerald F. Linderman, *Embattled Courage: The Experience of Combat in the American Civil War* (New York: The Free Press, 1987), p. 267.

17. Henry Kyd Dopuglas, *I Rode with Stonewall* (Chapel Hill: The University of North Carolina Press, 1940), pp. vii, 175; John B. Gordon, *Reminiscences of the Civil War* (New York: Charles Scribner's Sons, 1903), pp. 84-88.

18. J. L. Napier to Col. D. G. McIntosh, Nov. 30, 1896. Antietam Studies. Record Group 94. National Archives.

On September 5, The Army of Northern Virginia started to cross into Maryland in hopes of drawing the Federal Army of the Potomac out of Northern Virginia and of rallying Confederate sympathisers in Maryland to the South's cause. The Marylanders did not come to the Confederates' assist, which forced Robert E. Lee, the commander of the invading army, to press northwest, toward the Federal garrison at Harper's Ferry, Virginia. The "lost order", Special Order 191, accidentally fell into the possession of the Army of the Potomac at Frederick, Maryland.

With Major General George B. McClellan's much larger forces pursuing him, Lee split his forces. Thomas J. Jackson's Corps encircled Harper's Ferry, which surrendered on September 15, while the rest of the army spread itself along three major passes over South Mountain, Maryland. Fox's, Turner's, and Crampton's Gaps fell into Federal hands on September 14, 1862. Lee quickly pulled his defeated forces to the hills around Sharpsburg, Maryland and prepared to give battle.

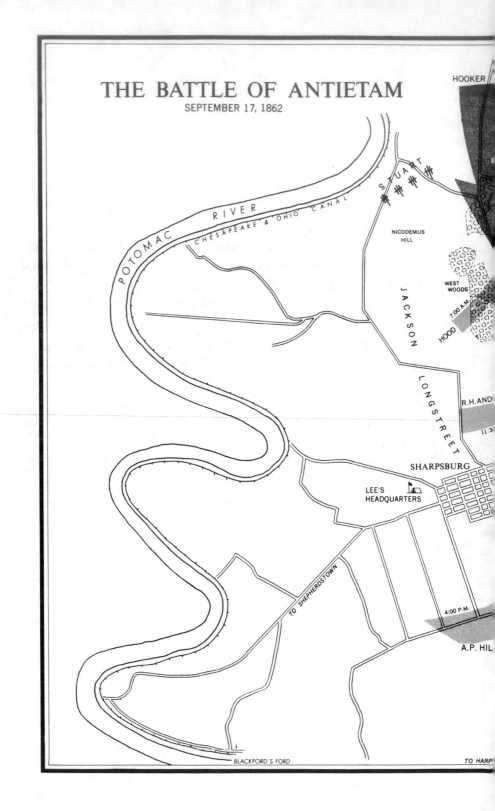

THE BATTLE OF ANTIETAM
SEPTEMBER 17, 1862

HOOKER

POTOMAC RIVER

CHESAPEAKE & OHIO CANAL

STUART

NICODEMUS HILL

JACKSON

WEST WOODS

7:00 A.M.

HOOD

LONGSTREET

R.H. AND

11:3

SHARPSBURG

LEE'S HEADQUARTERS

TO SHEPHERDSTOWN

4:00 P.M.

A.P. HIL

BLACKFORD'S FORD

TO HARP

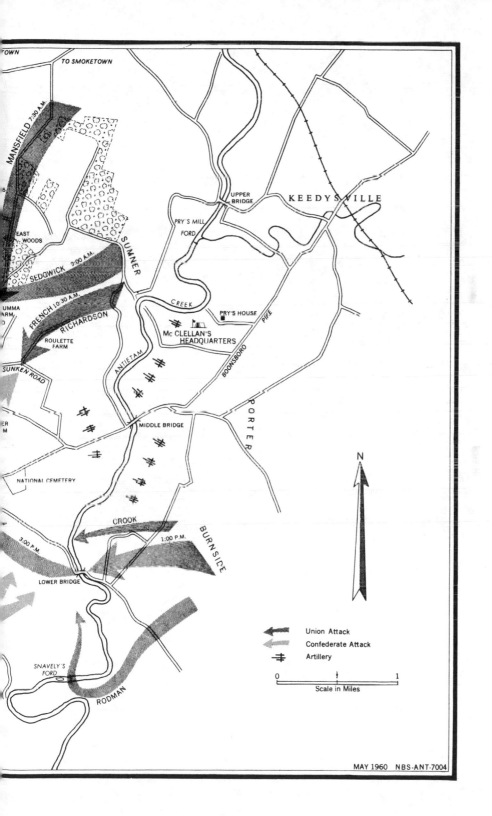

TO SMOKETOWN

MANSFIELD 7:30 A.M.

EAST WOODS

SEDGWICK 9:00 A.M.

FRENCH 10:30 A.M.

RICHARDSON

ROULETTE FARM

SUNKEN ROAD

SUMNER

CREEK

PRY'S MILL FORD

UPPER BRIDGE

KEEDYSVILLE

PRY'S HOUSE

McCLELLAN'S HEADQUARTERS

ANTIETAM

BOONSBORO PIKE

MIDDLE BRIDGE

NATIONAL CEMETERY

PORTER

CROOK

1:00 P.M.

3:00 P.M.

BURNSIDE

LOWER BRIDGE

SNAVELY'S FORD

RODMAN

N

Union Attack

Confederate Attack

Artillery

0   1
Scale in Miles

MAY 1960 NBS-ANT-7004

Antietam:
The Soldiers' Battle

CHAPTER ONE

"Many bulls have compassed me . . . ."

TUESDAY, SEPTEMBER 16, 1862

Samuel Mumma Farm

Over the three preceding days, the war had crept agonizingly closer to Samuel Mumma's farm, which lay nestled in a swale north of Sharpsburg, Maryland. The elderly German Baptist had listened to the dull, rolling boom of cannon and the clash of small arms fire as the opposing armies wrestled for control of the passes along South Mountain. The day before, he and his rather large family — one wife and sixteen children — had been ordered to leave their home for safer territory.[1] The Mummas had carried off what they could. The evacuation went smoothly despite a tense moment when one of his daughters snapped at a Rebel officer, who had offered his hand to assist her in getting over a fence.[2] Now, his richly blessed farm lay in the wake of a nasty rear guard action. All of his labors were about to pass for naught.

Mrs. Mumma had grown concerned about the family's present comfort. They had spent a rough night on the floor of a church without adequate covers. Samuel consented to send off two of their sons — Dan, the eldest boy, and Samuel, Jr. — and a friend to get their necessities. The three left in the afternoon. Four rough miles and thousands of soldiers were between the church and their home.[3]

The West Woods

Brigadier Generals Isaac R. Trimble's and Alexander R. Lawton's Brigades (Major General Richard Ewell's Division, Thomas J. Jackson's Corps) were among the first Confederate troops to stagger into the West Woods on September 15. The Georgians,

North Carolinians, and Alabamians of the two brigades flopped down among the fallen trees and the limestone outcroppings of the southern section of the woods.

The 21st Georgia (Trimble's Brigade) spent the night around the simple white washed brick church which occupied a slight hill in the clearing between the forest and the Hagerstown Pike, south of the Smoketown Road intersection.[4] Captain James Nisbet (H Co., 21st GA) ambled about the church grounds. No one dared to enter the church. General Robert E. Lee had issued strict orders against looting.

Since entering Maryland the men had lived off ripened corn and green apples. The heat, the diet, and the consequential onset of diarrhea had left many good men strewn along the roadside. The ranks seemed pitifully small at morning roll call. Lawton's Brigade (13th, 26th, 31st, 60th, and 61st GA) averaged under two hundred men apiece. Trimble's Brigade (15th AL, 12th and 21st GA, 21st NC with 1st NC Bttn. attached) could muster less than one hundred fifty men each.[5] James Nisbet did not like the percentages. The Federals outnumbered them three to one.[6] The average Yankee regiment carried three hundred to four hundred muskets.

The sky seemed to become more overcast as Nisbet walked back to his men.[7] A stranger in a foreign land, the captain pulled aside a curious civilian who had meandered into the regiment's bivouac. He had heard the fellow chatting with his soldiers about the Dunkers and their church.

"Who are the Dunkards?" Nisbet asked.

"They are the German Baptists. This is a German settlement."[8]

The reply confused the young Georgian. He did not know that many of his men were going to die on the property of a pacifist Christian sect.

The Dunker Church Ridge

Captain William Parker, whose Virginia battery had moved into the battalion park across the road from the church, did not agree with their pacifism. A devout Methodist and an ardent secessionist, the captain had forsaken his lucrative medical practice and his young, pregnant bride to lay down his life for his state.[9] He neither drank, nor smoked, nor cursed. Neither did he play cards or go dancing.[10] This good officer demanded unquestioned obedience and devotion to duty of himself and of his men, for whom he set the example.

The battalion (Colonel Stephen D. Lee's) had gone into bivouac on the southern slope of the curved ridge which ran east for about four hundred yards from the Dunker Church to Mumma's lane. A cornfield on the far side of the lane masked the right flank of the battery from any assault in that quarter.

The Smoketown Road, to the north, cut diagonally across Parker's front, running northeast into the East Woods, which was about six hundred yards to his right front on elevated ground. Another tall cornfield, bordered by a low worm fence, dominated the right side of the Hagerstown Pike about eight hundred yards north of his position. The ground from the Smoketown Road south to the sunken lane (to his rear) dipped into a swale, where it dropped abruptly in conformity to the bend of the Dunker Church ridge. Any infantry which approached from the northeast or the east, once it reached the swale, could charge the Pike unchecked, unless the north-ward facing battery, on the right, cut them down.

Parker's outfit would be lucky to crawl away under fire from the superior Federal artillery. Yankee field batteries, with their more reliable shells, would inflict their fair share of havoc, but the twenty pounders, which the Federals had planted on the far side of the Antietam, would cause them the most harm. He and his men had watched the blue coated engineers whacking away at the trees along the eastern ridge of the creek since first light.[11] The captain had a great deal on his mind. He had problems about which he could do very little. Had it not been for his tremendous inner strength, he should have collapsed from the strain of it all. William Watts Parker was an exceptional individual whose firm belief in Jesus Christ and in the tremendous power of prayer bolstered him greatly.

He had a great deal to pray about. His bride — a girl who was eighteen years his junior — was in her final month of pregnancy. She wrote to him constantly. The "Doctor", as she always called him, could not be near her in her most desperate hour.[12] He had meticulously stored all of her letters in the battery chest.

He also had two very worried parents complaining to the War Department about him. In both cases, the soldiers in concern were fifteen year olds who had, as the captain insisted, enlisted of their own free will.

Kenny Richardson's father claimed that his son had been coerced to enlist. Parker contested that the lad had signed up to serve with his older brother, Joseph, who was currently recuperating from a wound which he received a month earlier at the Second Manassas.

The widowed Mrs. Trueman argued that her son, Johnnie, had run away to fight. Parker rebutted that, despite the fact he had no written proof, Mrs. Trueman had known of and had consented to her boy's enrollment months before he had actually signed up. Further, the captain complained, he could not and would not "unenlist" either soldier. (As it was, the captain had privately resolved to hold both boys in reserve to shield them from needless risks.)[13]

His crews' diet for the past three weeks of green corn (raw or improperly cooked corn) and of ripened fruit had crippled most of them. Plagued by galled crotches, bleeding and ulcerated rectums, lice, and assorted vermin, they became quite weakened and irritable. Even the stoic doctor could not conceal his personal discomfort. He penned home that he felt "so unwell".[14] Unwell or not, he had to devote his total attention to the situation at hand.

The West Woods

All morning long, troops had sought welcome reprieve from the muggy air by bivouacking in the West Woods. Jackson's Corps (Brigadier Generals William E. Starke's, William B. Taliaferro's, Isaac Trimble's and Harry T. Hays' Brigades) and Colonels W.T. Wofford's and E. McIver Law's Brigades of Brigadier General John B. Hood's Division (Major General James Longstreet's Corps) had been resting some time.

James Steptoe Johnston, Jr. (11th MS), Colonel McIver Law's orderly, lost his enthusiasm for Maryland very shortly after the Army of Northern Virginia crossed the river into the state. The people had not rallied to the southern cause as he and so many of his comrades had anticipated.

"Instead of an outburst of overflowing joy, at the sight of their deliverers," he wrote to his future wife, "not one solitary soul had come to the River bank to see us cross or welcome us to the soil. The country looked as one might imagine Paradise did, after the expulsion. All nature looked verdant and delightful, but no one of the human family was to be seen to enoble it."

The ladies, generally, were cold and distant to the Confederates. They talked a big fight when it came to being loyal to the Union.[15] Orderly Sergeant Frank M. Mixon (E Co., 1st SC Vols.) recalled how one young lady, about sixteen years old, stood with a group of other girls and women in the doorway of Hager's store in Hagerstown and boldly waved a National flag at the Rebs as they passed.

"Why don't you fight under this flag?" she challenged them.

One of the South Carolinians shouted back, "Hagerstown, Hager's Store, Hager's daughter — hurrah for Hager." At that the entire column gave the ladies a rousing Rebel Yell.[16]

James Johnston noted that, while the townspeople usually shut their doors and shutters to their "deliverers" long before the soldiers reached their towns, a few of the ladies along the route sold them butter and milk, though not in large quantities.

"They neither one seemed surprised that a rebel could go 48 hours, without food, but thought it had become quite natural for us to starve," he complained. ". . . we were convinced that 'secesh' in Maryland was as near an humbug as anything of the day."

Sharpsburg

The small country hamlet of Sharpsburg seemed very uninviting to many of the men in Robert E. Lee's dirty, ragged army.[17]

The omens pointed toward a horrendous engagement within hours. Most of Thomas J. Jackson's weary brigades had been lounging among the limestone outcroppings of the West Woods since about daylight. Captain Michael Shuler (H Co., 33rd VA) used the first few minutes he could get to scratch in his diary, "Sept. 16th Tuesday Reveille a little over sunup. Waded the Potomac again and are in Maryland. . . . Marched 15 miles."[18] The night march from Harper's Ferry to Sharpsburg had left over half of the "Old Stonewall" Brigade strung out wheezing along the seventeen miles of country road. By the time the brigade had crossed the Potomac at Boeteler's Ford, barely two hundred fifty men could respond to morning call.[19]

They nearly lost Lieutenant Ezra E. Stickley (A Co., 5th VA) in the streets of Sharpsburg. Tempted to desert, he stayed by Colonel A. J. Grigsby's (C.O., Winder's Brigade) side until the brigade entered the town. At that point, the lieutenant begged leave to get some food and water from a nearby house.

As he dismounted near the gate to the yard, Stickley became increasingly nauseous. He nervously helped himself to some tomatoes and a little water, then raced after his command. It took all of his personal reserve to conquer his fear and not "disappear".[20]

The lieutenant was not alone in his sentiments. A large portion of Lee's army did not care to enter Maryland. Prior to invading the State, General Robert E. Lee issued a general order which allowed barefoot men to remain in Virginia with the wagons. Second Lieutenant Robert T. Hubard (G Co., 3rd VA CAV) watched grimy infantrymen deliberately remove their footgear and throw them away. He had never seen so many stragglers before. The army was going into this next engagement greatly below its normal strength.

Morale was low in that part of the Army of Northern Virginia which did not cross into Maryland. The hard summer campaign had exhausted many of the men. Corporal James B. Painter (K Co., 28th VA) grumbled loudly about the army. Rumor had it that the men might be ordered to fight under the Black Flag — give no quarter. He did not like fighting under the Red Flag — the Stars and Bars. When it came to crossing into Maryland, he turned up barefoot and content.

Even "Old Jack" (Jackson) thought the trek had been rather severe.[21] To the stern and pragmatic Jackson, the men's rest during the lull provided him with fresher troops to feed into the meat grinder of a general battle.

During the past months, his division had rightfully earned the reputation of being a hard marching and fearless outfit. Now, their ranks were terribly thinned by casualties, straggling, and blatant desertion. He would have to hurl his men against the allegedly better fed and better equipped Federal troops.

Off to the southeast, they could hear the terrible bellowing of the Federal long range guns. The reports were followed by the thunder of their own pair of twenty pounders. Pitiful — so pitiful. The giant in pursuit of the little tailor. A fairy tale written in blood.

The fairy tale became a terrifying reality for the citizens of Sharpsburg, particularly for those who lived near the center of the town. Confederate troops had been tramping through the village before dawn. Ambulances, most of them empty, creaked west in order to escape the host of enemy troops which had assembled along the eastern bank of the Antietam — about one and one half miles from the town.[22] Many of the town's inhabitants had taken refuge in their basements, where they huddled in fear of the inaccurate hostile shelling.

Major Heros Von Borcke, Major-General J.E.B. Stuart's chief of staff, and Dr. Jacob Grove's family found the clamor in the streets interesting.[23] The huge Prussian, like his idol "Beauty Stuart", had a knack for surrounding himself with the niceties which the average infantryman could only fantasize about — fine food, dry quarters, and women. Von Borcke had quartered himself in the doctor's big red brick home on the southwestern corner of the village square. The family clustered about the front windows to gape at the wounded who staggered past the house.

The major ushered the doctor and his womenfolk into the cellar when the shelling began. He then returned upstairs where he casually plopped upon the living room sofa. Von Borcke took out his journal and started to scratch down a few notes. It was about 11:00 A.M.

He had just begun to write when a shell struck the house. Within seconds, the ladies scurried upstairs to see what had happened. A second shell crashed through the attic! It sent the women running, skirts in hand, back to the basement. Once they went below, Von Borcke returned to his cushioned seat and to his writing. He apparently was trying to impress his hosts with his superb self-control. The room exploded! Plaster and wood whirled through the smoke choked room. The major and the rest of the furnishings skittered madly across the floor, the concussion leaving him in a heap.[24] Another round, simultaneously, burst through the attic and exploded with terrific effect in the courtyard. The dazed officer stumbled toward the shrieks of the mounts which his orderlies had tethered behind the house.

His aides quickly helped Von Borcke into the saddle. Noticing that one of the horses was a twitching mass of jelly, the major decided to clear out. He and his people bolted onto Main Street only to find it cluttered with overturned ambulances and wounded or dying men. The horses reared and hesitated at the smell of blood. The air seemed alive with sulfur and fragments.

The small band plowed through the crowd and made for a hill north of the town. Once there, they reined in to watch the firing. As Von Borcke congratulated himself upon making it away safe, a gasping orderly pointed toward the major's horse. A shell splinter had struck the animal in the right hind quarter.[25] The major's brush with artillery had cost him a fine mount.

During the shelling, several members of Captain M. B. Miller's Battery (3rd Co.) of the Washington Artillery wandered into the town from the West Woods. Skulkers hung about the street corners, on the watch for anyone who might be carrying whiskey. Most of the others, who thronged the streets, were either foragers or wounded men.

Miller's Louisianans scoured the town for a shopkeeper to sell them some sugar, coffee, and other luxuries. They finally coerced one frightened store owner into selling them what they wanted. They offered him the option of taking their greenback dollars or being looted. He took the cash.

One of the artillerists, Napier Bartlett, entered a nearby house to have his coffee ground. A soft, motherly voice greeted him as he stepped inside. An elderly lady was singing gently to herself as she rocked, in her chair, before a crackling fireplace. She did not get up and she hardly reacted to the Confederate's presence.

While he helped himself to her coffee grinder, she continued to sing. Occasionally, she would stop long enough to speak of her only child. He belonged to "Stonewall" Jackson's command. She described her boy with a gentle presence, undisturbed by the exploding shells outside. She said he was the bravest of Stonewall's men, which she felt certain marked him for death.

The filthy soldier noticed the despair in her face. The tantalizing aroma of the ground coffee filled the small house. Bartlett pleaded with her to take some of his ration but she declined. He left her home, knowing that she could not have taken his coffee for herself. She would have sent it to her son.[26]

The Middle Bridge

Captain Francis Edwin "Ed" Pierce (F Co., 108th NY, II Corps), whose black servant had disappeared the previous evening with his rubber overcoat, awoke in an evil mood. The evening "dew" had left him soaked and cold. His empty stomach growled and demanded immediate satiation. Angry and spiteful, he started beating the fence corners for his "contraband", whom he deprecatingly referred to as his "shade".[27]

Sixteen year old Sergeant Thomas Francis DeBurgh Galwey (B Company, 8th OH, 1[st Brigade]/3[rd Division]/II[Corps]) wanted to see the Confederates as dead and as bloated as those he had seen along the roadside at Fox's Gap the day before. The Rebels began the regiment's day with a solitary shell, which exploded over the sleeping color guard. When the smoke cleared and the half awake men rallied, Color Corporal William W. Farmer (D Co.) was not with them. The blast cleaved him in half. The drummers hastily dragged the mangled corpse away while the men restacked their arms and rekindled their old fires for hot coffee and hard crackers.

The intermittent whining and screaming of the shells serenaded them. Having been aimed at the gunners on the ridge to their right front, the projectiles passed harmlessly overhead and crashed into the fields beyond.[28] Some burst but most did not.

The boy sergeant wiped the sleep from his eyes and chatted casually with his messmates. The II Corps lay en masse by brigades on both sides of the Boonsboro Pike. Brigadier General Nathan Kimball's Brigade (14th IN, 8th OH, 132nd PA, and 7th WV) rested on the left of the road along the base of the eastern slope of the ridge.[29] The Irish Brigade (29th MA, 63rd, 69th, and 88th NY) lay down to the right front along the western base of the same hill on the northern side of the Boonsboro Pike. A field of corn along the creek masked its front.[30] (Map 1)

As the morning wore on, Lieutenant Colonel Franklin Sawyer ordered the men of the 8th Ohio to stay near their weapons because he expected the regiment to be called into action. By 11:00 A.M., the cannonading had increased in tempo and had become quite monotonous. Some of the more curious and foolhardy "boys", including the plucky Sergeant Galwey, "accidentally" got lost, only to find themselves on the ridge across the road, near the big guns.[31] The Irish Brigade, with its peculiar green flag, rested on its belly at the base of the slope while the German artillerymen fired over it at the Confederate lines. The excited Ohioans kept pointing toward the Rebel guns, which were in battery on a ridge about one mile distant.[32]

They had not been there long when a series of "huzzahs" rent the air from the fields behind them. Turning about, the infantrymen joined in the hubbub. "Little Mac" (Major General George B. McClellan) was trooping the lines along the Boonsboro Pike, sopping up all the ego inflating attention which he seemed to thrive on. The Johnnies shared in the hullaballoo by showering the crest with an exceptionally heavy barrage. The Midwesterners flattened out and hugged the heaving ground.[33] The Ohions, having seen enough gunnery practice for the day, raced back to their regiment.

The Lower Bridge Road Near Sharpsburg

The Federal artillery struck squarely in Brigadier General Thomas F. Drayton's Brigade (50th, 51st GA, and 15th SC) which was on the high ground immediately south of the Lower Bridge Road. One of the Federal Parrott shells bounded over the hill top and rolled, apparently harmless, into the cook fire of Lieutenant W. McFadden (E Co, 6th SC, Jenkins' BG). His messmates carried him away with a shattered leg.

On the northern side of the road, Longstreet posted his division batteries. Colonel George "Tige" Anderson's Georgia Brigade (1st Regulars, 7th, 8th and 9th GA) hugged the ground about ninety feet to the rear of the artillery pieces, whose caissons stood to their immediate front.

First Sergeant William H. Andrews (M Co., 1st GA Reg.) ruefully noted the Federal signal flag atop South Mountain not minutes before the shelling began. They could not afford to lose any men. Anderson's Brigade numbered about five hundred

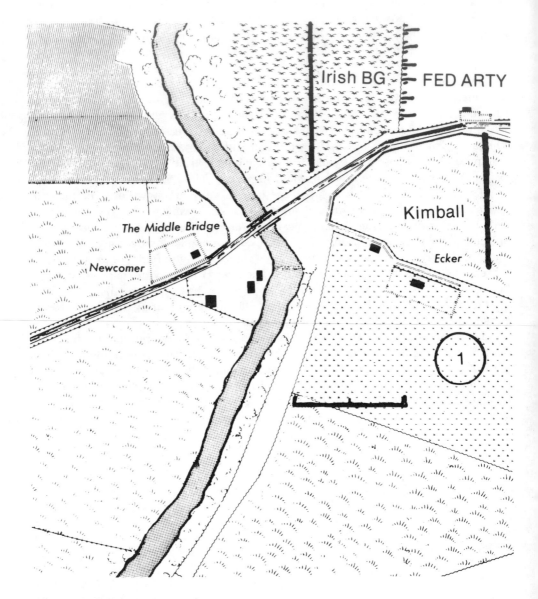

(Map 1) SEPTEMBER 16, 1862
Position of the Irish Brigade and Kimball's Brigade of the II Corps at the Middle Bridge.

men. The 1st Georgia Regulars counted about fifty soldiers. Besides himself, Andrews' M Company claimed one corporal and three privates. Those outnumbered Confederates believed they comprised the best of Lee's Army.

Longstreet's gunners responded immediately to the Yankees who shifted their pieces from Drayton to them. As the shells exploded in and around Anderson's Brigade the Georgians pushed themselves as low as possible to the ground. Their officers, however, remained afoot or mounted. Sergeant Andrews kept his eyes upon the division's field and staff officers.

During the height of the barrage Major General James Longstreet rode calmly behind the field pieces while scrutinizing the Yankee guns through his binoculars. He left the reins draped across the horse's neck and allowed the horse to quietly walk and graze toward the right of the brigade before heading into the village. Near the end of the bombardment, Brigadier General William N. Pendleton, Lee's Chief of Artillery, rode along the same route seemingly as relaxed as Longstreet.

Throughout the entire shelling, "Tige" Anderson trooped the brigade line with his hands clasped behind him. He seemed totally unaware of the explosions around him.

"Did you see that shell brush his coat tail?" one of the men chirped.

Others were too busy mocking the cowardice of the 1st Georgia's assistant surgeon, J. C. Farley. As he broke to the rear a Georgian piped, "Here is a safe place, doctor."

Turning about, Farley dodged in the direction of the "concerned" soldier when another hallooed, "Run here, doctor; here is a good place." Several shell concussions nearly flattened him before he abruptly changed course toward a more "safe" spot. No sooner did he reach the place from which the voice emanated than a third prankster from way down the line beckoned him. Unable to bear the infantrymen's cruel sport any longer, he raced to the protection of the small brook which flowed into the town's reservoir. Farley's antics literally left the infantrymen clutching their sides and roaring with laughter.[34]

The Middle Bridge

The Irish Brigade had lain upon its arms all night. The men were hungry and cross. The night had tingled and clanked its way into morning as braying mules and whining horses were led to the Antietam to drink. To worsen matters, bunglers in blue uniforms kept wandering across the road through their position to get cold water from the creek.[35] Invariably, they tramped upon the hands of many sleeping men.

With the dawn came the Rebel pot shots at the big guns behind the Federal line. Time and again the enemy's round shots sizzled harmlessly into the creek, which was about one hundred yards to the brigade's front. The men watched the near hits flatten the unharvested corn. By noon, the Confederates switched to shells and their twenty pounders started to rain upon the Yankees. Most of the rounds passed completely over the hill. One, however, did not.

Sergeant Matthew Hart (K Co., 63rd NY), with his company, watched a shell strike the crest of the hill behind them, directly beneath one of the huge guns. The projectile hesitated a moment. With its fuse burning painfully slow, the missile started to roll down the hill toward the center of the regiment. Not a whisper was heard as the men locked their hands over the backs of their heads and pushed their faces into the dirt. No one wanted to see his own demise.

After what seemed like an eternity, a man popped his head up and looked around. Matthew Hart lay very still, his knuckles white from their own grip. The big shell had come to a gentle stop against the soles of his feet. The fuse still sputtered. Within a moment, it had burned itself into the casing. The nervous sergeant pushed his face closer to the ground and waited. Nothing happened. The shell was a dud.

Hart nearly went berserk. He was alive. No one could shut him up. He jabbered the rest of the day about his personal miracle.[36]

Lieutenant Ira Bronson (I Co., 5th NH, II Corps) had been counting his blessings since the day before, when his regiment, while serving as the point for the II Corps, flushed an obstinate sniper from the eastern side of the creek near the Middle Bridge. His company had no sooner fanned out to either side of the Boonsboro Pike than a musket ball whistled past his head. As his men sprang forward, a second ball whizzed by and a tattered sniper kicked up dust and made for the bridge. With a swarm of lead buzzing close to him, the lone soldier stopped in the middle of the road, defiantly waved his hat at the Yankees, and made tracks for the safety of his own lines.

Ira Bronson quietly poked a finger through the matching holes in his tunic. Had he filled out his blouse more or had the Reb been a trifle more accurate, he would have been on some surgeon's butcher block.[37]

The barrage fell among the 108th New York. Captain Ed Pierce (F Co.) had just returned from the stream in Keedysville when the first projectile barrelled into the camp. Striking the ground about eighty feet from his company, which was drawing rations, it bounced another three hundred twenty feet, through the crotch of the tree under which they were issuing rations, and smashed into a hard cracker barrel. Flour dust scattered to the four points of the compass as the shell somersaulted several times then stopped — unexploded — in the field.

Two seconds later, the rest of the Confederate battery's shells screamed overhead. The New Yorkers hurled themselves, face first, into the dirt. Captain Pierce noticed how pale everyone became, himself included. None of the shells burst but they did kill five or six men from the brigade. "I saw one fellow's foot taken off very neatly," the Captain later wrote.[38]

Another near miss fell in the 61st/64th New York, while it lay on the eastern side of the ridge (south of Pry's House), and gutted Lieutenant Colonel Nelson Miles' horse but left him unharmed. A lucky shot could have snuffed out a post war hero.[39]

The Lower Bridge Road Near Sharpsburg

The stamina of Longstreet's artillery horses amazed Sergeant William H. Andrews (M Co., 1st GA Reg.) Emaciated and droop eared, they sleepily munched the grass at their feet with their eyes closed. They were too exhausted to run. Like their butternut clad masters, the beasts refused to succumb to starvation or wounds. One of them continued to walk about despite an ugly cannon ball hole in his neck.

A bugle blared, "Riders, prepare to mount!"

The horses' heads snapped up; their nostrils flared.

"Mount!" echoed across the ridge. The teams reared and pawed the ground.

"Limber to the rear!" The war horses wheeled their ammunition chests about and hauled the guns below the Federals' line of sight.

Looking about, the sergeant caught a glimpse of General Robert E. Lee, who was mounted on Traveler near the line, exchanging salutes with "Stonewall" Jackson. Andrews erroneously assumed that Jackson's Corps had just arrived upon the field.

The sergeant had no way of knowing that the stubborn Thomas J. Jackson had come to inform his commanding general that he finally concurred that the Army of Northern Virginia had to take a stand at Sharpsburg. "Old Jack" agreed, in view of the circumstances, it was better to give battle in Maryland, than to retreat without a struggle. Their decision to stay to "save face", for whatever reason, political or military, bore a high price in lives.[40]

The Upper Bridge (Eastern Bank)

The I Corps, like the II Corps, had already seen its share of fighting along South Mountain during the two preceding days. It had arrived in the vicinity of Keedysville late in the afternoon of September 15, 1862, several hours behind the II Corps. An unidentified member of the 12th Massachusetts (3/2/I) later recalled how confused and disorganized the village seemed. Dead mules intermittently lined the roadside along with discarded knapsacks, broken wheels, and incapacitated wounded men.[41] The Corps continued to pour into the town until late in the afternoon of the following day. By nightfall, September 16, 1862, the II and the IX Corps had completed the Federal line — a line which extended almost four miles north to south along the serpentine Antietam Creek.

The Upper Bridge (Western Bank)

Brigadier General Marsena Patrick's Brigade (21st, 23rd, 35th, and 80th NY, I Corps) had been on the alert since 4:00 A.M. — twelve nervous hours of waiting.[42] Around 4:00 P.M., the I Corps, with three companies of the 3rd Pennsylvania Cavalry in the advance, started moving north in an attempt to develop the Confederates' left flank.[43] Hot tempered Brigadier General George G. Meade took his division of Pennsylvania Reserves across the Antietam first, followed by Brigadier General Abner Doubleday's Division, with Brigadier General James B. Ricketts' Division bringing up the rear. The advance developed the "slows".

Once they crossed the creek, Companies C and I (3rd PA Cav.) probed west along M. Miller's farm lane, while Company H, under the command of Lieutenant William Miller turned north along the Williamsport Road to reconnoiter that flank. The two companies on the left flank moved south, then west. Company C led the probe, followed by I Company. Captain Edward S. Jones (C Co.) sent his squadron (about thirty-two men) and Lieutenant E. Willard Warren (C Co.), with his first platoon, west in a wide arc as skirmishers. (Map 2)

The second platoon under Sergeant Thompson Miller (C Co.), with Company I (Captain James W. Walsh), brought up the rear at the regulation distance. The cavalrymen flushed a few Confederate videttes from the fields around M. Miller's but drew no

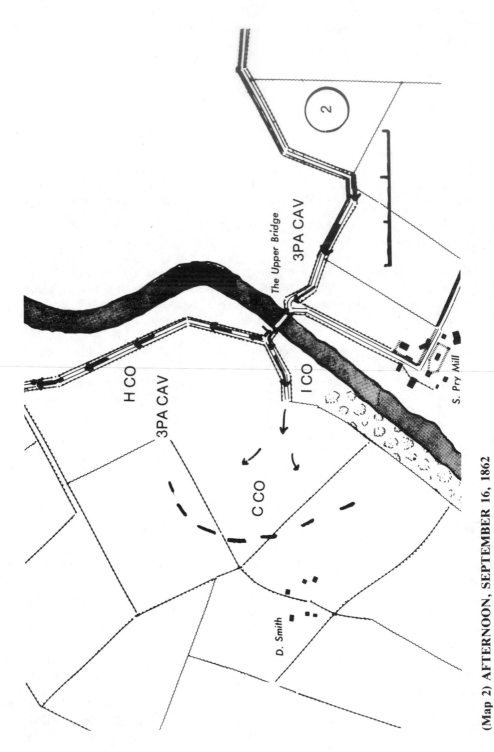

(Map 2) AFTERNOON, SEPTEMBER 16, 1862
The advance of Companies C, H, and I, 3rd Pennsylvania Cavalry at the Upper Bridge.

C COMPANY, 3rd PENNSYLVANIA CAVALRY

Taken in 1863, these pictures show some of the troopers who initiated the action in the East Woods on September 16.
(History of the 3rd Pennsylvania Cavalry)

fire. As they turned south on Morrison's farm lane, Lieutenant Warren's platoon came under sniper fire from the East Woods. Captain Jones immediately halted his small command. Captain Walsh (I Co.) galloped past Sergeant Miller's platoon to investigate the situation along the northern section of the woods.

The Confederate sharpshooters caught Miller's men, mounted and exposed, in the lane near Morrison's farm house. The sergeant ordered Private John McCourbie, his best marksman, to dismount and take out a couple of the bushwhackers. Four troopers responded. Without orders, they slipped up to the fence along the lane, took careful aim, and volleyed in unison into the tree tops to their left front.

Moments later, Captain Walsh clattered into Sergeant Miller's platoon.

"Who ordered those men to dismount?" he shouted in anger, the shots apparently having passed over his head. "This is no place for them to be off their horses!"

The sergeant disrespectfully retorted that he did not care to sit quietly by and be used for target practice and that it did not take too long to remount, whereupon, he ordered his men to their horses.

Things calmed down immediately as Major-General Joseph Hooker (I Corps) galloped into the group to survey the situation. It would not have been good for either the captain or the sergeant to continue their feud in the general's presence.[44]

The Upper Bridge (Eastern Bank)

By 6:00 P.M., Patrick's people still remained in column on the Upper Bridge Road. They were waiting to move. General Patrick had ridden off to find the division commander, Abner Doubleday. It seemed that someone had forgotten to tell Patrick what to do with his four regiments. Moments after he left, S. D. Lee's batteries near the Dunker Church, firing blind, sent a few erratic shells his way.[45] The column moved further north, out of range.

Corporal Austin "Jim" Stearns (K Co., 13th MA, 3/2/I), having consumed his daily "square" meal of hard crackers, potatoes, and salt pork earlier in the day, was hungry. Near dark, his brigade joined one of the five brigade columns which were moving on the enemy. He saw "Fightin' Joe" Hooker, I Corps commander, racing his horse at breakneck speed along the lines. He kept yelling at the men to get moving.[46] A private in the 12th Massachusetts (3/2/I) noticed the general cavorting about too, and he made a mental note of the officer's excitedness. Hooker was "all alive". His very looks spelled mischief. He was not the calm and immaculately dressed gentleman the soldier had seen sipping brandy and water the day before. Hooker seemed very unstrung.[47] There would be no cook fires that night and no dinner, either.

Hurry up and wait. Hurry up and wait. It took the 13th Massachusetts an hour to cross the ford below the Upper Bridge. Once across, it halted to await orders.[48] Soaked from the waist down, with fine grains of sand and tiny bits of gravel rubbing their feet raw, the bored infantrymen finally tramped north in an attempt to out-distance the Rebel shells from the West Woods.[49] To the southwest (their left front) the sharp reports of the Pennsylvanians' breech loading rifles and the terrible blasts of artillery rent the cool night air.

The Martin Line Farm

Law's Brigade (4th AL, 2nd and 11th MS, and 6th NC) deployed in skirmish order in the fields immediately north of Samuel Poffenberger's. They had been there since about 4:00 P.M. The Yankees stumbled into their perimeter an hour before dark.[50] At about the same time that Hooker rode into Captain Jones' Pennsylvanians (C Co., 3rd PA Cav.), Lieutenant William Miller (H Co.) turned his cavalrymen south onto the Smoketown Road, where it intersected the Williamsport Road. About one hundred yards to his front, he noticed a small body of Federal infantry moving by the left oblique. He recognized them as the Pennsylvania Reserves by the bucktails which they wore on their kepis.

Colonel Hugh McNeil (13th PA Res.), at the head of his command, crawled between the fence rails and met the lieutenant in the road. He cordially asked the cavalryman where he was going. Miller told him that he was ordered to find out where the Rebels were, at which point McNeil queried if he would like some company. Miller accepted and the colonel sent two companies to both sides of the Smoketown Road, behind the lieutenant's mounted videttes. Everything seemed so serene and quite.

The East Woods

Unknown to Lieutenant Miller, General Hooker had sent Lieutenant Willard Warren's and Sergeant Thompson Miller's platoons (C Co., 3rd PA Cav.) against the Confederates in the East Woods. The lieutenant and the sergeant dashed clear through the eastern end of the woods, well ahead of their men. As the two troopers neared the southern border of the trees, they stumbled into a Confederate artillery section (S.D. Lee's Bttn.). *(Map 3)*

At less than thirty feet, canister whistled about the Yankees and wounded one of their mounts. The scared cavalrymen wheeled about and headed back where they came from.

The Martin Line Farm

Simultaneously, to the north, Lieutenant William Miller (H Co., 3rd PA Cav.) and Colonel Hugh McNeil (13th PA Res.) walked into a large body of infantry. The woods several hundred yards south of Martin Line's house erupted in flame and sulfur. Miller's videttes doubled back upon the 13th Reserves who had just reached Line's farm lane.[51]

"Forward, Bucktails!" Colonel McNeil yelled, seconds before a bullet went through his heart.

Armed with muskets and conventional rifles, the Southerners reluctantly fell back toward the East Woods and its secure looking stacks of cord wood, huge trees, and limestone outcroppings. A fire fight, backed by Federal canister, erupted. The Union soldiers, with their breech loading Sharps rifles, never seemed to run out of ammunition. They fought in open order. Rather than attack with the traditional line, they advanced in echelon, with the prone units providing cover fire from the rear. The Pennsylvanians, who repeatedly ran a few yards then dropped, fought like Rebels.[52] *(Map 4)*

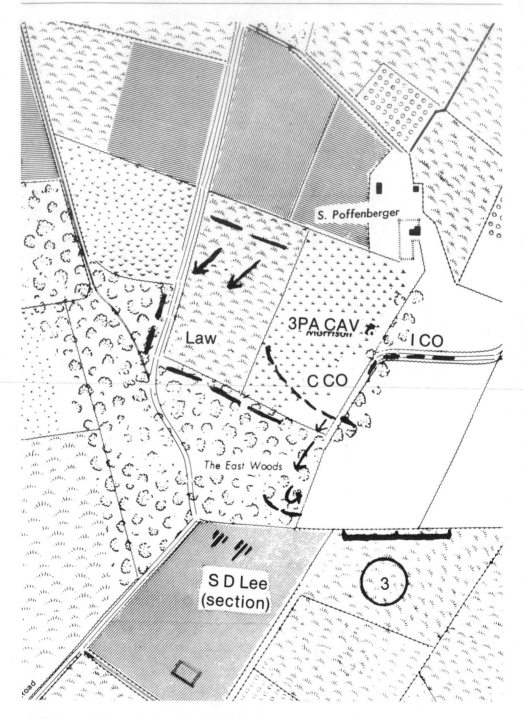

(Map 3) AFTERNOON, SEPTEMBER 16, 1862
C Company, 3rd Pennsylvania Cavalry, opens the fighting in the East Woods.

(Map 4) AFTERNOON, SEPTEMBER 16, 1862
The drive of the 1st Pennsylvania Rifles (13th Reserves) against Law's Brigade south of the Martin Line farm.

As the Confederates neared the eastern edge of the East Woods, the slow withdrawal devolved into a full scale stampede. A number of men threw down their arms and surrendered. The others bounded over the worm fence which bordered the near edge of the woods. More shots rang out from the Yankees and a Rebel yell, accompanied by a volley, responded. The 4th and 5th Texas regiments (Wofford's Brigade, Hood's Division) bolted into the woods from the west and the south, respectively. Private William R. Hamby (B Co., 4th TX) felt somewhat intimidated by the much larger Federal regiments which were converging on the East Woods in echelon. The Yankees' flags flapped vigorously in the breeze and their bugle calls resounded above the shelling and riflery.[53] *(Map 5)*

Taking the onrushing Yankees by surprise, they exchanged shots at point blank range.[54] Within moments, a section of howitzers from S. D. Lee's Battalion had pulled up close to the action and was ripping the tree tops into splinters.[55]

The West Woods

From approximately due west, at about seven hundred yards, Poague's three gun battery hurled round shot and shells into the rear of the Federal lines. William Poague's gunners, their pants still dripping from the river fording near Shepherdstown, Virginia, had hastily unlimbered in front of the eastern face of the West Woods. From their position they could see what appeared to be two lines of Federal infantry emerging from the East Woods.[56] Between them and the enemy lay Wofford's three remaining regiments (Hampton's Legion, 18th GA, and 1st TX). Demoralized Rebs came running from the trees. To the battery's immediate right Jones' (21st, 42nd, 48th VA, and 1st VA Bttn) and Colonel A. J. Grigsby's (4th, 5th, 27th, and 33rd VA) readied brigades rested on their arms. Both faced north to thwart any Federal attack from that area.[57]

The Yankee fire was very inaccurate. During the twilight, the Confederate gunners watched the fuses of the Federal shells trace reddish streamers through the sky like huge fireflies.[58] Poague's men were putting out a well paced fire when a newly promoted shavetail (2nd lieutenant) bounded into the battery from out of nowhere. He dashed his mount in and about the guns. "Let 'em have it! Let 'em have it!" he screamed.

Several "let 'em have its" later, the grimy artillerymen told him in no uncertain terms to get lost or they would "let him have it." Having known the men before his promotion, the former headquarter's orderly wisely quit the field for a safer spot.

Not long after, an unusually large officer with a sword came running into the battery from the east. At a full run, he dove for cover behind a log to the rear of Sergeant Edward Moore's piece. An uninvited twelve pound ball smashed into his hiding place and sent him tumbling into a heap in the field. Without breaking pace, he unrolled himself and disappeared at full speed into the West Woods.[59]

Mumma's Lane

Further to the east, near Mumma's lane, the Federal fire seemed more accurate and terrifying. Captain Parker's two twelve pounders and two rifled pieces held the right of S. D. Lee's line. Firing north into the East Woods, with his right masked by Mumma's cornfield, he tried to support the battalion's two forward guns.

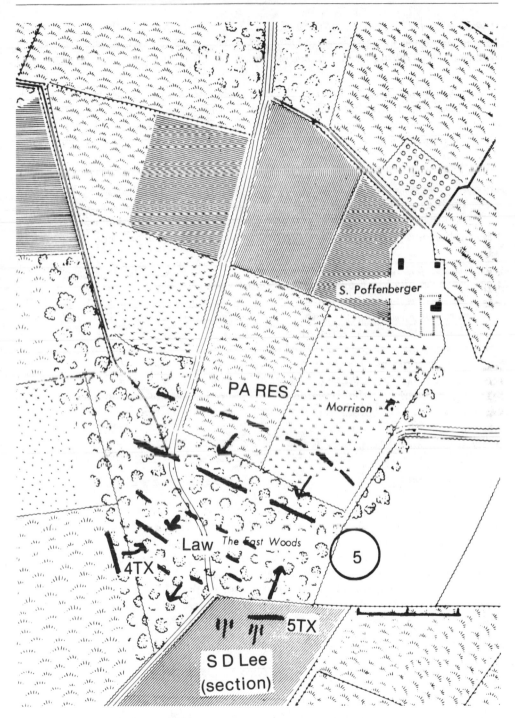

(Map 5) SEPTEMBER 16, 1862
The struggle for the East Woods before 8:00 P.M.

It was nerve-racking work to fire over the heads of his own soldiers. The big guns, across the creek, using the white Dunker Church as their mark, started to drop a tremendous plunging fire all along the lane.

A horrifying scream burst from the rear as the lead horses of Lieutenant Thompson Brown's one team pitched and reared into a bloody pile, both horses the victims of a single shell. Glancing back, the lieutenant saw Bobby Clarke, the driver, stretched out in a puddle of gore.

"Lieutenant!"

Brown wheeled about, his mouth agape in horror. Bobby Clarke stood there — an oozing mess of blood and membranes.

"My brains are out!" the sixteen year old screamed in despair.

Thompson Brown hesitated and a wry grin flickered across his lips as he turned back to his guns. "Then you have the biggest brains I ever saw!" he called over his shoulder.[60]

The boy dutifully wiped the nauseating mess off with his hands then returned to his post. He had two dead horses to cut loose.

The fighting lasted a little over two hours with neither side gaining a strategic advantage. By 8:00 P.M. all but the 4th Texas (Wofford's BG, Hood's Division) had fallen back to the West Woods. An hour later, as Lawton's and Trimble's Brigades came to their relief, the Texans retired to the woods to replenish their cartridge boxes and to draw some rations.[61]

Casualties had been light by comparison to their other engagements. Among them were several men from the Hampton's Legion and a stray captain from the 1st Texas. Somehow, he was captured in a picket skirmish by the 12th Massachusetts. He did nothing to raise the Yankees' morale by telling them that the entire Confederate army was around Sharpsburg.[62] *(Map 6)*

The East Woods

Death was not taken lightly. Chaplain H. W. Hatton (13th PA Res., 1/3/I) would have a difficult time explaining to Mrs. McNeil, the colonel's wife, why her husband had to die. As he sat beside his beloved commander's corpse, he tried to reorganize his thoughts. The brigade lost ninety-five men in killed and wounded in that charge across the open ground to the woods.[63]

Israel Washburn, the gray haired chaplain of the 12th Massachusetts barely escaped a similar fate. Having picked up a musket, the old man got involved in the skirmishing only to get knocked down by a ball in his chest. His pocket Bible absorbed the round's impact and saved his life.[64]

The Joseph Poffenberger Farm — The Nicodemus Farm

By 10:00 P.M. the field, with the exception of sporadic picket firing, had fallen silent. On the Federal side, Lieutenant Colonel Robert Anderson's and Colonel Albert L. Magilton's Brigades (the 9th, 10th, 11th, and 12th PA Res. and the 3rd, 4th, 7th, and 8th PA Res., respectively) held the North Woods, facing south. Patrick's Brigade

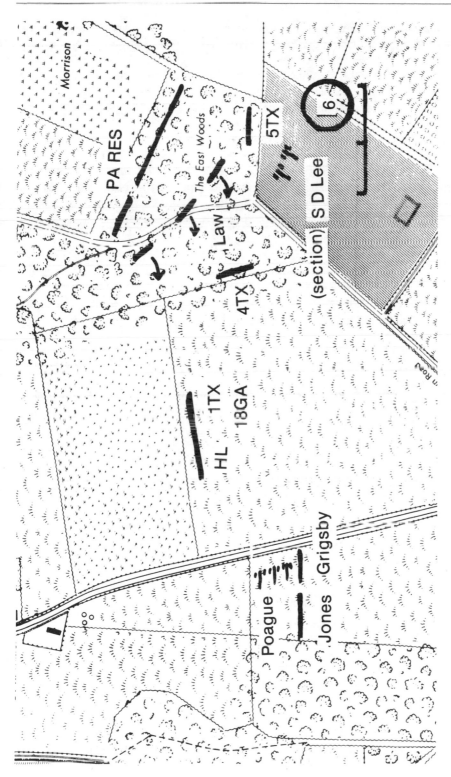

(Map 6) EVENING, SEPTEMBER 16, 1862
The end of the East Woods fight.

faced west along the Hagerstown Pike between Joseph Poffenberger's and Middle-kauf's lanes. Lieutenant Colonel J. William Hofmann's Brigade (the 7th IN, 76th and 95th NY and 56th PA) would come up on Patrick's left later in the evening. Brigadier General John Gibbon's and Colonel Walter Phelps, Jr.'s Brigades (the 19th IN, 2nd, 6th, and 7th WI, and the 22nd, 24th, 30th and 84th NY and the 2nd U.S. Sharpshooters, respectively) lay by in close support in columns of regiments. Ricketts' Division continued the line east from Joseph Poffenberger's lane to Samuel Poffenberger's orchard. Brigadier General Truman Seymour's Bucktails (the 1st, 2nd, 5th, 6th, and 13th PA Res.) held a portion of the southern and western section of the East Woods.

The 3rd Pennsylvania Cavalry advanced south in close column of squadrons to the vicinity of the Nicodemus and the D. R. Miller farms, just below the southern edge of the North Woods. The men stood by their mounts and listened to the Confederate pickets chatting with each other throughout the night.[65]

The men were tired and nervous. The I Corps' losses were very light. Patrick's Brigade, for instance, lost a few men in securing the North Woods under the fire of Poague's Battery.[66] A piece of canister brained a man in C Company of the 12th Massachusetts. A sergeant in G Company, who was AWOL from a Frederick hospital, quickly replaced him. The unarmed noncom fell upon that fellow's warm corpse before it stopped twitching. It was the only way he could procure a weapon.[67] Gibbon's "Iron Brigade" suffered temporary casualties among its Westerners. The victims of gluttony, they payed the natural consequences for having wantonly pilfered Sam Poffenberger's orchard.[68]

Corporal Jim Stearns (K Company), whose regiment, the 13th Massachusetts, bivouacked in a field just east of Magilton's Pennsylvanians, could not find a comfortable place to stretch out. He dozed off, sitting upright. Not long before, he had seen his major, J. Packer Gould, nearly get taken away by a round ball in Poffenberger's corn.

The cannon ball smacked into the corn mound right in front of the "old man's" horse. Stearns heard the major frantically urge his frightened animal to "Get up, get up. That was meant for us. Get up. Get up."[69] Shoulder straps did get scared after all, but Stearns couldn't have cared less. At that moment, he wanted to eat something warm, but fires were prohibited. The Brass did not want to let the Rebels know where they were.[70]

The West Woods — The Mumma Farm

On the Confederate side matters were somewhat better, particularly for the rear lines. For the first time in three days, most of Hood's starving and barefoot division cooked rations and spent the night with full bellies.[71] Jones' (Colonel Bradley T. Johnson, commanding) and Grigsby's Brigades (west to east, respectively) slept on their arms, about five hundred fifty yards north of the Dunker Church. Their left was in the West Woods; their right was anchored on the Hagerstown Pike. Lawton's Brigade, less the 31st Georgia, which was on picket in the East Woods, lay in the field to the right of the Pike, about two hundred yards south of Miller's cornfield. The line ran about fifty yards east, then turned southeast for about three hundred yards. To Lawton's right, the 12th Georgia formed the left of Trimble's line, while the rest of the Brigade held Mumma's lane below the family cemetary.

Brigadier General Roswell Ripley's Brigade (the 4th and 44th GA, and 1st and 3rd NC) rested in line about one hundred yards to the rear of Trimble. S. D. Lee's artillery battalion formed the reserve on the reverse slope of the Dunker Church Ridge. Hood's Division, with Brigadier Generals Jubal Early's, William E. Starke's, Harry T. Hays', and William B. Taliaferro's Brigades spent the night in the West Woods.[72] *(Map 7)*

The West Woods

Major Heros Von Borcke and Captain William Blackford, another member of Stuart's staff, had waited for the general for over an hour at the Dunker Church. When he did not materialize, they shrugged it off and leisurely rode to the artillery bivouac in the hayfield behind the West Woods. The two officers tethered their horses near the huge haystacks then strolled over to a nearby well, where they sat down to dine on some goodies which they had foraged in Pleasant Valley.[73] Their supper done, they crawled into a comfortable hay mound and dozed off, while their mounts nibbled away on their bed. Unknown to them, Stuart and his staff slept in a nearby stack. They were exhausted. The General and his bodyguard had used the entire day to reconnoiter the Army of Northern Virginia's left flank. During the East Woods fight, a solitary shell unhorsed James McClure (F Co., 10th VA Cav.), who was at Stuart's side. McClure, whom General Jackson had personally ordered to turn loose a captured mount several days before, found himself afoot. His beloved "Beelzebub" died from shell injuries. Nevertheless, he stayed by his commander's side.[74]

Captain Poague's men, who were trying to sleep in the neighboring field, stayed with their guns, pursuant to orders. In the distance, they heard Pleasants, their smithy, howling after his mules, which had been scattered into the darkness by one of the few Federal shells to fall into the battery.[75] Sergeant Edward Moore slept atop his caisson in a futile attempt to keep his newly "requisitioned" Yankee uniform reasonably clean.[76] He had done all right by the Yanks at Harper's Ferry.

The Dunker Church Ridge

Captain Parker's people dozed off in much the same manner as Poague's, either under their guns or on their limbers. Lieutenant Jordan C. Parkinson shared the ground beneath a caisson with his captain, whose earnest and loud praying awakened him not long after he fell asleep; he did not object to it. Only a miracle would keep them alive on the morrow. The man could pray his life away if he wished to.

As he lay on this back, with Parker's supplications wafting over him, the young lieutenant stared wonderingly at the sky. It seemed beautiful. His thoughts drifted toward home and family.

Many slept fitfully on both sides that night. The sporadic picket firing continued throughout the evening. At one point a loud burst seemed to illuminate the entire East Woods. The whole place seemed on fire. Parkinson thought it better to die awake by the guns than on his back asleep.[77] The light rain, which fell shortly after midnight, chilled many to the bone.[78] That would lead to pneumonia and infection for some of those unfortunate enough to catch lead.

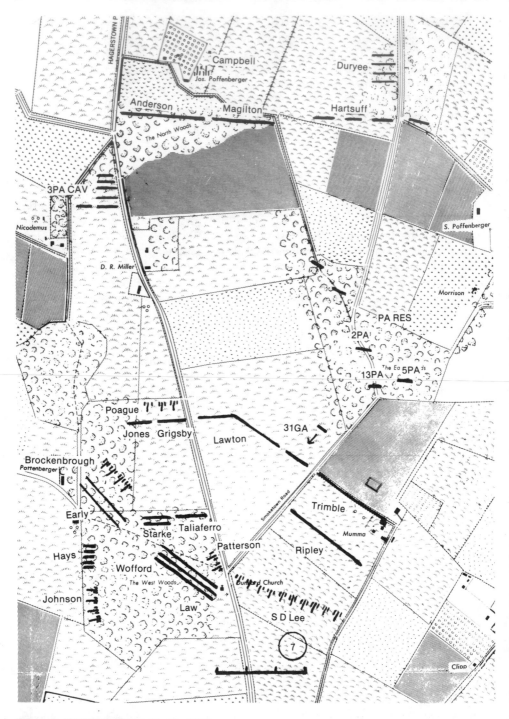

(Map 7) SEPTEMBER 16-17, 1862
Position of troops on the northern end of the field from midnight to dawn.

Around 11:00 P.M. Colonel A. J. Grigsby called over his aide-de-camp, Lieutenant Ezra E. Stickley (5th VA) and his orderly, a fellow named Cox.

"Boys," the colonel drawled, "no fight tonight. You can lie down here and get some sleep."

Stickley and Cox immediately prepared to bed in the open just east of the West Woods. Each man secured a stone for a pillow. The lieutenant, who had procured some new clothes and a pair of fine buckskin gloves in Harper's Ferry, carefully arranged the gloves on his rock. He then spread his blanket over them and on the ground. Tying the reins of their mounts to their feet, as was customary during a crisis, the two runners reclined side by side and covered themselves with the same blanket. Colonel Grigsby remained standing beside his mount. Stickley apparently had forgotten his death premonition.[79]

The Upper Bridge

The Federal troops did not rest at all for the better part of the night. McClellan kept strengthening his enormous camp along the creek. In the camps of the XII Corps, near Pry's house, regimental officers stole from tent to tent to awaken their men. They issued strict orders against loud talking and they prohibited all fires. The men groped about in the darkness like thieves in the night, blindly following their file leaders north toward the Upper Bridge.

It took him until 10:30 P.M. to get the XII Corps across the Antietam and moving west. Many of the soldiers had never seen the "elephant". They felt nervous about their initiation into combat. As the regiments crossed the Upper Bridge, they clutched their cups and canteens close to their bodies in an effort not to alert the Rebs to their presence.[80]

SERGEANT WILLIAM POTTS, F Company, 124th Pennsylvania He took command of his company when the captain quit the field and the lieutenants refused to assume control. *(History of the 124th Pennsylvania)*

Sergeant William W. Potts (F Co., 124th PA, 1/1/XII), a reluctant soldier by any standards, was already in a mutinous frame of mind by the time the outfit had gotten to Keedysville. During the night march over South Mountain, the men had continually tried to break column to forage food. Their brigade commander, Brigadier General Samuel Crawford, confronted one particularly whining group and barked at them to keep on going. He contemptuously called them "Pennsylvania cattle". Potts, who quite understandably belonged to that fractious bunch, said tongue-in-cheek that it was wrong to shoot one's own officer, then he coyly added that if the old man "accidentally" stepped between him and a Reb, he would not think twice about pulling the trigger.

Now, as Potts tried to quietly march across the stone bridge over the Antietam, he could hear cavalry sabres jingling against saddles. Artillerists swore at their obstinate teams. There he was, trying to steal into a bivouac like a beggar, while the rest of the army made enough racket to startle a deaf man.[81]

The Martin Line Farm — The Lower Bridge

By midnight, the XII Corps had arrived at the cornfields of Martin Line, where it bedded down in close order by column of companies. A field hospital had already gone into operation at the house — a grim reminder of the soldier's fragile state in life.[82]

The 125th Pennsylvania, another inexperienced regiment, which brigaded with the 124th Pennsylvania, sacked out near the log house. The men endured the horrifying shrieks and groans which echoed from within its walls as the surgeons probed and sliced into the morning hours. The men gawked at the litter bearers as they hauled in Colonel Hugh McNeil's corpse (13th PA Res.). They found it hard to believe that people really died in war.[83]

While the XII Corps sneaked into its grisly bivouac, the IX Corps, commanded by Brigadier General Jacob Cox, literally tiptoed into position on the far left of the line, near the Lower Bridge. (The Corps had acquired the new commander not two days before when it lost its beloved Jesse Reno at Fox's Gap.) It seemed ludicrous — thousands of armed and dirty veterans sneaking into their own lines like cat burglars. As Colonel Harrison S. Fairchild's Brigade (the 9th, 89th, and 103rd NY) crept into camp, a minor fracas nearly precipitated a mass panic.

The 9th New York (Hawkins' Zouaves) stacked their arms and laid down for a well deserved rest. In the still, muggy darkness, a member of the 103rd New York tripped over a mutt — the 9th's regimental mascot. The dog yelped! The startled soldier tottered backwards into a musket stack. Weapons clattered and crashed! Frightened soldiers cursed and swore as the two regiments sprang into a tangle of arms and legs. For several minutes, pandemonium controlled the field until the dazed men realized the Rebel guerillas had not attacked them.

With order restored, the 9th separated from the 103rd and stumbled over a nearby slope into a thin belt of corn which bordered the creek. From his place in G Company, Private David Thompson (9th NY) enviously studied the auroras from the Confederate fires as they radiated from the distant ridge beyond the creek. Thompson comforted his growling stomach by mixing his coffee and sugar ration in his hands then chewing them — dry. Considering that he might be a corpse on the morrow, eating such an unpalatable meal seemed most appropriate.[84]

That same evening, Private Samuel Compton (F Co., 12th OH, IX) could not eat. He lost his appetite that morning at Fox's Gap while watching the Federal burial crews disposing of the Confederate dead. The men, who were very drunk, took their picks and made four or five passes at the ground without breaking it.

They wanted to avoid handling the bloated and gray looking bodies as much as possible. The decomposing corpses polluted the air with their offensive, sickening odor. Compton did not fault the burial detail for solving their problem quickly. One by one, they picked up each dead Rebel by the belt, teetered over to a nearby well, and cast him down its shaft. Compton counted sixty bodies in all before he staggered away, nauseated.[85]

The Middle Bridge (Eastern Bank)

Sergeant Thomas Galwey (B Co., 8th OH) watched the flashes of musketry in the woods across the creek with a curiosity borne of inexperience; the eery silence which followed the action disturbed him, much like the silence before a downpour. Deep within himself, he sensed that the following day would rain death as he had never imagined it. He tried to sleep to escape his misgivings about himself.[86]

Lieutenant Joseph S. Harris, having just arrived in the bivouac of the 108th New York, brought a gift from Washington, D.C. — a new National flag. Captain Ed Pierce, since his F Company was the largest in the regiment, volunteered Sergeant George Goff and Private Tom McKibbins to form the nucleus of the color guard.

Shortly, thereafter, the quartermaster issued an additional forty rounds to each man. Ironically, few of the men, Captain Pierce included, suspected they were going into battle on the morrow.[87]

The afternoon's shelling killed and wounded several men in the neighboring 130th Pennsylvania. The untried regiment moved east with French's Division to get out of range. The men closed ranks en masse to wait out the evening.[88]

Across the creek, near Joseph Poffenberger's barn, First Sergeant William H. Harris (B Co., 2nd WI) tried to doze off with the distant shouts of Confederate officers on their picket lines echoing hauntingly in his ears. He slept very little. He shivered throughout the wet misty night; his spine tingled as if someone was continually running ice up and down his back. He later wrote of that evening, "I felt certain that there would be desperate fighting in the morning and that many of my comrades would fail to answer roll call when the morning sun had again sunk behind the western hills." He tried to pray himself to sleep, but in vain.[89]

The West Woods

An ominous spirit visited the Confederate camp also. Major Moxley Sorrel and the rest of "Pete" Longstreet's staff had just bedded down in a small wood west of the West Woods. The Jeff Davis Legion securely picketed its mounts along the northern perimeter of the trees while sentinals alertly tramped their beats. The night seemed quiet — deathly quiet. Shortly after midnight, an indescribable presence whispered along the picket rope. Horses whinnied and neighed! The rope snapped! The mounts shied and stampeded to the rear, nearly trampling the dozing officers into mush.

Moxley Sorrel, a devout Christian, hastily picked himself up from the dirt as the troopers frantically chased after their animals. Some spirit had frightened the horses. He could sense its presence. Weak from diarrhea and galled, the major lay down once again, disturbed to his soul by his narrow escape. He thanked God for his good fortune.[90]

The East Woods

Lieutenant Colonel William A. Christian's Brigade (26th NY, 94th NY, 88th PA, and 90th PA) got lost in the total darkness which engulfed the East Woods. "... we groped around in the woods for some time," Private John D. Vautier (I Co., 88th PA) bitterly complained, "but had to catch hold of one anothers coats." Vautier lost his grip on the man next to him and dejectedly threw himself down next to a tree to wait for daylight. He slept little.

Throughout the evening, Rebel pickets, who mistook the troops in the woods as their own, "walked into our lines and innocently asked what Regt. this was. They soon found out," Vautier scratched in his memoirs.[91]

As the battle opened, the opposing armies held the following positions. The Federal I Corps stretched from the North Woods to the northeast corner of Poffenberger's Lane, then turned south into the East Woods. The Confederates, part of Jackson's and Longstreet's Corps, occupied the ground from the West Woods, near the southwestern corner of the Cornfield, to the Mumma Farm. The Federals moved south to take the Confederate artillery on the ground east of the Dunker Church. The fighting swirled around the West Woods, the East Woods, and the Cornfield all morning.

CHAPTER TWO

"They gaped upon me . . . as a ravening and a roaring lion."

WEDNESDAY, SEPTEMBER 17, 1862

Dawn to 6:20 A.M.

The rain, which started falling as a gentle shower shortly after midnight, turned into a downpour by the predawn hours.[1] It rolled away by first light, leaving both armies soaked to their skins and feeling generally irritable.

The West Woods

Major Heros Von Borcke and Captain William Blackford (Stuart's staff) tumbled out of their haystack near the West Woods with the first sharp cracks of riflery. Von Borcke was a trifle piqued. He was damp because he had not burrowed deep enough into the haystack and he was hungry. The Yankees had not given him ample time to forage breakfast.[2] As he and Blackford set out toward the left flank and Stuart's guns near Nicodemus Heights, he noted the large numbers of barefoot men preparing for combat near the West Woods. No way, the gigantic Prussian thought, could these men successfully counter a Federal thrust.[3] Perhaps the heavy ground fog which smothered the low spots of the rolling pastures along their front would be worked to their advantage. Surprise — striking at point-blank range under the cover of the eery mist — could quite conceivably work to the defenders' favor.[4]

The Cornfield

The skirmishers began popping off rounds at one another around 3:00 A.M.[5] From the high ground near D.R. Miller's cornfield Private John Worsham (F Co.,

21st VA., Jones' Brigade, Jackson's Division and Corps) could see the Yankee signalmen on the eastern ridge along the creek wigwagging to their men on South Mountain.

Colonel A. J. Grigsby tapped Lieutenant Ezra Stickley (5th VA). The young officer and the brigade orderly, Cox, awakened instantly. Untying their sleeping mounts from their feet, the two rolled their blankets. In the flurry, Stickley could not find his right hand glove. The colonel immediately ordered him to trot the brigade line to rouse the troops with instruction for each man to recap his piece.[6]

Already, the big guns had started hurling shells into and around the brigade's position. Joined by the Federal field batteries, to the north, they filled the sky with sizzling metal.[7]

One of the projectiles, having passed over the West Woods, exploded in a wood stack behind the Confederate lines alongside the 3rd Virginia Cavalry as it moved, in column, by the flank toward Lee's extreme left flank. A chunk of cord wood smashed Lieutenant Colonel John T. Thurston's left arm. A fragment from the same shell killed another man's horse, seriously wounded the rider, and barely missed Captain Richard Watkins of K Company.

Private E. M. Price (K Co.) carried the colonel to a small house behind the lines, where Assistant Surgeon Alexander T. Bell promptly amputated the arm at the shoulder. (The Colonel died from blood loss the next day at dawn.)

The Martin Line Farm

No one knew who opened fire first. Corporal David Wilkinson (A Co., 124th PA., 1/1/XII) recalled that "As soon as daylight came, the ball was opened." It started with a single shot. One of his comrades, upon hearing it, stupidly remarked, "Some fellow is out shooting squirrels this morning." The volley which quickly erupted in the distance instantly hushed him. The time for jesting had ended.[8] The point of who fired first seemed irrelevant. Finding cover — getting so low to the ground that the concussions of incoming rounds ruptured eardrums — was all that mattered. Men screamed and shrieked. Horses panicked. The ground fog seethed with missiles and no one felt safe.

The West Woods

Poague's Virginia Battery fell in shortly before dawn. The captain considered the Federal guns with a very healthy respect. He disliked being fired on from the rear. The least the Yankees could have done was hit the white church near the West Woods, than overshoot it. "The enemy are not fighting fair," he later complained, but then he wryly concluded, "He is playing a game in which all things are fair."[9]

Sergeant Ed Moore, one of his gunners, also wished the Federals had plopped their shells elsewhere. No sooner had his drivers hitched up than an incoming round burst over his lead pair of horses. Driver Sam Moore (no relation) flew off the saddle like a twig in the wind while his horse floundered and dropped. Ed Moore ran into the confusion before the smoke cleared to check the damage. Sam was too far gone to help therefore his sergeant left him alone. The battery did not have time to waste upon a dying man. The sergeant glanced at the wounded horse, which had gained its feet. A fragment had sheared off one of its forelegs, but the animal refused to fall. Even after Moore replaced it, the mortally wounded horse stayed by its post, hobbling after the gun as it lurched into battle.[10]

The Dunker Church Ridge

Stephen D. Lee's Battalion had already rolled into its former position along the ridge from the church to Mumma's lane. The batteries had been there since first light. Jordan's Battery unlimbered facing northeast, immediately south of the Smoketown Road-Hagerstown Pike intersection. Parker, Rhett, and Woolfolk went into battery to the right respectively.[11] Captain Parker's men hastily loaded with shell and awaited orders to cut loose at the huge cornfield to the north.[12] (Map 8)

The Joseph Poffenberger Farm

The Union soldiers littered their previous night's bivouacs with their playing cards which they quickly chucked to rid themselves of Satanic instruments.[13] Major Rufus Dawes, second in command of the 6th Wisconsin (4/1/I), hurriedly organized his small regiment for the advance with the brigade. Small arms fire crackled to the south. In the distance, he heard the thunder of Parker's guns near the Dunker Church. His men got to their feet like the professionals they were supposed to be — including those who had gorged themselves on Samuel and Joseph Poffenberger's apples the evening before.[14]

The major knew his people. They were rough and dependable. Their brigade — the "Iron Brigade", as Major General Joseph Hooker dubbed it[15] — mustered a little over one thousand men between the four regiments.[16] Three days before, at Turner's Gap near Boonsboro, the Westerners had earned their sobriquet when they attempted to show Colonel Alfred H. Colquitt's Brigade (Major General Daniel H. Hill's Division, Jackson's Corps) "what fer" at a stone wall on the eastern slope of South Mountain. Two of the nervous Federal regiments accidentally volleyed into each other while flanking the wall. When the fighting ended at dark, the Yankees had not gained their objective — the old stone inn at the Gap's crest.

The casualties had been very disproportionate. The Confederates took out over three hundred men, including the Yankees who shot each other, while their aggregate casualties numbered less than a third of that amount.[17]

The brigade prepared to advance at the "common time" toward Meade's nervous Pennsylvania Reserves, who were posted in the North Woods, facing south. The Western regiments formed in columns of divisions (two companies on line). The 6th Wisconsin, with the 2nd Wisconsin to its immediate rear, placed its right flank against the post and rail fence on the eastern side of the Hagerstown Pike. The 7th Wisconsin, with the 19th Indiana to its rear, fell in behind the 2nd Wisconsin. Colonel Walter Phelps' small brigade (22nd, 24th, 30th, and 84th N.Y., and the 2nd U.S. Sharpshooters) then Marsena Patrick's New Yorkers finished out the column.[18]

By the time they started to move out, Poague's Confederate battery rolled onto the hillcrest south of D. R. Miller's barn. At first, First Sergeant William H. Harris

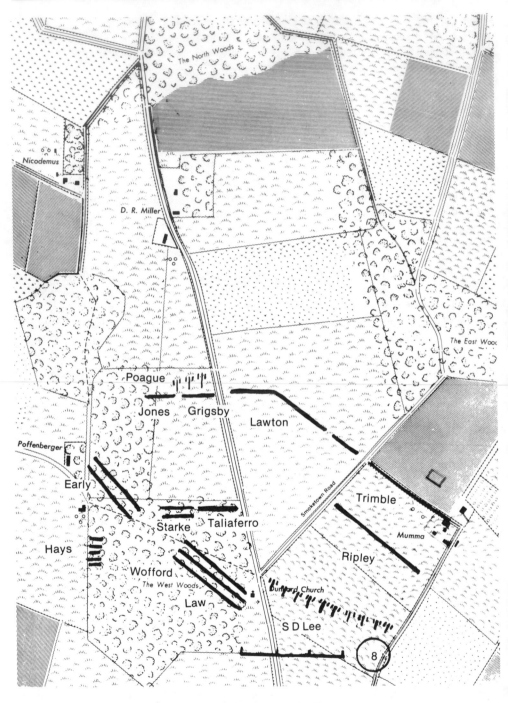

(Map 8) DAWN TO 6:20 A.M., SEPTEMBER 17, 1862

The Confederate troop disposition on the northern end of the field before the first Federal infantry assault.

(B Co., 2nd WI) mistook it for one of their own batteries. The scream of incoming shells shattered that illusion. As the line stepped off, two exploded simultaneously in the thick fog above the center of the Iron Brigade. A third, probably a percussion shell, burst in the rear line of the 6th Wisconsin.[19] Screams and moans rent the air as searing iron gouged a tremendous hole in the unsuspecting ranks. Captain David K. Noyes (A Co.) dropped with blood spurting from the stump where a foot had been.[20] Their brigade commander, Brigadier General John Gibbon, anxiously watched the soldiers calmly drag the wounded away before going any further. That single round struck down thirteen men.[21] Lieutenant Colonel Edward S. Bragg (6th WI) ordered his men to close ranks. As they advanced, parade like, toward the North Woods, the commands shifted into regimental fronts. The 2nd Wisconsin moved to the left of the 6th Wisconsin and the 7th Wisconsin filed left while the 19th Indiana moved into the open space next to the Hagerstown Pike. They left behind a number of dead, among them a terribly mangled soldier whose arms and legs were ripped from his body.[22] *(Map 9)*

Lieutenant Colonel J. William Hofmann's Brigade (7th IN, 76th and 95th NY, and 56th PA) simultaneously crossed the Hagerstown Pike toward the right flank of the Iron Brigade.[23] The intense skirmishing to the front, and the unrelenting, deadly rain of shells indicated some very severe fighting.

The Iron Brigade halted momentarily to realign itself after it passed Joseph Poffenberger's barn. Major Dawes (6th WI) dispatched Captain John Kellogg with I Company into the plowed field beyond the North Woods, and Captain Alexander Hooe with C Company to the far right, beyond the Nicodemus House, while the rest of the regiment and the 2nd Wisconsin swung into line on a regimental front.[24] The major looked back to observe the maneuver.

"Company E! On the right, by file, into line . . ."[25] Dawes shifted his attention over his shoulder as Captain Edwin A. Brown crumbled to the ground. The officer passed away without a sound, shot down in midsentence by a round through his open mouth.[26]

The men steadied and pressed forward. They passed through Meade's line at the North Woods and entered Miller's plowed field at the "common time". The front rank stepped off at "charge bayonets" and the rear rank at the "right shoulder shift".

As the skirmishers disappeared over a rail fence into the cornfield on Miller's farm, the 6th and 2nd Wisconsin regiments advanced to about the middle of the clover field to the left of the Miller house. They laid down, trying to make themselves inconspicuous targets for the Confederate skirmishers, whom they flushed from the white farm house on their right flank.[27]

The rest of the brigade went prone in the furrowed field to their rear. They also tried to mold their bodies into the freshly turned soil. The sky buzzed with deadly minies. Shells exploded incessantly. The ground heaved and rolled.

Dawes watched his skirmishers fall back to the edge of the cornfield where they flattened out, pinned by small arms fire and artillery fire from the right flank. J. E. B. Stuart's gunners on the heights across the pike hammered the Federals terribly.[28] The more time the major's men remained in the field, the more they would die without a chance to retaliate.

(Map 9) DAWN TO 6:20 A.M., SEPTEMBER 17, 1862
The deployment of Gibbon's Brigade in the North Woods.

John Gibbon, the Iron Brigade commander, realized the peril his soldiers were in. The gruff professional rushed Captain Joseph Campbell's Battery (B, 4th U.S.) into position behind the prone 7th Wisconsin and the 19th Indiana regiments. Within minutes, the six brass guns were returning fire above their troops' heads to the front and the right. Brigadier General Abner Doubleday, the Division commander, detached Lieutenant James Stewart's section (two guns) to the right rear of the Miller farm house to silence a Confederate gun which cut loose from a knoll about half way between the Pike and the East Woods.[29] The burly lieutenant, his nostrils flaring with the excitement of the battle, ordered his men to return fire.[30] Jordan's section (S. D. Lee's Battalion) ceased fire from that position within minutes. *(Map 10)*

The Dunker Church Ridge

Captain Parker's gunners, near the Dunker Church, were too enveloped in the smoke of their own pieces and of the incoming rounds to notice whether or not Jordan's section, which had unlimbered north of the Smoketown Road, had fallen silent.[31] His body shot through with adrenalin, Captain Parker darted his horse from one end of the battery to the other. All the while, he exhorted his men to respond to the Yankee fire with all the energy they could muster. During the excitement, the captain singled out Corporal James Darden, with whom he shared a political and spiritual affinity and whom he considered to be the coolest man in his battery.[32] While running from gun to gun, Parker screamed at the corporal, "If I am killed, tell my wife I was never happier in my life."[33] In the ecstacy of the moment, the normally reserved, close mouthed officer revealed a darker side of his personality — his blood lust.

William Parker's battery was getting plenty of Yankee attention. It seemed as if every field piece of the entire Army of the Potomac had trained upon his people. The enemy had gotten range with the first round they fired from one of the big guns across the Antietam.[34] The knoll became an inferno. The sky burst and thundered with successive concussions. It rolled and hissed with shell fragments. His boys started to drop with disconcerting regularity, their pitiful cries piercing the sulfuric cloud which shrouded their position.[35] Stray rounds were also taking men out.

Fifteen year old Davey Brown fell with a ball through the leg.[36] Corporal Newell was dead.[37] Lieutenant Parkinson was down with a shattered knee. Captain Parker dismounted and hurriedly operated on his prize officer in an effort to save his life. He wanted him back to his guns.[38] Bill Cook got leg shot — a minor wound. John Turnbridge caught one through the hand.[39] Horses pitched and screamed, frantic from the smell of blood.

The West Woods

Sergeant Edward Moore (Poague's Battery) went into action with his crew at the battery's old post, about three hundred fifty yards south of the Miller barn, just as Colonel Abram Duryee's Brigade (97th, 104th, and 105th NY, and 107th PA) neared the southern edge of the cornfield.[40] Moore's team rested at right angles to the rear of his gun, with the lead pair immediately behind the cannon.[41] The shooting had

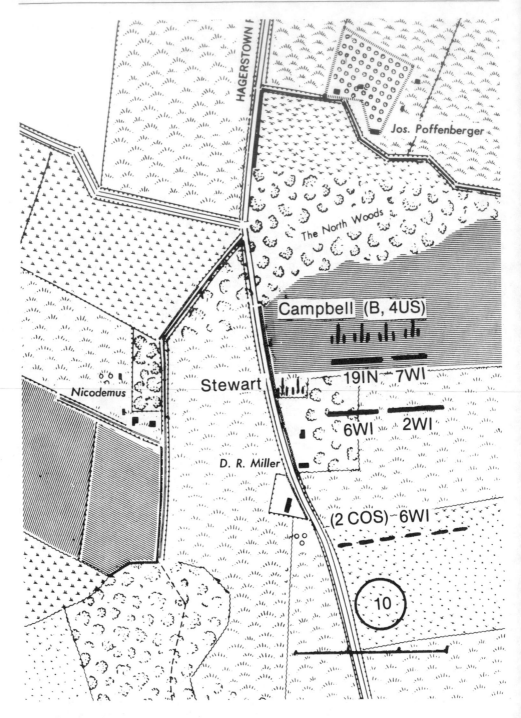

(Map 10) DAWN TO 6:20 A.M., SEPTEMBER 17, 1862

The Federal positions around D. R. Miller's farm.

gotten very hot. Poague ordered his crews to fire due north to silence a Federal section (Lt. James Stewart's section, Btty. B, 4th U.S.) which harrassed his position. The twenty pounders across the Antietam made his post very uncomfortable. A huge shell ricocheted off the ground behind Moore's gun and passed, unexploded, between the pants seat of his quick thinking lead driver and his saddle. The soldier had thrown himself upon his mount's neck without a second to spare.[42] Nearby lay the horse with three feet. Moore had blown out the loyal animal's brains with his service revolver to end its suffering. The battery, having quickly fired one round per gun, retired through Grigsby's waiting line.[43]

Jackson's very weary veterans caught their first glimpses of the advancing Federals as the sun broke through and the ground fog began to evaporate. Lieutenant Ezra Stickley (A Co., 5th VA) hardly believed what he saw. He and the men around him were awed by the spectacle before them. Over one thousand Federals advanced toward them at the "common time" as if on parade. The first rank carried its arms leveled at the waist. The rear rank carried its at the shoulder. The bayonets of Duryee's Brigade glistened ominously above the green corn.[44] To his left front, with its left flank partially concealed in the West Woods, lay Jones' Brigade with Grigsby's to its right. Both outfits were prone on the reverse slope of a slight ridge, well hidden by the tall grass and the worm fence which ran across their front.[45] Poague's gunners were working their pieces hard to the rear of the line.

Colonel Grigsby ordered his men up. "Forward, charge bayonets, common time! March!"

Ezra Stickley (5th VA) went to mount as a Federal battery rapidly walked three explosive rounds toward the brigade. The first struck about one hundred fifty yards to the south. The second fell seventy-five yards closer. The third burst in Stickley's horse as he prepared to mount. The explosion violently hurled the aide to the ground and splattered the horse all over the field.

Looking up from his gory puddle, the young man realized that what was left of his horse was going to fall on him. He immediately jumped up and stumbled into the horrified line of infantry, where two men caught him to keep him from collapsing.

As the grimy veterans supported the bloody lieutenant, he numbly realized the extent of his injuries. The shell had torn off his right arm, which dangled lifelessly by shreds of skin from his shoulder. It had also ripped the flesh off his right side, broken a rib, and bruised his lung. As the men shoved him onto the saddle of another horse to evacuate him, Stickley realized why his right glove had disappeared.[46]

Nearby, Lieutenant Alfred Kelly (21st VA) and his horse pitched sideways into a tree. A shell fragment slammed into his right leg above the knee and hurled them down as a body. The lieutenant crawled away, badly jarred but still ambulatory.

(His regiment fared much worse. Only nineteen of its sixty-eight men walked out of the fighting around the Cornfield.)[47]

The Mumma Farm

On the far right of the Confederate line, near Mumma's, Major Thomas C. Glover (21st GA., Trimble's Brigade) obtained permission to move his small regiment northeast to the high ground along the Smoketown Road, near the family cemetery. Captain James Nisbet (H Co.) commanded the left wing of the regiment, which lay behind a post and rail fence on top of a limestone outcropping. Since dawn, the soldiers had been popping off rounds at the 2nd and 13th Pennsylvania Reserves, neither of which would leave the security of the East Woods.[48] The brave captain anchored himself behind a rock ledge next to a red-headed Irishman named John C. Smith (H. Co.). "Smitty's" blood was up.

Every time he fired, he would roll onto his back and chirp in his brogue, "I got another one of those Blue Bellies that time!"

"Take care, Smith," the captain cautioned him, "they'll get you."

The stubborn private ignored the advice. About fifteen to twenty minutes later, a rifle ball glanced between the rocks behind which the two men had taken cover. Smith bounced away from the fence and flopped onto his back, screaming for a stretcher.

"I'm shot through the paunch," he cried.

Nisbet grimly noted the blood rolling from Smith's front and back as the litter bearers tossed his body onto their canvas pallet and hustled him away. The captain snatched up the soldier's idle rifle and defied military regulation by firing it. He had a bully time putting Smith's remaining cartridges to good use.[49]

The Cornfield

Duryee's Brigade had inadvertently become the advance unit of the Federal column while the Iron Brigade lay in Miller's field. By 6:00 A.M., it arrived at the southern end of the cornfield and the low Virginia rail fence which separated it from the clover field north of the Smoketown Road. Gibbon's Brigade had been advancing rather steadily, about one hundred twenty-five yards behind Duryee until Jackson's left brigade (Jones') rose en masse and fired into the 6th Wisconsin's five right companies as they crossed into the field west of the Hagerstown Pike.[50] Almost simultaneously, Lawton's Brigade stood up in the clover field to the front of Duryee's line and volleyed point-blank into the Federals. Men toppled like ten pins! Screams and curses rent the air. The Yankees retired and laid down behind the rail fence and exchanged volleys with the exposed Rebel line. (Map 11)

Lieutenant Colonel Bragg (6th WI) staggered in the wake of Jackson's first volley. While pulling his five companies back between the fence rows along the Hagerstown Pike, he sent Sergeant Major Howard J. Huntington bounding into the corn to find Major Dawes.

The sergeant major found Dawes and his line pinned by excessive musketry and shell bursts. Bullets pocked the dirt all around them.

"Major," Huntington screamed, "Colonel Bragg wants to see you, quick, at the turnpike."   .

Dawes loped after the sergeant only to hear the colonel mutter, "Major, I am shot" before he crumbled to the ground. Noticing a tear in the side of Bragg's great coat, the major ordered two enlisted men to carry him rearward. They rolled their colonel, whom they believed to be mortally wounded, onto a shelter half and stumbled north.[51]

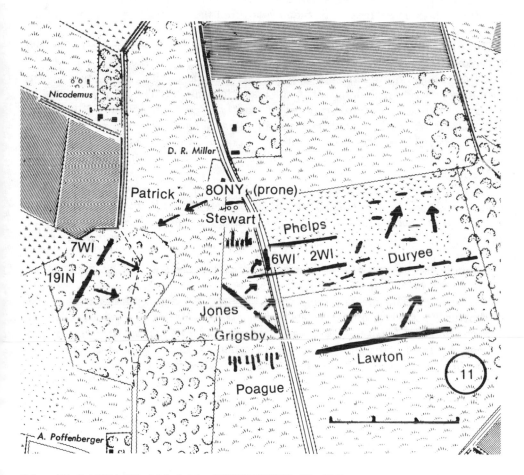

(Map 11) DAWN TO 6:20 A.M., SEPTEMBER 17, 1862
The initial fighting in the Cornfield.

As the soldiers disappeared deeper into the corn, Dawes spied a group of Confederate staff officers near the eastern face of the West Woods. Enlisted men handed him six rifles in rapid succession while the major, who used the top fence rail for support, snapped off rounds at the gathering and dispersed them.[52]

Bullets whizzed through the air from the front and the left. Confederate skirmishers slipped into the cornfield between the two leading Union brigades and picked off men at insanely close ranges. The 2nd Wisconsin lost Lieutenant Colonel Thomas S. Allen, who was wounded. His blood splattered the cornstalks about him.[53] First Sergeant William H. Harris (B Co., 2nd WI) dropped his rifle and stumbled rearward. Blood flowed freely from his left breast and the corners of his mouth. He mistakenly thought he was dying.[54]

Dawes hurriedly ordered his people to guide left, deeper into the relative security of the tall corn.[55] In so doing, he accidentally left the 7th Wisconsin and the 19th Indiana isolated in the northern most part of the West Woods, where Gibbon had sent them to secure the right from a possible flank attack.[56] The movement also uncovered Patrick's Brigade which had been detached west, across the Pike, to support the 19th Indiana.[57] Several batteries went into action east of Miller's and death was everywhere.

As the left wing of the 6th Wisconsin filed further into the corn, Dawes noticed that the right wing (three companies), under Captain Kellogg, did not follow. He immediately sent Sergeant Major Huntington to find the captain. The intrepid sergeant raced into the bullet-swept road and found the officer hugging the ground behind his men.

Huntington shouted, "If it is practicable, move forward the right companies, aligning it with the left wing."

"Please give Major Dawes my compliments," Kellogg replied, "and say it is impracticable; the fire is murderous."

The Sergeant Major nodded in agreement and bolted away into the swaying corn. Dawes was not impressed with the good captain's response and he again ordered the right wing into the corn. As Huntington double quicked a second time to the right, a bullet plucked him off his feet! Bruised and bleeding, the undaunted soldier painfully regained his feet and relayed his order to Kellogg.

The captain immediately obeyed only to have his men mown down like hay. He ordered them prone again. The rest of the brigade pressed forward with Phelps' small outfit until the two brigades were dangerously close to one another.[58]

The Pry House

From a bald hill on the eastern bank of the Antietam, near Pry's house, George McClellan and his small army of aides and the general staff assembled to safely observe what he hoped would be the complete destruction of "Bobby" Lee's ragtag army. Two civilians had just joined the general's coterie to share in the excitement of the day.

Frank Schell, special artist for "Leslie's", had awakened in Keedysville to the thunder of the opposing batteries. Mounting, he whipped his horse toward the Pry house. Once there, he dismounted and pushed his way through the throng of couriers about the headquarters. He wanted to get a grand view of the engagement. The knoll was alive with prancing horses and panting men. Not far off, he spotted McClellan with his close friend, Major General Fitz Porter, and several other officers. All were on foot. The reporter quietly edged himself into the milling group, hoping to catch a tasty bit of information.[59]

Nearby, unobserved by Schell, a matronly looking lady stood with a portly, balding general who sported great mutton chop whiskers.[60] Both had their glasses fixed upon the hills to the west.

It seemed as if everyone had their eyes transfixed on the unobtrusive white church and the arch of Confederate artillery which stretched eastward from it. The smoke billowing from their weapons rolled down the hills to the creek. It began as a series of huge sulfuric clouds which dissipated into stringy vapors as the morning breeze swept the smoke toward the Antietam. The Federal infantry was nowhere to be seen. The Confederate lines, which were apparently prone, were barely visible. Wisps of smoke from the West Woods and from the swale south of the Smoketown Road betrayed their positions.[61] The smoke rose in sheets from the ground like steam from a sewer on a chilly day.

The general with the mutton chop whiskers, without regard for the woman by his side, gave a court order to an aide and the fellow dashed away. Almost as hurriedly, the woman sheathed her binoculars and scurried away, skirts in hand, toward the Pry house. Her deep brown eyes were dark with worry.[62]

The West Woods

"Old Jack" (Thomas J. Jackson) sat astride his horse, south of Jones' Brigade, with his eyes locked upon the ground beneath his horse's feet.[63] To his right, in a very exposed position, Poague's Battery hammered the Federal guns above Miller's.[64]

Sergeant Ed Moore kept feverishly working what was left of his crew. A twenty pound shell gutted or mangled all the horses and the three outriders of one of his guns, among them the driver who had successfully dodged an earlier attempt upon his life. Moore felt ill. Between rounds, he snatched glimpses of Jackson. Rider and horse both had their heads bowed in apparent contemplation. The morose, stern officer seemed oblivious to the bullets which clipped the trees about his head. He ignored the considerable numbers of his men who were straggling rearward. When his thirteen year old orderly, Charles Randolph, nervously ran up to him and pointed frantically from one part of the field to another, the general listened, but still kept his eyes upon the ground.[65]

Presently, a shout went up from his old brigade. A shell exploded directly over the line. Men crumbled and the line bolted forward.[66]

The Cornfield

The Yankees faltered. Rebels successfully infiltrated the corn between the Federal brigades and were "using up" the enemy at very close range. The Yankees buckled momentarily, regrouped, then surged forward again.[67]

Jones' Brigade started to retire under the increased pressure. Men halted in small groups to fire, then dodge between the swaying corn stalks. Things were getting rough all over.

Lieutenant Alger M. Wheeler (B Co., 21st NY), while glancing to the left, along his company's front, noticed that Charlie Johnson (B Co.) seemed to be in convulsions. As he approached the enlisted man, he embarrassingly discovered that the private was giggling uncontrollably.

Johnson quickly shut his mouth to stifle himself, but his cheeks bulged out; he coughed and another peel of laughter erupted from him. Lieutenant Wheeler bared his sword to slap the private with the flat of the blade when General Patrick bellowed for the brigade to move by the right flank, across the Hagerstown Pike.[68]

Five Federal regiments dashed across the open ground, heading west toward the northern tip of the West Woods. These were the 7th Wisconsin and Patrick's four New York regiments. Part way across the open ground, the last regiment, the 80th New York (20th N.Y. State Militia) peeled away from the column and fell in on the reverse slope of the crest near Miller's barn, facing south. (The 19th Indiana was already in the West Woods.) Stewart's section (B, 4th U.S.) careened into the hay field, about fifty yards to the front of Jones Brigade.[69]

Patrick's Brigade and two of Gibbon's regiments (I Corps) moved into and toward the northern tip of the West Woods to secure the Corps' right flank. Stewart's section of Battery B, 4th U. S. Artillery moved onto the high ground east of them to provide support while the rest of the Corps pressed south and southwest from the Cornfield and the East Woods against the Confederates in the middle and southern sections of the West Woods and those near Mumma's.

CHAPTER THREE

"My heart . . . is melted in the midst of my bowels."

6:25 A.M. until 7:00 A.M.

The Pry House

Frank Schell snapped his eyes toward General McClellan when he called over Fitz Porter and pointed toward the West Woods. The other officers clustered around their commander-in-chief, chattering and clucking terribly.[1] The reporter locked his glasses upon the woods then shifted them toward the right. His heart thumped uncontrollably as a thrilling spectacle rolled across the fields to his front.

The Cornfield

Major Rufus Dawes (6th WI.) felt his heart racing too, but from fear. Blue coated soldiers from Duryee's Brigade were running back through the corn by squads, having withstood all that they could bear.[2] A huge gap stretched between the left flank of the 2nd Wisconsin and the East Woods, where Duryee's men had been. The small arms fire to the right slackened off a bit as the Federal batteries, in the fields to the north, slammed the West Woods. The Iron Brigade and Phelps' Brigade moved forward through the corn.

The 2nd Wisconsin right wheeled. The 6th Wisconsin, aided by its right wing which had finally moved into the corn, followed suit.[3] They left Captain Werner Von Bachelle's corpse (F Co.) in the Pike under the protective watch of his beautiful Newfoundland dog. The loyal animal, which the former French officer had taught to salute, refused to leave his master's side. (Two days later, the men found the dog — dead — across the captain's body. They buried them together.)[4] With the green jacketed 2nd U.S. Sharpshooters (Phelps' Brigade) as the hinge along the Hagerstown Pike, the entire brigade began to execute a grand right wheel through the corn toward the clover field above the Smoketown Road. Adjutant Lewis C. Parmelee (2nd US SS) and a private from A Company (2nd US SS) spotted a Confederate flag fastened to a fence post along the Pike. The lieutenant beat the enlisted man to the prize but was shot dead by the Rebels who were hiding behind the fence. He fell, struck by five rounds, which splattered his blood on the rails. The private wrenched the colors from the grasp of a Confederate who attempted to save them and headed north. Nearby, Lieutenant "Jack" Whitman was killed while trying to lead his men into the fray.[5] As the Yankees approached the low split rail fence which separated them from the Confederates, instinct overcame discipline. The men automatically popped their weapons off their shoulders into their sweating palms. The line halted, without orders, and ripped off a ragged volley at Lawton's Butternuts, who had risen and simultaneously unleashed a well directed volley.[6]

Corn stalks flew apart as if hit by a dull scythe. Men dropped or were hurled like discarded rag dolls to the ground, as Phelps' New Yorkers stampeded into the rear ranks of the Wisconsin regiments.

The outnumbered Confederates stubbornly retired toward the West Woods. The soldiers halted every now and then to load and fire. Hays' Brigade (5th, 6th, 7th, 8th, and 14th LA), having come to Lawton's support, also started to pull out. Ammunition had gotten too low to sustain combat.[7]

The Wisconsin regiments, their thinning ranks having been filled with the New Yorkers from Phelps' line, bolted the fence and advanced steadily, firing as they went. Officers and men alike feverishly tore cartridges, loaded, and fired. Wounded men passed their weapons to the uninjured around them. They kept getting closer to the batteries around the Dunker Church.

More and more Federals started to drop. With each additional casualty, a man or two turned tail and headed back to the corn.[8] The charge was losing its drive. The line fell back to the rail fence.[9]

The astonished Confederates hastily regrouped and, despite their dwindling numbers, rushed back to their former positions, which were not too difficult to locate. The corpses of their comrades in butternut clearly delineated their old battle lines.[10]

On the right, Trimble's Brigade, less the 21st Georgia, fell back, leaving a dangerous gap between Lawton's right and Ripley's left, which was on the lane north of Mumma's. Colonel H. B. Strong, commanding Hays' Brigade and part of Lawton's, ordered hs regiments into the still thick corn to the left of the prone 2nd Wisconsin in an attempt to curl up the Federal flank.[11] *(Map 12)*

The Mumma Farm

Major Thomas C. Glover (21st GA) sought out Colonel James Walker (C.O. Trimble's Brigade). He realized that his men were wasting their ammunition on the Yankees, who had retired beyond the effective range of their weapons. He asked Walker for permission to fill the void left by Hays' advance. Lawton's men absorbed two aimed volleys from the men on the southern edge of the cornfield and were getting used up fast.

Walker gave the order for the 21st Georgia to move out. As his aide delivered the command to the regiment, a ball struck Major Glover through the body and sent him to the ground — severely wounded.[12]

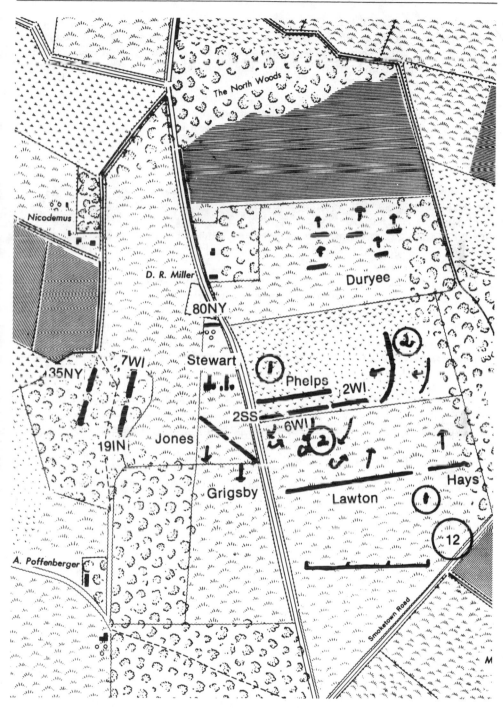

(Map 12) 6:25 A.M. — 7:00 A.M., SEPTEMBER 17, 1862
Lawton and Hays attempt to turn Gibbon's left flank.

Captain James Nisbet (H Co.), being the senior captain, immediately assumed command. He ordered the regiment to doublequick toward the left along the Smoketown Road. The rugged Georgians charged in open order toward the first of the two fences which bordered the road when a volley from the East Woods caught them on the front.

Men slumped over the fence rails — dead. Captain Nisbet never saw the bulk of his command scramble into the shallow depression cut by the road. As he swung his legs over the top rail of the worm fence on the southern side of the road, a round struck him square in the gut and sent him flopping into the packed dirt. More bullets kicked up the ground around him. He did not move.[13]

Brigadier General Roswell Ripley, whose regiments held Mumma's lane and orchard, quickly grasped the situation and responded immediately. Colonel William A. Christian's Brigade (the 88th, and 90th PA, and the 26th and 94th NY) having pushed deeper into the East Woods without their commander, who had deserted them from safer ground, tried to blast the socks off the 21st Georgia.[14] It also turned its attention upon Ripley's men.

Outnumbered, Ripley prepared for the worst. While his men fired into the advancing Blue Coats, the general ordered Colonel William L. DeRossett (3rd NC) to torch Mumma's house and barn. He had to deny the Federals any decent cover should he be forced to retire. *(Map 13)*

(Daniel Mumma, the family's eldest boy, with his younger brother, Samuel, Jr., and their friend had found the house a shambles when they stole into it on the afternoon of the 16th. The place had been ransacked. Sam and the other boy left Dan alone in the house that night.

Dan had bolted the door to discourage any further looting. Shortly after Sam left, he slipped through an open window on the ground floor and hid in the upper level of the spring house. By daylight on the 17th, he was long gone.[15])

Sergeant Major James Clarke and six other "volunteers" from A Company, 3rd North Carolina, pounded furiously against the door of the house. It would not budge. Bullets chinked brick fragments off the wall around the detachment. Armed only with torches from their morning cook fires, the seven Rebels felt very insecure. As they slipped around to a protected side of the house, they discovered the open window which Dan Mumma had forgotten to close during his escape.

One of the men flipped his torch into the empty room, while Clarke took the rest of the party toward the barn. A bullet struck the sergeant major in the arm, but did not drop him. He finished his assignment and returned his men, unscathed, to the regiment before he reported to Ripley, who immediately sent him with orders to the 4th and 44th Georgia regiments (Ripley's left regiments).[16]

Ripley's concentrated fire stymied Christian's advance. Hays' Brigade, which had rushed recklessly into

COLONEL WILLIAM DE-ROSSETT, 3rd North Carolina

He ordered a squad under the command of Sergeant Major James Clarke to burn Mumma's house and barn. *(Clarke, NC Regts.)*

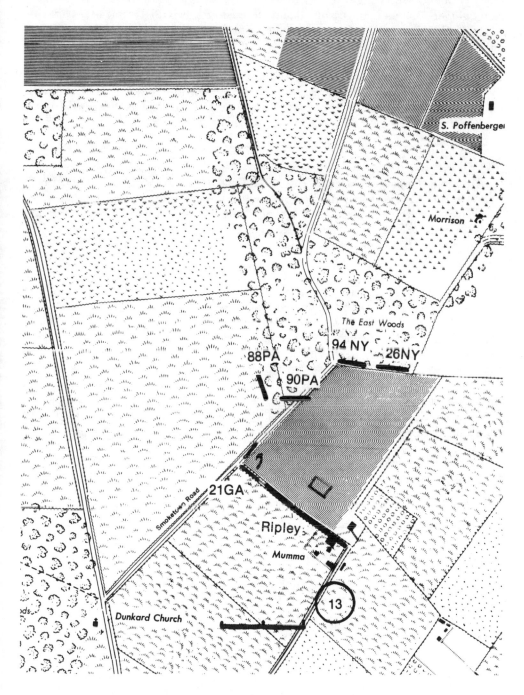

(Map 13) 6:25 A.M. — 7:00 A.M., SEPTEMBER 17, 1862
Christian's Brigade stalls Ripley and the 21st Georgia.

the fray, found itself caught in a vicious crossfire. Stuart's batteries, on Nicodemus Heights, were pounding the cornfield and the East Woods with a tremendous amount of shells. S. D. Lee's Battalion, including Jordan's advanced section, were thinning out the cornstalks to Hays' front. Matthews' gunners (F, 1st PA. Artillery) were pouring Federal shells into the clover field from the north. The 88th Pennsylvania (2/2/I) volleyed into Hays' right flank.[17] Ammunition was getting scarce.[18]

Huge gaps appeared in the line. Colonel H. B. Strong (6th LA) lay dead with his horse upon the field, near the western face of the East Woods.[19] Without warning, a new Federal brigade made its appearance from the north.

The North Woods

Brigadier General George L. Hartsuff's Brigade (12th and 13th MA, 83rd NY, and 11th PA, 2/I), less Hartsuff who was shot in the side as the brigade moved out, was closing on the cornfield from Joseph Poffenberger's woods. The 11th Pennsylvania, with the 12th and 13th Massachusetts regiments to its left, respectively, marched through the open ground above the cornfield with the 83rd New York on the left flank in the East Woods.[20]

Corporal Jim Stearns (K Co., 13th MA) fought to keep his bloodshot eyes open. As the brigade crossed Miller's plowed field and passed around Reynolds' Battery (L, 1st NY), he clearly saw Lawton's and Hays' men halted and waiting on the southern edge of what had once been a lush cornfield. He could also see S. D. Lee's guns along the Dunker Church ridge. They made themselves known immediately. As soon as the 13th cleared the North Woods, the cannons nearest the white church opened fire.

The first round whizzed safely overhead; the second fell closer to the line. As the regiment stepped over the split rail fence which separated the plowed and mown grass fields, Stearns cast an anxious glance to the rear and watched a third shell send a handfull of Magilton's Pennsylvanians to the ground while they hesitated near the southern edge of the North Woods.

The place reverberated with hundreds of explosions. Stearns advanced but a few paces into the cornfield when something struck him solidly on the right side. His sergeant watched him collapse into a quivering lump upon a corn hill.

The sergeant immediately rolled Stearns over. The dazed corporal could barely understand him. Before he knew it, Captain Charles H. Hovey (K Co.) had rushed up and asked him if he was hurt.

"Not much," Stearns painfully gasped as he clutched his bleeding side. "Lost wind."

Hovey told him to sit still until he was able to follow. A breath later, another shell exploded within a few feet of Stearns, which aroused the corporal and sent him scrambling after his regiment.

Rejoining his company, he stepped over the rail fence into the field above the Smoketown Road.[21]

The Cornfield

The 12th Massachusetts had fallen prone, while Thompson's Battery (C, PA) unlimbered and cut loose over the regiment toward Poague's Battery near the West

Woods. The Rebel fire did not slacken. Presently, the 12th rose to its feet and pressed on toward the corn, where it caught up with the 13th at the sturdy rail fence along the northern edge of the cornfield. A direct hit scattered rails and men through the grass.

The Massachusetts soldiers scrambled over the remaining sections of fence and pushed into the corn. As the 13th Massachusetts and the 83rd New York flushed Hays' Louisianans across the 12th's left front, the men fired scattered rounds after them.[22] (Map 14)

Remnants of Hays' and Lawton's Brigades had fallen into a line about halfway across the clover field south of the cornfield.[23] They saw the entire Federal line rise up by impulse along the southern edge of the cornfield as Hartsuff's men filled the gap between the Federal left and the East Woods. The Yankees' long bayonets glistened in the sun. The Confederates immediately fired and Hartsuff's three regiments in the corn began to return the fire.[24]

The Federals shot down the colors of the 13th Georgia. The severely wounded Colonel Marcellus Douglass (C.O., Lawton's BG), while glancing back to check on the Federals, happened to see the flag fall in a depression several yards south of the Cornfield. He immediately asked a boy in the ranks to recover it. The child soldier raced to within a few feet of Hartsuff's Yankees, snatched up the tattered standard, and ran back toward the colonel. Two bullets thudded into the youngster but he kept moving.

Colonel Douglass lived long enough to see the flag in his troop's possession. As the volunteer reached the thinning Confederate line, the colonel collapsed with his eighth and last gunshot wound.[25]

The West Woods

The right half of the Federal line did not halt. The 2nd U.S. Sharpshooters, the 6th Wisconsin, and the 2nd Wisconsin joined in the blood letting. The air reeked with death. The soldiers along the eastern side of the Hagerstown Pike went berserk. Many men shouted and cried. Some had tears rolling down their faces while they hysterically loaded and fired. Scores of them were struck down as they clamored over the split rail fence and right wheeled toward the Dunker Church.[26]

"Old Jack" finally sparked to life. What was left of his men were running from the field. Gathering his staff, he and Poague's gunners tried to halt them, but to no avail. Time and again, the general heard, "No ammunition. No ammunition."[27]

What remained of Jackson's old brigade was stubbornly holding its own original position. Suddenly, a section of Yankee artillery (Stewart's B, 4th U.S.) opened fire upon his front. Two rounds in quick succession burst overhead. General John R. Jones, his division commander, fell from his horse — unconscious.[28] A pair of very willing volunteers dragged him to the rear.

Starke's Brigade (1st, 2nd, 9th, 10th, and 15th LA, and the Louisiana Tigers) and Taliaferro's Brigade (47th and 48th AL, and the 10th, 23rd, and 37th VA) stepped out at the double quick from the West Woods near the Dunker Church to come to Jones' and Grigsby's aid. A courier from Jackson accelerated their pace. Jones was down. William Starke, now division commander, seized the flag of a retreating

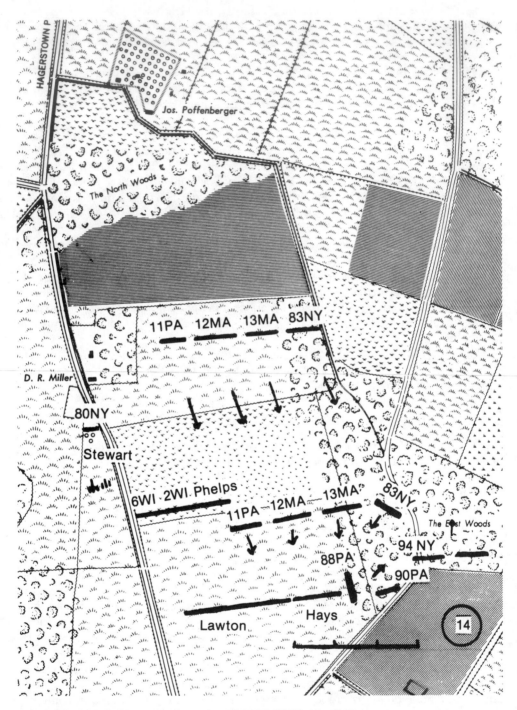

(Map 14) 6:25 A.M. — 7:00 A.M., SEPTEMBER 17, 1862
Hartsuff's Brigade saves Gibbon and Phelps in the Cornfield.

regiment in a futile attempt to rally it. A burst of small arms fire from the wheeling Yankees snuffed out his life. He fell dead upon the field, bleeding from at least four wounds.[29] The two Confederate brigades automatically changed front and charged into the Yankees along the Hagerstown Pike.[30] *(Map 15)*

The Federal riflery decimated both brigades before they reached the road. Second Lieutenant Richard P. Jennings (E Co., 23rd VA) led his seven man company into action. Five of them were hit before going a few paces beyond the West Woods. Jennings pulled a rifle and cartridge box from one of the corpses and dashed toward the Hagerstown Pike.

He dove to the ground alongside the road just as a Federal soldier mounted the fence rails above him. The lieutenant instinctively raised himself and fired upward. An exploding shell overhead obliterated the report of his weapon; a fragment struck him in the hip and knocked him to his hands. Rolling several steps to one side, Jennings took cover behind a large tree stump with Captain Thomas S. Michaels (F Co., 23rd VA) and a lieutenant from the 48th Virginia.

A corporal from one of the 23rd Virginia's other companies stood by the stump loading and firing deliberately. The three officers begged the enlisted man to lie down. He refused. Shortly after, a bullet passed over Jennings' legs and carried away the other lieutenant's knee caps. A second ball struck Captain Michaels' ankle. A third snuffed out the corporal. His lifeless hands clawed Jennings' face as his body toppled over the three of them.

"I am going out from here," Jennings blurted.

"Do not try it, Lieutenant," Captain Michaels insisted, "you will be killed before you can reach the timber."

R. P. Jennings bluntly told the captain he preferred to die game than lying where he was. With that, he painfully got to his feet and made for the West Woods. He had barely limped three steps when a burst of musketry, which flew around him "like a swarm of bees", jolted him to life.

"I just let out and ran like a deer," he recalled, "and made it to the timber, but I was almost scared to death when I got there."[31]

The Dunker Church

Wofford's Brigade (Hampton's Legion, 18th GA, 1st TX, 4th TX, and 5th TX) rested in a ravine along the southern and western sides of the West Woods. The commissary staff had finally issued three days' rations to the starving troops — a very small slab of bacon and a fistful of flour to each man. Private J. M. Polk (I Co., 4th TX) quietly hunkered down in front of a small fire to bake his bread. Not having a three legged skillet, he added water to his flour, kneaded it into dough and wrapped it around his ramrod. He had just put the rod over the flame when a bursting shell rolled the man near him into a ball with a snapped leg.

Immediately, the small brigade fell in and prepared to advance. Polk shakily noted that they were going into action with company sized regiments and a battalion sized brigade. He knew the odds had to be about four to one in the Yankees' favor.[32]

The West Woods

Lieutenant James Stewart's artillerists (B, 4th U.S.) had fired their third round of case at the clearing north of the Dunker Church when Starke's soldiers broke

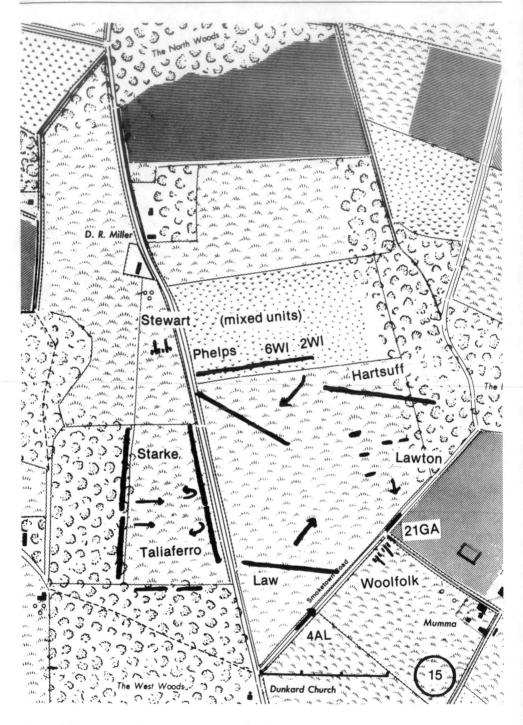

(Map 15) 6:25 A.M. — 7:00 A.M., SEPTEMBER 17, 1862
Phelps and Gibbon try to take the West Woods.

for the hollow to his front, then darted across the road into the corn.[33] His section was posted on the crest of Miller's southern hayfield to the immediate front of two huge hay mounds. The southern edge of Miller's cornfield was about one hundred twenty feet to his left front.[34]

The burly Scot prowled between his two crews. He was thinking fast. Captain Campbell, the battery commander, had sent him into a virtually untenable position. The 80th New York (Patrick's Brigade) was concealed in a deep creek hollow near Miller's barn to his rear, where Stuart's gunners had pinned it. The Federal troops in the West Woods to his right front, had disappeared into a swale, thereby greatly restricting his field of fire. Something had to be done soon. Rebel snipers, in the corn to his left, started harrassing his men. Within a couple of minutes, they cooly picked off three of his men as if they were at a shooting match.[35] His people could not do much to stop them. The Johnnies calmly propped their weapons on the fence rails along the Pike and squeezed off rounds.[36]

The North Woods

Things along the Federal line turned terribly sour. As Hartsuff's men started to pass through the North Woods, the Pennsylvania Reserves took a fearful drubbing. Minies whizzed through the air thick as bees. Frank Holsinger (F Co.), whose regiment, the 8th Pennsylvania Reserves, held the extreme left of the line behind the 3rd Pennsylvania Reserves, felt quite humbled by the awesome circumstances in which he found himself.[37] Shells burst in the tree tops, showering the men with cords of wood. The bullets, which whacked into the tree trunks, unnerved him, but he dared not crack.[38]

Major General George G. Meade, the division commander, paced his mount back and forth behind the line. His huge, protruberant eyes seemed more pronounced with his rage. As the 8th moved out with the rest of the brigade toward the southern edge of the North Woods, one man broke and ran for the safety of a big tree.

"Get that man in the ranks!" Meade commanded.

A sergeant ran over to the soldier and tried to urge him back into line but he was not forceful enough to suit the general.

"I'll move him!" Meade yelled.

Dashing his mount up to the tree, Meade whipped out his sabre and sent the shirker sprawling with a deliberate blow across his back.

Frank Holsinger (F Co.) held his place, trying to quiet his disgust for the evil tempered officer. He felt that it was bad enough to get rubbed out by the Johnnies, much less by his own people.

When the line halted in the clearing just on the northern fringe of the plowed field, Holsinger felt more queasy. The men stood at their arms. No cowards there. No lying down. Meade wanted men, not yellow bellies.

The soldiers grew more listless as the seconds wore into minutes. Some rested on one foot, then on the other, like children waiting for a pass to the outhouse. Someone prayed quietly. Only his lips moved. The occasional sickening thud of a round striking home punctuated the nerve-wracking silence along the line.

Suddenly, Private Joseph Maugle (F Co.), who stood near Holsinger, chirped up in his high nasal twang, "Damned sharp skirmishing in front."

A soldier laughed. Then another. Within seconds, the entire regiment had picked up on the absurdity of his crack. Smiles glimmered and faded. Dying seemed kind of humorous.[39]

The Cornfield

About 1,150 yards south of the North Woods, no one laughed as the magnificent charge of the Wisconsin and New York regiments died in its steps. Hartsuff's Brigade halted to exchange rounds with the 21st Georgia and Hays' pitiful handful of Rebels.

The Confederate infantry and their gunners were taking out Yankees in squads. The command of the 12th Massachusetts devolved upon a captain and the regiment's dead lay in piles.[40] Men went rearward, wounded in the hands from muskets which had been shattered by rifle fire. Shells gouged terrible furrows through the field, taking men down in groups. Canteens were shot away from their straps and haversacks were shredded to rags by the fierce musketry as men died by the score. Private Joseph Blake saw Corporal Dick Mann (B Co.), who was carrying the state colors, stagger off the field in a daze, the result of an untended wound which he received earlier in the fighting.[41]

Corporal Jim Stearns (K Co., 13th MA), his bruised side still thumping from his collision with a shell, found himself loading and firing mechanically. While loading, he noticed a good friend in D Company throw up his arms and flop to the ground. The man's body twitched once, before he died.

The corporal had gotten too involved in his work to see much of what was happening around him.

"Close up to the right," Captain Charles Hovey (K Co.) screamed.

Jim Stearns gasped. The men to his right were down — most of them dead. Instinctively, he passed the word to Henry Gassett (K Co.), the first man to his left.

As the corporal sidestepped, Gassett threw down his rifle and ran to the rear, shouting, "Jim, I'm hit."

Henry barely went seventeen feet before collapsing to the ground. Stearns trotted after him.

"Where ya hurt?"

Before Gassett could answer, the captain ran up, telling Stearns to take Henry to the rear. The regiment could not hold out much longer, he explained, and there was no sense in getting trampled to death.

Lifting Henry up, Stearns threw his right arm around the wounded man's waist and started toward the East Woods.[42]

The West Woods — The Cornfield

On the Federal right, near the Hagerstown Pike, the situation disintegrated from possible victory to a staggering rout. About half way through the clover field, the line abruptly halted. The Yankees' weapons were too fouled to use. Men had to pound the ramrods home to seat their shots.

A long, unbroken line of Confederates swarmed out from around the Dunker Church. They fired by files as they approached the trapped New Yorkers and

Westerners on the western flank. Men fell like grass beneath a scythe.

A panicked soldier shrieked, "Now save who can."

Rifles clattered to the ground as shoulder straps and enlisted men alike raced back to Miller's corn. Private Silas Howard (E Co., 2nd US SS) who had been shot several times, including once through the chest, defiantly jerked the firing block from his Sharps rifle and hurled it as far as he could. Since he expected to die, he was not about to give the Rebs a serviceable weapon. Major Rufus Dawes (6th WI) felt a sharp sting on the back of his calf, but kept on running.[43]

Hood's rugged Division (Law's and Wofford's Brigades), screaming like mad men, bolted into the high ground above S. D. Lee's Battalion and pressed for the Cornfield, while most of Starke's and Taliaferro's badly mauled units retreated to the West Woods. The soul chilling Rebel yell echoed across the smoke covered field as Hood's wild men charged across the bloodied ground between the Cornfield and the Smoketown Road. Law's men (the 2nd and 11th MS, and the 6th NC) moved toward the Federals in a northeasterly line, while his last regiment, the 4th Alabama, moved by the right flank down the Smoketown Road toward the East Woods.[44]

The Texas Brigade (the 18th GA, Hampton's Legion, and the 1st, 4th, and 5th TX) came up, close upon its heels. About halfway through the field, Law halted his people to meet Hartsuff's volleys. The 4th and 5th Texas regiments, which were right behind the 11th Mississippi, nearly collided with its rear rank. Lieutenant Colonel R F Carter (4th TX) immediately ordered his men prone and cautioned them not to fire until they could definitely identify the troops to their front as friend or foe.[45] Lieutenant W. H. Sellers, Hood's aide, simultaneously made the 5th Texas lie down.[46] The 18th Georgia, with Hampton's Legion and the 1st Texas raced across the Hagerstown Pike into the clover field.[47] The Georgians triggered a rolling fusilade from their hips into the remnants of the 6th and 2nd Wisconsin, which had halted to deliver one more volley before disappearing into the Cornfield.[48] The diminutive Hampton's Legion (seventy-seven effectives), as it brought up the left of the line to the eastern side of the Hagerstown Pike, ran directly into Lieutenant James Stewart's case rounds.[49] (Map 16)

Private Elliott Welch (Hampton's Legion), who stood near the colors, helplessly watched Herod Wilson (F Co.) go down. Color Corporal James E. Estes (E Co.), who ripped the flag from Wilson's death grasp, lay a few paces beyond. C. P. Poppenheim, a German from A Company, managed to stagger a few rods further with the colors before a bullet coldly snuffed him out. Major J. H. Dingle, Jr. feverishly snatched up the banner. Waving them wildly, he stepped out on foot, yelling, "Legion, follow your colors!" The South Carolinians, their blood up, rallied and darted insanely toward the southwest corner of the Cornfield.[50]

Lieutenant James Stewart (B, 4th U.S.) fumed with rage. In the few minutes he had been in Miller's hayfield, the Rebels knocked out half of his two crews.[51] Confederates seemed to be everywhere to his front and left. Minie balls zinged off the barrels and the gun carriages in a nerve-wracking staccato.

The entire I Corps started to bend like a twig. As Law's men struck toward the East Woods, the entire shebang snapped!

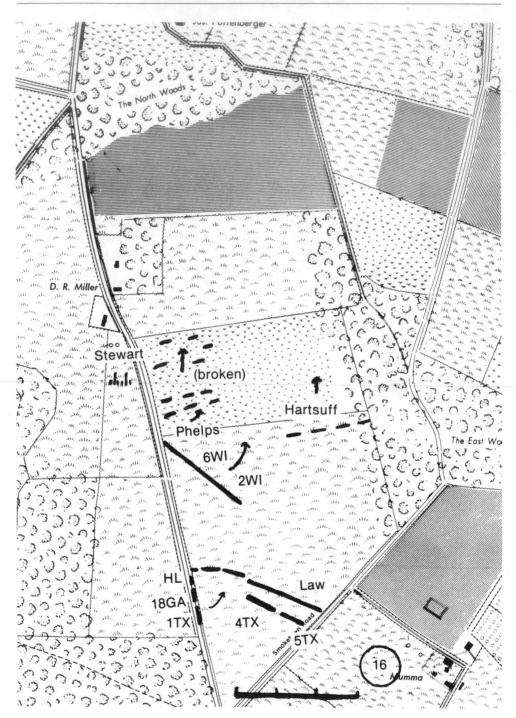

(Map 16) 6:25 A.M. — 7:00 A.M., SEPTEMBER 17, 1862
Hood's division thwarts the Federal charge from the Cornfield.

The Smoketown Road

"Crawl down here, Captain!"

James Nisbet (H Co., 21st GA) cautiously raised his thumping head. Through dazed eyes, he saw blurred arms frantically making obscure gestures at him. Dirt sporadically stung his face. His right side and stomach felt stiff.

As his head cleared, the badly bruised officer realized that something had knocked him off the fence into the dirt of the Smoketown Road and that there were bullets striking the ground about him. Rising on all fours, he scrambled drunkenly down to his pinned regiment only to have Lieutenant James Wesley Blevins, Jr. (H Co.) drop nearby with a round through his shoulder.

The lieutenant bled so profusely that Nisbet sent him to the rear to find a surgeon. As Blevins staggered off, Captain Merrill T. Castleberry (C Co.) scurried over to find out what was going on.

A ball struck him through his open mouth and exited through the back of his skull. He fell heavily against the bottom rail of the fence, with his head low and bent back. Nisbet pulled his friend's body around to elevate his head. As he propped the captain's bleeding skull upon a cartridge box to keep him from drowning in his own blood, someone down the line called out, "They are running!"

Nisbet darted an anxious glance through the fence. The 13th Massachusetts and its brother regiments were making tracks. The captain sent word to what he believed to be Lawton's right regiment that he wanted permission to advance. He then ordered the 21st into the field without receiving confirmation.[52]

The East Woods

Henry Gassett (K Co., 13th MA), his body torn by two additional wounds — the right shoulder and the left leg — begged Jim Stearns to leave him and save his own life. The corporal refused.

Skulkers filled the East Woods, two of whom had just refused to aid the corporal and his badly bleeding comrade. Shells knocked wood out of the tree tops by the cord. As he retreated to a huge Maryland oak, Gassett begged Jim to leave him die, but again Stearns refused.

Bullets started clipping through the trees. Jim Stearns saw the 21st Georgia loping toward the woods. Grabbing Henry's arm, he pulled him to his feet and limped northeast amidst a scattered rain of lead.[53]

The Dunker Church Ridge

Captain William Parker's battery had been catching rounds all morning. They seemed to materialize from the sulfuric canopy which totally engulfed his guns. Jordan's section had retired to the Dunker Church. Woolfolk's advanced section was in the northeast corner of Mumma's swale.[54] Screams and explosions echoed incessantly across the smoke darkened field.

Parker's men took their lumps. Ed Duffey, the outfit's wag and the captain's personal thorn in the flesh, limped away with a bullet wound in his left thigh.[55] Some distance to the rear of the battery, he found a surgeon who offered him some whiskey. The Irishman declined and asked for water from the doctor's canteen. Duffey took a swig or two, then the doctor quickly slit open his pants leg and cut the bullet out without any anesthesia.

George Jones had his eyebrows singed off when his gun prematurely discharged while he rammed a round home. Nearly blinded, he scrounged up a replacement sponge when a bullet shattered his original one, and he stayed by his gun. Johnnie Trueman, one of the children whom the captain refused to "unenlist", fell, writhing near his piece with a shattered knee. Near the southern crest of the ridge, the captain's other problem child lay in a bloodied heap. Kenny Richardson and Willie Evans had been called forward to assist with the guns. As the boys neared the crest, a low bursting shell killed Kenny.[56]

The main Federal thrust from the Cornfield failed as Confederate reserves poured from the lower part of the West Woods into the sector. The strike produced a series of counterattacks which caused the Cornfield to switch hands several times.

CHAPTER FOUR

". . . thou hast brought me unto the dust of death."

7:00 A.M. - 7:20 A.M.

The Federal line from the East Woods to the Hagerstown Pike scattered like quail before Hood's screaming men. Hartsuff's and Christian's Brigades, under the pressing circumstances, later insisted they had retired in good order. They suffered very high casualties.

The East Woods

The 90th Pennsylvania (Christian's Brigade), the victim of a vicious crossfire from Stuart's guns on Nicodemus Heights[1] and riflery from Law's men, left its acting brigadier, Colonel Peter Lyle, and ninety-eight soldiers strewn over the mowgrass near the East Woods.[2] The colors went down. Seventeen year old William Paul (E Co.) rounded up about ten men and raced into the clover field to recover them. A wild hand to hand fight ensued in which the young man lost seven of his people.[3] As the colors left the field in the hands of their third bearer and disappeared into the East Woods, Lieutenant Hillary Beyer (H Co.) remained upon the field to relieve the plight of the wounded. Bullets cracked and buzzed about his head. When the Rebs got too close, he slung a severely wounded man over his shoulder and staggered toward safer ground.

Private John D. Vautier (I Co., 88th PA) barely escaped death when a branch, which a cannon ball had severed, fell on his messmate Jess Tyson and killed him.[4]

The 12th Massachusetts (Hartsuff's Brigade) was thoroughly smashed. Of the three hundred twenty-five men who marched onto the field, only thirty-two escorted the colors from the battle.[5] Another sixty-nine wandered into the ranks by the next evening. Over 67% of their men fell that morning.[6]

The Cornfield

By the time the Confederates advanced half way through the clover meadow below the Cornfield, their stunning charge had fizzled into an embarrassing crawl. On the left, along the Hagerstown Pike, the Hampton's Legion, with the 18th Georgia to its right, left wheeled and smashed into the Cornfield. They drove the Federals almost to the Miller House.[7] Abruptly, the Legion left wheeled again, right into the post and rail fence where it ran past the southwestern corner of the Cornfield.

The regiment halted there to pick off some slow running Yankees. Private Elliott Welch (Hampton's Legion) threw aside his rifle, because it would not fire. He bent down and picked up another, but it would not shoot. Exasperated, he snatched up a third. It worked well.

The Confederates concentrated their riflery upon the fleeing Federal color bearers. "I fired every shot at the U. S. flags and as fast as they raised (them) they fell again," he wrote. They gunned down three Federal color bearers from behind.[8]

In the excitement, Private Welch forgot how many times he shot his rifle. Canister and shells raked the regiment from the right flank. "Never have I seen men fall as fast and thick," he told his parents, ". . . I never saw rain fall faster than the bullets did around us."[9]

A well aimed volley ripped into the regiment without warning from about one hundred yards away. A shell burst over Private Elliott Welch as he fired his fifth or sixth round. The concussion doubled him over and rendered him unconscious.[10] Major Dingle, on the left of the line, struck the ground, the regimental standard clenched in his dying grasp. Lieutenant Colonel M. W. Gary immediately pried the flag from the major's dead hands and passed it to Marion Walton (B Co.), who carried it the rest of the day.[11]

Brigadier General John Bell Hood, who realized that his left wing was in trouble, ordered the panting 1st Texas to file by the left flank to support the Legion. Part way through the field, a courier sent the Texans by the right flank (their original front) into the Cornfield. Lieutenant Colonel P.A. Work (1st TX) lost total control of his people as they disappeared among the battered cornstalks and entered the fray without any support.[12] The thick smoke and the incredible loudness which surrounded his men blotted out the location and the noise of his fast approaching relief troops which kept them from connecting with his line. Unknown to him, Law's Brigade once again was on the move. It was sweeping into the Cornfield to his right.[13] (Map 17)

Major Dawes (6th WI) and his men never bothered to look behind as the 18th Georgia herded them north. On a slight crest across the road the major noticed the reassuring muzzles of Campbell's Battery being leveled toward the heavily overgrown rail fence to his front. The scared Yankees cleared the obstacle with haste and scampered over the crest to the safety of the other side.[14]

Captain Joseph Campbell (Battery B, 4th U.S., commanding) deployed his four remaining guns not five minutes before the Wisconsiners and the New Yorkers appeared in the corn to his front. Sergeant Mitchell's piece, which faced southeast, was in the center of the Hagerstown Pike along a slight ridge. He held the left of the line.[15] The other guns stretched along the crest immediately south of the Miller barn. The gunners stood by their double shotted pieces, nervously watching their own men scramble through the corn toward the farm house.

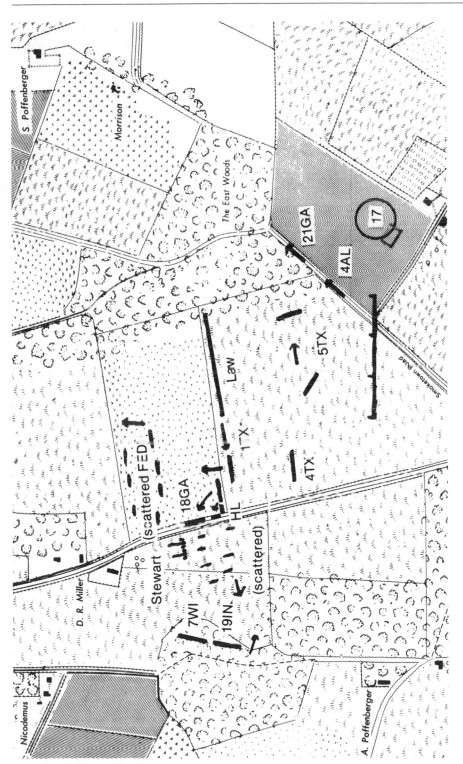

(Map 17) 7:00 A.M. — 7:20 A.M., SEPTEMBER 17, 1862

The Texas Brigade rushes into the Cornfield.

As the last Yankee rushed past them, the four Napoleons unleashed a point blank barrage into the fence along their front. The 2nd Mississippi dropped to the ground behind the fence to the left of the guns as did the 11th Mississippi and the 6th North Carolina to its immediate right.[16] The 1st Texas received the full blasts of the canister. Fence rails flew through the air like straws in the wind. The cornstalks were flattened or sheered off and men thrashed about on the ground like beached fish.

The angered Texans rallied despite their losses and returned fire into Campbell's Battery. Yankee gunners started to drop among their guns.[17] Sergeant West, who commanded the first cannon west of the road, crumbled, shot through the thigh. His anxious horse holder, Horace Ripley, a "detached volunteer" from the 7th Wisconsin, helped him back to Miller's house.[18] Sergeant Joseph Herzog (the company tailor, Stewart's section) was also down, gut shot.[19] Unaided, he dragged himself toward the house with his intestines tightly clutched in the fingers of one hand.[20]

Captain Campbell and his child aide, fifteen year old Johnny Cook, had just galloped up to Mitchell's gun in the road as the first rounds of canister clattered through the corn. A muffled scream reverberated from the position. Gunnery Sergeant Mitchell was under one of the wheels, the overloaded cannon having rolled over him in the recoil.[21]

Cook and Campbell dismounted. The sky exploded above them, obliterating the whine of the Texans' bullets. Pompey, the captain's roan, went down in the road, his mouth a mass of gore. He was bleeding from seven bullet wounds.[22] The boy went to yell something to his captain, but he was too late. The shell which burst in Pompey's mouth also struck down Captain Campbell. Fragments struck him in the neck, shoulder, and side.[23]

Johnny picked up the officer as best as he could and dragged him back to Miller's. Along the way, Campbell muttered to him to search out Lieutenant Stewart, and — if he was alive — tell him to assume command of the battery.[24] The weary boy turned his captain over to a battery driver and stumbled off to find the lieutenant. Stewart, who had always bawled at Johnny for riding a milk white pony along the firing line, would not be yelling at him to, "Get that damn ghost out of sight!" this time.[25]

By the time he found Lieutenant James Stewart, the section south of the barn had pulled out. Almost half of the original crews south of the Miller barn were out of action. A large percentage of the horses had been slain or wounded in their traces.[26] The two right guns had fallen silent. Only Henry Klinefelter's (Sergeant Mitchell's) Napoleon and Horace Ripley's piece remained in service and they fired fitfully.[27]

Henry Klinefelter and three other men manned the gun in the road following Sergeant Mitchell's accident. Every time the gun fired, the recoil sent it further northward until it had actually rolled below the crest of the slight ridge upon which it had been posted. In the excitement, none of the four men noticed that the elevating screw had worked itself so low with each discharge that the rounds were passing well above the heads of the Rebels to their left front.

Brigadier General John Gibbon happened to see this as he came upon the gun. He screamed at Klinefelter to adjust the elevating screw. The soldier, who could not hear him above the din, continued to load the piece. John Gibbon did not yell a second time. Leaping from his horse, he ran up to the cannon and cranked the screw himself until the muzzle nearly touched the ground to its front, then he ordered the gun fired. Cornstalks, fence rails, and pieces of bodies sailed through the air.[28]

Horace Ripley, to Klinefelter's right, lost both horses he was holding to rifle fire. His corporal brained the one whose lower jaw had been shot away, while he cut the traces to the one with the shattered thigh.[29]

Moments later, a ball cut the corporal down. Ripley and his comrade, Eldridge Packer, took the piece by themselves. Crawling on their hands and knees, they loaded and fired the heavy gun amid a rain of lead.[30] Neither one expected to survive the slaughter.

Meanwhile, Brigadier General George G. Meade was pushing his shaky Pennsylvanians toward the beleaguered battery. The racket from the Cornfield made it impossible to hear shouted commands. The ground heaved and rolled in continuous contractions. Artillery and small arms fire seemed to blend into a constant roar.[31]

Major Rufus Dawes (6th WI) managed to reorganize a pitiful remnant of his men in Miller's yard. Somehow, he had picked up the regimental colors.[32] The survivors' blood was up. They wanted to press the fight and regain their lost ground. Some had already gone to service the pieces of Campbell's crippled battery, but they were not the best of crews.

They almost proved to be more deadly to their own men than to the enemy. When loading double canister, the loader normally rapped the second charge against the gun's hub to break the powder cartridge free before pushing the load into the bore. The first time one of Stewart's "volunteers" tried the maneuver, he smashed his hand on the hub. With bullets pinging off the muzzle, the angry infantryman shoved the round, powder and all, down the barrel and told Lieutenant Stewart that he would have to fire it that way. Only a miracle kept the round which followed from exploding prematurely in the cannon.[33]

In the meantime, John Gibbon, his black mustache crusted with powder, raced over to Major Dawes and ordered his people into the field to secure the line on the right. The general disappeared into the smoke before the startled major could reply.[34]

BUGLER JOHN COOK,
Battery B, 4th U. S. Artillery

This fifteen year old won the Medal of Honor for assisting with one of the battery's guns. *(Deeds of Valor)*

Johnny Cook feverishly assisted Packer and Ripley at their gun. As he stepped back toward the caisson to get a round, General Gibbon handed him one and then sighted the piece after the boy rammed it home.[35] The general seemed to be everywhere loading, sighting, and cursing.

"Give them hell, boys!" he shouted repeatedly.[36]

Cook and his men received a great deal more hell than they dished out. With the Johnnies less than fifteen yards away, the young bugler yanked the lanyard to fire his final shot. Fence rails flew through the air like grass in the wind.[37] The roar and the flame of the cannon obliterated the screams of the men who were shredded by the canister. *(Map 18)*

Blue uniformed soldiers staggered across Cook's front toward the right, led by an

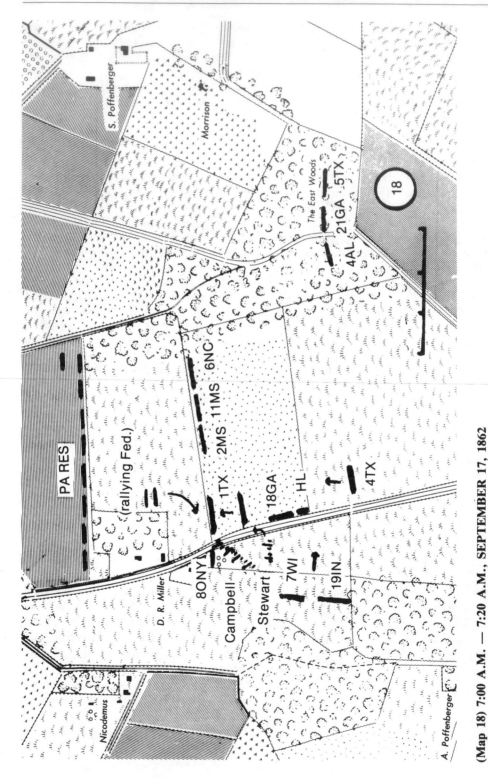

(Map 18) 7:00 A.M. — 7:20 A.M., SEPTEMBER 17, 1862
The Pennsylvania Reserves halt Hood's offensive in the Cornfield.

officer carrying the National colors. In its final moments of action, Cook's crew almost blew away what was left of the 6th Wisconsin.[38]

From the east, Yankees emerged from the smoke. Meade's Pennsylvanians had finally arrived. Before reaching Miller's, Meade sent the 10th Pennsylvania Reserves to the far right to relieve Patrick's 23rd New York. Shell fire from Nicodemus Heights and stray rifle fire seriously wounded several men, including the colonel, before the regiment reached its objective.[39] The rest of the brigade plunged headlong into the battle. Once the right connected with the regiments west of the Miller farm, the Federals would have a front ten regiments wide. They were going to smash the Confederates in the Cornfield.

The 9th Pennsylvania Reserves held the Pike, with the 11th, 12th, 7th, 4th, and 8th regiments strung out to its left across the fields into the East Woods.[40] The Pennsylvanians rolled past the silent guns of Battery B. The 7th Wisconsin, with the 19th Indiana on its right, simultaneously, broke from the West Woods and headed for the Cornfield. Two of Patrick's regiments, the 35th New York (behind the 7th Wisconsin) and the 21st New York (behind the 19th Indiana), left the limestone ledge, which ran north to south into the woods, and started across the smoke obscured field.[41]

A volley tore into the 9th Pennsylvania from the battered 1st Texas. The color guard collapsed, shot down to the man. Two regiments to the east, a bursting shell over the 7th Pennsylvania Reserves took out five men on the right of A Company. Private Leo Faller, who had received a slight head wound at the Second Manassas, perished along with Captain James Colwell and three other enlisted men, without firing a shot. Leo's brother, John, did not have time to check on him. The attack had thrown the entire Federal line into confusion.[42]

The sight of a much superior Federal force along his front prompted Colonel McIver Law to snap at his orderly, James Johnston (11th MS) to race south and find help immediately. Johnston dug his spurs into his already wounded horse's flanks and sped away.[43]

At the same time to the east, the 2nd and 11th Mississippi, and the 6th North Carolina, rose at a mere thirty feet from the 4th and the 8th Pennsylvania Reserves and panicked both regiments, which in turn stampeded the 3rd Reserves behind them.[44]

Frank Holsinger (F Co., 8th PA Res.) nearly soiled his pants when they stepped into the guns of the North Carolinians. The boys had just flushed some Rebels from the East Woods and were wildly pursuing them, when at the edge of the Cornfield, along the low rail fence, a motley line of butternut and gray rose up and leveled their muskets at the unsuspecting Federal line. In the uproar which followed, Private Holsinger lost his nerve. The volley knocked over one half of the regiment off its feet.[45] Dead and dying men lay all over the place.

The flag was down but not out. Corporal George W. Horton (F Co.), who had been wounded earlier at South Mountain, jabbed the staff into the ground and clung to it as he crashed to his knees.[46] The riflery completely shot away one foot. When one of his comrades rushed over to relieve him of his flag, he lashed out. No one would take those colors from him — no one. Moments later, he was killed — shot through the body. Nearby lay the North Carolinian who slew him. The Yankee lieutenant who snuffed him out was heading away from the field. The colors were nowhere to be seen.[47]

With the death of the man who had bragged that there was not a bullet made which could kill him, the 8th Reserves and the 4th Reserves — to its right — disintegrated. Private Holsinger (F Co.) did not intend to stop running until he reached a spot a considerable distance north of the Pennsylvania line.[48] The Rebs seemed invincible.

They were not. The morning's fights had decimated the Confederate ranks. Their ammunition was getting critically low. The Texan charge stalled momentarily about ninety feet from Campbell's Battery. The murderous Federal riflery was cutting down men by the handfuls. Private O. T. Hanks (K Co., 1st TX) latched his eyes onto a Federal soldier who was wearing a double breasted shirt. The man was hiding behind the worm fence on the northern edge of the Cornfield. He raised up on his knees to stare through two rails which had been propped on end to form a triangle. Hanks raised his rifle to shoot. He thought to himself, "If we whip (you) I am going to see if I killed you."

A bullet struck Hanks under his left arm and exited between his left shoulder blade and his spine. Dropping his weapon, he tottered south. A second ball cut through his hat rim over his right ear. A short distance to the rear a stretcher crew picked him up and carried him to a field hospital.[49]

Lieutenant Colonel P. A. Work (1st TX) found himself in a very bad fix. Almost half of his regiment was scattered through the corn. Rifle fire was coming in from the front and both flanks. In the confusion, he sent his adjutant, Sergeant W. Shropshire (D Co.), to find General Hood and get permission to retire. A volley from the unbroken 9th, 11th, and 12th Pennsylvania Reserves countermanded that decision. The 1st Texas began to inch its way south toward the swale east of the Dunker Church. As the regiment's fourth color bearer, Jimmy Malone (K Co.), stepped to the rear a burst of musketry killed him. The colonel saw six men dash after the colors. He saw the flag raised momentarily only to disappear in the corn and the smoke as the regiment kept moving rearward.[50]

Of the two hundred twenty-six men the Colonel led into the Cornfield, only forty came away unhurt. Many of the wounded fell into Federal hands. Lieutenant Tom Sanford (M Co.) was among them, downed with a bullet in the thigh from which he bled to death.

The four Perry boys in E Company did not get away either. Early O. Perry died in the corn and his brother H. Eugene dropped with a wound. Clinton Perry, who was not related to either of the other two, perished, while his brother, S. F. "Bose" Perry was shot but not killed. Captain F. S. Bass (E Co.) sacrificed eighteen of his twenty-one men in the Cornfield.

Not one of the six men who chased after the colors returned. The 1st Texas, in every sense of the phrase, was "used up".[51]

To the left rear of the 1st Texas, Private Elliott Welch (Hampton's Legion) regained consciousness. His head felt strange. He slowly realized that his right eye would not open, that his right ear was filled with blood and that he was lying in a pool of his own blood. His rifle was to one side of him and his cap to the other.

He numbly examined the kepi, heedless of the bullets which whistled around him. The shell fragment had ripped the lining apart inside, but had left the outside material in one piece. He later scrawled home, "It is really a mercy I was not torn to pieces."

Alone in his pain, he dazedly staggered rearward.[52]

When Lieutenant Colonel Gary (H.L.) observed the 7th Wisconsin, the 19th Indiana, the 21st New York, and the 35th New York making a bee line for his position, he realized that his twenty-two men could not defend the Pike. They skedaddled.[53]

Lieutenant Colonel S. Z. Ruff (18th GA) and his few men noticed the four Yankee regiments pressing toward his left flank also. He quit the field with his seventy-five remaining soldiers by running the gauntlet of fire along the Hagerstown Pike toward the West Woods.[54]

Lieutenant Colonel Carter (4th TX) had posted his outfit in the Pike along the inside sections of the fence which bordered the road.[55] His men had taken severe fire for what seemed like hours but actually had been only minutes. The air was filled with lead.

His wounded crawled in among the boulders which flanked the road on both sides, trying to protect themselves from more harm. The colonel could hear them crying as they were repeatedly struck by ricocheting bullets.[56] *(Map 19)*

"It was as near a knock-down and drag-out as anything I have ever seen or heard of," Private J. M. Polk (I Co., 4th TX) recollected. Corpses and wounded men blanketed the ground around him. After he fired his first shot, Polk merely picked up discarded rifles or muskets to fight with. He never loaded once during the engagement.

His friends disappeared in the smoke like spectral beings. He never saw Milt Garner (I Co.) or R. B. Paul (K Co.), the only Jew in the regiment, again. Within minutes only two officers and eight enlisted men remained unhurt in his company.[57]

Their ammunition dangerously low, his people tore through the pockets of their dead comrades looking for cartridges.[58] As the 18th Georgia filed past the 4th Texas, it joined in. Both units continued on toward the Dunker Church.[59]

The West Woods

James S. Johnston, Jr. (11th MS) dispairingly brought his horse to an abrupt halt in the clover field north of the Smoketown Road. No Confederate troops were anywhere to be found. He immediately urged his mount west across the Hagerstown Pike into the open ground bordering the West Woods, where he remembered that Jackson's Division had been earlier in the day.

Some of the men in the 19th Indiana noticed the lone horseman and turned to fire at him. Johnston had barely looked east to see which way Law's command was streaming from the field when a minie ball whizzed by his ears. Pulling his horse's head south, the orderly dug his spurs into its flanks and sent it careening down the Hagerstown Pike to safety.

He affectionately recalled, "The noble animal seemed to appreciate the exigencies of the case and despite his lamed leg carried me along the whole line with at least 1600 men shooting at me without faltering."[60]

Lieutenant Alger Wheeler (B Co., 21st NY) quickly scaled the fence along the western side of the Hagerstown Pike and, with a curse, jumped into the lane. Several feet from him, the regiment's color bearer waved the flag violently from side to side. When the Lieutenant asked him why he was doing that, he shouted that "he wanted to get a heap of bullet holes in it."[61]

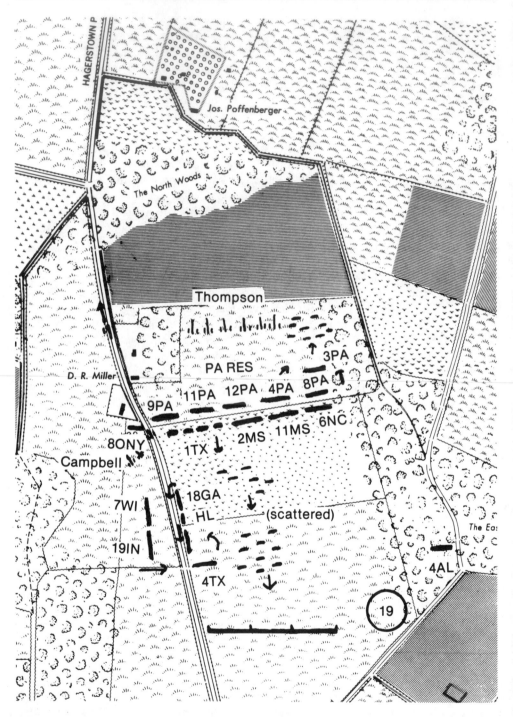

(Map 19) 7:00 A.M. — 7:20 A.M., SEPTEMBER 17, 1862
The decimation of the Texas Brigade in the Cornfield.

The Cornfield — The North Woods

Meanwhile, in the field north of the Cornfield, the Rebel counterattack ran amok. A boy from the 8th Pennsylvania Reserves abruptly halted amidst the route and turned about to face the onrushing Confederates. Holding his rifle in one hand and waving his kepi about with the other, he screamed, "Rally, boys, rally! Die like men; don't run like dogs!"

Frank Holsinger (F Co.) stopped. Shamed to the quick by a lanky kid who had more guts than he did, he ran back to the fellow, stood beside him, and began to calmly load and fire.[62] Others soon joined him. The shaky blue line began to hold its own. The Johnnies started to retire from the field.

Unfortunately for both sides, more Confederates were being fed into the meat grinder. Colquitt's Brigade (the 13th AL, the 6th, 23rd, 27th, and 28th GA) were rushing for Mumma's lane below the cemetary, while Ripley's Brigade (the 4th and 44th GA and the 1st and 3rd NC regiments) moved by the left flank toward the Cornfield.[63] What was left of Jackson's Division, with the 4th Texas, whose guns were empty, pushed toward the northern end of the West Woods.[64] There would be no respite for either side.

The Cornfield

Time slowed for the thousands of wounded. Their moans and shrieks mingled with the continuous thunder of artillery and the clatter of the musketry. Water was scarce. Canteens replaced ammunition in value among the injured, many of whom were beyond human help.

Robert Taggart (C Co., 9th PA Res.) saw his first sergeant, Robert Mahaffey, who had been wounded by shrapnel at South Mountain, bend over to give a drink to a wounded Rebel. A minie smashed into his face as he did so. His canteen flew through the air and the sergeant dropped to the ground with his mutilated face cupped in his hands. (Unable to bear his horrible disfiguration, he killed himself before the week was out.)[65]

At Miller's house a surgeon happened upon Sergeant Joseph Herzog of Campbell's Battery. He hurriedly examined the noncom's wound. The bullet had ripped open the sergeant's abdomen from one side to the other. The blood-splattered doctor coldly told Herzog that he had, at the most, a few hours to live.

"If that is the case, Doctor," Herzog cooly replied, "those few hours are not worth living."

As the doctor turned to leave, he heard the ominous double click of a hammer going to full cock. By the time he turned about, it was too late. Herzog jerked the trigger of his revolver. As the smoke cleared and the report of the pistol died away, the sergeant lay in a pool of his own blood and brains. He shot himself in the right temple to hasten the inevitable.[66]

In the Cornfield, a soldier from the 12th Massachusetts wrenched the colors of the 1st Texas from beneath the warm corpse of Lieutenant R.H. Gaston (H Co.).[67] Within touching distance of the flag lay thirteen Butternuts who had perished for the honor of their regiment.[68]

Two field surgeons found the horribly mutilated Lieutenant Ezra Stickley (5th VA) on the parlor floor of an abandoned farm house (probably A. Poffenberger's) and prepared to tie off the arteries in the stump of his profusely bleeding right arm.

The doctors abandoned him before completing the operation when the Federals hurled several shells through the house. Luckily, a straggler, whom the lieutenant knew, staggered into the room and asked if the lieutenant wanted anything. Water! Stickley needed water! He had a terrible thirst. Unable to find any, the soldier pulled the officer to his feet and dragged him southeast toward the Hagerstown Pike.[69]

The day was young. The Cornfield stank like a charnel pen. Suffering was multiplied by more suffering and death by more death. The sun had barely moved in the sky.

The Texas Brigade was driven from the Cornfield by Patrick's Brigade, the 19th Indiana and the 7th Wisconsin, which took up a line in the Hagerstown Pike, facing east. Simultaneously, the Pennsylvania Reserves pushed Law's Brigade from the Cornfield toward the West Woods. Ripley's Brigade, with Colquitt's in support, rushed north to fill the gap left by Wofford and Law in the Cornfield. At the same time, the Federal XII Corps was converging on the Cornfield and the East Woods to help the badly shot-up I Corps.

CHAPTER FIVE

"The assembly of the wicked have enclosed me."

The Martin Line Farm — The North Woods — The East Woods

The XII Corps approached the field from the northeast. Remnants of regiments were scattered all about the place, which was not very reassuring to the Corps' advance units. The Corps had been on the move for over an hour and in that time had covered a mere two miles. The morning passed terribly slow — move and halt — move and halt — without gaining any appreciable ground.

Chaplain Alonzo Quint of the 2nd Massachusetts (3/1/XII) longed for the coffee which he tossed away during the regiment's last hour long break. The men had just about gotten the pots boiling when an aide sent them forward. The soldiers hastily kicked out their fires and rushed into formation without their coffee as the regiment marched with its brigade toward the sound of cheering beyond the woods to its right front.[1]

Major General Joseph Mansfield, the XII Corps commander, heard the racket also, but he was not sure which side was doing the hoorahing. The only people he had seen of the I Corps had been the walking wounded and the stragglers. "Fightin' Joe" Hooker, the I Corps commander, had not sought out the elderly Mansfield to advise him of the battlefield situation. The XII Corps, therefore, deployed like a huge skirmishing party as Mansfield committed the Corps to the conflict piece meal.

Brigadier General George H. Gordon's Brigade (the 27th IN, 2nd MA [Pennsylvania Corps d'Afrique attached], 107th NY, 3rd WI, and the 13th NJ), followed by Brigadier General Samuel Crawford's Brigade (10th ME, 28th NY, 46th, 124th, 125th, and 128th PA), led the Corps, which was closed en masse, column of divisions

71

(two company front, fifteen ranks deep). Brigadier General George S. Greene's Division followed right behind.[2] As Gordon's Brigade passed an isolated body of woods to the northeast of the East Woods, the 13th New Jersey and the 107th New York, his two green regiments,[3] peeled off from the column to secure that flank against any Confederate thrust from the East Woods.[4] The four remaining regiments marched south by the front into the North Woods, where they halted to realign and unsling knapsacks.[5]

Captain Ezra Matthews' (F, 1st PA) and Captain Dunbar R. Ransom's (C, 5th U.S.) Batteries opened fire above the heads of the Pennsylvania Reserves, which had rallied and held their positions.[6] Gordon's people fell in behind those two batteries.[7] Captain John A. Reynolds' (L, 1st NY) and Captain James Thompson's (C, PA) guns, on the southern edge of the North Woods, went into a new position and prepared to give fire.[8] Scores of dead and wounded cluttered the field. Typically, error compounded error as the undirected Federal troops inched into the havoc of Miller's flattened Cornfield.

Crawford's six regiments developed the "slows" as they neared the clearing north of the East Woods. The unpopular Crawford commanded three relatively veteran regiments — the 46th Pennsylvania, 10th Maine, and the 28th New York. They all went into action with terribly reduced ranks. The 28th counted sixty effectives.[9] The remaining three regiments of the brigade were untried and very new to the service.[10]

The North Woods

The 124th Pennsylvania (Crawford's Brigade) veered away from the rest of the command and headed west toward the North Woods. Private George Miller (D Co.) tried to ignore the chaos around him as he trotted with his herd toward the far right. He wished that his nine month enlistment had expired. He had thirty weeks to go.[11] Having witnessed the gory aftermath of South Mountain, he lost his desire to become a hero.[12]

As the regiment double quicked past the badly rattled, but relatively unharmed 4th Pennsylvania Reserves, young Miller recalled the grisly cartload of freshly amputated arms and legs which the burial details left behind for the new men to gawk at as they tramped over the mountain.[13] Getting wounded and lying under a surgeon's knife worried him more than the chance of dying.[14] The 124th Pennsylvania continued west along Poffenberger's lane — away from the brigade.[15]

The East Woods

Simultaneously, the 10th Maine, still en masse, filed left, across the Smoketown Road to its eastern side. As it did so, a stretcher party carried the mortally wounded assistant surgeon of the 12th Massachusetts, Albert A. Kendall, past it. The 128th Pennsylvania moved in the same type of formation, south, to its right on the western flank of the road. The regiments were marching slow.

General Joseph Hooker (I Corps) galloped into the 10th Maine from behind and feverishly asked the line officers to which regiment they belonged. They told him, whereupon he blurted that the Rebs had broken through his lines.

"You must hold those woods!" he insisted, while directing the men south.

The regiment filed deeper into the plowed field before fronting to the right (south). The troops marched at the "common time" toward the East Woods. As they slowly descended into a gentle swale and inched up to the opposite crest, the column came under plunging fire from the Confederate skirmishers along the worm fence which bordered the northern edge of the woods.

With the lines so closely massed, Adjutant John Gould (10th ME) watched the men drop faster than he anticipated. In a few steps, the Confederates took out about one dozen soldiers.

"We were almost as good a target as a barn," Gould complained, ". . . it is terrible to march slowly into danger, and see and feel each second your chance of death is surer than it was the second before."

Colonel George L. Beal could not allow his men to be needlessly slaughtered. Without consulting General Mansfield, who apparently did not know that Hooker had deployed his people, the colonel ordered his soldiers to move by the double quick into regimental front.[16]

The three Confederate regiments in the East Woods anxiously waited for the overly cautious Yankees to parade into their ambuscade. The 4th Alabama (Law's Brigade) and the 5th Texas (Wofford's Brigade) held the left and right flanks, respectively.[17] They had both been sent to the woods during Hood's assault upon the Cornfield.

The Texans were nervous. Their ammunition was about gone. First Lieutenant W. II. Sellers (A Co., 5th TX), Hood's aide, failed in his attempt to bring up more cartridges from the rear lines. Within minutes, Crawford's Yankees would be upon their position. Captain Ike Turner and his one hundred seventy-five Texans would not be able to hold the line against such odds.[18]

Captain James Nisbet (21st GA), whose regiment occupied the Rebel center in the East Woods, sent his mauled command beyond the tree line to face the freshly arrived 10th Maine, which was crawling over the worm fence on the hill north of his line. When the New Englanders halted to reform, the wiley Nisbet immediately turned his men about and sent them scrambling for the cover of the woods. It was each man for himself as the regiment took shelter behind every available tree.

Nisbet, still eyeing the faltering New Englanders, shouted to his well concealed men, "If we draw their fire and they stop to shoot we can hold our position. If, however, they continue to advance we will fall back skirmishing as we are half way ahead of the rest of our line."[19]

The 10th Maine went for the bait. Nisbet's people let the Blue Coats get so close that both sides could clearly discern each other's head coverings.[20] Seconds after he gave the order to hold the line, the 21st Georgia opened fire. Several Federals dropped in the mow field. The Maine line staggered, apparently confused, while one or two companies unleashed a rattling volley before any order was restored.[21]

Company F, on the left of the 10th Maine, took cover behind a limestone ledge which parallelled a short portion of the northern edge of the woods. The right companies quarter left wheeled and jumped the fence. Using the woodstacks and trees for cover, the New Englanders formed a ragged line to fitfully volley into the Confederates.

A sniper's bullet smashed into the skull of Colonel Beal's horse. The colonel hastily attempted to dismount the plunging animal as it pitched and reeled around and
around, but a musket ball bored through both of his legs and sent him crashing to
the ground. In his agony, he released his grip on the reins.

COLONEL GEORGE BEAL, 10th Maine
Two Confederate bullets simultaneously
brained his horse and smashed both of his
legs during the fighting in the East Woods
(USAMHI)

As the regiment quickly loosed two
rough volleys, the dying horse careened
into Lieutenant Colonel James S. Fillebrown and stove in his chest and stomach
with two rapid kicks from its hind legs.
Major Charles Walker, who was desperately ill, assumed command. The
situation looked very bad.[22]

Meanwhile, the 28th New York,
followed by the 46th Pensylvania, moved
by the right flank and slipped into
Miller's field, where they both changed
to front and started toward the left of the
4th Alabama.[23] The 128th Pennsylvania,
in attempting to pass from the field north
of the East Woods into the Cornfield,
filed into a ravine near the right of the
125th Pennsylvania.[24] As the head of the
column neared the Cornfield, the 4th
Alabama shot it to pieces. Colonel
Samuel Croasdale fell from his horse —

dead. Lieutenant Colonel William H. Hammersla dropped with a shattered arm. The
men panicked. The minies seemed to fly from the tree trunks and the wood stacks
to the left of their line. Their division commander, Alpheus Williams, thundered
into the chaos and coerced them back into line. He started to pull the 128th out of
its fix.[25] *(Map 20)*

General Mansfield did not act nearly as cocky as he had an hour earlier, when,
in reponse to a cheer from Gordon's Brigade, he boasted, "That's right, boys; you
may well cheer. We are going to whip them today! Boys, we're going to lick them
today!"[26] The activities of the 10th Maine alarmed him. The regiment, while leading
Crawford's poorly deployed brigade, halted in the grassy field on the eastern side
of the Smoketown Road, near the northern edge of the East Woods.[27] He could not
believe what he saw. The men opened fire upon a company of stragglers. They were
driving their own men back to the shelter of the East Woods. He had to stop them.
The New Englanders were taking out their own men.[28]

Mansfield never saw the attack upon the 128th Pennsylvania. Passing behind
the 125th Pennsylvania, in the field, above the 10th Maine, he spurred his mount
toward the left wing of the New England regiment. His staff trailed after him. He
pushed his way through companies F, H, A, K, E, I, G, B, D, and C toward the right
of the line (which was inside the woods), and commanded the soldiers to cease fire.

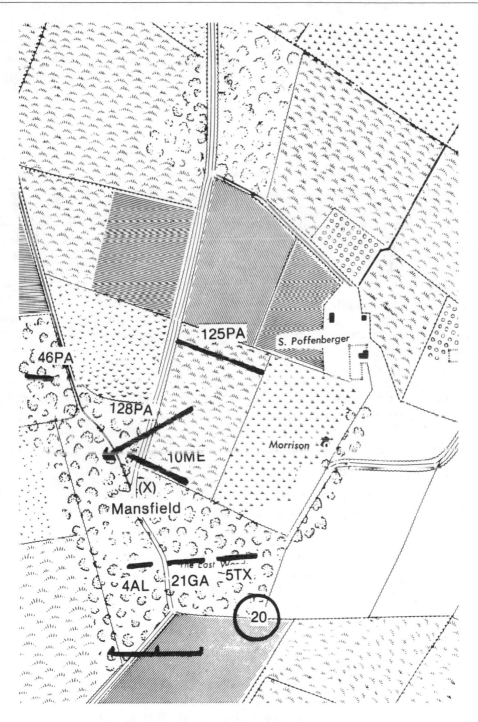

(Map 20) 7:20 A.M. — 8:00 A.M., SEPTEMBER 17, 1862
Crawford's Brigade pushes into the East Woods.

"You are shooting your friends," he screamed, "There are no Rebs so far advanced."[29]

Captain William P. Jordan and Sergeant Henry A. Burnham (C Co.) halted him and yelled that the general should see the Rebels' gray coats. They pointed momentarily toward the several snipers in the trees.[30]

The old man, his beard grimed by the powder of his own men, leaned forward in the saddle and squinted at the tree line.

"Yes, yes, you are right," he gasped.[31]

No sooner had Mansfield realized his error than the 4th Alabama and the 21st Georgia fired their disabling volleys into the 128th Pennsylvania and the 10th Maine. Mansfield's horse shuddered then turned to the tug upon its reins and made for the rail fence which the poor animal could not jump. *(Map 20)*

The general, tottering in the saddle, goaded the bleeding horse north along the Smoketown Road, away from the 10th Maine, until he came upon the right company of the 125th Pennsylvania. Captain Gardner (K Co.), who noticed that the general seemed ill, immediately called for some men to help the general dismount.

Sergeant John Caho (K Co.) and Privates Sam Edmunson (K Co.) and E.S. Rudy (H Co.), with two stragglers, gently eased the bleeding officer from his horse. Forming a chair with their muskets, the five men picked up Mansfield and carried him to a lone tree in the rear of their line, where they left him to await the arrival of a surgeon. They returned to their places in the ranks.[32] They had no time to mope over a dying man.

There were too many waning lives on both sides to be overly concerned about the comfort of the wounded, who had to fend for themselves. The weak would perish. The strong would muddle through.

The Cornfield

To the left of the Confederate line, the fighting had not abated in the bloodied Cornfield. Ripley's Brigade (the 4th and 44th GA, the 1st and 3rd NC) rushed by the left flank northwest from Mumma's onto the high ground above the Smoketown Road. As the 3rd North Carolina cleared the last rail fence along the road, the entire brigade faced right and charged toward the Cornfield.[33]

The line fired as it neared the southern edge of the Cornfield. The small arms fire caught the 19th Indiana on the right flank as it scrambled over the eastern fence along the Hagerstown Pike. Lieutenant Colonel Alois O. Bachman (19th IN) keeled over — dead. As he toppled into the road, nineteen year old Captain William W. Dudley (B Co.) assumed command.[34]

Finding his people under fire from the front, flank, and rear, the captain called to his men to pull out. The Yankees shot between the fence rails as they retired, leaving many corpses in their wake. With the remains of Jackson's Division having reoccupied the middle section of the West Woods, the Federal grudgingly yielded the field and headed for the security of the limestone ledge west of the Pike.[35] They had no way of knowing that most of the three hundred Confederates who held the woods had no ammunition for their weapons.[36] They only knew that some of them were striking down Federal soldiers. *(Map 21)*

The Hagerstown Pike

Within fifteen minutes, the 21st New York had lost about forty percent of its men. The regiment, unable to bear up under the pressure of Ripley's advance, started pulling out. Lieutenant Alger M. Wheeler (B Co.) waited until his small company had cleared the top rail of the fence along the western side of the Pike before he made tracks for the northern tip of the West Woods.

As he darted below the limestone ledge west of the road and headed onto the low ground near the woods, he recognized one of his men limping very slowly from the battle. With bullets kicking up the dirt around them, he threw his left arm around Charlie Johnson's waist and half dragged him to the safety of the West Woods.

A close examination revealed that a bullet had struck Charlie, who was the smallest man in his company, near his waist and had lodged very close to his spine. The boy with the case of the giggles was dying very slowly and very painfully.[37]

The Cornfield

The Yankees had knocked out their share of Butternuts. They disrupted Ripley's charge, forcing his men to close ranks before they went into the Cornfield. In Ripley's passing lay patches of wounded men, among them 3rd Lieutenant John Gay (B Co.) of the 4th Georgia.[38] Unconscious and breathing through a ghastly hole in his chest, he had fallen where he had stood as a file closer, three paces to the rear of the line.[39] He was completely unaware of the hell which swirled around him.

To the right, the Federal fire took out handfuls of men in the 44th Georgia. In C Company, Second Lieutenant Ashbury Hull Jackson meticulously noted their losses. Lieutenant Louis N. Johnson was dead. Captain William Haygood (C Co.) caught a bullet in the arm. A bullet struck George Kiting in the calf. William M. Elder dropped with a hip wound. Private William W. Hunt tottered rearward with a finger missing on one hand. Ripley's men, despite their increasing casualties, refused to give up the battle.[40]

Sergeant Major James Clarke (3rd NC) struggled to remain conscious. With the smoke from the burning Mumma buildings behind him, he stumbled across the clover field and past Parker's very badly shot up battery toward the West Woods. He was trying not to bleed to death before he reached the surgeons. He finally made his way to the field hospital in the grass field southwest of the West Woods. He could not recall how long he had gone unattended. At length, the most beautiful woman he had ever seen tended to him. She had raven black hair and deep dark eyes. As she bandaged his arm and he mentally ravaged her, the thought crossed his mind that she might have been one of the people who had lived in the Mumma house which he and his men had put to the torch.[41]

Sharpsburg

Miss Savilla Miller of Sharpsburg was no less courageous than Clarke's anonymous belle. Amidst a persistent rain of brick bats, shell fragments, and shards of glass, which the Federal shells sent in every direction, she remained upon her father's front porch to dole out glasses of cold water to the wounded in the town.[42]

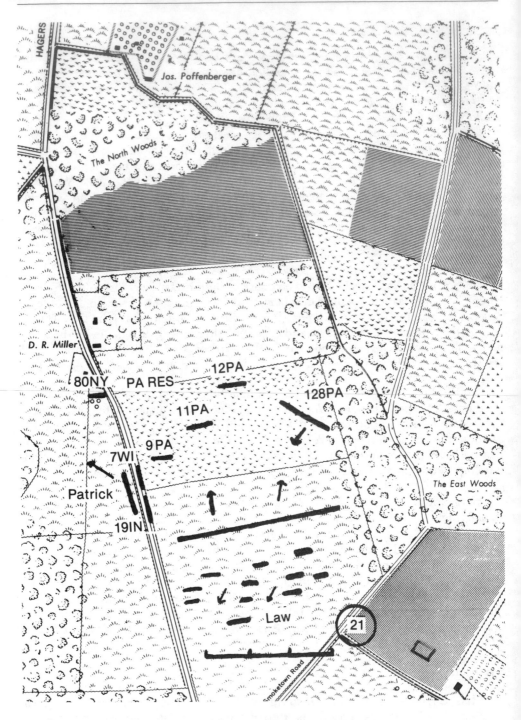

(Map 21) 7:20 A.M. — 8:00 A.M., SEPTEMBER 17, 1862
Ripley's counterthrust against the 19th Indiana and the 7th Wisconsin.

The East Woods

General Mansfield sat for a long time beneath that tree in Poffenberger's field, bleeding profusely from his severe wound. His own people had abandoned him so they could push the Rebs out of the very woods that he had insisted were not occupied. Two days as Corps commander and he sat alone, dying.[43]

The Dunker Church

Artillery could not be spared, particularly among the overworked gunners of S. D. Lee's Battalion. Woolfolk still had one section in the northeast corner of Mumma's swale, just inside the corner of the Smoketown Road and the farm lane intersection. Rhett's Battery had pulled out and redeployed on the west side of the Hagerstown Pike, facing northeast, about one hundred yards below the West Woods. Hardaway's guns held the western section of Mumma's cornfield to the right of his old line. Jordan's men remained across the road from the Dunker Church, but Parker's Battery and Woolfolk's remaining section were being pulled out. Moody's four pieces were rushing to Jordan's assist. Two guns rolled into battery to Jordan's right. The remaining two careened north after Ripley's Brigade to give it close support.[44]

Since the battle opened, the sky had rolled and rumbled incessantly from the continuous artillery fire. Ducking shells became futile. The Federals, who had gotten their range on S. D. Lee's Battalion since first light, were thumping his position mercilessly. Captain Parker's men ran a severe gauntlet of exploding shells as they raced with Woolfolk's section toward a more secure position about six hundred yards south of the Dunker Church ridge.

As Sergeant Joshua C. Hallowell's gun (Parker's Battery) wheeled about to move away, a solid shot ripped through the two lead horses. Sixteen year old George Warburton, the lead rider, went down under them. The shot crushed his legs.[45] A second round killed the two horses behind his within moments after the men dragged the boy away. The two remaining horses became frantic from the scent of blood and started thrashing about. Joe Hay hastily slashed their harnesses with his pocket knife while Rob Bryant leaped upon the wheel horse to haul the gun away. The sky exploded above his head and Bryant flew from the saddle — killed.

A naval officer on S. D. Lee's staff crumpled, also, bleeding to death from a fragment in the neck. Private George Goff jumped into the saddle and whipped the horses into a gallop, and saved the gun.[46]

Stephen D. Lee wept openly. His men had expended most of their ammunition. They had suffered exceedingly high casualties, and he ordered them to retire. He could follow their trail for they had clearly marked it with their discarded overcoats, letters, empty ammunition chests, and their dead. They dumped every nonessential item to increase their speed.[47]

The Cornfield

Campbell's Battery (B, 4th U.S.) had served to its limit. At about the same time that the valiant Captain Parker and his men were quitting the field, what was left of Battery B, 4th U.S. Artillery was also leaving the field. Lieutenant James Stewart, despite the loss of most of his horses and forty of one hundred men, took the guns down the Hagerstown Pike just as Ripley's Brigade tore into Patrick's Brigade and the 19th Indiana.[48]

As he headed into the plowed field north of Miller's, a staff officer ordered him back into line next to Ransom's Battery (C, 5th U.S.). Stewart complied. He sent one section and enough men for one crew to Ransom's right, while the other four guns headed north.

Shortly after, both his section and Ransom's Battery were sent to the southern edge of the North Woods, where neither could fire because the dense smoke to their front obscured their fields of fire. Stewart was piqued. The Rebs shot his horse twice in less than two minutes.[49]

The West Woods (Northern End)

General Marsena Patrick and three of his regiments (21st, 23rd, and 35th NY) occupied a rather precarious position. They secured the limestone ledge which paralleled the Hagerstown Pike north of the West Woods. With their backs to J. E. B. Stuart's guns and skirmishers, their right flank covered by Jackson's men, and their front subject to fire from Ripley's men in the Cornfield, they realized they could not hold that flank of the Union line without substantial assistance. Colonel William Rogers (21st NY) held the right wing of the brigade at the point nearest the West Woods. He felt quite vulnerable to an enfilade. When he requested that Major Dawes (6th WI) and Captain Dudley (19th IN) form their regiments in line at right angles to and north of his line, the two of them ordered their units off the field.

Abandoned, Patrick retired his men north to the reverse slope of the swale south of Miller's barn, where they joined with the 80th New York (their brigade). The weary Federal troops dug in and kept their heads low lest the Yankee artillerists behind them mow them down by mistake. The dirty veterans wasted no time in assessing their situation. They could not fight. They had no ammunition. A number of scavengers dragged in some of D. R. Miller's fence rails and started cook fires. Within minutes, coffee was boiling. They had not eaten anything since the previous evening.[50]

The Federal I Corps was "used up" by 8:00 A.M., which left the poorly deployed XII Corps to defend the Cornfield from Ripley's and Colquitt's Brigades. The XII Corps, without its own commander, Joseph Mansfield, had to conduct the battle on its own.

CHAPTER SIX

"Deliver my soul from the sword . . . ."

8:00 A.M. to 8:40 A.M.

The Cornfield

By 8.00 A.M. both sides had fairly well shot each other to shreds. The once tall Cornfield was reduced to scattered stands of stalks and bloodied stubble. Ripley's Brigade had been fragmented in its assault upon the field. Despite the fact that it turned back Patrick's Brigade and the 19th Indiana, it had gotten badly confused in the charge.

The 3rd North Carolina, numbering five hundred twenty officers and men, bore the brunt of the assault. Colonel William L. De Rossett, fell, shot through the bowels shortly after he ordered the regiment to change front to rear on the tenth company. With the regiment reformed at nearly right angles to the rest of the brigade line, Major S. D. Thurston, who assumed command, ordered the North Carolinians to charge.[1]

The 128th Pennsylvania regrouped and started to press Ripley's front.[2] The Pennsylvanians held their own and began to pour a telling fire into the Confederates. The 1st North Carolina faced the 128th Pennsylvania from the southwest. Private Calvin Leach (B Co.) watched the Yankees go prone behind the shattered worm fence which bordered the southern edge of the Cornfield. Every time gaps appeared in their line, the second rank of Federals quickly filled them. The "Stars and Stripes" waved defiantly from side to side.

Private Leach lost his captain, Thomas S. Bouchelle; they carried him away with a bullet in his mouth. Lieutenant Joseph W. Peden fell with a thigh wound nearby.

81

Leach tried to kill the men around the Federal colors but his rifle would not take a ball following the first shot. Picking up the weapon of the fellow who went down next to him, he feverishly loaded and fired at the Yankees. In the smoke and the confusion, he wondered if he killed any.

The Yankees were knocking down the North Carolinians by the squads. Fighting them and his shrivelled stomach, which he had hardly fed in the last four or five days, almost overwhelmed Calvin Leach. He wanted the day to end and the firing to cease.[3]

The Pennsylvanians killed and wounded three hundred twenty of the 3rd North Carolina, including twenty-three of its twenty-seven line officers, and over one hundred sixty of the 1st North Carolina. Only sixty-six men left the field unscathed.[4] Before the hour passed, however, the 128th Pennsylvania lost one hundred eighteen men.[5] To the east, the 10th Maine was pushing the three Confederate regiments in the East Woods to its southern fringe.[6]

The East Woods

The Confederates had a difficult time dealing with the New Englanders' unusually rapid fire. The Mainers were using experimental cartridges which did not have to be bitten open to combust. The caps ignited the paper and the charges simultaneously. Some of the Yankees did not bother to seat the rounds with ramrods. They merely slapped their musket butts on the ground to drive the charges home.

This rapid fire took its toll and kept the Confederates constantly dodging for cover. The Rebs were shooting low and quite accurately. Within minutes after they dropped both colonels, their riflery killed Captain Nehemiah Furbish (G Co.) and mortally wounded First Sergeant William Wade, I Company's acting lieutenant, who had foolishly perched himself on the fence rails, sword in hand to pounce upon any man who broke ranks. The minie struck him so hard that its thud was heard over fifty feet away in the right of H Company.

Sergeant George A. Smith (E Co.) was struck in the neck by an exploding bullet which left eighteen lead fragments in his throat. First Sergeant Edward Brackett (acting lieutenant, D Co.) fell shot through the bowels. Lieutenant Alfred L. Turner (B Co.) went down, leg shot. The air reverberated with the peculiar snaps of English explosive rounds.

Screams of, "Aim low!", "Give 'em hell!", and "Give it to the damn Yankee sons of bitches!" taunted the thinning New England line. The longer the Yankees sustained the fight, the more violently and frequently the Confederates swore. They were dying game.[7]

Captain Ike Turner (5th TX) was very worried. His ammunition was almost gone. His four attempts to contact Hood for relief failed and the Federals continued to take his people out. He had about ninety effectives left.[8] The New Englanders were less than fifty yards from his line.

Once again, the ground between the Dunker Church and the East Woods swarmed with Confederate troops. A section of Moody's Louisiana Battery burst north from the Smoketown Road ahead of the troops toward the southern portion of Miller's clover field, while Woolfolk's section threw in support from Mumma's farm. For fifteen minutes, Moody's artillerists kept the Federals pinned until relieved by infantry. To the left rear of the 5th Texas, Colquitt's Brigade (13th AL, 23rd, 27th, 28th, and 6th GA) started from Mumma's northern lane toward the Cornfield. Garland's Brigade (5th, 13th, 20th, 23rd NC) of D. H. Hill's Division (Jackson's Corps) moved into line along the post and rail fence south of Mumma's. What was left of Hood's Division regrouped around the Dunker Church.[9] Poague's Battery relocated to a new position above the Smoketown Road-Hagerstown Pike intersection and belched shells into the Cornfield.[10]

The Cornfield

The air reeked of sulfur and blood. It was hot and muggy and difficult to see the sun through the smoke which enveloped the area from Miller's to Mumma's. The noise had not abated since dawn. No one could be heard above a shout in the chaos which reigned.[11]

Brigadier General Alpheus Williams, having assumed command of the XII Corps, pulled the badly shaken 128th Pennsylvania from the Cornfield as Colquitt's lead regiment came into view from the southern corner of the East Woods. The Pennsylvanians went prone in a field north of their previous position, while the Confederates fell upon the Yankees near the Miller house.[12]

The Rebels bolted into a trap. They rushed into the concave of a "U" shaped Federal counterattack. The 3rd North Carolina, on the right of Ripley's Brigade, assisted by the 1st North Carolina, stayed in the fight, despite tremendous losses, until they exhausted their ammunition. Private R. H. Daniels (K Co., 4th GA), who was fighting on the left of the brigade, along the Hagerstown Pike, glanced over to his right in time to see those two North Carolina regiments fold up, which, in turn, panicked the 44th Georgia. The soldiers of the 4th Georgia, assisted by their officers who frantically rummaged through the corpses' cartridge boxes, took their one or two rounds at a time and sustained their position on the field for a few minutes more.[13]

What remained of Ripley's Brigade quit the place along with Moody's two guns, which limbered at the southern edge of the Cornfield and tried to make for the safety of the Dunker Church ridge. The 4th Alabama (Law's Brigade) retired from the East Woods, south, leaving the 6th North Carolina of its brigade to take its former post on the left of the 21st Georgia.[14]

The North Woods — D. R. Miller's

The 124th Pennsylvania had been in the North Woods for about half an hour, waiting to be committed to its first action. The men were tense — very tense. They nervously peeled off their knapsacks and dressed their line while stragglers and wounded men staggered through their ranks, trying to escape the shells from Nicodemus Heights.[15]

In the excitement, Sergeant William Potts (F Co.) forgot his premonition of being wounded or killed.[16] The company was in deep trouble. Some frantic officer galloped up to the regiment and ordered it into action. The shoulder strap sputtered something about his men getting cut to pieces.

Sergeant Potts and most of his command did not feel like doing battle that day, or any other day, for that matter. The choice was not theirs to make. As the regiment advanced on both sides of the Hagerstown Pike, heading south, the musketry became more intense. Captain Frank Crosby (F Co.) matter-of-factly told his men they could get killed if they wanted to, but things were getting too hot for him and he would "be damned" if he wanted to be part of it. He quit the field on the spot, leaving his green company without a commander. The company hesitated a moment. The lieutenants refused to take over. Potts, who had been the company drill master in more peaceful times, assumed control by default. He ordered the men to dress on the colors, which could be seen across the road behind a stand of corn, and step out.[17]

The regiment did not go far. As soon as the seven companies on the left entered the Cornfield, they laid down to meet the assault of Colquitt's left regiment. Companies A, D, and F tried to carry the line on the right, but without success. They got as far as the swale below Miller's barn, where they went prone behind the crest above Patrick's resting and weary men.[18]

Sergeant Potts and a fellow they called William T. "Bill" Daller (F Co.) darted across the open ground south of the swale, trying to determine which direction the rounds were coming from. They found out. When the pair got close to the rock ledge which Patrick had used earlier in the day, the Rebels opened fire.

Private Daller went down, curled up in pain from a blow to his midsection. Potts fell too, shot through the instep of his right foot. Daller threw his musket aside and painfully hobbled back toward the company. He was not bleeding. The ball bent the Bowie knife on his waist belt double.

Potts followed him, and the men mocked him for imitating Daller. Potts jammed his musket, bayonet first, into the ground and staggered north, away from his company, snapping back at them that he had enough to carry without it.[19] The right wing of the 124th stayed "pinned" for what seemed like a very long time.[20]

The Cornfield

Meanwhile, Colquitt's soldiers struck the Federals a glancing blow as they charged toward the Miller farm house. Screams and curses, barely audible above the roaring artillery fire, reverberated from the sulfuric cloud which engulfed the right of the Confederate line.

The 6th Georgia smacked into the 5th Ohio (1/2/XII).[21] The Ohions lashed out with a vengeance at the Georgians. Rifle butts cracked skulls and weapons roared at point blank range as the small Yankee regiment of one hundred eighty men wrested their tiny section of the East Woods from the stunned Confederates and pushed them into the Cornfield.[22]

Simultaneously, the two remaining regiments of the brigade (7th and 66th OH) took the field as Colquitt's Brigade volleyed obliquely at the 124th Pennsylvania. In the confusion, the 7th and 66th Ohio regiments believed that they were cut off from their own lines. Numbering less than four hundred effectives between them, they hesitated before advancing into the Cornfield, which was to their front.

Lieutenant Colonel Eugene Powell (66th OH) assumed command of both regiments without consulting the senior officer of the 7th Ohio. He hoped to take advantage of what appeared to be an excellent opportunity for a counter strike against the Confederates. The 27th Georgia went prone behind the shattered worm fence along the northern edge of the Cornfield to fire into the advancing 3rd Wisconsin and the 27th Indiana, which, unknown to Powell, were moving up to his right flank.[23] The excited colonel pushed his mount into his stymied line and ordered his men to cut loose into the unsuspecting Confederates.

Captain Orrin Crane, senior officer of the 7th Ohio, countermanded him. Powell, once again, ordered his troops to fire. Crane belayed the order. Those were Union men up there, he insisted. The two officers verbally wrangled for control of the two regiments.

Powell won out, presumably by "pulling rank". As he pushed further into his line, he commanded the men to volley. Flame and sulfur belched death along the fence row from the center to both flanks as the three Ohion regiments (5th, 7th, and 66th OH) shot point blank into the Rebels. Some of the shots thudded into the East Woods and cut down several soldiers in the right companies of the 10th Maine.[24]

At that instant, the Federals pounced upon Colquitt's line with a fury. The Yankees were dishing out more lead pills than they were receiving, and, for once, they were not yielding ground.

The 2nd Massachusetts held Miller's farm house by wrapping itself along the inside of the badly battered picket fence which enclosed the southern and the eastern boundaries of the orchard.[25] The thin slats offered nominal protection from the incoming rounds, but the men were much more secure there than if they had been in the open mow field with the 3rd Wisconsin and the 27th Indiana. Those two approaching Federal regiments did not fire en masse at first for fear of striking down the Ohions whom they saw darting about in the smoke to their front.

The volley from the 27th Georgia struck the two regiments with a terrible force, but did not rout them. Stubbornly and methodically, the Union soldiers loaded and fired into the smoke to their front while an equally determined enemy replied in kind. Weapons became intolerably hot among the ranks of the 27th Indiana.[26] Skin stuck to rifle barrels and faces were charred from premature discharges. Men were dropping too fast to count. Corporal Edmund Brown (C Co., 27th IN) was stunned by it all. A man near him burst out laughing, following a good shot. A second later, the man dropped. Another soldier turned momentarily to warn the fellow behind him not to fire so close to his face. Both fell, simultaneously.

The file closers faithfully performed their duties. The lines shifted to the center of the regiment as the men closed ranks by stepping sideways over the bodies of their own men.

Wounded soldiers refused to quit the field. A lanky Indiana private was seen staggering from the firing line with what appeared to be a serious wound. After stepping several yards, he turned his back to the fighting (as if to shield himself from another injury) and ripped open his blouse. The resigned expression on his face confirmed his situation. Realizing that he had "bought it", he stoically drawled, "Wall, I guess I'm hurt about as bad as I can be. I believe I'll go back and give 'em some more." He picked up a discarded weapon and walked back to his inevitable death.[27]

Things remained rough. Ammunition was getting very low. The musketry slackened as the men stopped to scrounge cartridges from the dead and the wounded.[28]

Around 8:00 A.M. Major General Joseph Hooker (I Corps) sent Captain Alexander Moore, a volunteer staff aide to Lieutenant William Miller's cavalrymen (H Co., 3rd PA Cav.), who were rounding up stragglers near D. R. Miller's. The captain requested and received ten well mounted men under Corporal Andrew J. Speese. Speese and his people reported to the general as he posted Captain E. W. Matthews' Battery (F, 1st PA) on the eastern end of Miller's mow grass field behind Brigadier General George H. Gordon's Brigade.

Within minutes, Hooker had dispatched all of his newly acquired orderlies, but Speese, to various parts of the field. As Colquitt's attack waxed particularly fierce, the general noted more and more of Gordon's men lying down, perhaps to protect themselves from the terrific musketry.

Hooker yelled at Corporal Speese to send the brigade forward with cold steel and take the Cornfield by the points of its bayonets. The enlisted man rode up to Colonel Thomas Ruger (3rd WI) (whose name he subsequently forgot) and relayed the command.

Colonel Ruger, having assumed command when General Crawford took over the division, refused to comply. His men were almost out of ammunition, he protested. If he was to charge, Hooker would have to deliver the command in person.[29]

The Colonel, in the meantime, asked Colonel George L. Andrews (2nd MA) to commit his men before the 3rd got "used up". Without hesitating, the New Englander ordered his right companies to left wheel into line. His men cleared the fence and swung around on a hinge formed by the left companies. The regiment fired by the right oblique into the left and the center of Colquitt's dwindling brigade.[30] In the East Woods, the 28th Pennsylvania poured a devastating volley into the right rear of the Rebel line.[31]

Simultaneously, General Hooker rode into the 3rd Wisconsin which held the center of Gordon's Brigade and asked why his command had not been obeyed.

"Attention!" echoed along the line and the soldiers got to their feet. "Fix bayonets, forward double quick!"

A parting volley splattered the line as it dashed down the crest from Miller's toward the Cornfield.[32]

Huzzahs echoed along the Federal front as the six regiments along the northern edge of the Cornfield charged with bare muzzles and bayonets into the demoralized Confederate line. Whooping like aborigines, the Yankees swept over the hotly contested ground. Confederate officers, brandishing swords, futilely tried to manhandle their men back into their ranks. It was no use.[33] The Confederates had taken enough. The further the Federal line chased them, the more it disintegrated as the Rebels' return fire felled men or as others stopped to pick up souvenirs. (Map 22)

Private Wendell Croom (C Co., 6th GA) remembered seeing Colonel Colquitt in tears. The brigade lost over 50% of its effectives.[34] Private Benjamin H. Witcher (K Co., 6th GA), glancing at the rows of butternut-clad troops lying in formation about him, however, realized he was not alone and decided to take a stand. A comrade screamed at him that those men were all dead! Witcher yelled back that they were not, at which point his friend discharged his weapon into one of the bodies point blank. The fellow did not twitch. Witcher retreated.[35] (The two hundred fifty man regiment left eighty-one dead, one hundred fifteen wounded, and about thirty "missing" upon the field.)[36]

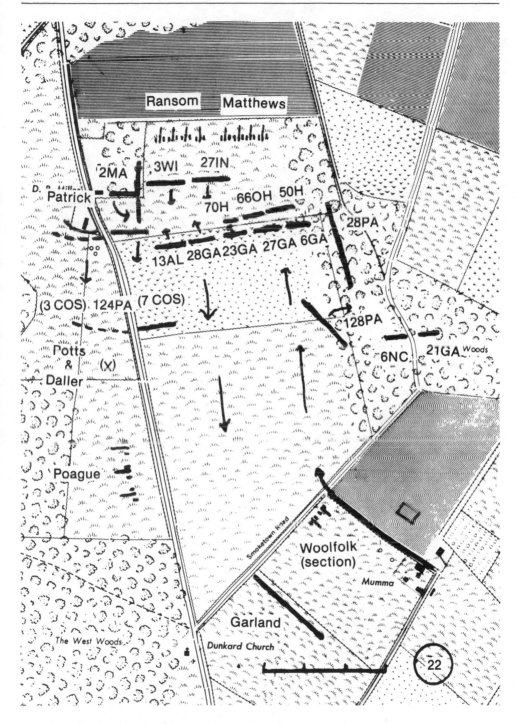

(Map 22) 8:00 A.M. — 8:40 A.M., SEPTEMBER 17, 1862
The final Confederate push against the Cornfield.

Confederate battle flags littered the ground, where several enterprising Yankees "captured" them. Private John Murphy (K Co., 5th OH) picked up the flag of the 13th Alabama. A moment later, he dropped, wounded.[37] Similarly, Sergeant Wheat (E Co., 3rd WI) snatched up the colors of the 11th Mississippi (Law's Brigade) while his regiment, led by Major General Joseph Hooker, drove toward the southern portion of the East Woods.[38]

The West Woods

The 124th Pennsylvania got caught up in the general movement. The seven left companies advanced cautiously to the southern edge of the Cornfield, where they laid down and fired into the backs of the fleeing Rebels. Captain Norris L. Yarnell (D Co.) assumed command when a round plucked Colonel Joseph Hawley from the saddle. The second in command, Major Isaac Haldeman, could not be found. Being "green", the captain decided to keep his people out of harm's way.[39]

Yarnell had other problems too. The three companies across the Pike had gotten pinned by Jackson's men. The firing became too rough for them as they left the swale south of Miller's barn. Corporal David Wilkinson (A Co.), who had just lost his kepi and part of the little finger on his right hand, caught a bullet in the leg after going but a few feet. He limped away.[40]

Private George Miller (D Co.) fared no better. As he advanced with his company, in open order, against the northern section of the West Woods, a bullet struck him with hammer force in the left side of his abdomen. Half dazed, George nervously glanced down at his frock coat. He was bleeding just below the rib cage. Without dropping his weapon, he instinctively slipped his free hand around his back. He could feel his blood flowing out the exit hole in his back. It felt hot and sticky.

Charlie Eckfeldt, (D Co.) whose rifle was shattered by a minie, looked over to see George staring blankly at his bloody hand. Charlie called out to him, then bolted over to help Miller strip off his belt and cartridge box. Miller absent-mindedly passed his rifle to Charlie and started to hobble rearward.

He was in shock and failed to notice if anyone helped him. The smoke, the head-jarring concussions of the exploding shells, and the shrieks of the wounded all went unnoticed. He did not hear them. A trail of blood and fecal matter followed after him.[41]

CAPTAIN NORRIS YARNELL,
D Co., 124th Pennsylvania

Following the wounding of his colonel, he assumed command of this hapless regiment.
(History of the 124th Pennsylvania)

The wounded Sergeant William Potts (F Co.) had barely passed to the rear of the line before two very willing volunteers fell out to assist him. Private John J. Chalfant (F Co.), his mess mate, was one of them. They hastily bound Potts up, who was bleeding profusely from his wounded foot, sat him on a musket between them, and made for the North Woods. On the way down the Hagerstown Pike, Chalfant cooly reminded the sergeant of his previous night's death premonition, but Potts did not want to hear it. A shell blew up in the road where they would have been had they not stopped to apply a tourniquet to his foot. Potts wanted to leave before some artillerist called his number.[42]

Poffenberger's Lane

Lieutenant William E. Barry (G Co., 4th TX), whom the Federals captured on the Hagerstown Pike when the Texas Brigade retreated to the West Woods, had been watching the fighting from a ridge along Poffenberger's lane, when the Ohions smacked the 6th and 27th Georgia regiments. He was the "guest" of the 12th Pennsylvania Cavalry, which belonged to the Union provost detachments.[43] Fresh Federal regiments swarmed the entire East Woods. It seemed as if the whole Confederate line had collapsed.

To his left rear in the mow field and the adjacent cornfield, no less than four Yankee regiments were converging on the "boys" in the East Woods. Stragglers and walking wounded streamed rearward unchecked. Their numbers far exceeded the cavalrymen's capacity to stop them. Major James Congdon (12th PA Cav., commanding), Lieutenant Barry's host, dismounted and was casually supervising the roundup of skulkers. He jabbed the Confederate officer in the ribs and, with a shout, pointed toward a party of Yankees who were jubilantly heading down the lane toward them. They were carrying a souvenir.

Major Congdon hailed the soldiers over and asked them where they captured the flag and if they knew whose it was.[44] The man who carried the colors grinned rather stupidly at the officer.

"I did not capture it, Major. I found it in the cornfield."

The major asked Lieutenant Barry if he could identify it. The lieutenant, his eyes welling with tears, quietly reached out for the staff as the Yankee soldier just as tenderly handed it to him.

"I know it well," Barry choked. "It is the flag of the First Texas regiment."

Kissing the stained and tattered banner with the reverence due an icon, he returned it to the enlisted man and haltingly asked where he found it. The soldiers told him that it lay within a hand's grasp of a cluster of thirteen dead Rebels and that he had to roll a dead Confederate officer off the flag to pick it up.

Lieutenant Barry soberly listened to the description of the deceased officer. He knew the man as Lieutenant R. H. Gaston (H Co., 1st TX), the brother of Captain W. H. Gaston (H Co., 1st TX) — Barry's friend.[45] Honor carried such a terrible price.

The East Woods

At about the same time that Colquitt's Brigade folded so did the Confederate right flank in the East Woods. With rounds coming in from the left front and the north, the three Confederate regiments which had stubbornly held the woodstacks and the oaks were forced to make a run for it. Their ammunition all but gone, and with no less than twelve Federal regiments converging on their sanctuary, they had no other alternative.[46]

The 6th North Carolina (Law's Brigade), on the left, fell back first under fire from the Cornfield and the woods, while the 21st Georgia and the 5th Texas retired under the creeping advance of the 111th Pennsylvania, the 3rd Maryland, the 102nd New York, and the 125th Pennsylvania. As they withdrew toward Mumma's, Captain Thomas P. Thomson (G Co., 5th NC) in Garland's approaching brigade also noticed the tremendous drive against the East Woods. "They are flanking us!" he screamed. "See yonder there's a whole brigade!" Before his brigade commander could reach the frantic captain, the entire outfit turned and streamed south.[47]

Captain Nisbet (H Co., 21st GA) and his men literally ran for their lives for the safety of the ridge north of Piper's farm. As they passed their former position on the Smoketown Road, Nisbet halted long enough to dispatch a couple of men to retrieve Captain Castleberry's corpse so they could properly inter it in Atlanta. Within moments, the panting men returned. The captain's body was gone.[48] Theirs would be gone too because they were skedaddling. Nisbet, who felt depressed and nauseated from his wound, lost no time in following after them.[49]

The East Woods — The Smoketown Road

Colonel Jacob Higgins (125th PA) moved his green regiment cautiously down the slope toward the northern edge of the East Woods.[50] Over to the left front, obscured from view by the dense smoke from the burning Mumma farm and the fighting in the general area, the 111th Pennsylvania, the 3rd Maryland, and the 102nd New York (east to west, respectively) pushed steadfastly toward the East Woods. Stragglers, wounded men, and riderless horses passed through and around the Pennsylvanians as if they were a rock in a swift flowing stream. A badly wounded boy wobbled unsteadily through B Company, on the far left of the line.

"Go in, boys! Go in, boys! Give them Hell!" he shrieked.

Private Miles Huyette (B Co.) ruefully noted the soldier's agony as he clasped his left forearm vicelike with his right hand and tried to stop the bleeding from his shattered wrist.

In the dense smoke, Huyette tuned his previously virgin ears to differentiate the distinctive "zipps" and "pings" of passing minies from the gut-wrenching "thuds" of those which struck bone and flesh. He occasionally snatched glimpses of the 6th North Carolina's rear guard, who, using the trees and woodstacks in the woods for cover, hastily fired off rounds then, seemingly, evaporated into thin air. As the smoke intermittently lifted, he could distinctly see individual Butternuts stop to load and return fire.[51]

Colonel Higgins, who was unable to locate the regiment he was supposed to relieve, right obliqued his men toward the western border of the woods. Many of the fleeting shadows, which not moments before had brought down some of his own people, came running toward the regiment with white handkerchiefs tied to the muzzles of their weapons. He sent them rearward under guard.[52]

The 125th Pennsylvania burst from the East Woods into the clover field. They ran into a suffocating wall of smoke from the Mumma buildings. B Company got pinned against the worm fence north of Mumma's cemetary and had to fall in behind A Company, which was to its immediate right. Small arms fire whistled into the company's right rear from the fighting to the north.

The men threw themselves prone upon the trampled clover.[53] The shells started coming in hot and close, forcing the regimental staff officers to hastily dismount. A round disabled Lieutenant Colonel Jacob Szink when it tore away his stirrup strap and sent his mount careening across the field.[54] Behind B Company, Adjutant Robert M. Johnston plucked the gloves from the corpse of Colonel Strong (6th LA) and waved them victoriously in the air.[55]

Amid the terror and confusion, a mounted staff officer set his spurs to his horse's flanks and came careening from the south along the rear of the regiment, heading for the right of the line. Miles Huyette (B Co.) rolled over onto his back to watch the show. The horse's neck was extended in full gallop; the reins dangled and bobbed loosely with the plunging animal. The officer (a lieutenant) reeled in the saddle in an apparent stupor. A shell exploded on the horse's left rear flank, sending it and its rider into a bloody pile. The infantrymen stared in awe as the lieutenant pried himself from his dead animal and staggered over to their line.

Half giddy, half stunned, he nonchalantly blurted to a nearby soldier, "It was a hell of a wonder I was not killed, and me so damned drunk." He reeked of whiskey.[56] The day seemed as if it would never end. (Map 23)

Some men and officers of the 10th Maine finally happened upon the unfortunate General Mansfield when their regiment retired from the fray. Sergeants Merritt, Storer Knight, and Adjutant Gould took a blanket and laid the painfully wounded officer on it. They also found a black cook from Hooker's Corps and coerced him to help them get the portly Mansfield into one of the waiting ambulances along Poffenberger's lane. As they rough handled the dying general into the wagon, Adjutant Gould looked across the field and noticed the 107th New York being led toward the East Woods by General Crawford.[57] Troops were everywhere.

A shell struck G Company of the 107th New York. Captain H. G. Brigham (G Co.) watched helplessly as it shredded eleven of his men. Amid the smoke and carnage, he heard sixteen year old Willie Everts shrieking and wailing. The explosion had ripped the boy's legs away. The regiment continued into the woods but the memory of Willie's pleas stayed etched in Captain Brigham's mind forever.[58]

The Martin Line Farm

Corporal "Jim" Stearns (K Co., 13th MA) and his badly wounded comrade, having escaped the East Woods, finally stumbled into the rapidly filling farm yard around the Martin Line house. Laying Henry Gassett in the front yard, Jim searched around back for some straw. He quickly averted his attention from the seriously hurt soldiers who littered the area toward the haystack near the barn. The injured men in the stack called out to him. They were from his regiment. Snatching up a considerable armful of straw, he shouted back that he would see to them after he had bedded down and fed Henry. He did not feel much like chatting.

Jim gently helped Henry onto his bed of fresh straw and then set about to find some scrap wood for a coffee fire. In the distance to the southwest, he heard the

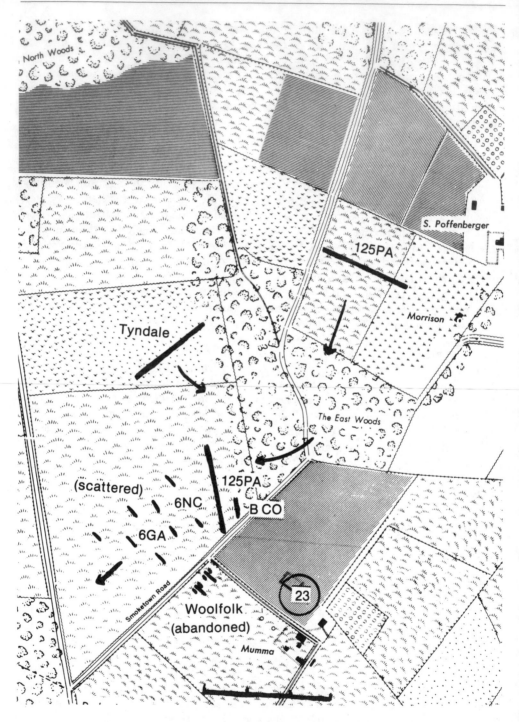

(Map 23) 8:00 A.M. — 8:40 A.M., SEPTEMBER 17, 1862
The 125th Pennsylvania cleans out the East Woods.

terrible rumbling of the battle. He wondered how the XII Corps, which they passed en route, was faring.

Within a short while he had given Henry a couple of cups of coffee and had washed his wounds. Things had gone bad for the regiment. Captain Charles H. Hovey (K Co.) had been shot, but held on. In the haystack, Jim found no less than twelve of his company — all wounded. One of the three company sergeants was head shot. A corporal with a wounded foot was there too. Private Charles A. Trask (K Co.) lay among them, bleeding to death from fragment wounds in the side and back. At least three of his friends were dead or left to die upon the field.[59]

The Federal Rear Lines

Lieutenant Alger Wheeler (B Co., 21st NY) helped a lieutenant, who had been shot in the head when the regiment withdrew from the field, to a farm house east of the Cornfield. The surgeons were too busy to treat a head wound so the Lieutenant walked his friend past the farm house toward a more comfortable spot in the garden. The wounded lieutenant nearly fainted at the sight of the grisly pile of amputated arms, legs, and hands which the doctors had callously chucked out the window into the yard. The stack was several feet high, almost level with the window sill.

Lieutenant Wheeler gently eased his injured comrade onto a bee gum in the farm's cabbage patch and proceeded to examine the wound. Luckily for the victim, a spent ball had only cut a quarter inch deep, two inch long furrow in his skull. The young man lowered his bleeding head into the palm of his left hand which accidentally jerked his sword scabbard against one of the cabbage leaves. He passed out.

Lieutenant Wheeler quickly glanced to the left of the unconscious officer. A freshly amputated foot, which Wheeler suspected some animal had dragged there to eat, lay naked under the disturbed cabbage leaf.[60]

The West Woods — The East Woods

It was about 8:40 A.M. The battle had run unabated since daylight. The fields were filled with dead and wounded. The air reeked of sulfur. The artillery continued to roar, making it nearly impossible to hear screams above the din. The Cornfield and the East Woods were finally in Federal hands, but the Confederates still held the West Woods and the ridge which commanded them. Only Ewell's, Jackson's, and Hood's depleted divisions secured the left flank of Lee's army. They were running low on warm bodies to commit to battle. Most of the regiments which remained upon the field mustered fewer than fifty to seventy men. In the 21st Virginia (Jones' Brigade, Jackson's Division), two men remained in F Company — Privates John Worsham and Reuben J. Jordan — and Jordan had been detached as a skirmisher to the northeast corner of the West Woods.[61] If the Federals had pushed their advantage, they could easily have rolled up the Army of Northern Virginia and carried the day.

The Federals, however, true to form, did just what Robert E. Lee hoped they would do. They halted to regroup around their newly won objectives.

The seven left companies of the 124th Pennsylvania pulled back and went prone in the Cornfield, about fifty yards south of Miller's house, while the three right companies across the Pike, exchanged shots with the enemy in the northern section of the West Woods. With almost sixty-four casualties and no orders to advance, the men saw no need to get seriously engaged.[62] The 13th New Jersey, 2nd Massachusetts, and 3rd Wisconsin (facing west, in line, north to south respectively) secured the East Woods with the 27th Indiana in reserve. The 107th New York was posted where the Smoketown Road entered the woods, facing south. The unit had not fired a single shot.[63] Tyndale's three Ohio regiments, which were running out of ammunition, raced south toward Mumma's.[64] Simultaneously, the 3rd Maryland, 102nd New York, and the 111th Pennsylvania converged on Mumma's from the east. The 125th Pennsylvania was the most advanced regiment in the Army of the Potomac. With both flanks in the air it was pinned on the high ground above Mumma's cemetary awaiting orders to move forward.[65]

Not only were the Union troops traveling blindly over unfamiliar terrain, but none of their general staff really knew what was going on. In the smoke and confusion, "Fightin' Joe" Hooker (I Corps) had no idea where the Confederates were or what regiments he had left to command.[66] *(Map 24)*

The Cornfield finally belonged to the XII Corps, which repelled Ripley's attack and routed Colquitt's demoralized brigade. It also held the East Woods and the untried 125th Pennsylvania advanced along the Smoketown Road to find a command which no longer remained in tact.

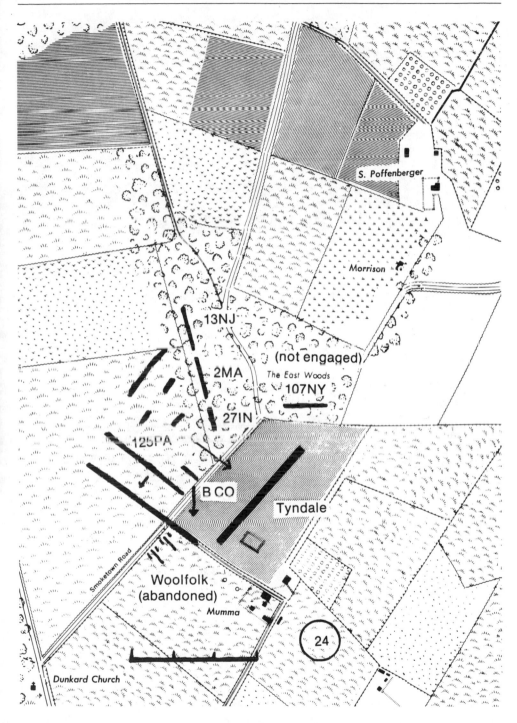

(Map 24) 8:00 A.M. — 8:40 A.M., SEPTEMBER 17, 1862
The XII Corps secures the East Woods.

CHAPTER SEVEN

". . . Be not far from me for trouble is near . . ."

Joseph Hooker and his aide, Corporal Andrew J. Speese (H Co., 3rd PA Cav.), were not the only confused people upon the field. No one knew exactly how their particular side fared. The field had changed hands too often. Commands had become terribly scattered.[1]

The Martin Line Farm

Frank Schell, the special artist for *Leslie's Illustrated*, arrived at the Martin Line cabin, but did not linger there because he found the surroundings too ghastly. He decided, instead, to head south toward the East Woods. He stayed for several minutes in the open gazing at the sky's deceptive tranquility. The bright sun and the virtually cloudless sky seemed so out of place. He felt very depressed.[2]

Hearing the jangling of sabres and harnesses to the east, he twisted about in the saddle and discovered the first units of the II Corps moving south, away from the Line farm. Major General Edwin V. "Bull" Sumner personally led his II Corps. The old cavalryman sat bolt upright in the saddle, as if on parade. His cavalry escort surrounded him as the three brigades of John Sedgwick's Second Division approached from behind in three parallel columns of four. Frank Schell sat astride his horse, enthralled by the spectacle of it all.[3] Once again, the Federals were going to assault the Confederates piece-meal.[4]

96

The West Woods

The Confederates, simultaneously, were feeding more men into the West Woods area. Captain William Blackford (Stuart's staff) had posted himself for the better part of the morning with John Pelham's horse artillery on Nicodemus Heights.[5] The twenty-five Confederate field pieces had been putting a tremendous plunging fire into the Cornfield and the North Woods since the battle began.[6] By 8:00 A.M., a line of thirty Federal guns, north of Joseph Poffenberger's, had started to respond with equal fury until a sulfuric cloud enveloped the entire hill. The Confederate position remained tenable as long as the ammunition held out and as long as the Yankees did not rush the position with a heavy column of infantry.

The seven battle flags which flapped in the breeze behind Pelham's gunners drew as much fire as the batteries did, and that is what Stuart wanted them to do. They were a feint — a clever ruse to mask the movement of Jubal Early's Brigade (13th, 25th, 31st, 44th, 49th, 52nd, and 58th VA) to the southwestern side of the West Woods.

Sergeant Samuel D. Buck (H Co., 13th VA) represented his entire company upon the field that day. The others had fallen out between Harper's Ferry and Sharpsburg during the night march of September 15. Fear of disgracing his family by deserting and a strong sense of duty kept him in the ranks. As the rest of Jubal Early's Brigade advanced upon the West Woods, J. E. B. Stuart deployed the small regiment of less than one hundred men in the cornfield east of Pelham's batteries on Nicodemus Heights.[7]

Sharpsburg

BRIGADIER GENERAL WILLIAM BARKSDALE, brig. commander, ANV

His Mississippians greatly assisted in the route of John Sedgwick's division from the West Woods. *(William E. Strong Collection, Duke U.)*

About one mile to the south, on Sharpsburg's main street, Brigadier General William Barksdale's Brigade (13th, 17th, 18th, and 21st MS) flopped down for a much needed rest. James Dinkins and W. L. McKee (C Co., 18th MS) gathered up their company's canteens and went for water at Michel's Spring.[8] They were exhausted. The brigade had covered the seventeen miles from Harper's Ferry in fourteen hours of straight marching. Along the road, hundreds of men collapsed from exhaustion. In Dinkins' company sixteen enlisted men and one lieutenant remained of an original complement of sixty soldiers.[9] They barely arrived with that number.

The Potomac River at Shepherdstown was swift and shoally. The men who had shoes held them with their cartridge boxes high above their heads as they tried to negotiate the crossing. Dinkins could still see plucky Tommy Brennan, the shortest man in C Company, attempting to ford. Brennan struggled to within sixty feet of the Maryland bank when he called out, "Boys, I am over dry sod."

At the same moment he slipped into a sink hole and disappeared completely from view. Seconds later, he clawed to the surface of the river and sputtered, "After I get some dry clothes on." Life never seemed to wear down that sprightly Irishman.[10]

James Dinkins wished they all felt as lively. The men had not sung one note since they took the right fork in the road south of Harper's Ferry. They all knew that they were going to see the elephant once again.[11] The men were professionals and realists who knew they had nothing to sing about.

The West Woods

Jubal Early's people did not feel too elated either. With the exception of Poague's Battery, which had moved along the eastern face of the West Woods to a point midway between the Cornfield and the Dunker Church, they were the only organized Confederate units in the West Woods.[12] When Early's Brigade arrived in the West Woods, it found about two hundred to three hundred men northwest of the Dunker Church. They were the remnants of the 27th Virginia and the 9th Louisiana (Grigsby's and Starke's Brigades, respectively).

Early, whom Stuart field promoted to division command to replace the wounded Lawton, immediately formed his brigade behind what was left of Jackson's Division. He ordered them to prepare to attack.[13]

The East Woods

Meanwhile, Frank Schell had not strayed very far from the Line house. As Sedgwick's Division doublequicked past him toward the East Woods, a panting staff officer charged at the reporter from the rear.

"Where in the name of God is General Hooker?" he screamed as he reined beside Schell. "Do you know anything about his whereabouts?"

"No," Schell replied.

The officer spurred away toward the hospital. Simultaneously, a shell burst directly over the house which threw the entire area into confusion. Two wheeled ambulances, loaded to capacity with wounded men, rumbled and jolted by and Schell heard someone shouting about moving to a safer farm — further north along the Smoketown Road.

The young artist decided to head toward the action. Wheeling his horse about, he raced to catch up with Sedgwick's men whom he eventually located near Morrison's cornfield as they maneuvered into battle lines.[14] Brigadier General Willis A. Gorman's Brigade (34th NY, 15th MA, 82nd NY, and 1st MN, south to north, respectively) formed in the cornfield forty paces in front of Brigadier General Napoleon J. T. Dana's Brigade, which had halted in the open behind the worm fence along the eastern border of the field.[15] Brigadier General Oliver O. Howard's Philadelphia Brigade fell in and faced west, forty paces behind Dana's regiments.[16]

Schell noticed the men were very feisty.[17] In fording the Antietam they had gotten soaked to the knees.[18] They did not halt to shake the gravel out of their shoes. As they stood in formation waiting to advance, they physically and verbally abused all stragglers who stumbled their way.

They cuffed and kicked the walking wounded — particularly those who showed no blood — when they hobbled too close to their lines. Sedgwick's men waxed particularly nasty with the demoralized zouaves of the 14th Brooklyn, who had been used up with the "Iron Brigade". (They lost thirty-one of less than one hundred men. Their bright red trousers made them conspicuous targets. One group of four unwounded soldiers wandered from the East Woods with an injured comrade between them. They wisely skirted around the Second Division's forming lines.[19]

The Smoketown Road

The situation was not ideal. Federal units moved about the field without direction because Union staff organization was a shambles. Joseph Hooker (I Corps commander) and Corporal Andrew J. Speese (H Co., 3rd PA Cav.) bolted south from the Cornfield looking for an organized regiment to command.[20] Near the southern point of the East Woods they noticed troops in new uniforms dashing through the smoke, who were moving southwest along the Smoketown Road. They spurred their mounts after them.

Colonel Jacob Higgins (125th PA) had just pushed his green regiment a few rods further along the Smoketown Road to give them better protection from the incoming rounds of Patterson's Battery, which was shelling the regiment from a limestone ledge east of the Dunker Church.[21] As the outfit rushed forward, B Company filed to the left and went prone in Mumma's lane, while the rest of the regiment flattened out in the clover field on the northern side of the road. The billowing smoke from Mumma's buildings obscured their vision to the front. The regiment was pinned.[22]

Private Miles Huyette (B Co.) and two other men from his company crawled under the fence rails toward one of Woolfolk's abandoned guns, south of the road. They wanted a good peek at the Rebel position. A twelve pound ball crashed through the wheels of the piece as the men neared it. With spokes and splinters flying close, Huyette and his friends rolled through the dirt and scrambled for cover. They could get a closer look another day.[23]

Amidst the confusion, General Hooker and his aide tore into the regiment's line.[24] They found Colonel Higgins kneeling behind a fence rail and cautiously peering at the West Woods.

"Colonel, what regiment is this? What is in front of you?" Hooker demanded.

Colonel Higgins answered, "125th Pennsylvania Volunteers — nothing but rebels."

Hooker, red faced and blustery, pointed dramatically toward the Dunker Church. "Advance and hold that woods." Snipers rudely interrupted the general's performance. His fine white horse reared in pain as several dying rounds thumped into its body.

"General," Higgins said, "You had better get out of this."

"Guess I had," the general numbly replied.

Within seconds, a ball whizzed over Colonel Higgins' shoulder and smacked into the general's left instep. Without muttering a word, Hooker wheeled his horse about and rode away.[25] This occurred approximately between 8:40 A.M. and 8:50 A.M. No one commanded the Army of the Potomac upon the field.

The East Woods

A short distance east of the 125th Pennsylvania, Hooker dazedly sent a freshly arrived courier to fetch Edgell's Iron Battery (1st NH).[26] He then weakly asked Corporal Andrew J. Speese (H Co., 3rd PA Cav.), who was to his right, to draw close to him. He told Speese he was wounded. Hooker looped his right arm around the enlisted man's neck and leaned heavily against him. It was all the corporal could do to manage the general's weight and handle both horses to get them to the East Woods.

As they neared the trees and a captured Confederate battery (identity unknown) which Gordon's Brigade had overrun in its drive through the Cornfield, the men, who were scampering over the guns and caissons like children, cheered him. The general weakly lifted his hat to them and continued on.

When one of the regimental surgeons noticed Hooker was bleeding, he offered him his canteen of brandy. "Fightin' Joe" declined it. The cavalryman and the surgeon lifted Hooker from the saddle and laid him on the ground.

Corporal Speese pulled the spur from the general's bloody boot and attempted to ease the boot off. The tugging caused too much discomfort. They cut the boot away. As they loaded Hooker into an ambulance, he ordered Speese to hunt out General George Gordon Meade and give him the command of the I Corps.[27]

Meanwhile, Edgell's Iron Battery (1st NH) smashed through the fence in front of B Company (125th PA) and went into battery facing the Dunker Church from Mumma's lane. A second battery, Monroe's Battery D, 1st Rhode Island, bounced and thundered down the Smoketown Road toward the high ground across the road from Edgell's. Their combined barrages silenced Patterson, forcing him to retire. The field became terribly silent, except for the occasional whine of a sharpshooter's bullet.[28]

Nicodemus Heights

Captain Blackford (Stuart's staff), who had gotten snatched up in the shelling on Nicodemus Heights, seemed aloof to the terrible racket caused by the heavy cannonading. Not everyone in the vicinity shared his tranquility.

The Nicodemus House, a beautiful square, white framed building, lay in a depression between the opposing lines. A roughly turned field separated the house from the Confederate left flank. Throughout the entire battle not a single round crashed through the house. The shells cleared the roof by a very safe distance.

The racket, however, unnerved a flock of women and children who had taken refuge there. Captain Blackford noticed the civilians during the latter moments of the bombardment. The gaggle burst from the house and ran pell mell toward Pelham's guns. The captain laughed out loud as they frantically scrambled through the deep furrows in the ground. The women's hair streamed out behind them. Every time a child fell over a clod, another bolted further ahead, thinking that a playmate had been killed.

Blackford's laughter dissipated quickly for he suddenly realized that if they continued on their present course, they would run directly into the thundering death they were so desperately trying to escape. He spurred his mount in among them and bawled at them to turn back.

They were too frightened to listen, therefore he quickly yanked several children onto his saddle and carried them to safer ground. Within moments, the guns ceased fire. Blackford would believe they had stopped to save the children.[29] Historians would attribute the relative silence to the mutual exhaustion of both sides. It was 8:40 A.M.[30]

The Smoketown Road

The sniper fire became quite hot along the line of the 125th Pennsylvania. The soldiers got as low to the ground as possible to keep from getting hit. A bullet flattened itself on a rock near a soldier's head, the concussion nearly knocking him out. A scared puppy, which belonged to an artillerist in Monroe's Battery, crawled down the blouse of Albert Robison (G Co.), and a canister ball cut down Corporal John Christian (G Co.). Things were getting very bad.[31]

Presently, Captain E. L. Whitman, from General Crawford's staff, dashed into the line and told Colonel Jacob Higgins, "The General sends his compliments and requests you to advance with your regiment into that woods and hold it at all hazards."

The Colonel ordered his regiment to its feet. The men right obliqued at the double quick to the right of Monroe's gunners. Riflery from the West Woods dropped some of B Company in the dirt as the soldiers scrambled over the double rows of fences along the Smoketown Road. Miles Huyette (B Co.) left several comrades draped limply upon the rails while he "made lively" to catch up with his company.[32] The regiment faced front (west) and passed around Monroe's Battery, heedless of a lone artillerist, Private Royal W. Caesar, who, not minutes before, lost his leg at the ankle to a solid shot.[33]

The Pennsylvanians advanced in beautiful order, driving scattered Georgians and North Carolinians from a long, northeasterly depression in the ground to their right. As they charged, their own wounded sought refuge in a swale to the left of the road.[34] The line abruptly halted to the right of the Smoketown Road-Hagerstown Pike intersection and laid down behind the badly shattered post and rail fence, which bordered the near side of the road.[35] *(Map 25)*

The West Woods

Captain William Poague's Virginia Battery did not retire with the rest of the Confederate artillery. During the lull in the fighting, his gunners poured shells and round shot across Miller's ground toward the East Woods and Tyndale's Ohions who were moving behind the 125th Pennsylvania toward Mumma's farm.[36] The captain could barely believe what he saw. The 125th Pennsylvania, while advancing on the Dunker Church, passed within fifty yards of his battery without molesting them. (He failed to recall that many of his men were wearing captured Federal uniforms.) Poague spurred his mount back into the West Woods, trying to warn any troops in the vicinity of the imminent attack.[37]

At the same time, G Company (125th PA) under Captain John McKeage fanned out from the right wing of the regiment and disappeared into the West Woods.[38] B Company, on the left, under the command of Captain Ulysses L. Huyette, secured the Dunker Church, which the men discovered was filled to capacity with wounded Confederates.[39] The rest of the regiment apprehensively watched the two companies take their objectives, while they hauled in a few Confederate prisoners. Colonel Higgins dismounted in the road to tend to the grievously wounded Lieutenant Colonel James M. Newton of the 6th Georgia. The dying officer begged for whiskey then morphine. Higgins had neither.

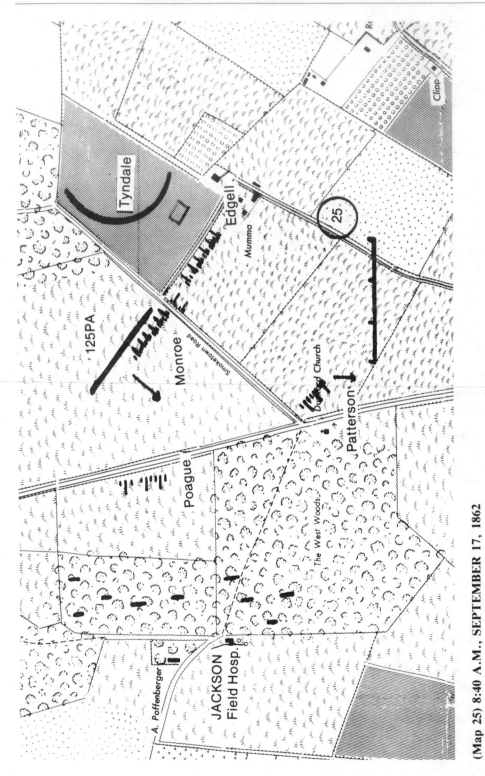

(Map 25) 8:40 A.M., SEPTEMBER 17, 1862

A temporary respite in the West Woods sector.

"I am shot through," Newton groaned. "Oh, my God, I must die."

The Confederate rolled over onto his stomach and expired. The Colonel immediately dispatched his prisoners to the rear under guard. One of the Georgians, while eyeing the long Federal line, blew through his teeth that his outfit had never been routed by a Yankee brigade, to which Higgins quipped that the Reb was looking at a regiment. Eyeballing the line one more time before being taken away, the Reb observed that it must be "a damned big regiment."[40]

Captain Poague happened upon Early's Brigade near the southwestern edge of the West Woods. He sought out Colonel William "Extra Billy" Smith (49th VA), the sixty-six year old who commanded the brigade in Early's absence.[41] The general had crossed the Hagerstown Pike south of the woods and was trying to scrounge up reinforcements from the right of the line.[42]

Poague asked the former postal clerk what they should do. "Extra Billy" bluntly told the captain that he intended to hold his own. He and his people were going to stay put.

"I am here yet," he arrogantly boasted.

As Poague slipped back through the woods, skirmishing erupted along his right flank.

"Well, I am afraid you won't be there very long, old fellow," he mused.[43]

Neither the Yankee skirmishers nor their main line noticed Poague as he slipped by their right flank to his anxious battery. By the time he arrived at his pieces the fighting around the church had become quite severe. He ordered his men to limber up and they feverishly complied.[44]

G Company (125th PA) very cautiously edged its way to the western border of the West Woods.[45] Private Reese Williams brought in a scared Georgian, who excitedly pointed toward the haystacks in the field to the west and alleged that Jackson's divisional hospital was there. A moment later, shots rang out. Private David R. P. Johnson was wounded.[46]

B Company, which had occupied the Dunker Church, heard the shots and braced itself for the collision which the men sensed would follow. Miles Huyette stared into the trees around the church. Dead and wounded men littered the woods like twisted mannequins. Shells had sheered off the tree tops and had gouged ugly holes in the church walls. Branches and limbs dangled bizarrely from the trees or lay in gnarled heaps upon the forest floor.[47]

The firing picked up in tempo. Early's Brigade took cover in a ravine to the right of G Company and started to pour a hot enfilading fire into the startled Yankees. Meanwhile Colonel "Tige" Anderson's (1st Reg., 7th, 8th, and 9th GA) and General Robert Kershaw's Brigades (2nd, 3rd, 7th, and 8th SC) rushed the southern edge of the West Woods with their arms at the right shoulder shift.[48]

Anderson's Georgians, being in the advance, got as far as the stubble field six hundred yards south of the Dunker Church before McKeage's skirmishers opened fire. The small brigade went prone while Kershaw's South Carolinians passed over it and double quicked toward the West Woods.[49]

Brigadier General Howell Cobb's Brigade (16th, and 24th GA, Cobb's Legion, and the 15th NC), to the rear, peeled off toward the western end of a sunken farm lane where it intersected the Hagerstown Pike.

Captain McKeage (G Co.) shouted for his men to retire. The soldiers scrambled back toward the regiment, which had taken position (facing south) just west of the church. In the confusion, the Reb whom Reese Williams captured turned on him and tried to reverse the situation, but Williams put up a good fight and escaped.[50]

As G Company retired toward the main line, B Company also fell back.[51] Kershaw's South Carolinians started to roll through the West Woods toward the Pennsylvanians' exposed left flank.

The Confederate brigade, in moving out without being properly aligned, accidentally triggered the attack.[52] As the Rebels neared the standing 125th Pennsylvania, they dropped their weapons into their hands and opened fire. The Yankees had not chosen a very good defensive position. The left wing of the regiment went into line on and to the left of the ridge west of the Dunker Church. The right wing stood slightly below the other half of the regiment, where the north-south limestone ridge nearly bisected the line.[53] Riflery from Early's men on the right began to take its toll as men on the crest fell from rounds which passed over the troops on their far right. *(Map 26)*

Kershaw's fire slashed into the regiment also. Miles Huyette (B Co.) watched the bullets make the leaves in front of him dance.[54] Captain William Simpson (F Co.) caught a round in the right shoulder.[55] Private Levi Decker (H Co.) was shot through the left shoulder while trying to shoot his rifle.[56] Private Dave Donnelly (B Co.) crashed to the ground in front of the Dunker Church with a paralyzing bullet in his left thigh.[57] Screams split the air, but could barely be heard above the tremendous musketry.[58]

Colonel Higgins, who had returned empty handed from the Smoketown Road, needed reinforcements. The Confederates were taking out his men very fast. He handed his mount to his brother, Joseph, the first lieutenant in B Company, and shouted at him to hunt out General Crawford (acting Division commander) and inform him that the regiment would be completely flanked without assistance. Lieutenant Higgins asked his brother where he might find the general. The last he saw him, the colonel said, was in the Cornfield. At that, the lieutenant took off at a full gallop, heading northeast.[59]

Captain Poague used the pandemonium to his advantage. With rounds thumping the trees about them, his crews hauled the three guns through the woods to the perimeter of the fighting and escaped toward Nicodemus Heights.[60]

The Cornfield

The West Woods and Mumma's fields became charnel pens. General Marsena Patrick's Brigade (I Corps) got to its feet as two fresh regiments from the XII Corps — the 60th and 78th New York regiments (Goodrich's Brigade) — ran south along the Hagerstown Pike toward the West Woods and the Dunker Church. They raced straight toward the fighting from the stranded 125th Pennsylvania.

General Patrick strongly advised their commanding officer, Colonel William Goodrich, to advance with extreme caution until he could fetch some reinforcements to back them up. Goodrich did not heed the warning. As Patrick spurred his horse across the Cornfield, he watched the two regiments disappear into the northern section of the West Woods, where hostile riflery killed Goodrich moments later.[61]

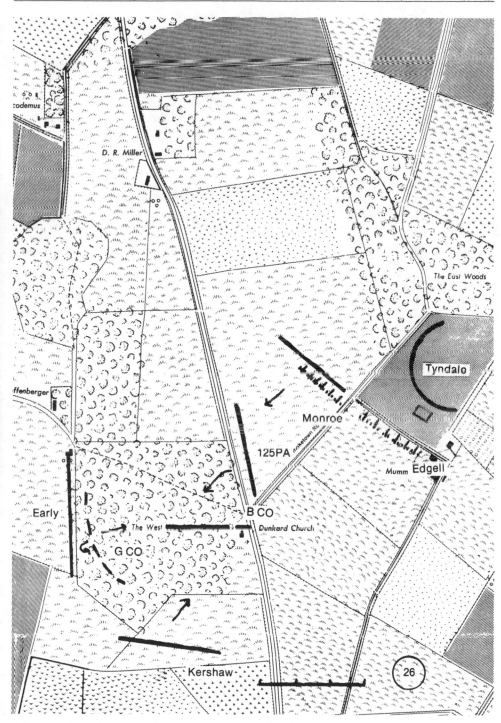

(Map 26) 8:40 A.M. — 9:00 A.M., SEPTEMBER 17, 1862
The 125th Pennsylvania temporarily secures the West Woods.

The East Woods

Meanwhile, Sumner's grand assault upon the West Woods had finally gotten under way, despite a very shaky start. Stuart's artillery on Nicodemus Heights, in conjunction with S. D. Lee's badly mauled crews, who had just gone into battery on a slight ridge about six hundred yards south of the Dunker Church, blindly cut loose upon the East Woods.[62] The shells struck home in Sedgwick's Division as it began to march, forcing most of the brigade and line officers to dismount for their own safety. Gorman's Brigade stepped out of Morrison's cornfield and made for the East Woods. General "Bull" Sumner and his staff rode to the immediate right rear of the line. A man in the 19th Massachusetts (Dana's Brigade, second line) saw them and noted how calm and serene the old man looked as he trotted, hat in hand, into battle. The breeze plucked at Sumner's long gray locks and he seemed to smile amid the racket and the gore which surrounded him.[63]

By the time the general reached the far side of the East Woods, his alleged smile had evaporated. He turned around in the saddle and scanned the woods. Generals John Gibbon (I Corps) and George H. Gordon (XII Corps) eyed Sumner as he kept pace with the right of Gorman's Brigade. The old man, who kept a steady eye toward his rear, did not notice either of the two general officers. He was looking for Dana's Brigade which had not left the woods yet.

"Where is my second line?" he spat.

John Gibbon immediately spurred to Sumner's side and offered his services as a courier.[64]

Dana's Brigade took a serious pounding from the Confederate batteries. The 19th Massachusetts, on the right of the line, faltered as it changed front by the right flank. Colonel Edward W. Hinks halted his shaky troops. "Colors and general guides on line, on centre dress" he ordered.

The 19th closed ranks and the colonel wheeled his horse about. He ran the regiment through the manual of arms for about a minute. The time, however, seemed much longer to the men in the ranks. Despite the stray minies which cut down men at intermittent intervals, the regiment calmed down. Meanwhile, the rest of the brigade had gone into the East Woods. Hinks cooly brought his men to "Parade Rest" before sending them at the double quick after the line.[65]

Sumner and the first line of the division continued across the bloodied Cornfield. Few of the men had seen such carnage before.[66]

Asa Fletcher joined the 15th Massachusetts (Gorman's Brigade) on the night of September 16. He belonged to Andrews' Company of Massachusetts Sharpshooters. The man had never seen combat before. He did not know how to march. He did not have the company's regulation telescopic rifle. Instead, he carried a small caliber Remington rifle. The captain, John Saunders, being a laid back fellow, did not seem too disturbed by Fletcher's inadequate training or inferior equipment.

Fletcher asked him about getting a military weapon. The captain casually told him, "Go in! Get under cover and do all the harm you can to the Johnnies; the first man killed in the company, if within your reach, take his rifle and cartridges."

Asa Fletcher did not appreciate the advice. As he stepped between and around the bodies in the Cornfield, he kept hoping that he would not be the first man to "loan" out his rifle. The contorted and swollen corpses unnerved him. He tried dodging every shot which whined by him. He felt completely unstrung. His hands trembled violently. The more nervous he became, the angrier he got with himself. He was ashamed of his own cowardice, but he was scared and rightfully so.[67]

No one could adequately describe the Dantean horror of the Cornfield. None of the survivors could. The overwhelming carnage innundated their minds. They had to watch where they stepped. First Lieutenant John P. Reynolds, Jr. (D Co., 19th MA) stumbled over the body of a Confederate color sergeant. He stopped long enough to rip the "Stars and Bars" from the staff. Rolling it into a ball, he passed the colors to one of Colonel Hinks' orderlies. The flag disappeared and the lieutenant lost his trophy.[68]

Sumner courted disaster. He and John Sedgwick marched the Second Division onto the field as if it were passing in review. It approached the West Woods at the common time on brigade front. The men marched in close order, with less than seventy-five paces separating the brigades. Gorman's Brigade led the attack. Dana's Brigade (19th MA, 42nd NY, 7th MI, 59th NY, and 20th MA, north to south) held the center of the formation. Howard's Brigade (71st, 106th, 69th, and 72nd PA, north to south) came last. Sumner did not bother to post skirmishers or flankers. None of his men understood the rationale behind such a rash formation. Their flanks were up in the air and they were too close together to maneuver against any assault. One survivor recalled that the formation was "very faulty".[69]

General Sumner rode ahead of Sedgwick's Division to reconnoiter the situation of the 125th Pennsylvania in the West Woods. He saw nothing of Lieutenant Joseph Higgins (B Co., 125th PA). Sumner asked the pinned Pennsylvanians for their regimental number and spoke briefly with Colonel Higgins before galloping away.[70]

The new regiment desperately needed help. Colonel Jacob Higgins feared that the Confederates would overrun his position.[71] He walked, bareheaded, into the woods along the front of his line to survey the situation. His men had held their own thus far, but he knew they could not withstand the incoming fire.

The right companies were getting shot to pieces. Bullets zinged past without let up. Captain William W. Wallace (C Co.) paced the line snapping at his men to be firm.[72] The Confederates charged the line three times and were repulsed.[73] The outfit needed an immediate assist. Private Stephen Aiken (D Co.) dropped with wounds to the face and neck when a minie shattered his jawbone. He lay unconscious on the ground.[74] Casualties continued to accumulate.

The Dunker Church — The East Woods

The minutes dragged on forever. Sumner intercepted Gorman's Brigade as it neared the middle of the Cornfield. He sent Brigadier General Willis A. Gorman to the 125th Pennsylvania. Gorman ordered Higgins, who had returned to his regiment, to maintain his post, saying that his own men were on the way, but that it would take a few minutes to bring them into line.[75]

Presently, the 34th New York peeled away from the left flank of Gorman's Brigade as Colonel James A. Suiter double quicked his men southwest toward the Dunker Church.[76] A portion of the 78th New York (Goodrich's Brigade, XII Corps), having left its dead commander in the northern section of the West Woods rushed upon the rear of the right wing of the 125th Pennsylvania at about the same time that the 34th New York fell in on the rear of the 125th's left wing. Only two companies of the 34th New York extended beyond the left flank of B Company. Colonel Higgins had plenty of help but his own men blocked their line of fire.[77] It was about 9:00 A.M. The 125th Pennsylvania had been under fire for about twenty minutes and it had about ten minutes left to stay in the West Woods. *(Map 27)*

The 125th Pennsylvania (XII Corps), in pursuance of Major General Joseph Hooker's orders, initiated the assault upon the West Woods in the vicinity of the Dunker Church. Hooker was wounded before making contact with General William Sumner (II Corps C. O.), who was then preparing to launch a grand assault upon the West Woods from the East Woods.

The 125th Pennsylvania, backed by the 34th New York, was ordered to hold back Early's and Kershaw's Brigades while Sumner used Sedgwick's Division to turn the Confederate left flank.

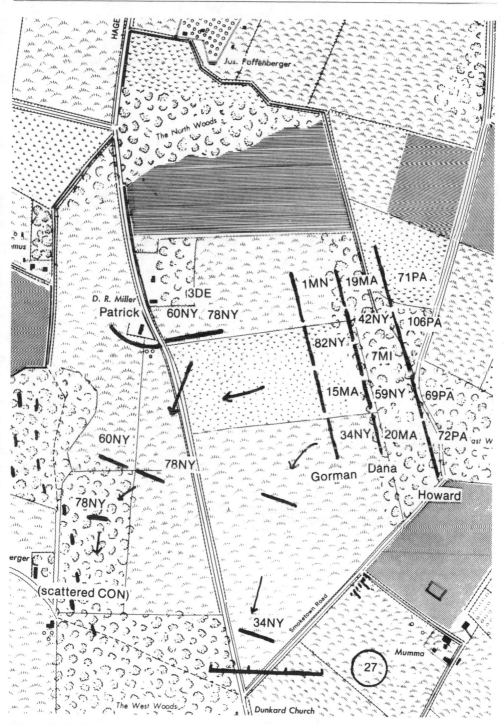

(Map 27) 8:40 A.M. — 9:00 A.M., SEPTEMBER 17, 1862
Sedgwick's Division begins its advance against the West Woods.

CHAPTER EIGHT

"My God, my God, why hast thou forsaken me?"

9:00 A.M. - 9:30 A.M.

The West Woods

By 9:00 A. M., S. D. Lee's gunners had expended nearly all of their ammunition.[1] Woolfolk had left two of his pieces on the ridge northwest of Mumma's farm. His men retired the other piece by prolonge.[2] Parker's Battery could not operate at all, because small arms fire around the Dunker Church had cut all of its rammers in half.[3] Everything the men owned was scattered between the Dunker Church and their new position, which was on the crest of a hill about six hundred yards south of the church. They had posted their guns in battery on the northern edge of a cornfield. Woolfolk's two serviceable guns rolled into position in a stubble field to their right.[4] The smoky ground to their front indicated severe fighting. The men could not shout above the din. The continuous noise of the musketry drowned out everything but the thunder of artillery from other sectors of the field.[5]

The fields to the left of Lee's Battalion surged with moving infantry formations. Kershaw's South Carolinians, in the West Woods, charged pell mell into the guns of the surprised 125th Pennsylvania, which forced the brigade to spend the better part of the last hour under the cover of the ridge which ran north to south through the West Woods. To the left rear, Barksdale's Mississippi Brigade (13th, 17th, 18th, and 21st MS) stumbled into position.[6]

110

South of the West Woods

Jim Dinkins and W. L. McKee (C Co., 18th MS) barely returned from the spring in Sharpsburg in time. They fell in as the brigade took off for a mile long run to the north. The brigade halted in a grove of large trees (probably south of the Reel farm). Brigadier General William Barksdale pranced his mount along the brigade's front as the companies came into line.

"The situation is desperate," he shouted. "The enemy is pressing the center. We must drive them back; Stonewall Jackson says so. I want every man to do his duty as a Mississippian. If any of you cannot, step out, and I will excuse you."

No one moved. Despite the urge to do so, it was not the appropriate time for an honest man to openly declare his desire to live. Federal shells burst overhead. Barksdale ordered his men to pile all of their nonessential equipment by one of the trees. It did not take long. Dinkins counted only seven or eight blankets by the tree — the brigade's entire ground cover.

While the men stood to arms, Major General Daniel H. Hill rode onto the field about one hundred yards to the north. He reined his big yellow horse to a halt to observe the fighting in the West Woods. Dropping the reins, he scanned the smoke to the front with his binoculars.

Dinkins stared in awe at the general. As his Adjutant General, Major Ratchford, rode up, a shell bored through Hill's mount. The horse dropped straight down upon its knees without so much as a twitch. Hill merely shook his feet from the stirrups and stepped away from the corpse without taking the field glasses from his face.

Major Ratchford dismounted and removed Hill's saddle and blanket from the dead horse, while the general swung onto his horse and rode away. Jim Dinkins considered Hill the coolest officer in the entire Army of Northern Virginia.[7]

The West Woods

Jubal Early did not feel quite as calm. He had returned to the West Woods to find his small brigade engaged in a fire fight with the stubborn Pennsylvanians around the Dunker Church. He sent his aide, Major Hale, back to Jackson, who was on the ridge west of the church, near Poague's Battery. The major returned with Jackson's promise of reinforcements.

The moment Hale finished his report, a battery cut loose from the high ground east of the West Woods. Monroe's Battery (D, 1st RI) had advanced along the Smoketown Road and gone into battery on the southern side of the road.[8] It was placing shots into S. D. Lee's batteries, west of the Sunken Lane.

An infantryman raced around the southern skirt of the woods to tell Major Hale that the guns along the Smoketown Road were Yankee. Hale refused to believe the man. He cautiously reconnoitered the area himself and confirmed the report. "Old Jube" Early refused to believe his aide. Not an hour before, he had seen Confederate field pieces in that area. The general skirted around the western and southern edge of the West Woods until he reached the Hagerstown Pike. What he saw took him aback. A heavy column of Federal infantry was rushing into the swale east of the Dunker Church.[9] Greene's Division of the XII Corps, having replenished its ammunition, was moving to support Monroe's Battery.[10]

Early's people had ideal cover. Most of the Federal rounds screamed over their heads. They had taken cover behind a second limestone ledge which parallelled the Hagerstown Pike. Most of the Federals could not see the Confederates who were shooting them down. On the Yankees' right, the 49th Virginia drove off some skirmishers from G Company, 125th Pennsylvania, with a nicely executed volley. Early's men needed help. In the smoke and the woods, they could barely tell what was going on beyond their immediate front.[11]

Tyndale's Brigade (2/XII) rushed to the base of the twisted ridge east of the Dunker Church. S. D. Lee's guns and Poague's Battery, which were on the ridge west of the Hagerstown Pike, put out enough fire to force the three Ohio regiments to lie down. The 5th Ohio, facing west, held the right with its right flank touching the Smoketown Road. The 7th Ohio lay to its left, to the immediate rear of Monroe's Battery. The 66th Ohio faced southwest along the same line.[12] The three regiments numbered less than five hundred eighty men combined. Captains commanded the 5th and 7th Ohio Regiments. Lieutenant Colonel Eugene Powell commanded the 66th Ohio; he had only two lieutenants to staff his regimental line. Man for man, the three diminutive regiments were adequate matches for Kershaw's men in the West Woods.[13] *(Map 28)*

No sooner had the Ohions taken cover below the crest of the ridge than Lieutenant Colonel Hector Tyndale (the brigade commander) brought up the 28th Pennsylvania to the left of the line.[14] The line shifted to the right to accommodate it.[15] Further to the left of the brigade, on the western side of Mumma's lane, Colonel Henry Stainbrook rushed his small brigade (3rd MD, 102nd NY, and 111th PA) to the support of the 66th Ohio. The 3rd Maryland and the 102nd New York went to the immediate left of the 28th Pennsylvania. The 111th Pennsylvania moved to the right front which blocked the line of fire for the 3rd Maryland and the 28th Pennsylvania.[16]

To the north, the entire Federal line was moving across the bloodied ground from Mumma's to D. R. Miller's. Sedgwick's Division started to penetrate the West Woods from the northeast. Gorman's and Dana's Brigades ran into skirmishers from Early's left flank and Stuart's front. Howard's Pennsylvania Brigade had not quite reached the woods. The advance slowed to a series of lurches. Each brigade halted in turn as Gorman's soldiers flushed Confederate "bushwhackers" from the far border of the West Woods. The limestone ledges which broke the ground also segmented the brigade lines which tried to maintain their close intervals in spite of the terrain. A full ten minutes passed before Howard's Brigade completely entered the woods. The officers halted their men and leisurely lit up cigars and pipes while they waited for Gorman's men to make some headway.[17]

Stray rounds took out indirect targets as bullets and shot, which either missed or passed through the front brigade, struck soldiers in the two brigades to its rear.[18] When the 19th Massachusetts (Dana's Brigade) descended the slope from the Pike into the woods, seventeen year old Ernest Nichols (C Co.) pitched forward from the line.

"Nichols is gone," someone called out.

The boy lay motionless on the ground — stunned. Moments later, having regained his breath, he staggered back to his place in line grumbling, "I'm not killed yet."

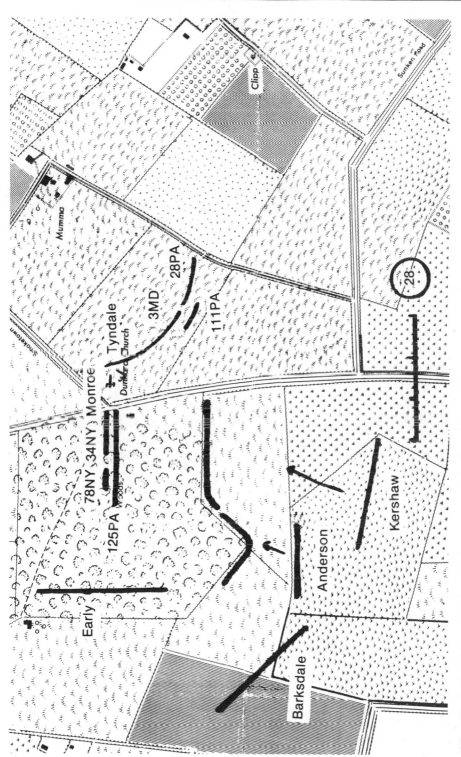

(Map 28) 9:00 A.M. — 9:30 A.M., SEPTEMBER 17, 1862.
The Federals' desperate attempt to hold the Dunker Church.

Major Edmund Rice, who heard the comment, muttered loud enough to be heard, "There's a brave man."[19] Bravery had its limitations. The Second Division had stepped into its own death trap.

Rifle fire smashed into the 15th Massachusetts (Gorman's Brigade) as it moved into the mow grass near A. Poffenberger's farm. The regiment halted to engage remnants of Ewell's, D. R. Jones', D. H. Hill's, and Hood's battered divisions. Less than forty-five feet separated the two forces. Canister and case shot clattered through the woods from Stuart's batteries which were still posted on Nicodemus Heights.[20] Tree limbs rained down upon the heads of the Yankee soldiers and bark chipped off the trees. On the Federal right, the 1st Minnesota and the 82nd New York advanced three times into the cornfield north of A. Poffenberger's. Three times the skirmish line which represented the 13th Virginia drove them back to the West Woods.[21]

Sergeant Ed Moore (Poague's Battery) remembered the dead run from the West Woods to Nicodemus Heights. Terribly mangled horses and destroyed caissons littered the route. The Federal twenty pounders, across the Antietam, made the new post very uncomfortable.[22] Poague's guns went into battery on the right of Raine's Lynchburg Battery. Brockenbrough's Maryland, then D'Aquin's Louisiana Batteries continued the line to the left. Poague's gunners could not see the West Woods, which was about five hundred yards to the east, through the suffocating smoke. The battery struggled to survive in its own pocket of battle — a post which seemed isolated because of the reduced visibility. Regimental battle flags from Early's Brigade poked above the skyline just to the rear of the guns,[23] while a stone wall separated the battery from the cornfield and the Yankees who were concealed in it.[24]

J. E. B. Stuart seemed to be everywhere among the field pieces and in the cornfield, with the black plume in his hat fluttering in the southeasterly breeze which wafted the smoke of the battle into the woods. He sang to himself, as was his habit, while personally leading his skirmishers against Gorman's line. Confederate canister and shot whistled over the tops of the cornstalks into the ridges of the West Woods.[25]

The artillery fire and the riflery shredded the Federal ranks. The first volley into Gorman's Brigade gouged huge holes in his line.[26] The 15th Massachusetts, in particular, took a fearful drubbing. Sergeant Johnathan P. Stowe (G Company) fell with a broken right leg. Whatever had hit him had almost unhinged his leg at the knee and he lay helpless on the ground with the shot and the minies singing all about him. Believing death was near, he pulled out his pocket diary and his pencil to leave a testament behind.

"Battle Oh horrid battle," he painfully scrawled, "What sights I have seen. I am wounded! And am afraid shall be again as shells fly past me every few seconds carrying away limbs from the trees . . ." His body shuddered as he continued, "Am in severe pain. How the shells fly. I do sincerely hope shall not be wounded again."[27]

There were scores of Sergeant Stowes in the 15th Massachusetts.

"Lie down! Every man on his own hook!"

Asa Fletcher (A Co., 15th MA) could hear Captain Saunders' words over and over again. He followed the captain's advice. Fletcher kneeled behind a large oak from which he could see Rebel skirmishers taking cover behind a big haystack to the right of A. Poffenberger's house. The sharpshooter found some courage welling up within him. He cooly counted his rounds — nineteen cartridges. Somehow, the whole business seemed a great deal like target practice. Taking careful aim with his Remington, he deliberately dispatched one Confederate and within a few minutes, he killed four more.

Fletcher's luck ran out as he rammed home his sixth shot. The small bore heated up and fouled, causing the ball to lodge in the barrel before it was properly seated. Without thinking, he stood up, unable to decide whether to extract the bullet or to discharge the piece as it was. For a second, he glanced at the haymound which was less than thirty feet away. He distinctly saw a skirmisher take steady aim and fire.

Fletcher, instinctively, dodged into the round which struck him in the chest. He crashed to the ground, unable to move, numbed from head to foot.[28]

Gorman's Brigade completely blocked the field of fire for the other two brigades. The 19th Massachusetts, which occupied the right of Dana's line, stood on a rise of ground just to the rear of the 1st Minnesota (Gorman's Brigade). The 42nd New York (Dana's Brigade), to its left front, had closed upon the rear of the 1st Minnesota.[29] The 7th Michigan, 59th New York, and the 20th Massachusetts (Dana's Brigade, north to south) continued the line west of the limestone ledge which ran through the woods toward the Dunker Church.[30]

Colonel Hinks ordered the 19th Massachusetts to lie down. The men could not return fire without hitting the Minnesotans. They admired how their colonel sat astride his mount near the center of the regiment with his arms folded across his chest while the bullets and slugs smacked into the trees around him. A smile seemed to flicker on his face as he tempted death.[31] (Map 29)

Death seemed to be everywhere. Twice, the 15th Massachusetts drove away the gunners from one of Stuart's batteries only to be forced back into the West Woods. In all, the New Englanders gained only thirty feet of ground that day.[32] The cornfield north of A. Poffenberger's lent itself to a debacle similar to the one which occurred in the Miller Cornfield. The 15th, which had seen the carnage of the morning's fighting, could also hear its own twenty pound shells rumbling overhead. The gunners across the Antietam were shooting by "guesstimation". They could not see through the pall of smoke which enveloped the West Woods to differentiate friend from foe. They merely placed the shells where they assumed the hostile projectiles came from. Their barrages proved to be unnervingly accurate. Bullets and shrapnel materialized from every quarter.

Nicodemus Heights

Sergeant Ed Moore (Poague's Battery) heard the terrible roar of a big round as it barrelled past his gun. He glanced behind him toward his limber chest as the huge shell burrowed a trench in the ground next to Moore's lead driver, Henry Rader, who was prone next to the swing pair of horses. The impact levitated Henry's body from the ground and slapped him down again. The horses shied, trying to stampede while Henry staggered to his feet and mindlessly stumbled to the rear. In an instant, Robert E. Lee, Jr., one of Moore's men, sprang at the horses. Snatching up their reins, he pulled the frightened team back to its position.[33]

The artillery captains fussed and griped at a courier who ordered them to limber up and follow Captain John Pelham's crews further to the left of the line. Pelham,

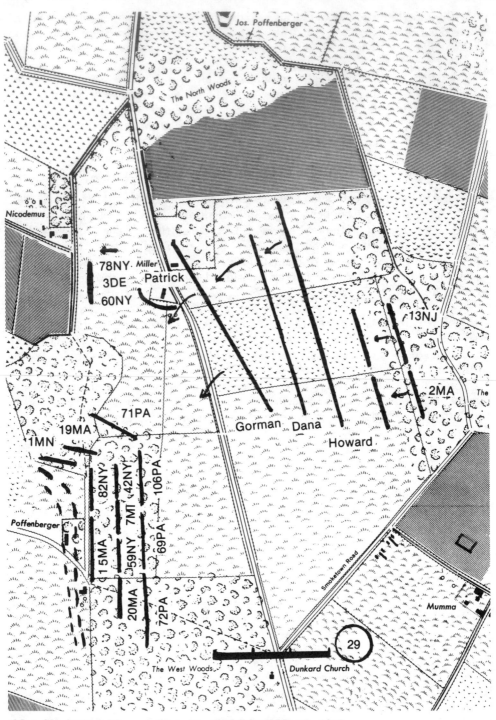

(Map 29) 9:00 A.M. — 9:30 A.M., SEPTEMBER 17, 1862
Sedgwick penetrates the West Woods.

who was something of a dandy like his idol, Stuart, wanted them to go to an exposed position without infantry support. The crews limbered up despite their misgivings
about the venture.[34]

Ed Moore assumed they were pulling out to avoid the severe fire from the
Yankees' big guns.[35] Like the others, he had no idea that Pelham intended to use
them to probe the Army of the Potomac's right wing for a weak spot.[36]

Several of the batteries began to pull out too soon. While asking his section commander, Lieutenant Archibald Graham, if his gun should limber up, a one inch
canister ball knocked him down like a ten pin. Lieutenant Graham, hastily surmis-
ing that Moore was dead, galloped off, leaving the sergeant for the burial parties.
The shot, which had gouged an ugly wound clear to the thigh joint, paralyzed Moore,
and left him on the ground in terrible pain. The sergeant watched the opposing fire
tear out clods of grass and earth, knowing full well that he would receive no succor
because of the general orders which forbade the evacuation of the wounded until
the artillery ceased fire. Shortly after his wounding, the pain subsided, but he could
not crawl away. His legs were completely numb. Time seemed to stop.[37]

Time dragged on at an interminally sluggish pace. So much happened in so little
time that the soldiers tended to capsulize their experiences into anecdotal fragments
which, later, relayed a false sense of slowness to the day's events. Time and again,
the combatants remembered that the sun appeared to stand still in the sky. This
was particularly true for the Confederate soldiers, most of whom had borne a larger
portion of the battle than the individual Federal participants.[38]

The West Woods

By approximately 9:20 A.M., the area around the West Woods had become a
whirlwind struggle as fresh Confederate brigades converged on Sedgwick's unsuspecting men and the 125th Pennsylvania. A gigantic trigger mechanism snapped,
unleashing an unimaginable blast of destruction through that sector of the battlefield.

The Dunker Church

Kershaw's and Early's brigades had their
hands full. Unknown to them, plenty of help
was hurrying toward them from the south.
Robert E. Lee personally posted McCarthy's
Richmond howitzers in reserve northeast of the
Hauser farm.[39] Riflery from the 15th Massachusetts kept the artillerists on their bellies, unable
to return fire. Private Hobijah L. Meade
watched two men go down under the severe
fire. He felt certain, that had their captain insisted upon manning their guns, none of them
would have survived.[40]

Colonel George T. Anderson's Brigade (1st
Reg., 7th, 8th, and 9th GA), with Barksdale's
Mississippians on its left, raced through the
fields south of McCarthy's Battery, heading
toward the left flank of Sedgwick's Division.
The Georgians flopped down behind the rail
fence along the southern border of the West

**BRIGADIER GENERAL JOSEPH
KERSHAW, brig. commander, ANV**
He lost a large portion of his South
Carolina Brigade in two reckless
charges against Tyndale's and Stainbrook's Brigades in Mumma's
swale. *(William E. Strong Collection, Duke U.)*

Woods while waiting for Kershaw's people to drive the Pennsylvanians from the Dunker Church. Tearing the rails down for cover, the Confederates buried their faces in the grass and waited to be fully committed. The bullets smacked into the fence with unnerving regularity. Sergeant William H. Andrews (M Co., 1st GA Reg.) nearly died from curiosity. He had barely stuck his eyes above the fence when a minie ball buried itself in the rail directly in front of his nose.

"Tige" Anderson could not let his men remain idle. Ordering them up, they filed at a run, with their arms at the right shoulder shift, down the fence line to the left. Once it cleared Kershaw's left flank, the brigade fronted and charged. As they bolted over the rails on the western end of the fence row, they fired en masse.[41]

Brigadier General Paul J. Semmes' Brigade (10th and 53rd GA, 15th and 32nd VA) swept toward Gorman's front from the south, to Barksdale's left rear. Ensign John T. Parham (C Co., 32nd VA) stood to the right of Captain Coke, awestruck by Barksdale's superb advance. When he commented that it was the grandest sight he ever saw, the captain somberly quelled his enthusiasm.

"Yes, John," he sadly noted, "it is grand, but look in our front, my boy, and see what we have to face."

Shells, shot, and minies literally furrowed the ground before them. Captains were ordered to the rear centers of the companies but Coke refused to move, electing to stay by the regimental colors. The young ensign advised him, for safety's sake, to go to his post.

The captain declined. "Yes, everywhere is dangerous here," he commented. Moments later, a round hit him above the knee and left him writhing upon the field.[42]

Orders rippled from the right of Semmes' line to charge. One by one, the small regiments filed by the right flank through the gate in the northeast corner of the field. Amidst all the carnage, Captain Edward M. Morrison (15th VA, commanding) noted the chestnut rail fence and the beautiful tree near the gate. Their rustic beauty contrasted so starkly with the horror around them. To the front, the captain saw officers darting back and forth through the smoke like ghosts.[43]

Brigadier General Robert Ransom, Jr.'s Brigade (24th, 25th, 35th, and 49th NC) trotted at the left oblique from the farmland north of Reel's farm toward Semmes' rear. Simultaneously, Colonel Van H. Manning's Brigade (46th, 48th NC, 30th VA, 3rd AR, and 27th NC) rushed toward the Dunker Church.[44]

The West Woods

The Federal line consolidated in the northern section of the West Woods. Sedgwick's three brigades had fairly well crammed themselves into that sector. Gorman's Brigade, which held the base of the plateau, fought along a country lane which ran through the woods from the Nicodemus farm part way to A. Poffenberger's.[45] Dana's Brigade stood in line about forty paces to the rear. Howard's Brigade secured the plateau near the Hagerstown Pike. The entire brigade was in the woods. The 72nd Pennsylvania (on the extreme left) stood in the forest just below the crest of the hill near the center section of the woods. From the base of the hill, most of Gorman's men could not see Howard's Brigade because Dana's line and the dense smoke obstructed their line of sight.[46]

The Hagerstown Pike

Sedgwick's advance picked up stray regiments from the XII Corps. The 2nd Massachusetts and the 13th New Jersey (south to north) of Gordon's Brigade approached the West Woods to the left rear of the 71st Pennsylvania. They had gotten caught up in the spectacle of the grand assault and had gone into action of their own accord. The two regiments crawled through the remains of the post and rail fence along the Hagerstown Pike and reformed on the road. Captain Charles F. Morse (2nd MA) took B Company across the second fence line into the field toward the Dunker Church. They could see troops milling about in the woods but they could not definitely identify them. In the smoke, they lost contact with Sumner and Sedgwick.[47]

The Cornfield

To the north, Marsena Patrick returned to discover that the Confederates had killed Colonel William Goodrich (brigade commander, 3/2/XII) and that the brigade was a shamble.[48] Three of the four regiments were on the northern edge of the West Woods.[49]

Patrick could not find any senior officer present, therefore, he tried to assume command. He ordered the three regiments (60th NY, part of the 78th NY, and 3rd DE) to man the rail fence which bordered the cornfield west of Nicodemus' plowed field. As the three regiments pushed ahead, Patrick saw two or three Confederate regiments crest the brow of a hill to their left rear. He tried to countermand his previous order, but the regiments, which owed him no allegiance, continued on. He was not their commander.[50]

The West Woods

Barksdale's Mississippians closed upon the West Woods. They halted in the plowed field south of Hauser's farm. The brigade stood to arms for about five minutes while Ransom's North Carolinians changed front and charged into the West Woods.

Jim Dinkins (C Co., 18th MS) watched the rifle and shell fire indiscriminately splinter the high post and rail fence along the regiment's front. The North Carolinians had run into strong opposition from the 15th Massachusetts and the 59th New York.

A spotted cow stampeded through the 18th Mississippi. With its tail raised high in the air, the frightened animal lumbered across the field like an awkward race horse. A shell exploded in front it. The cow disappeared into the resulting crater for a moment before it scrambled out and kept on running.

"Boys, she's a Confederate cow," Kit Gilmer (C Co.) shouted. "She's going south."

Kit should have gone with her because he went down shortly after when a bullet crushed his leg.[51]

The Dunker Church

Meanwhile, the 125th Pennsylvania, a part of the 78th New York, and the 34th New York had taken about all of the beating they could handle. "Uncle John"

Sedgwick rode away from his division to check on the situation at the Dunker Church, which he found untenable. He ordered Colonel James A. Suiter to pull the 34th New York out of the action, then he galloped away to turn Howard's left flank to face south. He triggered a holocaust.[52]

The 34th New York and the 78th New York stampeded northeast, leaving the 125th Pennsylvania on its own to face the four Confederate brigades in its sector. Kershaw's and Early's Brigades pressed the line from the front and the right.

Captain Ulysses L. Huyette (B Co.) stormed into the 125th Pennsylvania. The Rebs were closing in on the Dunker Church. He could not hold them back. Colonel Higgins frantically looked about him. Seeing no Federal supports anywhere, he ordered the regiment to retreat. The men, at first, refused to comply. He sent Adjutant Johnston toward the right of the line with the order to pull out, but a bullet killed him before he could execute the command. Suddenly, the Rebel Yell echoed along the regiment's front. Colonel Higgins responded with an oath, but to no avail.[53]

The Rebs were so close that they shouted at the Pennsylvanians to surrender. They ran, instead. The right of the line peeled back then disintegrated, dragging the left of the regiment with it, as the men, individually and in groups scattered toward the East Woods.[54] Private Fred Gerhard (D Co.) did not get the word. He stayed in the woods long enough to shoot his last round before he trotted down the Smoketown Road.[55] Miles Huyette (B Co.) received the shock of his life when he discovered himself standing alone near the Dunker Church with the Confederates less than fifty yards away. He made tracks toward Mumma's.[56] Privates J. George Lincoln and C. James McDivett (both C Co.) dragged Michael Brenneman (C Co.) out of the fray at great risk to their own lives.[57] The Confederates swarmed through the woods, shooting madly as they went. Federal soldiers scattered like quail. Having no time for the wounded, they left many of them behind. Two rounds simultaneously cut down the Simpson brothers (H Co.). Randolph dropped with a bullet in the breast. The color sergeant, George, caught one in the temple.[58] The colors went down repeatedly with five other members of the color guard, one of whom received five wounds before he gave them up. Fifteen year old Eugene Boblits (H Co.) snatched up the flag and carried it a short distance when a bullet knocked him down. Sergeant Walter Greenland (C Co.) took the standard from Boblits and bore it toward Mumma's.[59]

The fire was vicious. Bullets from both sides repeatedly struck the wounded men. A round bore through Private Levi Decker's (H Co.) already wounded left arm before he reached the Hagerstown Pike. As he staggered toward Monroe's Battery, which was posted on the limestone ledge east of the woods, another rifle ball hit him in the right hip. The impact hurled him to the ground. He could not move; his entire system went into shock.[60]

The bulk of the 34th New York fled to the north side of the Smoketown Road. The men ran for their lives, looking for some kind of artillery support. They intercepted Lieutenant George A. Woodruff's Battery (I, 1st U.S.) as it thundered down the Smoketown Road and went into the battery in the clover field north of Mumma's.[61] In the confusion, the caissons nearly trampled Private William R. Strickler (F Co., 125th PA) into mush. The gunners almost ran over him as he turned to fire a final shot at the Confederate line which was forming in front of the Dunker Church.[62] *(Map 30)*

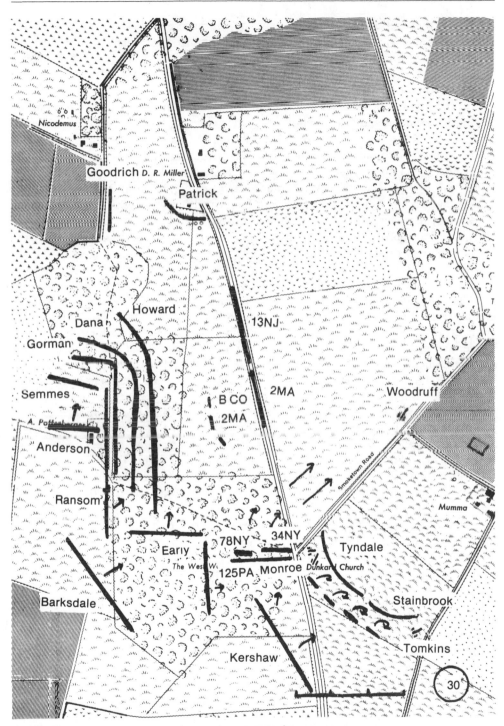

(Map 30) 9:00 A.M. — 9:30 A.M., SEPTEMBER 17, 1862
The collapse of the Dunker Church and the envelopment of Sedgwick's flank.

The events following the collapse of the southern end of the West Woods un-folded very quickly. To most of the men, the one hundred yard dash from the church to the cover of Monroe's Battery seemed much longer. The survivors of the 125th Pennsylvania found themselves trapped between Battery D, 1st Rhode Island Bat-tery and Kershaw's South Carolinians.

In the chaos, the Pennsylvanians smashed into and through the moving column of South Carolinians, many of whom were also wearing blue uniforms. As Colonel Higgins (125th PA) penetrated the Rebel regiment, he passed right by the colors and for a second contemplated snatching them away from the color bearer. Better judge-ment prevailed and he skedaddled for the protection of Woodruff's Battery. Miles Huyette (B Co.) saw Captain J. Albert Monroe sitting upon his horse behind his loaded guns. The captain calmly motioned with his sword for the frightened Yankees to lie down or move away from the muzzles of his battery. Miles Huyette skirted around the guns. Private Tresse (B Co.) did not. He flattened himself out and played dead.

The battery fired in unison as Kershaw's men bolted across the Hagerstown Pike toward them.[63] Woodruff's Battery (to the right rear) cut loose simultaneously but the South Carolinians, despite huge gaps in their ranks, refused to halt.

Sergeant Greenland (C Co., 125th PA) handed the colors to Captain Wallace, his captain, who stuck them in a tree stump behind Woodruff's guns as the Confederates concentrated their weapons upon him. Kershaw's survivors were amazed to see the officer standing, much less unhurt, following a volley of at least one hundred rifles at the regimental colors.[64] Captains McKeage (G Co.) and Wallace hurriedly rallied their men and ordered them prone behind the battery before they started to return fire.[65]

Tyndale's Ohions, to the rear of Monroe, prepared for the onslaught. A projec-tile exploded in the center of the 5th Ohio's color guard. The men quickly raised the standards as the brigade instinctively rose to its feet along the crest and fixed bayonets. Tyndale's line took aim as the South Carolinians neared the guns. At twenty-five yards, they fired. Kershaw's Brigade staggered, held for a few moments, then slowly retired to the West Woods, where joined by Ransom's Brigade, they advanced a second time.

At that moment, Brigadier General George Greene (Tyndale's Division com-mander) raced onto the field with Captain John A. Tompkins' Battery (A, 1st Rhode Island). The Ohions cheered as Greene rushed the battery through the left of the line and posted the pieces to meet Kershaw's assault. The general rose in the stir-rups and raised his hat to them.[66]

Kershaw's people started to close again on the Mumma farm. The brave Con-federates charged across the Pike right into the muzzles of the two batteries and another wall of flaming lead sent them reeling back to the West Woods. As the smoke cleared and that sector of the battlefield quieted, the Federal soldiers stared in hor-ror across the open ground to their front. The Confederate dead, mostly men from the 3rd and the 7th South Carolina regiments, lay in windrows in front of Monroe's and Tompkins' smoking guns.[67] The colors of the 7th South Carolina, having been shot from their staff, were draped across the still warm corpse of the last member of the color guard. Kershaw sacrificed over half of his men in the attack.[68]

Wounded men writhed upon the ground. Private Tresse (B Co., 125th PA) waited until the last Confederate trampled over him before he picked himself up from among the dead and casually ambled back to his regiment.[69] Private Fred Gerhard (D Co.) scrounged over the corpses behind the battery looking for a new weapon. He "swapped" his piece for a nicer one. While he was at it, he "appropriated" a leather case, containing a knife, fork, and spoon, from a dead Reb, whose eating days were over. He heard a wounded Rebel call out to him. Gerhard asked him what he wanted. The man asked to be put in the shade. Gerhard helped him to his feet and tried to carry the man off. When he discovered, however, that the Reb could not walk because he was partially disemboweled, he laid him back down. He saw no use in dragging a dying man to safety.[70] Many other soldiers also spent the lull in the fighting to collect souvenirs.

One of Tompkins' sergeants shaved the fried brains of a dead Confederate from the muzzle of Thomas M. Aldrich's cannon and kept them for a momento. Aldrich who was unable to leave his gun, dejectedly watched Corporal Jacob Orth (D Co.), whose regiment, the 28th Pennsylvania (with the 111th Pennsylvania) had defended Tompkins' right section from Kershaw's attack, unwrap the standard of the 7th South Carolina from the corpse of the last bearer.[71] (His action won him the Medal of Honor four years later.)[72]

Sergeant Edward Russ (D Co., 125th PA) fell, helpless, near the Hagerstown Pike. When a Confederate bent over him and started to rifle his pockets, Russ assumed he was going to be bayonetted and robbed. The Reb picked up an ambrotype lying by Russ' side.

"Is this yours?"

"Yes, that is my dear wife," Russ feebly replied.

The Confederate pressed the picture into Russ' hand. He gazed momentarily at the gut shot Yankee before he ran into the fray with Kershaw's men. During the Confederate retreat, six men from D Company chased after the fleeing Confederates and retrieved their sergeant's still warm body. Sergeant Russ defied the surgeon's prediction that he had not long to live. He died an old man.[73]

Captain J. Albert Monroe (Battery D, 1st RI) cooly spurred his bobtail into the West Woods in pursuit of the fleeing Confederates. Colonel M. W. Ransom's (35th NC) hastily regrouped veterans could not resist the urge to pluck him out of the saddle. A disorganized volley of about one hundred rounds whistled and zinged through the trees around the captain. Several rounds struck his bobtailed horse.

The undisturbed Monroe did not react to the small arms fire. Colonel Ransom, who admired the Yankee's superb self-control, immediately yelled at his men, "Cease firing; don't shoot that brave man."

Captain Monroe quietly and deliberately turned his horse about and returned to his guns. His crews were in desperate need of help and the cowering infantrymen seemed unwilling to assist them. Confederate sharpshooters were picking off his artillerists and killing his horses.

"Limber to the rear!" Monroe shouted.

As his men leaped to their duties, the survivors of Kershaw's Brigade stood up along the ridge west of the Dunker Church and volleyed. Lieutenant Ezra K. Parker, Monroe's junior lieutenant, and a man whom he had personal misgivings about, exhibited tremendous personal courage in hauling away four of the guns under a vicious fire. (He earned the Captain's undying respect.)

Lieutenant Stephen W. Fiske, his senior officer, tried to extricate his section from the rain of lead. It seemed as if every Reb in the West Woods had zeroed in on his two guns. One piece and its limber got away with little loss and joined Lieutenant Parker's column in the Smoketown Road. The other cannon, however and Stephen Fiske did not fare well at all.

A bullet slammed into the lieutenant's horse, but failed to disable it. The riflery cut down five of the six horses on the remaining limber chest as it swung about to receive the trail of the gun.

"Mr. Fiske," Monroe spat, "get some infantry quick — I'll fix the prolonge."

The lieutenant clattered away on his wounded horse as the captain yelled at the two remaining section members to manhandle their twelve pounder. The acting gunner laid hold to one wheel of the Napoleon, while the other grabbed the opposite wheel. He hugged it tightly and tucked his head against the rim, trying to shield himself from the Confederate bullets — a rather senseless tactic. The Rebs were to his back.

"Fix prolonge," Captain Monroe ordered.

The gunner leaned over the trail to pull the rope away, but the other, glancing up at Monroe, whined, "We don't know how, sir."

Two rounds smacked simultaneously into the officer's already wounded mount. Losing his temper at his thoroughly trained veterans, he raised his sword above the quaking artillerist and screamed, "Fix that prolonge, God damn you!"

The frightened cannoneer instantly sprang to the trail and inserted the toggle of the prolonge just as Lieutenant Fiske returned with about twenty infantrymen. They laid hold to the wheels and the drag rope and pulled the Napoleon away amidst the cheers of their own troops and of the Confederates, who momentarily ceased fire to honor their courage.[74]

During the brief half hour to forty minute struggle around the Dunker Church, casualties soared. The 7th South Carolina lost one hundred forty of two hundred sixty-eight engaged, including Colonel D. W. Aiken, who was wounded at the muzzle of Tompkins' guns.[75] The Federals suffered as terribly. The 111th Pennsylvania lost one hundred ten of three hundred present.[76] The Confederates took out two hundred sixty-eight effectives of the 28th Pennsylvania.[77] The 125th Pennsylvania counted two hundred twenty-nine casualties of about seven hundred engaged.[78] Tyndale's diminutive Ohion regiments accounted for about another seventy losses.[79] The Federals lost approximately thirteen men per minute in the assault on the Dunker Church.[80]

The Smoketown Road — The Hagerstown Pike — The West Woods

A general engagement from the Dunker Church to D. R. Miller's erupted moments after the 34th New York legged it from the Dunker Church toward the East Woods. General John Gibbon (Iron Brigade, I Corps) had just sent Woodruff's Battery careening into the clover field above the Smoketown Road when the entire West Woods, south to north, exploded with musketry. Gibbon immediately wheeled his horse about and sped toward the East Woods. Bullets whistled about him. One of them struck him somewhere about the body, but did not stop him.[81]

At about the same time, further to the right in the Hagerstown Pike, Colonel George L. Andrews (2nd MA) ordered the color sergeant, "Show your colors!"

Color Corporal Francis Lundy (B Co.) waved the flag. A volley burst from the tree line in response. One bullet snapped the flag staff in twain while another tore the socket from Lundy's belt. The volley knocked down about one fourth of the regiment. Colonel Andrews and his lieutenant colonel, Dwight Wilder, having just returned from the left of the line to the center of the regiment, were caught in the fire. A bullet thudded into the lieutenant colonel's left hip. He cried out about the intense pain only to get struck again, this time in the left wrist. He collapsed into the road as the regiment, with the 13th New Jersey, having no supports on either flank, retreated eastward.[82] *(Map 31)*

In the West Woods near A. Poffenberger's, the 15th Massachusetts had gotten into more trouble than it could handle. It repelled Ransom's North Carolina Brigade only to get hammered by Barksdale's and Semmes' Brigades. Bullets came in from all directions, including the rear.

Within minutes, Lieutenant Samuel J. Fletcher's H Company (15th MA) shrunk from sixty-two to ten men. A bullet slammed into his one brother's skull. James Fletcher died in his brother's arms. The lieutenant's other brother, George, flopped to the ground with an apparently fatal chest wound. A quick inspection revealed that George owed his life to the Harper's *Weekly*, which he had folded and stuffed into his blouse that morning. (The bullet passed through sixty four folds of newspaper and stopped short of his body.)[83]

The 59th New York (Dana's Brigade) volleyed point blank into the New Englanders' backs in a frenzied effort to stop the Confederate frontal assault. Lieutenant Colonel John W. Kimball (15th MA) hurriedly ferreted out General Sumner to tell him that the crazed New Yorkers were killing his men as fast as the enemy. The general, who was riding along the brigade's line, dashed into the 59th New York and profanely yelled at the men to cease fire.[84]

The 59th New York and Gorman's men temporarily stymied Semmes' advance. Captain Edward Morrison (15th VA, commanding) trotted up to Semmes, who was standing on a rock pile swinging his hat and cheering hysterically. The captain, who could not see the Federals through the smoke, shouted at Semmes, "General, are they retreating?"

"No," Semmes bluntly replied.

Embarrassed, Morrison returned to his shrinking regiment.[85] Within minutes, he lost three color bearers — one killed and two wounded.[86]

The charge across the field disrupted and scattered the brigade. The first rank of the 32nd Virginia moved too far ahead of the rear rank. Ten paces separated the lines, which forced them to close up to prevent the men behind from accidentally shooting those in front.

Bullets pierced the regimental standard seventeen times and cut the staff in two without touching Color Sergeant Bob Forrest. He stayed at his post in the center of the small regiment, apparently oblivious to the blood and brains of his comrades which splattered his jacket sleeves.

Ensign John T. Parham (C Co., 32nd VA), like his severely wounded friend, Captain R. I. Henley, picked up a musket and stood by the flag, returning fire like an enlisted man. Rounds clipped his wrist and foot, but he remained at his post.[87]

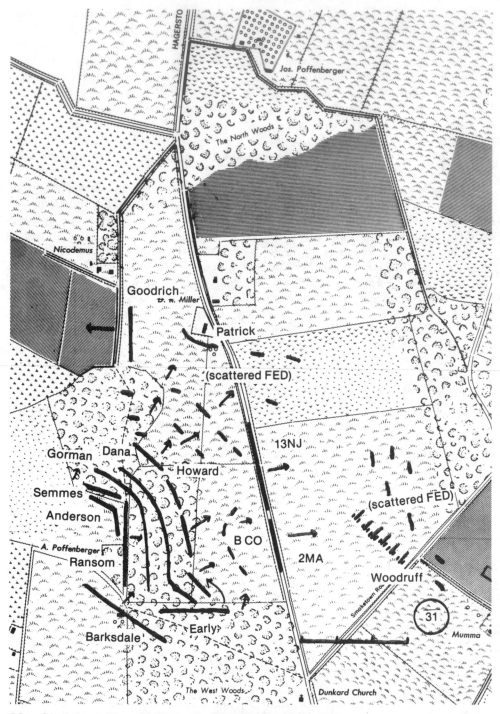

(Map 31) 9:00 A.M. — 9:30 A.M., SEPTEMBER 17, 1862
The route of the Federal right wing in the West Woods.

General Semmes and his two orderlies were running around the area like lunatics. In all the smoke and racket they could not tell exactly where the Yankees were. Once again, Captain Morrison (15th VA) dashed up to the general to find out what was going on. He found the Confederates regrouping and firing as if at drill into the woods to their front. Rebel yells split the air as they volleyed blindly into the trees.[88]

General John Sedgwick arrived in Howard's Brigade too late. He got there just as Manning's, Barksdale's, Semmes', Early's, G. T. Anderson's, and Ransom's Brigades swarmed the West Woods and swept toward the Hagerstown Pike. Their rolling volley plucked Sedgwick from the saddle with a ball in his leg. (Later, while rallying his men behind Woodruff's Battery, he received two more wounds.)[89]

Ensign Parham (C Co., 32nd VA) strained to hear what General Semmes was screaming at him. He wanted to know where the Yankees were. The young officer glanced across the seventy-five to one hundred yards which separated his men from the Yankees and pointed to the stone wall on the far side.

"Yes," Semmes yelled, "and they will kill the last one of us, and we must charge them."[90]

The Federal riflery decimated the 15th Virginia. Of the sixteen men and one officer in I Company, only two of them remained unhurt. Three died. Eleven were wounded, including First Lieutenant George P. Haw, the company commander, who had a shattered left arm.[91]

Semmes gave the command to attack. The Confederate regiments hurriedly realigned, mingling commands together. Color Sergeant Bob Forrest (32nd VA) advanced several paces to the front of the outfit and halted to wait upon the rest of the regiment which was still reforming.

Lieutenant Henry St. Clair (I Co.) bolted up to Forrest in a flurry.

"Bob Forrest," St. Clair cried, "why in the hell don't you go forward with the flag; if you won't" — He lunged for it — "give it to me."

Bob gripped the broken staff tighter and snarled back, "You shan't have it; I will carry this flag as far as any man; bring up your line and we will go up together."[92]

While rifle fire peppered the regiment as the men closed ranks, Captain Morrison (15th VA) continually paced the line, rifle in hand, as was customary with many Confederate officers, exhorting his people to keep up their rapid fire. He noticed a very muscular fellow from the 13th North Carolina (Garland's Brigade) clap his mouth in his hands and walk rearward.

The bullet passed through his mouth while he was giving the Rebel yell and missed his teeth. He stumbled through the 15th Virginia mumbling through his clenched teeth, "Boys, I'll have to leave you. Going to the rear to look for that damned ball. Give 'em hell and my compliments."

A little further down the line a lanky Georgian with a blanket roll with a huge knot in the middle of it halted as the troops regrouped. Slipping the roll off his shoulder, the fellow carefully unrolled the blanket and removed the imposing lump — a half gallon crock of apple butter. The famished soldier scooped the contents out by the handful and shoveled them into his grimy mouth. When the line bolted forward, the Georgian shoved the rest of the apple butter into his mouth and raced into the fray with a dirty face.[93]

Sergeant William H. Andrews (M Co., 1st GA Reg.), who slipped off the top fence rail during Anderson's first advance, picked himself up and nervously "drew trigger" on the color bearer of the 1st Minnesota. Sixty yards to the north, the flag rippled gently in the breeze and the sergeant wanted the singular honor of dropping it. As his sights leveled on the breast of Color Sergeant Samuel Bloomer (1st MN), he fired. Nothing happened! Andrews bitterly fumbled for his nipple wrench and pick. Unscrewing the nipple, he cleaned out the vent at the breech, tapped fresh powder in from another cartridge, replaced the nipple, and recapped. By then, however, the brigade had advanced into the woods.

Lieutenant G. B. Lamar (F Co., 1st GA Reg.) waved his sword from the front of the line, beckoning his men forward. Andrews ran through the ranks to join him lest he be accused of cowardice.[94]

Riflery splattered the 1st Minnesota. Color Sergeant Samuel Bloomer, who was resting on his flag staff, crumbled to the forest floor when a minie ball penetrated his right leg just below the knee cap. Crawling to the southern side of a big Maryland oak to protect himself from friendly fire, he feverishly tore his trousers off to inspect the wound. The bullet, in exiting, had ripped the back of his leg to a pulp. Bloomer quickly tore a long strip of cloth from his blanket to cut off the blood flow above his knee.[95]

Meanwhile, on the Federal right, the 42nd New York started to scramble up the limestone ledge into the ranks of the 19th Massachusetts. A few men to the south tried to deliberately aim in the direction of Howard's line. About four hundred yards to the left, Captain Oliver W. Holmes, Jr. (A Co., 20th MA) saw an Irishman in G Company face rearward and drop to his knee to shoot. The captain screamed at the man, but he continued to take aim and fire.

"You damn fool!" Holmes shrieked as he struck the soldier with the flat of his sword across the base of the neck and prostrated him.[96]

"What are you doing?" someone exclaimed. "Don't you know any better than to fire into our third line?"

One of the New Yorkers retorted, "You had better look back and see if they are the third line."

Simultaneously, Major Chase Philbrick (15th MA) cried out, "See the Rebels!"

"Bull" Sumner broke off his conversation with Lieutenant Colonel Kimball (15th MA) and shot a startled glance at the ridge where his third line was supposed to be. He followed Philbrick's quaking finger in the direction of the Hagerstown Pike.

Brigadier General Oliver O. Howard, whose men could not see the Confederates through the smoke to their front, saw General Sumner riding frantically toward his brigade.

"My God, we must get out of this!" Sumner shouted but Howard could not hear him above the shooting.

The stunned general wildly signalled Howard to swing his line back by the left flank, and he tried to attempt a turning movement. It was too late.[97] The 72nd Pennsylvania (Birney's Zouaves, Howard's Brigade) disintegrated and streamed toward the East Woods.[98] The 69th Pennsylvania, while trying to face south, collapsed, which, in turn, broke the 106th and the 71st Pennsylvania regiments. Sumner spurred into the 106th regiment. His eyes flashed and his long white hair streamed out behind him as he waved his hat in the air and called, "Back boys, for God's sake move back; you are in a bad fix." The Pennsylvanians panicked and ran from the field.[99]

Dana's Brigade had no rear to fire into.[100] The 20th Massachusetts, on the left of Dana's Brigade, retired in good order, but not before the Confederates shot down a large number of men.[101] A volley shattered the 59th New York from the rear and its colors went down. Colonel William Tidball immediately snatched them up. Riding from one end of the regiment to the other, he yelled, "Rally on the colors!" It was futile. The regiment, having lost two thirds of its men, had already begun to quit the field.[102]

The 15th Massachusetts tried to maintain some semblance of a regimental line as it loaded and fired by the numbers. Most of the rounds passed well over the heads of the Confederates who were raking its left flank from a ravine. A bullet knocked down Lieutenant Colonel John W. Kimball and his mount. The state flag went down. Sergeant Charles Frazer (C Co.), who carried the national colors, snatched the downed state flag from its bearer and carried both until a round picked him off his feet.[103]

On the right, the 60th and 78th New York, and the 3rd Delaware (Goodrich's Brigade, XII Corps) defied Marsena Patrick's warning and went into the plowed field south of the Nicodemus farm. Semmes' Confederates volleyed into their left flank.

Patrick immediately pulled his men back to the ledge which they had secured earlier in the day, where they anxiously waited out the attack. They tried to rally as many men as possible, however, with Confederate battle flags getting closer to the right rear (southwest), the New Yorkers, upon command, retired toward the North Woods. The soldiers marched off as if on parade.[104]

The West Woods had turned into a bedlam as regiment after regiment retreated from the chaos. Wounded men on both sides staggered blindly between the trees. Color Sergeant Samuel Bloomer (1st MN) was still propped against a tree and was calmly pouring water over his broken right leg as Anderson's Georgians tumbled over the rail fence in front of him.[105]

Blue uniformed men blanketed the woods all along Anderson's front. Sergeant William H. Andrews (M Co., 1st GA Reg.) believed he could have walked east to west in the woods without touching ground. The Yankees resorted to bushwhacking. The fighting devolved to taking pot shots from tree to tree by individual soldiers or by squads.

Within fifteen minutes, Anderson's Georgians had driven the Federals through the forest to its northern and eastern borders. An officer dashed along their front and ordered them to pull back. Sergeant Andrews pursued the Yankees a short distance further then retired to the safety of the woods.[106]

During his withdrawal, Andrews stumbled upon Samuel Bloomer. The Georgian cautiously approached Bloomer and dove for cover as a shell exploded between them. Bloomer, who laughed at the Reb for acting so foolish, continued to bathe his smashed leg. Recovering his composure, the Confederate properly introduced himself. Andrews and the Yank spent several minutes exchanging amenities. The Yankee told the Reb he had been shot early in the fight and he mused how he had carried the flag since the First Manassas. "Some of you boys were too sharp for me this morning," Bloomer remarked. As they chatted, Andrews realized that "We were no longer enemies, but American soldiers who believe in extending a helping hand to those in distress." A shell buried itself in the tree right above the Yankee's head, which prompted Andrews to leave him, not knowing that they would hear from each other again.[107]

Before he left, the sergeant and his comrades constructed a makeshift barricade of cordwood around Bloomer to protect him from stray rounds.[108] He assumed that a man with a leg broken below the knee like Bloomer's faced an unmerciful death.[109]

Captain Penrose Hallowell (D Co., 20th MA) clutched his shattered left arm close to his body and wandered north through the Confederate lines as if they did not exist. Bullets thunked into the trees around him. A minie thudded into the back of a fleeing Union soldier in front of him. As the man flopped to the ground, Hallowell dazedly stumbled past him.[110]

His good friend, Captain Oliver W. Holmes, Jr. (A Co.) lay on the forest floor in a puddle of his own blood. A ball struck him about a fraction of an inch off center in the back of the neck and exited through the front, barely missing his jugular vein and windpipe. He was still alive, but in a great deal of pain.[111]

The 15th Massachusetts fell back about one hundred yards to the northeast, where it faced about and volleyed to check a Confederate advance from the West Woods. The regiment, which entered the fight with five hundred eighty-two men, left over three hundred seventy of them upon the field.[112] The 1st Minnesota, whose right company hinged on the right company of the 19th Massachusetts, backed out of the fighting toward the northwest, firing in volleys to the south and the southwest as it moved. Crossing the front of the 19th Massachusetts (which was facing southwest) it aligned its left company on the right flank of the New England regiment. The maneuver completed, Colonel Hinks ordered the 19th Massachusetts to face front to rear on the first company, which brought its rifles to bear east. Together, the two regiments volleyed into the Confederates who were moving in for the kill from the front, flank, and rear. They fired twice before retreating to the plowed field south of the Nicodemus farm.[113] *(Map 32)*

Captain Morrison (15th VA) fired all the cartridges in a dead man's box and stepped a few yards away from the firing line where he picked up another and rejoined the fighting as was his habit. He shot two rounds and was preparing to fire the third one when something knocked him unconscious. About a minute later, he came around as four of his men lifted him onto a stretcher and started rearward with him. A projectile prostrated the stretcher party. The fragments splattered Charlie Watkins' brains all over Morrison, causing him to release his grip and dump the captain while he struck the ground with a sickening thud. "Billie" Briggs, another stretcher bearer, crashed to the earth with a broken thigh. The third man in the party lost the second and third fingers on a hand and the fourth one was also wounded. Within seconds, several men ran over to carry Morrison off, but he sent them back into the ranks, where they were really needed.

The captain watched the regiment bolt into the woods near the Nicodemus farm, then very slowly hobbled and crawled to one of the huge haymounds near the West Woods. A mess of blood and brains from head to foot, the captain listened to his blood slosh over his feet as it rolled down his pants legs into his boots.

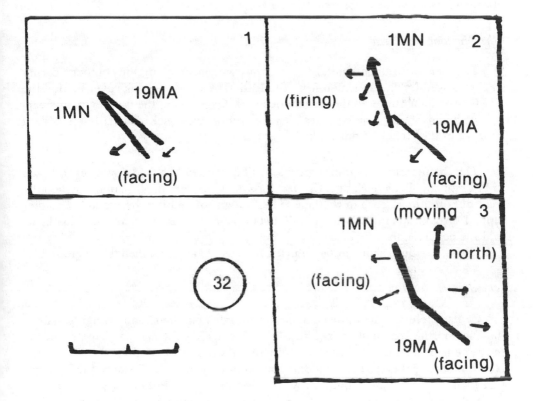

(Map 32) 9:30 A.M., SEPTEMBER 17, 1862

The difficult withdrawal of the 1st Minnesota and the 19th Massachusetts from the West Woods.

Among the wounded in the hay stack, he found Lieutenant John Nussell (15th VA). The lieutenant had no mark other than a large dark blue lump on his breast about the size of a child's fist. He immediately tended to Morrison, whom he considered more seriously hurt than he. Nussell cut away Morrison's right coat sleeve to stop the bleeding at its source. He discovered that the shell fragment had carried away the captain's right shoulder joint. He was going to bind up the wound when one of the men in the stack screamed that it was on fire.

The injured men scattered as fast as they could. Morrison crawled into a fence corner to await what he believed to be the inevitable.[114]

The Nicodemus Farm

The Yankees rallied behind a stone wall which ran along the southern corner of the plowed field. A few men from the 19th Massachusetts took cover behind the rail fence which bordered the Nicodemus lane. Once again, the two regiments peppered the advancing Confederates. Several times, they picked off a few standard bearers in the Rebels' front ranks.[115]

The Confederates fired into their left. Their volley knocked down several men in H Company. Private Nathan Bartlett Jordan, while capping his rifle, watched the man next to him drop into the lane. The thought of helping the wounded soldier zipped through his mind when a bullet slammed into his chest between his heart and his collar bone.

"Boys, I've been shot," Jordan blurted in disbelief as he crashed to the ground.[116]

Nicodemus Heights

Captain John Pelham moved some of the guns on Nicodemus Heights a short distance north. Poague's Battery and three other crews which participated in the movement, came under fire immediately from the massed Federal guns north of the North Woods. Pelham's men could not pinpoint their location because the Yankees had planted their guns behind a row of trees on Joseph Poffenberger's farm.

Pelham's officers protested taking on such an immense force. The boyish major quipped, "Oh we must stir them up a bit and then slip away." The Confederates "stirred up" the Yankees more than a little bit for the Yankees stirred out Pelham's guns with a vengeance.[117]

Captain John Pelham selected a section of twelve pound Napoleons to flank the Union right at the Nicodemus farm. As they pulled out, north across the plowed field, the teams and limbers got bogged down in the soft mud. Pelham immediately brought in the 13th Virginia from the cornfield east of his position to manhandle the field pieces up the slope to the crest west of the barn.

Sergeant Samuel D. Buck (H Co.) found himself, since he was the only man present in his company, assigned to K Company. With approximately fifty men to each artillery piece, the infantrymen slung their weapons and shouldered and dragged the guns and their limber chests into battery.

CAPTAIN JOHN PELHAM,
Stuart's Horse Artillery, ANV

During the morning of September 17, he attempted to stir up the Union right wing in the vicinity of the Nicodemus house. The Federals stirred him out, instead.
(William E. Strong Collection, Duke U.)

His guns deployed, John Pelham ordered the infantrymen to fan out and commence firing into the retreating 19th Massachusetts and 1st Minnesota, which were retiring from the West Wood onto the farm.[118]

In the process, the Confederates rousted out the Yankees in and around the Nicodemus farm. When a charge of canister burst in the road south of the farm house, it sent the snipers from the 19th Massachusetts scurrying for safer ground. Another charge exploded over the main body of the regiment, shattering Captain George W. Bachelder's leg (C Co.). Private James Heath (C. Co.) dragged his beloved captain through the plowed field to the safety of a wheat stack near the barn.

Colonel Hinks (19th MA) also went down with an abdominal wound and a fractured right arm. Lieutenant Colonel Albert F. Devereaux took over the regiment despite the loss of his favorite horse and a bullet wound in his arm. A minie ball smashed half of John Barry's (C Co.) upper jaw, carrying away part of his nose. Lieutenant Albert Thorndike (H Co.) left the field with a gut wound which would plague him for years. The ball, which entered one vest pocket, was spliced in half by Thorndike's watch chain. One half of the bullet exited through the other vest pocket. (Years later, he voided the other half and his watch chain.)[119]

The sharpshooters of the 13th Virginia and Captain John Pelham's artillerists made the position of the 19th Massachusetts too hot to hang onto. The guns, which were double shotted with canister, pounded the New Englanders' flank unmercifully.

Every time the Yankees attempted to move, the Virginians drove them to cover. At one point, an intrepid soldier mounted the fence in a foolish act of bravado. Sergeant Samuel D. Buck (H Co., 13th VA) leveled his rifle on the man and fired. The Yankee toppled into the farm lane. The Sergeant, realizing that at the least twelve other men sighted in on the dead man, never boasted about his "kill".[120]

The two retreating Federal regiments could endure no more. They retired north through the Nicodemus barnyard to a hollow beyond, well below the Confederate artillery fire. From there, they were recalled to W. Middlekauf's, above the North Woods, where they remained until dark in support of a battery. They were the last two Federal regiments to leave the West Woods.[121]

The D. R. Miller Farm — The East Woods

The struggle around the West Woods had been a battle within a battle. In twenty minutes two thousand two hundred ten Yankees of some five thousand engaged were injured or killed.[122] Few of the men were as cocky upon leaving the woods as they had been upon entering it.

Turner Gustavus Morehead, the snowy haired colonel of the 106th Pennsylvania (Howard's Brigade), had gotten thoroughly miffed with the Confederates during the route. A round toppled his horse, pinning him beneath it. Three enlisted men pulled their colonel free. The badly bruised "old man" hobbled north with them a short distance until he realized that he had left his sword in the saddle scabbard. His men could not dissuade him from going back for it.

"Yes, I will," he protested. "That sword was given to me by my men and I told them I would protect it with my life and never see it dishonored, and I am not going to let them damn rebels get it."

The colonel rushed to the horse and retrieved his sword. Morehead took off at a limping gait while the Confederates shouted for him to surrender. With bullets whizzing by his ears from yards away, the stubborn officer made off with his sword and his life. He staggered into D. R. Miller's bruised but alive.[123]

Private Frederick W. Oesterle (E Co., 7th MI) did not stop running until he was well into the northern part of the East Woods. The Rebels had cut his company to mincemeat. Only fifteen of the original thirty-six men and none of the noncommissioned officers came out of the West Woods unscathed.

In less than thirty minutes he had escaped death four times. The first ball plucked the cap from his head. The second punched through his blouse pocket, shredding his pocket dictionary to pieces. The remaining two grazed his leg above the knee and his right arm. He felt fortunate to still be breathing.[124]

Captain J. Albert Monroe (D, 1st R) mercifully dismounted from his severely wounded horse after he joined the battery near the East Woods. As he pulled the saddle and the blanket off his horse he happened to notice that the majority of the six bullet wounds were grouped in the area where his left leg had been. Not a superstitious man by nature, Monroe recalled how he had dreamed the night before that he had lost his left leg. The fact that the Rebels had almost fulfilled his premonition did not alarm him in the least. He merely turned his horse loose, then ordered one of the battery's buglers to pull the saddle and reins from his own mount so the captain could replace them with his accoutrements.

While one very disgruntled bugler straggled to the rear with his saddle hanging uncomfortably from one shoulder, Corporal Charles C. Gray picked up a musket and a full cartridge box from a nearby corpse and advanced toward the reforming Federal lines. The Rebels had picked off four of his Number Ones (the loaders) and he wanted to return the favor. Lying down, he calmly sniped at any movement he could see about the West Woods. When the return fire got too hot, the corporal coldly pulled a couple of bodies in front of him to use for cover. He continued sniping until called into action again.[125]

To the west, the Confederates repelled Sedgwick's Division of the II Corps. Another action was developing, simultaneously, to the south along what would be called the "Bloody Lane".

CHAPTER NINE

"Oh my God, I cry in the daytime but thou hearest not . . ."

9:00 A.M. - 9:30 A.M.

The East Woods — The Roulette Farm

Frank Schell, Leslie's special artist, listened apprehensively to the Rebel yells which drifted across the smoky fields from the southwest. He cautiously slipped away from the rear of Sedgwick's Division; as it stepped into the fields west of the East Woods, he headed south to what he hoped would be a safer spot.[1] Stumbling into the southwestern corner of the woods, he came across the casualties from the morning's engagement. Bodies lay strewn among the rocks like discarded rag dolls. Schell hastily noted that the majority were Confederates — Georgians, Texans, and North Carolinians. Union stretcher bearers had already begun to clear away their own men.[2]

The carnage affected him deeply as he edged among the shattered bodies of the 21st Georgia.[3] He wanted to find a more secure place to work — some place away from the stray minies which still clipped the bark and leaves from the trees around him. The woods had gotten too "hot" for him to dally.[4]

Moving east, then south, he steered clear of Morrison's cornfield, which was swarming with squads of frightened soldiers. Schell descended into the rolling meadows east of Mumma's, all the while trying to get further away from the nerve tearing Rebel yells which reverberated from the West Woods, where, unknown to the artist, Early's men were attacking the 125th Pennsylvania.[5] The young man crouched on a ridge immediately east of Roulette's huge white barn. An immense hay mound flanked the barn's northern side. To the east and the south, he carefully noted the carriage house and the farm buildings, which were bordered on the south

135

by a substantial orchard. Confederates darted in and about the buildings and the haystack thick as bees around a hive.⁶

Frank Schell unwittingly stumbled into remnants of Colquitt's and Brigadier General Samuel Garland's brigades (D. H. Hill's Division), which occupied the Roulette farm. William Roulette, the owner, had confined himself in the cellar of their home since the battle opened.⁷ His farm offered the battle weary Rebels a haven from the scathing combat of the West Woods and Miller's Cornfield, and they helped themselves to his house and his orchard, but left his bee hives alone.⁸

The Confederates did not appear very anxious to abandon the place. Schell watched litter bearers casually carry off wounded men while snipers, using the huge hay mound near the barn for cover, calmly fired to the north and northwest.⁹

BRIGADIER GENERAL ROBERT RODES, brigade commander, ANV
His misunderstood command to face the right wing of the 6th Alabama east triggered the collapse of the Bloody Lane.
(William E. Strong Collection, Duke U.)

The bulk of Garland's and Colquitt's battered commands had retreated to a country lane which intersected the Hagerstown Pike about six hundred yards below the Dunker Church. They arrived at the section between the Pike and Mumma's lane about the same time that Brigadier Generals Robert E. Rodes' (26th, 12th, 3rd, 5th, and 6th AL) and George B. Anderson's (2nd, 14th, 4th, and 30th NC) Brigades filed into the eastern portion of the same lane.¹⁰ The 2nd North Carolina stood in line to the right of the 6th Alabama. The 6th covered a small section of the lane where it turned southeast at about a forty-five degree angle to the rest of the lane. The 2nd North Carolina secured the eastern angle of the apex, with Roulette's lane bisecting its front.¹¹

The Bloody Lane

Captain John Calvin Gorman (B Co., 2nd NC) nervously glanced along the nine hundred yard long Confederate position. He knew very well that D. H. Hill's three brigades stood little chance against a strong Federal assault. The 2nd North Carolina numbered about three hundred muskets.¹² The 4th North Carolina, further to the right, mustered eighty men.¹³ On the far left, the 12th North Carolina (Garland's Brigade) counted between twenty-seven to thirty-two armed bodies. Company C of that regiment had only seven privates and no officers present. Captain Gorman figured the odds at about four to one in the Yankees' favor.¹⁴

That undulating sunken lane became the key to Robert E. Lee's center. With the bulk of his army engaged near the West Woods, he had few men to spare in that sector of the battlefield. Shortly before 9:00 A.M., he and D. H. Hill toured the road, where he paid particular attention to Colonel John B. Gordon's 6th Alabama, which held the most advanced portion of the road.[15] The regiment rested on a crest about midway between the extremities of the lane. To Gordon's left, the lane leveled off and the bank became less steep on both sides of the road.

A snapshot of the BLOODY LANE, looking down hill and east of the position of the 6th Alabama. Roulette's lane appears off to the left where the fence crosses the road. *(Manuscript Dept., Duke University).*

To his right, the lane dipped sharply then climbed to a long plateau for several hundred yards. Erosion had cut the road bed six to eight inches deep from the front of the 2nd North Carolina to the far end where the 30th North Carolina was posted.[16] At some points, the surrounding farm land stood three to six feet above the road bed.[17]

COL. JOHN B. GORDON, 6th Alabama

He pledged to General Robert E. Lee that his men would hold their position in the Bloody Lane until the sun went down. He thought it would never set that day. *(William E. Strong Collection, Duke U.)*

The anxious Confederates hastily tore down sections of the fence rail on the southern bank and strengthened the split rail fence to their front.[18] They constructed a tentatively formidable barrier to any Federal onslaught. Captain Gorman (B Co., 2nd NC) did not feel all that secure.[19]

Colonel John Gordon (6th AL) did not share his pessimism. When Lee and Hill inspected his regiment, Gordon, who was by nature a firebrand and a warhorse, gallantly and honestly assured the generals that his men would hold the line while any of them lived. "These men are going to stay here, General, till the sun goes down or victory is won!" he proudly boasted to Lee. Within the next few hours, he would wonder if that same sun would ever set.[20] The two generals continued along the lane toward the Hagerstown Pike to supervise the reorganization of the rest of Hill's Division which was reeling from the latest Federal push into Miller's Cornfield.

Captain Gorman walked with his colonel, Charles C. Tew, toward the crest of the knoll to the right front

**COL. CHARLES C. TEW,
2nd North Carolina**

**A bullet in the head killed
him during the opening
actions along the Bloody
Lane.** *(Clarke, NC Regts.)*

of the 2nd North Carolina. As they stood there, Colquitt's and Garland's skirmishers fanned out into the swales near Mumma's and Roulette's to impede the next Federal attack.[21] Boyce's Battery rolled into position, facing northeast, in front of the sunken lane to the right of Mumma's lane.[22]

The Confederates in the sunken lane braced themselves for combat. It seemed as if the entire area to their left front was caught up in a whirlpool of blood and sulfur. They stared in awe as Tyndale's Brigade and the 125th Pennsylvania drove their men across Mumma's to the West Woods.[23]

Frank Schell got lower to the ground as the firing increased. A Confederate officer raced up to Roulette's barn and halted. The reporter watched the man gaze intently to the north then gallop away. To the west, Schell watched blue uniformed soldiers (Tyndale's Ohions) move onto the crest across from the Dunker Church, about nine hundred yards from him. Suddenly, Confederate artillery slammed into the Federals as they neared the top of the hill, where S. D. Lee's Battalion had been earlier in the day and Schell carefully marked each yellowish burst from the guns as they opened fire from their new position near the sunken lane-Hagerstown Pike intersection. The crawling, writhing blotches of blue he believed were wounded. One man, who lay on his back, listlessly waved his arms in the air, beckoning like a Captain Ahab for others to follow him to the grave. Nearby, Schell thought he saw another soldier trying to inch below the hill to get away from the gunners.

The Confederates at Roulette's started to shoot to the northwest and the east. A feeble reply rattled from a hill about three or four hundred yards south of Schell. He could not tell which side fired the volley.[24] (They were probably Colquitt's and Garland's skirmishers from the sunken lane.)

The East Woods

At approximately 9:00 A.M., Brigadier General William H. French's Division of the II Corps came upon the field. The Division entered from the north, along the ridge above Roulette's and Mumma's farms. Brigadier General Max Weber's Brigade (1st DE, 5th MD, and 4th NY, west to east), led the attack, followed by Colonel Dwight Morris' Brigade (14th CT, 130th PA, and 108th NY, west to east) then Brigadier General Nathan Kimball's Brigade (14th IN, 8th OH, 132nd PA, and 7th WV, west to east).

The shelling temporarily undid the wet and inexperienced troops as they entered the East Woods. Huge branches showered them from above and round shot shrieked through the air as the men faced left (by the rear rank) and attempted to form a battle line. Morris' Brigade staggered; the men stumbled awkwardly about, obviously confused.

At that moment, Brigadier General William French rode into the mess. "For God's sake, men," he screamed, "close up and go forward!"

Lieutenant Colonel Sanford H. Perkins (14th CT) got his men into line, along with the rest of the brigade, and followed Weber's soldiers onto the descending ground between Mumma's and Roulette's.[25]

Schell caught his first glimpse of Weber's men as they swept around him and Roulette's barn toward the sunken lane. Their fresh regimental colors snapped lively in the breeze. Officers, waving their swords like the Scots at Culloden, cheered their men on. The martial spirit snatched Schell up as the first Federal line marched forward with the precision borne of constant drilling. Allaying his natural aversion to death, particularly when it seemed most likely to be his own, the young artist nestled further into his secure spot to observe his first real battle.[26]

The Bloody Lane

The Confederates in the lane gazed in amazement at the massiveness of French's column. They too noticed the martial splendidness of Weber's well trained men, but with noticeably less enthusiasm than Frank Schell. The front of each Federal Brigade covered the same distance as Hill's two brigades combined.[27] The sunken lane was to become a Confederate Thermopolae.

Colonel Tew (2nd NC) ordered his men to lie down and the other regiments followed suit. Only the officers remained on their feet, trying to inspire their men by their examples. Their brigadier, George B Anderson, realistically assessed their situation. He shouted at an aide to rush after General D. H. Hill and "for God's sake to send us reinforcements."

Captain Gorman (2nd NC) stepped with Colonel Tew over the rails and strolled to the crest of the ridge, some fifty feet to the regiment's front. The captain's heart nearly stopped when he beheld the spectacle which extended across the farm land before him. Anderson's plea rang in his ears above the violent palpitations in his chest.

Yankee soldiers, three battle lines in depth, and at close intervals, stretched as far as he could see to either side of the Roulette farm. He watched them steadily advance until he could clearly distinguish the stars on the blue fields of their national colors.

Gorman, who had checked his watch when Anderson sent his courier off, looked back at his battle tested veterans who crouched in the lane behind him. Their unflinching determination, which he read in their eyes, encouraged him. At that moment, about 9:15 A.M., he believed that he and his stalwarts would earn great honors for the State of North Carolina, regardless of his morbid suspicion that none of them would outlive the day.[28]

The Roulette Farm

Weber's Brigade (French's Division, II Corps) did not successfully route all of the Confederate skirmishers from Roulette's and the surrounding fields.[29] His line moved in nearly perfect formation — the front being slightly convexed — through and around the farm without paying any serious attention to the outbuildings, which still sheltered over twenty Rebels.[30] Morris' Brigade, which was about one hundred yards behind, had to contend with them as it came onto the farm.[31] The 14th

Connecticut (Morris' Brigade) had calmed down considerably. In its approach through Mumma's orchard, Sergeant William B. Hincks (A Co.) and several enlisted men from A Company leisurely helped themselves to some apples. The regiment, with the exception of B Company, which halted on the left to clear Roulette's spring house of sharpshooters, narrowed the distance between itself and Weber's 1st Delaware. The 108th New York, on the left flank, bypassed the farm buildings entirely and left them directly in the path of the 130th Pennsylvania.[32]

Private Edward W. Spangler (K Co., 130th PA) had trouble keeping up with his regiment. The inflamed carbuncle on his right knee slowed him considerably. The captain told him to stay behind because his leg was too stiff to walk on, but when his comrades chided him for showing the "white feather", Spangler determined to "see the elephant" despite his disability. He caught up with the regiment on the northern edge of Roulette's farm.[33]

**PRIVATE EDWARD SPANGLER,
K Company, 130th Pennsylvania**

During the fight for the Bloody Lane, he shot away his ramrod and had to procure a new weapon from a corpse.

(My Little War Experience)

Private S. M. Whistler (E Co., 130th PA) had seen all of Maryland that he cared to. His soaked trousers clung uncomfortably to his legs. The waist deep Antietam had washed sand and gravel into his shoes which worked through his socks to his feet. Most of the regiment was grumbling about the provost guard which had not allowed them to wring out their socks. The 130th, having not been in the service a month, had a great deal to get accustomed to.[34]

Frank Schell noticed how twisted Morris' Brigade became as it negotiated Roulette's.[35] The 14th Connecticut pressed ahead as did the 108th New York. Roulette's barns and outbuildings snagged the 130th Pennsylvania, which had already lost momentum in crossing the post and rail fence along the pasture northwest of the farm.

The Rebel skirmishers, who had evaded Weber's people, popped out of the sheds and the barn to harass the untried Pennsylvanians. The 130th handled itself well. The outgunned Confederates beat a hasty retreat back to their shelters as the Yankees closed in on them. Within minutes, they had fairly well routed most of the Confederates out and sent them rearward. Some lingering soldiers from B Company (14th CT) helped Sergeant Samuel Ilgenfritz (I Co., 130th PA) stir out about twenty disillusioned Rebels from the spring house. While he escorted his prizes away, the rest of the regiment rushed south. In their haste, the inexperienced soldiers left the barn lofts and the main house's basement untouched.[36]

The Pennsylvanians foolishly tried to climb over the tall picket fence and stone wall which extended southeasterly from the carriage house to the eastern branch of the farm lane. Frustrated by the effort, the men laid hands on the support posts and the top rail, and jerked the fence flat. In the process, it fell on Theodore Boyles (E Co.). His friend, John Hemminger, gaped unbelievingly as the regiment and Colonel Henry I. Zinn, who was mounted, crossed the downed fence over the top of Boyles. In their enthusiasm to draw Confederate blood, they crushed a couple of Boyles' ribs and inflicted internal injuries on him.

PRIVATE JOHN D. HEMMINGER, E Company, 130th Pennsylvania

He and two other soldiers saved their corporal's life while under severe fire along the Bloody Lane. (USAMHI)

Rushing across the open ground, the 130th Pennsylvania quickly smashed the picket fence bordering the orchard to splinters with its rifle butts. The air buzzed and whirled with thousands of enraged honey bees, after the bumbling Pennsylvanians disturbed their hives on the eastern end of the lane. The bees, as Private Hemminger put it, "urged" them forward.[37] The regiment reassembled in the orchard south of the farm house with its left flank bordering the farm lane, then moved on.[38]

William Roulette, unaware of whose troops were tramping over his farm, stepped out of his cellar. The moment he recognized a squad from the 14th Connecticut escorting a few more Rebels from his spring house, he went wild. "Give it to 'em!" he screamed. "Drive 'em! Take anything on my place, only drive 'em!" The last the New Englanders saw of him, he was heading rearward.[39]

Brigadier General Nathan Kimball's new brigade followed Morris' men at about one hundred yards.[40] The rough and rocky ground in the woods north of Roulette's broke up his regiments as they faced by the left flank and started over the high ground toward Roulette's swale. Some of Hooker's men stampeded past the right flank of the 8th Ohio toward the Antietam.[41]

The 14th Indiana, with the 8th Ohio to its left, steadily sprayed around the farm buildings,[42] while the 132nd Pennsylvania and the 7th West Virginia moved southeasterly, creating an inverse angle on the brigade line.[43] The green 132nd Pennsylvania regiment left several trembling men in the fields above the farm because the file closers were not doing their duty. The fretful soldiers, shamed by their excusable cowardice, rested until they recovered their composure, then chased after the regiment. Lieutenant Frederick L. Hitchcock, the adjutant of the 132nd Pennsylvania, felt very uncomfortable. His feet were still soaked from the crossing, and he kept grumbling to himself about his waterlogged trousers as he entered his first action. He was trying to mask his real fear of being wounded or killed. Like so many soldiers, he imagined death to be preferable to wounding and eventual surgery.[44]

The Bloody Lane

The Confederate officers continued to stare at Weber's beautifully aligned brigade. The front rank carried their weapons at "charge bayonets", while the rear rank and Morris' Brigade marched with their arms at the "right shoulder shift."[45] Colonel Tew (2nd NC), standing on the hill to the left front of the 1st Delaware, watched Colquitt's and Garland's skirmishers waiting in front of Weber's Brigade as the regiment entered Clipp's plowed field.[46] Boyce's Battery limbered up and pulled out to the south as the 1st Delaware neared it.[47] The Rebel infantrymen in the lane were on their own. A mounted officer (probably Colonel John W. Andrews, 1st DE), who rode in the front of his regiment, waved his hat in salute to the Confederate officers, who were in full view. Colonel Tew responded in kind. Within moments, the Confederate skirmishers cut loose then retired by files. They fired as they went, until their officers ordered them back to the safety of the lane.[48]

John Gordon (6th AL) admired the discipline of those new Yankee troops. Their clean, almost bright blue uniforms and white gaiters fascinated him as did their regimental band, which he heard urging them forward with a bright air. The Yankees' unfaded colors snapped smartly in the breeze, as the 1st Delaware marched forward, in step.[49]

"What a pity," Gordon thought, "to spoil with bullets such a scene of martial beauty!"

The colonel casually stepped into the sunken lane knowing full well that his men had to twist the Yankees' fantasy of war into a cruel reality.[50]

The Confederates in the sunken lane held their fire until the Federals crested the hill to their immediate front, heedless of some impetuous souls who wanted to cut loose on their own.[51] Weber's regiments, each one moving shoulder to shoulder and at the "common time", topped the ridge simultaneously. They crawled over the worm fence, reassembled, and marched forward. The Rebels waited until they were sixty feet away, then fired in unison. Through the tremendous cloud of smoke and flame they could see Yankee soldiers getting lifted off their feet and slammed to the ground.[52]

The 4th New York, on the far left, retreated until it collided with the 108th New York along the eastern branch of Roulette's lane. The new troops turned their bayonets on the fleeing troops and forced many of them back to the front.[53]

The mounted officer in front of the 1st Delaware went down with his dead horse.[54] Brigadier General Max Weber fell in the volley, also wounded.[55] Almost the entire color guard of the 1st Delaware, along with about one third of the regiment's nine hundred soldiers were either killed or wounded in front of Rodes' Alabamians.[56] (Map 33)

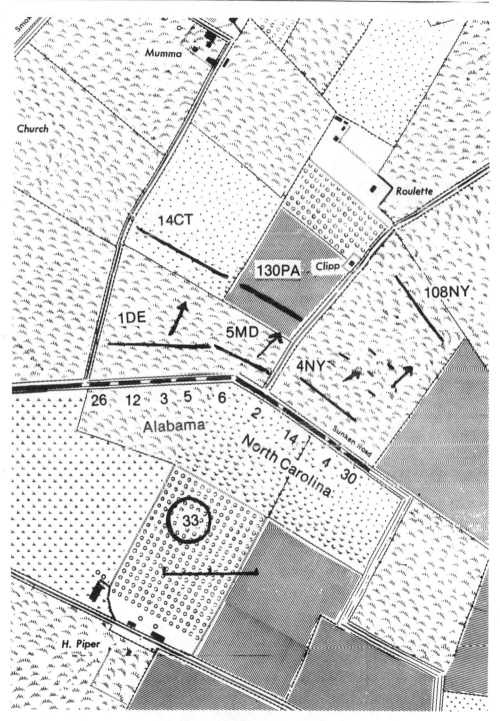

(Map 33) 9:00 A.M. — 9:30 A.M., SEPTEMBER 17, 1862
The first Federal repulse at the Bloody Lane.

ADJUTANT FREDERICK L. HITCHCOCK, 132nd Pennsylvania

During the assault on the Bloody Lane, he was ordered to get the 108th New York moving or shoot its colonel, Oliver Palmer.
(War From the Inside)

Lieutenant Frederick L. Hitchcock (adjutant, 132nd PA) became more apprehensive as the regiment entered Roulette's meadow. The Confederate volley sounded like shot rattling against a tin plate as it struck down soldiers in the first brigade.[57] Men collapsed by the squads on the brow of the ridge to the front of his regiment. An anonymous officer toppled to the ground under his wounded mount.[58]

The Mumma Farm — The Roulette Farm

Private S. M. Whistler (E Co., 130th PA) in the second brigade noticed the hot breeze, which seemed too close to breathe.[59] He was not the only man having a hot time of it. Weber's Brigade, for all intents and purposes, was "hors de combat". Sergeant Thomas Galwey (B Co., 8th OH, Kimball's Brigade) strained to see what was going on through the heavy smoke which rolled from the sunken lane into Roulette's lane. The 14th Connecticut halted on the southern edge of Mumma's cornfield and fired wildly in the direction of the Confederates, whom they could not see. In the process, they cut down some of Weber's men as they streamed pell mell into their line. The right wing and the center of the untried regiment panicked and broke. Frenzied officers bullied their men into line.[60] They lost precious time restoring order and realigning themselves before advancing again.

The Bloody Lane

The extra minutes gave Hill's men ample time to reload for another volley. John Gordon (6th AL) cooly observed the pinned officer in front of the 1st Delaware extricate himself from beneath his dead horse and run back to his shocked men, whom he rallied beyond musket range for another charge.[61] He admired the Yankee's spunk — no matter how foolhardy it was.

Weber's and Morris' combined brigades, less the 108th New York which would not budge from the northern slope of the first ridge east of Roulette's, tried to double quick over the ridge along the sunken lane right into the muzzles of Hill's veterans.[62]

Color Sergeant Thomas J. Mills (H Co., 14th CT) thudded to the ground, mortally wounded. In the chaos, about a dozen men from the 14th Connecticut misunderstood an order from Captain Isaac Bronson (I Co.) and dashed into the open ground north of the sunken lane with the rallied 1st Delaware and the 5th Maryland. Nine of the men retreated immediately when they realized they were alone. Another, Sergeant

Benjamin Hirst (D Co.), hightailed it when Rodes' Alabamians rose to rush after the fallen colors of the 1st Delaware.

Sergeants William B. Hincks and William H. Hawley (A Co.) fired a couple of rounds before they noticed that their regiment had retreated deeper into Mumma's corn. Behind them, Captain Jarvis E. Blinn (F Co.) crumbled with a bullet through his heart. "I am a dead man!" he gasped as he collapsed. When the Rebel fire punched through the Federal charge like an awl, the two brigades stampeded back toward Roulette's, leaving their wounded and dead in the smoke. Once again, the center and the right of the 14th Connecticut were temporarily routed.[63]

On the western part of the ridge, in front of Rodes' Brigade, the 1st Delaware retreated one hundred yards into the cornfield on the southern end of Mumma's lane. The first volley had taken out almost one third of the regiment, including the lieutenant colonel, who was wounded. The regimental colors were on the ground about sixty feet from the Confederate position. The Confederates sacrificed a large number of men to the pinned 5th Maryland and the 1st Delaware as squads broke from the sunken lane and attempted to make off with the Yankee standard.

With a company of the 5th Maryland providing cover fire from the left, Captain James Rickards (C Co., 1st DE) and thirty volunteers charged from the corn into the open to retrieve the flag. As the party neared the colors, Sergeant John Dunn (C Co.), who was next to Captain Rickards, noticed a wounded Confederate limping toward them. He was using his musket for support.

"I'll drop that fellow," Dunn spat.

Captain Rickards slapped the sergeant's weapon down.

"You wouldn't shoot a wounded man!" he exclaimed.

Within seconds, the Rebel brought his weapon to his shoulder and shot Rickards. Instantly, several muskets roared. The soldier died where he stood and minutes later, the captain expired.[64] Second Lieutenant Charles Tanner (H Co.), angered by the death of his comrade, screamed for more volunteers. He and his small group bolted into the clearing between the 1st Delaware and the Alabamians. They got to within ninety feet of the dead color guard before the Confederates drove them back.[65]

Meanwhile, Chaplain Henry S. Stevens (14th CT), having left some wounded with William Roulette in his basement rejoined B Company on the left of the 14th Connecticut. Captain Elijah W. Gibbons (B Co.) asked the chaplain if he had seen the colors. Stevens told him they had been at the center of the line not moments before. The rattled officer dashed through the corn to the center of the regiment and demanded that the new color bearer, Sergeant George A. Foote, raise them. Foote showed the captain the bullet snapped staff and the decapitated brass eagle on the top and told him that he had been ordered to lower the colors to quit drawing fire. Captain Gibbons raged at the sergeant to lift them up. Up they went, not to be sheathed again.[66]

The 130th Pennsylvania advanced steadily behind the 5th Maryland until it reached the high worm fence which bordered the southern end of the plowed field. They had no protection whatsoever from the Confederates in the lane.

The line halted to tear down the fence in preparation for a charge. Casting three or four rails aside, Corporal John Strickler (E Co.) had stepped over the remaining four rails with private John D. Hemminger (E Co.) when a shell fragment struck him in the shoulder and hurled him backward into the plowed field. Before any of his men could reach him, a minie ball ripped through one of his legs, both of which were still draped over the fence.

William Hamilton (E Co.) and John B. Woodrow (E Co.) snatched the corporal by the shoulders while John Hemminger grabbed his legs and tried to pull him away to safety. The moment they picked him up, a ball smashed through Strickler's other leg. Pulling his feet free from the fence, the three privates dropped the corporal in the dirt and dove for cover along the firing line.[67]

Simultaneously, about twenty men from the 2nd North Carolina filed into Roulette's lane in an attempt to flank the 130th Pennsylvania from the left. The Pennsylvanians slaughtered them.[68]

Kimball's Brigade developed the "slows" at the farm. The men could see the two front brigades streaming by squads toward the flanks of their line, the last volley having shattered them like crystal. Kimball spurred his mount along the rear of the 8th Ohio, which occupied the farm.

"Now boys," he cautioned, "we are going and we'll stay with them all day if they want us to!"[69]

The 132nd Pennsylvania tottered forward like an unstable toddler. The right wing double quicked through the eastern section of Roulette's yard, trampling the family garden to dust. The men smashed into a row of white washed crates on the southern edge of the yard and upset them. They knocked over Roulette's bee hives and the angered bees swarmed the regiment. Soldiers broke and ran with the bees in pursuit. Kimball's staff and their own officers hurried after the panicked Pennsylvanians. It took them several minutes to rally the stung soldiers and get them back into the ranks.[70]

John Gordon (6th AL) walked the line behind his men, encouraging them to remain steadfast. On several occasions he had come out of a fight with a perforated uniform but no wounds or with body scrapes but no show of blood. His men believed that he possessed some kind of supernatural charm — a type of immortality. The colonel, who was caught up in his own legend, made no effort to seek cover.[71]

The collapse of Sedgwick's command in the West Woods left the western section of the battlefield in Confederate hands. Tyndale's and Stainbrook's Brigades (XII Corps) occupied the western side of Mumma's swale, waiting for another Confederate charge from the West Woods.

Federal attacks against the Bloody Lane intensified while Federal troops rallied in the northern end of the field.

CHAPTER TEN

". . . be thou not far from me, O Lord."

The West Woods

Captain Norwood "Pen" Hallowell (D Co., 20th MA) staggered about eight hundred yards northwest from the West Woods to the Nicodemus house, with his bloodied right hand still clamped to the artery in his shattered left arm.[1] Wounded and dying men filled the farm yard.[2] Intermittent artillery fire still roared overhead. Hallowell picked his way through the men and went into the house where he settled for a spot in the parlor along the wall beneath a pendulum clock. Wounded soldiers were sprawled all around the room.[3]

Stunned though he was, the captain did not lose his wits. He knew that the Confederates would be quick to take him prisoner because he was an officer. Luckily, he had gone into action wearing the dark blue blouse and the sky blue trousers of an enlisted man. (His baggage had not caught up with him at the time of the battle.) He calmly removed his sword and shoulder straps, the only items which indicated his rank, and tucked them under a nearby blanket, which probably saved him from a long stay in Libby Prison.

Captain Oliver W. Holmes, Jr. (A Co., 20th MA) picked himself up amid the carnage of Sedgwick's debacle and started running, somewhat unsteadily, in the general direction of the rest of the shattered division. Blood coated the seam in his tunic at the middle of the collar and at his throat in front. He felt feverish and hot, but he was not incoherent.[5] As he wobbled through the woods, dodging rocks and bodies, he chuckled to himself. Recalling how *Harper's Weekly* had reported his wounding at Ball's Bluff when it bragged, "Massachusetts hit in the breast", Holmes now thought to himself, "This time I am hit in the back, and bolting as fast as I can — and it's

147

all right — but not as good for the papers." (The captain would note in retrospect that the 20th ran only on General Sumner's orders.)[6]

**ADJUTANT
WALTER CLARK,
35th North Carolina**

He got medical assistance for the crippled Colonel Francis Palfrey of the 20th Massachusetts in exchange for the colonel's pistol and sword. *(Clarke, NC Regts.)*

Not everybody experienced his lightheadedness. Holmes' colonel, Francis W. Palfrey, lay on the forest floor with a crippling wound. Unable to move, he called for help until a Confederate, Adjutant Walter Clark (35th NC, Ransom's Brigade) crawled to his assist. Clark agreed to help the wounded officer receive medical attention, but for a price — Palfrey's pistol and sword. The trade saved the Yankee's life.[7]

The hapless Asa Fletcher (Andrews' Sharpshooters, 15th MA) could not roll onto his back. The round in his chest temporarily paralyzed him and he lost all track of time. He felt as if he had lain upon the field all day. A frightened horse nearly trampled him to death. Not long after, several Rebels happened across his body and, finding that he was not dead, they threatened to bayonet him. Asa insisted they had to take him prisoner. They soundly cursed him and moved on. Their laughter, mingled with scattered rifle shots, echoed ominously in his ears. Some less compassionate Rebels were murdering wounded Federal soldiers who moved or who were too alive for their liking. Fletcher lowered his head to the ground and played dead rather than risk a bullet through the back of his head.[8]

Nicodemus Heights

Sergeant Ed Moore (Poague's Battery) had spent what seemed the longest time upon the ground, still paralyzed by the cast iron shot which had lodged against his right thigh joint. Eventually, some enlisted men, who mistook him for an officer because he wore a white shirt, dragged him to a field hospital, about fifty yards to the rear of his position. Two surgeons from a badly depleted regiment treated him quickly and kindly in consideration of his "supposed" rank. The young soldier owed his life to his "biled" shirt.[9]

The Joseph Poffenberger Farm

Clara Barton, the matronly looking woman who observed the flight of the I Corps from Pry's hill, had left General Ambrose Burnside several hours before. She and her orderly pulled their wagon into the cornfield across the lane (southwest) from Joseph Poffenberger's farm house. They unhitched their mules in a swale south of the stone wall which separated them from the thirty field pieces which Hooker had massed west of Poffenberger's orchard. The tall corn and the North Woods, to the south, masked their wagon from the Confederates.

Carrying as many bandages and stimulants as she could manage, Miss Barton hurried along a path through the corn toward the house. As she crossed Poffenberger's lane, she collided with Pennsylvania surgeon, James Dunn, at the small wicker gate which opened into the yard. After a stunned, silent moment, the kind doctor, who was a friend of hers, threw up his hands.

"God has indeed remembered us!" he exclaimed. "How did you get from Virginia so soon? And again to supply our necessities! And they are terrible. We have nothing but our instruments and the little bit of chloroform we brought in our pockets."

He continued to ramble on while helping her carry the desperately needed supplies to the farm house. "We have torn up the last sheets we could find in this house. We have not a bandage, rag, lint, or string, and all these shell wounded men bleeding to death."

Miss Barton hastily scanned the farm yard around the house. At least three hundred wounded men were strewn about the place. Four tables were set up on the front porch of the house, each with its own patient and attending surgeon. Bunches of corn leaves, which replaced the depleted bed sheets for bandages, were heaped at the foot of each table. She had arrived just in time.[10]

The Nicodemus House

Captain Oliver W. Holmes, Jr. (A Co., 20th MA) staggered into the Nicodemus living room in a daze. The shock of his wounding was starting to affect him, however, he tried to compensate for it by acting overly calm. He believed he was dying.[11]

"Holmes!" he heard a pained voice rasp out.

The captain searched the faces about the room until he happened upon "Pen" Hallowell who was still slouched against the wall beneath the octagonal pendulum clock.

"Have you seen my brother, Ned?" Hallowell gasped.

Holmes, whose swollen throat made talking nearly impossible, slowly turned his head from side to side — "No" — as he slumped down beside his friend and listened disinterestedly, to the clock's loud ticking.[12]

Outside, artillery shells and round shot plowed through the injured men in the farm yard, mangling them further.[13]

A short distance to the south, the 1st Minnesota and the 19th Massachusetts were putting their last volleys into Semmes' and Anderson's Brigades before leaving the fighting.[14]

Holmes pulled a pencil and a piece of scrap paper from inside his blouse. Fearing that he would pass out and die — an anonymous corpse — he feverishly scrawled, "I am Capt. O. W. Holmes, 20th Mass. Son of Oliver Wendell Holmes. M.D. Boston."[15] (Within days, he would nonchalantly pen home that he was not as badly injured as it had at first seemed.)[16]

By 10:00 A.M., Confederate soldiers had pushed into the Nicodemus farm yard. Captain Hallowell heard Confederate officers inquiring among the wounded if there were any officers among them. They hauled a few officers away. They paroled enlisted men. As the "usual luck" — Holmes' favorite expression — would have it, only one Rebel poked his head through the broken panes of the living room.

"Yankee?" he shouted.

"Yes," someone groaned.

"Wounded?" he asked, perhaps relieved that no one was in good enough shape to kill him.

"Yes," came the reply.

"Would you like some water?"

The Rebel whirled his canteen into the room and dashed off to join his men at the skirmish line north of the house.[17]

A Confederate officer and his men found Nathan Jordan (H Co., 19th MA) propped against one of Nicodemus' wheat stacks. When the officer saw how pale and blood soaked the New Englander was, he curtly told his men, "He's done for," and left him to die. Nathan Jordan refused to succumb to his fate.[18]

The North Woods

John Gibbon, having posted Woodruff's Battery (I, 1st U.S.), raced his mount north along the western face of the East Woods toward his brigade's jumping off point. He saw stampeded and confused Federal soldiers everywhere. Squads stopped sporadically to return fire upon the Confederates, whose charge had been broken up in the West Woods. He found his badly shot up brigade (Iron Brigade, I Corps) in the North Woods, in line facing south along the Hagerstown Pike. The men stoically gained their feet and fell into regimental front when Gibbon ordered them to stem any route in their area — a very noble gesture, considering that his brigade barely covered one hundred yards. In a melodramatic display, Gibbon rode to the front of his command, and, centering himself on it, he tried to heroically draw his saber only to find out that he could not. The sword would not budge from the scabbard. (The round which hit him while he was escaping down the Smoketown Road bent his sword at the hilt.) Foiled at his attempt to bare steel for the first time during the war, he commanded his men to halt and reform all stragglers. They complied and succeeded to a limited extent.[19] The fighting, as compared with that of the morning, was over in the northern section of the battlefield.

The Nicodemus House

There were some limited counterattacks which consisted of the Federal batteries near the North Woods ferreting out pesky snipers and skirmishers in the upper section of the West Woods. During one of these encounters, the gunners drove the Rebels out of the Nicodemus farm. They had only been on the ground about fifteen minutes.

The Rebel who loaned his canteen to the wounded in the house poked his head through the window again, and shouted, "Hurry up there! Hand me my canteen! I am on the double-quick myself now!"

One of the disabled Yankees chucked the canteen at him and he disappeared, leaving the soldiers in and about the farm to the mercies of both armies, whose shell blasts rattled and shattered the windows of the house but did not pass through it.[20]

The West Woods

Six of Barksdale's Mississippians broke away from their brigade to pursue the downed colors of a Yankee regiment near Sedgwick's left flank. Moments before they reached them, a Yankee ran back to the woods, snatched the colors by a corner, slung them over his back, and raced across the Hagerstown Pike with the flag staff dragging the ground behind him.

Simultaneously, they drew canister fire from Woodruff's Battery (I, 1st U.S.), which was trying to strike the larger concentration of Confederates in the woods. Within seconds, three of the six men were knocked down. Lieutenant John M. Jennings and Hamp Woods died instantly. Jesse Franklin crawled away with a ball in his thigh. The three survivors, C. C. Cummings, Jerry Webb, and Bill McRaven, hurled themselves to the ground behind a small section of stone wall which ran in front of the Dunker Church on the western side of the road. For a few uncomfortable minutes they sniped at the battery.

Presently, Bill McRaven dropped his rifle and double tracked back into the West Woods. The other two followed right after him. C. C. Cummings caught McRaven as he turned to bayonet a frightened Yankee drummer who had taken shelter behind a tree stump. Cummings, who snatched the fifteen year old away from him on the grounds that he saw him first, wanted to attract more Yankee fire. He sent his comrades back to the wall to provide cover.

Grabbing the Yankee by the back of his jacket collar, Cummings shoved the drummer ahead of him as a shield. The Yankee battery loosed a single charge of canister at the church with no effect.

The musician, having pleaded for his life on the grounds that his father was serving in the Confederate ranks, wriggled free from the Reb as he tried to cross the stone wall. The Yankee prostrated himself along the eastern base of the fence seconds before a third round of canister burst forty feet in front of him. A bouncing shot clipped Cummings in the side and sent him backwards over the wall and left him gasping for air next to Jerry Webb. (McRaven had run away again.)

As he came around, the frightened Mississippian worked his legs to see if they still could move. Satisfied that they would still support his weight, he advised Jerry to survey the Federal lines before they made a run for it.

Webb poked his head up in time to see Tyndale's Ohions bracing themselves for another counterthrust, which, unknown to him and Cummings, was developing south of the woods. At Cummings' request, Jerry Webb dashed toward the far side of the Dunker Church to draw musketry. The theory was that the slower running Cummings, could follow while the Yankees reloaded. A number of bullets buzzed and zinged close by Jerry's body and missed. E. E. Cummings, who was determined never to go flag chasing again, hobbled safely after him. Together, they disappeared into the West Woods.[21]

Meanwhile, part of Manning's Brigade (46th NC, 30th VA, and 48th NC, north to south) emerged from the West Woods. The Dunker Church split the 48th North Carolina in half. Many of the North Carolinians took cover behind the trees and refused to advance into the open. Those few that did step out momentarily halted to realign themselves with the 30th Virginia, which had also halted. Colonel E. D. Hall threw the 46th North Carolina across the Hagerstown Pike in an attempt to take the Smoketown Road, which was barely visible in the dense smoke. The regiment staggered and fired a wild volley before falling back. The 30th Virginia rushed at the oblique to fill the gap on the left, while the reformed 48th North Carolina bolted due east.[22]

Tyndale's Brigade poured a tremendous volley into the two Confederate regiments as they crossed the Hagerstown Pike.[23] Captain George H. Payton (A Co., 30th VA) slipped and fell off the top rail of the fence along the Smoketown Road;

he lay badly bruised in the road as Tyndale's volley splintered the fence rails above him. Private Joe Haislip (C Co., 30th VA) threw himself to the ground. Breaking a cartridge open, he smeared his face with powder to feign an injury and crawled to the rear. He would try to kill Yankees another day.[24] The Virginians, despite the terrible musketry, delivered a couple of volleys into Tyndale's line while taking a severe beating. The Yankees, besides shooting away an entire corner of the regimental flag, also put fifteen holes in it in less than five minutes.[25]

As the 48th North Carolina crossed the fence into the Hagerstown Pike, a terrific fire lashed into its ranks. Men blatantly deserted westward. Lieutenant Colonel Samuel H. Walkup (48th NC) brandished his pistol and futilely threatened to shoot anyone who broke ranks. Colonel Van Manning, the brigade commander, rode into his rapidly disintegrating regiments and begged the North Carolinians to go back into the maelstrom. Bullets struck him, simultaneously, in the left arm and in the breast. He toppled into the road where some volunteers picked him up and carried him rearward. Walkup scrambled over the second fence into the open ground east of the road only to see what remained of the regiment break up and retreat madly into the woods.[26] *(Map 34)*

Tyndale's line rose to its feet and rushed after Manning's retreating regiments. The 102nd New York (Stainbrooks's Brigade) remained in Mumma's swale, but the 13th New Jersey and the Purnell Legion (3/2/XII) which had just advanced from the East Woods and Miller's Cornfield, respectively, fell in on the right rear of the line.[27] A last volley from the West Woods spattered the line as it surged over the crest of the Dunker Church ridge.

Lieutenant Colonel Eugene Powell (66th OH), a man who had had his coat shoulder shot through three times and had had his collar shot away not seconds before, turned his head to the left to observe the spectacle down along the sunken lane when a round slammed into his head. The ball knocked him unconscious. His body swayed back in the saddle, while his hand convulsed on the reins. Powell's horse responded to the tug and wheeled about, taking its rider to the rear and the safety of the East Woods.[28]

Lieutenant Colonel Walkup (48th NC) could not rally his panicked men. Colonel R. C. Hill streamed by him with half a company. No one listened to the officer. Soldiers from the 2nd South Carolina, having taken cover in the ravine at the western base of the woods, begged Walkup and his people to stand by them. Captains Turner and Richardson, and Lieutenant Witherspoon with part of D Company tried to stand but the tremendous Federal fire cut too many of them down. They ran down to the stone wall along A. Poffenberger's lane to reform.[29]

The charge penetrated the West Woods almost as far as the ridge about one hundred yards west of the church, where the formation contracted and formed an arc — along the ridge formerly held by the 125th Pennsylvania, toward the southwestern corner of the woods to the Hagerstown Pike.

The left of the brigade, in flushing the Confederates out of the West Woods, ran into opposition from Patterson's Battery and Manning's two remaining regiments, the 27th North Carolina and the 3rd Arkansas, both of which had just arrived to support the guns.[30] The two regiments moved up the rise behind the battery as it began to retire. The 27th North Carolina went prone behind a worm fence along the northeastern portion of a cornfield behind a ridge about six hundred yards south of the

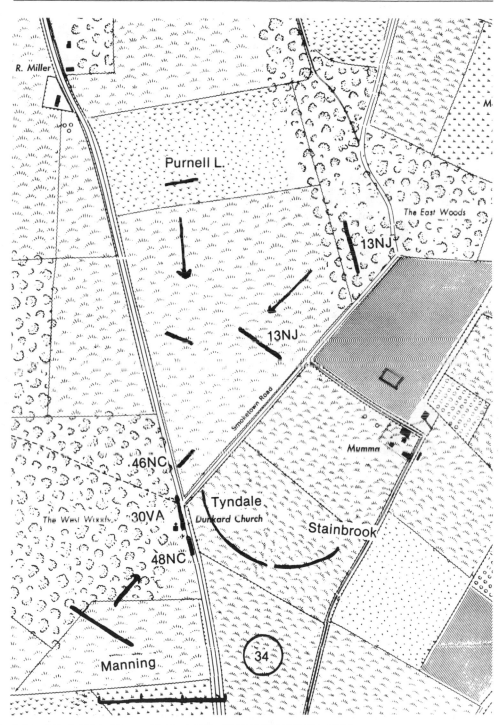

R. Miller

Purnell L.

The East Woods

13NJ

13NJ

Smoketown Road

46NC

Mumma

Tyndale

The West Woods   30VA   Dunkard Church   Stainbrook

48NC

34

Manning

**(Map 34) 9:30 A.M. — 10:30 A.M., SEPTEMBER 17, 1862
Tyndale and Stainbrook hurl back Manning's assault.**

COLONEL JOHN R. COOKE, 27th North Carolina
When complimented by General Longstreet for
holding his advanced position without any ammuni-
tion, he replied that he would stay where he was
or go to Hell trying.
(Miller's Photographic History)

Dunker Church. The 3rd Arkansas, commanded by the 27th's impetuous John Cooke, advanced on the right in full view of the Federals along the Dunker Church ridge. For half an hour, the two outfits took fire from that sector. *(Map 35)*

Colonel Cooke posted the Arkansans in a stubble field about one hundred yards to the right front of the North Carolinians.[31] When the Yankees charged Manning's three regiments and Manning went down severely wounded on the Hagerstown Pike, Cooke calmly ordered his men to fall back to the ridge and the cornfield south of their line.[32] Companies F, K, and G (left to right) of the 27th North Carolina laid down behind the worm fence which bordered the cornfield, facing north, while the rest of the two regiments formed along the northeasterly section of fence which followed the ridge.

Cooke pulled the right of the line back twenty paces and commanded it to lie down in the corn, leaving the three wing companies to concentrate their riflery upon the West Woods. From their position on the ridge, the men in the 3rd Arkansas peered under the smoke which enveloped the West Woods. They could only identify the troops, which milled about the area, from the knees down.

The withdrawal, which was designed to lure the Yankees into a charge, attracted a hail of lead instead. Captain James A. Graham (G Co., 27th NC) noted, with a bit of understatement, that the movement caused severe suffering.[33] Cooke ignored the minies. He stood boldly upon the hill crest next to a lone hickory tree, inspiring his men by drawing more fire.[34] Private Will Summerville (I Co., 3rd AR), however, while leaning against that tree, next to Cooke, was shot and killed instantly. His shocked comrades gawked at his lifeless body as it teetered for several moments before keeling over.[35]

Cooke's musketry sufficiently thwarted any further drives against the Confederate left. Brigadier General George Greene, who followed the two Federal brigades into the West Woods, did not know what the situation was like on his right flank. He erroneously assumed that Sedgwick's Division still occupied the northern section of the West Woods, therefore, he did not allow his two flanking regiments, the Purnell

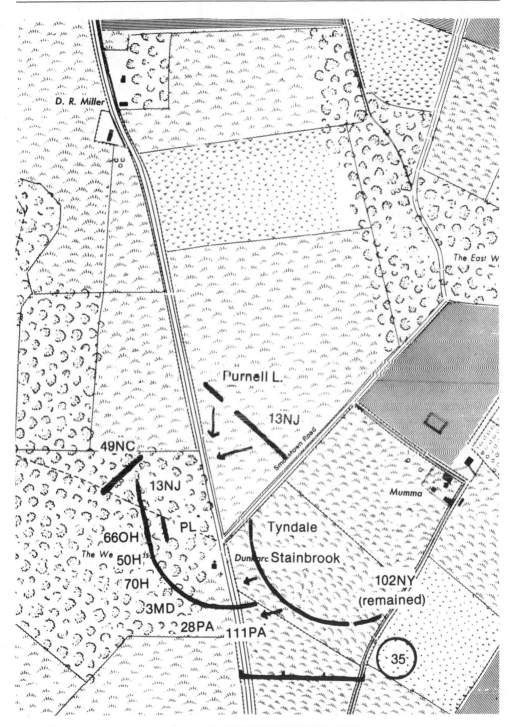

(Map 35) 9:30 A.M. — 10:30 A.M., SEPTEMBER 17, 1862
Tyndale and Stainbrook gain a foothold around the Dunker Church.

CAPTAIN JAMES A. GRAHAM, G Company, 27th North Carolina

He left behind a very detailed account of John R. Cooke's assault upon the Federal right flank at the Bloody Lane.
(Clarke, NC Regts.)

Legion and the 13th New Jersey to fire north of their position near the Dunker Church.[36] Unknown to him, the 49th North Carolina (Ransom's Brigade) was on that flank.[37]

Lieutenant Colonel Samuel H. Walkup (48th NC) managed to gather about one hundred men at the stone wall near A. Poffenberger's lane. Presently, another fifty, which represented the 2nd South Carolina, fell in with them. Within fifteen minutes Colonel R. C. Hill (48th NC) returned from points due west with less than fifty soldiers. They hugged the ground to wait out one of the worst shellings they had experienced to date.[38]

The Bloody Lane

Meanwhile, the situation at the sunken lane became more confused as French's first two shattered brigades fell back upon Nathan Kimball's Brigade and fragmented it. Kimball's troops shifted their front. The 14th Indiana anchored its left flank on the western side of Roulette's lane and advanced uphill toward the front of John Gordon's 6th Alabama. The 8th Ohio moved to its immediate left and made for the 2nd North Carolina. The 132nd Pennsylvania continued the line to its left with the 7th West Virginia completing the eastern flank of the formation.[39]

Young Sergeant Tom Galwey (B Co., 8th OH) helplessly watched as the Confederates in the sunken lane rose up at their leisure and fired into his regiment. The 8th had no shelter of any kind. The men charged with their heads bent down as if in a driving rain. Gaps appeared in the ranks as the Confederate volleys took out files of men. Galwey had never seen such killing before.[40]

The Confederates at the apex fired as if they were picking off squirrels — cooly, and with deliberate aim. The advancing Federals, cheered on by their excited officers, let out a feeble "huzzah" and charged the crest in front of the 6th Alabama and the 2nd North Carolina.[41] Those two regiments unleashed a horrendous volley as the 14th Indiana and the 8th Ohio came over the rise about fifty yards from their barricades.[42]

The carnage stunned Sergeant Galwey. Hundreds of men dropped in the soft, white speckled clover north of the lane. His orderly sergeant, a man named Fairchild, remained in the formation despite a terrible head wound which left his face covered with blood. Jack Sheppard (B Co.), his messmate, toppled without muttering a sound — killed by no less than one dozen hits. "Happy Jack" had boasted not long before that the Rebs had not molded the bullet which could kill him.[43]

The Federal line recoiled and went prone on the reverse slope of the ridge.[44] The air rolled and thundered with explosions as Confederate artillery on the high ground west of the lane and Boyce's Battery, which had pulled back to Piper's orchard, poured every bursting projectile they could into the ridge.[45]

The blades of grass around him vibrated so violently, that Galwey stupidly remarked to a comrade that they were being swarmed by crickets. The soldier laughed. Spent bullets — not crickets — were skipping through the grass.

Confederate reinforcements tumbled into the lane from Piper's cornfield.[46] Brigadier General Ambrose Wright's Brigade (44th AL, 3rd, 22nd, and 48th GA) piled into the rear of the North Carolinians nearly causing a route. Colonel Carnot Posey's men (12th, 16th, and 19th MS, 2nd MS Bttn) plowed into the lane. Brigadier General Roger A. Pryor's Brigade (14 AL, 3rd VA, 2nd, 5th, and 8th FL) and Colonel W. A. Parham's eighty-two men (6th, 12th, 16th, 41st, and 61st VA) went into position in Piper's orchard. For a few minutes it appeared as if the Confederate center would collapse by its own hand. Wright, who was quite drunk, tried to send the 4th North Carolina and the 30th North Carolina over the fence to meet the Federals head on, but their line officers refused to comply, insisting that their brigadier general had told them to let the Yankees come after them. Fate decided the issue. The Federals, who had laid down behind their ridge, started to reply with small arms fire and wounded both Wright and George Anderson, the latter mortally. The brigade's command devolved upon Colonel Charles C. Tew (2nd NC).[47] *(Map 36)*

The fighting became a bloodied slug fest — a contest of attrition. Despite mounting losses in the sunken lane, the Confederates poured a devastating fire into the 14th Indiana and the 8th Ohio.

General Kimball pranced his horse from one end of the line to the other mumbling, "God save my poor boys!" Tom Galwey (B Co., 8th OH), who overheard him and who had been watching the regimental front drastically contract as the men shifted toward the center to fill gaps in the line, thought, "Well ought he to pray." Someone shouted that Lieutenant William Delaney (B Co.) was gut shot. Lieutenant John Lantry (B Co.) died near the boy sergeant when a shell fragment blew the top of his skull off. Another friend, Jim Gallagher (B Co.), rolled down the crest into Roulette's lane, coiled up in a ball with a severe head wound.[48]

Casualties were mounting in the 132nd Pennsylvania which was to the left rear of the 8th Ohio. Colonel Richard Oakford died in the first volley when a ball penetrated his left shoulder and severed an artery.[49] Captain Robert A. Abbott (G Co.) spat out a mouthful of blood and teeth, when a bullet shot away his lower jaw. As he stumbled rearward, Assistant Surgeon George W. Hoover, who was fresh out of medical school, hauled him behind a large haymound and saved his life with on-the-spot surgery.[50] The Pennsylvanians fired individually, with each man crawling beneath the crest of the ridge to reload.[51] As the soldier beside Lieutenant Frederick Hitchcock (Adjutant, 132nd PA) inadvertently stood up, a minie ball struck his rifle in the forestock and prostrated him. Regaining his senses, the fellow discovered he was only bruised. He picked up another gun and returned to the line.[52]

To the right, in E Company of the 130th Pennsylvania, casualties continued to escalate. Corporal John Strickler's pitiful pleas became unendurable to his comrades, John Hemminger, William Hamilton, and John B. Woodrow. They picked him up and carried him off.

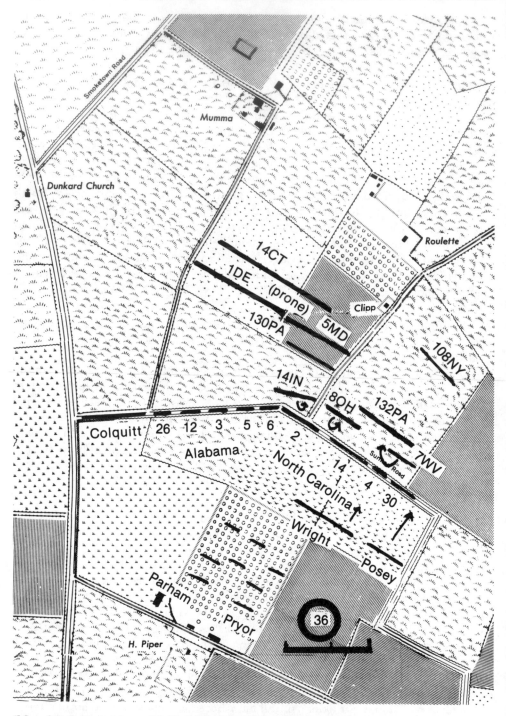

(Map 36) 9:30 A.M. — 10:30 A.M., SEPTEMBER 17, 1862
The Confederates thwart the second Federal assault upon the Bloody Lane.

They got as far as Roulette's spring house. Strickler begged for water only to get struck a fourth time by a spent musket ball which carried away the heel of one shoe.

"My God," he screeched, "I must be killed by inches!"

The three soldiers hastily hauled him further to the rear to the Division's field hospital. They dropped him among the wounded and headed back to the regiment.[53]

The East Woods — The Roulette Farm — The Bloody Lane

In the din and the smoke, the soldiers in the front ranks could see little beyond their own sector. Help for French's Division was on the way. Major General Israel B. Richardson's Division (II Corps), with the Irish Brigade (29th MA, 63rd, 69th, and 88th NY) in the lead, had forded the creek around 9:30 A.M. and was preparing to join in the attack upon the Confederate center.

Corporal William L. D. O'Grady (C Co., 88th NY) did not take his shoes off to ford the hip deep Antietam at Pry's Ford.[54] Like many of the others in the 88th New York, he had not had his shoes off for a week and he feared that he would not be able to get his swollen feet into the shoes once he removed them. The men were ordered to wring out their socks and fill their canteens before falling in; those who chose to, and who still had socks, complied.[55]

Petty jealousies and interpersonal feuds for the patronizing favor of its brigadier, Thomas Meagher, who allegedly doled out what few promotions there were to cronies, had injured the brigade's morale. Meagher was a primper, who that very morning sported a fancy blue uniform with a gold shoulder sash. The 18 year old O'Grady overheard the general tell his orderly to carefully brush off the uniform, to which the corporal mentally quipped, "We'd all have a brush soon."[56]

The brigade set out from the ford in columns of four with the 69th New York in the lead, followed by the 29th Massachusetts, the 63rd New York, and the 88th New York, respectively.[57] As they double quicked west toward a belt of woods directly north of Roulette's, they passed Israel Richardson, their division commander, who, noticing the emerald green flags of the 88th New York, rose in the stirrups and belted out, "Bravo 88th. I shall never forget you!" to which the 88th responded with three resounding "huzzahs".[58]

Charging into Roulette's swale in column, the four regiments ran through remnants of French's command and halted below a section of split rail fence atop a steep bank which parallelled Roulette's lane where it turned northeast from the orchard.[59] The column quickly swung into battle formation by the flanks with the 69th New York on the right and the 88th New York on the left.[60]

Meagher ordered the men down and called for volunteers to tear down a second fence along the edge of a plowed field about three hundred yards from the lane.[61] Private Samuel Wright (E Co., 29th MA) and seventy-six others stepped forward. Snipers in the tree tops along the farm lane picked off a few of the Irishmen as they bolted the hilltop.[62] Several sharpshooters from the 88th New York, who "found" rifles to replace their muskets with their buck and ball loads, provided cover fire for the volunteers. They eliminated their Rebel harassers within a few minutes. Those few men who reached the fence ran into a galling hail of lead from the sunken lane. Bullets literally snatched rails from their hands. A few of the wounded managed to stagger back to the brigade. Private Wright tore away what rails he could then raced back to his regiment, leaving most of the volunteers shredded and dead upon the fence. Wright caught two rounds in the back as he reached his men.[63]

William Roulette, who had turned back to his house at the sound of the renewed firing, ran out of his cellar and stared at his rescuers. He stood motionless, seemingly dumbfounded as he gaped at the hastily forming brigade, then he ran back to Chaplain Stevens of the 14th Connecticut, and the wounded, who were still huddled in the basement of his house.[64]

Meagher, his aides, and the two brigade chaplains, Fathers Ovellet and William Corby rode along the front rank. Before he and the other priest dismounted, Corby bestowed a conditional absolution upon all who would fall that day, except those who displayed cowardice.[65] They followed in the wake of the charge to administer the Last Rites to the dead and dying. *(Map 37)*

With the fence down, Meagher rose in the saddle and cried at his men, who were already taking a beating, "Boys! Raise the colors and follow me!"[66]

The Irishmen dashed into the riflery from the sunken lane with their heads lowered.[67] They caught Posey's Brigade on the flank as it bolted the lane and turned the left wing of the 7th West Virginia. Their attack nearly annihilated the 16th Mississippi, and they drove the Confederates back to the security of the sunken lane. The Irish Brigade moved into the space vacated by the 7th West Virginia as it retired to replenish its ammunition. The Federal front now extended from the left of the 8th Ohio nearly to the far corner of the Confederate position.[68]

The Yankees closed to within fifty yards of the Confederate line which brought them within range to use their muskets to maximum effect. They left an appalling number of casualties in the three hundred yard stretch from the fence row to the ridge above the Confederate defenses. A single volley decimated the brigade's front rank and sent every regimental color to the ground.[69] Before the hour was out, regimental losses in Meagher's Brigade would average 60%.[70]

The Irish fought in grand style — upright as if on parade.[71] Every time a man went down, another stepped over him to close ranks. Their buck and ball loads took their toll on the Rebels as did those of the other Federal regiments. Captain John Gorman (B Co.,

**THE 7TH WEST VIRGINIA REGIMENT
before its engagement at Antietam. *(USAMHI)***

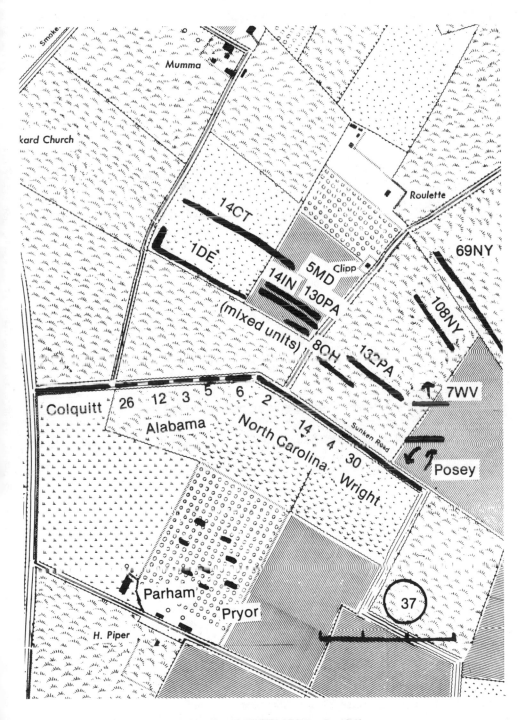

(Map 37) 9:30 A.M. — 10:30 A.M., SEPTEMBER 17, 1862
Posey and Wright reinforce Anderson's North Carolinians in the Bloody Lane.

2nd NC) recalled that the "lead was flying thick", making it "too hot" to allow reinforcements to come up.

The Confederates were too tightly packed together to prevent multiple woundings
and many died while loading or aiming.[72] A bullet through the heart froze one man
in the act of tearing open a cartridge. The reporter, Charles C. Coffin, found him
as he had died, with the cartridge clenched tightly between his teeth.[73] Even the
seemingly indestructable Colonel John Gordon (6th AL) could not evade fate.

Around 10:00 A.M., as the Irish Brigade burst from Roulette's, the first volley
from the 8th Ohio and the 14th Indiana caught him and Colonel Charles C. Tew
(2nd NC) while they were conversing behind the Rebel firing line. Tew slumped to
the ground with a minie ball in his brain. Gordon staggered from a round through
his right calf.[74]

The vigorous colonel limped along his line, refusing to yield to his wound. Injured men risked certain death to scramble over the bank behind them and escape
into Piper's cornfield.[75] John Gordon encouraged his men not to balk as he watched
them, with admiration for their superb bravery, fall on both sides of him. They kept
firing away at the Yankees as if they were at a Sunday turkey shoot, and the Yankees,
for their part, seemed as equally determined not to relenquish the field. Minutes
after his first wounding, a second ball struck him again in the right leg, a short distance
above the other hole. Luckily, neither bullet struck bone. Gordon refused to go to
the rear. He hobbled, albeit slower, but steadfastly, from one flank of his regiment
to the other, while his blood pumped into his trouser leg with each painful step.[76]

The Federal line grew stronger while the Confederate position diminished in
strength.[77] Brigadier General John C. Caldwell's Brigade (Richardson's Division, II
Corps) was inching up the steep slopes northeast of the 88th New York toward the
right flank of the 30th North Carolina. The 64th/61st New York led the column,
followed by the 7th New York, the 81st Pennsylvania, and the 5th New Hampshire,
respectively.[78]

The 61st New York halted near a solitary tree on the hillside. Sergeant Charles
A. Fuller (C Co.) noticed a fully leaved, bigger tree off to the left front. Several rifle
shots burst from that tree's top and a few men went down with wounds. Within a
minute, Captain Manton C. Angell (E Co.) collapsed with a bullet in his skull. His
death shocked Sergeant Fuller, who instantly recalled the captain's earlier remarks
that he would die in this fight. Colonel Francis Barlow (64th/61st NY) screamed for
a half dozen volunteers. Their rifle fire dropped two sharpshooters to the ground.[79]
(Map 38)

Colonel John R. Brooke's Brigade (2nd DE, 52nd, 57th, 66th NY, and 53rd PA)
went prone north of the Irish Brigade, along a steep ridge east of Roulette's. Sergeant
Gilbert H. Fredericks (C Co., 57th NY) saw Caldwell's people halt near the eastern
corner of the sunken lane, where it turned south. Bullets whistled past the men's
ears. A loud thumping noise alarmed Sergeant Fredericks until he realized that it
was his heart. He was scared and impatient. Were he to die that day, he wanted
to get it done with quickly.[80]

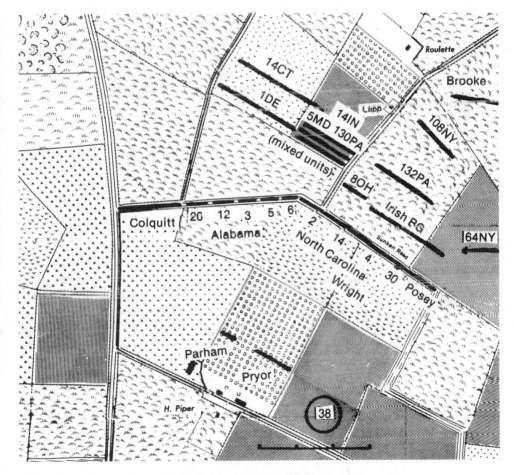

(Map 38) 10:30 A.M. — 12:00 P.M., SEPTEMBER 17, 1862
The Irish Brigade stabilizes the Federal left along the Bloody Lane.

The Pry House

For so many of the men, it seemed as if the day had gone on forever, even for the newly arrived VI Corps. The Corps, with William F. Smith's Division in the lead, arrived in Keedysville around 10:00 A.M. Having left Crampton's Gap on South Mountain at dawn, it marched part way down Pleasant Valley toward Harper's Ferry when word arrived that the town had fallen to the Confederates, whereupon, the Corps about faced and double quicked north.

Private Benjamin Franklin Clarkson (C Co., 49th PA, Hancock's Brigade) looked across the Antietam from the ridge top near Pry's house toward the sunken lane plateau. The battle's roar echoed ominously in his ears and, as the sun shown above the smoke, the oppressive heat engulfed him. He stoically noted, as the men neared Keedysville and as the sounds of battle increased in volume, that the card players in the regiment were tossing their decks aside — to shreave themselves of their Satanic devices.[81]

The East Woods — The Mumma Farm — The Cornfield

Sedgwick's soldiers, for the most part, scattered like chaff in the breeze toward the safety of the North and the East Woods, where many of the regimental historians alleged — years later — they supported undefended batteries. In reality, the batteries supported them. The guns deterred the Confederate drive into the open ground beyond the West Woods. Tompkin's Battery (A, 1st RI) faced southwest along the ridge west of Mumma's cornfield. Woodruff's guns (I, 1st U.S.) trained upon the West Woods from a position north of and immediately across from Mumma's lane where it intersected the Smoketown Road. Cothran (M, 1st NY) formed a hinge on his right in the clover field, facing due west while Captain Joseph E. Knap (E, PA) went into battery on the southern edge of the Cornfield, with the East Woods a few yards to his rear. Monroe's Battery (D, 1st RI) was nearby with five guns.[82] Bruen's Battery (10th NY) finished the line to the right by facing west from the eastern edge of the Cornfield.[83] By 10:30 A. M., besides the motley XII, II, and I Corps units in the East Woods, they were all that stood between the Confederate left and their own demoralized right wing.

The slug match along the Bloody Lane continued unabated while both the Confederates and the Federals fed new troops into the area.

Greene's Division (XII Corps) held the Dunker Church area of the West Woods against regrouping Confederate forces.

To the east, across the Antietam, the VI Corps had arrived upon the field from Pleasant Valley, Maryland.

CHAPTER ELEVEN

"O my strength, haste thee to help me."

10.30 A.M. - 12:00 P.M.

The Pry House

The newly arrived VI Corps lost about half an hour in marching and counter marching south, then north, then south again on the Boonsboro Pike to protect McClellan's supposedly weak center and threatened right flank.[1] The Corps finally halted in the road, east of Samuel Pry's house. The men sweltered in the heat while they awaited further orders to deploy.[2]

The trot from Pleasant Valley fatigued Major Thomas Hyde, the twenty-four year old commander of the 7th Maine (Irwin's Brigade, Smith's Division). He had seen nothing of the route except the dust which the 77th New York (Irwin's Brigade) kicked up in his face. The heat and the asphyxiating, powdery dirt which enshrouded the column forced a number of men from the forward regiments to fall out along the roadside. Hyde prided himself that the 7th Maine lost only one seriously ill man that way. He also took pride in the fact that he had memorized the name of every man in his command — all one hundred eighty-one of them — since leaving Alexandria, Virginia in August. The major honestly boasted that he "knew" his men both literally and figuratively. Veterans of the Peninsula and Williamsburg, where they distinguished themselves under the direction of Winfield Scott Hancock, the Mainers would follow their gutsy major anywhere. They knew him to be a man of few words, who expected to be obeyed, and who would go into the thick of any action with them.[3]

Brigadier General Winfield Scott Hancock, who did not command Hyde's Brigade in this campaign, was "all alive". Hancock's brigade (6th ME, 5th WI, 43rd NY, 49th and 137th PA) would lead the attack of the Corps onto the field that day and he tried to steel the men for what lay ahead.

MAJOR THOMAS HYDE,
7th Maine

Following his futile push into Piper's swale, he cried himself to sleep. *(USAMHI)*

"Boys," Hancock wildly spat, while prancing his mount from one end of the 49th Pennsylvania to the other, "do as you have done before, be brave and true, and I think this will be your last battle."

Private Benjamin Clarkson (C Co., 49th PA) suspiciously eyed Hancock from the regiment's front rank. The boy, who served under the general when he commanded the 49th early in the war, solemnly reflected upon the last phrase about "your last fight", and like others who heard similar exclamations, he knew that for many it would, indeed, be their last battle. Clarkson mentally added that many more would have to face combat after this engagement.

The private glanced about him. Not a single New Testament or Bible was among the scattered playing cards which littered the road. He consoled himself that, despite the terrible circumstances in which he found himself, no one had openly tested God by desecrating His book. The boy soldier spent the few remaining peaceful minutes he had left in prayer and contemplation.[4]

The East Woods — The Mumma Farm

The situation had changed little in the vicinity of Mumma's and the East Woods since the Ohions smashed Manning's three regiments. Snipers, sharpshooters, and artillerists controlled the fields for both armies.

The Federal gunners shifted their guns about the place like chessmen to protect the Army of the Potomac's right wing from intrepid squads of Confederate infantrymen who harassed the disorganized regiments in the East Woods. Bruen's (10th NY) and Woodruff's (I, 1st U.S.) Batteries left the field to be replaced by Captain John D. Frank's (G, 1st NY) and Knap's (Independent E, PA Light) Batteries, respectively.

Private James P. Stewart (Btty. E, PA Light) hated the battery's position. So many dead and wounded lay in their path that Captain Joseph M. Knap ordered his artillerists to clear them out of the way before he posted his six 3 inch rifles in battery north of Mumma's lane.

While performing this onerous duty, Private Stewart snatched a button and one brass star from the corpse of a Confederate whom he erroneously assumed to be Lieutenant Colonel James M. Newton of the 6th Georgia. All around him the wounded pleaded to be dragged off or to be given water. He could do nothing for them.[5]

Lieutenant Evan Thomas' (A and C, 4th U.S.) Battery rolled into position east of Mumma's lane to Knap's immediate left.[6] They discouraged the Confederate infantry from leaving the security of the West Woods.

The West Woods' debacle utterly crushed Union morale in the Army of the Potomac's right wing. Edwin Sumner, due to his own cautiousness, would not advance any of his troops, able bodied or not, across the bloodied ground to support anything, even his precious guns.[7]

The discouraged soldiers from the I, II, and XII Corps lounged in dejected clusters throughout the East Woods. The maps would later represent their positions in neat, solid black lines — a "fact" not borne out by the evidence. Soldiers meandered throughout the woods without direction. Officers could not find their commands and, in at least one case, the disgruntled soldiers did not try to find any officers to control them.

Private Edward T. Harlan (E Co., 124th PA) retired with all due haste during Sedgwick's rout with his regiment to the East Woods where the Smoketown Road entered it. The exhausted and frightened soldiers threw themselves down upon the corpse strewn ground, heedless of the carnage which surrounded them. They had "seen the elephant" — been in combat — and had gotten thumped. There was not an officer alive who could send them into the open again. None of their officers were going to try and commit them to action again, either. They felt secure behind Cothran's six rifled pieces and they saw no need to disturb their relative tranquility. Private Harlan found himself a comfortable spot very close to the group which represented the more stalwart portion of the regiment and nestled down for a rest.[8] He wanted the war to come to him rather than he go to it.

Frank Schell, Leslie's artist, stole away from his nest when the hill above Roulette's barn became too uncomfortable and personally dangerous, and loped toward the East Woods. Cutting a northwesterly path through Roulette's cornfield and Mumma's plowed ground, he dashed across the Smoketown Road and took cover along a remnant of the worm fence which bordered it.

He peered through the smoke which drifted into the woods from Mumma's. Swarms of litter bearers, risking death at the hands of snipers or from random shells, scoured the fields about the farm to rescue helpless men. Ambulances lined the Smoketown Road where it turned north.

The artist, once again finding his spot too hazardous, pushed north. Wounded and dying men were all about the woods. Some screamed for help. Their pitiful croakings and squeals sliced him to the marrow of his soul.[9]

As he crossed the left of the 21st Georgia's former line, he stumbled over a wounded Confederate. The man lay at the base of a scarred oak, with his shattered left leg bound in corn leaves. His right hand was draped across his brow; he weakly begged Schell for water. The nervous reporter had none. The Georgian implored Schell to pull his dead comrade off his body, because he wanted to be dragged away before his men returned to retake the woods. Frank Schell gently pulled the corpse off the man's chest. Hastily glancing about him, he noticed that the stretcher crews had removed only Yankee casualties. They were not bothering with the Confederates yet.

The artist did not want to get involved with either the Rebel or any possible battle line. He left the man and moved a short distance west, toward the Cornfield. He paused long enough to speak briefly with a tall, gangly Georgian who was sitting upright with both hands clasped tightly about his bruised right ankle. The boy kept his eyes fixed upon the bearded corpse which was stretched out on its back at his feet. Schell peered into the grimy face hidden beneath the small brimmed, conical hat. The powder stained lips numbly mumbled something about the dead man being a relative — the boy's father.[10]

Frank Schell, the man, had seen enough of the rampant inhumanity to last a lifetime, but Frank Schell, the artist, a young man who made his living by selling pictures to a war ravenous public, had a distasteful duty to fulfill. He quickly sketched the two wounded Georgians then left them to themselves and continued west.

The stench and the gore of the Cornfield overwhelmed him. He did not want to step onto its blood soaked ground. He stood still, gaping at the bloated and blackened bodies. At one point, he caught a glimpse of what appeared to be an entire Confederate regiment — lying in formation. In the suddenness of their deaths, they had flung their weapons and accoutrements in every direction. Unable to bear the ghastliness of the field, he bolted into the East Woods.[11]

Pry's Ford

The VI Corps finally received orders to move out around 11:00 A.M.[12] "Bull" Sumner intercepted the head of the column and the Second Division commander, Major General William F. Smith, as they plunged into the knee deep water at Pry's ford. While Hancock's Brigade fell into regimental front, Sumner ordered Smith to move his people north to Joseph Poffenberger's to secure the Army's batteries along the Hagerstown Pike. At that moment, Lieutenant Colonel Joseph H. Taylor (Sumner's staff) galloped up to two of the generals and blurted something about Cothran's (M, 1st NY) and Frank's (G, 1st NY) Batteries needing immediate support.[13] General Smith ordered General Hancock to move out his first two regiments, the 49th Pennsylvania and the 43rd New York, to save those guns.

Hancock, once again, staged some rather melodramatic histronics in front of the 49th Pennsylvania.

"Men, I am about to lead you into the presence of the enemy," he boasted as he trotted to the center of the regiment, "but stand by that old flag to-day" — He emphatically pointed to the regiment colors — "and it will be all right!"

The regiment's rousing cheer echoed against Hancock's back as he turned his horse about and spurred toward the East Woods without them. The two regiments slowly fell into columns of four, shouldered their weapons, and marched, by the quick time, west in pursuit of their energetic brigadier, who had already disappeared over the brow of the hill onto M. Miller's farm lane.

The panting soldiers could not believe what they rushed into. Private Benjamin Clarkson (C Co., 49th PA) had never witnessed such pandemonium. The bursting shells, the shrieks of the wounded, and the "whizzing" of the solid shot appalled him. From the farm lane, he stared off to his left, where long lines of professionally aligned Federal troops cautiously advanced across the open, undulating fields toward the sunken lane. Confederate musketry and artillery fire punched random holes in their formations, but they held.

Wounded men staggered or crawled across their path, disrupting the Pennsylvanians' column. Blood stained, powder smeared, some of them mangled beyond description, they tried to stop individual soldiers for water or for direction to the nearest field hospitals.[14] The veterans however, could be of no assistance. They carefully passed around and among the wounded as they hurried toward the East Woods and their impatient general.

The Bloody Lane

Colonel John Gordon (6th AL) gaped weakly at the September sun as it inched its way toward the noon azimuth and he wondered if it would ever set that day. The blood soaked trousers clung to the calf of his right leg. Knowing that his men might falter if he quit the field, the colonel summoned every emotional reserve he could muster and stayed afoot. Even when a musket ball tore through the upper part of his left arm, horribly ripping out the tendons and mangling his flesh, he refused aid. With blood trickling, dark red, down over his hand and between his fingers, he reminded himself that he would not be moved. He had personally promised Robert E. Lee that he would stay, and Honor, with the help of his vigorous constitution, kept him to that pledge.[15]

On the northern side of the lane, what remained of French's three brigades tenaciously poured lead into the Confederate ranks. The 130th Pennsylvania (Morris' Brigade) had gone on line west of Roulette's lane with the 14th Indiana (Kimball's Brigade). The 8th Ohio, the 132nd Pennsylvania (Kimball's Brigade) and the Irish Brigade (Meagher's) continued the line to the east of the farm lane.[16] Only the 108th New York (Morris' Brigade) remained frozen on a crest to their rear.

Ammunition had gotten too low to sustain prolonged combat. Having fired his eighty rounds, Private Edward Spangler (K Co., 130th PA) rolled over a private from the 1st Delaware, who had lost the top of his skull, and rifled ten Enfield cartridges from his waist box. They fit down the bore of his Springfield, so he used them.[17]

To the left of the two prone Pennsylvania regiments, on the rise above Roulette's lane, the 8th Ohio's fire slackened. Their ammunition nearly depleted, the Ohions began to take more deliberate aim, trying to score with every shot. Sergeant Tom Galwey (B Co.) noticed the musketry momentarily cease to his front. All along the line, the noise dwindled considerably as several Confederates in the 6th Alabama and the 2nd North Carolina tied white handkerchiefs to their ramrods and cautiously poked them above the fence rails to signal they had had enough. A number of brave, if not foolhardy, Yankees stood up and strutted down toward the lane to accept their surrender.[18]

The 6th Alabama and its stalwart colonel, John Gordon, had taken about all the beating they could stand. Within minutes after his third wounding, a bullet passed through Gordon's kepi. Very shortly, he caught a fourth ball while directing fire on the left of his line. This one nailed him in the left shoulder, leaving its wooden base plug and a wad of clothing in its track. The impact staggered him but did not drop him. He remained upright but considerably less ambulatory. Again, the thought of leaving the battle entered his mind. He suppressed it. His men repeatedly begged him to retire, but the man seemed bent on dying for the sake of Honor. He could not expect his men to remain steadfast if he did not set the example.

While tottering toward the right of his regiment, he came upon the dying gray haired Joseph A. Johnson (G Co.) among the tangled corpses which filled the lane, lying protectively beside the lifeless body of a much younger man.

"Here we are," the bleeding man feebly gasped to Gordon. "My son is dead," he whispered, as if he were tucking the boy into bed, "and I shall go soon, but it is all right."

There was no conceivable way that John Gordon could abandon devoted troops as Private Johnson and his son, Fourth Sergeant Edward M. Johnson, at such a critical hour.

Through his pained eyes, however, Colonel Gordon noticed a commotion of sorts toward the right of his line; in the hollow across from Roulette's lane, the men appeared to waver.

He called for a volunteer and a Private Vickers responded immediately. The colonel falteringly told the boy to remind those troops of their pledge to General Lee. Vickers bolted like a jumped deer toward the right flank and had gone but fifty yards when a bullet, striking him in the side of the head, jerked him off his feet and slammed him — dead — into the lane.

Shocked by the boy's death, and, apparently, unwilling to risk another man's life or weaken his firing line, the colonel very unsteadily inched his way toward the regiment's right flank.[19]

Private Edward Spangler (K Co., 130th PA) drew a bead upon a large Confederate officer who was waving his sword in an attempt to keep his men from wavering. In his excitement, he forgot to remove the ramrod from the bore of his Springfield. The ramrod rang through the air with no effect. Moments later, he saw the officer collapse in the lane, shot down by one of the men in the 130th Pennsylvania.[20]

Scores of battered corpses and wounded men cluttered the lane. John Gordon (6th AL) tottered a few painful steps when a ball struck him square in the face, just below the left eye. The impact violently snapped his head, which hurled his kepi, top first, to the ground. He thudded loudly onto his face, unconscious.

The stretcher crew found him layed out like a mannequin with his face immersed in his blood filled kepi. They hurriedly rolled him onto his back and rough handled him onto their stretcher. Blood pumped violently from the huge exit wound on the right side of his neck with each labored breath. One of the rescuers, apparently, noted that had the Yankees not put a hole through his cap, Gordon would have drowned in his own blood.[21] They carted him off and the line held — without him.

The Confederates waited until the careless Yankees were too close to escape before they dropped their surrender flags and opened fire.[22] The unfortunate men had no chance of escaping, and they died within arms' reach of the lane. On the right, some members of the 4th North Carolina foolishly tried to flank the Irish Brigade during the confusion and were mown down.[23] Simultaneously, the 8th Ohio cut down the color bearer of the 2nd North Carolina. Man after man snatched up the standard in rapid succession and insanely waved it from side to side in defiance of the Yankees, who coldly dispatched them like moving targets in a shooting gallery. The Ohions deliberately concentrated their fire on specific targets, like any Confederate who stupidly exposed himself. At one point, Sergeant Tom Galwey (B Co.) saw one Rebel break for the southern bank of the lane and disappear in the smoke. He was the only enemy soldier the Irishman saw desert during the engagement.[24] The 130th Pennsylvania noticed him too. They shot him through the rear as he tried to scale the fence along the southern bank of the road.[25]

The cry for ammunition echoed all along Kimball's line. While Galwey and his comrades rummaged through the cartridge boxes of the dead and wounded for more rounds, he heard a loud murmuring off to the left in what he thought was the Irish Brigade.[26] The Rebels had reduced the Irishmen to a miniscule remnant of their former strength, making it difficult, in the smoke, to distinguish them from the average size regiment.

The humming — men passing the command to charge — rippled along the entire ridge, clear to the 130th Pennsylvania. Steel clinked against steel as individual squads furtively fixed bayonets for a fourth attempt to take the lane.[27]

The Roulette Farm

In the meantime, Brigadier General Nathan Kimball, knowing that his brigade needed support, scanned the hills east and northeast of his position for the rest of Richardson's Division (II Corps), only to find them still clinging to the swales while the Rebels devastated his ranks. He also discovered, to his ire, that in the tumultuous advance to the now Bloody Lane, the 108th New York (Morris' Brigade) remained on a hillside southeast of Roulette's. He searched the hillock where the 132nd Pennsylvania was lying and spied Lieutenant Frederick Hitchcock (Adjutant, 132nd PA) on the high ground, in the open, arguing with an enlisted man rather than paying attention to his duties.

Private George Coursen (K Co., 132nd PA) refused to fight with the rest of the men. He would not lie down. Instead, he perched himself on a boulder which rose above the top fence rail and started shooting from there. He kept shouting, "Come over here, men, you can see them better." Adjutant Hitchcock had been fulfilling his duties as file closer until he discovered Coursen, who was coldly and deliberately picking off Rebels in the lane, despite the bullets which buzzed around him. Hitchcock ordered the private to dismount and join the ranks. Coursen refused. The lieutenant was about to continue the dispute when General Kimball shouted at him to leave Coursen alone and tend to his needs.

Kimball told Hitchcock to inform the colonel of the 108th New York that his people were needed immediately on the brigade line. The inexperienced lieutenant felt very awkward about telling a superior officer what to do, but he feared Kimball's wrath more.

Suppressing his desire to desert, Hitchcock sprang across the bullet swept clover field to the 108th New York, where he found Colonel Oliver H. Palmer, its commander, cowering on his belly behind the prone regiment. Lieutenant Hitchcock yelled at Palmer to get his soldiers to the front. Colonel Palmer, whose head was turned away from the lieutenant, slowly, mutely raised his head and twisted it until his eyes met Hitchcock's. He stared mindlessly at the young subordinate and made no attempt to relay the command to his regiment.

A curse reverberated across the clover field above the musketry. Hitchcock, trembling because he did not know how to coerce the colonel into compliance, snapped his eyes back toward the knoll west of Roulette's lane. Nathan Kimball had locked his gaze upon the 108th New York and from his position on the ridge, he had witnessed the futile exchange between the two officers. The general screamed at the lieutenant to return immediately. This time, he ordered the adjutant, "Get those cowards out of there or shoot them."

Lieutenant Hitchcock anxiously returned to the New Yorkers. He unsnapped his holster flap and went for his service pistol.

Major George B. Force (108th NY), who was standing next to Hitchcock, vainly tried to rally his men by shouting and waving his cap. They would not budge. A cannon ball struck him full in the head and decapitated him. The impact hurled his body to the ground as if he were a toy. Suddenly, the officers of the 108th New York leaped up and demanded their men to do likewise. As some two hundred of the shaky New Yorkers dashed toward the right of the line, the very relieved lieutenant secured his weapon and trotted after them, leaving the quaking Colonel Palmer to wallow in his shame.[28] The remainder fled north to the safety of the upper fords of the Antietam.[29]

The 108th New York did not get to the sunken lane in time to assist the smattering of men who attempted to take it with the bayonet. The Alabamians in front of the 132nd Pennsylvania, upon seeing the powdered blackened Yankees in their soiled new uniforms charge their line, cried out, "Go back there, you black devils," before they quickly dispatched them with a wall of lead.[30]

By approximately 11:30 A.M., it appeared as if the Federals would never take the Bloody Lane. Caldwell's Brigade, with Brooke's Brigade to its rear, was still prone behind the Irish Brigade, waiting for orders to go into action. Their brigadier, John Caldwell, mysteriously disappeared when the brigade got too close to the shooting and the men would not advance without him.[31]

The East Woods

Private Edward Harlan (E Co., 124th PA) would have forgotten the war for a longer amount of time had not an immaculately uniformed officer, sporting a well groomed goatee and mustache, nearly trampled him to death.

"To what regiment do you belong?" the officer loudly demanded.

"The 124th Pennsylvania."

"Where is your colonel?" the officer excitedly snapped.

"He is wounded and taken from the field," Harlan replied.

"Where is your lieutenant colonel?"

Private Harlan, who was apparently rattled, inadvertently lied, "Our regiment is divided and he must be with the other part." (The regiment went into combat without a lieutenant colonel.)

"Where is your major?" the officer impatiently shot back.

"Don't know," Harlan shrugged.

The officer exploded. "Who in the hell has command of you?"

"Captain Yarnell."

"Send him to me."

Private Harlan fetched D Company's captain, who noticing the bright silver of a brigadier's star upon the officer's shoulder, snapped to attention and saluted.

"Have you command of these men?" the general growled.

"Yes, sir."

"You are Pennsylvania men and I am General Hancock, a Pennsylvania man, and if you are not with your command, I will take charge of you, and will ask you to support my battery."

Winfield Scott Hancock promptly reformed the drowsy Pennsylvanians and delivered one of his finer theatrical performances. Parading, as usual, from one end of the line to the other, he sonorously informed them that he had never lost a piece and he did not want to lose one that day. He said he would not call the 124th unless he needed it (much to their relief, no doubt) but that if he did, come! and come a yelling! The Rebs, he bragged, were the devil for shot, but they could not stand a bayonet charge.

With that, Hancock wheeled about and disappeared in a cloud of dust to seek out Major General William Smith, who was then leading the rest of his division (VI Corps) upon the field.[32]

"Double-quick Forty-ninth!"

Lieutenant Colonel William Brisbane's voice echoed over the column and the regiment accelerated its pace. Striking the Smoketown Road, the 49th Pennsylvania and the 43rd New York (Hancock's Brigade, VI Corps) followed it north to Poffenberger's lane, where it moved by the left flank, maneuvered into regimental front and crashed through the East Woods into the mow field north of the Cornfield toward the right of Frank's Battery (G, 1st NY). As the 49th passed around the splintered trees in the woods, they stepped over a large number of Sumner's men who lustily cheered on Hancock's Pennsylvanians and New Yorkers. The two regiments trotted into position abreast of the battery.

Bullets flew about their ears, Confederate batteries showered the line with shells, causing more racket than harm. Benjamin Clarkson (C Co., 49th PA) anxiously stood at his post in the front rank on the far left of the line. He clearly saw a heavy Confederate skirmish party advancing from the middle section of the West Woods toward the Cornfield, to the regiment's left front. Neither of the two regiments had cover of any sort and they could not expect any help from the troops in the woods behind them. Those men insisted they had no ammunition.

Several minutes later, the unmistakeable thundering of an approaching battery rumbled over the regiment from the East Woods. Lieutenant Colonel Brisbane quickly obliqued the 49th Pennsylvania to the right for about sixty yards, leaving a big gap between his people and the 43rd New York.

Captain Andrew Cowan's 1st New York Battery of 3 inch rifles rolled into position to the left of the Pennsylvanians and began to unlimber while the remaining three regiments of Hancock's Brigade (6th ME, 5th WI, and 137th PA) double quicked onto the field to extend the Federal line to the right of Cothran's Battery (M, 1st NY), near the Smoketown Road. Acting Major Thomas Huling (49th PA) advanced C Company into Miller's mow field and dashed it left — in front of Cowan's pieces, where he ordered the men prone. (Map 39)

Private Clarkson (C Co., 49th PA) felt very uneasy. His half of the company went to ground among the bloating corpses and waited for the Confederate skirmishers to leap frog closer. The rest of the regiment, including the right wing of his company, could not commence firing at the encroaching Rebels without striking his wing.[33]

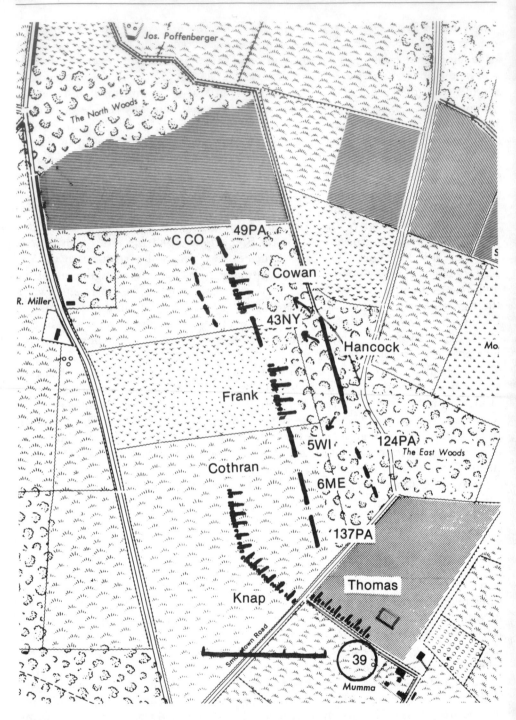

(Map 39) NOON — 1:00 P.M., SEPTEMBER 17, 1862
Hancock's Brigade reinforces the Federal line in the East Woods.

Lieutenant Colonel Brisbane, for some unaccountable reason, did not countermand the order. (He must have been somewhere else.) It was a bad day for misplaced officers. Major Huling mysteriously disappeared from the regiment immediately after he posted Clarkson's Company.

Benjamin Clarkson had never witnessed such desolation before. Desperately wounded men along with the corpses of soldiers and horses were everywhere. The pungent stench of burned powder irritated his nostrils and made his eyes water. Cannon balls skittered across the open ground like huge marbles, scooping up dirt by the buckets and brutally crushing any flesh they bounded into. Shell fragments, red hot and hissing, showered the Pennsylvanians and the East Woods. The incessant racket paled him. He started to pray.[34]

The North Woods

Clara Barton heard the increased commotion to the south. She checked the sun. It was almost noon. The smoke from the Federal batteries drifted across the hollow from the north and obscured her view. She had far more to worry about than whether she could see where the battle was going on. She was waging her own warfare — one against time and the elements.

The hot, sulfuric air robbed the skin of moisture. Besides their injuries, the men contended with sandpapery throats and cracked, bleeding lips. Wayward shells exploded randomly in the hollow while Miss Barton worked her way from soldier to soldier.

Kneeling down, she cradled a soldier's head in her right arm and tenderly raised a canteen to his parched lips. The water barely touched his tongue when something burning hot tugged on her left sleeve and passed through the man's chest from shoulder to shoulder. His entire body jerked violently for a second as the water, untasted, trickled down over his lifeless face. Clara Barton numbly lowered the dead man's head to the ground. The stray ball, which had passed through her sleeve and brutishly slain him, would leave a permanent scar upon her heart. (She never patched the hole in her dress.)[35]

The West Woods

Captain David Guy Maxwell (H Co., 35th NC) could hardly believe Private William S. Hood's (H Co.) story. Not long after Monroe's Rhode Island Battery quit the field, Colonel Matthew W. Ransom (35th NC) asked for a volunteer to check out the disposition of the Federal troops. The fearless, 18 year old Hood, who was barefoot because his feet were too raw to wear shoes, unhesitatingly leaped up and took off at "trail arms".

The once fair complexioned soldier disappeared for at least one hour which led Maxwell and Colonel Ransom to believe he was not coming back. Around 11:00 A. M., approximately an hour after he left, the black haired, filthy young man returned and immediately reported to the colonel. He explained why he was so late getting back.

CAPT. DAVID G. MAXWELL
H Co., 35th North Carolina

He sent private William Hood on a private reconnaissance which the private used to procure coffee.
(Clarke, NC Regts.)

While wandering among the dead and wounded in the Hagerstown Pike, Private Hood stumbled across a wounded Federal officer who was begging for water. The poor man, in desperation, offered the private his gold watch and chain, and all of his greenback Federal dollars if Hood could arrange for the Confederates to carry him off. The teenager politely declined. Instead, he devised a strategy to scout the Federal lines and be humane at the same time.

Not far from the Pike, William Hood hailed over some Federal pickets whom he led to the seriously hurt officer. As a stretcher crew carried the "shoulder strap" away, the videttes invited the Confederates to their outpost for coffee. The ragged private graciously accepted. The Yankees kindly allowed him to return to his own lines after they filled his haversack with fresh coffee and his memory with information.[36]

Sergeant Edward Moore (Poague's Battery) could not stay long at Jackson's field hospital on A. Poffenberger's farm. As the battery inched past the hospital, Captain Poague sent Moore's crew to fetch him. They found their aching sergeant and placed him atop a caisson before pulling out after the rest of the battery.

William Poague was very carefully trotting his pieces toward the Hagerstown Pike. He had limped away from the cornfield west of the Nicodemus farm with only one reliable gun. The two remaining artillery pieces could fire, but they were too shot up to withstand the strain of rapid or sustained movement. The Yankees crippled most of his crewmen and shot down the bulk of his teams.[37]

General Robert E. Lee and his staff, who were dismounted, intercepted the battery on a knoll about six hundred yards below the Dunker Church, west of the Hagerstown Pike. Lee hallooed Poague and motioned him over. The captain halted his teams and rode up to the general to offer his services. Bob Lee, Jr., the commanding general's son, and several other crew members wandered over and clustered around the officers.

Poague saluted, whereupon, Lee, his face solemn and unflinching, asked the captain about the battery's condition and ammunition supply. The grimy officer told Lee that he had only one full team left. The other guns could serve, he added, but not for any great length of time.[38]

The general blankly studied the group of enlisted men, passing over his son without a sign of recognition. He ordered Poague to dispatch his one good piece with a salvaged crew and his best horses to the front. The others were to go to Sharpsburg, refit, and return to the line as soon as possible.[39] The captain, after saluting, turned to mount when Bob Lee, Jr. stepped out of the knot of dirty enlisted men and approached his father. The general stared momentarily at his son before he congratulated him for not being hurt. He apparently had not recognized the soldier with the blackened face.

Bob, Jr. dejectedly groaned, "You are not going to put us in the fight again in our crippled condition, are you?"

Robert E. Lee, the general, not the father, pointed his bandaged right hand toward the Bloody Lane and the stalemated Federal lines.

"Yes, my son, I may need you to help drive those people away." The general, facing his son, managed a smile and exchanged a few pleasantries with him before he turned his attention back to the battle. Bob Lee, Jr., the soldier, shuffled downcast back to his crew.[40]

Leaving the good team behind, the two remaining gun crews rolled slowly toward Sharpsburg. A short distance away, Moore's men halted as all fixed their attention upon the village. Edward Moore hardly recognized the place. Flames seemed to envelope most of the houses. Shell burst after shell burst sent flocks of maddened pigeons fluttering about from roost to roost as they stubbornly or stupidly refused to surrender their nests to an obviously superior enemy.[41]

Moore did not give a second thought to the psychological import of his observation, but the rousted pigeons and the Army of Northern Virginia had a great deal in common in relation to the Yankees. Much like the beleaguered pigeons of Sharpsburg, the Army of Northern Virginia was preparing to rearrange its lines of defense against a numerically superior foe. Like the birds, they were not prepared to give up their roosts without a severe fight.

Robert E. Lee continued to feed his battered troops from the morning's fight into the line along the Hagerstown Pike. The 1st North Carolina, which mustered sixty-six men, having spent a few hours resting in a hollow southwest of the West Woods, replenished their empty cartridge boxes and trooped east toward the Hagerstown Pike. As they passed by General Lee and his staff, he personally directed them onto the field.

"Go in cheerful, boys," the twenty year old Calvin Leach (B Co.) recalled Lee saying, "they are driving them back on the right and left and we need a little help in the center."

As the North Carolinians took cover behind the stone wall along the Hagerstown Pike, Private Leach stared up at the bright sun. "I often looked at the sun," he wrote, "and longed for night to come as the firing would cease."[42]

The VI Corps secured the East Woods while Robert E. Lee personally directed troops onto the field to support his weakening center along the Bloody Lane. Casualties climbed in that section of the field as the Federals continually hammered the stubborn Confederate line.

CHAPTER TWELVE

"Strong bulls of Bashan have beset me round."

NOON - 1:00 P.M.

The West Woods

By noon, Tyndale's hodge podge, eight regiment "brigade", in the West Woods, had expended most of its ammunition.[1] Lieutenant Colonel Tyndale did not allow his two right regiments, the 13th New Jersey (Gordon's Brigade, XII Corps) and the Purnell Legion (Goodrich's Brigade, XII Corps), to fire north of their position for fear of striking Union troops which General Greene, his division commander, erroneously informed him were still in that part of the West Woods.[2] Unknown to either officer, the 46th North Carolina (Manning's Brigade), with the 25th, 35th, and 49th North Carolina regiments (Ransom's Brigade) used the hour and one half of relative quiet to marshal their forces in the wooded ravines north and northwest of the Purnell Legion, Tyndale's anchor regiment.[3]

The Confederates, in an attempt to envelop the Yankees' right flank, carried their arms at "the trail". The shaken troops of the 13th New Jersey, who believed that the Rebels meant to surrender, allowed them to pass to their right. Adjutant Hopkins (13th NJ) and another officer quickly reassessed the situation and turned the right company (D Co.) to meet the assault.[3]

Captain Joseph Knap's Battery (E, PA Light), which was in the clover field immediately north of Mumma's lane, had been under fire since about 10:30 A.M. So far, the Confederate gunners had smashed one limber's wheel and had killed one horse and two men in Thomas' Battery (A and C, 4th U.S.), which was across the Smoketown Road from his left gun.[4]

Shortly before noon, Colonel Tyndale came out of the West Woods to Knap's

Battery. Pulling out his spy glass, he directed Lieutenant James D. McGill to focus in on the West Woods. Private David Nichol (Knap's Battery) overheard the officers saying something about the 28th Pennsylvania needing help. Presently, McGill snapped at his section (two guns) to limber and move out.

". . . it was no place for Artillery," Nichol later wrote "but the Lieut[enant] had to obey orders."

The two rifled pieces raced into Mumma's swale toward the southern end of the West Woods.[5]

The section had barely pulled away when the Confederates struck hard and rousted the startled Purnell Legion (MD) and the 13th New Jersey out of the West Woods with a vengeance. One by one, in rapid succession, Tyndale's demoralized regiments began to stream from the woods toward Mumma's swale.[6] The formerly valiant 13th New Jersey raced pell mell down the Smoketown Road toward the protection of the rest of Knap's (E, PA Light) and Thomas' (A and C, 4th U.S.) Batteries above Mumma's lane.[7] The 3rd Maryland, 111th and 28th Pennsylvania on the left of the 66th Ohio tried to maintain their lines. Only their color guards and a smattering of men attempted to rally with Crane's three Ohio regiments (66th, 5th, and 7th OH) below the crest of the Dunker Church ridge.[8] Tompkins' Battery (A, 1st RI) hitched up to make room for Captain C. D. Owen's Battery (G, 1st RI) as it rumbled down Mumma's lane into the swale.[9]

Owen's gunners quickly reined to a halt below the Confederates' line of sight. They apparently were going to smash Rodes' Alabamians, who were less than three hundred yards south of their position.[10]

Colonel John R. Cooke (27th NC), having watched the Yankees flush from the West Woods, excitedly noticed how the Ohions cowered below the Dunker Church ridge, some five hundred yards northeast of his two regiments. Like a race horse chafing at the gate, he nervously anticipated the charge which his fallen brigade commander, Colonel Van H. Manning, had given him carte blanche to execute should the occasion arise. When Knap's guns stole onto the horizon, Cooke took advantage of the situation by immediately rushing the three left companies of the 27th North Carolina from the northern edge of their cornfield to the northeastern side. The Tar Heels took steady aim and loosed a perfect volley.

The cheers of the 28th Pennsylvania had barely died away when Cooke's men cut down several horses of the section's Number Two rifle, while the artillerists attempted to manhandle the gun into battery. The Yankees panicked, abandoned their gun and limber, and ran for their lives. The air around them sang with flying lead. Colonel Tyndale fell mortally wounded with a bullet in his head. James Marshall (E, PA Light) let out a piercing shriek an fell dead from a bullet in his side, near James Stewart's cannon. Samuel Clark came in with a shoulder wound. William H. Anderson lost part of his elbow. Sergeant Adam Shaw was down and John Lewis, the color bearer, was severely wounded in three places. A recruit named Joseph Klinefelter disappeared altogether. The Number One gun turned about and stampeded what remained of the 3rd Maryland, 111th and the 28th Pennsylvania on the brigade's left, scattering them toward the numerous haymounds which dotted Mumma's mow grass.[11]

Cooke saw his chance. Enlivened with the opportunity for glory, the colonel screamed for his two regiments to rise up and "Prepare to charge!"[12] The 27th North

Carolina (on the left) and the 3rd Arkansas (on the right) enthusiastically got to their feet and formed in battle line.[13]

A slightly built man in the 3rd Arkansas timidly approached his captain with an unusual request as the men closed ranks.

"Sir," he drawled, "would it be all right if I kinda give the boys a tune as they move out? I got my fiddle with me."

The officer blurted that he could play as long as it was a particular mountain square dance tune.

"Swing your partner! Doe see doe! Granny, will your dog bite? Hellfire no!" squealed overhead and mingled incongruously with the sounds of battle as Cooke's command of one thousand untried souls stepped over the splintered worm fence to their front into the stubble field bordering the Hagerstown Pike.[14]

The fiddling attracted a few annoying rounds from the 1st Delaware, which lay in the cornfield to Owen's (G, 1st RI) left. An inebriated Confederate colonel galloped up to Lieutenant Colonel Richard W. Singletary as he centered himself on the front of the 27th North Carolina.

"Come on, boys!" the colonel slobbered as he wildly slashed the air with his saber. "I am leading this charge!" Singletary bitterly confronted him. "You are a liar, Sir! We lead our own charges."

The drunken officer reined his mount aside and sallied forth against hallucinatory enemies while the two inexperienced regiments took off at a dead run toward Mumma's smoldering ruins.[15] *(Map 40)*

The Bloody Lane

Further east, the Federal position along the Bloody Lane seemed to deteriorate despite the Confederates' appalling losses. For a long while, Caldwell's Brigade had helplessly watched the Confederates whittle the Irish Brigade away. Time and again, the men in the 61st New York saw the Irishmen's colors drop and rise again. Sergeant Charles Fuller (C Co., 61st NY) heard Brigadier General Thomas Meagher frantically plead with Colonel Francis Barlow, "Colonel! For God's sake come and help me!"

Barlow yelled back that there was nothing he could do. He would advance as soon as Caldwell ordered him to.[16]

The Irish Brigade, a mere remnant of its former self, ran out of ammunition. It ceased fire and rose to its feet. Forming in columns of four, at the right shoulder shift, the shot up regiments defied the incoming Confederate rounds and prepared to leave the field with a professional arrogance. Meanwhile, the 14th Connecticut retired to Roulette's, where it went into line along the farm lane, east of the house.[17]

Caldwell's Brigade (64th/61st, 7th NY, 81st PA, and 5th NH), which had lain in the trough behind the Irish Brigade for over an hour, would not move to their comrades' assist. Neither would Colonel John R. Brooke's Brigade (2nd DE, 52nd, 57th, and 66th NY, and 53rd PA) budge. It nestled against the reverse slope of a "safe" crest to their rear, and, likewise, stayed undeployed, while the Confederates shot Meagher's Irishmen into a bloody pulp.[18]

A snag developed in the withdrawal as the Irish filed off to the right rear of Colonel Francis Barlow's 64th/61st New York regiments. The 69th New York, followed by the 29th Massachusetts executed perfect right wheels and double backed

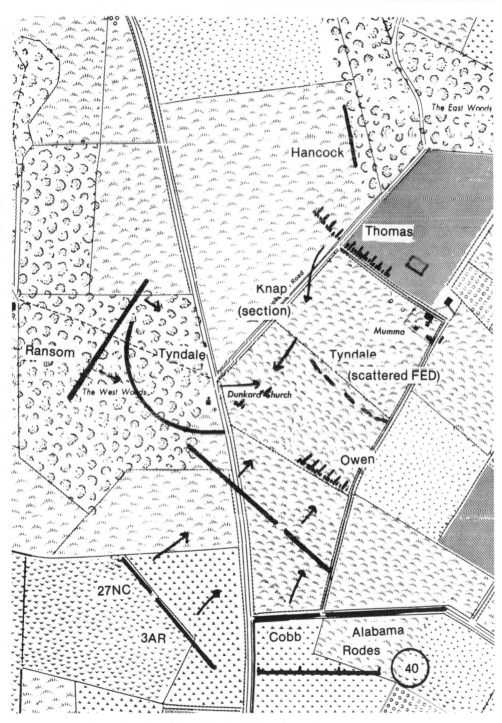

(Map 40) NOON — 1:00 P.M., SEPTEMBER 17, 1862
Ransom and Cooke throw Tyndale's Brigade out of the West Woods.

fours toward Roulette's amidst the cheers of the 57th New York, as they passed its right flank.[19] The badly shot up 63rd New York, however, became entangled in its own maneuver and halted momentarily to straighten itself out. Its left and right wings bent at right angles to each other, which exposed the color guard. *(Map 41)*

A well directed volley from the 4th North Carolina ripped through the Irishmen and punched huge holes in Companies C and F on the right flank of the 88th New York. The two New York regiments pulled back, leaving a big gap in the line along their former front.[20]

Tying a frightened musician to each end of his belt sash so he would not lose them, Colonel Francis Barlow (64th/61st NY) stormed at his two combined regiments to rise up. The reluctant New Yorkers gained their feet and snapped to right shoulder shift. Right obliquing his men into the open field closer to the lane than the Irish Brigade had been, Barlow ordered his people to direct their fire into the right flank of the 4th North Carolina. They were so close, the Confederates had to hug the northern bank of the road to keep from getting hit.[21]

Simultaneously, the 2nd Delaware (Brooke's Brigade) moved into the line on the right of the 7th New York (Caldwell's Brigade).[22] Once again, it looked as if the Federals were going to die piecemeal.

On the far left of the line, Colonel Edward Cross (5th NH) paced to and fro behind his line. A red bandana covered a nasty scalp wound on his bald head and his eyes seemed to flame as he ranted at his men, "If any man runs I want the file closers to shoot him. If they don't, I shall myself."

Lieutenant Thomas Livermore (K Co., 5th NH), who feared his irate colonel as much as the Rebels, hugged the ground with his men. Shortly after Barlow's soldiers moved out and the 2nd Delaware came onto line, the regiment stood up.

The New Englanders fired and loaded by files from the right as they prepared to advance toward the knoll to within ninety feet of the Bloody Lane. Lieutenant Livermore, who thankfully observed that the Irish Brigade had fairly well "used up" the Rebels to his front, posted no objection to the light opposition from the Confederate ranks.[23]

Their riflery hit Colonel F. M. Parker and Adjutant Phillips of the 30th North Carolina. A bullet, which cut a deep groove in the Colonel's head, exposed, but did not damage, the membrane that encased his brain. He staggered out of the fight severely but not mortally wounded.[24]

"Where's General Caldwell?" a familiar voice bellowed from behind.

Thomas Livermore turned his face toward the right rear only to hear a few men shout back, "Behind the haystack!"

"God damn the field officers!" the voice exploded.

Israel "Greasy Dick" Richardson, the division commander, had again come upon the field. Afoot, sword in hand, his face blackened by powder, the general personally posted Captain William Graham's Battery (K, 1st U.S.) near the eastern corner of the Bloody Lane before he stormed into Caldwell's Brigade.[25] He did not like what he saw — stagnant battle lines and rapidly escalating casualties. *(Map 42)*

The East Woods

Private Benjamin Franklin Clarkson (C Co., 49th PA) lay, terrified, with the left platoon of his company in Miller's mow field, directly in front of Cowan's 3 inch

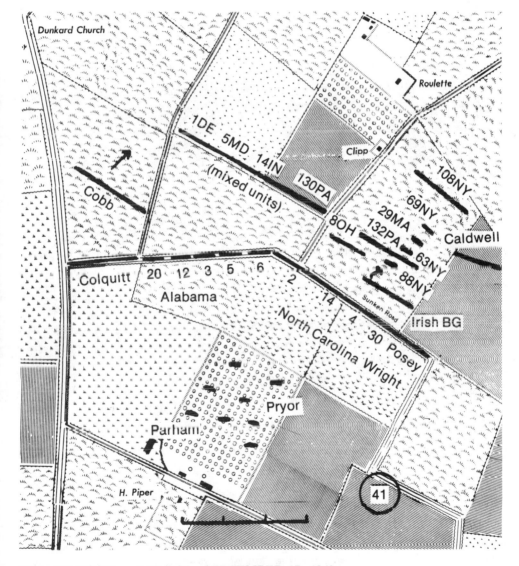

(Map 41) NOON — 1:00 P.M., SEPTEMBER 17, 1862
The Irish Brigade retires from the Bloody Lane.

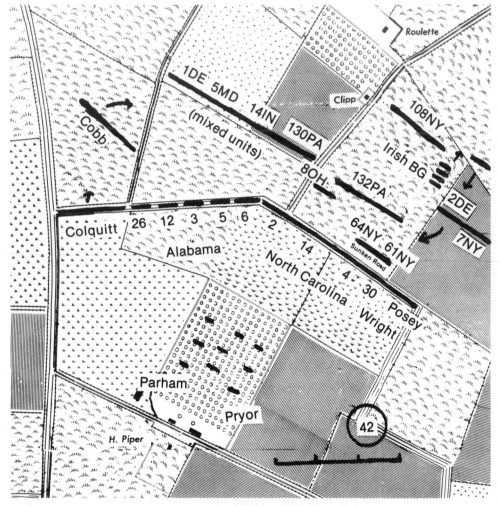

(Map 42) NOON — 1:00 P.M., SEPTEMBER 17, 1862
Barlow's 64th/61st New York keeps the Confederates in the Bloody Lane in check.

ACTING MAJOR THOMAS HULING,
49th Pennsylvania

General Winfield Scott Hancock
dressed him down in front of his men
for putting a company in front of
Cowan's Battery and for hiding behind
an oak tree in the East Woods.
(History of the 49th Pennsylvania)

rifled pieces. He trembled as Ransom's Brigade and a portion of Early's Division pursued Orrin Crane's men to the open ground east of the West Woods and pelted the 49th with rounds intended for the Purnell Legion and the 13th New Jersey.

Moments later, in the wake of Cooke's charge, two Confederate batteries (unidentified) rolled onto the open ground south of the Dunker Church and fired upon Hancock's extended brigade with shell and round shot. Clarkson felt absolutely helpless.

Suddenly, General Winfield Scott Hancock materialized along the front of Company C. Clarkson stared up at the general, whose excited horse kept dancing from side to side a few paces away from his head.

"His horse was all excitement, his head erect and nostrils distended," the private recalled, as were the general's at the moment.

"Men, who put you out here?" Hancock demanded.

"Our Major!" someone called back.

"Where is your major?"

"He is behind that large white oak tree at the edge of the woods in our rear."

"Tell your major to come here, instantly," Hancock growled.

A runner broke from the ranks and ferretted out Acting Major Thomas Huling from the security of an immense oak on the border of the East Woods.

The general verbally abused the quaking major in front of his men, while Clarkson, a God fearing soul, mentally erased all but the conclusion of the blasphemous reprimand.

". . . . Do you want your men all cut to pieces?" Hancock raved. "What do you mean? . . ."

"Come away from here, general, you ought not to be here."

The general snapped his eyes upon one of his still panting aides who had overanxiously interrupted his superb performance.

"The enemy is coming right toward us!" the officer exclaimed while pointing a badly shaking finger toward Cooke's screaming line as it crossed the Hagerstown Pike.

"Damn them!" Hancock spat. "Let them come! That's what we are here for. Step back, men, step back."

The general, while cooly inching back Clarkson's platoon, lost track of Acting Major Huling, who used the distraction to slip away — out of sight, out of mind.

Benjamin Clarkson, having become so engrossed in Hancock's tantrum, temporarily transferred his anxiety for his own personal safety to that of his hyperactive general whom he expected to see killed at any moment. The private nervously shuffled back to his post, a few paces from the hub of Cowan's right gun, never once taking his eyes off the prancing Hancock.

"Now, men, stay there until you are ordered away; this place must be held at all hazards!" the general thundered.

Clarkson watched Hancock calmly pull a mental flask from inside his blouse, plug it into this dry mouth and take a lingering draught. The thirsty private, who knew better than to suppose that Hancock carried water in the bottle, knowingly brushed the drink aside as "something". He would not find fault with his idol.

Hancock capped his bottle and tucked it away. Turning to Captain Andrew Cowan, he confidently ordered, "Now, Captain, let them have it!"

The general dashed for the East Woods before the gunner had yanked the lanyard on the first gun.[26]

The West Woods

The boldness of Cooke's assault completely undid the Ohions and Owen's Battery. The 27th North Carolina with its bright red battle flag slapping defiantly in the sky from the charge's momentum, completely overran the Yankees in the swale, while (on the right) the 3rd Arkansas with Cobb's Brigade (16th and 24th GA, and 15th NC) from the western end of the Bloody Lane pushed the 1st Delaware deeper into Mumma's cornfield, away from the lane.[27]

Captain James Graham (G Co., 27th NC) hardly believed the drive's success. Shouting at the Ohions to surrender and behave as prisoners of war by lying down, the Confederates raced through the demoralized Yankees and continued, unimpeded, toward the smoking ruins of the Mumma farm. The astonished captain incredulously watched the Federals throw down their muskets and start to trudge south toward the Confederate lines without any escorts, while the haystacks in Mumma's mow field bristled with makeshift surrender flags — white rags or handkerchiefs hastily tied to bayonets or musket barrels. Some two or three hundred Yankees were quitting without a fight.[28]

Colonel John R. Cooke and his men were in their glory despite the fact that the five regiments became more unmanageable as the attack progressed. Cooke had to double quick to catch up with his color bearer, Corporal Harry H. Campbell (G Co.), who had gotten too far in front of the line and who was leading the 27th North Carolina directly toward the muzzles of Thomas' Regular Battery (A and C, 4th U.S.). Having caught up with the overly exuberant standard bearer, the colonel screamed at him to slow down.

The already hoarse Campbell glanced over his bobbing shoulder and rasped out, "Colonel, I can't let that Arkansas fellow get ahead of me!"[29]

He did not either. Cooke merely aimed him further to the east toward Roulette's lane, where he hoped to escape Thomas' deadly canister, which had pounded his two regiments since they crossed the Hagerstown Pike.

The impetuous and inexperienced colonel mistakenly assumed that Ransom's North Carolinians, who had herded the Yankees into Mumma's swale, would silence those guns on his left flank.[30] They did not. Ransom's people demonstrated only momentarily in front of the West Woods before the Yankee artillerists across the fields from them got their range. They absorbed several shells and took casualties before melting into the West Woods.[31]

Within a minute or two, Generals Thomas J. Jackson and J. E. B. Stuart rode into Ransom's prone line, which they found at the base of the wooded slopes west of the Dunker Church. First Lieutenant William Hyslop Sumner Burgwyn (H Co., 35th NC) noticed Jackson's worn and filthy uniform. "Little Sorrel", the general's horse, seemed better groomed than the general, who was somberly peering beneath the brim of the floppy slouch hat which he had pulled down over his forehead.

"Old Jack" rode over to Colonel Matthew W. Ransom (35th NC), whom he found standing, and said he wanted the North Carolinians to take the battery (Knap's) which was still north of Mumma's lane.

The colonel replied he would try, if ordered, but the attempt would fail. The general, who had not ridden up the hill to the Hagerstown Pike, retorted that, having just witnessed the regiment's last charge to the edge of the West Woods, he believed the assault would succeed.

The powder grimed colonel countered that the regiment tried to gain the crest but that when the men reached the Pike they saw what he believed to be the bulk of McClellan's army in support of the guns.

"Have you a good climber in your command?" Jackson growled.

Colonel Ransom called for volunteers and the barefoot Private William S. Hood (H Co.) jumped up immediately.[32] Jackson sent Hood shinnying up a tall hickory tree for a "looksee". The general told the boy to count the Federal battle flags in the fields east of the East Woods. The obedient Hood clung tightly to the tree trunk while bullets clipped off the bark beneath his feet; he nervously scanned the Yankee lines.

"Who-ee! there are oceans of them, General!" he howled.

"Never mind the oceans, count their battle flags," Jackson sternly shouted back.

The private methodically told off every set of flags he could see. When he reached thirty-seven or thirty-nine, Jackson told him, "That will do, come down and we will get out of here."

William Hood won an orderly's spurs, which he later strapped to his calloused feet, and Jackson recalled Ransom's regiments, which left the gallant 27th North Carolina and 3rd Arkansas to face the fast approaching VI Corps on their own.[33]

At about the same time, Private C. A. Richardson (B Co., 15th VA), who was standing in line awaiting orders, happened to glance skyward. Judging by the position of the sun, he assumed it was noon. A commotion down the brigade's front attracted his attention. A stately, gray haired soldier, who was mounted on a superb horse, trooped the line asking the officers if they knew where he might find General Jackson. Richardson, who could not understand why they treated an enlisted man with such respect, approached one of his officers about the fellow. The private was taken aback somewhat when he learned that the respectable looking gentleman in the plain gray uniform was Robert E. Lee, his commanding general.[34]

The Bloody Lane

Second Lieutenant Charles B. Tanner (H Co., 1st DE) did not care about the fighting in Mumma's swale to the right of his regiment. He had other things on his mind. The regimental colors were still on the ground sixty feet in front of the

LIEUTENANT CHARLES TANNER, H Company, 1st Delaware
While rescuing the regimental colors in front of Rodes' Alaba-
mians, he suffered three wounds.
(Deeds of Valor)

Confederates. Major Thomas A. Smyth (1st DE) offered to gather up twenty-five of the regiment's best shots and instruct them to fire above the colors if Tanner would run forward to snatch them up.

"Do it," Tanner cried, "and I will get there!"

Twenty volunteers responded to Tanner's call and sprang with him into the bullet sprayed open ground. As he reached the colors and tugged them free of the standard bearer's corpse, he ruefully noticed they were splattered with blood. A second later, a minie ball shattered his right arm. Not waiting for another wound, he clenched the flag in his bloodied right hand and set the record for the eighty yard dash. Two more bullets slammed into his body but did not drop him. He staggered into the regiment as it prepared for Cooke's charge against its right flank. Major Smyth immediately promoted the profusely bleeding Tanner to first lieutenant then ordered the regiment to pull back its right flank to meet the Confederate attack.[35]

At the bend in the Bloody Lane, for the last ten minutes, Barlow's two New York regiments (64th/61st NY) had brutally pinned the 4th North Carolina. The New Yorkers kept the Rebs down but not without problems of their own. Private Barney Rogers, an Irishman (A Co., 61st NY), went into combat with a worn out strap for a belt. When the regiment crawled over the fence northeast of the lane to engage the Rebels, his "belt" snapped. Unable to hold onto his pants, and simultaneously, load and fire, he released his grip on the waistband. The trousers fell down around his ankles and hobbled him like a horse.

As his sergeant, Charles Fuller (C Co.), paced the line in performance of his duties as file closer, Barney called over his shoulder, "Charley, cut the damned things off!" Fuller pulled out his large pocket knife and slit the pants from waist band to ankle on one side.

"You can kick the other leg out," Fuller shouted.

A few jiggles later, and the Irishman was in the fight unhindered. A southerly breeze cleared the smoke along the regiment's front and sent the Irishman's shirt tail flapping in its wake. Laughter echoed in the air behind Barney Rogers when Sergeant Fuller hauled aside Captain Ike Plumb (C Co.) to gawk at his bare backside. The illiterate private was naked from his socks to his waist.[36]

Captain William Graham's Battery (K, 1st U.S.) fired over and into the Confederate line from the eastern corner of the lane. The Rebels' fire slackened perceptibly with every artillery discharge. They started to waver, particularly in the 2nd North Carolina, which held the ascending ground in the apex of the Bloody Lane. Orderly Sergeant James Shinn (B Co., 4th NC), whose regiment occupied the line two regiments to the east wondered how much longer his men could endure the small arms and the gunnery fire which pounded the regiment from all directions but the rear.[37]

In Piper's orchard, Lieutenant Colonel W. A. Parham (C. O., Mahone's Brigade) pulled aside Lieutenant William W. Chamberlaine (G Co., 6th VA), who was reforming what he could find of his regiment.

"Lieutenant," the colonel yelled, "go back a little, try and find General R. H. Anderson, explain to him the situation and ask for reinforcements."

The lieutenant set off immediately for the Hagerstown Pike.[38]

Lieutenant Colonel J. N. Lightfoot (6th AL) haled over Brigadier General Robert E. Rodes as he approached the regiment's left wing from the mow grass south of the lane. Lightfoot gestured toward his enfiladed right wing, which was masked by the northwestern corner of Piper's cornfield. Rodes impatiently yelled at Lightfoot to pull his right wing out of the road into the corn, then galloped back toward Piper's farm without waiting to see the command executed.

J. N. Lightfoot stepped behind the center of the skeletal regiment and called, "6th Alabama, about face, forward march."

As the powder stained survivors leaped and clawed their way over the bank behind them into the corn, Major E. L. Hobson, commanding the 5th Alabama, on Lightfoot's left, rushed over and asked if the whole brigade was to retire. Lightfoot, having misunderstood the original command in the din of the battle, merely replied, "Yes."

One by one, first in squads, then by platoons, Rodes' five regiments shattered and streamed rearward. The general, who did not know what had transpired until it was too late, had fallen with a canister shot in the thigh while tending a wounded aide.[39]

The 130th Pennsylvania rose up and pursued the Rebels into the lane,[40] while the 64th/61st New York stood up and right wheeled, throwing its left flank into the lane between the 4th North Carolina and the 14th North Carolina.[41] The New Yorkers literally jumped over the heads of the Confederates. Quickly, they unpiled the corpses and laid each man out individually then handed their canteens to the wounded Confederates.[42]

Captain Thomas B. Beall (I Co., 14th NC) could barely see through the dense smoke which engulfed his small regiment. A withering fire from the 8th Ohio, on the left front, and the 132nd Pennsylvania, to the right front, literally swept away the men on both flanks, including the rest of the forty-five man C Company. In the terrible confusion a Confederate officer dashed into the North Carolinians from the right and screamed at Colonel Risden Tyler Bennett (14th NC) that the Yankees had flanked them and were preparing to enfilade the regiment from the rear.

Captain Beall shot a frightened glance over his right shoulder and noticed that the 64th/61st New York had overlapped the Bloody Lane in a north-south line. The Yankees, moving like a door on a hinge, were closing in on them from behind.[43]

Part of the 108th New York plunged into the lane, trampling dead and wounded Confederates under them.[44] Rebel and Yankee troops became too entangled to get clear fields of fire. The North Carolinians could not hold the lane any longer. Those who could broke and ran through the corn south of the road. Bullets and canister gouged the Confederates from the north and the east. Men dropped rapidly. Others were brutally hurled through the corn. Commands disintegrated into frightened and confused squads. (The regiment lost two hundred seventy-eight of five hundred twenty-three officers and men engaged.)

Captain Thomas B. Beall, Lieutenant Hanny, Private Preston D. Weaver (I Co.), and Colonel R. Tyler Bennett (14th NC), finding themselves separated from their regiment, made tracks, west toward the Hagerstown Pike.[45] It all happened so quickly that no one really knew quite what was going on except within their own range of sight.

In the center, some soldiers of the 132nd Pennsylvania, noticing that the Confederate fire had slackened drastically, trotted down to the lane. They stumbled upon the severely wounded Lieutenant Colonel R. B. Nisbet of the 3rd Georgia and gently carried him back to their regiment.[46] As they bore him back through the Pennsylvanians, Lieutenant Frederick Hitchcock (Adjutant 132nd PA) stepped over to shake his hand as a farewell courtesy. (Hitchcock assumed Nisbet was dying.)

"God bless you, boys, you are very kind," the fair complexioned colonel gasped. Asking to be laid down in a sheltered spot, he continued, "I have but a few moments to live. You have killed all my brave boys; they are there in the road."

Hitchcock wrote down the embroidered rank and insignia on Nisbet's collar as he slipped to the top of the knoll to inspect the carnage in the sunken lane. It appalled him.[47]

At about the same time, a curious private in the 8th Ohio found the dying Colonel Charles C. Tew (2nd NC) propped in a sitting position against the southern bank of the lane. The Ohioan scanned the officer from head to foot. Blood still streamed steadily from Tew's temple and he clenched his sword in both hands across his knees. As the private cautiously stretched out his hand to snatch the sword, the colonel instinctively pulled the prized weapon toward his body then pitched over — dead — at the Ohion's feet.[48] Further to the left, Private Henry Niles (K Co., 108th NY) helped round up one hundred sixty-eight prisoners, and in the process picked up the colors of the 14th North Carolina. While headed rearward with the standard, an officer from the 64th/61st New York stopped him.

The officer advised him, "You'd better give me those colors, boy. You're liable to be shot by one of your own men."

The frustrated private handed over the flag and dejectedly trudged north to his regiment and his less than heroic colonel.[49]

The 64th New York herded an additional one hundred Confederates rearward while the 61st New York claimed three battle flags, one of which went to Second Lieutenant Theodore Greig (C Co.), who jerked them from the hands of their color bearer of the 4th North Carolina and got shot through the neck in the process. (Colonel Barlow later recorded that his men lost one of their battle trophies.)[50]

On the far left, the 5th New Hampshire bolted ahead of the rest of its brigade toward the Bloody Lane. As they swept forward, the New Englanders shot down the remaining Confederates, who were rapidly throwing down their weapons and falling to their knees with their hands raised.

Lieutenant Thomas Livermore (K Co.) thought they had killed them to a man when one of the Rebs, who was playing "opossum", sprang up from among the corpses and dashed for the rail fence behind him. Shots followed him and he slumped dead over the top rail. As the 5th New Hampshire pushed a short distance into Piper's cornfield, the lieutenant had to urge several men forward. They lagged behind to maliciously shoot and bayonet the already bullet riddled corpse. The rest of the men crouched among the bloodied cornstalks and were blindly shooting through the low hanging smoke toward the rapidly disappearing Confederate line.[51] (Map 43)

The Piper Farm

The Confederates did not run far. At the base of Piper's swale, about six hundred yards south of the Bloody Lane, regiments from every brigade present merged

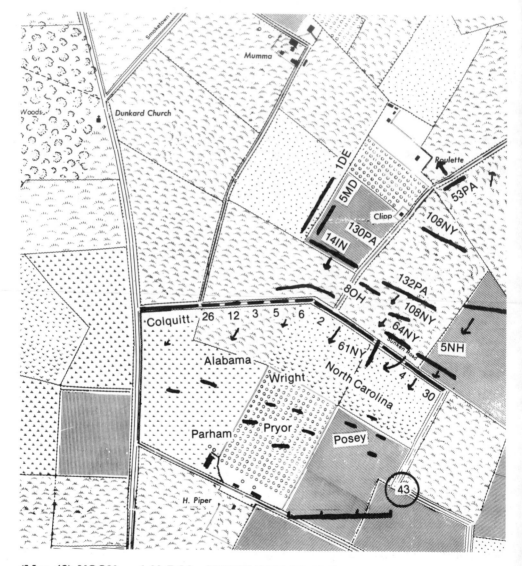

(Map 43) NOON — 1:00 P.M., SEPTEMBER 17, 1862
The Bloody Lane Collapses.

**LIEUTENANT THOMAS LIVERMORE,
K Company, 5th New Hampshire**
**He watched his men brutally bayonet and
shoot a Confederate corpse when they
crossed the Bloody Lane.**
(History of the 5th New Hampshire)

into mixed commands. Officers and enlisted men rallied despite tremendous desertions and prepared for the Federal onslaught; but the Yankees did not venture far below the lane.[52] Once again, the methodical Yankees wasted precious time to reform. On the left, Boyce's Battery rolled onto the slope near the farm house.[53]

The Hagerstown Pike

Lieutenant William Chamberlaine (G Co.), the dandy of the 6th Virginia, found an officer in the Hagerstown Pike who told him that General Richard H. Anderson was wounded. At that moment, a horde of retreating Confederates, many of them from Parham's Brigade, flooded Piper's lane. Both officers rushed into the throng and began to rally them behind the western face of the stone wall along the Pike.

The lieutenant asked a boy to stand with them.

"I have been shot in the hand," he protested.

Chamberlaine pleaded, "We must whip them to-day. Give me your gun, I will load it."

Taking the musket, the lieutenant charged the piece and was returning it when a ball struck the soldier again.

"Ah," he spat bitterly as he staggered away, "if you had not stopped me."

A short distance to the north, Chamberlaine spotted an abandoned six pound smoothbore cannon from Huger's Battery. Near it stood a wounded battery horse, which was still hitched to the limber. With the help of four infantrymen, the lieutenant started to manhandle the gun south.[54]

Captain Thomas D. Deall (I Co., 14th NC) and his small party of two officers and one enlisted man, who had bounded the stone wall, came to their assist. Together, they wheeled the gun and its limber to the mouth of Piper's lane.[55] A soldier galloped up to them as they wheeled the piece to face east and asked them what they were doing. The infantrymen shouted the obvious — they were going to shoot it. Without a moment's hesitation, the soldier, who identified himself as Major Fairfax of Longstreet's staff, leaped from the saddle and assisted in the loading. Taking the lanyard from Lieutenant Chamberlaine, he yanked it as the skirmishers from the 66th New York entered the lane near the barn.[56] The blast sent the New Yorkers to the ground. As Major Fairfax leaped into the saddle and spurred away, several men hallooed, "Over here is the place for that gun." Officers and enlisted men alike shouldered the piece to the high ground, about fifty yards north of the lane.[57]

The Piper Farm

Sergeant Tom Galwey (B Co., 8th OH) came to a stop in the cornfield a "stone's throw" from the Piper orchard, which swarmed with "Graybacks". He clearly saw D. H. Hill, whom he mistook for "Stonewall" Jackson, frantically urge his men forward to within pistol shot of the 8th Ohio. Glancing to the right rear, Galwey grimly noticed what appeared to be two Confederate regiments overrunning the right of the Federal line in Mumma's swale. The order passed through the regiment to fall back. Man by man, the 14th Indiana, which had no ammunition, the 8th Ohio (with about three rounds per man), and the 130th Pennsylvania tried to retire slowly to Roulette's lane. The withdrawal devolved into a mad scramble for safety.[58]

Mumma's Swale

Cooke's North Carolinians and Arkansans, with Cobb's men, pushed head first into an indefensable position. The charge dispersed both regiments and their comrades from Cobb's Brigade over a front from the cornfield north of Roulette's to the cornfield along the Bloody Lane.[59] The fields behind the Confederates writhed with over two hundred "paroled" Yankees who had willingly surrendered and were trying to avoid Thomas' guns (A and C, 4th U.S.) and the plunging fire of several Confederate batteries which had moved to the high ground south of Piper's.[60]

On the right flank, Captain Bart Johnson (A Co., 3rd AR) and his men did not find the resistance so light. As they raced into Mumma's swale, some of the Ohions and skirmishers from the 1st Delaware pitched into them with a fury. The Yankees put up a stout fight and for several minutes, the two lines became entangled in a vicious hand-to-hand encounter.

The Federals, however, could not sustain their position. They broke and ran into the corn east of Mumma's lane with the Razor Backs close behind.

Captain James Graham (G Co., 27th NC) halted his small segment of the regiment in the corn above Roulette's, while some of his men occupied the farm's outbuildings. Small arms fire became more intense along his front, while the canister on the left flank ceased altogether because Thomas could not bring his guns to bear on the 27th North Carolina for fear of cutting down the Federal troops in that area. To worsen matters, a fresh Yankee regiment, the 53rd Pennsylvania (Brooke's Brigade) advanced into the cornfield and fell in behind a stone wall on its eastern border.[61]

Their ammunition nearly gone, the hard pressed Confederates ransacked Yankee cartridge boxes only to discover that the rounds were too large for their own weapons.[62] The charge had taken out over two hundred of their men in less than ten minutes.[63] Pressured on the front by the rapidly reforming Yankees, their musketry dwindling from lack of rounds, and their ranks thinning quickly, Colonel John R. Cooke kept his men in the struggle as long as he could. Valor, however, could not compensate for sheer lack of numbers. *(Map 44)*

Roulette's Lane

Squads from the 8th Ohio, 14th Indiana, and 130th Pennsylvania ran the gauntlet along Roulette's lane in single file, ducking low to avoid the shells and bullets which splintered the fence rails on their left. The 8th Ohio, which had lost over one hundred

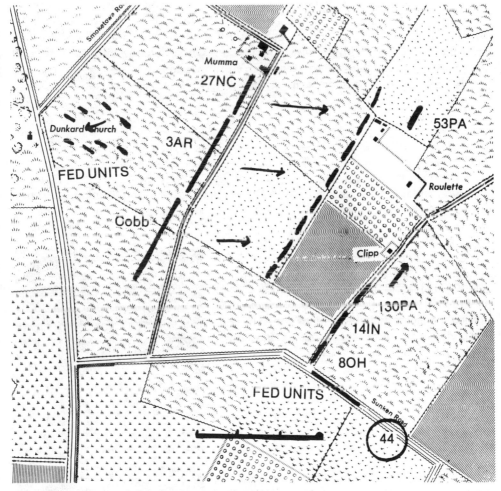

(Map 44) NOON — 1:00 P.M., SEPTEMBER 17, 1862
Cooke and Cobb pressure the Federal right in Roulette's lane.

men, took quite a few casualties there.[64] The Indianans, halting, gathered up cartridges from the dead and wounded and tied up the narrow lane to exchange rounds with the 3rd Arkansas and the 27th North Carolina, who were also busily looting corpses for ammunition.[65]

Young Sergeant Tom Galwey (B Co., 8th OH), while stooping to offer some precious water to a wounded Confederate in the Bloody Lane, was distracted by a loudly groaning man nearby. Glancing about, he latched his attention upon a helpless Confederate captain whose eyes had been shot away by a single bullet. The sergeant, not having time for any more humanitarian efforts, took off at a low trot then broke into a run down the farm lane toward Roulette's. A shout echoed into the valley from the East Woods ridge. Galwey looked up, while dodging bullets, in time to see two immense Federal lines emerge from the woods, then he kept on running for the protection of the northern cornfield.[66]

Mumma's Swale

Colonel William Irwin's Brigade (7th ME, 20th, 33rd, 49th, and 77th NY) of the VI Corps, which arrived on the field on the heels of Hancock's Brigade, was moving into Mumma's swale to drive out Cooke's pesky Confederates. Colonel William Irwin, whom Major Thomas Hyde (7th ME) later accused of being drunk, rashly committed his regiments piecemeal to the battle without properly deploying them.[67] He personally wheeled his largest regiment, the 20th New York, onto the Smoketown Road on the far side of the East Woods.[68]

Colonel Ernest Von Vegesack, the volatile Swede who replaced the regiment's cowardly German colonel following the outfit's poor performance during the Peninsular Campaign, pushed his eight hundred Germans into a shaky line and double quicked them south, then south west toward the Dunker Church plateau.[69] Shrapnel and canister knocked men down by the handful. The regiment shuddered until the colonel yanked out his revolver and dashed along the rear rank popping off rounds at any apparent skulkers.[70] Suddenly, the colors moved out in the center of the line. The Germans leveled their rifles with their menacing saber bayonets and tried to keep pace with the color sergeant.[71] Heads down, their high conical black hats looking awkwardly out of place, the regiment charged into an increasingly heavy artillery barrage and did not, for the first time in its military career, break and run for the rear.[72]

Irwin sent the 77th New York, which was to the Germans' immediate rear, toward the Hagerstown Pike as skirmishers.[73] Major Hyde

**COLONEL WILLIAM IRWIN,
brigade commander, VI Corps**

He ordered the 7th Maine into Piper's swale despite Major Thomas Hyde's objections.
(History of the 49th Pennsylvania)

(7th ME), whose command was third in the column, watched in awe as the long convex line of Germans rushed off at the oblique into the fields southwest of his fast approaching regiment.[74] Captain Long, Irwin's aide, sidetracked Hyde's one hundred eighty-one man regiment to the left before it could catch up with the 77th New York.[75]

Thomas Hyde, while rushing past a portion of the 10th Maine, took a few moments to inquire about two acquaintances of his in that outfit. He went into battle with a heavy heart. Both men — Colonel Beal and Lieutenant Colonel Fillebrown — had fallen to Confederate fire not three hours before the 7th Maine arrived upon the field.

The small New England regiment left wheeled, pushed through the woods, and broke into Mumma's plowed field north of the family cemetary. One by one, the men feverishly tore down each fence rail in their path as they worked their way toward the left flank of the 27th North Carolina.[76]

Colonel Cooke, who finally realized that his terribly outnumbered soldiers could not withstand the odds, hollered at his men to pull back. The Rebels, who heard the order, fired one last volley into the fast approaching 20th New York, then panicked and "double-quick timed" (according to Captain James Graham, G Co.), back toward their original position — right into the waiting and leveled weapons of a large number of their armed "prisoners" who had decided to "unquit" the war.[77]

The 3rd Arkansas came to a sudden halt as the regrouped Federals in Roulette's lane leveled their weapons and fired into them. Men slammed to the ground by squads. Fred Worthington (A Co.) collapsed next to Captain Bart Johnson — dead. Within seconds, about half the regiment was down.

Bullets now came in from all directions, in many instances at ranges under sixty yards as the 27th North Carolina and the 3rd Arkansas retreated directly across the front of the 20th New York, which was too busy charging toward the guns along the Hagerstown Pike to pay any attention to them.[78]

Major Hyde (7th ME) saw the bulk of the frightened Rebs break across his front — east to west — at a safe distance from his struggling troops and decided to liberally interpret Captain Long's directive to connect with Von Vegesack's left flank. The major sent his soldiers scrambling southeast into the cornfield to roust the Confederates lingering in Roulette's buildings, an action which cost him twelve men and a few minutes.[79]

Meanwhile, the rest of Irwin's mishandled brigade stampeded into combat. The four hundred man 49th New York swung left and followed on the rear of the 20th New York at about one hundred yards. The regiment stepped into the clover field south of the Smoketown Road at the double quick with their muskets at the right shoulder shift and sprayed around Mumma's burned out barn where some comrades from the 21st New York (Patrick's Brigade, I Corps) called after them, "You will find a hot time of it in there, boys!"[80]

The 33rd New York (about one hundred fifty men) which brought up the tail end of the column, stumbled into line on the left rear, less B Company which Vanneman's Battery (B, MD) cut off from the regiment as it passed through the line en route to the Cornfield.[81]

The very disorganized brigade raced through a rain of exploding shells toward the western most section of the Bloody Lane. About half way through Mumma's swale, Captain Long, at General William F. Smith's request, ordered the 33rd New York away from the left flank of the 49th New York. Lieutenant Colonel Joseph W. Corning faced his command by the right flank and double quicked them toward the right flank of the 49th New York, which threw it across the Hagerstown Pike into the West Woods, immediately south of the Dunker Church.[82]

In the meantime, Colonel Irwin pulled the small 77th New York (one hundred seventy-five men) off picket near the Hagerstown Pike and sent it careening by the left flank, by files, down the Hagerstown Pike toward the Dunker Church. The New Yorkers ran south, with their rifles on their shoulders to catch up with the 33rd New York, whose right wing had just penetrated the West Woods.[83] *(Map 45)*

The Hagerstown Pike and the Dunker Church

Colonel John Cooke's panting soldiers threw themselves behind the rail fence in the cornfield and prepared to die. Simultaneously, General Robert E. Lee, despite his injured hands, galloped up to their line.

"Boys," he shouted, "you must hold the center or General Lee and the Army of Northern Virginia will be prisoners in less than two hours."

At that, he wheeled about and spurred away. He had barely gone when General James Longstreet and four staff officers thundered onto the field behind Cooke's line. The officers hurriedly rolled an abandoned field piece into position, loaded it, and put one round into the advancing 20th New York before remounting and tearing southeast toward Piper's.

Once again, tremendous bloodshed became the medium of exchange for gallantry and foolhardiness. The rest of the Confederate batteries on the ridge six hundred yards south of the Dunker Church and Cooke's hastily reorganized regiments unleashed a hellish barrage into Von Vegesack's Germans. Monstrous gaps appeared in the line, leaving a gory wake in its path as it neared the southern edge of the West Woods.[84]

Captain Long, Irwin's aide, and Lieutenant John Carter (B Co., 33rd NY), with his detached company, could not believe what was unfolding before them. As they approached the 77th and the 33rd New York, respectively, both men noticed that the West Woods seethed with Rebel troops. Lieutenant Carter and Captain Long did not reach the two regiments in time.[85]

Lieutenant William W. Chamberlaine (G Co., 6th VA) and his mixed crew fired one round at Irwin's men. The shot bounded so poorly along the undulating ground east of the Dunker Church that the "artillerists" at Colonel R. Tyler Bennett's (14th NC) suggestion, rolled the cannon back toward Piper's lane.[86] While the rest of the Confederate artillery below the Dunker Church stalled the 20th New York, Ransom's North Carolina Brigade rose and slammed into the 33rd New York and the 77th New York simultaneously from the north and the west. Bullets plowed into the 33rd New York from the rear, taking out about forty officers and men.[87] The 77th New York lost about twenty-five effectives, including Color Sergeant Joseph Murer, who fell with a ball in his head.[88] Both regiments professionally faced about and delivered two well executed volleys into the West Woods. Falling back to the

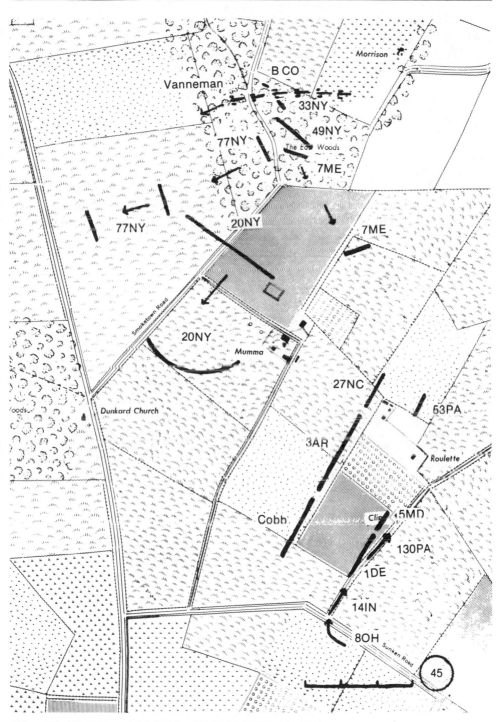

(Map 45) NOON — 1:00 P.M., SEPTEMBER 17, 1862
Irwin's Brigade, VI Corps, flanks Cooke and Cobb in Mumma's swale.

Dunker Church ridge, they went to earth behind the crest and hugged the ground for their lives.[89] *(Map 46)*

General D. H. Hill raced up to Colonel R. Tyler Bennett (14th NC) in the Hagerstown Pike and screamed at him to reform the unattached soldiers who swarmed the area. The colonel complied. Assisted by Captain Thomas B. Beall (I Co., 14th NC), he led the soldiers forward in a "forlorn hope". The New Yorkers' volley shattered the formation and sent the survivors streaming for cover. Not long after, a shell burst severely wounded the colonel.[90]

Mumma's Swale

The 7th Maine rushed through Mumma's cornfield, east of the farm lane, passing over deceased Confederates, which burned an indelible picture of butternut and gray clad file closers and of ranks stretched out in near perfect formation in Thomas Hyde's mind. They had died suddenly, without a chance for escape. Their bloating corpses, which contrasted sharply with the bodies' light colored or reddish hair, remained ghastly spectres in the young major's consciousness until he died over thirty years later.[91]

The New Englanders went prone behind the rail fence on the left of Von Vegesack's Germans, who had fallen back to the swale. The 20th New York was bent at right angles, with its colors forming the hinge, where the Dunker Church ridge turned east to north.[92] The 49th New York, 77th New York, and 33rd New York, respectively, continued the line to the north. A battery, not twenty yards to the left front of the 77th New York, raked its position with canister and solid shot.[93]

Major Hyde's soldiers took cover behind the large boulders which dotted the landscape to their front. Looking to the right, the major saw men streaming away from the pinned 20th New York. Including Lieutenant Emery (7th ME), who was rolling about the ground gut shot, his regiment had taken thirteen casualties in the charge from Roulette's. The Germans were faring far worse. They seemed insistent upon drawing fire. Thomas Hyde, a pragmatic man, could not condone such foolish bravado. Crouching low to avoid sniper fire from the West Woods, he trotted over to Colonel Von Vegesack, who was still mounted, and yelled at him to lower his colors — to stop the Rebs from singling out his regiment.

"Let them wave," the Swede vainly exploded. "They are our glory."

Before the aghast Hyde could mutter a reply, Von Vegesack had spurred away, pistol in hand to pick off shirkers.[94] The major left the colonel to enjoy his day of glory, while he returned to his relatively quiet section of cornfield. *(Map 47)*

The Piper Farm

The fighting in Piper's cornfield lapsed only momentarily as Israel Richardson's Division collected itself for a drive against D. H. Hill's rallying Confederates. While Irwin's men blundered onto the battlefield, the 5th New Hampshire (Caldwell's Brigade) and a portion of Brooke's Brigade were moving recklessly into Piper's valley, directly into the muzzles of Miller's Washington Artillery.[95]

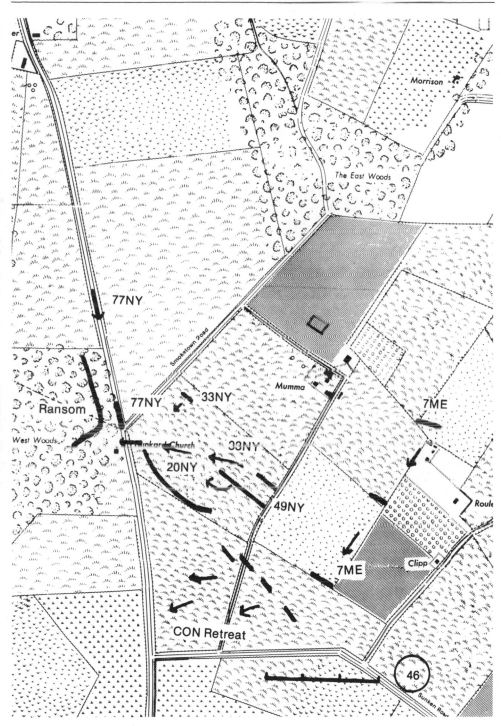

(Map 46) NOON — 1:00 P.M., SEPTEMBER 17, 1862
Irwin's Brigade, VI Corps, drives Cooke and Cobb from the field.

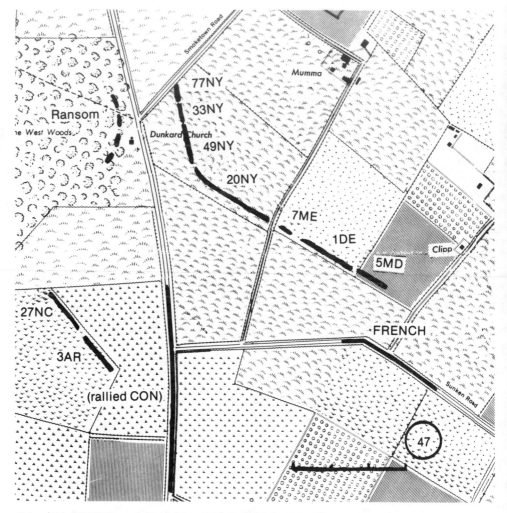

(Map 47) NOON — 1:00 P.M., SEPTEMBER 17, 1862
Stalemate near the Dunker Church.

Barlow's 64th/61st New York, in conjunction with the 5th New Hampshire, crashed through Piper's cornfield in pursuit of D. H. Hill's disorganized commands.[96] The 57th and the 66th New York (Brooke's Brigade) bolted across the grisly Bloody Lane, to Barlow's rear, and made directly for Piper's house and farm buildings.[97] The 7th New York (Caldwell's Brigade) followed on the left.[98] Within minutes, the fighting reached a crescendo. Bullets and canister clattered through the corn, splattering Yankee blood over the green leaves. The Confederates were far from whipped. Major General James Longstreet and his staff galloped into Miller's section to supervise the action. The carpet slippered Longstreet, his cigar still tightly clenched between his teeth, sat sidesaddle on his mount, with one leg thrown across the pommel. He irked Captain M. B. Miller's artillerists by directing their fire and constantly encouraging them in their work.

At one point, he offered to give the sweating crews a hand but he had injured his right hand earlier in the day. Napier Bartlett bitterly remembered that the general's wounded hand worked well enough to plug a metal flask into his mouth. The thirsty enlisted man longed for a shot of whiskey himself.[99]

The guns bucked ten to twelve inches from the ground with each blast. Nearby, D. H. Hill seized a flag, gathered fifty men and rushed for the high ground on the left of the 5th New Hampshire.[100]

"Tige" Anderson's Georgians leaped the stone wall along the Hagerstown Pike and advanced in open order about one hundred feet onto the high ground west of Piper's barn. The color bearer frantically waved his flag from side to side and gave "heart" to the reorganizing Confederates in the area.

Down in Piper's lane, Lieutenant William W. Chamberlaine (G Co., 6th VA) and his "gunners" wheeled their junk cannon to face northeast toward Piper's cornfield and orchard.

They fired three rounds in rapid succession at the New Yorkers and forced them back into the corn. Twice more, the Federals regrouped only to be driven back by six more well placed shot.[101]

The entire Federal line buckled. Sergeant Hugh Montgomery, color bearer of the 61st New York, miraculously escaped death. The Rebs shot twenty-nine holes in his flag and snapped his flag staff twice, but missed him entirely.[102] The 57th New York, which had already lost three standard bearers before crossing the lane, sacrificed its fourth, Lieutenant Colonel Philip Parisen. A bullet knocked him from the saddle of his charger, "Dick", when the regiment tried to flank Miller's left section in Piper's orchard. His men abandoned his peaceful looking corpse and fell back with the 66th New York toward the Bloody Lane.[103]

To the left, in Piper's corn, the 7th New York (Caldwell's Brigade) found itself under fire from the front and the right flank, which forced it to file left. The movement brought it directly across the path of regrouped Confederate infantry and the muzzles of Miller's section.

Private Henry Gerisch (A Co., 7th NY) gaped unbelievingly at the Confederates as his regiment fronted at less than seventy-five feet from their position. In seconds, he saw the gunner load and sight the one field piece directly at the colors. Being in the front rank, fifth man from the flag, Gerisch knew that he was as good as dead.

The field piece leaped from the ground, shrouded in flame and sulphur. The canister killed six, wounded nine more, and punched an ugly hole in the 7th New York. The blast reeled Gerisch a good thirty-five feet, where he collapsed — unconscious.[104]

The double canister missed the 64th/61st New York, which was to the left rear of the 7th New York, in the corn north of the orchard. The New Yorkers fought it out toe to toe with the Confederate infantry despite the canister which whistled about them.

The Confederates suddenly retreated, leaving a lone soldier by himself. The poor fellow feverishly dashed across the furrowed ground (south) in an attempt to outrun the bullets which pocked the dirt around his feet.

Sergeant Charles Fuller (C Co., 61st NY) futilely begged his men not to gun the fellow down. He wanted to reward the man for his courage with his life. A bullet jerked the Reb off his feet just before he got out of range.

The canister, which miraculously missed his combined regiments, dropped Colonel Francis Barlow. The men carried him rearward with wounds to his face and groin.[105]

The Yankees put on a defiant show. Plucking apples as they retired from the fray, they leeringly munched on them between shots in the faces of the Confederates who had not been allowed to plunder the trees for themselves.[106] Major H. A. Herbert (8th AL) nearly ordered his entire command to shoot a rude, but undeniably heroic Yankee. The fellow deliberately lagged behind his men during the retreat until he fired every round in his cartridge box. His ammunition gone, the cheeky soldier turned his back to Herbert's men, bent over, and nastily patted his backside before skedaddling for the security of the Bloody Lane. Herbert and his soldiers, though angered by the invitation to kiss the Yankee's rump, refrained from killing him in recognition of his bravery.[107]

While the smoke cleared in front of Lieutenant William W. Chamberlaine's (G Co., 6th VA) six pound gun, a lone Federal halted to deliberately fire at him. The ball struck the ground in front of his feet but did not harm him.[108]

The Bloody Lane

A cry bounced off Charles Fuller's (C Co., 61st NY) head. Turning about, the sergeant watched the bare buttocked Private Barney Rogers (A Co.) crawl off the field like a wounded dog. The middle aged Irishman clumsily stumbled away on two hands and one leg. The other, he kept extended full length behind him. (Unknown to Fuller, a ball glanced off a rock beneath Rogers' foot and bounced upward through the private's big toe.)[109]

As Richardson's men retreated through the corn their lines became entangled. One the far left, the 5th New Hampshire split into two wings and was nearly flanked by Hill's small party. *(Map 48)*

Colonel Edward Cross angrily regrouped his New Englanders below the muzzles of William Graham's twelve pound Napoleons (K, 1st U.S.), which were firing ineffectively toward the high ground south of the Dunker Church. Thomas Livermore (K Co.) peered through the smoke, which engulfed the regiment, trying to pinpoint

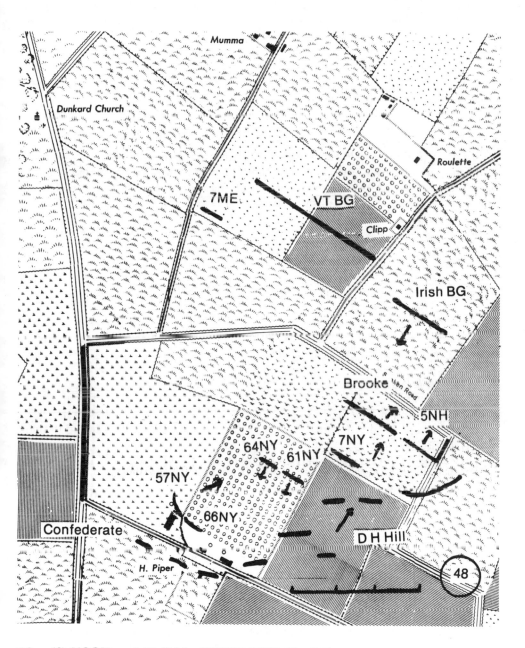

(Map 48) NOON — 1:00 P.M., SEPTEMBER 17, 1862
The Confederates hold their own in Piper's swale.

the Confederates who had rushed under Graham's guns to a fence several yards south of the line (along the far border of the cornfield). As the 5th New Hampshire stepped backwards through the corn toward the lane, Colonel Cross separated it from the troops to the right and reunited the two wings.

Once in the lane with the rest of the brigade, the 5th New Hampshire knelt on the bloodied Confederate corpses and braced themselves for a counterattack. They could see little movement through the tall corn. Presently, a sharp eyed soldier cried aloud that the Rebs were moving in on the regiment from the left. Bending his regiment at right angles, facing east and south, Edward Cross filed part of his command to the left and counterflanked the Confederates.

A terrible firefight erupted at point blank range. Artillery shells from the far southern ridge above Piper's farm exploded indiscriminately in the mass of writhing soldiers. A single burst in G Company killed or wounded eight of the nine men in the 5th New Hampshire's color guard. Simultaneously, the Rebels dashed for the third successive time into the muzzles of the Federal line.

Lieutenant Livermore felt the blood in the lane ooze into his knees. A darting glance to the right, where the fighting still raged unabated, told him that no help would come from that quarter.

"Shoot the man with the flag!"

The shout echoed emptily in the lieutenant's ears. Less than fifteen yards away, a Confederate standard bearer, who was semaphoring the colors from side to side, disappeared in a burst of riflery.

Colonel Cross, bare headed, his wounded scalp still streaming red through his red bandana and down over his powder stained face, maniacally paced his line.

"Put on the war paint!" he screamed.

The New Englanders tore open cartridges and smeared their sweating faces with powder before loading.

"Give 'em the war whoop!" the colonel blustered.

Shrieking and chattering like lunatics, the soldiers of the 5th New Hampshire began firing rapidly into the corn. Screams, curses, and yelps reverberated in their sector of the field.

"Fire! Fire! Fire faster!" some men prattled.

Thomas Livermore got caught up in the madness. Searching the ground around him, he pried a Belgian musket from the waxen hands of the Rebel corpse beneath him. A quick inspection showed him the antique was capped and probably loaded.

Despite orders to the contrary, the lieutenant snapped the smoothbore to his shoulder and pulled the trigger. He liked it. The thrill of a musket recoiling into his shoulder invigorated him. He dropped to all fours and started hunting for another piece when Colonel Cross stepped into his path.

Cross boomed, "Mister Livermore tend to your company!"

The lieutenant quickly obeyed.[110]

The 132nd Pennsylvania, which had remained on the slope during that final charge, heard a louder ruckus from the rear. Once again, General Thomas Meagher, aboard his white charger, led his men at the double-quick toward the Bloody Lane. As the general neared the Pennsylvanians' left flank, he toppled from the saddle. Getting to his feet, he staggered and reeled about, "swearing like a crazy man", Adjutant Hitchcock (132nd PA) wrote. (The enlisted men insisted that Meagher was drunk.)

The sweep continued without him, with many of the Pennsylvanians taking part in it. Hitchcock had more to worry about than one supposedly drunken officer. The stout, balding, unkempt Major General Israel Richardson clumped past the lieutenant en route to Graham's Battery (K, 1st U.S.) and shouted, "You will have to get back. Don't you see yonder line of rebels is flanking you?"

The lieutenant followed the general's quaking hand to the right. John R. Cooke's two regimental flags and those of Howell Cobb's Confederates flapped in the breeze in the fields west of Roulette's lane. Hitchcock's mouth dropped open momentarily until Irwin's Brigade descended wildly into Mumma's swale and drove the Confederates back.[111]

Meanwhile, the Irish Brigade, which had replenished its ammunition, returned to the Bloody Lane.[112] The 81st Pennsylvania (Cross' Brigade) moved into Piper's corn on the left of the 5th New Hampshire to mop up.[113] Brigadier General W. T. H. Brooks' Vermont Brigade (2nd, 3rd, 4th, 5th, and 6th VT) of the VI Corps went into line to the left rear of the 7th Maine, and the 14th Connecticut filed in column of files uphill to support Graham's Battery (K, 1st U.S.) from the east.

A shell exploded in Company D, two files behind Sergeant Benjamin Hirst (D Co.). Turning about, he saw no less than a dozen of his men stacked in a gory heap. Private William P. Ramsdell was the first corpse he recognized in the pile. Not ten minutes before, Ramsdell had quietly told Hirst that were he to get hit, he wanted to have the top of his head blown off. He got his wish.[114]

Lieutenant Colonel Nelson Miles (64th/61st NY) sent Sergeant Charles Fuller (C Co.) with Porter A. Whitney (C Co.) and George Jacobs (C Co.) halfway into the trampled corn to scout what the Confederates were doing. The three men took cover behind some cornstalks, which they stood up to shield them from view. They observed several mounted Confederate officers off to their right front. After debating whether to pick them off or not, Fuller detached one of the men back to the regiment, who presently returned to order Fuller and the remaining soldier to retire. Their reticence to shoot down the officers probably saved James Longstreet's life.[115]

The fighting, with the exception of sporadic artillery and sniper fire, was over in the Bloody Lane — West Woods sector, but at a terrible price in personnel and staff officers. On the Confederate side, Generals Ambrose Wright, George B. Anderson, Richard H. Anderson, and Robert Rodes had fallen — seriously wounded. The Federals listed Generals Thomas Meagher, Max Weber, and Israel Richardson down and about eight regimental commanders — fifty percent of them among the Irish Brigade.[116]

Ironically, Israel Richardson fell while retiring Graham's Battery (K, 1st U.S.) to a safer spot north of the Bloody Lane. A shell fragment mortally wounded him in the shoulder while he was talking to Captain Graham. Stretcher crews evacuated him across the creek to the Pry house, where he died six weeks later in a great deal of pain.[117]

The East Woods

While the action seesawed in its final moments along the Bloody Lane and Irwin's Brigade made its stumbling entrance and meteoric withdrawal, the Confederate batteries also pounded Hancock's Brigade along the face of the East Woods.

Private Benjamin Clarkson (C Co., 49th PA) stared nervously into the eyes of the boy standing to his right. The soldier had turned deathly white.

"Poor fellow," Clarkson thought to himself, "you're frightened. I wish you were away from here." Then, he mentally checked his own state of mind and silently concluded, "If he should look into my face it would look as white to him as his did to me."

Moments later, during a shelling fit, a canister ball knocked the pale soldier down. A very willing party hauled him back to the East Woods. Simultaneously, a cannon ball carried away Gus Heller's foot in B Company. Thirteen year old Drum Major Charlie King (F Co.) collapsed into a comrade's arms with shrapnel in his body. Andrew Spear (C Co.), Henry Laub (A Co.), and Thomas Huston (C Co.) dropped in quick succession and were taken to the rear. Clarkson, who was anxiously watching his comrades fall about him, expected to die at any moment. He wanted to go home — immediately.

The officers finally ordered the regiment to lie down. Clarkson, who was next to Cowan's right gun, bounced off the ground with each discharge, and gravel and dirt pelted the line with the explosion of each incoming round. The air screamed and hissed with shot for what seemed like ages.

Ben Clarkson's mind meandered to his home, his devotion to duty, and his faith in Christ. Having resigned himself to death, the private raised his face from the dirt. Just then, a cannon near the Dunker Church fired a random shot.

Clarkson fixed his attention on the gun's report in time to see the cannon ball as it bounced and skittered into the field several rods in front of him.

"No! You were ordered to stay here until ordered away," he reminded himself as he buried his face in the earth to avoid seeing himself splattered all over creation.

The twelve pound ball passed within inches of his skull, lifting the hairs on the back of his head in its flight. The man behind him groaned. Thinking the worst had happened, Ben Clarkson rolled over to check the damage only to discover that the shot had missed the fellow too. He followed the ball's path to the East Woods, where it lodged with a terrific thud into a huge white oak. Out popped Acting Major Thomas Huling from behind the tree. The startled officer kept running further east. The men saw no more of him that day.

Seconds later, a Confederate caisson exploded with a horrendous blast, followed by a towering column of black smoke — so high that the troops down by the Lower Bridge could see it. Resounding huzzahs echoed all along the Federal lines, followed by a feeble Rebel yelping.[118]

Having evaded two mounted officers who were violently rousting out skulkers in the East Woods, Frank Schell, the meandering artist, stole north into Miller's plowed ground, where a captain from the 72nd Pennsylvania (Howard's Brigade, II Corps) dejectedly told him about Sedgwick's rout. Everywhere, exasperated soldiers fruitlessly tried to rally defeated squads of the I, II, and XII Corps. Now, as Irwin's Brigade stupidly rushed into Mumma's swale, he headed south toward the firing. At the edge of the Cornfield he lingered long enough to rough sketch Vanneman's sweating gunners (B, MD) who were working their Parrotts in their shirt sleeves. An exploding shell disabled one of the battery horses and sent Schell on his way.

The reporter froze as he edged away from the artillerists. A cold chill raced through him as he became sickeningly aware that a musket was trained on him. Turning about slowly, he came face to face with a kneeling Confederate who had been killed while in the midst of firing. A cornstalk kept his stiffening body from collapsing.

Frank Schell loped toward Mumma's smoking buildings. The farm yard swarmed with stretcher crews. As he neared the barn, which Irwin's Brigade converted into a field hospital, the cry, "Canister!" exploded behind him.

Schell hurled himself against the barn's charred wall as did the stretcher party nearest him. For a second or two shot rattled like hail against glass, then the crewmen went back to retrieve their wounded man, whom they unceremoniously ditched in their run for cover. He was dead — killed by the canister. Nearby lay one of their own soldiers. Callously rolling the corpse into the dirt, they picked up their new charge and carried him to the surgeons. Schell did not follow them into the barn. For twenty minutes, he hugged the stone wall until the Federal artillery silenced the Confederate batteries south of the Dunker Church.[119]

Roulette's Cornfield

Sergeant Thomas Galwey (B Co., 8th OH) joined what was left of his regiment in the cornfield north of Roulette's and helped count their losses. His company had about thirty-two men down.[120] The regiment had a more one hundred ninety men present of an original three hundred forty-one.[121] As the rest of the brigade assembled in the corn, it became apparent they had "seen the elephant". The 14th Indiana lost one hundred eighty of three hundred twenty; the 132nd Pennsylvania counted one hundred forty-two casualties, and the 7th West Virginia lost one hundred sixty-three.[122]

For all intents, Kimball's Brigade had become "hors de combat". The men knew it, and so did their division commander, Brigadier General William H. French, whom the men saw unashamedly crying. They also overheard the rattled "Bull" Sumner blubbering something about them being the "Gibraltar Brigade". Their rock, it seemed, was shattered somewhat.

Kimball's people rested long enough to fill their canteens then they shuffled north, where they laid down in relative safety along the cornfield's border. A bursting projectile sent Galwey and another enlisted man into a heap. The young Englishman got up with a ringing head and a ruptured right ear drum. Joseph Lloyd, his comrade, caught a shell splinter in the thigh. Four volunteers from the 7th Ohio (Tyndale's Brigade) quickly picked up Lloyd and stumbled down the hill toward Roulette's. They had gone but a few feet when several shells exploded directly overhead. The men dropped Lloyd like a scalding iron as one of them, a sergeant, collapsed with hot fragments in both thighs.

The three remaining soldiers called over another man and hustled their bleeding sergeant to a surgeon who later removed both of his legs. Sixteen year old Tom Galwey had to tend for Lloyd on his own.

The boy hobbled into a nearby ravine with his wounded comrade and plopped down on his behind, too fagged to carry on. Lloyd, who was quite frightened, begged the boy sergeant to bear him further. He was married! A father too! He had responsibilities which Galwey, who was single, could not know anything about!

Thomas Galwey listened, dumbfounded, to Lloyd's rantings. When the married man bluntly told Galwey that his life did not matter as much as his, the boy erupted into a gut wrenching laugh. He sat there guffawing at Lloyd's absurd remarks.[123]

The North Woods

Clara Barton had nothing to laugh about. She found a man with a severe facial wound lying near the door of Poffenberger's barn. As she tried to brush past him into the barn, he tugged at her skirt.

"Lady," he mumbled, "will you tell me what this is that burns so?"

Miss Barton told him she would fetch a surgeon.

"No! No!" he painfully insisted, while pulling at her arm. "They cannot come to me. I must wait my turn, for this is a little wound. You can get the ball. There is a knife in your pocket. Please, take the ball out for me."

Clara insisted that she could not help much. She had never performed surgery before.

He pleaded with her. "You cannot hurt me, dear lady, I can endure any pain your hands can create. Please do it. It will relieve me so much."

Kneeling down, she pulled out her pocket knife and carefully selected her sharpest blade. As she raised the boy's head to cut the ball out of his jaw bone, a wounded sergeant, who was sitting nearby, offered to help.

The sergeant, who had been shot through the fleshy part of both thighs, shoved himself along on his buttocks and secured the boy's head in his lap, while she carved the piece of lead from his mouth.

Having washed and bandaged the soldier's mangled face, she tenderly helped the sergeant, who had assisted her, onto his back. She proceded about her work.

Half an hour later, she found the noncom crying, not from his wounds, but for his captain. A comrade had just informed him of the officer's death upon the field.[124]

Sharpsburg

Private Bird Wright (B Co., 8th FL) lay mortally wounded somewhere in Sharpsburg. Four days before the battle, he had written his last letter to his wife, Anne Barineau Wright. She never received it. Unknown to him, she had died on August 24. (He passed away on September 25.)[125]

A mile beyond the Dunker Church, in the yard of a brick cottage, Sergeant Ed Moore (Poague's Battery) found himself next to Captain John Carpenter of the Allegheney Roughs. Moore felt warmed as he drained the last ounce from the officer's two ounce whiskey flask. Both had leg wounds — Moore in the thigh — the captain in the knee.

When one of the surgeons informed Carpenter he would lose the leg, the officer moaned, "You see that?" He pointed to a pistol by his side. "It will not be taken off while I can pull a trigger."[126]

The doctor wisely did not pursue the matter.

It seemed as if both armies had decided to do the same. It was 1:00 P.M. From the Bloody Lane north to the North Woods the fighting came to a standstill. Nine Federal batteries were in position in that area of the battlefield. They continued to exchange occasional rounds with the Confederate batteries at Piper's and the Dunker Church. The "good fight" having been fought, the men were ordered to fire only in defense and not to encourage another general engagement.[127]

What many historians have traditionally referred to as the Morning and the Midday Phases of the battle ended with the last shots in the Cornfield — West Woods area and the Bloody Lane, respectively. The Third or Afternoon Phase centered around the Middle and the Lower Bridges.

CHAPTER THIRTEEN

"All they that see me laugh me to scorn . . . ."

The Middle Bridge

Little had occurred on either bank of the Antietam near the Middle or Lower Bridges since the hostilities opened during the previous day. The 4th U.S. Infantry sent four companies across the Middle Bridge during the early afternoon of September 16 to secure the Boonsboro Pike around Newcomer's barn. Before dark, under sporadic and inaccurate sniper and artillery fire, Companies G and K advanced about half a mile west to the eastern side of a high ridge, which ran south of the Pike across from Newcomer's house, and suffered only four wounded in the process. That night Companies D and E, 1st Battalion, 12th U.S. Infantry crossed the creek to relieve the four companies of the 4th Infantry, which rejoined their regiment on the eastern bank.[1]

Throughout the night, the 1st Battalion, 12th Infantry kept relieving its picket force, two companies at a time, at two hour intervals. The night passed rather quietly until around 8:00 P.M.

Lieutenant Thomas Evans, D and E Companies commanding, had just finished stretching his forty-five men from the right side of the Boonsboro Pike in an arc west to the large cornfield which bordered the creek, when a shout, followed by scattered shots, erupted from the western side of the bridge. Evans spun around and stumbled into a huge hole near the creek bank. Scrambling out, he limped north toward the bridge where he heard horses' hooves clattering over the hardened road surface. The panting lieutenant found the sergeant of the guard in a panic. He blurted something to Evans about a squad of Rebel cavalry on reconnaissance. Evans, a

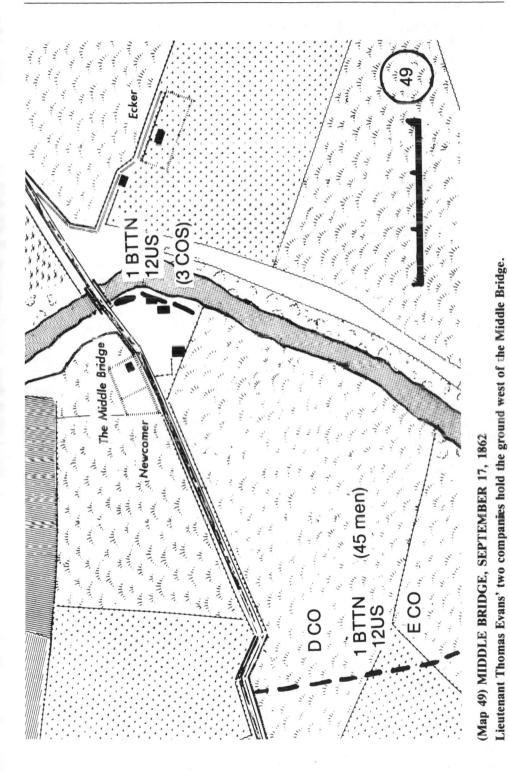

(Map 49) MIDDLE BRIDGE, SEPTEMBER 17, 1862
Lieutenant Thomas Evans' two companies hold the ground west of the Middle Bridge.

somewhat unflappable Welshman, said he was not so sure. More than likely, a band of horses spooked the guard.[2] *(Map 49)*

The Regulars were not there to precipitate a general engagement. All battalions of the 12th and the 14th Regulars, combined, did not have nine hundred men between them.[3] They were in no shape, following the Peninsular Campaign to engage in severe combat. They were there to protect the Middle Bridge solely. Unknown to them, McClellan's cautious crony, Major General Fitz John Porter, V Corps commanding, believed that Lee would try to penetrate the Federal center and he vowed he would hold his post at all costs.[4]

Lieutenant Evans and his men finished their duty at 10:00 P.M. They recrossed the creek and spent the night without incident. At 9:00 A.M., Wednesday, the lieutenant took his forty-five men out on picket again and spread them out over the same ground that they had covered the day before, at the same ridiculous intervals — one man per ninety feet. The remaining three companies of the 1st Battalion took cover along the creek bank behind Newcomer's barn.[5]

The Regulars wisely made every effort to avoid the prying sights of Nathan Evans' Independent Brigade (17th, 18th, 22nd, and 23rd SC, and Holcombe's Legion), which occupied the fence rows along the high ridge to their front.[6] The Rebs observed every move the Federals attempted to make from the tops of some hay mounds on the ridge, about three hundred yards southwest of Lieutenant Evans' most advanced man.[7]

Thomas Evans believed that the Rebs posted a battery somewhere to his front but he could not pinpoint it through the tall corn which dominated the last ridge before the town. The Confederates failed to roust out his overly dispersed command. Occasionally a canister shell or a case shot harmlessly pelted sections of his "line"; several rounds burst "well in D Company", his original command, without effect. Most of the solid shots screamed overhead toward Captain Stephen H. Weed's battery (G, 5th U.S.) on the ridge across the creek, where they splintered trees half way up the slope or sizzled loudly into the creek.[8]

The lieutenant and his people behaved as discreetly as possible. They had to protect the bridge and nothing more. He had no way of knowing that his small skirmish party equalled the strength of many of the opposing Confederate units.

The Boonsboro Pike

Lieutenant William "Big I" Wood (A Co., 19th VA, Garnett's Brigade) was very hungry. His regiment had not eaten since the previous morning and no rations seemed forthcoming, either.

Brigadier General Richard Garnett's small brigade of about three hundred men (8th, 18th, 19th, 28th, and 56th VA) deployed in extended order — one man every six feet — from the Boonsboro Pike to the Lower Bridge Road.[9] The left of the line anchored itself behind the first fence row, about two hundred yards east of the Lutheran Church, just below the brow of the hill which overlooked Newcomer's house. The right flank lay in a mow field, on the far end of the same ridge, immediately east of the town's spring. Bachman's German artillery, with Squires' Battery to its left along the Pike, hurled shells over the cornfield to their front toward the creek.[10]

Lieutenant Wood, from his post near the brigade's right, watched columns of Federal infantry moving, tortoise like, toward the Lower Bridge. He felt less than enthused about the entire situation.[11]

The Lower Bridge

To Wood's right, on the opposite side of the Lower Bridge Road ravine, Jenkins' (1st, 2nd, 5th, 6th SC, and 4th SC Bttn), Drayton's (51st GA, 3rd and 15th SC), and Kemper's (1st, 7th, 11th, 17th, and 24th VA) Brigades of Jones' Division occupied a four hundred yard stretch which extended to the southern flank of a small cornfield.[12] The three brigades mustered about nine hundred muskets between them.[13]

Brigadier General James L. Kemper's Brigade probably accounted for about one third of the soldiers present, despite the terribly depleted ranks of two of his regiments — the 1st and the 17th Virginia. Private John Dooley (D Co., 1st VA) counted seventeen people present for duty in his regiment — eight officers and nine enlisted men. Private Alexander Hunter (A Co., 17th VA) noted a mere fifty-six officers and men were in his outfit. Counting himself, his company mustered one lieutenant and two rank and file.[14]

Most of the 17th Virginia, on Kemper's far right, went into line behind a brand new post and rail fence on the eastern edge of a small cornfield while the rest of the regiment, with the brigade, advanced some one hundred fifty yards to the front and took cover behind a stone wall bordering an orchard.[15] A long swale, about sixty yards wide from crest to crest, separated them from another ridge which paralleled theirs at a slightly lower elevation. The men went prone, resting their muskets on the bottom fence rails and waited for the Yankees to come to them.[16] They would have a long wait. Private John Dooley (D Co., 1st VA) smirked as he surveyed their defenses. The general expected them to take on the numerically superior and better equipped Federal troops with a skirmish line.[17] The appearance of a section of J. S. Brown's Virginia Battery twenty paces from the brigade's right flank did not allay any doubts he had about surviving the ensuing ordeal. The battery's apparently questionable reputation had preceded it to the front.[18]

The Porterstown Road

The Federal IX Corps, across the Antietam, had been lurching about since daylight when Confederate batteries in the vicinity of the Boonsboro Pike started to lob rounds at the Federal heavy artillery on the bluffs near the Middle Bridge. A few casualties resulted but most of the projectiles turned out to be duds. The monotonous whizzing of the shells lulled some of the men to sleep.

Brigadier General Samuel Sturgis' two brigades were on the eastern and western sides of the Porterstown Road, nearly six tenths of a mile south of Porterstown.[19] Colonel Edward Ferrero's Brigade (21st and 35th MA, 51st PA, and 51st NY) had spent the night west of and parallel to the road in column of regiments. The colonel set up his brigade headquarters in a small woods near the road, while placing the brigade in a hollow behind a ridge. The men had watched some fine artillery demonstrations during the previous evening.

Lieutenant John Williams Hudson (D Co., 35th MA), one of Ferrero's aides, left his regiment, which held the rear and most secure post in the brigade formation, to enjoy the show from the crest of the ridge. Battery and counterbattery fire flashed and reverberated from north to south from the far bank of the Antietam. The lieutenant and a few of his men, like children enthralled by a fireworks display, excitedly noted the time lapses between the muzzle flashes, the shell bursts, and the sounds of the explosions — which followed many seconds later.[20]

The Confederates began the brigade's morning with an artillery barrage along the entire length of the creek. A shell exploded in the midst of the 21st Massachusetts, prostrating the entire color guard as it gathered in a group to read a worn copy of the hometown paper. The men calmly picked themselves up, dusted themselves off, and continued their reading as if nothing had happened.[21] Round shot fell among the brigade also, inflicting negligible damage. One "respectable" shot, however, bounded through a corner of the woods and lazilly rolled to a stop beneath the headquarters' mounts which were picketted along the edge of the woods. Colonel Ferrero's "attache" — a Black waif named Johnny — ranted and carried on among the staff about how that ball "passed right under his horse."[22]

The Middle Bridge

Morrell's Division of the V Corps, which had bivouacked in the swales north of the IX Corps, by 9:00 A.M., had marched and countermarched since daybreak without gaining any appreciable ground. The division crossed to the north side of the Boonsboro Pike to a knoll within clear view of the Pry house to fill the gap left by Richardson's Division (II Corps), which was fording the Antietam to support Sedgwick.

Private Robert G. Carter, whose regiment, the 22nd Massachusetts (Barnes' Brigade), had been in the field only one week, quietly rolled onto his back to observe the shells land behind the lines. Captain Charles Kusserow's (D, 1st Bttn, 1st NY), Captain E. Taft's (5th NY), and Weed's (G, 5th U.S.) heavy batteries, on the ridge to the west, thundered furiously against the Confederate positions. Carter glanced to the southeast toward the square, bricked Eckel house. His mind absently roamed over the large yard with its quaint garden, shrubs, and fruit trees. A horse (or mule) — Carter could not distinguish clearly which it was — serenely munched on the shrubbery while tethered to the garden fence. When a projectile killed it, the new soldier recalled the carnage he had seen as he passed through Turner's Gap. The regiment, in its new uniforms, seemed so out of place among the bloated, corrupting corpses of Colquitt's dead Confederates. War did not seem so glorious as it had been portrayed.

Curiosity nudged Carter and a few of his comrades to climb the hill and watch the Yankee long range guns pound the Rebels. The artillerists laughed at the skittish infantrymen as they frantically dodged what they perceived to be "close" shots, until a twenty-pound Confederate shell slammed into the gun's position. The crew instantly dove for cover only to find that a dud had landed among them. The sweating gunners loped back to their piece amid the jeers and the taunts of the "beetle crunchers", who would not have been alive to scorn them had the projectile exploded.[23]

From their excellent observation post, the New Englanders could see the fighting along the Bloody Lane. Someone noted the advance of the Irish Brigade with its emerald green standards flapping in the breeze; moments later, they helplessly watched a tremendous Confederate volley scythe down the Irishmen like mow grass.[24]

The artillerists enjoyed the panoramic view also. From their vantage point they could and did fire rounds at selected locations all across the fields from the corner of the Bloody Lane to the West Woods. Not half an hour before Carter and his friends climbed among the batteries, Captain Stephen H. Weed (G, 5th U.S.) had placed a memorable round.[25]

The Boonsboro Pike — Sharpsburg

Shortly before 9:00 A.M., Generals Robert E. Lee, James Longstreet, and Daniel Harvey Hill moved to the eastern side of Sharpsburg to observe the movement of Hill's troops toward the Bloody Lane. As they neared the first crest beyond the town, north of the Boonsboro Pike, Longstreet suggested they dismount lest they appear too conspicuous a target for the Yankee gunners across the creek. Lee and Longstreet dismounted. Hill, with typical bravado, remained aboard while the three officers at "safe" intervals walked to the top of the ridge.

One mile away, Major Alfred Woodhull, with Weed's Battery, spied a Confederate officer on a gray horse through his glasses and informed Captain Weed, who wanted to try his hand at sharpshooting. The captain carefully laid the piece, stepped aside, and yanked the lanyard.

"Pete" Longstreet, upon hearing the report, snapped his head up in time to see the muzzle puff. He immediately advised Hill that the shot was homing in on him. Hill, who kept his eyes upon Rodes' regiments, which were moving toward the Bloody Lane, ignored him. The shell roared in low and sheered off the horse's forelegs. The animal dropped onto its bloodied stumps, leaving the general in a near fetal position in the saddle. Longstreet limped over on his carpet slippers and quietly helped him from the horse. Finding another mount (a golden colored one), his fourth that morning, Hill moved on with Lee toward the Bloody Lane. He lost that new horse by 10:30 A.M.[26]

The Lower Bridge

The IX Corps was scattered from Pry's house to N. Rohrbach's, one mile below Porterstown. Orlando Willcox's Division lay closer to South Mountain than to the creek.[27] The Corps was not prepared at all to assault the southern flank of the Army of Northern Virginia. With the exception of scattered picket firing near the creek and an overly cautious foray around 9:00 A.M. by Companies F and I of the 11th Ohio (Crook's BG, Scammon's Div.) into the plowed field across from the Lower Bridge, the morning had passed rather quietly in that section of the field.[28]

The Porterstown Road

The day promised to be a long, hot one and the regimental commanders in Sturgis' Division (IX Corps) ordered their men out by squads to fill all available canteens. Hundreds of men broke ranks and streamed like scattering cockroaches toward the nearby wells.[29] The rapid exodus and the milling about attracted the attention of the Confederate batteries across the creek.

Richardson's and Eshelman's Batteries, from a ridge west of Otto's lane, and Squires' and Bachmann's gunners, south of the Boonsboro Pike, opened fire upon the swarm despite the extreme range.[30] Their aim, though inaccurate, put the ambulance train in the fields east of the Porterstown Road to flight, but did not discourage the thirsty infantrymen in the midst of their water details. Two unidentified privates from E Company, 9th New Hampshire, almost "bought the farm" in a small orchard near the ambulance park when an incoming shell burst directly in front of them. The projectile hurtled over their heads with a horrendous scream and crash, which ripped the apple trees to splinters. Hard, green apples pelted the men like hail, forcing them to dive for cover. Crawling from beneath a blanket of apples, the two men limped after their water, filled their canteens, and returned, bruised, but successful to their regiment.[31]

Across the Porterstown Road, opposite Brigadier General James Nagle's Brigade, the 35th Massachusetts joined the trek for water too late. Their runners, who were loaded down with canteens, returned to the regiment slightly before 10:00 A.M. The sweating men received the warm, muddied water as if it were priceless. They were lucky to have that, because the hordes of thirsty soldiers had about dried up the wells.[32]

By 10:00 A.M., heavy firing erupted near the Lower Bridge. Within minutes, Ferrero's Brigade staggered to its feet and joined the division column.[33] By the time they got under way, however, the small arms fire had died away, leaving only the reports of an artillery duel echoing along the creek banks.[34]

The Lower Bridge

Lieutenant Colonel William R. Holmes (2nd GA, Toombs' BG, D. R. Jones' Div.) vowed to "Stonewall" Jackson that his men would hold the heights overlooking the Lower Bridge or die in a ditch trying.[35] The Confederates, though short on men, had more than their share of determination. The 2nd Georgia (about 125 men) and the 20th Georgia (225 men) held the heights along the creek and the Lower Bridge Road for about eight hundred seventy-five yards, which placed one man about every eight feet.[36] Richardson's and Eshelman's Batteries covered the Georgians from a ridge about five hundred yards west of the bridge.[37] The 50th Georgia (210 men), with one company from Jenkins' South Carolina Brigade and a battalion (five companies) from the 11th Georgia (G. T. Anderson's BG) occupied the bluffs from the right of the 2nd Georgia, at the quarry, south to the big bend in the creek, then west to a spot directly north of Snavely's Ford. The distance of over one thousand six hundred fifty yards greatly strained their defensive capabilities. They, probably, numbered a little over three hundred men.[38] Benning's (Toombs') Brigade, which normally had two other regiments with it, had left the 15th and the 17th Georgia with the other half of the 11th Georgia on provost duty with the Army's wagon train on the Virginia side of the Potomac.[39] The Georgians took cover behind trees, rock outcroppings, and fences along the bridge road and the western bank of the creek. Many shinnied up trees to cover the bridge from better vantage points.[40] *(Map 50)*

By 9:00 A.M., they had repulsed the cautious probe by two companies of the 11th Ohio.[41] An hour later, the 11th Connecticut, under the command of Colonel Henry W. Kingsbury, was sent from Harland's Brigade (Rodman's Div., IX) against the bridge. The Yankees burst over the twin knolls east of the bluffs in extended

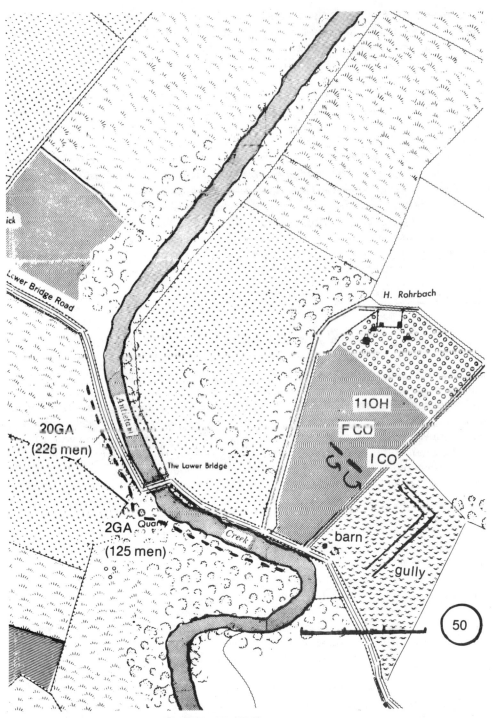

(Map 50) 9:00 A.M., SEPTEMBER 17, 1862
Two companies of the 11th Ohio make a half hearted foray against the Lower Bridge.

order. Benning's Georgians fired madly into the onrushing Yankees as they reached the rail fence and the stone wall to the south and the north of the bridge, respectively. For ten minutes the New Englanders put out a tremendous fusillade. Their men lay sprawled about the stubble field behind them. Others were draped over the stone wall.

Captain John Griswold (A Co., 11th CT) leaped the stone wall, followed by several men and plunged into the creek only to find it swift flowing and four feet deep in the center. A burst of small arms fire caught the party there. A few men plunged into the stream — dead. The others, Griswold excepted, turned back. The captain, who was already mortally wounded, staggered to the Confederate side of the creek where he collapsed on the muddy bank and bled to death.[42]

The Georgians forced the New Englanders back to the safety of the knolls. They inflicted one hundred thirty-nine casualties upon the Yankees, including their colonel, who left the field — dying.[43] He perished at the hands of men under the command of his beloved brother-in-law, Brigadier General David R. Jones.[44] The Confederates let their heated gun barrels cool and saved their rapidly depleting ammunition supply for further assaults.[45] *(Map 51)*

The Porterstown Road — H. Rohrbach's

Sturgis' Division, having heard the firing, started to slowly get under way. Nagle's Brigade (2nd MD, 6th and 9th NH, 48th PA) took the lead through the fields parallel to the lane which led to H. Rohrbach's. Ferrero's Brigade (51st NY, 51st PA, 21st and 35th MA), moving by the left flank in four columns of files, followed.[46] The march did not set any speed records. Neither brigade commander possessed any genuine knowledge of their precise location and depended on guides from their brigade headquarters, who were barely familiar with the local topography themselves. Lieutenant John W. Hudson (35th MA), Ferrero's aide, at the head of the column with Lieutenant Colonel Sumner Carruth, guided Ferrero's four regiments by the left flank through the undulating fields east of Rohrbach's for about one thousand fifty yards.[47] He stopped the column often, not to rest, as he later explained, but to await further instructions. The wooded ridges along the route shielded the two brigades from direct fire but not from an occasional overshot — that particulary disconcerting type of plunging fire which killed by accident.

Nagle's Brigade moved through the ravine west of H. Rohrbach's house above the farm lane to avoid that plunging fire. Private William H. Wilcox (I Co., 9th NH) and a handful of men from his company, not liking their limited view, broke ranks and dashed toward the wooded crest on their right flank to get a better view of the creek. They covered the few rods easily, then scampered on all fours toward the summit, which they almost reached. A solid shot struck the tree in front of Wilcox, just above his forehead, and splintered the trunk. Branches rained down upon their heads as the startled infantrymen rolled and slid down the hill in a panicky bolt for shelter.[48] *(Map 52)*

The column moved through the ravine after a few minutes' delay and filed by the right flank over the ridge into Rohrbach's southern cornfield.[49] To the south of the four infantry columns, Captain Asa M. Cook's 8th Massachusetts Battery fired west toward Eshelman's Battery. At the same time, a section of Captain Seth

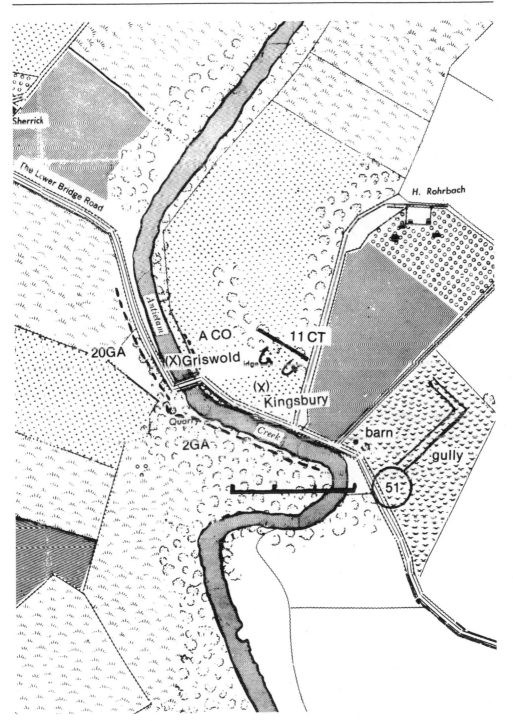

(Map 51) 10:00 A.M., SEPTEMBER 17, 1862
The 11th Connecticut loses heavily in its try for the Lower Bridge.

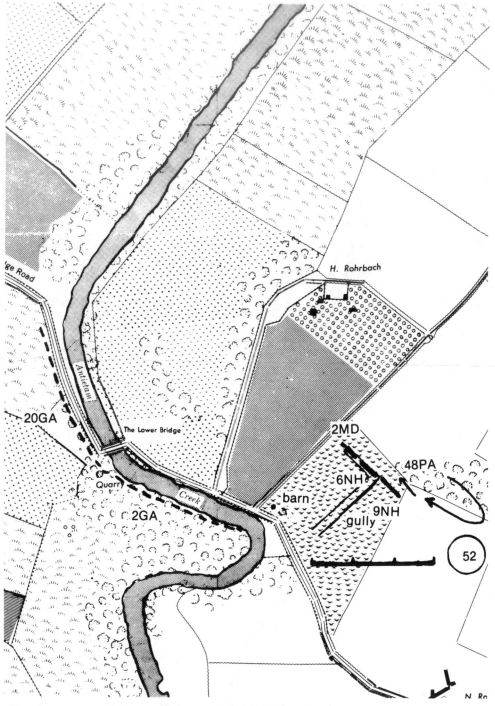

(Map 52) 10:30 A.M. — NOON, SEPTEMBER 17, 1862
Nagle's Brigade prepares to attack the Lower Bridge.

Simmonds' Kentucky Battery hammered away from the high ground in front of Rohrbach's orchard.[50] The 2nd Maryland, followed, respectively, by the 6th New Hampshire, 9th New Hampshire, and the 48th Pennsylvania, advanced by the right flank through the tall corn toward the short length of an "L" shaped gulch which cut easterly uphill from the creek bottom before turning north near the top of the cornfield.[51]

The Lower Bridge

Doctor Theodore Dimon, the Acting Surgeon of the 2nd Maryland, having become alarmed at the increased artillery fire, left his hospital staff in the woods northeast of Nagle's Brigade and hurried along the rear lines toward the cornfield. As he passed along Ferrero's men while they rested in the wooded ravine east of the cornfield, he quickly exchanged amenities with his good friend Colonel Robert Potter (51st NY) and kept on. Cresting the ridge above the cornfield, he found the 2nd Maryland prone in the gulch where it paralleled the hilltop. The rest of the brigade was stretched out in the corn on a north-south line which extended from the angle in the "L" of the gulch. To the northwest, behind the cover of another corn studded hill, he spied the Divisional headquarters. The doctor felt very relieved that the regiment had not gone into battle yet. He settled down to chat with Lieutenant Colonel Eugene Duryea, who was informally squatting behind his men with his blouse unbuttoned.

An aide ordered the colonel down to Sturgis, the Division commander. The doctor futilely strained his neck to overhear the brief "confab", as he referred to it. Moments later, Duryea strode back to the surgeon, buttoning up his blouse as he walked, which the doctor correctly interpreted as signifying that "work was now at hand."

"Unsling knapsacks," the colonel growled.

As the regiment struggled to free itself of its excess accoutrements, Dimon asked Duryea to give him the story. Duryea bluntly told him that Sturgis asked him if he wanted a star — a promotion to brigadier general. The colonel did not hesitate to tell him, "Yes."

" 'Well' ", the colonel continued, quoting Sturgis, " 'there is a bridge around the other side of this hill, and the Lieutenant Colonel of the 6th New Hampshire thinks his regiment too small to head the assault on it, so I offer it to you.' All right, General, I'll make a try for that star anyhow."[52]

Without wasting any time, the colonel solemnly led his regiment, by the left flank, down the gulch toward the creek, the rest of the brigade following as they had come upon the field.[53] Doctor Dimon trailed after his Marylanders as they approached the bottom land and the country road which followed the contours of the creek bank toward the Lower Bridge.[54] (Map 53)

Lieutenant John Williams Hudson, Ferrero's junior aide, stood to the right of his brigade which had just halted in columns of files part way over the crest into the cornfield. From his post, he observed Nagle's men put on a good military show as the 2nd Maryland, and the other regiments, in their own good time, fronted individually and volleyed blindly into the high bank across the creek from them.

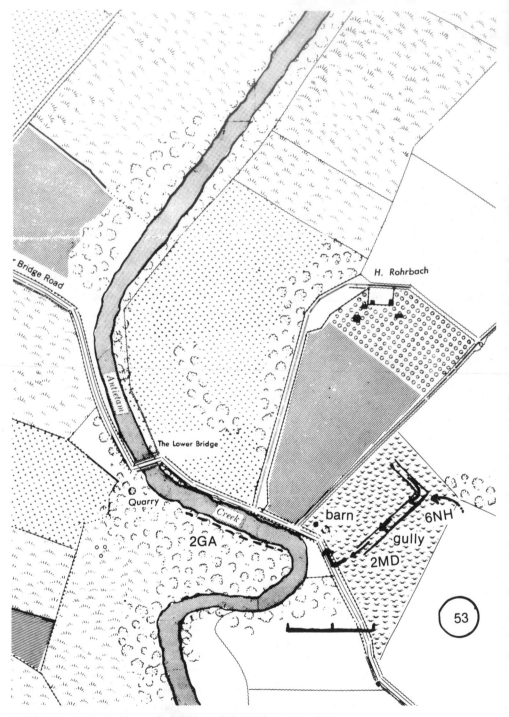

(Map 53) 10:30 A.M. — NOON, SEPTEMBER 17, 1862
Colonel Duryea leads the 2nd Maryland into the fray.

He attempted to act rather fearless himself. The staff had taken a post on the eastern end of a country lane which ran down to the creek. It gave them a complete view of the plowed field to the left and of the cornfield to their right. The twenty-nine year old lieutenant cautiously stole into the open ground above the lane with the rest of the officers rather than seek the safety of a nearby tree. The racket of the artillery and the occasional incoming rounds disturbed him but he did not want to appear to be unnerved.[55]

The 2nd Maryland, in the meantime, was rushing northeast, across the Lower Bridge Road, toward the plowed field below the bridge. While the head of the column halted to feverishly tear down a section of the post and rail fence which blocked their approach, Doctor Dimon spotted a dilapidated pole barn with a thatched roof in the northwestern corner of the cornfield. A pool of clean looking water bordered it on the south. Walking over to it, he stooped down, unhitched his tin cup from his canteen strap and kneeled down to sample the water. As the cup touched the surface of the pond, a tremendous exchange of artillery explosions, punctuated by the cracking of small arms fire, startled him. He raised his head up to find himself being gawked at by an isolated and apparently confused, group of enlisted men, whom he assumed were skirmishers.

The doctor immediately ordered the men to prepare the barn for casualties. They were to stack all available straw or hay and the barn door against the western and northern walls to protect the wounded from stray rounds from the bridge. They were also to fill up their canteens and keep them for the injured.

The doctor quickly tried to find out what was happening to the 2nd Maryland. A hasty glance into the plowed field saddened him. Blue uniforms seemed to thickly dot the area. The regiment was pinned between the road and a very well constructed fence section along Rohrbach's southern lane. The Marylanders twisted and writhed, trying to individually evade the tremendous riflery from the tree tops across the creek. Shells snapped branches off above the stream and sent them crashing into the water below. Above the din, Doctor Dimon distinctly heard Colonel Duryea's piercing voice scream, "What the hell you doing there? Straighten that line there, forward," as he viciously threw the last fence rail aside and bolted into the stubble field east of the bridge. The regiment snapped into files by the right flank and staggered after their ferocious colonel.[56]

The 6th New Hampshire filed through the openings on the heels of the 2nd Maryland. With bayonets fixed, the two regiments charged in columns of four toward the bridge. The Georgians on the opposite bank cut loose with a scathing fire. Bullets materialized from the trees and the barricades, rapidly knocking down Marylanders and New Englanders. A number of men huddled on the lower end of the bridge but did not stay there long.[57] The two regiments withdrew to the relative safety of a pair of rocky knolls about one hundred yards to their rear. (Map 54)

The remaining two regiments of Nagle's Brigade tried to provide cover fire but went awry. The 48th Pennsylvania, on the far left, went prone along the Lower Bridge Road and shot wildly into the cliff on the opposite bank. The 9th New Hampshire, while crossing into the plowed field below the bridge, ran into severe artillery and musketry fire and was forced to run for cover along the post and rail fence which

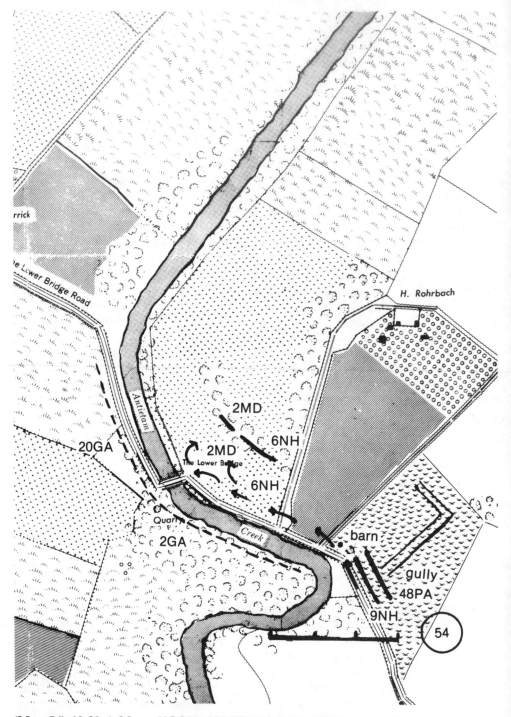

(Map 54) 10:30 A.M. — NOON, SEPTEMBER 17, 1862
The 2nd Maryland and the 6th New Hampshire assault the Lower Bridge for the first time.

bordered the road. The Confederates, it seemed, were throwing everything they could jam into the muzzle of an artillery piece at them — including railroad iron. A fifteen inch long section of track whirled through F Company as it ran toward the road. The startled soldier, whose head it barely missed, gaped at the twirling iron as it struck the ridge behind him and tumbled end over end down the hill toward him.[58] The horrendous noise and the apparent thought of dying from scrap metal totally unstrung another man in F Company. As the line neared the fence, he collapsed, face first, into the freshly turned ground.

"Get up!" Captain Andrew J. Stone commanded.

"I can't," the soldier whimpered.

He could not move. The exasperated officer finally detailed several men to carry the fellow behind the lines. They layed him under the bank near the big bend in the creek.[59] The New Englanders took a very bad beating as they fired over the bottom rails of the fence. Officers dismounted and went prone with the men. Lieutenant Colonel Titus took a weapon from the corpse of a man from the 6th New Hampshire, who had just been killed beside him, and, contrary to protocol, joined in the fighting like an enlisted man.[60]

The hospital staff immediately established a field hospital in the pole barn to the left rear of the regiment.[61] The chaplain and bandsmen stoically braved bullets to drag wounded men from the firing line to their surgeon, William A. Webster.[62]

Within minutes, stretcher crews carried off Captains Smith Whitfield (G Co.) and John Cooper (K Co.), both of whom were severely injured.[63] Private Edward M. Messenger (I Co.) stood up to get a better shot and was about to fire when a ball clipped off his left thumb, passed over his rifle barrel, and struck him in the forehead above his right eye. The impact hurled him to the ground. His comrades screamed for a bandsman to take his corpse away from the line. With blood pulsating from the entry wound and the exit wound, in front of his right ear, the men erringly counted Messenger as their first fatality for the day.[64] The casualty list climbed by the minute, but the men held.

Colonel Fellows, his palm leaf hat bobbing conspicuously with every move, crawled from man to man along the line, encouraging each one to do his duty.[65] Private George Russell (G Co.) rolled over in a ball — shot through the intestines.[66] The incoming rounds from the tree tops and the opposite bank were producing particularly ugly wounds among the Yankees. (By approximately 11:30 A.M., when Ferrero's Brigade finally began moving on their flank, Nagle's men had expended most of their ammunition and had taken heavy losses, among them Lieutenant Colonel Titus. He fell with a bullet in his side.)[67] (Map 55)

Ferrero's people spent at least half an hour waiting for Nagle's men to shuffle upstream from the cornfield. Finally, around 11:00 A.M., he ordered Lieutenant Hudson to send the 51st Pennsylvania, the 51st New York, and the 21st Massachusetts, respectively, down the slope, through the gulch, into the cornfield to fill the gap left by the 48th Pennsylvania, which was moving past the creek bend.

The 48th Pennsylvania, marching by the right oblique, stomped deliberately into the cornfield, taking a rather indirect route toward the twin knolls to support the 2nd Maryland and the 6th New Hampshire in another assault.[68]

Dr. Dimon and Dr. Reber (48th PA) were amputating the shattered leg of Captain James A. Martin (E Co., 2nd MD). Dimon and Reber were standing opposite

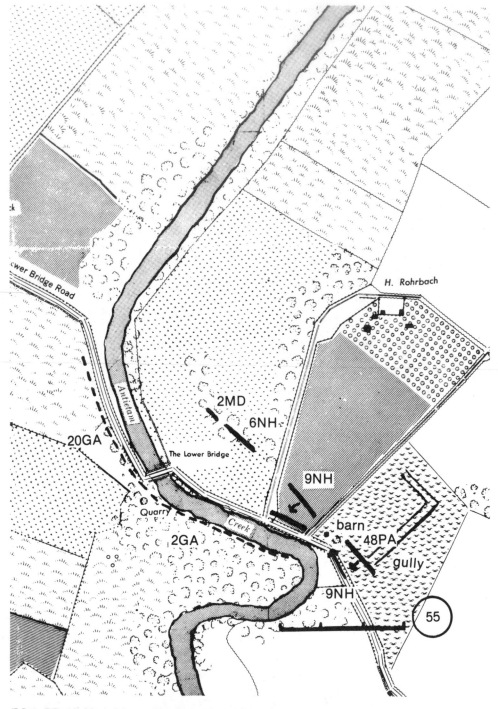

(Map 55) 10:30 A.M. — NOON, SEPTEMBER 17, 1862
Nagle's Brigade becomes fully committed to the battle.

each other. Doctor Dimon severed the officer's leg and tossed it aside. He had just clamped an artery in the forceps while the Pennsylvania surgeon was adjusting the ligature in it to stop the bleeding when a shell burst directly overhead. Fragments peppered the straw roof; one of them fell directly between the doctors' bowed heads, their hands and the leg stump into the bloodied straw at their feet without touching them or their patient. Undisturbed by the sizzling shrapnel, the two surgeons tried to finish their grisly work.

Vehement cursing and swearing temporarily distracted Dr. Dimon. Furtively glancing up from the captain's leg, through the double doors which opened east into the cornfield, he noticed Samuel Sturgis, the Division commander, loudly dressing down Lieutenant Colonel Joshua K. Sigfried of the 48th Pennsylvania.

"God damn you to hell, sir, don't you understand the English language?" Sturgis bellowed, "I ordered you to advance in line and support the 2nd Maryland, and what in hell are you doing flanking around in this corn?"

The 48th moved down in front of the barn and advanced diagonally to the northeast to its assigned position.[69]

Ferrero's three older regiments, marching by the left flank as Nagle's Brigade had, descended into the corn, a short distance east of the Lower Bridge Road, where they fronted, facing the creek. Lieutenant Hudson, who was afoot, waited until the rest of the brigade had formed in column of regiments before he sent for the 35th Massachusetts. The regiment was very "green" and at South Mountain, while under fire, "... had not gained any credit for efficiency ..." and "..., nobody cared to have

COLONEL EDWARD FERRERO, brigade commander, IX Corps

He won a general's star, at a personal cost of two barrels of whiskey, for the taking of the Lower Bridge. *(USAMHI)*

any part of the day depend on it," the aide recalled after the battle. (By "nobody", Hudson meant Colonel Ferrero.) As Lieutenant Colonel Carruth led his shaky New Englanders into combat for a second time, Hudson ran down through the corn to find Colonel Ferrero.

Leaping over the fence rows bordering the Lower Bridge Road, he found the colonel standing in the flat open space at the creek bend. The colonel meditatively observed the creek and the speed of its current. Ferrero told Hudson that as soon as the brigade moved onto the level ground behind them, he intended to cross the Antietam, which he believed fordable at that point.[70]

Another ear shattering volume of musketry burst upstream as the 2nd Maryland and the 6th New Hampshire, in columns of four, with the 48th Pennsylvania in support, charged the bridge again. The heated firing did not last long. The Georgians broke the two lead regiments and their reserve and sent them streaming back to the knolls.[71] At about the same time, the

9th New Hampshire, its ranks very thinned and low on shot, shifted northeast toward the knolls to take cover with the rest of the brigade.[72] *(Map 56)*

The wounded men who stumbled eastward through the corn did not deliberately treat the nervous men of the 35th Massachusetts badly. As they filed between the rows of stalks, they greeted the "fresh fish" with a gory parade of mangled arms, legs, or stumps which left very dark stains on the leaves and the corn mounds. The New Englanders had walked into a house of horrors. For almost an hour they had watched men disappear into the corn, where they heard screams, and shouts, and the roar of artillery and small arms fire, but they had not seen any of it.[73] They knew they were descending into a Valley of Death.

The soldiers noticed as they neared the level ground along the Lower Bridge Road that men were dying not one hundred yards to their right. They could hear their agonizing screams, but no hostile bullets were coming into their sector at all. The Rebels did not take so much as one pot shot at Ferrero's Brigade. The air seemed hot, suffocating. Their sweaty uniforms clung uncomfortably to them.[74]

Colonel Ferrero, after sending Lieutenant Hudson back into the cornfield to search out General Sturgis and to obtain permission to ford the stream, mounted his horse, passed through an opening in the fence and headed into the corn. He rode up to the 51st Pennsylvania, his lead regiment and commanded, "the 51st to forward" then trotted off without waiting to see the order executed. Neither Colonel Robert Potter (51st NY) nor Colonel John Hartranft (51st PA) paid any attention to their dancing master turned warrior. Hartranft deliberately turned toward his regiment with a sarcastic smile as if nothing had been said.

A very short time later, Colonel Ferrero spurred along the front of the Pennsylvanians in a rage.

"Why in the hell don't you forward?" Ferrero yelled.

John Hartranft, who considered himself a better man than his commander, nonchalantly replied, "Who do you want to forward?"

"The 51st Pennsylvania," the colonel spat.

Hartranft glared up at his brigadier and cooly answered, "Why don't you say what you mean when you want me to move?"

At that Ferrero wheeled his horse about and headed for the flat, open space west of the Lower Bridge Road. The brigade, led by the obstinate Colonel Hartranft, followed.[75]

Meanwhile, Sturgis stumbled across Hudson instead and bluntly informed him that Major General Ambrose Burnside, himself, had instructed him, "Send down the 2nd Brigade — I know they will take it." Hudson loped back to the creek and relayed the Division commander's reply to Ferrero, who rather bitterly replied that Nagle (1st Brigade) ought to do it. The 2nd Brigade was too used up from the recent campaigning for the task. (Ferrero wanted to ford the stream with his "used up" troops rather than lose them in a suicidal frontal assault.)

Once again, the energetic, but tiring Lieutenant Hudson disappeared into the corn to argue his commander's cause only to be told more emphatically by Sturgis to "Go on" and take the bridge. Ferrero, upon receipt of this command, sent his "gofer" back through the corn again for a final directive.[76]

The third exchange got very loud between the general and the aide, both of whom had about reached their boiling points. Enlisted men in the still forming 35th

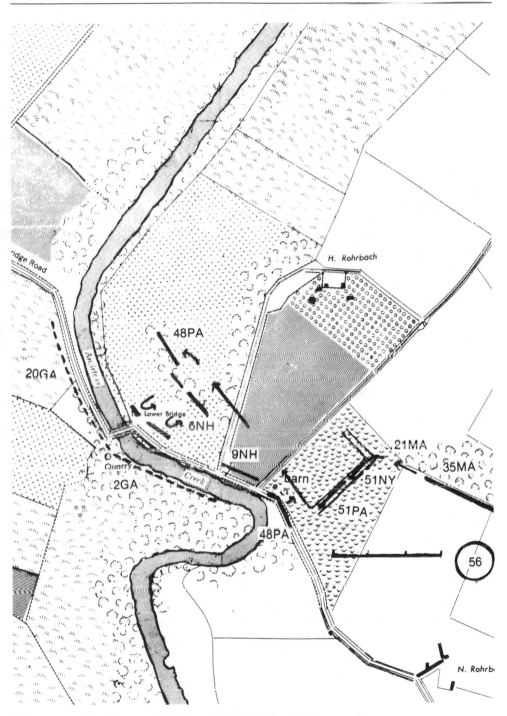

(Map 56) 10:30 A.M. — NOON, SEPTEMBER 17, 1862
The 2nd Maryland and the 6th New Hampshire fail in their second charge against the Lower Bridge.

Massachusetts overheard the two men above the shell concussions upstream. When Hudson asked Sturgis where he wanted Ferrero to put his brigade, the general exploded, "Have him move those regiments down to the stream immediately and take the bridge!"

Hudson, knowing that he meant the brigade's three veteran regiments, yelled, "And what with this new 35th Massachusetts?"

"Tell him," Sturgis blustered, "to move it across the bridge and up the hill in line of battle. There must be no delay. General Burnside is waiting for it to be done now."

The lieutenant, who listened to the artillery thundering down the creek from the bluffs, shouted back, "Isn't that artillery aimed at the position?"

"Yes, but it shall be stopped."[77]

Hudson ran back to Ferrero, who was still at the creek bend, and gave him the final order. Before the colonel could respond, the lieutenant queried, "Colonel, if you send the 35th to take the bridge, may I go with my company? They've but one officer."

"No, I can't spare you," Ferrero shot back.

John Hudson knew that the colonel had no intention of risking his career by sending the 35th Massachusetts into the field ahead of his seasoned troops.[78] Colonel Ferrero swung into the saddle again and shouted, "Attention, second brigade!"

The soldiers quickly formed ranks as their brigadier pranced before their colors.

"It is General Burnside's special request that the two 51sts take the bridge. Will you do it?"

Corporal Lewis Patterson (I Co., 51st PA), a known teetotaller, shattered the silence with, "Will you give us our whiskey, Colonel, if we take it?"

Ferrero, who had reached his limit with the contentious Pennsylvanians, turned on the corporal.

"Yes, by God!" he called. "You shall have as much as you want, if you take the bridge. I don't mean the whole brigade, but you two regiments shall have just as much as you want, if it is in the commissary or I have to send to New York to get it, and pay for it out of my own purse; that is if I live to see you through it. Will you take it?"

A resounding "Yes" echoed from the ranks along the creek bank.[79]

The tension rippled through the line as the colonel started to shift his impatient brigade about. The 51st Pennsylvania, following the diagonal approach taken by Nagle's men, passed northeast behind the 9th New Hampshire toward the right rear of the twin knolls. The 51st New York stayed in place while the smaller 21st Massachusetts filed right into the plowed field which the 9th New Hampshire formerly occupied.[80] The 21st Massachusetts behaved poorly in moving out. In small groups and singly, rattled soldiers rose up sporadically from their prone line and shot wildly through the light brush on their side of the creek into the opposite bank. They were firing "by guess", Hudson recounted, for which some got "a good rifle ball to pay for their wisdom.[81] (Map 57)

Colonel Ferrero heatedly "suggested" to Colonel William S. Clark (21st MA) that he calm down his herd. The colonel yelled at his men to rise up. Despite the lead which splattered into the line, the New Englanders gained their feet.

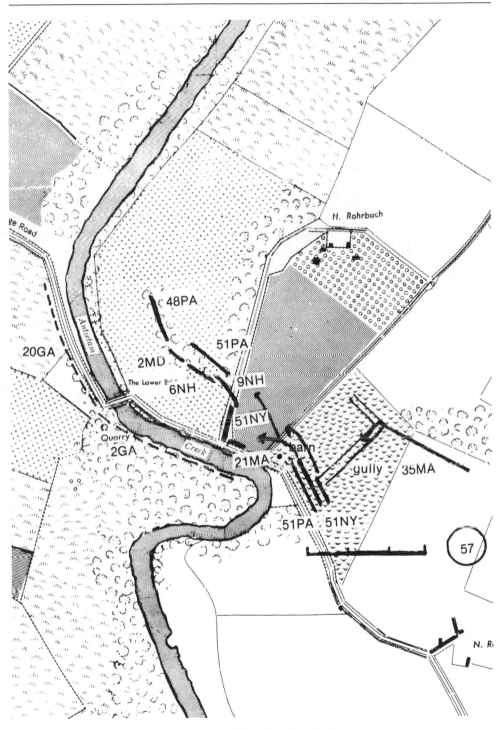

(Map 57) 10:30 A.M. — NOON, SEPTEMBER 17, 1862
Ferrero's Brigade gets into the fighting.

"Right dress! Front!" echoed across the plowed field.

"Rear rank, ready, aim, fire! Load at will. Load!"

Clark repeated the command for the front rank. Within a minute both lines were calmly shooting at will. Lieutenant Hudson, who stood behind them, could not see anyone on the opposite bank but he assumed some Rebels were dying just as some of the 21st Massachusetts were at that moment.[82]

Ferrero immediately posted the 51st New York at right angles to the 21st Massachusetts in the plowed field, facing the bridge, then he and his staff prepared to move behind the first knoll to direct the actions of the 51st Pennsylvania.

Only the 35th Massachusetts remained undeployed. Having advanced into the road at the creek bend, it stood there awaiting orders. The water looked cool, dark, and inviting to the perspiring soldiers as they stood at ease beneath the widespread branches of a large tree which dominated the creek bend. The hot noon sun bathed the surrounding fields in an innervating heat. Minutes seemed like hours as the men ditched their blanket rolls, knapsacks, and haversacks beneath the tree and posted a guard over them. The order rippled down the line to fix bayonets. The men solemnly steeled themselves for battle.[83]

The Federal attempts against the Lower Bridge were repeatedly stalled by a numerically inferior Confederate force. Lack of coordinated and coherent Federal leadership also hindered success at the bridgehead. General Ambrose Burnside, commanding the Army of the Potomac's Left Wing, had no real knowledge of the terrain. He personally insisted that the IX Corps take the bridge, which he did not see until after it was taken, by frontal rather than flank attack.

CHAPTER FOURTEEN

"They cried unto thee and were delivered."

NOON TO 1:00 P.M.

The Middle Bridge

General Robert E. Lee, who had been constantly reconnoitering his lines from the West Woods to Cemetary Hill, did not like the situation along the Lower Bridge Road. Shortly before noon, he calmly walked over to Colonel J. B. Walton, commander of his First Reserve Artillery Battalion, Captain Charles Squires, and First Lieutenant William M. Owen. He held his field glasses in his right hand. His injured left arm was still in a sling.

"Well, Colonel," Lee said, "what do you make of the enemy: what is he going to do?"

"They seem to be moving a battery more to our right," Walton replied.

Almost immediately, a courier reined to a halt near the officers. He handed a message to Lieutenant Owen, who quickly opened and read it.

"The enemy is moving a six-gun battery to our right, evidently with the intention of covering with it their crossing." Signed, "Johnson, Engineer Officer."

"Yes," Lee said, "I see they are. Colonel, can you spare this young officer to ride for me? None of my staff are present."

Walton consented. Lee turned to Lieutenant Owen, who felt like he would explode from such an honor.

"Go to General D. R. Jones, and tell him I wish that battery —" He pointed south with his field glasses "— moved further to the right to cover the lower ford, where the enemy will soon endeavor to cross. Let it be done at once."

Saluting, Owen leaped into the saddle and spurred down into the Lower Bridge Road ravine and up the opposite side into the orchard south of the road, where he found General Jones.

235

"Where is my chief of artillery?" Jones blurted upon receiving the order. No one who was present knew. "This is bad; the battery must be changed at once; Lieutenant, won't you do it for me?"

William Owen remounted and raced south past Richardson's Battery, which was shelling the bridge. Delivering the command to Captain B. F. Eshelman, he immediately wheeled about and returned to Squires' Battery.

He dismounted and reported to Lee personally that the order had been obeyed. Lee seemed very cordial, "I see it has. Thank you, *Captain*."

The freshly promoted lieutenant felt taller than he ever had.[1]

The Lower Bridge

Colonel Ferrero commanded Lieutenant Hudson to send for the 35th Massachusetts, which he did immediately. While the green regiment double quicked obliquely, northeast, toward the knolls east of the bridge, the 51st Pennsylvania made its move toward the bridge.

Lieutenant Hudson, who stopped to join Ferrero watch the 21st Massachusetts waste a "good quantity of ammunition" on the brush covered western bank, turned his head toward the right as a half hearted cheer reverberated from the crest of the wooded knolls. The exhausted Pennsylvanians walked and staggered in columns of platoons toward the creek. Lieutenant Hudson wryly noted, "we saw the 51st Pennsylvania rush (not very fast — tired soldiers don't go very fast)." Tired or not, the hard drinking bunch dove for cover behind the abutments of the bridge and the stone wall which parallelled the creek north of it.[2] The 51st New York clambered over and through the rail fence to its front and left obliqued through the stubble field to the rail fence which bordered the creek to the left of the bridge.[3] The 48th Pennsylvania, simultaneously, made for both flanks of the bridge with a small part of the 6th New Hampshire.[4] All four regiments started to pour a terrific fire into the opposite bank. They saw Confederates in pairs and threes dodging about through the smoke to escape their bullets.[5]

Captain James Wren (B Co., 48th PA) ordered his people prone among the 51st New York and they cut loose "at will" into the leafy foliage and the Rebel barricades across the stream. Captain Wren was cooly directing their musketry when an enlisted man from the 6th New Hampshire meandered over to him complaining that the Rebs had shot off the trigger finger on his right hand. He shouted that he still had forty rounds in his cartridge box and that he did not want to go to the rear.

The captain, succumbing to the thrill of the moment, and realizing that the bridge had to be taken on this assault, turned deliberately on the man and blurted, "Now you bite the ends off these cartridges and I will fire them cartridges of yours." Putting down his sword, he took the man's musket and carelessly stood up to shoot offhand.[6]

Three balls in rapid succession zinged close by the captain's ears. His men shouted to him to get down because the Rebs had his range. At that moment, Wren saw a Confederate leisurely step from behind a large tree next to the bridge, take careful aim, and squeeze the trigger. The bullet whistled just above his head. The captain ducked for cover.

Propping his musket on a fence rail, Wren sighted in on the tree. As the Reb exposed himself for another shot, the captain jerked the trigger and missed. Hastily reloading, he sighted in again, determined to draw blood. The next time the Confederate stepped out to shoot, the captain fired. As the smoke cleared, he thought he saw his target double over and drop. Assuming that he had hit the man, because no more rounds came in from that direction, Wren promised himself to check his kill if he lived to cross the creek. With the musket's barrel growing hotter with each shot, he continued to plug away at the Rebel barricades.[7]

The noise at the bridge reached a nerve shattering crescendo as musketry, shrieks, and curses mingled with the exploding shells and rattling canister from Simmond's Kentucky Battery, which was firing over their heads into the Confederate positions.[8] Time seemed to stop indefinitely as the Federal assault stymied into a slug fest.

Some of Colonel John Hartranft's men (51st PA) scrambled over the post and rail fence, which bordered both sides of the road south of the bridge, and took cover behind the lower wing of the abutment. The colonel, who was with the colors, used the upper abutment for shelter; he ordered his people to tear the rails out of the fence where it passed directly across the mouth of the bridge.[9] He anxiously watched the New Yorkers, New Englanders, and Pennsylvanians take a terrible flailing from the Confederates. The fence offered them nominal protection.[10] *(Map 58)*

From behind the knolls, Colonel Ferrero, who had caught up with the 35th Massachusetts, could not understand why the 51st Pennsylvania had not crossed the stream as ordered. The dapper dancing master impatiently ordered the ever present John Hudson to go down and find out why Colonel Hartranft had not done as commanded. The fact that their own artillery might destroy the advancing column apparently never occurred to him.[11] He simultaneously detached A Company from the right of the 35th to assist the left flank of the 21st Massachusetts.

Lieutenant Hudson glanced about as he, pursuant to the colonel's desire, started down the slight valley toward Hartranft's pinned soldiers. Members of the 2nd Maryland and the 6th New Hampshire fired sporadically toward the creek.[12] Colonel Enoch Fellows (9th NH) periodically poked his head over the sparsely wooded crest to observe the fighting. While he bobbed about, his head protected from the bright sun by a palm leaf hat, his tiring soldiers, for the most part, kept their skulls below the line of fire.[13] Before he trotted into the corn stubbled valley, the normally cautious John Hudson asked the New Englanders, some of whom hid too much for his liking, not to shoot him in the back.[14]

Taking off at a steady trot, the lieutenant dashed into the line just south of the bridge. The men pointed him in the direction of the northern parapet. Hudson darted across the bridge's mouth, stooping low to keep his back well beneath the road crest in the middle of the bridge. Prone Pennsylvanians, who were using the road hump for cover, busily peppered the west bank with a steady fusilade. He found Colonel Hartranft and his color guard huddled below the north wing of the bridge wall. As the aide approached the colonel, a "drop short" from Simmond's Battery exploded in the creek and sprayed water over the men behind the stone wall.

Hudson screamed at the colonel, ordering him to cross the bridge.

"Does he desire it?" Hartranft incredulously shouted back.

"Yes, sir," Hudson replied.

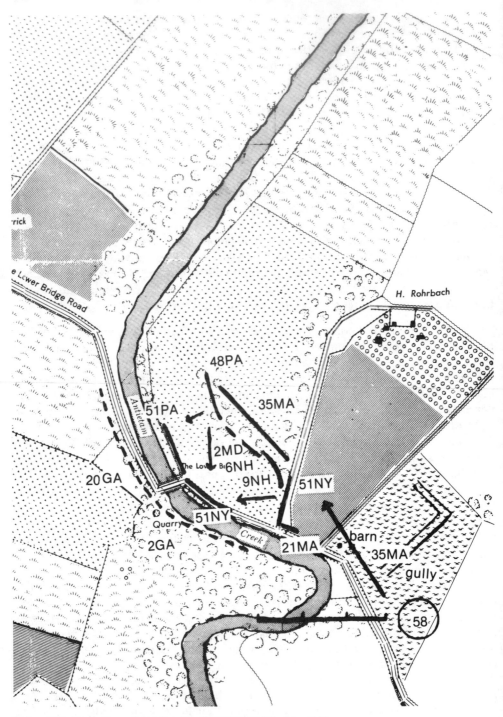

(Map 58) NOON — 1:00 P.M., SEPTEMBER 17, 1862
The 51st Pennsylvania and the 51st New York gain a foothold at the Lower Bridge.

"Very well," Hartranft replied.

The two officers headed south together. Hartranft and his color guard worked their way into the crowd on the bridge while Hudson sought out Colonel Robert B. Potter (51st NY) and told him to follow the Pennsylvanians across.[15] Potter shouted at his men to move and bolted onto the parapet where he was seen standing atop one of the walls cursing and swearing like a madman.[16] Lieutenant Hudson hurriedly raced back to the safety of the knolls. As he explained it later, "having on straps & sword & pistol, I was willing to keep moving," lest he be found too close to the bridge should the assault fail or should some Confederate sharpshooter single him out as a prize target. At the moment, the Confederates had more than one stray Yankee lieutenant to worry about.[17]

Colonel Henry L. Benning, commanding the Georgians at the bridgehead, found his position, which his soldiers had so valiantly held for so long, becoming more untenable. For no apparent reason to Benning, the 50th Georgia disappeared from his immediate right flank (which, perhaps, explains why the 35th Massachusetts received no incoming fire at the creek bend). The morning attacks left his men physically exhausted. Their fire dwindled perceptibly as the Yankees down at the bridge began to stir. Benning's good fortune had run its course along with his ammunition supply. He started to pass the word along the crest to fall back.[18]

They managed to drag away some of their wounded as they retreated, including one of them whom they should have left behind to die. The Georgians refused to abandon the gut shot Johnnie Slade (H Co.). (He died four days later in Sharpsburg.)[19]

Part of D Company of the 2nd Georgia did not hear the command above the crashing of the Federal artillery fire. Benning immediately sent First Sergeant Henean H. Perry (D Co., 2nd GA) to retrieve the rest of the command. He arrived as the company shot away its last rounds of ammunition.[20] *(Map 59)*

The riflery at the crossing seemed hot enough to Captain William Allebaugh (C Co.) and the color guard of the 51st Pennsylvania, who, with their colonel, were trying to rouse their men to action. Despite the ricocheting bullets from the trees and the hillside, the captain with First Sergeant William Thomas, three color bearers and one of the color guard, bolted across the bridge and planted the colors in the road at its mouth.[21] Simultaneously, Colonel Hartranft, hat in hand, and screaming at the top of his lungs, rushed to join them, followed by his excited men.[22] They effectively clogged the twelve foot wide roadway as soldiers halted to shoot at snipers in the tree tops or stumbled over the casualties in their paths.

The incoming riflery ceased suddenly as the Pennsylvanians reached the middle span.[23] A short distance to the left, some men of the 51st New York, who had forded the stream and scaled the quarry to the crest of the hill, flanked the reforming 2nd Georgia.[24] The riflery cut down Lieutenant Colonel William R. Holmes, Jr. (2nd GA) as he stepped away from the line with the intention of scrounging ammunition for his men. Instinctively, First Sergeant Henean Perry, Second Sergeant James G. Burton, Private W. R. Cox (all D Co.), and Captain Abner Lewis (B Co.) snatched up his corpse to carry him away. The captain and Sergeant Burton dropped, wounded by a second volley from the 51st New York.[25] The colonel died, sword in hand, five paces behind his color guard while attempting to fulfill his vow to hold the bridgehead or die in a ditch trying.[26]

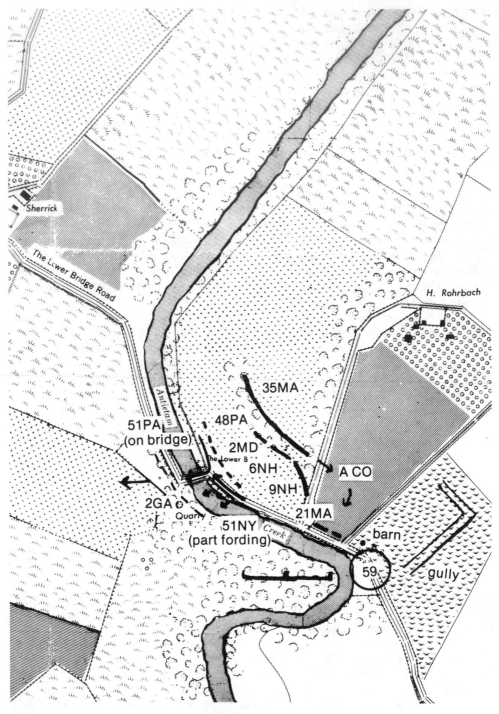

(Map 59) NOON — 1:00 P.M., SEPTEMBER 17, 1862
The 51st Pennsylvania and the 51st New York force a crossing at the Lower Bridge.

Lieutenant Hudson, in the meantime, reported to Ferrero, who directed him back to the bridge with orders for each regimental commander to form in the road along the western bank of the creek then occupy the crest above the bridge. By the time John Hudson responded, the scene at the crossing had become thoroughly muddled. The 51st Pennsylvania halted in the road at the entrance to volley at an enemy which was not there.[27] Colonel Hartranft leaned against the upper abutment, weakly fanning his hat as if to speed his men forward.

"Come on, boys," he panted, "for I can't halloo any more!"[28]

The 51st New York jammed the entire length of the bridge. Men shouted and screamed at one another as they pushed and shoved like so many runners on a big tread mill. Individuals halted to load and fire into the tree tops. They made a great deal of motion but no headway.[29] To the left rear, the 48th Pennsylvania and the 21st Massachusetts with A Company of the 35th Massachusetts continued to volley into the far bank.[30]

John Hudson got stuck in the middle of the mob. As he elbowed his way through the frantic herd, he repeatedly pleaded, "Make way for an aide." The struggle so exhausted him that when he came within hailing distance of the acting lieutenant colonel of the 51st New York, he blurted the commands to him with the request, "Will you pass it to your Colonel along the line?" The officer, a new acquaintance of Hudson's, politely, but with a hint of exasperation in his voice, retorted, "That is part of your duty, sir."

Hudson, who cooly and insubordinately apologized, continued to worm his way through the human roadblock. Finding the commanders of both lead regiments, the aide delivered his message and slowly worked his way back to Colonel Ferrero, who was still at the knolls.

The colonel appeared rather piqued. When Hudson returned from the creek, the tail end of the 51st New York still clogged the bridge while the rest of the regiment and the 51st Pennsylvania blocked the road on the western bank to volley.[31]

Dense, sulfuric clouds engulfed the entire creek bank as the frustrated Federals repeatedly fired at random at any individual Rebels who happened to pop from cover. ". . . Nothing like an uncovered rank of rebels was discernible, or indeed, existed," Hudson observed.[32] Only corpses, wounded men, and the crude lunettes composed of piled up fence rails marked the presence of any hostile force. Occasional potshots still came in from the tree tops but there was no genuine Confederate opposition left.[33]

Snavely's Ford

To the south, where the creek turned west, Fairchild's (9th, 89th, and 103rd NY) and Harland's Brigades (8th, 16th CT and 4th RI) had spent two hours on an open bluff listening to the sounds of the battle.

Lieutenant Matthew J. Graham (A Co., 9th NY) could not understand how their soldiers could stand, exposed as they were, without receiving any fire.[34] Only G Company of his regiment was deployed — among the tall trees which bordered the edge of the bluff, and which shielded them from the Rebels in the woods on the other side of the creek.[35] He recalled seeing a skirmish line approaching those woods. Muhlenberg's Battery (A, 5th U.S.) lobbed one round at them and received no reply. The line seemed to evaporate.[36]

Brigadier General Isaac Rodman (the Division commander) joined them. Together, through telescopes, they watched the 2nd Maryland and the 6th New Hampshire make two attempts on the bridge, which they could not see because the trees at the creek bend north of them obstructed their view. Graham noted how still the dead lay, with their heads downhill, toward the creek.[37]

Private David Thompson (G Co., 9th NY) still chafed at the officer he had seen checking his watch as if he had some appointment to keep. That was about two hours before. An order rippled down the line to move out. G Company fell back on the regiment to lead the advance down to the creek.[38] The Division started by the left flank down a narrow trail to the water's edge, where it filed right to the ford.[39]

The anxious soldiers plowed by twos into the waist deep cold water. Rifle shots spattered the surface about them. Lieutenant Graham immediately cocked his head toward the reports which reverberated from the bluffs in front of them. To the left front, behind a stone wall which crossed the top of a ravine which ran to the creek, he saw what appeared to be two companies of infantry (the 50th Georgia — two hundred twenty effectives). They fired a heavy but scattered volume of fire at the helpless New Yorkers, who were not allowed to return fire lest they stall the column. While Graham struggled with what he remembered as a very strong current, he lost two men to the Confederates.[40] Ahead of him G Company lost one soldier. This scared Private Thompson so much that he did not notice that he was soaking from the waist down.[41]

The 9th New York crossed quickly, still filing to the right along the creek bank, until it was directly under the shelter of a high wooded bluff east of the ravine. Screened from the Confederate regiment, the New Yorkers faced north and started grabbing at tree roots and tree trunks to pull themselves up the escarpment. Isaac Rodman, who had forded the creek afoot, was with them in the ascent.[42] While the New Yorkers strained up the slope, the 103rd and the 89th New York, respectively, began to crawl up behind them.[43]

The New Yorkers laid down on the edge of a mow field, awaiting the rest of their brigade. Lieutenant Graham suddenly noticed that they were not coming under fire. A rattling volley from the ravine caught his attention. Glancing to his left he recognized what he thought was the 4th Rhode Island bolting up the hillside. Led by a member of Burnside's staff, a theatrical fellow named Major "Happy" Tom Lyon, the New Englanders fired as they moved. They hastily drove the Confederates from the wall and secured the Division's left flank.

Lyon, who was putting on a fine "military show", had a difficult time controlling his pitching mount. Graham, while admiring the officer's bravery, thought the Confederates probably wounded the animal before skedaddling.[44]

The Lower Bridge

Meanwhile, the assault at the bridge stymied somewhat. The 28th Ohio, unknown to the New Yorkers or the Pennsylvanians, forded the creek above the bend in the Lower Bridge Road, where it turned toward Sherrick's farm, in an attempt to flank the Georgians from the north.[45] Simultaneously, a large number of impatient Yankees forded the stream at the big bend and scaled the quarry south of the 2nd Georgia.[46] The 51st Pennsylvania and the 51st New York retired below the creek bank to the water's edge to avoid any enfilading fire from the heights along the Boonsboro Pike, and to leave room for any reinforcements when, and if, they should arrive. Colonel Hartranft, who was about three hundred feet up the road, sent Lieutenant Colonel Thomas Bell south to fetch reinforcements. The few minutes his men expended taking the bridge had seemed much longer.[47]

Colonel Ferrero fumed as he bitterly watched his lead regiment, the 51st Pennsylvania, move upstream and go down under the shelter of the creek bank rather than ascend the heights.[48] Coffee fires with their tell-tale smoke were soon kindled.[49]

"Hudson," the colonel's sharp voice stung his ears, "tell your colonel to cross the bridge immediately, move along the road to the right, form in line and advance up the hill."[50]

The lieutenant delivered the order to Lieutenant Colonel Carruth, who immediately got the 35th to its feet. The regiment double quicked in column of files through the saddle between the knolls down to the creek.[51] The movement triggered a chain reaction as Colonel Fellows (9th NH) jumped to his feet, straw hat in hand, screaming, "Forward, Ninth New Hampshire! Follow the old palm-leaf!" The 6th New Hampshire and what could be found of the 2nd Maryland joined in the advance, which almost trampled itself to death when Lieutenant Colonel Carruth, in a moment of indecision, tried to front his regiment to fire across the creek. He changed his mind mid-command and unexpectedly moved his herd by the right flank onto the bridge.[52] The 51st New York had just edged Hartranft's Pennsylvanians further down the road to the right and extended its wing to the quarry ravine on the left.[53]

It looked as if each regiment's personal honor depended upon it being the first unit to cross the creek. The 21st Massachusetts ceased fire and merged with parts of the 48th Pennsylvania, the 6th New Hampshire, and A Company of the 35th Massachusetts in the impatient throng on the bridge.[54]

The tumult dislodged a very large sow and her litter. As the shooting died, she came squealing from beneath the bank south of the bridge. Bounding about and over corpses, her gluttonous piglets in close pursuit, she made straight for the 9th New Hampshire as it neared the rail fence east of the bridge. The maddened sow charged through a gap in the rails and tried to negotiate the opening between the legs of one of the advancing New Englanders. She proved to be too wide and he too low. The sow plucked the frightened soldier off his feet and carried him, screaming for his life, rearward.[55]

The 35th Massachusetts with the 21st Massachusetts hurriedly filed onto the Lower Bridge Road and formed in line in front of the two remaining regiments of their brigade (51st NY and 51st PA). They were quite excited. During the crossing a couple of men dropped snipers out of the trees near the bridge. One sharpshooter, in particular, left an indelible impression upon them. As he fell from his perch in the tree top, his one arm snagged a branch, from which he dangled before plummetting into the creek.[56] *(Map 60)*

Second Lieutenant Farquhar McCrimmon (H Co., 20th GA) and sixteen survivors of the 2nd and the 20th Georgia realized they could not withstand the onslaught of two Federal brigades and the soldiers who had succeeded in flanking them from the north. They came down the slope near the left of the 35th Massachusetts, which was moving in battle line up the hill. With hands raised or waving filthy white rags or pieces of newspaper on the ends of their ramrods, they were herded toward the

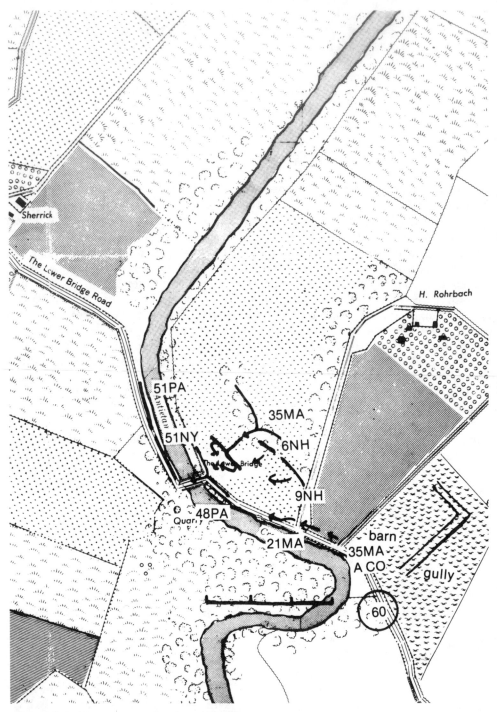

(Map 60) NOON — 1:00 P.M., SEPTEMBER 17, 1862
The rest of Nagle's and Ferrero's Brigades close on the Lower Bridge.

bridge where some of Hartranft's angry Pennsylvanians surrounded them. The frustrated Yankees started closing in on the defenseless Confederates.[57] Lieutenant Colonel Thomas Bell (51st PA), having turned about upon seeing the reinforcements arrive, rode into the seething group and calmed down his angered men. With the prisoners safely en route to the rear, Bell dismounted and cooly led his horse down the road toward the water for a drink.[58]

The 35th Massachusetts after struggling over the post and rail fence along the road wheezed and crawled part way up the hill toward the crest before changing into column and moving by the right flank with the contour of the ridge as it followed the bend in the road west.[59] Climbing over the split rail fence on the hilltop east of Otto's farm, the regiment continued to advance by the right flank into full view of Sharpsburg.[60] Richardson's Battery in Otto's stubble field opened fire immediately before limbering to escape capture. One shell burst over D Company wounding its corpulent commander, Lieutenant James Baldwin in the leg and several other places.[61] A second shell plowed through one file in the company killing David W. Cushing and Luther F. Read, who was cut in half. The line halted momentarily then started to withdraw toward the fence.[62]

At the same time a Confederate battery on the heights along the Boonsboro Pike, having noticed so many Federals moving toward the Lower Bridge, and the smoke from their fires, also fired. Lieutenant Hudson, once again upon an errand for Colonel Ferrero, sauntered across the bridge with an order for Colonel Hartranft (51st PA). The moment he cleared the eastern abutment, a shell exploded and sent fragments whizzing along the steep hill in front of him. A second burst along the creek bank to the right, then a third blew up close to the trail followed by the first projectile.[63] A fragment struck a tree rousting out Lieutenant Green (I Co., 9th NH), who was calmly leaning against its southern side.

The severely quaking lieutenant picked himself up and pointed excitedly to the spot three feet off the ground where the fragment impacted. "Mein Gott, boys, see vere I haf been sitting!"[64]

The barrage caught Lieutenant Colonel Thomas Bell (51st PA) about fifty yards from the bridge. He slapped Private Hugh Brown (I Co.) on the shoulder as he passed him on the road.

"We did it for them this time, my boy!" he exclaimed.

Barely two steps away, a ball from the second case shot glanced off his left temple. The impact whirled him around in a circle and slammed him full length onto his side. The men rushed to his aid as he rolled down the creek bank into the regiment's stacked muskets.[65]

Sergeant Edwin Bennett (D Co.) dashed to the creek bed with three other men. Pulling the colonel to his feet, they asked him if he was hurt badly.

The Colonel, the left side of his face quickly reddening with blood, put his left hand to his temple and calmly replied, "I don't think it is dangerous." He paused momentarily. "Boys, never say die."

His soldiers gently lowered him onto a blanket and, grabbing each corner, they struggled to carry him to safety.[66]

A regiment (probably the 48th Pennsylvania) started to scale the steep bank at the bridge entrance while Hudson strode north along the road, searching for Colonel Hartranft (51st PA). A considerable distance upstream, he found the left wing of the 51st Pennsylvania sprawled out along the creek bottom. Calling down to some enlisted men, he asked, "Where is your Colonel?"

"He passed out that way."

Hudson strained to locate the colonel in the direction the soldier pointed, but not seeing him, he shouted, "Where is your Lieutenant Colonel?"

"There he is, sir. Wounded."

Looking back, the lieutenant's eyes fell upon a stretcher being borne toward the abutment. The officer on board stared fixedly in the lieutenant's direction as he was carried south. His dimming glance, which locked upon Hudson, hurt the aide deeply. Hudson stared at the ugly blue bruise on the lieutenant colonel's left temple. Bell, a newly made friend, was dying.

"There is the Colonel," one of the Pennsylvanians hallooed.

Hudson abruptly turned about, met the colonel in the road, and asked why he had not advanced to support the 35th Massachusetts.

"I've no ammunition," Hartranft snapped.

The two frustrated officers stood there at a loss for words. They both had to answer to the moody Ferrero.

Hudson eventually ventured, "Shall I tell the Colonel so?"

"If you please."

The aide wheeled about and jogged toward the bridge.

"Lieutenant! Lieutenant!"

He impatiently turned around at the entrance to the bridge. He saw three men from his old company (D Co., 35th MA) struggling with a very heavy man on a blanket. A quick glance at the hat and the way the men tried to tenderly treat the officer told him that the fellow was Lieutenant James Baldwin of his company.

"You must excuse me," he called out, "I've something to do across the bridge." With that Hudson hurried off to deliver his message to Ferrero, who was still on the knolls.[67]

Lieutenant Colonel Joshua K. Sigfried (48th PA), upon crossing the bridge with the 21st Massachusetts, immediately detached Captain James Wren and his B Company as skirmishers with orders to cover the quarry and the ridge to the right. The plucky captain and a couple of his people detoured slightly to check on the Confederate they thought he had shot. He found a dead man lying beside the tree he had aimed at.

One of the men chimed in, "Captain, that is your man."

The thought that he had killed a soldier in combat thrilled him. As his men fanned out and began to scramble up the hill, Wren passed a tree with two cannon balls in it. The idea occurred to him that he ought to have it cut down and sent home, but he had other work to do, so he continued after his men.

As the ground widened, Wren sent back for more skirmishers. General Sturgis, who was then on the western bank, approved the request and sent E Company (Captain William Winlack) to his assist. As they neared the crest and the skirmish line widened further, he asked for more help. Sturgis — over Nagle's objections — dispatched Captain Oliver Bosbyshell with G Company.

At this point Wren sent a runner back for Captain Daniel Kaufman, the acting major to take command. Kaufman refused to come, which left Wren in control of three companies.

The skirmishers scrounged the hillside for souvenirs as they proceeded.[68] They discovered the remains of the 2nd Georgia in a slight entrenchment near the top of the hill. Over forty of the Rebels had fallen as a unit in near perfect formation. Lieutenant Colonel William Holmes lay five paces behind his color guard, riddled with bullets.[69]

Soldiers set upon the colonel's beautiful dress uniform like vultures. One man stole Holmes' expensive gold watch. Others cut the gilt buttons off his tunic. Captain Joseph A. Gilmour (H Co.) claimed a shoulder knot. Two men pulled the polished boots off his feet then callously flipped a coin to see which would have the complete pair.

Corporal Dye Davis (B Co.) happened upon a dead Confederate whose haversack bulged with Johnny cakes. Dye coldly jerked the haversack free and poured its contents into his own sack. He started munching on a chunk of the captured corn-bread as the company moved out. A friend reprimanded him, commenting that he could not eat anything which came from a corpse.

"Damn 'em, man," Dye retorted through a mouthful of bread, "The Johnny is dead but the Johnny cakes is no dead." He kept eating away.[70]

While the small 21st Massachusetts went northwest up the slope to connect with the left of the 35th Massachusetts, a couple of men in K Company fell out to examine some Confederate corpses. Harry Aldrich rolled over a dead Confederate sergeant to rifle the man's pockets. He helped himself to the Reb's wallet and the few five dollar gold pieces he found in it. His comrade, James Stone, stumbled across another dead Rebel near the crest of the hill. The fellow had bled to death while staring at a photograph. Stone pried it from his stiffening fingers. The Reb would see his children no more.[71]

The rest of Nagle's worn out brigade fell in on the western side of the Lower Bridge Road to make room for the Division's artillery, which was preparing to go into the creek valley. In the 9th New Hampshire, Wesley Simonds (I Co.) wandered about shod on one foot and bare on the other. When a bullet carried away the sole of one shoe earlier in the day, Simonds solved the problem by removing the upper shoe. Now, as the regiment maneuvered into line of battle, his comrades heard him repeatedly sing songing, "One shoe off and one shoe on, my son, John."[72]

Sergeant Henry E. Hubbard (I Co., 9th NH) kept griping about his near brush with death. As they took cover behind the knoll the stray ball which passed through and killed George D. Fox (I Co.) struck Hubbard square in his midsection and winded him. When Captain John W. Babbitt (I Co.) rushed over to inspect his "death wound", the sergeant painfully gasped, "I guess I'm a goner this time, Cap."

The officer carefully rolled Hubbard over and discovered that the bullet had mortally wounded the sergeant's cartridge box but had not penetrated the man himself.

As the regiment formed in the road on the west side of the creek, Hubbard kept growling about how it was "a mighty mean piece of business to pound a man most to death and not draw a drop of blood to show for it!"[73]

The Middle Bridge

Lieutenant Thomas Evans (D and E Cos., 1st Bttn., 12th U.S.) stayed with his men by the Middle Bridge while four batteries of the 2nd U.S. Horse Artillery swung into action on the ridge about five hundred yards from the creek. Captain John C. Tidball's gunners (A Btty.) with Lieutenant Peter C. Hains (M Batty.) roared away from the northern side of the Boonsboro Pike while Captain Horatio Gibson's batteries (C and G) opened upon the Confederates along the pike near Sharpsburg.[74] The ground literally heaved and rolled as the artillerists hurled shell after shell toward the village. Simultaneously, a squadron of the 4th Pennsylvania Cavalry conducted an insane charge across the Middle Bridge toward the valley beyond the artillery pieces. Several rounds struck the column about one hundred yards west of the span, killing its colonel, Benjamin Childs, and knocking down the better part of the squadron. The cavalrymen behind it hastily dismounted. Shaken troopers unsnapped their carbines and, using their horses for cover, slowly edged their way toward the ravine in front of the batteries.[75] While the rest of the 4th Pennsylvania filed into the field to the right of the Pike, the remainder of Brigadier General Alfred Pleasonton's Cavalry Division wheeled left and right and filled the low ground along the creek.

Within fifteen minutes, the Pennsylvanians' skirmishers came under what they considered severe riflery from three of Nathan Evans' South Carolina regiments (18th, 22nd, and 23rd SC), which commanded a Virginia rail fence between two plowed fields on a ridge seven hundred fifty yards from Tidball's and Hains' Batteries. The cavalrymen held their ground and spread out in an extended arch which conformed to the huge swale from Newcomer's house almost to the creek bank.[76]

Minutes after a shell fragment knocked him down, Lieutenant Warren Pursley (G Co., 18th SC) regained his senses. Soldiers streamed past him. He could not walk. Every breath hurt him severely. "Bullets pouring about like hail. Shells bursting round and over me. Throwing dirt on me," he recalled. "Looked impossible to escape." He lay there waiting to die.[77]

Captain Tidball (A, 2nd U.S.) began complaining to the Regulars across the creek that he needed more support. He would have to wait.[78] V Corps commander, Major General Fitz Porter, apparently had made it clear to his divisional officers that he needed them where they were. They had to keep the Middle Bridge from falling into Confederate hands.[79] *(Map 61)*

Captain Charles W. Squires (1st Co., Washington Artillery — LA), whose battery was on the first ridge immediately west of the Federal horse artillery, was taking fire from three directions — north, east, and south. The position seemed untenable. He felt isolated and hopeless. Below the ridge, west of his guns, Garnett's pitiful excuse for a brigade huddled, not daring to rise into the Federals' line of sight. The Yankees were shelling the position very severely.

To worsen matters, Robert E. Lee had insisted on hanging around his position for what seemed, to the captain, like the better part of the day. The commanding general was piqued while he surveyed the front east and north of the Middle Bridge.

"Captain, our men are acting badly," Lee grumbled.

Taken aback, Captain Squires dramatically pointed toward his sweating artillerists, who were working their pieces superbly.

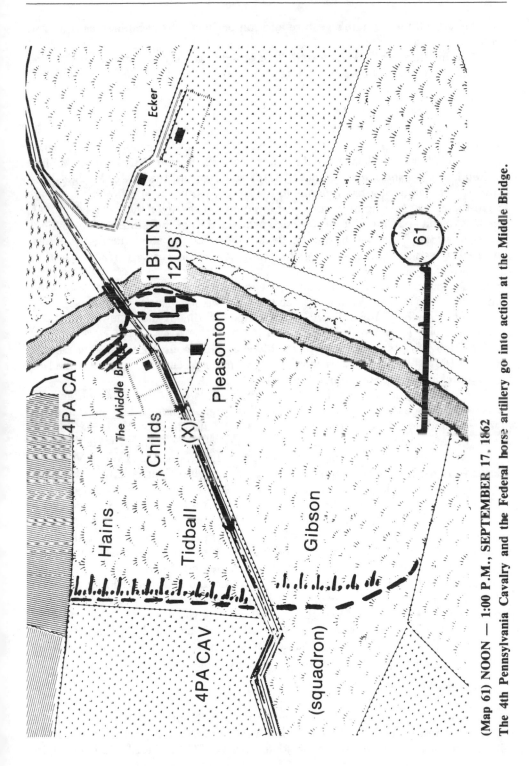

(Map 61) NOON — 1:00 P.M., SEPTEMBER 17, 1862

The 4th Pennsylvania Cavalry and the Federal horse artillery go into action at the Middle Bridge.

Lee noticed the Captain's gesture and somberly chastised Squires as if he had been insubordinate.

"The infantry, sir," Lee retorted, "are straggling, they are straggling."[80]

Shortly thereafter, the commanding general mounted and rushed toward his left wing.

The Lower Bridge

While that single squadron of the 4th Pennsylvania Cavalry cautiously "protected" Pleasonton's horse artillery, Captain James Wren (B, E, and G Cos., 48th PA) had worked his skirmishers seven hundred yards southwest of the Lower Bridge. They came across smoldering hay mounds in the mow field bordering the dense woods above the creek. A sickening, gut churning odor drifted over the Pennsylvanians. The legs of charred Confederate wounded protruded from the still smoking remains of one haystack. They had burned to death when Federal shells torched the hay. The Pennsylvanians gingerly dragged the unrecognizable corpses clear of the fires and continued south.

In so doing, Captain Wren captured two Confederate officers and took their swords as prizes of war. Wren inspected the weapons for inscriptions. He was quite lucky. The one bore the following inscription on the blade: "Lieutenant J. W. Shoemaker, 4th Regiment P.R.V.C., 33rd P.V.".

The Reb officer said he captured the blade at the Second Manassas. The captain later boasted in his diary, ". . . recaptured by Captain Wrens skirmis line at the Battle of Antetam Bridg September 17th 1862."[81]

The jubilant James Wren defied incoming rounds from Eshelman's Maryland Battery, which opened on Fairchild's assembling brigade from the high ground about eighteen hundred yards west, and connected with the 9th New York.[82] He found the regiment lying below the crest of the highest of three terraces which marked the ascent from the creek. Some soldiers on the right flank asked Wren who commanded his regiment before hunting out their colonel, Edgar A. Kimball.[83]

The entire brigade (89th NY, 103rd NY, and 9th NY, south to north, respectively) stretched from the haystacks to the wooded bluff above the bend in the creek. Their officers, who dragged their mounts up the hill, remounted on the narrow steppe (about ten feet wide) behind the line. Well below the line of sight of the Confederate gunners, they watched the round balls and canister ricochet off the crest at the heads of their prone men and crash into the tree tops behind them.[84]

Lieutenant Colonel Kimball rode over to Wren and commanded him to report back to General Sturgis with word that Rodman's Division had forded the creek two miles below the Lower Bridge and that all was well.

James Wren's three companies closed ranks while he called in his skirmishers. Turning by the right flank, they double quicked back toward the bridge, leaving Rodman's Division without any security on that wing.[85]

The 40 Acre Cornfield

Colonel H. L. Benning with the two hundred remaining men from the 2nd and the 20th Georgia made a frantic dash southwest toward a huge forty acre cornfield which dominated a hillside above the southern end of Otto's lane.[86] As his soldiers raced for their lives, Richardson's Battery, having loosed a parting barrage at the 35th Massachusetts, limbered up and rumbled north toward the Lower Bridge Road. Simultaneously, the 50th Georgia, less one hundred twenty-five of its two hundred twenty men, and the battalion from the 11th Georgia, double quicked from the stone wall at the top of the ravine near Snavely's Ford.[87] The four wheezing regiments stumbled into each other in the western part of the cornfield. The harried Benning quickly tried to deploy his defenseless men behind the stone wall which bordered the western side of the field. They would defend the right wing of the Army of Northern Virginia with their clubbed muskets. Considering they had no ammunition, there remained no other choice in their minds.

Colonel Benning did not have long to wait. Within minutes, Brigadier General Robert Toombs (commanding David R. Jones' Division) rushed the rest of Benning's Brigade (15th and 17th GA, and 5 cos. 11th GA) to his assist.

A shell screamed over the top of the 15th Georgia, as it approached Sherrick's cornfield, and fired a barn to the rear of the regiment. The small unit quickly dove for cover in the swale along the western side of the corn. A second shell, which exploded over the colors, tore one man to pieces, shredded the color bearer to a bloody pulp, and mortally wounded a third soldier. Scattered shots from the 9th New York clattered through the corn. One struck H. B. Seals (K Co.) in the skull and killed him.

The exhausted Confederates, having spent the bulk of their day eating dust while protecting the Army's supply wagons from marauding Federal cavalry, collapsed in formation along the stone wall. Toombs retired Benning's people toward the Harper's Ferry Road where they could replenish their ammunition and fill their growling stomachs. Henry Benning settled down with his grimy replacements to face two fresh Federal Brigades. It was about 1:00 P.M.[88] *(Map 62)*

Having taken the Lower Bridge, the IX Corps wasted hours to assemble and resupply in preparation for a counterattack which the Confederates were in no shape to conduct. Ironically, the Confederates in that sector braced themselves for an assault which never seemed to materialize.

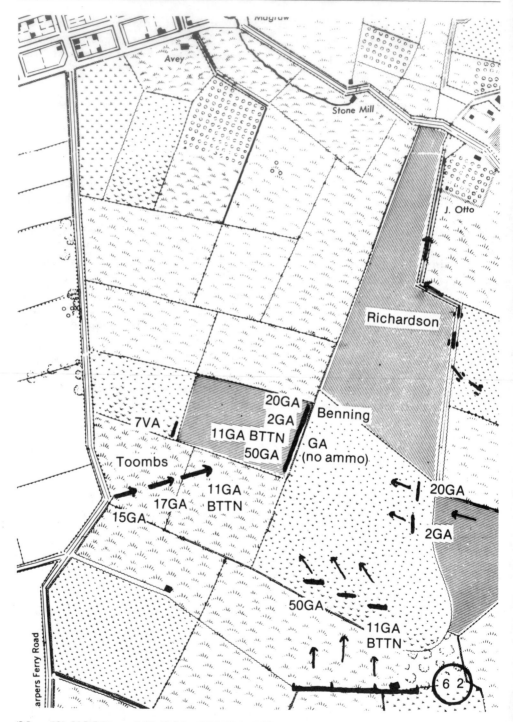

(Map 62) NOON — 1:00 P.M., SEPTEMBER 17, 1862
Benning's Georgians regroup on the western edge of the 40 acre cornfield.

CHAPTER FIFTEEN

"Why art thou so far from helping me . . ."

1:00 P.M. - 4:20 P.M.

The Harper's Ferry Road

Private Alexander Hunter (A Co., 17th VA) and the rest of Kemper's Brigade (less the 7th Virginia which was detached to the southeast edge of a cornfield several hundred yards to the right) had been on their stomachs since the first cannonading erupted down at the Lower Bridge that morning.[1] The barrage began with a horrendous blast while batteries on both sides of the creek unleashed at each other in unison. Hunter listened apprehensively as the batteries continued to fire by files. He stared at the sun as it inched its way west in the autumn sky. It glowed an ominous crimson red and appeared gloomy as it glared at him through the dense sulfuric clouds of burned powder which encircled him. Moments later, Federal "Hotchkiss shells" whined over their line, and exploded in the vicinity of the Harper's Ferry Road. The incoming rounds, with their particularly ear shattering scream, forced the Confederates to cringe behind the fence rails and get as low as possible to the ground.

As the hours wore on toward noon, the artillery fire subsided and a fierce musketry echoed westward from Benning's Georgians. Before an hour passed, those stalwarts came stampeding from the huge cornfield southeast of Kemper's Brigade toward the security of Sharpsburg. They seemed inordinately cheerful as they passed rearward.[2]

The Lower Bridge

One mile to the east, Captain James Wren (B Co., 48th PA) and his withdrawing Pennsylvanians "drew fire" from their brigadier, James Nagle. The general verbally ripped into Wren for pulling back without orders. The impudent captain snapped at Nagle, "I had not don that" and left the general fuming as he trotted down to the bridge where Brigadier General Samuel Sturgis was deploying his brigades. Captain Wren reported, as ordered, to his Division commander, who loudly thanked him and praised the Pennsylvanians for their well established skirmish line.

Nagle, who overheard Sturgis, smoldered a while before approaching Wren. He apologized, saying that he erroneously believed that the captain had retired from the field without orders and that Wren, considering how far he had gone beyond the main body of troops, had to rely upon his personal judgement. James Wren stubbornly and self-righteously accepted his superior's apology when he responded that he understood the general's behavior even if it was very impudent.[3]

Colonel Edward Ferrero hastily deployed the remainder of his tired brigade. The 21st Massachusetts went into line to the left of the still exposed 35th Massachusetts while the 51st New York and the 51st Pennsylvania continued the line almost to the woods

BRIGADIER GENERAL JAMES KEMPER, brigade commander, ANV

His small brigade stalled a considerably larger Federal force until Robert Toombs and A. P. Hill brought up reinforcements which saved the Confederate right wing. *(William E. Strong Collection, Duke U.)*

on the heights above the bridge.[4] The men pilfered the corpses' cartridge boxes and grimly laid down just below the crest. They were determined to put up a good show should the Confederates try to push them across the creek. Their brigadier and his loyal aide, Lieutenant John Hudson, hurried along the hilltop, attempting to organize their lines and to place the two batteries which they had at their disposal.[5]

Captain Joseph C. Clark's Battery (E, 4th U.S.) rumbled along the slope to the steppe behind Fairchild's New Yorkers, who had finally shifted their line to the front of the mow field southwest of the quarry. The gunners went into park on the second terrace behind the line then manually shouldered their pieces onto the slope of the ridge between the 103rd and the 9th New York regiments. The artillerymen tried to open fire, but every time they stood up the Confederate Battery (probably Brown's) pinpointed their location and drove them to cover.[6]

Lieutenant Matthew Graham (A Co., 9th NY) could not believe the Confederates' unerring accuracy. The air sizzled constantly with shrapnel and railroad iron. Casualties mounted. One man crawled away with nine punctures in his right arm. A round ball slammed into the ground in front of one of the ten pound rifled Parrotts with a loud thud, bounded over the piece and the artillery park on the lower level behind it, and crashed through the woods. Lieutenant Graham rolled onto his back and studied the severed tree tops. They teetered uncertainly before toppling toward the creek. The slow, unincumbered solid shots fascinated him as they leaped and skittered across the fields at leisurely paces which masked their death dealing potential.[7] Propped on his elbows, his eyes transfixed upon the bursting shells overhead, the lieutenant contemplated inching a finger into the air to see how high he could get it before losing it to the incoming rounds.[8]

Having posted Clark's Battery (E, 4th U.S.) on the left with Fairchild's Brigade and a section of Captain George W. Durrell's Battery (D, PA Lgt.) on the knoll immediately east of the Otto farm house, Lieutenant Hudson began to pull back the 35th Massachusetts from its north-south position to the creek side of the ridge, facing south.[9] Not all the men retired with the line. Rather than get mistaken for Confederates by the troops mustering along the creek, they let the colonel lead those who would follow to allegedly "safer" ground.[10] A Federal battery on Rohrbach's farm detected the regiment's movement and hurled a shell into the hillside behind the line. Dirt clods pelted the men from the rear.

Lieutenant Colonel Carruth frantically waved his hat. Fearing the batteries could not recognize him he quietly told his color sergeant, "Unfurl those colors, quick and wave them." His regiment had only the dark blue national standard and the Massachusetts State flag. He apparently did not want to be mistaken for an enemy by either side. "Steady! Not too high," he cautioned.[11] The Yankee artillerists let the shaken New Englanders crawl over the rail fence along the crest and laid down in the dried grass.[12]

Lieutenant Hudson wasted "quite a time" with Lieutenant Colonel Carruth, as commanded by Colonel Ferrero.[13] Sporadic projectiles continued to harass the line. One shell, coming in from the right on the ridge near Sharpsburg, skimmed along the top of the hill and ripped the knapsack from the back of one man, carrying it to the creek below. The soldiers laughed as the fellow's belongings sailed through the trees along the bank.

To the far right (northwest) they had a clear view of the haystack dotted hills which rolled from Sherrick's farm house up to the village. The firing from the right wing and the center of the line seemed to have lost all of its earlier ferocity as the field for the second time that day yielded to sniper fire and harassing artillery shots. To the south a thin line of skirmishers advanced into the fields surrounding Otto's huge cornfield.[14]

Lieutenant Colonel Edgar Kimball (9th NY) sent I Company into the open ground north of the big cornfield. The fighting and shouting rose to a fevered crescendo within moments, then gradually died away as the New Yorkers drove Kemper's skirmishers back to the stone wall three hundred yards west of Otto's farm lane.[15]

The Harper's Ferry Road

The relative silence all along the line from the Lower Bridge to the Middle Bridge lulled weary soldiers on both sides to sleep. Alexander Hunter (A Co., 17th VA) had lain for hours behind the new post and rail fence waiting for the Yankees to attack their position on the far right of the Confederate line. His legs were cramping from their constrained position. A few shells screamed horribly over the brigade line followed by a smattering of small arms fire from the 9th New York's skirmishers as Brown's Battery thundered in reply.[16] By then the men had grown nominally accustomed to the ear ringing pitch of the Federals' Hotchkiss shells.[17]

The man next to Hunter tuned in on the occasional rifle shots which zinged overhead. His mind drifted to prewar times when he had pursued musical studies.

"I caught the pitch of that minnie that just passed," he absently drawled to Hunter. "It was a swell from E flat to F, and as it retrograded in the distance receded to a D — a pretty fair change."[18]

Hunter listlessly rested in the grass and waited for an enemy who never seemed to attack.

The Lower Bridge

The Federal regiments down by the creek acted like vanquished troops. The stubborn Georgians, besides holding an entire Corps at bay, inflicting severe casualties, and causing frustrated Yankees to needlessly expend an inordinate amount of ammunition upon inferior numbers, had scored an emotional victory.

Dr. Theodore Dimon, the Acting Surgeon of the 2nd Maryland, remorsefully traced the regiment's path from the pole barn on the eastern side of the creek to the bridge. He found the adjutant, Thomas Matthews, slightly wounded at the head of a column of dead in the road near the bridge's mouth. Nearby, he discovered Captain Malcom Wilson's (F Co.) mutilated corpse. A twelve pound round shot struck his dear friend in the forehead and blew away the entire top of his head. Further on he came upon the 2nd Maryland resting along Rohrbach's lane where it ran into the Lower Bridge Road. The Georgians took out sixty-seven of the regiment's one hundred eighty-seven effectives.[19]

Across the creek on the ridge to the far right, ennui overtook the 35th Massachusetts. Many men slumbered undisturbed by the occasional artillery shells. Others gnawed on aged hard crackers. The line hummed with the idle chatter of a bored mob. Here and there groups of soldiers broke ranks to amble down to the Antietam for water.[20]

Lieutenant John Hudson, who wearied of the inactivity with his regiment, asked leave of Lieutenant Colonel Carruth (35th MA) on the pretense of reporting the regiment's activities to their brigade commander, Colonel Ferrero. The lieutenant took half an hour to "find" the colonel, during which time he scoured both the pole barn, near the creek bend, and the Rohrbach farm house in a luckless attempt to locate the corpulent Lieutenant Baldwin (D Co., 35th MA).

Ferrero dismissed Hudson with his typical "Very well." The lieutenant strolled to the bridge and hoisted himself onto the northern parapet next to Colonel Clark (21st MA). The two sat there, facing downstream, their legs dangling idly like school boys gone fishing, and mindlessly talked with the cluster of staff officers who gathered around the mouth of the bridge.

Moments later, a shell exploded overhead, sending hot fragments about them. A second round rapidly followed the first. Hudson watched it skim the slope to the right as he dove for cover behind the northern abutment of the bridge. The round bored through the middle of a slow moving gray horse, leaving an ugly hole in him. The mortally wounded animal staggered to the road, rolled down the embankment into the Antietam, and drowned.

Hudson, following the shouted advice of the bulk of Ferrero's staff, darted into the road then cut a sharp left and ducked behind the southern parapet of the bridge. The Confederates vigorously shelled the Lower Bridge from the heights along the Boonsboro Pike, effectively keeping ammunition wagons and troops from approaching from either east or west. Unknown to them, they trapped about fifty Federal soldiers — privates, servants, aides, a regimental commander, and Colonel Ferrero (a brigade commander) at the crossing site. While shells burst in the tree tops all around them the Federals lounged about munching on whatever rations they had with them.[21] Hudson, who later brushed aside the tense situation as nonsense, had no idea how seriously the Confederates were pounding the entire Federal position along the ridge.[22]

By 3:00 P.M., twenty-seven Federal regiments had crossed the Antietam and aligned themselves for a grand assault upon the tenuously held Confederate position along the ridge east of Sharpsburg. Colonel Hugh Ewing's three Ohio regiments (12th, 30th, and 23rd) forded the creek, near the bend where Ferrero had wanted to cross. The water, particularly for the shorter men, proved somewhat hazardous.

The very small Private Samuel Compton (F Co., 12th OH) nearly drowned as he plunged into what was for him armpit deep water. He wisely held his haversack and cartridge box above his head to keep them dry. The regiment went into line on the lowest terrace behind Harrison Fairchild's New Yorkers. Colonel Edward Harland's green brigade (8th, 11th, and 16th CT, and 4th RI) lay below the crest of the hill to the Ohions' left front. The 9th New Hampshire, 48th Pennsylvania, and the 6th New Hampshire were to the 23rd Ohio's immediate right in prone column of regiments. Ferrero's Brigade (the 51st PA, 51st NY, 21st and 35th MA) carried the line from the woods above the bridge to the Lower Bridge Road where it turned due west.

Colonel Thomas Welsh maneuvered his men (45th and 100th PA, 46th NY, and the 8th MI) into position from the hill behind Otto's farm house, south across the front of Ferrero's, people who had pulled back below the crest.[23] As his soldiers trampled over the 35th Massachusetts, which was on the hillside parallel to the Lower Bridge Road, a number of men tried to remain with the New Englanders, but their officers goaded them ahead.[24]

On the left, the 45th Pennsylvania clawed its way up the bluff to replace the 51st Pennsylvania, whose ammunition was exhausted. The men were still chaffing and cursing the Confederates for the death of Colonel Bell (51st PA) and the severe wounding of Captain William J. Bolton (A Co.), who was critically injured by a minie ball which struck him in the face. (The ball penetrated his right cheek, passed down his throat and lodged in his right shoulder.)

Colonel Hartranft (51st PA) stayed with the colors while he issued the command for the regiment to retire. It was each man for himself. In pairs or singly — as each man chose — the soldiers back slid, belly slid, ran or tumbled down the precipice to the creek bottom. The evacuation took twenty minutes. When it was over, only seventeen men and one line officer, Captain George W. Bisbane (I Co.), reported to the colonel and the color guard for duty.

A shell fragment snapped off Captain Bisbane's sword six inches below the hilt as he rose to descend the slope. (He kept the sword as a momento of the occasion and used it for all official formations for some time after the battle.) As the day progressed, more men straggled in to the regiment until there were enough present for a respectable picket force.[25]

The 100th Pennsylvania (Welsh's BG) fanned out into the swale west of Otto's farm house in a beautiful skirmish formation while across the road to the north, the 79th New York (Christ's BG) spread out to protect the three remaining regiments of its brigade (17th MI, 28th MA, and 50th PA) which had just forded the creek and taken cover in the trees along the bank.[26]

The Middle Bridge

Robert E. Lee strengthened his terribly thin line by shuffling his artillery from the West Woods area to the Boonsboro Pike. He had already sent for Lieutenant Thompson Brown's section (Parker's Virginia Battery) and a section from Jordan's Battery with orders to report to the crest east of the Pike in support of Moody's section and Garden's and Squires' Batteries which were heatedly throwing shells, round shot, and canister into the Federals from the Middle to the Lower Bridge.[27]

In the 19th Virginia on the far right of Garnett's Brigade, near the Lower Bridge Road, Lieutenant Nathaniel Wood stared at the well drilled Federals as they fell in along the creek to prepare for a general advance. Along his position, Confederate officers sheathed their swords and picked up muskets.[28] They needed every man they could muster.

The Lower Bridge

Private David Thompson (G Co., 9th NY) gazed wearily across the undulating farm land between the regiment and Kemper's skirmishers whom I Company were driving back to a breast high stone wall, which ran south to north from the corner of a very big cornfield. He hoped that there was no truth to the rumor they were going to attack the battery (J. S. Brown's Virginia Battery) which had plagued them for two hours.[29]

"Get up the Ninth!"

Lieutenant Matthew Graham (A Co., 9th NY) quickly rolled from his back to one side and gawked incredulously at Lieutenant Colonel Kimball. He thought the man had lost his senses. They would not last one minute upright under the shells which screamed overhead. The colonel seemed to lock his glare upon the astonished lieutenant as he repeated the command, "Get up the Ninth!"[30]

Most of the New Yorkers, in their distinctive dark purple uniforms and fezzes, quickly stripped off their knapsacks and rose to their feet. With a shout, the regiment dashed forward — into the post and rail fence along its front, which destroyed its formation entirely.[31] An explosive round splintered the fence on the right of the line as A Company scrambled over it.[32] The dash toward Otto's lane caught the flank of the Confederate skirmishers, which the 9th New Hampshire flushed across its front from the right.[33]

The Harper's Ferry Road

Five hundred yards away, from the southeastern corner of a small cornfield, the 7th Virginia (Kemper's Brigade) watched the fence and their brigade's sharpshooters disrupt the 9th New York's gallant charge. The small regiment fell back to the western side of the cornfield then filed into the drainage ditch which bordered the eastern side of the Harper's Ferry Road. (It took cover about three hundred fifty yards south of its former position.) The soldiers cautiously propped their muskets on the dilapidated board fence to wait out the new attack.[34]

Captain Philip S. Ashby, their commander, prowled behind the line, with his sword drawn.

"Men, we are to hold this position at all hazards. Not a man leave his place," the Mexican War veteran warned. "If need be, we will die together in this road."

The veterans peered uncertainly across the stubble field into the thin belt of corn behind their brigade line.[35] *(Map 63)*

The Lower Bridge — The Harper's Ferry Road

The impetuous New Yorkers inadvertently dragged the rest of their brigade and Harland's untried Brigade with them. The 103rd New York with the 89th New York to its left, continued the line to the left of the 9th New York. The 16th Connecticut (Harland's BG) advanced into the forty acre cornfield to its front with the 4th Rhode Island on its left. An aide sent the 8th Connecticut into the meadow to the left rear of the 89th New York while the 11th Connecticut remained along the edge of the woods above the creek.[36]

Simultaneously, on the far right of the line, Welsh's and Christ's Brigades advanced very slowly over the rolling farm land north and south of the Lower Bridge Road toward the high ground around Sharpsburg. Lieutenant Nathaniel Wood (19th VA) watched the Confederate artillery gouge holes in the two Federal brigades as they pushed toward the orchard and the stone mill several hundred yards down the ridge from his men. The Federals wavered, regrouped, and pushed on despite their losses. They were not going to be stopped. Garnett's Confederates readied themselves for an assault they could not repel.[37]

Private John Dooley (D Co., 1st VA) distinctly saw the Yankee battle flags bobbing above the crests of the ridges east of his regiment. The numerically superior Federals, whom he estimated to be around two thousand strong, seemed to crouch in the swales between the lines.[38] Time ceased as the Confederates continued to wait.

"Quick, men, back to your posts!" an officer shouted.

Alexander Hunter (A Co., 17th VA) and the rest of his forty-six man regiment instantaneously forgot about stamping the cramps out of their legs and dove for cover behind the post and rail fence as the Federals advanced Clark's (E, 4th U.S.) and Durrell's (D, PA Lgt.) Batteries into line east of Otto's lane.[39]

The two batteries mercilessly pounded Kemper's position and seemed to pay particular attention to J. S. Brown's gunners to the right of the brigade, who, unknown to Hunter, the Yankees could not see. A shell struck ten feet in front of the 17th Virginia, leaving Private Appich (E Co.) a shuddering lump of mutilated flesh. A second Hotchkiss round struck the prone line and two more men were carried off. The soldiers kept their faces in the grass as the short falling rounds threw a great deal of dirt over them.[40]

A little further to the north an enthusiastic officer on Kemper's staff named Beckham, raised himself up in the stirrups as Brown's artillerists shot back its first round in reply. Waving his hat madly about his head, he lustily cheered until a shot threw him from his horse and mangled his foot. Kemper and his staff trailed after the still yelling officer as a stretcher crew evacuated him toward Sharpsburg.[41]

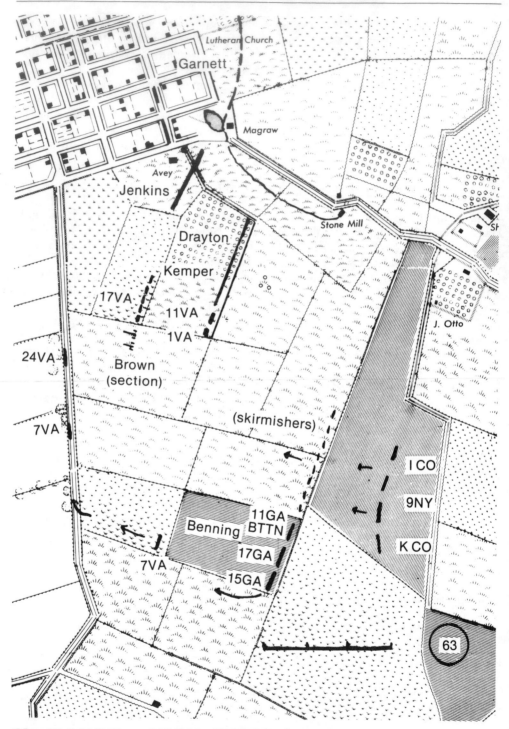

(Map 63) 1:00 P.M. — 4:20 P.M., SEPTEMBER 17, 1862
The 9th New York pressures the Confederate right.

The "splendid" Federal charge lurched to a halt east of Otto's farm lane to reform their lines while Clark's (E, 4th U.S.) and Durrell's (D, PA Lgt) ten rifled Parrotts provided cover fire. Brown's Battery, to the front, and Confederate skirmishers in the tall corn to the left of Fairchild's Brigade started taking out men by the squads as the New Yorkers struggled over the split rail fence along the farm lane. A portion of the 9th New York raced downhill toward a gap in the fence, cutting off the 9th New Hampshire (Nagle's BG), which had just left wheeled to pass through the same spot. A round ball struck the fence as the New Yorkers neared it, shearing off one of the support rails at a corner of the fence. The weathered wooden stake whirled inches above the New Yorkers, forcing them to duck low as they charged for the plowed field west of the lane.[42]

Private David Thompson (G Co.) threw himself prone on the freshly turned dirt west of the lane and waited for the rest of the command to claw its way through the furrows for reprieve from the savage Confederate plunging fire.[43] The panting Lieutenant Graham (A Co.) glanced at the regimental line, which had narrowed perceptibly with each rush. Men had fallen at every step. As he scanned the blue and purple dotted fields behind him his mind wandered. The dead and the wounded, who for the most part, lay head forward toward the enemy, reminded him of a field of flattened corn waiting to be plowed under for fertilizer.[44] David Thompson (G Co.) entertained no thoughts of being turned under. He was very uncomfortable. Moving to the front was suicide. Running away was cowardly. He hated being where he was, yet he stayed put, trying to forget the sickening sound of round balls cracking skulls.[45]

The regiment had no place to go but forward. As Brown's Battery fired, the New Yorkers rushed a few hundred feet ahead to another undulation in the plowed field and once again hurled themselves into the dirt.[46] Lieutenant Colonel Kimball paced up and down his badly mauled line euphorically clapping his hands or rubbing his palms together. "Bully Ninth! Bully Ninth!" he exclaimed. "Boys, I'm proud of you! every one of you!"

"Get down, Colonel!" and "Don't expose yourself that way!" the men repeatedly called out.

"Don't mind me, boys, I'm all right!" he called back.

Someone protested, "Wait till we're ready to advance!"

Kimball ignored him. "If you want a safe place stick close to me," he bragged. "Bully Ninth!"[47]

Brown's battery depressed its barrels and opened fire with round ball and canister upon Fairchild's Brigade. Private David Thompson (G Co., 9th NY) glanced over his shoulder and saw a mounted officer hunched low over his horse's neck galloping diagonally across the field toward the creek. He wished he were with him.

A rolled overcoat with the shoulder straps attached hurtled past the private's head. Snapping his eyes to the front, he saw a boy lying face down, motionless in the dirt. The canister shot plowed a groove from front to back in his skull and ripped his great coat from his shoulders. Nearby a man vehemently cursed a dying comrade for rolling onto him when he was hit.[48] Lieutenant Graham's (A Co.) harried mind meandered back to school days as he helplessly listened to the hail of canister fracture arms, legs, and skulls all around him. He bitterly recalled Jean Lannes' (one of Napoleon's marshalls) comments about Austerlitz, "I could hear the bones crash in my division like glass in a hailstorm."[49]

The Harper's Ferry Road

The artillery duel ended abruptly when the Yankee gunners dismounted one of Brown's pieces and slaughtered all of the mounts of another gun. The remaining artillerists hitched up and hauled out for safer ground.[50] As they thundered toward the west they shouted at the 17th Virginia that they needed ammunition. The beleaguered infantrymen grumbled about the gunners' alleged "cowardice" and grimly prepared to die.[51]

Kemper's, and Drayton's Brigades spent an anxious fifteen minutes waiting for the Federals to come up from Otto's farm lane. Alexander Hunter (A Co., 17th VA) loathed the silence. The men around him looked so terribly pale as they propped their weapons on the bottom fence rails.

Their officers cautioned them, "Steady men! steady, they are coming. Ready!!"

Hammers clicked back to full cock. They could not see the Yankees, whom they heard clanking up the hill.[52] On the left, the seventeen man 1st Virginia fired by files at any Yankee who popped his head over the horizon.[53]

"Steady, lads, steady!" Colonel Montgomery Corse cautioned the 17th Virginia. "Seventeenth, don't fire until they get above the hill."

Each man sighted for two feet above the crest. They studied the gilt eagle atop the colors of the 89th New York bob up and down until the stars and stripes became clearly visible.

"Keep cool, men — don't fire yet," Colonel Corse shouted.

Hats and faces jerked into view accompanied with the typical Yankee "huzzah".[54]

Captain David McIntosh's Pee Dee Battery arrived on the field via the Miller's Saw Mill Road. Having been rushed into action to a position to the right of the Blackford house, it fired about three shots at a large column of Federal infantry which appeared to be moving by the left flank toward the Confederate right.

Captain Adams of A. P. Hill's staff, suddenly galloped into the battery.

He shouted, "General Hill says, limber up your guns and go at a gallop to the left of that cornfield and support General Kemper."[55]

The battery swung left onto the Harper's Ferry Road with the twelve pound Napoleon in the lead. The column halted at an opening in the fence, several yards north of the small cornfield to Kemper's right flank, to allow J. S. Brown's battered crews to file out.

The second the Virginians cleared McIntosh's path, his men trotted his three largest pieces into the open ground to the left of the cornfield and swung into position. They abandoned the twelve pound howitzer and the caissons to provide enough men to man the rest of the battery. Everyone, the drivers, Captain McIntosh, even the color bearer, Baxter Rollins, sprang into action. McIntosh manned the trail of one gun and sighted it himself. Rollins planted his flagstaff between two of the guns and ran to assist James L. Napier with his Napoleon, next to the cornfield.

Fairchild's Federals were crossing the field at the right oblique, about two hundred fifty yards from the battery, toward Kemper's brigade, which was to McIntosh's left front. Within a minute, the artillerists had their range and were hurling double canister into the Yankee formation.[56]

Fairchild's Brigade charged en masse upon Kemper's and Drayton's small brigades. As the regiment crested the hilltop sixty yards from the Confederates, they fired in unison. The volley staggered the Yankees and soldiers fell in squads.[57]

The soldier immediately in front of Private David Thompson (G Co., 9th NY) cursed, dropped his musket, and threw his hands into the air. He fell with a thud, wounded behind the ear.[58] Company A went down almost to the man. Lieutenant Matthew Graham crumbled with a canister ball through his body. The tremendous reports of Kemper's and Drayton's volleys echoed loudly in his ears. The dazed officer hurriedly scanned his line. The regiment had dwindled to companies of twelve to fifteen men. The colors were down in front of him. One or two men died in futile attempts to regain them. Within a minute twelve men, among them Lieutenant Myers, had dashed forward and frantically raised the standards only to get cut down.[59]

On the left, the 103rd New York and the 89th New York closed ranks and, despite their losses, stubbornly returned the volley. The musketry splintered the post and rail fence along Kemper's front, taking out twenty-one of the remaining fifty-three men and officers in the 17th Virginia. The Confederates put up a splendid yet faltering resistance for another ten minutes as the New Yorkers approached to within ninety feet of their position and loosed several more well aimed volleys into them. Minutes later Colonel Corse (17th VA) was wounded in the foot. Thirty-five men were dead or wounded. The Federals could not be stopped.[60]

What was left of Kemper's Brigade bolted west toward the Harper's Ferry Road as the 103rd New York and the 89th New York overran them and turned southwest toward McIntosh's Battery.[61] The South Carolinian artillerists continued to unload double canister into the Yankees at less than one hundred yards. Yankee riflery killed or wounded most of the battery's horses and took out three of its twenty-one men, before the gunners could swing the limbers around to escape. The Southerners

**COLONEL MONTGOMERY
CORSE, 17th Virginia**

He fell into the hands of the 9th New York with a wounded foot and was recovered by his own men when the New Yorkers quit the field.
(Miller's Photographic History)

feverishly cut loose their dead animals and, at McIntosh's command, pulled out with the Yankees a bare fifty paces away. Abandoning their guns, they ran toward the Harper's Ferry Road.[62]

The 1st Virginia (about nine men) snapped off their last rounds and ran back through the cornfield behind them like flushed rabbits. The frail John Dooley (one hundred thirty pounds) could not seem to run fast enough, weighted down as he was by his cartridge box and musket which he never thought of casting aside. He attempted in vain to keep pace with the long legged, unincumbered captain, who kept turning around to lope backwards, lest he fall with a "disgraceful" wound. Private Dooley, taking advantage of his captain's awkwardness, won the "not so credible race" at the risk of getting shot in the back.[63]

Simultaneous with the assault of the 103rd and the 89th New York regiments, Captain Adolphe Libaire (E Co., 9th NY) snatched up the fallen regimental colors. The normally very Christian officer was quite livid. Waving the flag about his head, he commanded his company, "Up, damn you, and forward!"

What was left of the regiment scrambled to its feet, trampling dead and wounded alike and rushed Drayton's Confederates at the stone wall along the orchard. The wounded Lieutenant Graham (A Co.) saw Colonel Kimball with Captain Libaire, Lieutenants James Horner (B Co.) and Robert McKechnie (H Co.), who had his fez on the point of his sword, mount the wall with their men and go over. It all happened "in a flash" Graham recalled.[64]

The Middle Bridge

From the Lower Bridge Road to the Boonsboro Pike, the assault continued less dramatically. A small company of Regulars (I Co., 2nd U.S.) led by First Sergeant Francis E. Lacey purportedly drove a Confederate battery from the brow of the high ridge to the front of the Newcomer house. He would have maintained his advantage had his men not run out of ammunition and been fired upon by their own artillery.[65] The Confederates simply did not give the Federals much to shoot at. Captain Charles W. Squires, whose battery defended the hilltop immediately south of the Middle Bridge Road, just east of the Lutheran Church, had used up all of his ammunition. He needed infantry supports desperately. The only brigade present (Garnett's small force) had not moved as a body to the crest all afternoon. Only the 19th Virginia, on the right, and Jenkins' pitiful brigade, had done any firing in support of Garden's Battery, which was on the hill west of the stone mill's orchard.

Squires asked Colonel Stephen D. Lee, who was with him on the hill, if the infantry would attack.

"Squires," Lee said, "see General Garnett, he is a game man and will no doubt charge."

The general consented. As the infantry rose to attack, Squires began to pull his battery out. The sight of thousands of Federals in the valleys to the east undid the formation to a man. The line literally turned about and headed rearward without firing a shot.[66]

Three of Evans' regiments (18th, 22nd, and 23rd SC) streamed west toward Sharpsburg. By then, the painfully wounded Lieutenant Warren Pursely (G Co., 18th SC) had gained his feet but could not walk. A soldier with all of his fingers shot off wrapped his good arm around the Lieutenant and half dragged him to safety.[67]

As the Union troops advanced, the Holcombe Legion and the 17th South Carolina, which were on the farm lane west of Sherrick's, and the 19th Virginia fired a ragged volley then broke and ran for the hollow below the brow of the ridge in front of Sharpsburg where they quickly regrouped. The 79th New York (on the right) of Christ's Brigade advanced into the fields beyond the farm lane which cut across (north to south) from the Boonsboro Pike to the Sherrick farm on the Lower Bridge Road.[68] With their ammunition becoming critically low, and their ranks heavily damaged by artillery fire, they saw no need to overextend their lines.

The Lower Bridge

Colonel Thomas Welsh's Brigade (8th MI, 46th NY, 45th PA, and, 100th PA) kept pace with Fairchild's men. Their riflery drove Drayton's skirmishers away from the stone wall on top of the hill south of the mill house. The 100th Pennsylvania climbed the hill and closed in on the mill and its adjacent orchard. Using the haystacks for cover, they opened on Garden's Battery at very close range and forced the crews to retire the guns by hand.[69]

Jenkins' South Carolinians (1st SC Vols., 2nd, 5th, and 6th SC, 4th SC Bttn., and Palmetto Sharpshooters) stared anxiously at the two Federal brigades (Christ's and Welsh's) as they converged in formation, once again, for the mill. The order rang out to charge.

Darling Patterson, the color bearer of the 1st South Carolina Volunteers, darted ahead of his men with the battle flag extended fully above him. A mad race ensued with the Confederates rushing like madmen around Garden's retreating guns toward the stone mill's orchard while the Yankees closed in from the east and the south in parade ground formations.

The charge cost the 6th South Carolina its commander, Captain E. B. Cantey, who fell wounded and gave the regiment to Captain James E. Coker (E Co.). The Confederates reached the stone fence on the eastern edge of the orchard and drove the 17th Michigan back. Darling Patterson defiantly planted his colors behind the wall while Orderly Sergeant Frank Mixon (E Co., 1st SC Vols.) retired to the western side of an apple tree to feed his aching stomach.[70] *(Map 64)*

The Confederate artillery chewed up the 100th Pennsylvania a little with railroad iron and canister and inflicted less than forty casualties.[71] The Yankees crouched below the crest and easily dodged the projectiles. Welsh's men later claimed that they had used most of their cartridges.[72] Privates Frederick Pettitt and John Wilson (C Co., 100th PA), without orders, joined Fairchild's men in the drive against the Harper's Ferry Road, while their regiment, which, according to Pettitt, "was not ordered from the brow of the hill", kept well out of the line of sight. Pettitt, who was caught up in the excitement, did not notice that Wilson was missing until the Confederates drove the attack eastward.[73]

Typical of the events for the day, the Federals thwarted their own success. It was around 4:00 P.M. Fairchild's badly mauled brigade closed ranks to the right and laid down in front of the stone wall they had taken to await further orders.[74] A number of foolhardy individuals from the 9th New York, finding themselves in a hollow near the town, were flanked on the left by Confederates along the Harper's Ferry Road and retreated back to their own lines with warnings about a large body of Rebs descending upon them.[75]

The Harper's Ferry Road

Brigadier General Isaac Rodman noticed how contracted his front was and snapped at Colonel Edward Harland to bring up the 8th Connecticut of his brigade while he led up the 16th Connecticut and the 4th Rhode Island (Harland's BG) to bolster his line. At that instant, a bullet struck Rodman in the chest, fatally wounding him. He fell southeast of the stone wall.

Harland immediately assumed command and dispatched an aide to bring the first two regiments up.[76] A bullet dropped Harland's horse as he galloped east to get the 8th Connecticut. Dismounted, the colonel staggered to the New England regiment in the meadow just above the northeast corner of the big cornfield. He sent it careening up the hill to the left of the 89th New York.[77] The aide crashed into the tall field of Indian corn, located the other two regiments and told them to advance, thereby setting the stage for another debacle.[78] *(Map 65)*

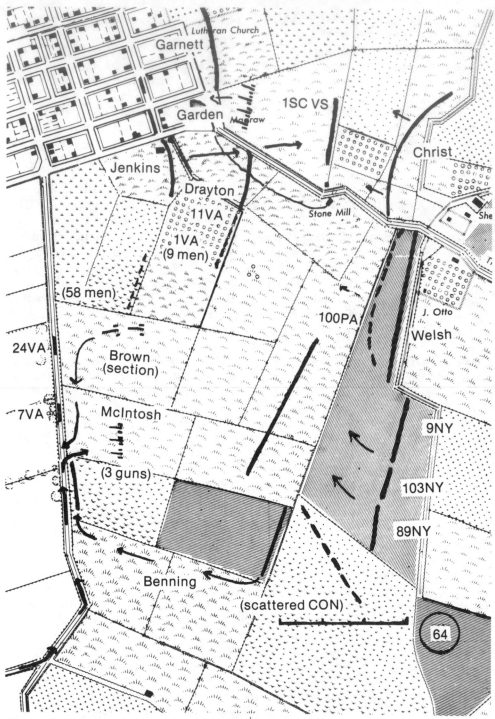

(Map 64) 1:00 P.M. — 4:20 P.M., SEPTEMBER 17, 1862
The IX Corps moves against D. R. Jones' Division.

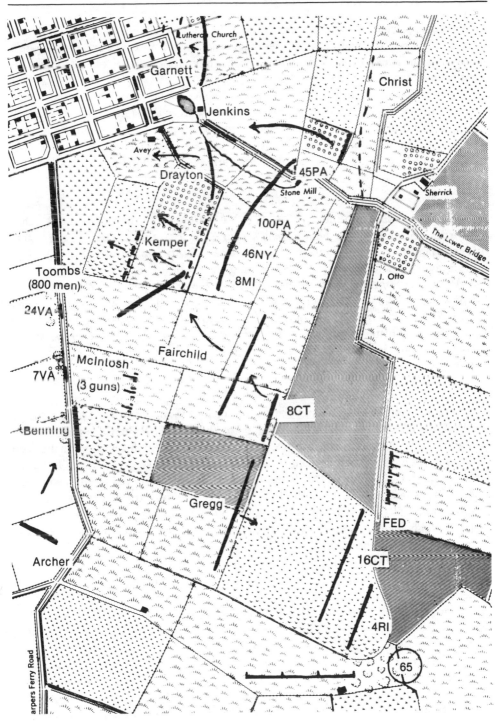

(Map 65) 1:00 P.M. — 4:20 P.M., SEPTEMBER 17, 1862
Jones' Division buckles under increased pressure.

Harland started to reconsolidate his lines. Skirmishers were called in and fronts dressed.[79] Fairchild's walking casualties staggered toward the creek and litter bearers from the ambulance corps selectively weeded out wounded officers from among the hundreds of stricken men.

Private David Thompson (G Co., 9th NY) discovered about one dozen of his regiment, all injured, lying in the hollow a short distance from the stone wall. His sergeant major hailed him over and ordered him to remove his blanket roll and help carry a wounded lieutenant to the rear.[80] A little distance away two ambulance corps men from the 9th New York pulled Lieutenant Matthew Graham (A Co.) to his feet and dragged him away from the fighting.[81]

Private Alexander Hunter (A Co., 17th VA) threw up his hands with two other men from his regiment as the Yankees swarmed around them. Two New Yorkers nudged them to their feet and herded them east. Casting a forlorn glance behind him, Hunter dejectedly noted the 17th lying in formation as it had fought.

About one hundred yards to the east the five men happened upon a cluster of Union officers who were gathered about their surgeon and a desperately wounded colonel.[82] The 8th Connecticut continued on without their lieutenant colonel, Hiram Appleman.[83] A bitter grin flickered across Alexander Hunter's face as he stared momentarily at the pale New Englander. His boys' fire for the most part had hit hard.[84]

Kemper's and Drayton's stubborn resistence in conjunction with superb artillery work had stymied the two Ohion brigades to the rear of Fairchild's and Welsh's Brigades. Only two regiments from Crook's Brigade, the 28th Ohio, with the 36th Ohio to its right rear, ventured into the meadow field above Otto's lane. The 23rd Ohio (Ewing's BG) occupied the depression in the plowed field above the southern end of Otto's lane, while the 30th Ohio (Ewing's BG) moved toward the tall corn to support the 16th Connecticut.[85] One of the Ohio regiments (probably the 23rd Ohio) refused to advance beyond the hollow. Captain John Shephard (Adjutant General, Fairchild's BG) snatched one of the regimental flags from a surprised color bearer and vainly urged them forward. The Ohions would not budge. Even the wounded Lieutenant Graham (A Co., 9th NY), who was carried past them, could not stir them to action. With feigned cheerfulness, he told them the fighting was over. All they had to do was move forward and take part in the "greatest victory of the war." The Ohions stared mutely at him, their unbelieving expressions denouncing everything he said. They would not believe him. (Map 66)

Forlorn over his failure to rouse the Midwesterners, the two men silently carried their lieutenant further into the swale east of Otto's lane. The battle seemed to cease; only an occasional minie ball zinged overhead. Once they crossed over the path of Fairchild's charge they came upon no more Federal dead or wounded, except Captain Barnett to whom Lieutenant Graham spoke while the captain bandaged his wounded hand.[86]

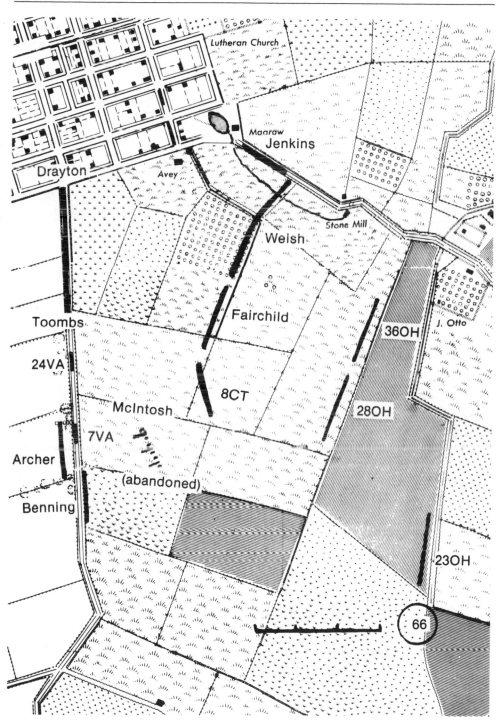

Lutheran Church

Maaraw

Jenkins

Drayton

Avey

Stone Mill

Welsh

Fairchild

36OH

J. Otto

Toombs

24VA

8CT

28OH

McIntosh

7VA

Archer

(abandoned)

Benning

23OH

66

(Map 66) 1:00 P.M. — 4:20 P.M., SEPTEMBER 17, 1862
The IX Corps halts to cheer itself for its conquests.

Once again a successful Federal counterattack died in its own tracks as the IX Corps halted to regroup. The Confederates were driven off but not demoralized or beaten. The Federals seemed to suffer from short sighted command objectives.

CHAPTER SIXTEEN

"I am poured out like water . . ."

4:20 P.M. - DARK

The Harper's Ferry Road

Brigadier General Maxcy Gregg's South Carolina Brigade (1st, 12th, 13th, 14th SC and 1st SC Rifles) with Brigadier General James J. Archer's Brigade arrived on the field via Miller's Saw Mill Road about the same time that the Federals moved out from the heights west of the bridge. Archer's Brigade (the 19th GA, 1st, 7th, and 14th TN) fell in along the plank fence parallel to the Harper's Ferry Road to support four of Toombs' regiments (2nd, 20th, 50th GA and 11th GA Bttn.). Admonishing his small brigade to curb its aggressiveness, Archer ordered his men prone behind the cornfield immediately west of Kemper's former position. As the Yankee sharpshooters picked off a couple of Tennesseans through the fence rails, Felix Motlow (1st TN) sarcastically noted that the Yankees were mean shots as long as they were not being sniped at. Gregg's men headed directly into the fields south of the advancing Federal line.[1]

The 14th South Carolina, in the lead, relieved Colonel H. L. Benning's three Georgia regiments (the 15th, 17th, and 11th GA Bttn.) behind the stone wall near the western section of the forty acre cornfield. Holding back the 1st South Carolina Rifles, Gregg sent his three remaining regiments into the corn.[2]

An aide rushed H. L. Benning and his Georgians further west, parallel with and in sight of the charging Federal forces who were about six to seven hundred yards north (right) of them. Benning snatched only a quick glimpse of them as his men picked up their pace and ran behind a small cornfield which bordered the Harper's Ferry Road. Striking the road, the staff officer immediately commanded the colonel to charge north, into the village. Benning asked, "Why?". The Yankees, he was informed, had Sharpsburg. *(Map 64-66)*

With Benning in the lead, the three small regiments cautiously slipped to the northwest corner of the cornfield. The colonel halted his column to personally reconnoiter the situation. What he saw as he quietly poked his head around the corner of the tall corn stunned him. McIntosh's three abandoned artillery pieces stood isolated in the open field about fifty yards from him. Fifty yards behind them, stood the reforming Federal line. The Yankees, whose line stretched clear from his cornfield to the orchard on the Lower Bridge Road, were standing at order arms "huzzahing" as if they had just won a baseball game. Benning slipped back to his men and prepared to strike.[3]

The Lower Bridge

The two ambulance corps men from the 9th New York half dragged, half carried Lieutenant Matthew Graham (A Co.) through the swale behind the Ohio regiments, trying to avoid spent bullets which occasionally dropped around them from the high ground to their left (west). The lieutenant thought for the moment he was in another world. As they neared the end of the small valley where it ran into the Lower Bridge Road, he was struck by the Sunday like quietness and serenity of the battlefield. They stumbled across only two or three soldiers, one of them a member of the 79th New York.

The "Cameron Highlander" was strolling along at ease with himself. From one hand he munched a pilfered apple; on the other shoulder he carried a stretcher. Graham's two "bandits", as he affectionately referred to them, accosted the fellow, and spoke a few hasty words with him before relieving him of the stretcher. The lieutenant expected to ride in comfort to the field east of the bridge.[4]

The 40 Acre Cornfield — The Harper's Ferry Road

The Confederate counterstroke could not have been better synchronized if it had been planned. Gregg's small brigade slipped past the Federal left flank unnoticed by nearly all the Yankees except a few of the wounded. Private Almon L. Reed (F Co., 89th NY) crashed to the ground in front of Kemper's line with a musket ball in his right knee. As he writhed on the ground, he glanced over to his left (south) and noticed what apparently was Gregg's Brigade rapidly marching toward Sherrick's forty acre field of Indian corn.[5] In the distance, the Confederates appeared to many like a Federal column. A large portion of them wore undyed Federal uniforms which they stole from the captured garrison at Harper's Ferry. They also flew captured National colors.[6] Almon Reed did not realize they were Confederates. Neither did Major Edward Jardine (89th NY) who, while strutting about with a captured Confederate flag in his grip, shouted loudly, "For God's sake, don't fire on our own men!" He quickly realized his error and seconds later screamed, "At them, Boys, they are under false colors! Give them Hell!"[7]

Benning's men on the western edge of the small cornfield along the Harper's Ferry Road checked their weapons and listened carefully to the colonel's hastily delivered instructions. A few of the soldiers were to stay in the corn as support; the rest were to move by the right flank and fire by files (two's) from the rear rank as they charged into the open. He hoped to create an illusion of greater numbers.[8]

To the southeast, Maxcy Gregg quietly but inefficiently positioned his sweaty troops in Sherrick's corn. The 13th South Carolina, on the left, took cover behind a section of stone fence on a hillock in the corn because Colonel O. E. Edwards (its C.O.) thought he was to play a defensive role and not an offensive one. To the right, Colonel Dixon Barnes (12th SC), believing he was to attack, sent his regiment into the swale toward a second stone wall, while the 1st South Carolina struggled to keep abreast on his right.[9] Both Gregg and Benning took the Federals by complete surprise at about the same time. (As a point of honor, Benning contested twenty-three years later that he had smashed the Yankees single handed.)[10]

Colonel Edward Harland's orderly crashed through the corn to the right flank of the 16th Connecticut, which was facing south by files, and breathlessly told Colonel Francis Beach to advance his large regiment (about nine hundred men) at the double-quick to the left of the Federal line. As he spurred away, the colonel shouted, "Attention!".

Instantly, the 12th South Carolina (about two hundred fifty men) volleyed into the unsuspecting regiment from a stone wall which was about ten feet away. Before the smoke cleared the rattled colonel cried, "Change front forward on the 10th company!" an impossible command for the untried soldiers to comprehend, much less perform.[11] The New Englanders valiantly tried to behave professionally. Rather than return fire, they staggered and crashed into each other in an attempt to execute the complicated maneuver. Barnes' South Carolinians unloaded several exceptionally well aimed volleys into the 16th Connecticut, while simultaneously waving their set of National colors and shouting not to shoot at "friends". Too many of the startled Yankees complied. In a matter of minutes, the beautiful new regiment left three hundred two casualties in the bloodied corn as it broke and ran toward the Antietam.[12]

**LEONARD G. MORRILL,
G Company, 16th Connecticut**

He was captured during Maxcy Gregg's counterthrust against the Federal left flank south of Sharpsburg. *(USAMHI)*

At the same time, H. L. Benning's three regiments (15th, 17th, and 11th GA [Bttn.], south to north) broke into the open from the Harper's Ferry Road, firing by files as they cleared the corn. Captain David McIntosh (Pee Dee Battery), upon hearing the shooting from the cornfield behind him, yelled at his orderly to bring up the howitzer and caisson he left parked west of the Harper's Ferry Road. Turning about, he ran into the corn to find out who was doing the shooting.[13] Unlike Gregg's men, the colonel's Georgians shot too low. Many of their rounds struck the ground at the feet of the 8th Connecticut. The New Englanders fired too high. For several minutes the two lines shot "spiritedly" but ineffectively at each other, until the Georgians raised their sights and gouged holes in the Yankee formation.[14] *(Map 67)*

Kemper's, Drayton's, Archer's, and the rest of Toombs' rallied Brigades (about eight hundred men) prepared to join in the fray. "Old Pete" Turney (Colonel, 1st TN) climbed the top rail of the board fence along the Harper's Ferry

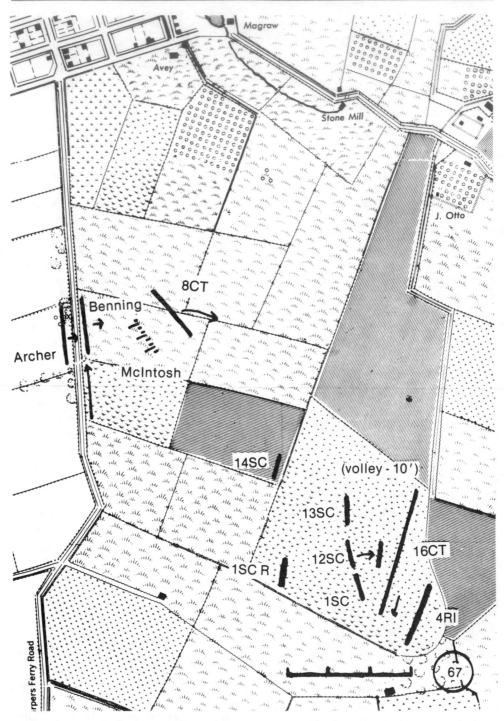

(Map 67) 4:20 P.M. — DARK, SEPTEMBER 17, 1862
Benning and Gregg launch their counterattacks.

Road. Private Felix Motlow wondered how the old man escaped death as he perched himself in the open amidst a storm of lead.

"Hog drivers, advance!" the colonel whooped.

The brigade leaped over the fence into the corn and merged with the other three brigades in a wild charge toward Harland's and Fairchild's reorganizing Federals.[15] In so doing, they cut across the 7th Virginia's front and blocked its line of fire.[16]

When they came abreast of Benning's troops, they halted to volley repeatedly at close quarters into the Federal troops who were doing some fine stand up fighting.

Robert Toombs frantically pranced his mount up and down the firing line, exhorting the men to stand firm. The general dispatched an orderly to scrounge up some field pieces.[17] Outnumbered as

MAJOR G. MOXLEY SORREL,
Longstreet's staff, ANV

He assisted Miller's section along the Harper's Ferry Road in the repulse of the IX Corps.
(Miller's Photographic History)

CAPTAIN NEWTON MANROSS,
K Company, 16th Connecticut

He died in the forty acre cornfield south of the town. *(USAMHI)*

he was, he needed the artillery to snap the Yankee line.

The Yankees on the ridge held out longer than the New Englanders in Sherrick's corn. Those five to ten extra minutes meant the difference between success or failure for either side. Private John Dooley (D Co., 1st VA) sarcastically noted in his diary that the Yankees were no "paragons of bravery". They should have easily crushed the diminutive Rebel forces.[18]

Men dropped in increasing numbers on both sides as the troops calmed down and improved their aim. The Federals started wavering on the left of the line as volley after volley flamed into their ranks.

John Dooley (D Co., 1st VA) heard a section of artillery (Miller's Battery) rumble into position to the right rear of his regiment.[19]

Simultaneously, James Longstreet and his staff charged up behind the two field pieces. When he noticed that the

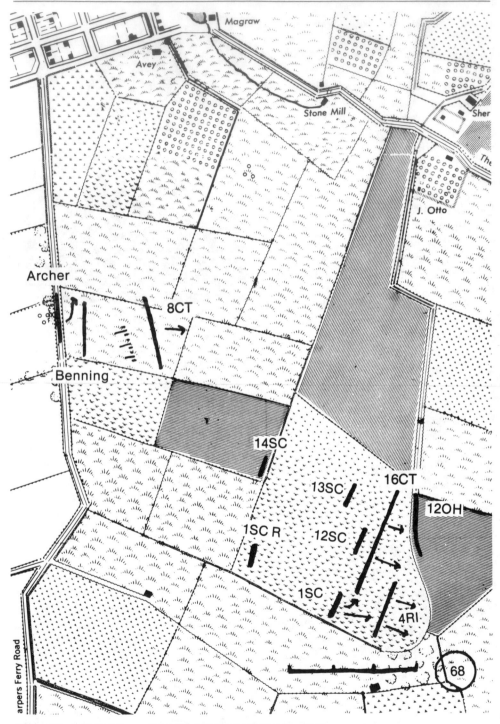

(Map 68) 4:20 P.M. — DARK, SEPTEMBER 17, 1862
Benning and Gregg roll up the Federal left wing.

crews were too exhausted to properly handle the guns, the general and his three officers, Captain Osmun Latrobe, Major Moxley Sorrel, and Major John W. Fairfax, dismounted and vigorously loaded both weapons. Fairfax, who seemed childishly overjoyed, clapped his hands and ran back to the ammunition chest for a round, while Longstreet sighted and primed the pieces himself.

Seconds later, the general yanked the lanyard on one cannon, then the other. His staff loaded a couple of more rounds. To the right front, Colonel H. L. Benning snapped his eyes skyward to follow the scream of the shells as they passed above him and slammed into the ground in front of the 8th Connecticut. The New Englanders scattered, forcing the rest of the Federal regiments to contract their flanks and retire to the north.[20] (Map 68)

The Lower Bridge

Private Alexander Hunter (A Co., 17th VA) and his captors halted momentarily on each ridge before reaching the creek to catch glimpses of the undulating landscape. He was somewhere near the last swale east of Otto's lane when Gregg's Brigade smashed the 16th Connecticut. The disordered Yankee lines streamed eastward from the cornfield as the Confederates shot into them from close quarters. When a Yankee half carried a wounded Confederate officer past Hunter and his escort, he asked what caused the panic.

" 'Stonewall' Jackson has just gotten back from Harper's Ferry; those troops fighting the Yankees now are A. P. Hill's division," the officer painfully informed him.

The Union soldiers ushered Hunter and his comrades further east, with the quickly setting sun glowing a forboding bright red upon their backs.[21]

A. P. Hill's timely counterattack catapulted the Federals west of the Lower Bridge into utter confusion. As McIntosh's artillerists raced back to their abandoned pieces, Richardson's, Pegram's, and Braxton's Batteries (south to north, respectively) swung into battery from Kemper's right to Miller's Saw Mill Road.[22] Their combined fire power threw the Federal bridgehead into nearly total chaos.

The barrage caught Lieutenant Matthew Graham (A Co., 9th NY) and his rescuers entirely by surprise. Two full ammunition wagons and a section of Clark's Battery (E, 4th U.S.) thundered around the steep road bend behind them, making for the narrow bridge. Stray minies plopped heavily from the trees and shell fragments sizzled into the creek as the drivers lashed their horses and mules and forced wounded men to scatter for protection along the roadside.

Colonel Ferrero's small party of about fifty enlisted men and officers, who were feeling rather silly for having loitered an hour or more behind the southwestern abutment of the bridge, started to emerge into the road when the first burst of artillery fire sent them diving for cover again. The cautious Lieutenant John Hudson (Ferrero's aide) poked his head around the end of the bridge only to see the division commander, Samuel Sturgis, calmly trotting down the road from the position of the 35th Massachusetts.

A shell exploded almost on top of him; splinters flew everywhere but the general continued riding toward the cowering staff officers as if nothing had happened.

Ferrero immediately "volunteered" Hudson to step into the open and meet the general. The lieutenant informed him of Burnside's plans for Ferrero's Brigade for the balance of the day.

The brigade was to move upstream to be relieved. Sturgis dismounted in the road, much to Hudson's dismay while the rounds burst in the tree tops, and listened patiently to the lieutenant. They both waited out the bombardment which had gotten quite heavy.[23]

Lieutenant Hudson anxiously watched the Confederate projectiles "walk" down the Lower Bridge Road paces in front of the wagons. One burst directly on top of one teamster, the report nearly deafening the lieutenant. The driver whipped his mules harder and escaped unscathed until he got jammed on the bridge with another wagon.[24] Lieutenant Graham (A Co., 9th NY) had never felt as discouraged as he was then. He tried excusing the apparent cowardice of the artillery crew upon exhausted ammunition supplies.[25] John Hudson, who had seen the wagons cross not minutes before, knew that the teamsters had not had enough time to unload their ammunition crates before turning back. The Confederates, while killing no one, had once again made the bridge impassable.[26]

When the artillery fire died away, several minutes later, Sturgis dispatched Hudson north to the 35th Massachusetts with orders to pull them back.[27] The regiment, according to Ferrero's previous directive, straddled the Lower Bridge Road to round up stragglers.[28]

As he delivered his command, the lieutenant noticed the regiment left wheeling to face south along the crest which paralleled the bend in the road and asked the colonel about it.

"Yes, sir," Carruth replied, "but you see I've got another order from that Brigadier General, and I suppose I must execute it."

The frustrated aide glanced in the direction the colonel nodded and saw a full brigadier astride his horse atop the hill, fully exposed in the setting sunlight; he was studying the hills to the west.

Hudson grumbled that he probably was Jacob D. Cox, the Corps commander, and he supposed the colonel should execute the order. Telling Carruth he would report first to Cox, then to Ferrero, Hudson dashed across the open ground to the general's side.

The tiring aide, who discovered he was addressing Cox, in person, advised him of Burnside's plan, apparently because he believed that Cox, who was Burnside's subordinate, would have to comply.

"Yes, I know that," Cox firmly answered, "but the regiment must move at once; you see the need of haste."[29]

A quick glance westward at the general's "you see" sent Hudson down to his haunches. Confederate skirmishers, silhouetted starkly against the skyline with the sun an evil red upon their backs, were already to the brow of the swale along the stone wall west of Otto's lane. Minies zinged overhead. Bidding good-bye, his conversation done, the lieutenant trotted into the creek valley at a crouch. He wanted to be nowhere near a mounted officer at that moment.[30]

The 40 Acre Cornfield

To the south, Gregg's South Carolinians were using the darkening sky, the corn, and their "requisitioned" Federal uniforms to every advantage. The 12th South Carolina advanced too far to the front in pursuit of the 16th Connecticut.[31] The 4th

Rhode Island, to the left rear of the fleeing New Englanders, could not determine where the lines were. They had opened fire into the corn along their front when the first refugees from the 16th Connecticut slammed into their right flank. Once again, the Confederates called out, "Cease firing, you are firing upon your own men." Colonel William P. Steere (4th RI) ordered his men to comply.[32] Lieutenant Colonel Joseph B. Curtis (4th RI) detected only U.S. colors bobbing about in the corn to his right and front. He immediately called for volunteers to reconnoiter the hillside. Lieutenant George E. Curtis and George H. Watts disappeared into the corn with the regimental color corporal and the standard.[33]

The 1st South Carolina, to the right rear of the 12th South Carolina, advanced to meet the three soldiers and fired into them when they were about twenty feet in front of the 4th Rhode Island. The colors flew from the corporal's grasp as he fell — dead from several wounds. Lieutenant Curtis snatched the flag and raced back through the corn with Lieutenant Watts. The moment they joined the regiment, the Rhode Islanders opened fire and tried to charge, unsupported, uphill, deeper into the corn.

The raw New Englanders surprised the South Carolinians as much as they were surprised. Private Berry Benson (1st SC) said the Yankees suddenly rose up in front of his regiment, then broke and fled from the corn with the Confederates at their heels.[34] The 1st South Carolina left wheeled in its pursuit, herding the Yankees northeast toward the bridge.[35]

The disorganized Yankees ran to the northeastern side of a limestone ledge which bordered the southern end of Otto's lane. They cowered there, too scared to run through the ravine to their rear toward the Antietam, while the Confederates kept them pinned with excellent drill manual volleying.

Major Alston (1st SC) stood behind the center of his regiment cooly delivering the commands, "Right wing — ready — aim — fire!", then "Left wing — ready — aim — fire!"

The display of military precision awed Private Berry Benson, who later recalled that the regiment had never fired by the numbers before or after that day. Their concentrated shooting pushed the Yankees by twos and threes across the swale northeast of the cornfield. Their lifeless bodies marked their places.

Presently, a lone Union officer on a splendid black horse, galloped from the woods, along the crest east of Otto's lane, and headed directly toward the panicky New Englanders. Brandishing his sword, he valiantly rode to and fro behind them, trying to get them to reform. Almost immediately, the 1st South Carolina drew beads on him and fired. Several times, the brave man escaped death only to get killed by a random shot.

When his master toppled from the saddle, the black horse galloped a short distance away, then returned. Standing by the officer's side, the horse gently nuzzled the corpse in an attempt to revive it. The South Carolinians cut it down because it was there and it was living.

Scattered fire peppered the 1st South Carolina as well. Sam Wigg, who stood next to the colors, collapsed. His friend, Berry Benson, saw him go down but did not try to help him up. Benson could tell by Wigg's lifeless expression that he was dead.[36]

Colonel Hugh Ewing's three Ohion regiments finally mobilized. As the 4th Rhode Island streamed from the cornfield, the 12th Ohio marched toward the 1st South Carolina's right flank.[37]

In moving into its position, it passed around scattered groups of the 16th Connecticut and Cook's Battery (8th MA Lgt.). The regiment advanced into the southern edge of the corn on the low ground east of the right wing of the 1st South Carolina and volleyed blindly in the direction of the Confederate rifle smoke.[38] The bullets clattered through the corn and scattered the Southerners westward. The Confederates ran uphill through the corn. The Yankees were too close to attempt a counterfire.[39]

A tremendous volume of hostile canister and small arms fire crashed through the corn from the high ground to the west but passed harmlessly over the Ohions' heads. The rattled stragglers of the 16th Connecticut, in the hollow behind the 12th Ohio, however, mistakenly thought the incoming rounds came from the edge of the corn. Consequently, they leveled their weapons and shot into the rear of the Ohions. Cook's Battery also cut into them.

Private Ephraim Snook (F Co., 12th OH) dropped behind Sam Compton (F Co.). A Yankee bullet splattered the brains of the man to his right all over his sleeve. A canister ball shattered the shoulder blade of the man to his left.[40]

The 30th Ohio, to its right, charged into the cornfield, heading due west while the 23rd Ohio cautiously moved over Otto's lane into the plowed field.[41] They were trapped within minutes.

The 23rd Ohio ran into musketry from the rallied Confederates from Kemper's, Drayton's, and Toombs' Brigades (about eight hundred men), and Archer's freshly arrived brigade (numbering less than three hundred fifty men between four regiments). It quickly withdrew from the field as did the 30th Ohio when it rushed into flank and front fire along the far western edge of the cornfield.

The 30th Ohio chased the Confederates away from the southern face of a stone wall in the cornfield and bolted into front and flank fire from part of Gregg's and Archer's Brigades. The regiment halted to volley back which gave the Confederates ample time to right wheel and attack them from the rear.

Lieutenant Colonel Theodore Jones (30th OH) screamed for the men to retire before a bullet brought him down. The left of the regiment did not get the word until Confederate riflery spattered it from the rear.

Private Edward Schweitzer (I Co.) got a nasty start when the regimental adjutant collapsed three paces behind him. Frantically glancing about, he saw his regiment shatter as the soldiers scattered like flushed quail in every direction. It was "Every man for himself" he recalled, himself included. The frightened Ohion, being totally confused by the minie balls which clattered through the field from all sides, ran like a jumped deer to the front. He suddenly skidded to a halt. The sight of armed Confederates not twenty paces in front of him, convinced him that he was running the wrong direction, and he blindly crashed east. He hoped to get out of the corn, and, eventually, Maryland alive.[42]

As the 1st South Carolina retreated, Private Berry Benson semi-deliberately attempted to lag behind. Under less trying circumstances, the private normally tried to maintain his personal honor by being the last man off the field but the Ohions were raking the line too severely to dally.

His Federal sky blue trousers, which he captured during the Second Manassas, nearly proved his undoing. They had split part way up the ankle of the left leg, and in fording the Potomac, they had gotten thoroughly soaked. As he retreated, the wringing wet leg split higher and higher from its own weight with each step. Every time he threw his foot forward, the momentum wrapped the flapping pants leg around his right leg. Running seemed impossible.

The distance had increased considerably between him and his regiment when a bullet smacked him on the right side of the skull. The impact sent a chill through his entire body. Stopping, he ripped his pants leg off at the groin and escaped in his drawers after his men.[43] *(Map 69)*

General Gregg sent Captain Perrin and his 1st South Carolina Rifles into the left flank of the 12th Ohio and sent them reeling to the swale west of the bridge.[44] Meanwhile, the 1st South Carolina jumped into a gully west of their former line, fronted, and waited for the Yankees who they did not know were not there to attack.

As they waited, Private Berry Benson gingerly peeled off his slouch hat. The spent round left a black mark in the gray felt just above the brim but did not dent his skull. A friend asked Benson if he had a hole in his long johns. The private found two holes in the leg — one in the front and one in the back above his left ankle. He unrolled his drawers, which were considerably too long for him to discover that a single bullet had gone through three folds of his underwear without drawing blood.[45]

The Federal left flank was gradually getting rolled up. Private David Thompson (G Co., 9th NY) returned to the hollow east of Kemper's former position during Benning's counterattack. He found about one dozen — mostly wounded — men from the 9th New York crouching in the bottom of the depression. All pleaded for water. One, in particular, John Devlin (G Co.), begged for a drink. A round ball had carried away one of his arms at the shoulder. He bled to death minutes after Thompson's arrival.

For over an hour, Thompson watched the bullets shred bark, leaves, and branches off the young locust tree on the lip of the hollow. As the fragments showered them, he wanted nothing more than to run away.[46]

In the midst of the brief encounter, Sam Compton (F Co., 12th OH) and Sergeant John Snook (F Co.) were sent to the rear to drag in a box of ammunition from a supply wagon on the ridge above the creek. Bullets whacked into the wagon and zinged about the two men but they grabbed a cartridge crate and headed for the regiment, which had gone prone a few hundred yards to the south.

Snook, being much taller than Compton, raised the ammunition box so high that the cartridges shifted to the right and nearly buckled Compton to the ground. As he struggled to keep his balance and walk, he gave the appearance of a man who was doubled over in pain. The Confederate snipers suddenly ceased fire. (Forty years later, Snook ran into an old Rebel who told him they stopped shooting because, in the poor light, it appeared that Snook was carrying off a wounded man.)[47]

By 5:00 P.M., every Federal regiment except the 9th New York had retired to Otto's swale or to the western creek bank north and south of the Lower Bridge Road.[48] In the encroaching darkness, soldiers groped through the fields searching for downed friends or seeking refuge from the defensive oriented Confederates.[49]

Most of the Federals complained they had run out of ammunition and eagerly retired down the Lower Bridge Road to safety. The 9th New York, having shifted

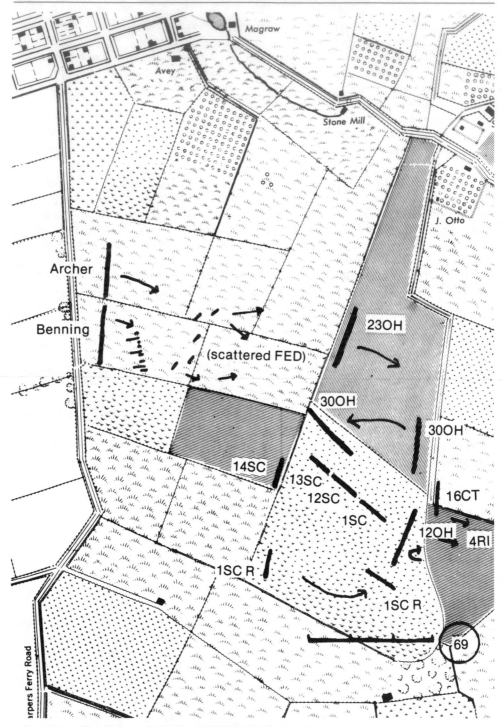

(Map 69) 4:20 P.M. — DARK, SEPTEMBER 17, 1862
The 30th Ohio attempts to save the IX Corps' left flank.

what was left of its men to the right, anchored its right flank on the road near the mill house and orchard.[50] Brigadier General Orlando Willcox, who received orders to fall back from Cox, relayed the command by courier to Lieutenant Colonel Kimball (9th NY).

Kimball curtly snapped, "We have the bayonets. What are they for?"

General Willcox personally ordered the regiment from the field. As the New Yorkers fell in on the road and marched east toward the bridge, Kimball boasted to Willcox, "Look at my regiment! They go off the field under orders. They are not driven off. Do they look like a beaten regiment?"[51]

The 9th New York was not beaten but badly mauled. They lost two hundred thirty-five casualties of three hundred seventy-three engaged.[52] As one of the New Yorkers, upon discovering how many were hit, tearfully blubbered to John W. Hudson the next day, "We shall soon be as few as we were before."[53]

Had not Nagle's and Ferrero's Brigades, in particular the 35th Massachusetts, gone into battle as the Confederates reached the western crest of Otto's swale, the bulk of Rodman's and Willcox's Divisions would have been cut off and routed. The 51st Pennsylvania, followed to the north, respectively, by the 51st New York, 21st Massachusetts, and the 35th Massachusetts, descended into Otto's swale heading for the snake fence along the farm lane.[54]

J. F. J. Caldwell (officer, 1st SC) studied their well organized, steady advance with admiration. Having served in Austria and France before the war, he had never seen such fine marching.[55]

Felix Motlow (1st TN) witnessed the Ohions' feeble attempt to hold Otto's stone wall. They fled, along with Lieutenant Coffin's two howitzers, when Colonel Peter Turney (1st TN) stepped in front of his wild Tennesseans and led them toward the swale. His men used the rifles, which they acquired from the Yankees at the Second Manassas, with terrible effect. Blue uniformed bodies plopped to the ground in large numbers along their front.[56]

Otto's Lane

As the 35th Massachusetts filed left along the ridge, Lieutenant John N. Coffin's section of 12 pound howitzers (Cook's 8th MA Lgt.) crashed full speed through the right of the regiment toward the left of Crook's Ohio regiments, which were retreating.[57] The 51st New York and the 21st Massachusetts dropped back near the crest, leaving the 35th Massachusetts on its own.

The New Englanders calmly realigned themselves then bolted over the crest toward the left of Coffin's unsupported section. Second Lieutenant Augustus Pope (I Co.) did not know what was going on. He could not understand why the Ohions were retreating. Musketry peppered their line from the stone wall on the opposite side of the swale. The color guard went down to a man. Captain William King (K Co.) seized the colors and carried them into the swale.[58]

Lieutenant John W. Hudson responded to the firing by making a bee line from the bridge, where he could not find Ferrero, toward the hilltop west of the creek. Struggling over the rail fence partway up the hill, Hudson waddled toward the crest with a gait "like that of an old hen". He took cover behind the north-south line of an "L" shaped stone wall, the southeast corner of which marked the southeastern corner of Otto's stubble field. He was not alone. Second Lieutenant Alfred Walcott (B Co., 21st MA), Ferrero's other aide, had gotten there first.

As he positioned himself near the angle in the wall to observe the action on both sides, Hudson asked Walcott where Colonel Ferrero was. The other aide "thought" he was on the hillside below them with the brigade, but he did not know for sure. A nervous look over the wall toward the bullet swept valley convinced Hudson that he should stay where he was and observe the fighting. A live aide could serve Ferrero better than a dead one.[59]

The 35th Massachusetts would have preferred to have been there too. It found itself isolated along Otto's lane with Companies C, K, and G, on its left wing, turned back at right angles, where the fence ran south, and faced south. The rest of the brigade pulled back partway up the eastern slope of the swale because it had little ammunition. The brigade's three left regiments temporarily laid down in the stubble and the grass with fixed bayonets which exposed the left companies of the 35th Massachusetts to the Confederate infantry in the cornfield, to the south, and those massing along the stone wall bordering the plowed field two hundred yards west of the lane.

Privates Marcus A. Emmons and James M. Stone (K Co., 21st MA) felt quite abandoned as they lay behind a rail fence on the crest to the left rear of the 35th Massachusetts. The regiment, which had expended thirty of its forty rounds prior to crossing, had been ordered to hold the line with cold steel. Bullets zipped and zinged closely overhead. Round shot bounded and crashed into and over the hillside. A cannon ball hit the prone Lieutenant Henry C. Holbrook (K Co.) and tore him to pieces. His horrible death stunned James Stone and left an impression on him which he would vividly recall fifty-six years later.[60]

The Yankees feared being overrun. They probably would have been driven to the creek if Brigadier General David R. Jones, the Confederate division commander in that sector, had allowed his generals to attack beyond the stone wall. Around dusk, as Ferrero's soldiers rushed to the defense of Otto's swale, he ordered both Robert Toombs and Ambrose P. Hill, who outranked him, not to drive the Federals into the Antietam, but to hold the hills protecting Sharpsburg.[61] He honestly thought that his command was too scattered to continue. He apparently reported that to General Lee, who allowed him not to press the Federals any further.[62]

Consequently, Hill called his brigade officers together along the stone wall on the hillside above Otto's lane to give them their instructions and to assess the combat situation.[63] Brigadier General L. O'Brien Branch brought his brigade (7th, 18th, 28th, 33rd, and 37th NC) over the crest behind Archer's and Jones' reformed commands.[64] Branch joined the physically ill Archer at the wall and was surveying the Yankee lines through field glasses when he sent a runner to fetch Colonel James Lane of the 28th North Carolina.

Lane rushed from his command to the stone wall. While searching about in the encroaching darkness for his brigadier, he stumbled upon Major Englehard, one of the general's staff.

"Where is General Branch?" Lane inquired.

The major's voice sounded very shaken and emotional as he told the colonel, "He has just been shot; there he goes on that stretcher, dead, and you are in command of the brigade."

**BRIGADIER GENERAL
L. O'BRIEN BRANCH,
brigade commander, ANV**

A stray bullet killed him near the southern end of Otto's lane just as the battle ended on September 17. *(William E. Strong Collection, Duke U.)*

The words echoed emptily in Lane's ears as his eyes followed the corpse from the field. A blind shot had struck Branch in the head and instantly killed him seconds after he called for Lane.[65] *(Map 70)*

The Confederates had no intention of overwhelming the Federals.

The cornered 35th Massachusetts bore the brunt of the Confederate counterattack with Lieutenant John N. Coffin's section. The Rebel artillery seemed to concentrate on the regiment, which, numbering around eight hundred men, must have appeared as large as a brigade. The New Englanders went prone and returned fire as fast as they could. File closers and line officers, pursuant to regulations, remained upright and tended to their lines. Following the first disorganized volley, the shooting devolved to firing at will.

Ramrods clattered fitfully down bores. Men cursed between rounds. Others screamed when they were hit. A sulfuric cloud enveloped the entire position. A bullet ripped through Lieutenant Colonel Carruth's neck very close to the jugular vein. Captain Stephen H. Andrews (A Co.), senior captain, immediately took over as Carruth staggered up the hill toward the bridge.

On the left, in K Company, all three officers were wounded. Over fifty percent of the company's sixty men were casualties, among them Privates Roscoe Bradley, who had boasted before going into action that he would come out unscathed, and his comrade, Sergeant William N. Merserve. They dropped simultaneously.

"Merserve I'm hit," Bradley blurted.

"So am I," shouted Merserve, as two bullets struck him in quick succession in the left arm.

Seconds later, Bradley cried, "Merserve I'm killed."

He collapsed, dead, in his sergeant's arms. The sergeant quietly put his friend down and started to tie off his arm above the elbow.

At one point, Captain William S. King (K Co.), the acting major, picked up a musket and shot at a cluster of Confederate flags behind the stone wall. His men cheered him feebly. They were too busy to worry about an officer's bravado.

Rifle barrels overheated. Forestocks smoldered. Cartridges jammed partway down fouled bores but the men triggered the pieces anyway without properly seating the bullets. They fired at every opportunity. Being "green", their officers did not have the sense to retire when common sense dictated to do so.

By dusk, as the casualties mounted and ammunition became harder to find, the regiment's rate of fire diminished perceptibly. Captains John Lathrop (I Co.) and William King (K Co.), who was severely wounded, crawled among the dead and

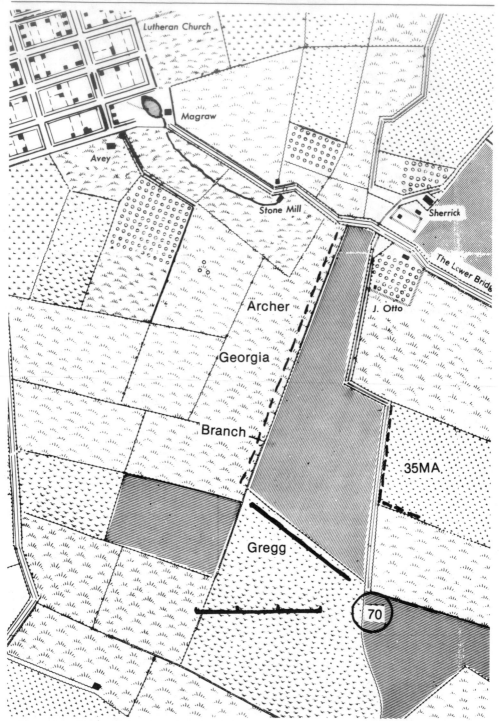

(Map 70) 4:20 P.M. — DARK, SEPTEMBER 17, 1862
The 35th Massachusetts shows its mettle.

injured, scrounging for cartridges. Above the racket they occasionally heard Captain Tracy Cheever (C Co.) advising his people to, "Pop away! boys, Pop away!" The left wing continued to get pounded mercilessly, while the right, under the protection of Coffin's section, took fewer hits.[66]

The Harper's Ferry Road

Lieutenant Coffin's section scored a direct hit on Captain David McIntosh's Battery. A bursting shell struck down the battery's teenage color bearer, Baxter Rollins, just as the Napoleon, which he was manning, fired. His feet slipped, and he fell under the wheel of the recoiling artillery piece. A couple of men tried to carry him to the Harper's Ferry Road, but he would not hear of it.

"Don't carry me to the rear, boys," he protested, "carry me to my flag. I know I must die and I want to die by my flag." They complied. He died peacefully.[67]

The Lower Bridge

From his position on the hilltop to the regiment's left rear of the 35th Massachusetts, Lieutenant John Hudson observed the fighting with Lieutenant Alfred Walcott (B Co., 21st MA). Neither ventured into the bullet riddled valley. While they were there, Adjutant Nathaniel Wales (35th MA) hobbled up to them from the creek.

ADJUTANT NATHANIEL WALES, 35th Massachusetts

Protected by body armor, he went into the fight near Otto's farm to "get a lick" at the Rebels. They got him first. (USAMHI)

Having deserted a sick bed at the regimental hospital, he donned Lieutenant James Baldwin's breast armor, picked up his Sharp's rifle, and headed for the fighting. He asked Hudson for the regiment's location, commenting that he wanted "to have a lick at the rebs." Going to the right, he climbed over the wall and tottered down to the regiment. The Rebs licked him first. A ball struck him in the left breast, immediately below the heart and knocked the wind out of him. Bruised by the dented armor, the lieutenant staggered away from the fighting.[68]

The adjutant of the 21st Massachusetts scrambled up the hillside from the battle, where he joined Hudson and Walcott behind the stone wall. He wanted to know where Colonel Ferrero could be found. The regiment had no ammunition and needed to be relieved.

At that point Walcott ran down toward the bridge to ferret out his ever elusive brigadier. Hudson and the adjutant settled down for a seemingly endless wait.[69]

The Middle Bridge

The Yankee advance against Garnett's Brigade nearly cost S. D. Lee his guns. As Garnett's people retreated, leaving the batteries along the Boonsboro Pike unprotected, Lee went berserk. Snatching a regimental flag, he heroically waved it from one side to the other, all the while screaming for the men to rally.

"I will stand by you."

The voice of a solitary infantryman by his side jolted him into reality and he retired with the rest of the brigade while the batteries north of the road stymied the Federal advance.[70]

The Lower Bridge

A tall Georgian captain bounded into the mill house orchard from the west and accosted Orderly Sergeant Frank Mixon (E Co., 1st SC Vols.), whom he found standing under one of the trees with an apple in his mouth.

"Where is your gun?" the captain demanded, "and why are you not shooting?"

"I am the colonel's orderly," Mixon rudely retorted.

The captain asked where the colonel was. Mixon told him that no one commanded the regiment at the moment.

The officer screamed at the South Carolinians to pull back. The rest of the brigade had retreated to an east-west line on the Lower Bridge Road and had flanked Welsh's Brigade from the north. The 1st South Carolina was isolated.

In the racket, Sergeant Mixon failed to notice what was going on around him. A glance to the right at the Yankees' closing in on the mill's barn brought him around.

"First South Carolina, retreat," he called.

The few Confederates left in the regiment bolted like jumped rabbits. Skirting around the front of the 45th Pennsylvania, they barely escaped capture. They left behind Captain Twiggs and ten men from the Holcombe's Legion (Evans' BG) in the mill house.

Half way up the hill toward the town, Frank Mixon (E Co., 1st SC Vols.) happened upon Talt Best. Talt lay on his back with a thigh wound. Extending both hands toward his sergeant, he pleaded to be carried off.

"Frank," he begged, "don't leave me here to die."

Mixon hailed over Sid Key (1st SC Vols.) and they dragged the man to safety.[71]

Sharpsburg

Captain Squires pulled his guns south along the top of the ridge to evade the Federal shells along the Boonsboro Pike. In so doing, he crossed the front of Welsh's Brigade (45th, 100th PA, 46th NY, and 8th MI) which was halted near the mill house on the Lower Bridge Road. The captain stared mutely at the silent Yankee formation, which stood about one hundred yards away. The Yankees made no attempt to fire at him. Counting his blessings, he slipped his crew into Sharpsburg to restock their ammunition chests.[72] W. R. Garden's battered guns followed him. Turning right onto the Lower Bridge Road, they continued to the Boonsboro Pike, then moved west into the Pike.

Not long before, Lieutenant Thompson Brown's crew (Parker's Btty.) reached the base of the hill where the Hagerstown Pike crosses Sharpsburg into the Lower Bridge Road. Colonel S. D. Lee halted them. He could see how terribly small they were — just enough artillerists to man two guns.

"You are boys," he stated truthfully enough, "but you have this day been where only brave men dare go. Some of your company have been killed; many have been wounded, but remember it is a soldier's duty to die, now, every man of you who is willing to return to the field, step two paces to the front."

They all did. Each one believed that the fate of the Army of Northern Virginia depended on him personally.

No sooner had they crossed the intersection than Squires' and Garden's Batteries rumbled down the Boonsboro Pike, away from the fighting. Lieutenant Brown tried to pass the guns on the side of the road, but Captain Charles Squires hailed him over.

"Who are you, and where are you taking those two guns?" the captain demanded.

"To take the hill you are leaving," Thompson Brown shot back.

"I can't hold it with two batteries, how can you with two guns? Return with me," Squires insisted, "or you will be cut to pieces."

"We are occupying this particular hill under special orders of Colonel Stephen D. Lee," the lieutenant shouted.

The fatigued and filthy artillerists nearly died from shock as they swung onto the brow of the hill three hundred yards north of the Boonsboro Pike. Besides a squadron of Pleasonton's overly cautious 4th Pennsylvania Cavalry and Sykes' Regulars, most of whom stayed fairly well in the ravine west of their own guns, the newly arrived Confederates could see the hills to the southeast swarming with blue uniformed troops.[73] Lieutenant Thompson Brown (Parker's Btty.) and his two crews immediately deployed into battery and threw a round of canister into the Yankee lines along the Boonsboro Pike. With each shot, the guns recoiled further west until they were below the crest of their ridge. As the cannons rolled more and more below the horizon, the gunners increased their elevation to drop charges, somewhat ineffectively, into the Federal ranks. They were not driven away from the fighting by First Sergeant Francis E. Lacey (I Co., 2nd U.S.) and his men but by the recoil of their own pieces, which the fatigued and rattled artillerists could not manhandle back to their original positions. By dark, one gun was lodged firmly against an ice house at the base of the hill. The crew loosed several rounds from there before calling it quits.[73] One of them, Private Willie Evans, passed out by the gun from exhaustion. He did not awaken until the battalion adjutant nudged him to tell him to pull out.[74]

The Middle Bridge

In the darkness, Captain Hiram Dryer (4th U.S., commanding) mounted up and quietly rode down the Boonsboro Pike into the Confederate lines. He quickly discovered that two regiments (Garnett's Brigade) and a single battery (probably Jordan's) connected Lee's flanks. Stealing back to his own lines he scrawled a note, the contents of which he cleared through the senior officer upon the field (Cpt. Matthew M. Blunt, 1st Bttn., 12th U.S.), to Lieutenant Colonel Robert Buchanan, his brigade commander.

An aide clattered across the Middle Bridge to the colonel, who was chatting with Captain Thomas M. Anderson (2nd Bttn., 12th U.S.). Buchanan read the note and returned it to the aide with orders to run it to Brigadier General George Sykes, the Division commander.

As the courier galloped south to relay the message to Sykes, Buchanan turned to Anderson and informed him that Dryer proposed that his 4th U.S., Blunt's 1st Battalion, 12th U.S., and Captain Harvey Brown's 1st Battalion, 14th U.S. launch a night assault upon Lee's center. The two officers realized how vulnerable the Army of Northern Virginia was at that point and that the V Corps had an opportunity to crush "Bobby" Lee before he crossed into Virginia.

They carefully observed Sykes discussing the message with Fitz Porter (V Corps) and George B. McClellan (Army of the Potomac). All three were mounted about one hundred yards to the south between Taft's (5th NY, Indpt.) and Weed's (I, 4th U.S.) Batteries. They saw the note being passed in the bright moonlight between the officers but could not hear the conversation. As usual, the idea died at the highest level of command. Nothing happened.[75]

Fitz Porter deliberately ignored Captain Dryer's communique. His reserve of approximately eleven thousand men could not operate independent of George McClellan's direct orders. The Commanding General had already sent two of Brigadier General Charles Griffin's brigades toward the Pry house to strengthen Sumner's battered Corps. Brigadier General Gouverneur K. Warren's Brigade was to the south to reinforce the IX Corps should it need help.

"*I* commanded the Reserve," Porter later noted. "At no time did I receive any order to put troops in action on the 17th — or even a suggestion."

With a force of less than three thousand soldiers at the Middle Bridge, he firmly believed he could not risk committing them to action.

"My orders were to keep my men to protect the bridge — covering our main supplies, protect batteries, and be ready to be sent away when called for by McClellan," Porter insisted over twenty years later.

Both he and his commanding general feared being overrun by the numerically inferior Army of Northern Virginia.[76] *(Map 71)*

Sharpsburg — Bloody Lane — West Woods

The 21st Georgia (Trimble's BG) spent the entire afternoon straddling the Boonsboro Pike near the village square. During that time General Robert E. Lee spoke several times with Captain James Nisbet (acting C.O.), giving him specific instructions on reforming stragglers.

"Captain," he said, "don't let any pass but wounded men. Halt all other, and form them into line to your rear. Let the wounded go on to Shepherdstown."[77]

Nisbet and his small band of about seventy-five men performed their duty as faithfully as possible. Nisbet, who likened Lee to George Washington, adored the commanding general. It distressed him tremendously to see Lee so downcast and melancholy.[78]

Lee had a great deal to worry about, particularly from his own soldiers, who found it very difficult to remain in the ranks while surrounded by so many bountiful orchards. Hundreds of parched and starving men wandered about the battlefield pilfering food.

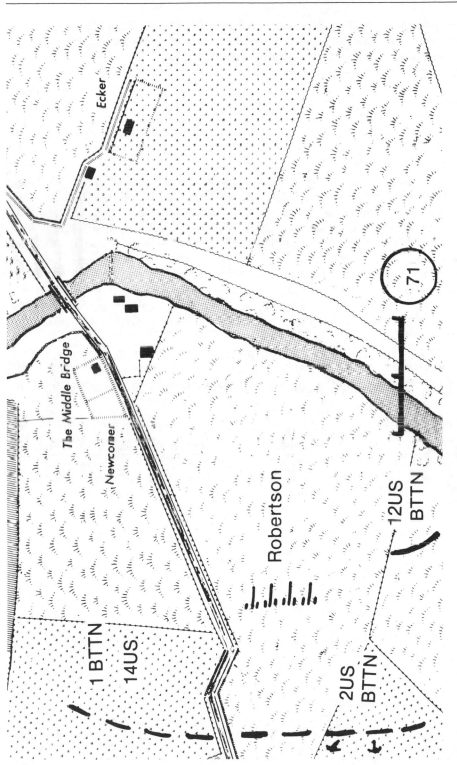

(Map 71) 4:20 P.M. — DARK, SEPTEMBER 17, 1862
The final disposition of the U.S. Regulars at the Middle Bridge.

Sergeant William H. Andrews (1st GA, Anderson's BG) left the West Woods with his brigade to a new position southwest of Piper's farm, along the Hagerstown Pike. The thirsty soldier walked away from his regiment down the pike toward a water pump near the town. An apple orchard on a corner lot detoured him.

The famished soldier, rifle in hand, bolted the post and rail fence on the western side of the pike. The trees were loaded with apples. Apples blanketed the ground. Within a few minutes his pockets and haversack bulged with stolen fruit. Not satisfied, the gluttonous Georgian snatched a discarded knapsack from nearby, plopped under a tree with one eye inattentively cocked on his brigade, and went to work. He wanted the food just to have it.

Two or three minutes later, a noise from very close by startled him. He found himself staring up the muzzle of Lee's horse, "Traveler". General Robert E. Lee glared icily down upon him from the saddle. The General was about ten feet away but to the frightened sergeant, he may as well have been standing on him.

Andrews dropped his incriminating knapsack, picked up his rifle, and snapped to "Attention". He instinctively brought the rifle to the "carry" and executed a proper rifle salute with his left forearm across his breast.

His precise military bearing did not impress the irate general. As the Regulars' provost guard surrounded the sergeant, Lee gave him a searing tongue lashing. So many words burst from the general's mouth that the sweating Andrews remembered only three of them.

"Straggler", "thief", "coward" Sergeant Andrews knew he was guilty of all three: straggler — he was not with his regiment; thief — his knotted trousers and stuffed haversack betrayed him; coward — he was scared to death. The general was livid.

"What command?" Lee snapped.

"Anderson's Brigade," Andrews blurted.

The general barked at the provost guard to escort the sergeant to the front lines. He then reined "Traveler" aside and cornered a barefoot looter nearby.

The man cried and begged so loudly that the provost detachment abandoned Andrews and encircled the soldier. The sergeant used the opportunity to scramble over the fence and return safely to the 1st Georgia.[79]

Intermittent riflery and artillery fire kept the troops along the Bloody Lane and the northern end of the Hagerstown Pike uncomfortably alert and jittery. Around 4:30 P.M., the Federals rolled Captain John Wolcott's (A, MD Lgt.) Battery into Mumma's swale, west of the farm lane and the cornfield. They were in the rear of the prone 7th Maine. Their presence immediately attracted sniper fire from Piper's haymounds.[80] The Confederates shot down twelve of Wolcott's people within half an hour.[81]

The Yankees contributed their share of havoc too. Private Knox (7th ME) crawled into some boulders paralleling the western end of the Bloody Lane shortly after 1:00 P.M. Over an hour later, Major Hyde (7th ME) inched to Knox's side on the crest of Mumma's swale to observe his handiwork. He was picking off gunners at an artillery section somewhere on the Piper farm. A Confederate general and some staff officers galloped onto the hill south of Piper's to survey the field when Knox squeezed off a round. An officer's horse plummeted suddenly to the ground and the others disappeared over the ridge.[82]

A cannon ball struck Major John W. Fairfax's stallion, "Saltron", underneath the tail, nearly tearing away the horse's genitals. The beautiful gray thoroughbred thudded loudly to the ground, throwing the elegant Major Fairfax from him with equal force.

The very excitable gentlemen limped over to General James Longstreet, the Corps commander. Longstreet, who was grimly observing the battle toward the Middle Bridge, did not appear too concerned about his major.

"General, General, my horse is killed," Fairfax cried in desperation, "Saltron is shot; shot right in the back!"

Longstreet stared rather queerly, almost unbelievingly at Fairfax, and bluntly silenced him with, "Never mind, Major, you ought to be glad you are not shot in your own back!"[83]

Privates James Dinkins, Billy McKee, Sam Finley, Lieutenant William McKie, and the two other enlisted men who comprised all that remained of Company C, 18th Mississippi (Barksdale's BG) passed the afternoon gorging themselves on apples in the orchard near the Nicodemus House. Yankee skirmishers eyed them for hours from the protection of D. R. Miller's stone wall along the Hagerstown Pike. Every now and then an artillery piece near the western edge of the East Woods dropped a round into the tree tops, pelting the powder stained veterans with more food.

About 4:00 P.M., Dinkins and Billy McKee, loaded down with empty canteens, and under the cover of twilight, edged their way to the small stream which flowed down into the West Woods from the southwestern corner of the Cornfield. Three generals — J. E. B. Stuart, Joseph B. Kershaw, and Howell Cobb — stood with Captain John Sims (21st MS) about fifty yards to the north, observing the Federals at Miller's.

A shell exploded among the group. Captain Sims fell backwards and thudded heavily upon the ground. James Dinkins immediately dashed to the captain's side. As he placed the canteen to the officer's mouth, Sims clutched it and tried to drink unassisted. His trembling hands clattered the mouth of the canteen against his teeth which spilled the water over his face.

Sam Finley (C Co., 18th MS) ran up to Dinkins. Each man grabbed one of the captain's arms and dragged him down the hill to cover. The powder burned generals followed. As a litter crew carried Sims to the rear, they returned to the limestone ledge along the Hagerstown Pike to continue their vigil.[84]

Captain Michael Shuler (H Co., 33rd VA) had seen enough killing to last him for a lifetime. Begging leave from his command because he felt ill, he trod south. He needed to escape the nauseating smell of death which permeated the area.[85]

The Nicodemus Farm

An unwounded comrade, probably a skulker, slipped up to Nathan Jordan (H Co., 19th MA) as he lay against one of Nicodemus' wheat stacks, and gave him a swig of wine from his canteen before he moved off. The wine brought Jordan around and seemed to make him more alert.

Realizing that if he remained upon the field after dark that he would probably never be found again, he decided to walk to safety. He painfully gained his feet and staggered east toward the Hagerstown Pike. A sentry near D. R. Miller's barn, with the help of some nearby pickets, helped him over the stonewall which bordered the Pike then sent him north. A civilian with a wagon filled with wounded picked him up a short distance down the road and took him to Hagerstown.[86]

CAPTAIN JACOB HAAS,
G Company, 96th Pennsylvania

He lost two men to one cannon ball in a "Quiet" sector near the East Woods. *(USAMHI)*

The East Woods

Confederate artillerists did their fair share of damage too. They sporadically dropped rounds into the Yankees to make their presence felt. A solitary round ball from the West Woods bounded into the 49th Pennsylvania (Hancock's BG) in the early afternoon and struck between Cowan's right gun (1st NY Indpt.) and the left flank of C Company.

Neither Private Benjamin F. Clarkson (C Co.) nor the horse holder he was conversing with knew of the ball's approach until it slammed into the lead horse's head and passed between them. Bone and brains splattered both of them. The artillerist, who was holding the horse's bridle, "was terribly splattered and was a sight to behold," Clarkson noted with understatement.

The blood and brains dried on Clarkson during the afternoon when the fighting cooled off in the East Woods sector. He heard the musketry and artillery from the IX Corps' assault and hoped it would not spread any further. The Confederates rolled a battery into the cornfield north of Nicodemus' house and opened fire. Captain Cowan immediately shifted his four three inch rifles northwest and replied with equal force. It ended in less than half an hour with the Confederates retreating.

As the battery withdrew, Confederate skirmishers, who had been feigning death amoung the corpses between the lines, leaped up and darted toward the West Woods. Company C cheered them on while sending a few harmless rounds at their backs. With darkness coming on, they did not care to start the battle anew.[87]

Not far to the south, behind the 5th Maine (Hancock's Brigade), the 96th Pennsylvania (Bartlett's Brigade), went into line on the eastern edge of the Cornfield. The carnage utterly shocked Captain Peter Filbert (B Co.). As he lay in the open, to the right of G Company, he counted forty corpses within a ten yard square area.

His brigade drew the attention of the same battery which pestered the 49th Pennsylvania. One of the 12 pound solid shot skittered into his prone regiment. Cutting over B Company, it grazed Captain Filbert and smashed into Captain Jacob Haas' Company G. The ball tore away Frank Treon's hands and one leg and ripped a leg from McCoy Sargent. Captain Haas immediately had both men carried to the rear. A short while later, the regiment retired to the East Woods.[88]

Mumma's Swale — The Piper Farm

Major Hyde (7th ME) wanted to see no more fighting, either. Wolcott's Battery (B, MD Lght.) of three inch rifles obscured the late afternoon sky in sulfuric clouds as they opened fire upon Lee's crews along the Boonsboro Pike.

Private Knox stole into the regiment shortly after the battery commenced firing. Showing Hyde the shattered breech of his target rifle — the effects of an aberrant Rebel shell fragment — he "borrowed" a couple of cartridge boxes and Windsor rifles from the regiment's few wounded before crawling back to his position along the Bloody Lane.[89]

Around 4:45 P.M., Captain Emory Upton, the First Division's artillery chief, and Colonel William Irwin, the brigade commander, rode into the battery to inspect the situation. Captain Wolcott complained bitterly to Colonel Irwin that Confederate snipers in the haymounds south of the Bloody Lane were taking out his crews.

Irwin rode over to Major Hyde (7th ME), whom he found lying below the crest of Mumma's swale.[90] The major had just sent a company as skirmishers, at Irwin's previous command, into the Bloody Lane to drive the snipers out, when Irwin accosted him.

"That is not enough, sir; go yourself; take your regiment and drive them from those trees and buildings," the colonel blustered.

The major, while rising and saluting, asked Irwin to repeat the command and point out the buildings.[91]

"Major Hyde," the colonel insisted, "take your regiment and drive the enemy away from those trees and buildings."

Thomas Hyde tried to avoid what he believed was a "forlorn hope".

"Colonel," he persisted, "I have seen a large force of rebels go in there, I should think two brigades."[92]

The colonel, who posted the batteries to break up the troops which he knew were massing in Piper's swale, ignored the major.[93]

"Are you afraid to go, sir?" Irwin spat. A string of oaths blistered Hyde's ears as the colonel reiterated the command and added, "Those are your orders, sir."

The major, rather than lose face or risk being cashiered for insubordination, shouted, "Give the order so the regiment can hear it, and we are ready, sir."

William Irwin screamed the order a fourth time.[94]

Lieutenant Lyman M. Shorey (F Co.) never forgot the command. Every officer and enlisted man knew that the Confederates had at least a brigade sized force in Piper's swale.[95] Thomas Hyde bawled his small regiment to "Attention". As the men fell into regimental front, the major told his two teenage guidon bearers — the boys who carried a small flag to mark the flanks of the line — to go rearward. Downcast, the two stepped off very slowly toward Mumma's house. They slipped back into the

LIEUTENANT LYMAN SHOREY,
F Company, 7th Maine

He was shot in the foot during Thomas Hyde's assault upon the Piper barn.
(Manuscript Dept., USAMHI)

ranks when the major was not looking. Hyde also instructed Color Corporal Harry Campbell to surrender the colors to Sergeant Perry Greenleaf but the corporal pouted so much that Hyde let him retain them.[96]

Lieutenant Butler and his fifteen man company fanned out beyond the Bloody Lane, driving the Rebs from Piper's orchard.[97] Meanwhile, the rest of the regiment filed by the left to the open crest paralleling the Bloody Lane, south of Mumma's cornfield, and faced front.

The New Englanders gingerly stepped among, over, and on the mangled Confederates in the lane before crawling up the opposite bank into Piper's cornfield, where they realigned. Adjutant Haskell, mounted upon the colonel's white horse, "Whitey", covered the left rear of the line. Major Hyde, on his Virginia thoroughbred, controlled the right wing. Hyde wheeled the regiment southwest and sent it crashing through the corn toward the right of Piper's barns at the double quick with leveled bayonets.

Wolcott's Maryland Battery (B, MD Lght.) fired over the Mainers as they descended into Piper's swale. In the dimming light the gunners dropped a couple of their canister shots too low. The first round struck down four Yankees on the right flank. The second knocked down Lieutenant Haskell and the colonel's "Whitey".

A cast iron ball struck Color Corporal Campbell in the right arm. As he thrust the bloodied hand up to give the colors to Hyde, the major shouted, "Take the other hand, Harry."[98] The regiment halted two times to volley before reaching the barn.[99]

Simultaneously, Private Westwood A. Todd (A Co., 12th VA) peered over the stone wall along the Hagerstown Pike in time to see Colonel William Gibson, in his shirt sleeves, trying to lead some of "Tige Anderson's" Georgians into Piper's swale. A Federal shell roared across his rear end; it carried away his shirt tail, and left the seat of his pants smoldering.[100]

Warmed, but not hurt, the old man threw his arms in the air and screamed, "Forward men, the whole line forward."

G. W. Edmontson (6th VA), the color bearer for Parham's small brigade, went down with a shattered knee cap. The flag fell to the ground and two quick thinking soldiers, grabbing Edmontson by the armpits, dragged him backwards over the wall along the Hagerstown Pike.[101]

The Confederates near the barns and the haystacks scattered, throwing aside their flag as they ran up the slope southwest of the buildings toward the Hagerstown

Pike.[102] Thomas Hyde spurred to the front of his wheezing line, trying to pick up the colors ahead of them. He rode into an ambuscade. As he topped the rise, twenty feet in advance of his men, a line of Confederates rose up and loosed a volley at them from the right and the front, while another body of Rebels ran toward the regiment's left flank. Within moments, they dropped about ten to twelve line officers and about two thirds of the regiment. Lieutenant Lyman Shorey (F Co.) limped back toward the Federal lines with a mangled foot.[103] The retreating Confederates, realizing that they outnumbered the 7th Maine, halted abruptly, reformed, and turned to countercharge.

Hyde instantly ordered his people to charge by the left flank which sent them careening away from the riflery. Cutting east on Piper's lane, the Yankees swarmed over and through the post and rail fence bordering the cow yard. The soldiers slipped through easily but the major's horse got pinned against the fence.

Sergeant Benson tore away the rails to let the major pass. Canister ripped through his haversack, scattering hard crackers everywhere. Hyde and the sergeant laughed as they made for the apple orchard on the hillside.

Part way up the slope the regiment came under fire from the ridge south of Piper's. Several volleys peppered the Yankees, then the Rebels charged.

Major Hyde's horse reared in pain. The major slipped out of the saddle to inspect the damage while the regiment hastily regrouped. Discovering that buck and ball loads had merely hit the horse in the rear and had knocked out its rear teeth, he remounted.

Barely one hundred yards away, the Confederates swarmed through the fence opening. His men cut them down with a good volley then retired up the slope.

Harry Campbell, the color bearer, screamed in pain. Hyde wheeled about, and rode south to retrieve the flag only to discover that the Confederates had worked through the orchard between him and his men. They were so close that Hyde could clearly discern "Manassas" on a battle flag in the darkness.

He turned his horse north and wove through the trees toward the northwestern corner of the high picket fence which bordered the field on three sides. The regiment crossed the fence at that point into the cornfield, but the major's thoroughbred could not negotiate it. He presently found himself surrounded by no less than one dozen Rebels.

"Rally, boys, to save the major," rang out in the night.

The New Englanders shoved their rifles through the fence slats and fired while Sergeant Hill cut an opening in the pickets with his saber bayonet which allowed Hyde to escape. Musketry slammed into the regiment's back and Federal canister clattered through the corn stalks as the Yankees stubbornly reformed. Three officers and sixty-five enlisted men gathered around the colors, which the only surviving member of the color guard — Corporal Ring — had saved before Hyde could reach them. One hundred one of the men lay scattered about the swale.[104]

As the regiment appeared on the open ground along the Bloody Lane, Brooks' Vermont Brigade rose up and cheered it. Colonel Irwin, who was apparently trying to round up reinforcements, breathed a sigh of relief. When the 7th Maine fell into its old position, Major Hyde curled up under a blanket with three of his officers — Channing, Weber, and Nickerson. The four cried themselves to sleep.[105] *(Map 72)*

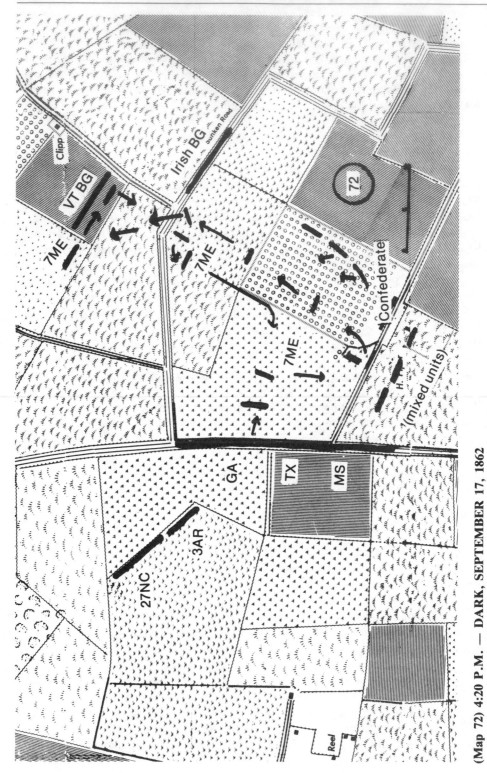

(Map 72) 4:20 P.M. — DARK, SEPTEMBER 17, 1862

The 7th Maine makes a desperate charge into Piper's swale.

The Hagerstown Pike

Major General James Longstreet, while witnessing the 7th Maine's gallant charge toward his vulnerable center, dispatched Major Moxley Sorrel to the high ground about six hundred yards south of the Dunker Church to Colonel John R. Cooke and his two regiments, the 3rd Arkansas and the 27th North Carolina. Since Irwin's Brigade of the VI Corps repulsed his drive at noon, Cooke's stalwarts had held their key position without any ammunition. The colonel repeatedly begged for cartridges, but there were none to be had.

"Major," Longstreet commanded, "go down to that regiment with my compliments to the colonel. Say he has fought splendidly and must keep it up. We are hard pressed and if he loses his position there is nothing left behind him; his men have made noble sacrifices, but are to do still more."

A stray bullet wounded Sorrel's horse as he cut across the fields to the hill and Cooke's post. There were many dead and disabled along the Pike and the Federal musketry roared and clashed incessantly.

Sorrel, a very devout Christian, never forgot the bold Cooke's heated response. It burned indelibly in his mind.

"Major, thank General Longstreet for his good words, but say, by God almighty, he needn't doubt me! We will stay here, by Jesus Christ, if we must all go to hell together! That damn thick line of the enemy has been fighting all day, but my regiment is ready to lick the whole damn outfit. Start away, Major, or you'll be getting hurt too, exposed as you are on that horse."

Their hands barely parted when an exploding shell knocked Sorrel from his horse, unconscious. Colonel Cooke had bearers carry the major off while he braced himself for what seemed like a Federal attack.[106]

It took some time for the artillery fire to subside on both sides. Lieutenant William W. Chamberlaine (G Co., 6th VA) and two of his men, George M. Todd and Chandler W. Hill (both from G Co.) still manned their six pound brass gun in Piper's lane. The lieutenant was scanning the terrain to the north with field glasses when something struck him across his face with tremendous force.

Blood gushed all over him. Not knowing whether he was mortally wounded or just grazed, he clapped a hand across his nose and stumbled toward Sharpsburg with George Todd.[107]

The Lower Bridge

Lieutenant John W. Hudson (Ferrero's aide) and the adjutant of the 21st Massachusetts became very concerned over Lieutenant Alfred Walcott's (B Co., 21st MA) absence. Hudson finally loped down to the bridge where he found Walcott and General Samuel Sturgis. When the general, who had just arrived, asked Walcott about the situation along Otto's lane, the aide blurted, "General, our regiments can't hold that position any longer; to my certain knowledge they are mostly out of ammunition, and some have been quite so nearly an hour."

Sturgis stood a moment, deep in thought. "By God, they must hold it; we've nothing else to hold it with." At that Lieutenant Hudson returned to the stone wall to wait out the battle.[108]

The battered 35th Massachusetts could not withstand the pressure. Captain John Lathrop (I Co.) told his men that three regiments were coming to their relief — after Captain William S. King (K Co.) disappeared while trying to locate them.[109] Coffin's artillery section retired shortly after dark. The Rebel riflery and canister increased as the day became darker and more troops poured into their ranks. With most of their ammunition gone and casualties increasing, the New Englanders withdrew up the hillside. Their promised reinforcements never arrived.

The 21st Massachusetts, less forty-five of its original one hundred fifty men, retreated with them. Their ammunition exhausted, they had spent the last half hour alone in support of their fellow New Englanders. Private Marcus Emmons (K Co.) bitterly complained that their brother regiments, the 51st New York and the 51st Pennsylvania, abandoned them when they ran out of bullets.

The 35th Massachusetts left behind its dead and their non-ambulatory wounded, surrendering the field to the Confederates, whose flashing rifles and muskets resembled fireworks in the night. Their battle was over.[110] In the darkness, the two regiments scattered all over the field. Lieutenant Albert Pope (I Co.) had no idea where his men were. All he knew was that he was in the waist deep Antietam heading for safer ground.[111]

Neither side had gained an advantage of any sort. Only the wounded, the dead, the dying, and the looters possessed the fields.

Both armies consolidated their lines much as they had been that morning. The Army of Northern Virginia still occupied the West Woods. While it had stubbornly forfeited the Lower Bridge, the Bloody Lane, and Mumma's swale, it still had kept the Army of the Potomac from breaking through its link to Virginia, the road to Shepherdstown, Virginia. Battered, but not broken, the Confederates contracted their lines and prepared to give battle again.

CHAPTER SEVENTEEN

"They look and stare upon me."

EVENING, SEPTEMBER 17, 1862

The Lower Bridge

When the exhausted New Englanders reached the summit above the Lower Bridge they could not believe what they encountered. Regiment after regiment was drawn up in battle front on the hillside and in the valley along the creek. Those soldiers who remained of the 35th Massachusetts pulled themselves into column and marched down to the creek where many of them fell out to scrub the blood and powder from their faces and uniforms.

Reforming in what looked more like squads than companies, they marched north on the road toward their former position. A commissary sergeant stood at the bend in the road with a partially filled barrel of boiled beef. As each soldier dragged himself past the barrel, he fished his hand in for a chunk of meat. On the top of the ridge the regiment filed by a waiting ammunition wagon and replenished their cartridge boxes. By then the field had been yielded to the pickets on both sides. The regiment stacked arms and counted its losses. The 21st Massachusetts remained along the creek bank. In the descent, twenty men lost themselves in the darkness. The adjutant counted only eighty-five men present for duty.[1]

Private Alexander Hunter (A Co., 17th VA) halted on the hilltop west of the Lower Bridge to gaze for a final time upon the battlefield. The village looked aflame with the brilliant red of the dying sun flickering across the distant window panes. The battle seemed over.

Turning east, the party came across the same troops as the 35th Massachusetts. One of his comrades gasped that there were not less than ten thousand Yankees gathered there.

301

Trotting down to the bridge, they passed a field hospital. Hunter found a Georgian cut in half by a round ball and four Yankees — victims of a single shell — piled together in a heap.

He crossed the creek and was put into a large herd of about five hundred Confederate officers and enlisted men. The tired soldier bedded down on the ground with the prisoners and fell asleep without a cover.[2]

C. A. Forney (I Co., 30th OH) felt chilled as he tried to sleep among the disorganized Ohions west of the bridge. The regiment had no blankets. The men lying next to him had one, so Forney decided to "share it". Without asking, he reached over to snatch the cover when his fingers came in contact with the cold lifelessness of a corpse. Completely unnerved, Forney crawled to another spot to sleep.[3]

The Harper's Ferry Road

Private Almon L. Reed (F Co., 89th NY) played dead throughout the evening as McIntosh's Battery fired over his head. All evening long Confederates repeatedly rifled his pockets looking for money or souvenirs.[4]

Private David Thompson (G Co., 9th NY) and the eleven wounded men in the hollow east of Otto's lane surrendered to the 15th Georgia. They followed their captors back to the Harper's Ferry Road and bivouacked on the ground without blankets.[5]

The 40 Acre Cornfield

Private Berry Benson (1st SC) hunkered down in the ditch in the forty acre cornfield and tried to forget his hand in the bloodletting that day. He could not erase the brutal slaying of that noble Yankee officer and his mount. He consoled himself with the fact that the officer died a short time after he had fired his last round at him. He felt ill and blamed it on a previous ailment.[6]

A short distance to the east, in the same cornfield, Private Edwin B. "Ned" Lillie (C Co., 16th CT) regained consciousness. A ball, apparently, had broken one of his legs above the ankle when the regiment fled from the field. He quickly pulled out his handkerchief and tied it around his wound, which for some reason, was not bleeding badly.

Nearby, within arm's reach, he found his friend, John Loveland (C Co.), in a semiconscious state. Lillie dragged himself to Loveland's side and dripped what water he had left in his canteen over his comrade's shattered leg. The sixteen year old unselfishly jerked the handkerchief from his own wound and tied up Loveland's leg with it. The pressure temporarily revived his friend.

Looking about, Ned attempted to sort out the hundreds of wailing voices which he heard pleading for water. He locked his stare upon one boy who was propped upright against a cornstalk.

The sun had blistered the poor soldier's face and had swollen his tongue until it protruded between his teeth, like a dog's. "Water, water," he listlessly moaned.

Lillie inched his way to the child and handed him an ear of corn which he found on the ground beside him. The boy bit into it. Blood suddenly gushed from his chest wound and he died with the cob in his mouth. Ned Lillie crawled back to the mortally wounded John Loveland to await what he believed to be his own inevitable death.[7]

In the darkness, Private Frederick Pettitt (C Co., 100th PA) stumbled upon John Wilson of his company in the saw mill orchard. Wilson calmly plucked the buckshot out of his knee while Pettitt kindled a small fire for some coffee. There was no way they could find the hospital that night. They bedded down among the trees.[8]

Otto's Lane

For what seemed like hours, Corporal Frank Whitman (G Co., 35th MA) remained among the tangled bodies of his regiment with another uninjured comrade. As they rose to leave, they each fired a parting shot at the Confederate pickets who were silhouetted along the stone wall. A sudden volley killed Whitman's friend.

The corporal flopped among the bodies and started groping about in the shadows for more unwounded men. The dying and the wounded who surrounded him screamed and moaned pitifully as he worked among them. Pleas for water emanated from everywhere. He discovered two other unharmed men, and for several hours they crept among the injured, trying to relieve their suffering before they stole up the hillside to look for their regiment.[9]

Corporal Whitman found Captain Lathrop (I Co.) and Lieutenant Hudson (D Co.) around midnight and, with about fifteen volunteers, recrossed the ridge. Colonel Hartranft's Pennsylvanians (51st PA) would not allow the enlisted men beyond their perimeter on the western side of the crest. The colonel permitted Lathrop and Hudson to proceed about halfway down the slope to get four men who had crawled a short distance out of the swale.

The rescuers had to be careful. The moon was very bright and Confederate sentries were beyond the position formerly held by the regiment. The two officers dragged three of the wounded back. (The remaining one died before they reached him.) For a few hours longer they assisted with carrying in the wounded who had crawled into the picket line. Using blankets as stretchers they bore soldiers into the creek valley to the field hospitals.

Meanwhile, Corporal Whitman (G Co.) persuaded the Pennsylvanians to let him into the valley to bring back a wounded man from his company. The intrepid soldier crept between the Confederate sentries and found his friend, whose leg was shattered.

Whispering to the fellow to be quiet and cooperate, the corporal slowly and agonizingly pulled the helpless man up the steep hill. It seemed like it took forever to get the fellow to the pickets.

The exhausted corporal rejoined his regiment and collapsed in the grass — sound asleep. Lieutenant Hudson (D Co.) curled up on the muddy creek bank near the western end of the bridge. He had no covers.[10]

The Lower Bridge

At midnight, the 48th Pennsylvania retired, under increased pressure from the Confederate skirmishers, to the hilltop west of the creek. The afternoon's scrap cost Captain James Wren's B Company three enlisted men — Fred Knittle, Matthew Hume, and Laurentus Moyer — all of whom were severely wounded.

An hour later an ammunition wagon pulled up to the base of the hill and resupplied the regiment's empty cartridge boxes. Falling in battle formation again along the crest, the men nestled down on empty bellies for a damp night.[11]

The J. F. Miller Farm

Dr. Theodore Dimon (surgeon, 2nd MD) established a field hospital at J. F. Miller's house, approximately eight hundred fifty yards northeast of N. Rohrbach's. After rousting stragglers and an idle driver with his ambulance from the barn, which was attached to the house, he tended to the slightly wounded. He appointed them cooks and nurses.

The 35th Massachusetts comprised a large portion of his severely wounded. Shortly after the doctor established himself in the house, three enlisted men staggered in with a "fat lieutenant, who was in great agony", slung between them on a blanket.

A quick examination revealed that the lieutenant, James H. Baldwin (D Co., 35th MA), had one hole in his leg and four or five "fat" wounds, none of which proved dangerous. Doctor Dimon untwisted the tourniquet around Baldwin's pudgy thigh which relieved most of his discomfort.

An hour or so later, while making his rounds, Dimon dropped in on the lieutenant, whom he had bedded down in one of the house's bedrooms.

Stripped, sponged, bandaged, and pillowed down, the officer was very distressed about his injuries. The surgeon quickly cheered him up by telling him he would probably be home on furlough within a few weeks.

"Oh," Baldwin joyfully beamed, "isn't this rich! Only a month away from home and back there again with wounds; get in a big battle, and victory; and all the girls running after me, and all the fellows envious."

The doctor left the lieutenant bubbling in his own joy. He scrounged up a few lanterns and put them in the barn, which was filled with wounded. He put himself to bed "in a regular bed" around midnight — worn out, but comfortable.[12] Private Charles F. Johnson (I Co., 9th NY) lay on the house porch, too crippled to move. The walk from Kemper's ridge to the Miller house — about one and one half miles — left him nearly paralyzed and terribly hungry. The two fist sized chunks of meat he snatched from a company cook, who was en route to the front, did not satiate his empty stomach. A friendly red legged and turbanned Zouave from the 5th New York (Warren's BG, V Corps) fetched Johnson all the apples he desired. Unattended, with a musket ball lodged in the flesh of his left hip, the nineteen year old private slipped into a tormented sleep.

He found himself unharmed, but hopelessly trapped in the vortex of a monstrous whirlpool. Rattlesnakes, demons, fire, brimstone, cannon balls, railroad iron, bayonets, and pitchforks, bathed in black powder and sulfuric smoke, darted, poked, and spun insanely around him. A sharp pain in his stomach jolted him to consciousness — cramps from too many apples. He stayed awake the better part of the night.[13]

The Middle Bridge

The bulk of the U.S. Regulars pulled back across the Middle Bridge with all of Pleasonton's Cavalry Division and the horse artillery between 7:00 P.M. and 8:00 P.M.[14] Companies D and E (1st Bttn., 12th U.S.) remained as skirmishers on the ridge west of the bridge. In the bright moonlight Lieutenant Thomas Evans cautiously observed the Rebels moving about on the hill east of the Lutheran church. The flames from the burning houses silhouetted them against the horizon. He passed the night on duty, and slept undisturbed.[15]

Sharpsburg

Captain James Nisbet (H Co., 21st GA) took a moment to relax. He felt very nauseous, the after shock of being struck in the side that morning. Bill Stewart (A Co., 6th GA), who was slightly wounded, helped Nisbet unroll his blanket and rubber ground sheet. A flattened minie ball dropped out of the folds onto the ground. After reporting to a surgeon, Nisbet with Captain Henry Battle (C Co., 21st GA), who was shot through the calf, limped down the Boonsboro Pike. They were heading toward Boeteler's Ford and Shepherdstown.[16]

They joined a portion of the Army of Northern Virginia's ambulance train. The semiconscious Lieutenant Ezra E. Stickley (5th VA) bounced along in one of the ambulances. He left more than just his personal belongings and a fine horse upon the field. When Doctors Sawyer and Black (Grigsby's brigade surgeons) removed his right arm and finally tied off his arteries, they carelessly left his arm under a kitchen table. At that moment, the lieutenant was grateful to be alive.[17]

Major Moxley Sorrel came around with the taste of whiskey in his mouth. Major John Fairfax, forgetting some personal feud between them, was pouring liquor, as delicately as the circumstances permitted, down the teetotaler's throat. Fairfax gently assisted Sorrel examine his wounds. A severe purple bruise extended from the base of his right shoulder blade down to his waist. Sorrel thanked God he was not paralyzed as he had originally feared.[18]

The Road to Shepherdstown, Virginia

West of the town, Lieutenant William W. Chamberlaine (G Co., 6th VA), his face swollen and terribly bruised, stretched out in a huge haymound west of the town. With the exception of a groove cut across the slightly fractured bridge of his nose, he had come away from the fighting in relatively good health. He slept, unmolested, throughout the night.[19]

Across the river in Shepherdstown, Virginia, Private Elliott Welch (Hampton's Legion) stumbled into the home of a Mr. and Mrs. Criswell. The couple's hearts went out to the starving wounded man and several of his injured comrades. When the filthy and exhausted soldiers asked Mrs. Criswell to cook a little meat for them, she also baked fresh bread and set out preserves from her pantry. As the soldiers wolfed down her gifts, she invited them to come back again before leaving the town. Elliott Welch, who had spent the better part of the day looking for a surgeon to bind his head up, never forgot her hospitality.[20]

The West Woods

Confederate soldiers scrounged among the corpses looking for loot and for friends — in no particular order. Private Asa Fletcher (A Co., 15th MA) begged the Rebel stretcher crew to carry him off. They cleaned out his pockets and grudgingly bore him to a nearby barn. Bedded down in the straw and given water, the Yankee felt much relieved. He asked an attendant when he would be treated. The nurse concluded his curse with "when we uns are taken care of."[21]

Brigadier Generals John Walker and William Barksdale gingerly wove their horses through the West Woods. As they approached the worm fence on the eastern edge of the woods they heard a feeble plea, "Don't let your horses t-r-e-a-d on me-e!"

The two officers reined their horses short and peered over their pommels into the darkness. A body was across their path.

"Who are you?" Walker asked.

"I belong to the 20th Mas-sa-chu-setts reg-i-ment. I can't move — I think my back's broken."

The two officers had an ambulance brought up and the man was cared for properly.[22]

Color Sergeant Samuel Bloomer (1st MN) found his leg swelling terribly. By dusk, the leg had completely buried the tourniquet beneath a taut mass of blackened flesh. With his water gone, Bloomer felt like giving up to what he believed was his certain death.

The sound of an approaching horseman attracted his attention. General Thomas J. Jackson, who was patrolling the West Woods on a private reconnaissance, rode up to the critically wounded Minnesotan and asked to which regiment he belonged. The general's compassionate words touched Bloomer deeply. Before he rode away, Jackson ordered several men, who were tending Federal prisoners, to see to the sergeant's needs.

A North Carolinian officer, presently, dismounted and offered his canteen to Bloomer. While the Yankee eagerly swallowed a mouthful of the warm water, the officer very kindly tried to bolster the wounded man's morale. He wanted to convince Bloomer that he would recover from his ugly injury. After a few minutes, the officer remounted and trotted off, leaving the Yankee to fate.[23]

The East Woods

Private Benjamin Clarkson (C Co., 49th PA) returned in the darkness from Roulette's spring where he washed the caked blood and brains from his clothing and face. A comrade, having appropriated one of Roulette's ruined bee hives, handed him a handful of honey comb and honey. The private gorged himself on hard crackers and honey, the sweetest meal he ever had in the army. There was no coffee. The officers would not permit fires because they expected a renewal of the contest in the morning.[24]

The West Woods

For several hours, Colonel J. M. Smith (13th GA) gingerly walked his horse through the clover fields north and west of Mumma's farm. He was looking for the living among the dead. In the blackness, he came across the severely wounded Second Lieutenant Robert T. Bowie (G Co.) of his regiment.

The young officer was so badly shot up that the ambulance surgeon told him he would have to bleed to death. That was several hours earlier. The still conscious Bowie begged the colonel to take him off. Smith agreed to lift him onto his horse, but they would have to swim the Potomac to get to a hospital.

The colonel, as gently as possible, pulled Lieutenant Bowie onto the animal's rump. Bowie thought he was going to die. (He did not.)[25]

Colonel McIver Law's orderly, James S. Johnston, Jr. (11th MS), gently cut the minie ball from his horse's leg and pocketed it. He owed his life to the animal's stamina. He therefore intended to do all he could to keep it alive as long as possible. "The bullet I saved for my horse's sake," he informed his sweetheart, Mary M. Green, "for as a soldier always preserves the bullet that is cut from him, who knows but that my horse may desire to see his bullet after the war."[26]

The North Woods

Clara Barton set her thirty volunteers to making gruel from the corn meal they found packed in their last three boxes of medicinal wine. As night came on, she ordered lanterns hung in Poffenberger's yard and barn.

She found the chief surgeon, bloodied and frustrated, sitting at the kitchen table with his chin propped in his hands. He stared at the flickering stub of a candle which was melting away in the center of the table.

Stepping up silently from behind, she tenderly asked, "Are you tired, Doctor?"

"Tired!" he exploded. "Yes, I am tired, tired of such heartlessness, such carelessness!" He wheeled angrily about to face her. "Think of the condition of things. Here are at least one thousand wounded men, terribly wounded, five hundred of whom cannot live till daylight without attention. That two inches of candle is all I have or can get. What can I do? How can I endure?"

Clara Barton took the harried doctor by the arm and led him to the door. She silently pointed toward the glowing lanterns in the barn.

"What is that?" he gasped.

"The barn is lighted and the house will be directly."

"Who did it?"

"I, Doctor," she replied.

"Where did you get them?"

"Brought them with me."

"How many have you?" the surgeon appreciatively enquired.

"All you want — four boxes."

Puzzled and amazed, he gaped another moment into the illuminated yard then turned away. From that moment on he treated Clara Barton very special.[27]

Not very far away, a very exhausted Lieutenant Alger M. Wheeler (B Co., 21st NY) grumbled in his journal, ". . . we were told that a great victory had been gained — we wondered where, when, and how."[28] There were thousands like him who never considered they had won anything except a reprieve from the killing.

Sharpsburg

While his crews replenished their ammunition chests, Captain Charles Squires reported to General Robert E. Lee as ordered. The general, who was on foot among several other officers, seemed curt.

"Captain Squires," he said, "gather up every rifled gun you can find, take them wherever you find them and proceed with them to General Toombs of Georgia."

The exhausted captain scrounged nine rifles but did not remember where or how he found them. He was too worn out to care, as his men hauled their pieces through the town, south toward the Harper's Ferry Road.

It was about dark. The village was ablaze, an uncomfortable inferno through which to pull full ammunition chests. He wanted to get away from the fighting to sleep.

He found General Toombs after the fighting ended. Seeing no need to loiter where he was not needed, Captain Squires asked to return to Sharpsburg. He promised General Toombs he would refill his battery's ammunition chests and return in the morning. When the general finally consented, Squires asked what he should report to Lee.

Robert Toombs stared intently into the exhausted captain's eyes.

"Squires, what was said of me at headquarters?" he queried, in reference to his recent arrest by Longstreet.

The captain told him that headquarters had buzzed with the report that his two regiments — the 2nd Georgia and the 20th Georgia — had kept an entire Federal Corps at bay.

"Then tell General Lee," Toombs boasted, "that I hold the same ground that I held this morning, I am burying my dead, caring for my wounded and have about 75 Yankee prisoners which I wish he would order me to hand to these cornstalks."

Squires withdrew with his guns, trying to think how he could break his promise of returning.

General Lee listened patiently to Captain Squires' report. Without a reply, he turned coldly to the already depressed General David R. Jones and said, "Do you hear that, General Jones?"

He received no response. The icy silence cut the general to his marrow. Jones never resumed command of his division again.[29] Captain William Owen found him the next morning in the orchard south of the Lower Bridge Road. Prisoners had told him of the mortal wounding of his brother-in-law, Colonel Kingsbury (11th CT). He had lost his will to command.[30]

Lee had lost a large chunk of his army — about forty percent — while trying to defend Sharpsburg. He had seen blatant straggling among his infantry and he did not feel in the best frame of mind. Headquarters buzzed with conciliatory remarks concerning the dour "Stonewall" Jackson. "What a pity," the officers murmured that he had not turned the Federal right flank.

Lee did not want pity. He wanted results. He knew that he had not truly beaten McClellan and he did not like stalemate.

A. P. Hill and D. H. Hill were present at his headquarters in the grove northwest of the village. John Hood, Jubal Early, and D. R. Jones were there along with numerous officers of lesser rank.

"But where is Longstreet?" Lee asked.

"I saw him at sundown, all right," Colonel Venable interjected.

Simultaneously, Longstreet, his cigar finally lighted, trotted up to the cluster of officers and dismounted. Lee stepped forward and greeted "Old Pete" with his right hand.

"Ah! here is Longstreet; here's my old war-horse! Let us hear what he has to say."

Drawing themselves together, with their backs to the other officers, the generals started discussing the combat situation among themselves. Using that as a clue to leave, Captain William Owen, who had just turned his prewar comrade, Lieutenant Colonel Theodore Jones (30th Ohio) over to the provost guard, and Colonel John B. Walton retired to the fringe of the headquarters with the surgeons.

The doctors gave them a cordial sip of whiskey; they filled their pipes and quietly sat down to rest before scrounging up dinner.[31]

The West Woods

In the darkness, J. E. B. Stuart began retiring his cavalry toward Shepherdstown. Private P. J. White (5th VA Cav.) dreaded the withdrawal. The cavalrymen trampled the dead and wounded, the latter of whom pleaded for mercy but could not receive it.[32]

During the retreat, a small party of stragglers, under a field officer, stumbled across Color Sergeant Sam Bloomer (1st MN). The Reb officer was in an evil mood. He seemed to delight in taunting the exhausted Yankee. He verbally assaulted Bloomer to the point of calling him a "nigger thief". Unable to control his anger, the sergeant carelessly went for the revolver and short sword he had hidden under the rubber ground sheet by his side.

"Disarm that man!" the officer yelled.

His men, apparently upset over his demeanor, reluctantly obeyed. The half conscious sergeant pleaded for the sword. His captain, Louis Muller, had given it to him as a gift. Too bad. The Rebels abandoned him. Dead Yankees did not need side arms.[33]

SEPTEMBER 18, 1862

The Lower Bridge

Around midnight a drenching rain fell which continued briefly into the next day. Samuel Compton's (F Co., 12th OH) wet clothes seemed to freeze to his skin as the air became cooler. His teeth chattered and his body shook from exhaustion and the cold. He tried to ignore his discomfort but around midnight, when he could no longer endure it, he slipped into the swale between the lines to "find" a discarded blanket or two.

About one hundred feet out, he came across a blanket draped over a mound. He pulled it away only to find two corpses — one, shredded to a bloody lump by a shell, the other cut in two by a cannon ball. He quickly dropped the winding sheet and ran a short distance to another blanket. As he stooped to carry it off, he became terribly aware that it was saturated with blood. The next find proved no better.

Nauseated by the gore and the sickening sweet smell of the blood, which permeated the low ground, he retreated back to his bivouac. He shivered throughout the night.[34]

Sometime after midnight, a female Army nurse wandered into the ranks of the 21st Massachusetts, which was still enjoying its coffee ration. Without asking for their regimental number, she sought out volunteers to fetch several stranded Federal wounded who were trapped along the Lower Bridge Road near Otto's and Sherrick's. They had to work quickly because the Confederate pickets held that ground. Several of the New Englanders willingly departed with her.

The rescue detail successfully carried in the injured men despite drawing Rebel picket shots. The nurse finally asked the volunteers where they came from. When they told her Worcester County, she seemed deeply moved. That was her home county. She hailed from Oxford. Clara Barton delightfully shook every man's hand before they left her to return to their regiment.[35]

In the morning skirmishing was again renewed along most of the battle lines. The 48th Pennsylvania lost two men between 11:00 A.M. and 12:15 P.M. to sharpshooters while picketting in Sherrick's cornfield. The one man — Alexander Prince (B Co.) — died, in Otto's swale, trying to rescue a wounded soldier from the 6th New Hampshire. The other, John Robinson, was shot below the navel while trying to kill his third Rebel skirmisher.[36]

Both sides picked off soldiers who tried to bring in the wounded. Private John Dooley (D Co., 1st VA) bitterly referred to the Yankees as "barbarous soldiers" because the pickets shot at any man from Kemper's Brigade who tried to drag off the injured of the 9th New York. They finally terminated all retrieval operations when a sharpshooter killed a man from the 7th Virginia during a rescue attempt.[37]

The Harper's Ferry Road

Private Almon Reed (F Co., 89th NY) crawled behind McIntosh's Battery to avoid Yankee sharpshooters. A stretcher crew, later that afternoon, carried him to a barn in a hollow near the village. They left him there, unattended, among other wounded Yankees. They received no water, no food, and no assistance until the following day when their own soldiers found them.[38]

Shepherdstown, Virginia

Across the river in Shepherdstown, Virginia, the wife of a local pastor, Mrs. Charles Wesley Andrews, plopped into a chair next to her parlor window. Her house had become a hospital for Colonel Philip Liddell (11th MS), a sixteen year old boy on Nathan Evans' staff, and a third soldier whose name she could not remember. Ambulances filled the street; wounded lay everywhere.

She started to write to a sickly relative who apparently was planning a visit. ". . . in your weak state," she thoughtfully advised, "Anne Ellen & myself have agreed that if you cannot come later (with Anne) you had better not start now."

The suffering which surrounded her innundated her soul and troubled her deeply.[39]

The Lower Bridge — The Middle Bridge

During the late afternoon, Colonel James Barnes' Brigade (2nd ME, 18th, 22nd MA, 1st MI, 13th, 25th NY, 118th PA, and 2nd Co., MA SS) crossed the Antietam and occupied the heights west of the creek north to Sherrick's.[40] The rest of Morrell's Division (V Corps) crossed the Middle Bridge and took up the posts formerly held by the Regulars. The brand new 118th Pennsylvania (Corn Exchange Regiment) went into line along the crest south of Sherrick's house, where it immediately came under sniper fire from a house on the outskirts of town.

The Pennsylvanians fired a couple of volleys at the house which temporarily silenced the sharpshooter in the attic. Their shooting attracted General Ambrose Burnside, who was reconnoitering the Lower Bridge Road. He trotted into the right wing of the 118th Pennsylvania without an escort.

One of the green soldiers, noticing Burnside's pleasant demeanor, inquired, "General, are there any rebels still about here?"

"Still about?" The general laughed, "Why, there are thousands of them just over the hill, and they will be coming for you pretty soon." He paused, still smiling. "In the meantime I am going to get out of this, as it is no place for me — I don't want to see any more of them."

Laughing out loud, he turned about, waved and rode away.[41]

Corporal Sanford (E Co.) mounted the fence, behind which he was hiding, to get a clear shot at a Confederate sharpshooter in the gable of a house on the edge of town. A bullet smashed his thigh and cost him his leg.[42]

In the fields to the west, the 100th Pennsylvania lost fifty-two men in some very heavy skirmishing. The men shot away over one hundred rounds each before dark. Across the Lower Bridge Road, west of Sherrick's, Lieutenant Schwenk (A Co.) of the 50th Pennsylvania (Christ's Brigade) took his skirmishers against Jenkins' South Carolina Sharpshooters. They also expended better than one hundred rounds apiece. (The lieutenant won a captaincy for his bravery.)[43]

The Bloody Lane

Major Thomas Hyde (7th ME), risking death at the hands of snipers, dashed into Piper's orchard. He and other Union soldiers were looking for more of their wounded. He found George Williams, one of the guidon bearers, dead. He also came upon the still warm corpse of Color Corporal Harry Campbell. He was propped against an apple tree with his pipe by his side. With bullets clipping the trees around him, the major rushed back to the safety of his own lines.[44]

At about the same time, General John Gibbon (Iron BG, I Corps), with a lone staff officer, rode down from the Dunker Church swale to the hill overlooking Piper's barn. A puff of smoke rolled from the top of the barn, followed by the distinctive crack of a rifle and the whistle of a bullet. In an instant burial detail dove for cover as the pickets on both sides cut loose. Gibbon spurred away thoroughly embarrassed and literally shaken by the experience.[45]

Privates Cleve Rowan and J. Warren Richmond (F Co., 2nd MS), John H. Darrah (12th MS), and a stray soldier from the 4th Texas left the security of the second floor in Piper's House and scurried into the apple orchard when the Federals retired to the Bloody Lane. Crawling to the northern end of the orchard, they took cover behind the trees which were the closest to the battered fence along the edge of the field, and continued their sniping. To their front, among the crushed cornstalks south of the lane, they spied about half a dozen Yankee pickets who were foolishly standing in the open along the road bank on the hilltop west of the bend in the lane.

The four Confederates opened fire simultaneously. The Federals dove, in succession, into the Bloody Lane. As the smoke cleared, Cleve Rowan stuck his head up to investigate the situation.

While waiting for the shooting to stop, Private F. H. Venn (19th MS) crawled across a riddled Yankee corpse. The weary Confederate morbidly fingered the man's wounds. He had been shot seven times. The sudden cease fire attracted his attention.

A white flag waved fitfully above the rim of the picket post. Without a moment's hesitation, Rowan jerked the new white handkerchief (which he had purchased at Harper's Ferry) from inside his blouse, tied it to the end of his ramrod, and semaphored a response to the Yankees.

Couriers from both armies cautiously ventured halfway into the open ground west of the orchard, parleyed momentarily, then wandered back to their respective lines. Not long after that a Federal officer, with an aide, and General Roger Pryor, with his orderly, stepped into the clearing for a conference.

Cleve Rowan and F. H. Venn used the general's presence as an excuse to stand up and amble toward the enemy's flag of truce. Venn left his rifle in a fence corner and moved to within earshot of the general and the Yankee lines. The presence of so many enemy flags in such a constricted area unnerved him. When Pryor retired to cover, so did he.

BRIGADIER GENERAL ROGER PRYOR, brigade commander, ANV

On September 18, he held a parley with a Union officer along the Bloody Lane as the result of a "false flag" of truce. *(William E. Strong Collection, Duke U.)*

Rowan, however, continued into the Yankee picket post. The soldiers in the shallow portion of the lane invited the Mississippian in for a "confab". The six Blue Coats, who belonged to the Irish Brigade exchanged small talk and jokes with him and gave him part of their rations as a gesture of professional courtesy. As Cleve Rowan stuffed the precious sugar, coffee, and tobacco into his haversack, he noticed a Federal general and his cavalry escort trotting into view.

"There is your Commander," the Rebel blurted nervously. "I will run; don't shoot me!"

While the Confederate dashed back to the orchard, one of the Irishmen chirped in a thick brogue, "Run, Johnny, we'll not harm ye."

Rowan slid to the ground beneath an apple tree to breathlessly await a new outburst of riflery. Instead, he heard another of the pickets cry out that the flag was a "false truce", which meant that the high command had not authorized it.[46] Shortly thereafter, the snipers in Piper's barn commenced firing upon the Yankees north of the Bloody Lane.

The Dunker Church

Shortly after dawn, Richard H. Watkins (K Co., 3rd VA Cav.) wrote to his wife, "Thanksgiving day darling and with all my heart do I thank God for his many distinguishing mercies to us . . . . Oh how I long for peace and pray that God would remove his afflicting hand from us and restore to us our liberties."

The fighting on the 17th cost the command two additional casualties, Mac Venable, who was severely wounded, and Pat Fitzgerald, who had a foot wound. Watkins told his wife, Mary, to write him often. The bugler sounded the "Assembly" and the officer hastily closed his letter, "So good day precious one I love you with my whole heart. Your own R_____ "[47]

At first light, Captain Bart Johnson (A Co., 3rd AR) tied his handkerchief to a severed hickory switch, and headed toward the West Woods. Crossing the picket line of the 48th North Carolina near the Dunker Church, he approached Irwin's prone brigade, which was below the ridge, east of the church.

Five Yankee pickets hauled him aside within plain view of the Confederate sentries. Captain Johnson immediately, and loudly demanded to see the officer of the guard. A major confronted him.

"What are you doing here with that flag?" he demanded.

Bart Johnson replied that he was going onto the field to retrieve Fred Worthington's watch to send home to his father.

"Don't you know you are in our lines and a prisoner?"

The Captain insisted that under the circumstances the major should let him go.

The Yankee officer asked the Rebel what his people were going to do that day.

"Fight on," Johnson firmly replied.

"I believe you fellows naturally love to fight," the major began. "We are tired of it over here; it is enough to disgust any civilized people to see the Battlefield. 12000 men killed and murdered and nothing gained — you may return."

As the Captain stepped away, Colonel E. D. Hall (46th NC) boldly approached the major and engaged in an extended conversation with him. Minutes later, hundreds of men from both armies crossed their picket lines and mingled in "No Man's Land".

The 48th North Carolina, which rested in the West Woods along its eastern face near the Dunker Church, retrieved many of their dead and wounded. Burial parties broke ground in the fields nearby while other soldiers collected gum blankets, hammocks, and other luxuries from the corpses, which had no need for them. Everywhere, soldiers tenderly gave water to their own and the Federal wounded.

Lieutenant Colonel Samuel H. Walkup (48th NC), who had the picket duty beyond the Hagerstown Pike, allowed the Yankees to recover their injured from the Confederate lines. He even took the time to chat with several Union officers.

When they started to talk about their war weariness and the Union cause, Walkup cut them off.

"That was not a subject we could hold discussion [on]," he recalled, "however glad we would be for the war to end."

The Yankees, he ruefully noticed, took better care of the Confederate wounded than the Confederates took of the Federal casualties.[48]

Many of the bodies were mutilated beyond recognition. The sight of the countless decapitated corpses sickened Private Samuel Johnson (1st MA Indpt. Lgt. Arty.) as he wandered among the dead of the Cornfield. Weapons, arms, legs, swords, gutted horses, and gory clumps of what had once been human beings littered the ground as far as he could see. The horror stunned him.[49] The men of the VI Corps, having not borne the brunt of the battle, had, consequently, suffered minimal casualties, and did not want to stir up a general battle. They appeared more than willing to be amenable to the Confederates.

The West Woods

Sam Bloomer (1st MN) found himself in a barn (probably Nicodemus') surrounded by over one hundred Federal wounded. Some Rebels had carried him there shortly before dawn. Not long after he lost his weapons, the North Carolinian officer who had shared his water with him found him again. The gentleman filled his canteen with fresh water from his own and left him for good. Bloomer still had the water but it would do his leg no good. The veteran had seen enough combat to know that he was going to forfeit it.[50]

The Cornfield

Late in the afternoon, the Confederates sent an officer into the picket line in Miller's Cornfield. Federal officers from the VI Corps honored the Confederates' request for a twelve hour cease fire.

Under flags of truce, parties from both sides met on the bloodied ground between the East and the West Woods to care for their wounded and dead. The soldiers ". . . chatted as pleasantly as though they had never done each other harm," James S. Johnston, Jr. (11th MS) penned. "The sentiment of all parties was for peace and many of them said that the pen would eventually have to settle the matter. The sword could not . . . . All the Yankees that have to do the fighting are getting tired of it . . ."[51]

The Bloody Lane

Along the Bloody Lane, the Confederates also asked for and received an unofficial cease fire to bury their dead.

Private Calvin Leach (B Co., 1st NC) commented on the irony of the situation. "It seemed very curious to see the men on both sides come together and talk to each other when the day before [they] were firing at each other."[52]

When no Rebels attempted to retrieve their dead and wounded from Piper's to the North Woods, the Union soldiers mistakenly believed that the Confederates had abused a privilege of "civilized" warfare and had used the time to slip away unmolested. Captain Charles C. Morey (2nd VT) noted in his diary that the generals commanding both armies never authorized a truce.)[53]

Sharpsburg

General James Longstreet ordered Colonel J. B. Walton to provide one battery to cover the withdrawal from Sharpsburg. Consequently, the Colonel dispatched Captain William M. Owen to find a battery in the town to perform the duty. The Captain, who was almost to Shepherdstown, Virginia, wearily turned his horse back toward Sharpsburg.

A dense fog blanketed the area. The bonfires which the soldiers had lit to mark their line of retreat filled the road with blinding smoke.

Troops, in retreat, streamed around his horse constantly and every time he happened to nudge one of them, they hurled curses and insults at him. Someone bitterly spat that Owen was a "cavalryman going after buttermilk."

Owen got as far as he intended to go. He reined his horse to a halt and waited. Presently he distinctly heard the jangling and clanking of a battery in the eerie mist east of him.

"Whose battery is that?" he called out.

"Captain Reilly's."

"Ah, Captain! — just looking for you," Owen replied as the guns lurched into view. "The chief of artillery directs you to halt here, and report to General Stuart as he comes by with the rear-guard."

"Devil take it now," Reilly growled in his thick brogue, while Owen slipped his pocket flask to his mouth, "can't somebody else do this? My men are tired out — let me get beyond the river —"

"Couldn't think of it, Captain," Owen teased, "this is the post of honor. Report to Stuart. Good-by, and good luck to you."

At that, the newly promoted captain wheeled his horse around and disappeared into the thick fog while Reilly verbally assaulted him from behind with mild oaths and "dang all 'posts of honor.' "[54]

The day passed in spasms of small combat and ended with an extremely loud clash of arms west of Sherrick's house. A squadron of Federal cavalry, on reconnaissance, moved in on a house on the north side of the Lower Bridge Road.[55] Around 8:30 P.M., they accidentally rode into Robert Toombs' Brigade after he had retired his pickets to take part in the withdrawal. When the Confederates halted the horsemen, the Yankees, who stupidly assumed the infantry which surrounded them were their own, called out their regimental number. Rifles roared and pistols snapped in the darkness. Toombs went down with a bullet in the hand and the cavalrymen skedaddled.[56] The battle was over for all but the wounded.

Epilogue

Commissary Sergeant Ephraim T. Stetson (G Co., 1st ME Cav.) had never witnessed such slaughter before. "They are fighting every day now," he informed his brother, "The woods and fields are full of the dead for miles around and the houses and barns are full of wounded in some places they lay in piles . . . . We are in hopes this will be the last fight. I hope so . . . ."[57]

Left in the town to care for the wounded, Surgeon James Mercer Greene (17th MS) tried to erase his grisly work from his mind. It drifted to prewar times and an attractive young woman, Miss Annie R. Shoemaker, from Harrisburg, Pennsylvania. As he carved and probed through the long hours, he resolved to write her at the first opportunity.

The mere thought of her seemed ". . . like resuming another life — once enjoyed but now long set aside and the very memory of its joy almost forgotten. I have been in this unnatural strife since its commencement . . ."

He realized how he had changed since the First Manassas. "My head had whitened and my very soul turned into stone," he later told her by letter. "A long vista of human blood shuts out the dearest past and a boundless expanse of the same crimson fluid stretches before us in the future. I see no end to it_____."

The gentle doctor with the aesthetic soul of a poet felt overwhelmed by the inhumanity which surrounded him.[58]

Less than ten months later, the Army of Northern Virginia, en route to Gettysburg, Pennsylvania, passed through the once verdant farmland around Sharpsburg. Private George K. Harlow (D Co., 23rd VA), out of morbid curiosity, visited the battlefield. What he saw nearly undid him emotionally.

"Dear Father Mother and Family,

. . . . I have been this morning over the old Sharpsburg battle field this morning and have witnessed the most horrible sights that my eyes ever beheld I saw dead yankees in any number just lying on the top of the ground with a little dirt throwed over them and the hogs rooting them out of the ground and eating them and others lying on the top of the ground with the flesh picked off and their bones bleaching and they by many hundreds! oh what a horrible sight for human beings to look upon in a civilized Country! When will this horrid war ever end; God grant the time may spedily [sic] the time may soon come that piece [sic] may return to our once happy Country and our lives may be spared to meet each other again on earth; may the Lord take care of you all and shield you from all harme [sic] is the prayer of your unworthy son and Brother.   G. K. Harlow"[59]

APPENDIX A

The following key of abbreviations must be referred to when reading this chart:

MG = Major General
BG = Brigadier General
Col. = Colonel
LTC = Lieutenant Colonel
Maj. = Major
CPT = Captain
LT = Lieutenant
KIA = Killed in Action
MIA = Missing in Action or Captured
WIA = Wounded in Action
B & L = Battles and Leaders, Vol. II.
Div. = Division
Brig. = Brigade
H = Howitzer
N = Napoleon
P = Parrott
R = Rifle
SB = Smoothbore

Federal and Confederate brigades and divisions are listed by the names of their original commanders. If another officer had command, his name is listed to the left of the original commander's last name and is enclosed in brackets.

In the space to the left of each brigade I have listed the main area of the battlefield where the brigade or individual regiment(s) were engaged.

Unless otherwise noted, Federal troop strengths on brigade, division and corps level come from Ezra Carman's statistics, a copy of which may be found in Edward J. Stackpole's *From Cedar Mountain to Antietam*. All Confederate strengths on brigade, division, and corps level, unless otherwise noted, are from Walter H. Taylor's *Four Years With General Lee*. The tables used at the end of each division which summarize the losses of the Army of Northern Virginia are the losses cited in *Battles and Leaders of the Civil War*, Volume II.

Unless otherwise stated, all regimental losses shown are those from the *Official Records*,

Artillery information came from Joseph Mills Hanson's, "A Report On The Employment Of The Artillery At The Battle Of Antietam, MD.", 1940.

I reconstructed the charts based upon the casualty figures given in *Battles and Leaders*. The authors estimated that the Confederates lost 20% of their casualties in the Maryland campaign in the battles along South Mountain. By deducting that amount from the *OR* figures by brigade I have developed a fairly accurate table of actual casualties sustained at Antietam, exclusive of the other battles in the campaign.

An * indicates that losses at South Mountain and at Crampton's Gap have been deducted.

This appendix may only be considered as a preliminary study of the numbers of troops present at Antietam. To obtain nearly perfect accuracy, obviously, one would have to study the daily reports of every regiment which took part in the engagement and that would evolve into a separate book. This study is an approximate chart of losses and strengths between September 16-18. I preferred to use the *Battles and Leaders* casualty numbers because they were printed prior to Ezra Carman's study and, in most cases, they very closely follow the *OR*'s accounting for dead and wounded, which did not tally Confederate missing.

317

Confederate strengths are as fallible as the records from which they came. They cannot be interpreted as one hundred percent accurate. When trying to tabulate their numbers, one has to remember that the Confederates listed their numbers as "officers and men", "muskets" (men), and as "men" (which sometimes included officers as well). Exact accuracy was not attainable. It is also advisable to note that Colonel Taylor (Lee's staff) made it his lifelong ambition to prove that the Army of Northern Virginia was always hopelessly outnumbered throughout the war. In case of Antietam, I have used, wherever possible, troop strengths from other sources as well as Taylor's.

Troops present for the Confederate forces apply to those reporting for duty September 16-18, 1862 and not those at South Mountain or at Shepherdstown.

The Army of Northern Virginia: General Robert E. Lee

	Unit	Pres.	KIA	WIA	Total
MG James Longstreet	Corp	—	0	2	2
MG Lafayette McLaws	Div.	2893	1	0	1
BG Joseph B. Kershaw	Brig.	832[1]	—	—	—
	2 SC	253	17	77	94
(West Woods and Mumma's Swale)	3 SC	266	7	73	80
	7 SC	268[2]	23	117	140
	8 SC	45	2	17	19
			49	284	333
BG Howell Cobb	Brig.*	—	—	—	—
	16 GA		18	66	84
(Western End of Bloody Lane)	24 GA		10	116	126
	15 NC		14	54	68
	Cobb's Legion	83[3]	13	114	127
			55	350	405
BG Paul J. Semmes	Brig.*	569	—	—	—
	10 GA	147[4]	12	55	67
(West Woods)	53 GA	134[5]	9	50	59
	15 VA	128[6]	9	50	59
	32 VA	160[7]	12	46	58
			42	201	243
BG William Barksdale	Brig.	858[8]	—	—	—
	13 MS	202	8	55	63
	17 MS	270	11	82	93
(West Woods)	18 MS	186	10	73	83
	21 MS	200	6	56	62
			35	266	301

Division Artillery: Maj. S. P. Hamilton
Cpt. Basil C. Manley: Manley's Batty (NC)
    1 - 3"R   2 - 12#H   3 - 6#SB
Cpt. P. W. Read: Pulaski Arty. (GA)   Pres. = 78[9]
    1 - 10#P   1 - 3"R   1 - 6#SB   4 (KIA)   10 (WIA)[10]

Cpt. M. C. Macon: Richmond (Fayette Arty.) (VA)
    2 - 10#P   4 - 6#SB
Cpt. E. S. McCarthy: 1st Co., Richmond Howit.   Pres. = 33[11]
    2 - 10#P   2 - 6#SB
Cpt. H. H. Carlton: Troup Arty. (GA)
    2 - 10#P   1 - 12#H   2 - 6#SB
24 guns

	KIA	WIA	MIA		KIA	WIA	MIA
B&L	90	455	6	B&L*	61	254	362
Kershaw	-49	-284	-0	Cobb	-55	-350	-96
	41	171	6		6	-96	266

	KIA	WIA	MIA		KIA	WIA	MIA
B&L	35	272	4	B&L*	45	219	34
Barksdale	-35	-266	-0	Semmes	-42	-201	-0
	0	6	4		3	18	34

Total:	KIA	WIA	MIA		KIA	WIA	MIA
Staff	1	2	0	B&L	2	10	0
Kershaw	49	284	6	Read	-4	-10	-2
Barksdale	35	266	4		-2	0	-2
Cobb	55	350	266				
Semmes	42	201	34				
Read	4	10	-2				
Artillery	48	185	0	(Losses not in *OR*.)			
	234	1298	308				

Present: 2893 (100%) - 1840 (64%) = 1053 (37%)

	Unit	Pres.	KIA	WIA	Total
MG Richard H. Anderson	Div.	3500	—	1	1
[Col. Alfred Cumming] Wilcox BG			—	—	—
	8 AL		12	63	75
(Piper's Orchard)	9 AL		12	42	54
	10 AL		10	53	63
	11 AL		3	26	29
			37	184	221
[Col. W. A. Parham] Mahone BG*		184[12]	—	—	—
	6 VA		3	15	17[13]
(Piper's Orchard & Hagerstown Pike)	12 VA		2	29	32[14]
	16 VA		—	4	4
	41 VA		1	6	7
	61 VA		(Not Reported)		
			6	54	60
[Col. Carnot Posey] Featherston BG			—	—	—
	12 MS		6	53	59
(Eastern end of Bloody Lane)	16 MS	228[15]	27	100	127
	19 MS		6	52	58
	2 MS Bttn.		5	55	60
			44	260	304
BG Lewis Armistead	Brig.		—	—	—
	9 VA	50[16]	(Not Reported)		
(Very Lightly Engaged Piper's Orchard)	14 VA		—	7	7
	38 VA		2	14	16
	53 VA		3	8	11
	57 VA		—	1	1
			5	30	35
BG Roger Pryor	Brig.	300[17]	—	—	—

	Unit	Pres.	KIA	WIA	Total
	12 AL		2	43	45
(Piper's Orchard)	2 FL		6	43	49[18]
	5 FL		15	39	54
	8 FL		13	56	69[19]
	3 VA		3	16	19
			39	197	236
BG Ambrose Wright	Brig.		—	—	—
	44 AL		4	65	69
(Eastern End of Bloody Lane)	3 GA		9	57	66
	22 GA		2	19	21
	48 GA		1	46	47
			16	187	203

Artillery: Major J. S. Saunders
Cpt. Victor Maurin, Donaldsonville Arty. (LA)
      2 - 10#P   1 - 3"R   3 - 6#SB
Cpt. C. R. Phelps, Huger's Norfolk Btty. (VA)
      1 - 10#P   1 - 3"R   2 - 6#SB

Cpt. Marcellus N. Moorman, Lynchburg Btty. (VA)
      (Composition Unknown)
Lt. J. H. Thompson, Grimes' Portsmouth Btty. (VA)
      (Composition Unknown)
10+ guns

		KIA	WIA	Total
(Phelps)		1	2	3[20]
(Moorman)		1	7	8[21]
(Thompson)		3	2	5[22]
		5	11	16

	KIA	WIA	MIA		KIA	WIA	MIA
B&L	34	181	29	B&L*	6	74	102
Cumming	-37	-184	-6	Parham	-6	-54	-0
	-3	-3	23		0	20	102

	KIA	WIA	MIA		KIA	WIA	MIA
B&L	45	238	36	B&L	5	29	1
Posey	-44	-260	-22	Armistead	-5	-30	-1
	1	-22	14		0	-1	0

	KIA	WIA	MIA		KIA	WIA	MIA
B&L	48	285	49	B&L	32	192	34
Pryor	-39	-197	-0	Wright	-16	-187	-0
	9	88	49		16	5	34

Total:

	KIA	WIA	MIA
Staff	0	1	0
Cumming	37	184	23
Parham	6	54	102
Posey	44	260	14
Armistead	5	30	0
Pryor	39	197	49
Wright	16	187	34
Artillery	5	11	0
(9 & 61 VA, Artillery)	26	113	—
	178	1037	222

Artillery was not counted separately in B&L.

Present 3500 (100%) - 1437 (41%) = 2063 (59%)

	Unit	Pres.	KIA	WIA	Total
BG David R. Jones	Div.	3400	—	—	—
[Col. Henry L. Benning] Toombs BG		585	—	—	—
	2 GA	120[23]	6	37	43
(Lower Bridge and Harper's Ferry Road)	15 GA	115[24]	6	30	36
	17 GA	130[25]	—	12	12
	20 GA	220[26]	4	33	37
			16	112	128
BG Thomas F. Drayton	Brig.*		—	—	—
(Snavely's Ford and Lower Bridge Road)	50 GA	220[27]	23	78	101
	51 GA		1	6	7
	15 SC		21	67	88
	3 SC Bttn.			(Not Reported)	
			45	151	196
[BG Richard B. Garnett] Pickett	Brig.*	268	—	—	—
	8 VA	22[28]	3	7	10
(Boonsboro Pike to Lower Bridge Road)	18 VA	75	4	30	34
	19 VA	54[29]	6	30	36
	28 VA	77	6	43	49
	56 VA	40	1	15	16
			20	125	145
BG James Kemper	Brig.*		—	—	—
	1 VA	17[30]	—	6	6
(Harper's Ferry Road)	7 VA	100[31]	2	8	10
	11 VA	85[32]	2	30	32
	17 VA	58[33]	5	24	29
	24 VA		—	2	2
			9	70	79
[Col. Joseph Walker] Jenkins	Brig.*	530[34]	—	—	—
	1 SC Vols.	106[35]	2	30	32
(Lower Bridge Road near Saw Mill)	2 SC Rifles		2	11	13
	5 SC		4	21	25
	6 SC		6	41	47
	4 SC Bttn.			(Not Reported)	
	Palmetto Sharpshooters		7	44	51
			21	147	168
Col. G. T. Anderson	Brig.*	500[36]	—	—	—
	1 GA Reg.		1	23	24
(All but 11 GA in West Woods &	7 GA		2	7	9
Hagerstown Pike)	8 GA		2	14	16
(Lower Bridge and Harper's Ferry Road)	9 GA		2	11	13
	-11 GA		—	8	8
			7	63	70

Artillery:
Cpt. J. S. Brown, Wise Artillery (VA)
(Composition Unknown)   1   4   1 MIA[37]

	KIA	WIA	MIA		KIA	WIA	MIA
B&L	16	122	22	B&L*	66	224	143
Benning	-16	-112	0	Drayton	-45	-151	-0
	0	10	22		21	73	143

	KIA	WIA	MIA		KIA	WIA	MIA
B&L*	24	159	26	B&L*	12	82	22
Garnett	-20	-125	-0	Kemper	-9	-70	-0
	4	34	26		3	12	22

	KIA	WIA	MIA		KIA	WIA	MIA
B&L*	22	157	10	B&L*	6	64	5
Walker	-21	-147	-0	Anderson	-7	-63	-1
	1	10	10		-1	1	4

Total:

	KIA	WIA	MIA	
Benning	16	112	22	
Drayton	45	151	143	
Garnett	20	125	26	
Kemper	9	70	22	Artillery not reported separately in B&L.
Walker	21	147	10	
Anderson	7	63	4	
Wise	1	4	1	
(3 & 4 SC, Artillery)	29	140	—	
	148	812	228	

Present 3400 (100%) - 1188 (35%) = 2212 (65%)

	Unit	Pres.	KIA	WIA	Total
BG John Walker	Div.	3200	—	—	—
[Col. Van H. Manning] Walker	Brig.	1600	—	—	—
	3 AK	675[38]	27	155	182
(West Woods and Mumma's Swale)	27 NC	325[39]	31	168	199
	46 NC		5	60	65
	48 NC		31	186	217
	30 VA	236[40]	39	121	160
			133	690	823
BG Robert Ransom, Jr.	Brig.	1600	—	—	—
	24 NC		20	44	64
(West Woods)	25 NC		2	13	15
	35 NC		3	23	26
	49 NC		16	61	77
			41	141	182

Artillery:
Cpt. Thomas B. French, Stafford Btty. (VA)

			KIA	WIA	Total
3 - 10#P	3 - 12#H	6 guns	1	1	2[41]

Cpt. James R. Branch, Petersburg Btty. (VA)

			KIA	WIA	Total
1 - 10#P	3 - 12#H	6 guns	2	3	5[42]
			3	4	7

	KIA	WIA	MIA		KIA	WIA	MIA
B&L	140	684	93	B&L	41	141	4
Manning	-133	-690	-6	Ransom	-41	-141	-0
	7	-6	87		0	0	4

Total:

	KIA	WIA	MIA
Manning	137	690	87
Ransom	41	141	4
(Artillery)	3	4	0
(Misc.)	4	0	0
	185	835	91

Present 3200 (100%) - 1111 (35%) = 2089 (65%)

	Unit	Pres.	KIA	WIA	Total
BG John Bell Hood	Div.	2332	—	—	—
[Col. W. T. Wofford] Hood	Brig.*	858[43]	—	—	—
	18 GA	176	10	58	68
(The Cornfield and Piper's Orchard)	1 TX	226	42	132	174[44]
	4 TX	204	11	110	121[45]
	5 TX	175	4	62	66
	Hampton's Legion	77	5	38	43
			72	400	472
Col. E. McIver Law	Brig.*	1474[46]	—	—	—
	4 AL		6	30	36
(The Cornfield and East Woods)	2 MS		22	102	124
	11 MS		6	77	83
	6 NC		6	94	100
			40	303	343

Artillery: Major B. W. Frobel

	KIA	WIA
Cpt. W. K. Bachman, Charleston German Btty. (SC)	2	2
4 - 12#N		
Cpt. H. R. Garden, Palmetto Btty. (SC)	0	9
1 - 12#N 1 - 12#H 2 - 6#SB		
Cpt. J. Reilly, Rowan Btty. (NC)	2	8
2 - 10#P 2 - 3"R 2 - 24#H	4	19

14 guns

	KIA	WIA	MIA		KIA	WIA	MIA
B&L*	55	334	50	B&L*	42	312	20
Wofford	-72	-400	-83	Law	-40	-303	-0
	-17	-66	-33		2	9	20

	KIA	WIA	MIA
B&L	4	19	0
Artillery	-4	-19	-0
	0	0	0

Total:

	KIA	WIA	MIA
Wofford	72	400	-33
Law	40	303	20
Artillery	4	19	0
Misc.	2	9	0
	118	731	-13

Present: 2332 (100%) - 836 (36%) = 1496 (64%)

	Unit	Pres.	KIA	WIA	Total
[Col. P. F. Stevens] Evans	Brig.*	280[47]	—	—	—
	17 SC	59[48]	14	39	53
(North of Boonsboro Pike)	18 SC		2	31	33
	22 SC		6	51	57
	23 SC		11	53	64
(Sherrick's) Holcombe Legion		41[49]	—	14	14
			33	188	221

Artillery:
Cpt. R. Boyce, Macbeth Arty. (SC)
     (Composition Unknown)   2   17   19[50]

	KIA	WIA	MIA
B&L*	32	148	52
Evans	-33	-188	-41
	-1	-40	11

Total:

	KIA	WIA	MIA	
Evans	33	188	11	(Artillery, included.)

Present 550 (100%) - 232 (42%) = 318 (58%)
Corps Artillery (1st Reserve Bttn.) Col. J. B. Walton
Present 300[51]
Cpt. Charles W. Squires, 1st Co., Washington Arty. (LA)
        1 - 10#P   2 - 3"R
Cpt. J. B. Richardson, 2nd Co., Washington Arty. (LA)
        2 - 12#H   2 - 12#N
Cpt. M. B. Miller, 3rd Co., Washington Arty. (LA)
        2 - 12#N
Cpt. B. F. Eshelman, 4th Co., Washington Arty. (LA)
        2 - 12#H   2 - 6#SB   **4 KIA**   **28 WIA**   **2 MIA**[52]
13 guns
Corps Artillery (2nd Reserve Bttn.): Col. Stephen D. Lee
Present: 292[53]
Cpt. Pichegru Woolfolk; Ashland Btty. (VA)
        (Composition Unknown)
Cpt. T. C. Jordan, Bedford Btty. (VA)
        2 - 3"R   1 - 12#H   1 - 6#SB
Lt. William Elliott, Brooks' (Rhett's) Btty. (SC)
        2 - 10#P   2 - 20#P
Cpt. George V. Moody, Madison Btty. (LA)
        2 - 3"R   2 - 24#H
Cpt. J. L. Eubank, Bath Batty. (VA)
        1 - 3"R   1 - 12#H   1 - 6#SB
Cpt. William W. Parker, Richmond Btty. (VA)
        2 - 3"R   2 - 12#H

19+ guns

	KIA	WIA	MIA		KIA	WIA	MIA
B&L	4	28	2	B&L	11	75	0
1st Bttn.	-4	-28	-0	2nd Bttn.	-11	-75	-0
	0	0	2		0	0	0

Total:

	KIA	WIA	MIA
1st Bttn.	4	28	2
2nd Bttn.	11	75	0
	15	103	2

Present 592 (100%) - 120 (20%) = 472 (80%)

	Unit	Pres.	KIA	WIA	Total
MG Thomas J. Jackson	Corps	—	—	—	—
[BG A. R. Lawton] Ewell	Div.	3400	—	2	2
[Col. M. Douglass] Lawton	Brig.	1150	—	—	—
	13 GA		48	169	217
(The Cornfield)	26 GA		5	10	15
	31 GA		11	39	50
	38 GA	123 [54]	45	55	100
	60 GA		11	48	59
	61 GA		16	91	107
			136	412#	548
BG Jubal Early	Brig.	1225 [55]	—	—	—
	13 VA	100 [56]	—	5	5
(West Woods)	25 VA		2	21	23
	31 VA		2	10	12
	44 VA			22	22
	49 VA		5	73	78
	52 VA		3	36	39
	58 VA			(Not Reported)	
			12	167	179
[Col. James A. Walker] Trimble	Brig.	700	—	—	
	15 AL		9	75	84
(Cornfield, East Woods, Mumma's Swale)	12 GA		13	49	62
	21 GA		4	72	76
1 NC Bttn. w/21 NC			1	—	1
			27	196#	223
[Col. H. B. Strong] Hays	Brig.	550	—	—	—
	5 LA		10	40	50
	6 LA		18	29	47
	7 LA		6	63	69
	8 LA		7	84	91
	14 LA			(Not Reported)	
(# indicates 1 man WIA at Shepherdstown)			41	216	257

Artillery:
Cpt. John R. Johnson, Bedford Btty. (VA)
        (Composition Unknown)
Cpt. L. E. D'Aquin, Louisiana Guard Btty. (LA)
        1 - 10#P   2 - 3"R
3 guns

	KIA	WIA	MIA		KIA	WIA	MIA
B&L	106	440	21	B&L	18	167	9
Douglass	-136	-412	-30	Early	-12	-167	-0
	-30	28	-9		6	0	9

	KIA	WIA	MIA		KIA	WIA	MIA
B&L	27	202	8	B&L	45	289	2
Walker	-27	-196	-0	Strong	-41	-216	-0
	0	6	8		4	73	2

Total:

	KIA	WIA	MIA
Douglass	136	412	-9
Early	12	167	9
Walker	27	196	8
Strong	41	216	2
(21 NC & 58 VA)	10	107	—
	226	1098	10

Present 3400 (100%) - 1334 (39%) = 2066 (61%)

	Unit	Pres.	KIA	WIA	Total
MG Ambrose P. Hill	Light Div.	1900[57]	—	—	—
BG L. O'Brien Branch	Brig.		—	—	—
	7 NC			(Not Reported)	
(Harper's Ferry Road & Otto's Lane)	28 NC			(Not Reported)	
	33 NC			(Not Reported)	
	37 NC			(Not Reported)	
BG Maxcy Gregg	Brig.	1000[58]	—	—	—
	1 SC		4	30	34
(The 40 Acre Cornfield)	1 SC Rifles		3	9	12
	12 SC		20	82	102
	13 SC		1	14	15
	14 SC			(No Casualties)	
			28	135	163
BG James J. Archer	Brig.	350[59]	—	—	—
	19 GA			(Not Reported)	
(Harper's Ferry Road & Otto's Lane)	1 TN			(Not Reported)	
	7 TN			(Not Reported)	
	14 TN			(Not Reported)	
[Col. J. M. Brockenbrough] Field	Brig.		—	—	—
	40 VA[60]		1	6	7
(Picket Duty Evening 9/17 Otto's Lane)	47 VA			(Not Reported)	
	55 VA			(Not Reported)	
	22 VA			(Not Reported)	
			1	6	7
BG Wm. D. Pender	Brig.		—	—	—
	16 NC			(Not Reported)	
(Otto's Lane)	22 NC			(Not Reported)	
	34 NC			(Not Reported)	
	38 NC			(Not Reported)	

Artillery: LTC R. L. Walker

Cpt. W. G. Crenshaw, Richmond Arty. (VA)

				KIA	WIA	Total
1-12#H	1-12#N	2-6#SB		1	3	4[61]

Cpt. Carter M. Braxton, Fredericksburg Btty. (VA)

				KIA	WIA	Total
2-3"R	4-6#SB			1	2	3[62]

Cpt. D. G. McIntosh, Pee Dee Btty. (SC)

				KIA	WIA	Total
1-10#P	1-3"R	1-12#H	1-12#N	1	2	3[63]

Cpt. W. J. Pegram, Richmond (Purcell) Btty. (VA)

			KIA	WIA	Total
2-10#P	2-12#N		1	2	3[64]
18 guns			4	9	13

	KIA	WIA	MIA		KIA	WIA	MIA
B&L	21	79	4	B&L	28	135	2
Branch	-0	-0	-0	Gregg	-28	-135	-0
	21	79	4		0	0	2

	KIA	WIA	MIA		KIA	WIA	MIA
B&L	15	90	0	B&L	2	28	0
Archer	-0	-0	-0	Pender	-0	-0	-0
	15	90	0		2	28	0

Brockenbrough and artillery not reported separately in B&L.

Total:	KIA	WIA	MIA
Branch	0	0	4
Gregg	28	135	2
Archer	0	0	0
Pender	0	0	0
Brockenbrough	1	6	0
(Losses B&L)	37	191	0
	66	326	6

Present: 1900 (100%) - 398 (21%) = 1502 (79%)

	Unit	Pres	KIA	WIA	Total
[BG John R. Jones] Jackson	Div.	1600	1	1	2
[Col. A. J. Grigsby] Winder	Brig.	200[65]	—	—	—
	4 VA		3	21	24
(The Cornfield & West Woods)	5 VA		2	26	28
	27 VA		3	5	8
	33 VA		3	16	19
			11	68	79
[Col. E. T. H. Warren] Taliaferro	Brig.	500[66]	—	—	—
	47 AL		6	30	36
(The Cornfield & West Woods)	48 AL		5	33	38
	10 VA	110[67]	(Not Reported)		
	23 VA		8	35	43
	37 VA		9	45	54
			28	143	171
[Col. Bradley T. Johnson] Jones	Brig.	250[68]	—	—	—

	Unit	Pres.	KIA	WIA	Total
	21 VA	68[69]	Lost 49		
(The Cornfield & West Woods)	42 VA	98[70]	10	36 (+1 MIA)	47
	48 VA		(Not Reported Separately)		
	1 VA Bttn.		(Not Reported Separately)		
			10	37	47
BG William E. Starke	Brig.	650[71]	—	—	—
	1 LA		14	49	63
(Hagerstown Pike & West Woods)	2 LA		10	49	59
	9 LA		25	57	82
	10 LA		17	34	51
	15 LA		4	15	19
	1st LA Bttn.		(Not Reported)		
			70	204	274

Artillery: Maj. L. M. Shumaker
Cpt. Joseph Carpenter, Alleghany Arty. (VA)

			KIA	WIA	Total
2 - 3"R	1 - 12#N		1	9	10[72]

Cpt. J. B. Brockenbrough, Brockenbrough's Btty. (2nd MD)

			KIA	WIA	Total
1 - 3"R	1 - 12#N	2 Blakely's	0	8	8[73]

Cpt. G. W. Wooding, Danville Arty. (VA)

			KIA	WIA	Total
2 - 10#P	1 - 3"R	1 - 12#N	2	3	5[74]

Cpt. William Poague, 1st Rockbridge Arty. (VA)

		KIA	WIA	Total
2 - 10#P	1 - 12#N	0	6	6[75]

Cpt. Charles J. Raine, Lee Btty. (VA)

		KIA	WIA	Total
3 - 3"R	1 - 12#H	0	5	5[76]

Cpt. W. H. Caskie, Hampden Arty. (VA)

		KIA	WIA	Total
1 - 10#P	3 - 6#SB	3	31	34

23 guns

	KIA	WIA	MIA		KIA	WIA	MIA
B&L	11	77	0	B&L	41	132	0
Grigsby	-11	-68	-0	Warren	-28	-143	-11
	0	9	0		13	-11	-11

	KIA	WIA	MIA		KIA	WIA	MIA
B&L	(Not Reported)			B&L	81	189	17
Johnson	9	62	0[77]	Starke	-70	-204	-15
	9	62	0		11	-15	2

Total:

	KIA	WIA	MIA
Staff	1	1	0
Grigsby	11	68	-11
Warren	28	143	0
Johnson	9	62	0
Starke	70	204	2
Artillery	3	31	0
(Not Rptd)	24	9	0
	146	518	-9

Present 1600 (100%) - 655 (41%) = 945 (59%)

	Unit	Pres.	KIA	WIA	Total
BG Daniel H. Hill	Div.	4593[78]	—	—	—
BG Roswell Ripley	Brig.	1349[79]	—	—	—
	4 GA		22	119	141
(The Cornfield)	44 GA		17	65	82
	1 NC	226[80]	18	142	160
	3 NC	547[81]	46	207	253
			103	533	636
BG Robert E. Rodes	Brig.*	750[82]	—	—	—
	3 AL		(Not Reported)		
(Bloody Lane)	5 AL [83]		7	32	39
	6 AL		52	104	156
	12 AL		17	57 (+27 MIA)	101
	26 AL		6	37	43
			82	257	339
[Col. D. K. McRae] Garland	Brig.*	756[84]	—	—	—
	5 NC		(Not Reported)		
(Mumma's & Western End of Bloody Lane)	12 NC	32[85]	(Not Reported)		
	13 NC		33	119	152[86]
	20 NC		9	24	33[87]
	23 NC		14	28	42[88]
			56	171	227
BG Geo. B. Anderson	Brig.*	1153[89]	—	—	—
	2 NC	300[90]	9	49	58
(Bloody Lane)	4 NC	80[91]	5	42	47
	14 NC	523[92]	23	141	164
	30 NC	250[93]	8	50	58
			45	282	327
Col. A. H. Colquitt	Brig.*	1320[94]	—	—	—
	13 AL	330[95]	(Not Reported)		
(The Cornfield, East Woods &	6 GA	250[96]	8	8 (+2 MIA)	18[97]
Western End of Bloody Lane)	23 GA		11	51	62[98]
	27 GA		12	71	83[99]
	28 GA	200[100]	9	50	59[101]
			40	182	222

Artillery: Maj. S. F. Pierson

Cpt. R. A. Hardaway, Alabama Btty. (AL)	KIA	WIA	Total
2 - 3"R 1 - Whitworth	0	9	9[102]
Cpt. J. W. Bondurant, Jeff Davis Btty. (AL)			
2 - 3"R 2 - 12#H	1	8	9[103]
Cpt. William B. Jones, Peninsula Btty. (VA)			
(Composition Unknown)	1	25	26[104]
Cpt. T. H. Carter, King William Btty. (VA)			
1 - 10#P 2 - 12#H 2 - 6#SB	2	3 (+1 MIA)	6[105]
12+ guns	4	45 (+1 MIA)	50

	KIA	WIA	MIA		KIA	WIA	MIA
B&L	110	506	124	B&L*	50	132	21
Ripley	-103	-533	-27	Rodes	-82	-230	-157
	7	-27	97		-32	-98	-136

	KIA	WIA	MIA		KIA	WIA	MIA
B&L*	30	137	187	B&L*	38	135	173
McRae	-56	-171	-60	Anderson	-45	-282	-154
	-26	-34	127		-7	-147	19

	KIA	WIA	MIA		KIA	WIA	MIA
B&L*	113	444	177	B&L*	3	24	2
Colquitt	-40	-180	-2	Artillery	-4	-45	-21
	73	264	175		-1	-21	-19

Total:

	KIA	WIA	MIA
Ripley	103	533	97
Rodes	82	230	-136
McRae	56	171	127
Anderson	45	282	19
Colquitt	40	180	175
Artillery	4	45	1
(5/12/14 NC, 3 AL, Arty.)	73	264	-20
	403	1705	263

Present 5328 (100%) - 2367 (44%) = 2961 (56%)
Reserve Artillery: BG William N. Pendleton
Present 621[106]

	KIA	WIA	Total
Cutts' Bttn.: LTC A. S. Cutts			
Cpt. J. A. Blackshear, Bttn. D, Sumpter Bttn. (GA)			
3 - 12#H 3 - 6#SB	1	7	8[107]
Cpt. J. Lane, Btty. E, Sumpter Bttn. (GA)			
2 - 20#P 3 - 10#P 1 - Whitworth	0	2	2[108]
Cpt. G. M. Patterson, Btty. B, Sumpter Bttn. (GA)			
(Composition Unknown)	1	5	6[109]
Cpt. H. M. Ross, Btty. A, Sumpter Bttn. (GA)			
3 - 10#P 2 - 12#H 1 - 12#N	0	18	18[110]
Jones' Bttn.: Maj. H. P. Jones			
Cpt. R. C. M. Page, Louisa (Morris) Btty. (VA)			
2 - 3"R 1 - 12#H 3 - 6#SB	2	7	9[111]
Cpt. J. Peyton, Richmond (Orange) Btty. (VA)			
1 - 3"R 1 - 12#H 3 - 6#SB	0	8	8[112]
Cpt. W. H. Turner, Goochland Btty. (VA)	4	47	51
(Composition Unknown)			
Cpt. A. Wimbish, "Long Island" Btty. (VA)			
(Composition Unknown)			

	KIA	WIA	MIA
B&L	4	47	0
Both Bttns.	-4	-47	-0
	0	0	0

Present 621 (100%) - 51 (8%) = 570 (92%)

	Unit	Pres.	KIA	WIA	Total
MG J. E. B. Stuart (Cav.)	Div.	1600	—	—	—
BG Wade Hampton	Brig.		(Not Reported)		
	1 NC				

	Unit	Pres.	KIA	WIA	Total
(West Woods)	2 SC				
	10 VA				
	Jeff Davis Legion				
BG Fitzhugh Lee	Brig.		(Not Reported)		
	1 VA				
(West Woods)	3 VA				
	4 VA				
	5 VA				
	9 VA				
[Col. Thomas Munford] Robertson	Brig.		(Not Reported)		
	2 VA				
	7 VA				
	12 VA				
	17 VA Bttn.				

Stuart Horse Artillery:
Cpt. R. P. Chew, "Ashby" Btty. (VA)
 (Composition Unknown)
Cpt. J. F. Hart, Washington Btty. (SC)
 (Composition Unknown)
Cpt. John Pelham, "1st Stuart" Btty. (VA)
 (Composition Unknown)

	KIA	WIA	MIA
B&L	10	45	6
(Entire Div.)	-0	-0	-0
	10	45	6

Total:

	KIA	WIA	MIA
Cav. & Arty.	0	0	0
(Misc. Cas)	10	45	6
	10	45	6

Present 1600 (100%) - 61 (4%) = 1539 (96%)

Corps	Div.	Pres.	KIA	WIA	MIA	ST	Survivors
Longstreet							
	McLaws	2893	232	1298	310	1840	1053
	R. H. Anderson	3500	178	1037	222	1437	2063
	D. R. Jones	3400	148	812	228	1173	2227
	Walker	3200	187	834	91	1112	2088
	Evans	280	33	188	11	232	48
	1st Bttn. Arty.	300	4	28	2	34	266
	2nd Bttn. Arty.	292	11	75	0	86	206
	Hood	2332	118	731	-13	836	1496
Jackson							
	Ewell	3400	226	1098	10	1334	2066
	A. P. Hill	1900	66	326	6	398	1502
	J. R. Jones	1600	134	425	-9	550	1050
	D. H. Hill	5328	403	1705	263	2367	2961
	Reserve Arty.	621	4	47	0	51	570
	J. E. B. Stuart	1600	10	45	6	61	1539
		30646	1754	8649	1127	11530	19116

Present 30646 (100%) - 1754 (6%) - 8649 (28%) - 1127 (4%) = Casualties 11530 (38%)
With Survivors 19168 (62%)
Comparison Between B & L and this study

	KIA	WIA	MIA	Total
Study	1754	8649	1127	11530
B&L	-1512	-7816	-1844	-11172
	+ 242 (+)	+ 833 (+)-	717	= + 358 difference

The Army of the Potomac: MG George B. McClellan

	Unit	Pres.	KIA	WIA	MIA	Total
MG Joseph Hooker	I Corps	14856				
BG Abner Doubleday	Div.	3245	(Engaged)			
Col. W. Phelps	Brig.	425[113]				
	22 NY		2	28	0	30
(The Cornfield)	24 NY		3	15	1	19
	30 NY		6	5	1	12
	84 NY	69[114]	6	21	0	27
	2nd US SS	264[115]	13	51	2	66
			30	120	4	154
LTC J. Wm. Hofmann	Brig.					
	7 IN		0	4	0	4
	76 NY	45[116]	0	4	0	4
(Nicodemus)	95 NY		0	1	0	1
	56 PA		0	1	0	1
			0	10	0	10
BG Marsena Patrick	Brig.	824[117]				
	21 NY	150[118]	12	57	2	71
(The Cornfield)	23 NY		4	35	3	42
	35 NY		8	55	4	67
	80 NY	135[119]	6	40	8	54
			30	187	17	234
BG John Gibbon	Brig.	1028[120]				
	19 IN	210[121]	12	59	0	71
(The Cornfield)	2 WI	314[122]	19	67	0	86
	6 WI	314[123]	26	126	0	152
	7 WI	190[124]	10	23	5	38
			67	275	5	347

Artillery:	KIA	WIA	MIA	Total
Lt. F. M. Edgell, 1st NH, Independent Light				
6 - 12#H	0	3	0	3
Cpt. J. Albert Monroe, 1st RI, Btty. D				
6 - 12#N	3	7	8	18
Cpt. J. A. Reynolds, 1st NY, Btty. L				
6 - 3"R	0	5	0	5
Cpt. Joseph Campbell, 4th US, Btty. B				
6 - 12#N	9	31	0	40
24 guns	12	46	8	66

Total:

	KIA	WIA	MIA
Phelps	30	120	4
Hofmann	0	10	0
Patrick	30	187	17
Gibbon	68	275	5
Artillery	12	46	8
	140	638	34

Engaged 3425 (100%) - 812 (24%) = 2613 (76%)

	Unit	Pres.	KIA	WIA	MIA	Total
BG James Ricketts	Div.	3158				
BG Abram Duryee	Brig.					
	97 NY	203[125]	24	74	9	107
(The Cornfield & East Woods)	104 NY		7	60	15	82
	105 NY		9	54	11	74
	107 PA	190[126]	19	43	0	04
			59	233	35	327
Col. Wm. A. Christian	Brig.					
	26 NY		5	41	20	66
(The Cornfield & East Woods)	94 NY		0	12	1	13
	88 PA		10	62	5	77
	90 PA		13	82	3	98
			28	197	29	254
BG Geo. L. Hartsuff	Brig.	1000[127]				
	Staff		0	1	0	1
(The Cornfield & East Woods)	12 MA	325[128]	49	165	10	224
	13 MA		14	119	3	136
	83 NY		6	105	3	114
	11 PA	235[129]	13	107	4	124
			82	497	20	599

Artillery:
Cpt. F. W. Matthews, 1st PA Light, Btty. F

		KIA	WIA	MIA	Total
4 - 3"R		3	8	0	11

Cpt. James Thompson, PA Light, Btty. C

	KIA	WIA	MIA	Total
4 - 3"R	0	11	2	13
8 guns	3	19	2	24

Total:

	KIA	WIA	MIA
Duryee	59	233	35
Christian	28	197	29
Hartsuff	82	497	20
Artillery	3	19	2
	172	946	86

Engaged 3158 (100%) - 1204 (38%) = 1954 (62%)

	Unit	Pres.	KIA	WIA	MIA	Total
BG Geo. G. Meade	Div.	2855	(engaged)			
BG Truman Seymour	Brig.					

	Unit	Pres.	KIA	WIA	MIA	Total
	1 PA Res.		5	22	0	27
(George Line Farm &	2 PA Res.		3	21	0	24
East Woods)	5 PA Res.		3	7	0	10
	6 PA Res.		8	61	0	69
	13 PA Res.		5	20	0	25
			24	131	0	155
Col. Albert Magilton	Brig.					
	3 PA Res.	200[130]	12	34	0	46
(The Cornfield)	4 PA Res.		5	43	0	48
	7 PA Res.		12	60	0	72
	8 PA Res.		12	44	0	56
			41	181	0	222
LTC Robert Anderson	Brig.					
	9 PA Res.		17	66	0	83
(The Cornfield)	10 PA Res.		0	9	0	9
	11 PA Res.		7	15	0	22
	12 PA Res.		13	46	2	61
			37	136	2	175

Artillery:
Lt. J. G. Simpson, 1st PA Light, Btty. A

	Unit	Pres.	KIA	WIA	MIA	Total
4 - 12#N			1	3	0	4

Cpt. J. H. Cooper, 1st PA Light, Btty. B

4 - 3"R			0	2	0	2

Cpt. Dunbar R. Ransom, 3rd US, Btty. C

4 - 12#N			2	13	0	15
			3	18	0	21

12 guns

Total:

	KIA	WIA	MIA
Seymour	24	131	0
Magilton	41	181	0
Anderson	37	136	2
Artillery	3	18	0
	105	466	2

Engaged 2855 (100%) - 573 (20%) = 2282 (80%)
Present I Corps 14856 (100%) - Engaged 9438 (64%) = Not Engaged 5418 (36%)

	Unit	Pres.	KIA	WIA	MIA	Total
MG Edwin V. Sumner	II Corps	18813				
	Staff		0	2	0	2
Escort 9 NY Cav., Cos. D & K			0	1	0	1
MG Israel B. Richardson	Div.	4029	(Engaged)			
	Staff		0	2	0	2
BG John G. Caldwell	Brig.					
	5 NH		8	102	1	111
(Bloody Lane & Piper's Farm)	7 NY		15	46	0	61
	61 NY	100[131]	6	34	1	41
	64 NY	250[132]	8	42	0	50
	81 PA		7	44	0	51
			44	270	2	316

	Unit	Pres.	KIA	WIA	MIA	Total
BG Thomas F. Meagher	Brig.					
	Staff		0	1	0	1
(Bloody Lane)	29 MA		7	29	3	39
	63 NY	341[133]	35	165	2	202
	69 NY	317[134]	44	152	0	196
	88 NY	302[135]	27	75	0	102
			113	422	5	540
Col. John R. Brooke	Brig.					
	2 DE		12	44	2	58
(Bloody Lane & Piper's Farm)	52 NY	119[136]	4	12	2	18
	57 NY	309[137]	19	79	3	101
	66 NY		11	91	1	103
(Roulette's Lane) =	53 PA		6	18	1	25
			52	244	9	305

Artillery:
Cpt. R. D. Pettitt, 1st NY Btty. B

6 - 10#P			1	0	0	1

Lt. Evan Thomas, 4th US, Btty. A & C

6 - 12#N		-	0	3	0	3
			1	3	0	4

12 guns

Total.	KIA	WIA	MIA
Staff	0	5	0
Caldwell	44	268	2
Meagher	113	422	5
Brooke	52	244	9
Artillery	1	3	0
	210	942	16

Engaged 4029 (100%) - 1168 (29%) = 2861 (71%)

	Unit	Pres.	KIA	WIA	MIA	Total
MG John Sedgwick	Div.	5437	(Engaged)			
	Staff		0	2	0	2
BG Willis A. Gorman	Brig.					
	15 MA	582[138]	57	238	23	318
(West Woods)	1MN	435[139]	15	60	15	90
	34 NY	311[140]	33	111	10	154
	82 NY	339[141]	21	92	15	128
	1st Co. MA SS		8	17	1	26
	2nd Co. MA SS	42[142]	0	21	3	24
			134	539	67	740
BG Oliver O. Howard	Brig.	2169				
	69 PA	486[143]	19	58	15	92
(West Woods)	71 PA	510	26	95	18	139
	72 PA	681	38	163	36	237
	106 PA	492	10	63	4	77
			93	379	73	545

	Unit	Pres.	KIA	WIA	MIA	Total
BG Napoleon J. T. Dana	Brig.					
	Staff		0	2	0	2
(West Woods)	19 MA		8	108	30	146
	20 MA		12	84	28	124
	7 MI		39	178	4	221
	42 NY	345[144]	35	127	19	181
	59 NY	381[145]	48	153	23	224
			142	652	104	898

Artillery:
Cpt. J. A. Tompkins, 1st RI Light, Btty. A

6 - 10#P			4	15	0	19

Lt. G. A. Woodruff, 1st US, Btty. I

6 - 12#			0	6	0	6
			4	21	0	25

12 guns

Total:

	KIA	WIA	MIA
Staff	0	2	0
Gorman	134	539	67
Howard	93	379	73
Dana	142	652	104
Artillery	4	21	0
	373	1593	244

Engaged 5437 (100%) - 2210 (41%) = 3227 (59%)

	Unit	Pres.	KIA	WIA	MIA	Total
BG William H. French	Div.	5740	(Engaged)			
BG Nathan Kimball	Brig.					
	Staff		0	1	0	1
(Bloody Lane)	14 IN	320[146]	30	150	0	180
	8 OH	341[147]	32	129	0	161
	132 PA	750[148]	30	114	8	152
	7 WV		29	116	0	145
			121	510	8	639
Col. Dwight Morris	Brig.					
	14 CT	1015[149]	20	88	48	156
(Bloody Lane)	108 NY		26	122	47	195
	130 PA		32	146	0	178
			78	356	95	529
BG Max Weber	Brig.					
	Staff		0	2	0	2
	1 DE	900[150]	62	356	32	450
(Bloody Lane)	5 MD		25	123	15	163
	4 NY	540[151]	44	142	1	187
			131	623	48	802

(Add 220 more casualties not in the *OR*.)

	Unit	Pres.	KIA	WIA	MIA	Total
Artillery:						
Cpt. J. D. Frank, 1st NY Light, Btty. G						
4 - 12#N			1	4	0	5
Cpt. C. D. Owen, 1st RI Light, Btty. G						
6 - 3"R			0	5	0	5
			1	9	0	10

Total:		KIA	WIA	MIA		
	Kimball	121	510	8		
	Morris	78	356	95		
	Weber	131	623	48		
	Artillery	1	9	0		
		331	1498	151		

Engaged 5740 (100%) - 1980 (35%) = 3760 (65%)
II Corps: Present 18813 (100%) - Engaged 15206 (81%) = Not Engaged 3607 (19%)

	Unit	Pres.	KIA	WIA	MIA	Total
MG Fitz J. Porter	V Corps	12930				
BG George Sykes	Div.	2274	(Engaged)			
LTC Robt. Buchanan	Brig.					
(Middle Bridge)	4 US		3	29	0	32
	1st Bttn. 12 US		1	3	0	4
	1st Bttn. 14 US	178[152]	0	2	0	2
	2nd Bttn. 14 US	121[153]	0	1	0	1
			4	35	0	39

3rd, 4th, 12th US (2nd Bttn.) = NO CASUALTIES

		KIA	WIA	MIA	Total
Maj. Charles S. Lovell	Brig.				
(Middle Bridge)	2 & 10 US	8	46	1	55
	11 US	0	1	0	1
		8	47	1	56

1st & 6th US, 17th US = NO CASUALTIES

	Unit	KIA	WIA	MIA	Total
Artillery:					
Cpt. Stephen H. Weed, 5th US, Btty. I					
4 - 3"R		0	3	0	3
Reserve Artillery:					
Lt. Bernhard Wever, 1st Bttn., NY Light, Btty. A					
4 - 20#P					
Lt. A. Von Kleiser, 1st Bttn., NY Light, Btty. B					
4 - 20#P					
Cpt. Robert Langer, 1st Bttn., NY Light, Btty. C					
4 - 20#P					
Cpt. Charles Kusserow, 1st Bttn., NY Light, Btty. D					
4 - 3"R (Combined Losses)		1	0	1	2
Cpt. William M. Graham, 1st US, Btty. K					
6 - 12#N		4	5	0	9
		5	8	1	14

26 guns

Total:

	KIA	WIA	MIA
Buchanan	4	35	0
Lovell	8	47	1
Artillery	5	8	1
	17	90	2

Engaged 2274 (100%) - 109 (5%) = 2165 (95%)
V Corps: Present 12930 (100%) - 3224 (25%) = Not Engaged 9706 (75%)

	Unit	Pres.	KIA	WIA	MIA	Total
MG Wm. B. Franklin	VI Corps	12300				
	Staff		1	0	0	1
MG Henry W. Slocum	Div.					
Col. Alfred T. A. Torbert	Brig.					
	1 NJ		0	6	0	6
(Plowed Field North of Mumma's)	2 NJ		2	7	0	9
	3 NJ		0	1	0	1
	4 NJ		0	3	0	3
			2	17	0	19
Col. Joseph Bartlett	Brig.					
	5 ME		0	5	0	5
(East Woods)	16 NY		0	2	0	2
	96 PA		1	1	0	2
			1	8	0	9

27th NY = NO CASUALTIES

	Unit	Pres.	KIA	WIA	MIA	Total
BG John Newton	Brig.					
	18 NY		0	4	0	4
(East Woods)	31 NY		0	3	0	3
	32 NY		0	4	0	4
	95 PA		1	9	0	10
			1	20	0	21

Artillery:
Cpt. J. W. Wolcott, 1st MD Light, Btty. A

	Unit	Pres.	KIA	WIA	MIA	Total
6 - 3"R			1	11	2	14

Lt. E. B. Williston, 2nd US, Btty. D

	Unit	Pres.	KIA	WIA	MIA	Total
6 - 12#N			0	2	0	2
			1	13	2	16

Total:

	KIA	WIA	MIA
Staff	1	0	0
Torbert	2	17	0
Bartlett	1	8	0
Newton	1	20	0
Artillery	1	13	2
	6	58	2

There are no figures available to compare numbers engaged with the numbers lost for this division.

	Unit	Pres.	KIA	WIA	MIA	Total
MG William F. Smith	Div.	2585	(engaged)			
BG Winfield S. Hancock	Brig.					
	6 ME		0	2	0	2
(East Woods)	49 PA		1	4	0	5
			1	6	0	7

43rd NY, 137th PA, and 5th WI = NO CASUALTIES

	Unit	Pres.	KIA	WIA	MIA	Total
BG W. T. H. Brooks	Brig.					
	2 VT		0	5	0	5
	3 VT		1	3	0	4
(Bloody Lane & Mumma's Swale)	4 VT		0	6	0	6
	5 VT		0	2	0	2
	6 VT		0	8	0	8
			1	24	0	25
Col. Wm. H. Irwin	Brig.	1706				
	7 ME	181[154]	12	63	20	95
(Dunker Church, Mumma's &	20 NY	800[155]	38	96	11	145
Piper's Swales)	33 NY	150[156]	6	41	0	47
	49 NY	400[157]	2	21	0	23
	77 NY	175[158]	6	26	0	32
			64	247	31	342

Total:	KIA	WIA	MIA
Hancock	1	6	0
Brooks	1	24	0
Irwin	64	247	31
	66	277	31

Engaged 2585 (100%) - 374 (15%) = 2211 (85%)
VI Corps: Present 12300 - Engaged 2585 (21% +) = Not Engaged 9715 (79% +)

	Unit	Pres.	KIA	WIA	MIA	Total
BG Jacob Cox	IX Corps	13819				
BG Orlando D. Willcox	Div.	3248	(Engaged)			
Col. Benjamin Christ	Brig.					
	28 MA		12	36	0	48
(North of Lower Bridge Road)	17 MI		18	89	0	107
	79 NY		5	27	0	32
	50 PA		8	46	3	57
			43	198	3	244
Col. Thomas Welch	Brig.					
	8 MI		4	25	2	31
(South of Lower Bridge Road)	46 NY	278[159]	5	11	0	16
	45 PA		1	36	1	38
	100 PA		9	48	1	58
			19	120	4	143

Artillery:
Cpt. A. M. Cook, MA Light, 8th Btty.

			KIA	WIA	MIA	Total
6 - 12#H			0	1	0	1

Total:	KIA	WIA	MIA
Christ	43	198	3
Welsh	19	128	4
Artillery	0	1	0
	62	327	7

Engaged 3248 (100%) - 396 (12%) = 2852 (88%)

	Unit	Pres.	KIA	WIA	MIA	Total
BG Samuel D. Sturgis	Div.	3254	(Engaged)			
BG James Nagle	Brig.					
2 MD		187[160]	17	47	3	67
(Lower Bridge)	6 NH		4	13	1	18
	9 NH		10	49	0	59
	48 PA		8	51	1	60
			39	160	5	204
Col. Edward Ferrero	Brig.	1620				
	21 MA	150[161]	7	41	0	48
(Lower Bridge)	35 MA	800[162]	48	160	6	214
	51 NY	335[163]	19	68	0	87
	51 PA	335	21	99	0	120
			95	368	6	469

Artillery:
Cpt. George W. Durrell, PA Light, Btty. D

		KIA	WIA	MIA	Total
6 - 10#P		0	3	0	3

Cpt. J. C. Clark, Jr., 4th US, Btty. E

		KIA	WIA	MIA	Total
4 - 10#P		2	1	0	3
		2	4	0	6

10 guns

Total:

	KIA	WIA	MIA
Nagle	39	160	5
Ferrero	95	368	6
Artillery	2	4	0
	136	532	11

Engaged 3254 (100%) - 679 (21%) = 2575 (79%)

	Unit	Pres.	KIA	WIA	MIA	Total
BG Isaac Rodman	Div.	2914	(Engaged)			
	Staff		1	0	0	1
Col. Harrison Fairchild	Brig.	943				
(Harper's Ferry Road)	9 NY	373[164]	45	176	14	235
	89 NY	368[165]	18	77	8	103
	103 NY	202	24	68	25	117
			87	321	47	455
Col. Edward Harland	Brig.					
(Harper's Ferry RD)=	8 CT		34	139	21	194
(Lower Bridge)=	11 CT	440[166]	36	103	0	139
(40 Acre Cornfield)=	16 CT	940[167]	47	177	78	302
	4 RI		21	77	2	100
			138	496	101	735

Artillery:
Lt. C. P. Muhlenberg, 5th US, Btty. A

		KIA	WIA	MIA	Total
6 - 12#N		0	3	0	3

Cpt. James R. Whiting, 9th NY, Co. K

		KIA	WIA	MIA	Total
2 - 12#Dalghren Rifles			(Not Reported Separately)		
		0	3	0	3

8 guns

Total:

	KIA	WIA	MIA
Staff	0	1	0
Fairchild	87	321	47
Harland	138	496	101
Artillery	0	3	0
	225	821	148

Engaged 2914 (100%) - 1194 (41%) = 1721 (59%)

	Unit	Pres.	KIA	WIA	MIA	Total
Col. Eliakim P. Scammon	Div.	3154	(Engaged)			
Col. Hugh Ewing	Brig.					
(40 Acre Cornfield & Otto's Lane)	12 OH		7	26	0	33
	23 OH		8	59	2	69
	30 OH		13	49	18	80
			28	134	20	182

Gilmore's Co. WV Cav. & Harrison's Co. WV Cav. Not Engaged = NO CASUALTIES

Artillery:
Cpt. L. W. Robinson, 1st OH Light, Btty. L
   6 - 10#P   (No Casualties)

	Unit	Pres.	KIA	WIA	MIA	Total
Col. George Crook	Brig.					
(Lower Bridge & Otto's Lane)	11 OH		4	12	5	21
	28 OH		2	19	0	21
	36 OH		2	21	2	25
			8	52	7	67

Artillery:
Cpt. Seth Simmonds, KY Light Arty. Simmonds' Indpt.

			KIA	WIA	MIA	Total
4 - 10#P 2 - 20#P			0	6	0	6
6 guns			0	6	0	6

Cavalry: Chicago Dragoons   (Not Engaged)

Total:

	KIA	WIA	MIA
Ewing	28	134	20
Crook	8	52	7
Artillery	0	6	0
	36	192	27

Engaged 3154 (100%) - 255 (8%) = 2899 (92%)
IX Corps: Present 13819 (100%) - Engaged 12570 (91%) = Not Engaged 1249 (9%)

	Unit	Pres.	KIA	WIA	MIA	Total
MG Jos. K. F. Mansfield	XII Corps	10126				
	Staff		1	0	0	1
BG Alpheus S. Williams	Div.	4735	(Engaged)			
BG Samuel Crawford	Brig.					
(East Woods) =	10 ME		21	50	1	72
(The Cornfield) =	28 NY	60[168]	2	9	1	12
	46 PA	150[169]	6	13	0	19
	124 PA		5	42	17	64
(West Woods) =	125 PA		28	115	83	226
(The Cornfield) =	128 PA		26	86	6	118
			88	315	108	511

	Unit	Pres.	KIA	WIA	MIA	Total
BG George Gordon	Brig.					
(The Cornfield) =	27 IN	340[170]	18	191	0	209
(The Cornfield & West Woods) =	2 MA	488[171]	12	56	2	70
	13 NJ		7	75	19	101
(East Woods) =	107 NY		7	51	5	63
Corps d'Afrique PA (w/2 MA)			0	2	1	3
(The Cornfield) =	3 WI	312[172]	27	173	0	200
			71	548	27	646

Total:	KIA	WIA	MIA
Staff	1	0	0
Crawford	88	315	108
Gordon	71	548	27
	160	863	135

Engaged 4735 (100%) - 1158 (25%) = 3576 (75%)

	Unit	Pres.	KIA	WIA	MIA	Total
BG George S. Greene	Div.	2504	(Engaged)			
LTC H. Tyndale	Brig.	1201[173]				
(The Cornfield, Mumma's Swale,	5 OH	180[174]	11	35	2	48
& West Woods)	7 OH	115[175]	5	33	0	38
	66 OH	120[176]	1	23	0	24
	28 PA	786[177]	40	210	88	338
			57	301	90	448
Col. H. J. Stainbrook	Brig.	523[178]				
(Mumma's Swale & West Woods)	3 MD	148[179]	1	25	3	29
	102 NY	145[180]	5	27	5	37
	111 PA	230[181]	26	76	8	110
			32	128	16	176
Col. W. B. Goodrich	Brig.	777[182]				
(West Woods)	3 DE	126[183]	6	11	0	17
	Purnell Legion MD	204[184]	3	23	0	26
	60 NY	226[185]	4	18	0	22
	78 NY	221[186]	8	19	7	34
			21	71	7	99

Artillery:
Cpt. G. W. Cothran, 1st NY Light, Btty. M

6 - 3"R			0	6	0	6

Cpt. Joseph M. Knap, PA Light, Btty. E

6 - 3"R			1	6	1	8

Cpt. Robert B. Hampton, PA Light, Btty. F

4 - 3"R			0	3	0	3
			1	15	1	17

16 guns

Total:	KIA	WIA	MIA
Tyndale	57	301	90
Stainbrook	32	128	16
Goodrich	21	71	7
Artillery	1	15	1
	111	515	114

Engaged 2504 (100%) - 740 (30%) = 1764 (70%)
XII Corps: Present 10126 (100%) - Engaged 7631 (75%) = Not Engaged 2495 (25%)

	Unit	Pres.	KIA	WIA	MIA	Total
BG Alfred Pleasonton	Div.	4320	(Present & Engaged)			
Maj. Charles J. Whiting	Brig.					
	5 US		0	1	0	1
Col. John F. Farnsworth	Brig.					
	8 IL		0	1	0	1
	3 IN		0	5	0	5
Col. Richard H. Rush	Brig.					
	4 PA		3	7	0	10
	6 PA		0	3	0	3
Artillery:						
Cpt. J. C. Tidball, 2nd US, Btty. A						
6 - 12#N			1	3	0	4
Lt. P. C. Hains, 2nd US, Btty. M						
• 6 - 3"R			2	3	0	5
Unattached: 15 PA Cav. (detachment)			1	0	0	1
			7	23	0	30

12 guns
Engaged 4320 (100%) - 30 (1%) = 4290 (99%)
[Cavalry division was engaged and deployed around Newcomer's barn near the Middle Bridge.]

SUMMARY:	Pres.	Engd	KIA	WIA	MIA	ST	Survivors
I Corps	11856						
Doubleday		3125	140	638	34	(812) =	2613
Ricketts		3158 ·	172 ·	946 ·	86	(1204) =	1954
Meade		2855 ·	105 ·	466 ·	2	(573) =	2282
II Corps	18813						
Richardson		4029 ·	210 ·	942 ·	16	(1168) =	2861
Sedgwick		5437 ·	373 ·	1593 ·	244	(2210) =	3227
French		5740 ·	331 ·	1498 ·	151	(1980) =	3760
V Corps	12930						
Sykes		2274 ·	17 ·	90 ·	2	(109) =	2165
VI Corps	12300						
Slocum		(Unknown)	6 ·	58 ·	2	(66) =	N/A
Smith		2585 ·	66 ·	277	31	(374) =	2211
IX Corps	13819						
Willcox		3248 ·	62 ·	327 ·	7	(396) =	2852
Sturgis		3254 ·	136 ·	532 ·	11	(679) =	2575
Rodman		2914 ·	225 ·	821 ·	148	(1194) =	1720
Scammon		3154 ·	36 ·	192 ·	27	(255) =	2899
XII Corps	10126						
Williams		4735 ·	160 ·	863 ·	135	(1158) =	3577
Greene		2504 ·	111 ·	515 ·	114	(740) =	1764
Cavalry	4320	4320 ·	7 ·	23 ·	0	(30) =	4290
	87164	53632 ·	2157 ·	9716 ·	1009	(12882) =	40750

The Army of the Potomac				The Army of Northern Virginia
	87164	Present ?		
	53632	Engaged	30646	
(4% of engaged)	2157	KIA	1754	(6% of engaged)
(18% of engaged)	9716	WIA	8649	(28% of engaged)
(2% of engaged)	1009	MIA	1127	(4% of engaged)
(24% of engaged)	12882	TOTAL	11530	(38% of engaged)

Chapter One

1 William A. Frassanito, *Antietam, The Photographic Legacy of America's Bloodiest Day*, Charles Scribner's Sons, NY, 1978, p. 109.
 Francis F. Wilshin, "Antietam Historic Structures", National Park Service, Department of the Interior, August 28, 1969, p. 6.

2 Freeman Ankrum, *Sidelights of Brethren History*, The Brethren Press, Elgin, OH, 1962, p. 105.

3 Frassanito, p. 109.
 Wilshin, p. 6.

4 James Cooper Nisbet, *Four Years on the Firing Line*, Bell I. Wiley, (ed.), McCowat-Mercer Press, Inc., Jackson, TN, p. 102.

5 Walter H. Taylor, *Four Years With General Lee*, James I. Robertson, Jr., (ed.), Indiana University Press, Bloomington, 1962, p. 71.
 Lawton had 1,150 present. Trimble (Colonel James A. Walker, commanding) had 700 men. Averages were: Lawton—192/regiment and Trimble—140/regiment. Bear in mind also that the Confederates counted only those personnel who bore "muskets", whereas the Federals not only included officers but noncombatants as well in their musters.

6 James A. Murfin, *The Gleam of Bayonets*, Bonanza Books, NY, 1965, p. 297.

7 John W. Schildt, *September Echoes*, The Valley Register, Publishers and Printers, Middletown, MD, 1960, p. 76.

8 Nisbet, p. 102.

9 Robert K. Krick, *Parker's Virginia Battery C.S.A.*, Virginia Book Company, Berryville, VA, 1975, p. 347.

10 *Ibid.*, p. 348.

11 *Ibid.*, p. 50.

12 *Ibid.*, p. 347.

13 *Ibid.*, p. 49.

14 *Ibid.*, p. 51.

15 James Steptoe Johnston, Jr., Letter 9/22/62, Mercer Green Johnston Collection, Manuscript Division, Library of Congress.

16 Frank M. Mixon, *Reminiscences of a Private*, The State Co., Columbia, S. C., 1910, p. 27.

17 James Steptoe Johnston, Jr., Letter, 9/22/62, Mercer Green Johnston Collection, Manuscript Division, Library of Congress.

18 Michael Shuler, Diary, 9/16/62, Vol. I. M. Shuler Collection, Manuscript Division, Library of Congress.

19 John H. Worsham, *One of Jackson's Foot Cavalry*, James I. Robertson, Jr., (ed.), McCowat-Mercer Press, Inc., Jackson, TN, 1964, p. 84.

20 Ezra E. Stickley "Battle of Sharpsburg," *CONFEDERATE VETERAN*, VOL. XXII, 1914, p. 66.

21 Robertson, *Stonewall*, p. 156.
 Robert T. Hubard, Notebook, 1860-1866, p. 141, 10522, "Damnation of Vancouver" and "Turvey" Manuscripts. Manuscript Department, University of Virginia Library, Charlottesville, VA.
 James B. Painter, Letter to Brother, 10/5/62, James Barney Painter Letters, 10661, Manuscript Department, University of Virginia Library, Charlottesville, VA.

22 Heros Von Borcke, *Memoirs of the Confederate War for Independence*, Vol. 1, Peter Smith, NY, 1938, p. 228.

23 Henry Steele Commager, (ed.), *The Blue and the Gray*, The Bobbs-Merrill Co., Inc., Indianapolis, 1950, p. 165.

24 Von Borcke, I, p. 227.

25 *Ibid.*, p. 228.

26 Napier Bartlett, *A Story of the War Including the Marches of the Washington Artillery*, New Orleans, Clark and ?. 1874, p. 136-137.

27 "Civil War Letters of Francis Edwin Pierce of the 108th New York Volunteer Infantry," *ROCHESTER HISTORICAL SOCIETY PUBLICATIONS*, XVII, "Rochester in the Civil War," Rochester, NY, "1944, p. 151.

28 Thomas Francis Galwey, *The Valiant Hours*, The Stackpole Co., Harrisburg, PA, 1961, p. 37.

29 *Ibid.*

30 William F. Fox (comp.), *New York at Gettysburg*, Vol. II. J.B. Lyon Co., Printers, Albany, 1900, p. 499.

31 Galwey, p. 38.

32 *Ibid.*, p. 37.

33 *Ibid.*, p. 38.

34 William H. Andrews. "Tige Anderson's Brigade at Sharpsburg", *CONFEDERATE VETERAN*, VOL. XVI. p. 578.
 James L. Coker, *History of Company G. Ninth S. C. Regiment, Infantry, C. S. Army and of Company E. Sixth S. C. Regiment. Infantry, C. S. Army*, The Attic Press, Inc., Greenwood, SC, p. 109.

35 Galwey, p. 37.

36 Fox, II, p. 499.

37 Frassanito, p. 80.

38 *ROCHESTER HISTORICAL SOCIETY PAPERS*, XVII, p. 152.

39 Charles A. Fuller, *Personal Recollections of the War of 1861*, News Job Publishing House, Shirburne, NY, 1906, p. 57.

40 Andrews, CV, XVI, p. 578.
  Robert E. Lee, Letter to Mrs T. J. Jackson, 1/25/66, Letterbook of Robert E. Lee, VA Historical Society, Richmond, VA.
41 Benjamin F. Cook, *History of the Twelfth Massachusetts Volunteers (Webster Regiment)*, Twelfth Webster Regiment Association, Boston, 1882, p. 70.
42 Marsena Randolph Patrick *Inside Lincoln's Army*, David S. Sparks, (ed.), Thomas Yoseloff, NY, 1964, p. 146.
43 Alan T. Nolan, *The Iron Brigade*, MacMillan Co., NY, 1961, p. 132.
  Regimental History Committee, *History of the Third Pennsylvania Cavalry, Sixtieth Regiment Pennsylvania Volunteers in the American Civil War*, Franklin Printing Co., Phila, 1905, p. 121.
44 *3rd PA Cav.*, p. 121-122.
45 Patrick, p. 146.
46 Austin C. Stearns, *Three Years With Company K*, Arthur A. Kent, (ed.), Farleigh Dickinson University Press, Rutherford, 1976, p. 124.
47 Cook, p. 70-71.
48 Patrick, p. 146.
49 Stearns, p. 125.
50 Joseph B. Polley, *Hood's Texas Brigade, Its Marches, Its Battles, Its Achievements*, Morningside Bookshop, Dayton, OH, 1976, p. 115.
51 *3rd PA Cav.*, p. 121-122.
52 Edwin A. Glover, *Bucktailed Wildcats, A Regiment of Civil War Volunteers*, Thomas Yoseloff, NY, 1960, p. 156.
53 W. R. Hamby, "Hood's Texas Brigade at Sharpsburg", *CONFEDERATE VETERAN*, VOL. XVI. 1908, p. 19.
54 Polley, p. 118.
55 Krick, *Parker's*, p. 50.
56 Edward A. Moore, *The Story of a Cannoneer Under Stonewall Jackson*, J.P. Bell Co., Inc., Lynchburg, VA, 1910, p. 147.
57 Worsham, p. 86.
58 William Thomas Poague, *Gunner With Stonewall*, Monroe F. Cockrell, (ed.), McCowat-Mercer Press, Jackson, TN, 1957, p. 45.
59 Moore, p. 149.
60 Krick, *Parker's*, p. 50.
61 Polley, p. 118.
62 Cook, p. 71.
  Elliott Stephen Welch, Letter to Parents from Winchester, VA, 9/22/62, in the Elliott Stephen Welch Papers, 1862-1865, Manuscript Department, Duke University Library, Durham, NC.
63 Glover, p. 156.
64 Cook, p. 71.
65 Cope, Map 1.
  3rd PA Cav., p. 123.
66 Patrick, p. 146.
67 Cook, p. 71.
68 Nolan, p. 134.
69 Stearns, p. 125.
70 Patrick, p. 146.
71 Polley, p. 118.
72 Cope, Map 1.
73 William Willis Blackford, *War Years With Jeb Stuart*, Charles Scribner's Sons, NY, 1945, p. 149.
74 Von Borcke, I, p. 229.
  "War Record 1861-1865 of Dr. James McClure," p. 6-7, Sarah Traverse Lewis Anderson Papers, VA Historical Society, Richmond, VA.
75 Moore, p. 150.
76 *Ibid.*
77 Krick, *Parker's*, p. 51.
78 Patrick, p. 147.
79 Stickley, CV, XXII, p. 66.
80 Oliver C. Bosbyshell (comp.), *Pennsylvania at Antietam*, Harrisburg Publishing Co., State Printer, Harrisburg, PA, 1906, p. 134.
  Edmund R. Brown, *The Twenty-Seventh Indiana Volunteer Infantry in the War of the Rebellion, 1861 to 1865*, Butternut Press, Gaithersburg, MD, p. 238.
81 Robert M. Green, (comp.), *History of the One Hundred Twenty-fourth Regiment Pennsylvania Volunteers*, Philadelphia, 1907, p. 120.
82 Bosbyshell, p. 134.
83 Miles C. Huyette, *The Maryland Campaign and the Battle of Antietam*, Hammond Press, Buffalo, NY, 1915, p. 28.
84 Robert Underwood Johnson and Clarence Clough Buel, (eds.), *Battles and Leaders of the Civil War*, Vol. II, part 2, Grant-Lee Edition, The Century Company, NY, 1888, p. 660.
85 Autobiography, Samuel W. Compton, p. 108, in the Samuel Wilson Compton Papers, 1840-1925, Manuscript Department, Duke University Library, Durham, NC.
86 Galwey, p. 38.
87 *ROCHESTER HISTORICAL SOCIETY PAPERS*, XVII, p. 152-153.
88 John D. Hemminger, E Co., 130th PA, Diary, 9/16/62, Michael Winey Coll., USAMHI, Mss. Dept., Carlisle Barracks, PA.
89 George H. Otis, *The Second Wisconsin Infantry*, Alan D. Gaff, (ed.), Morningside Bookshop, Dayton, OH, 1984, p. 260.

[90] Moxley G. Sorrel, *Recollections of a Confederate Staff Officer*, Bell I. Wiley, (ed.), McCowat-Mercer Press, Inc., Jackson, TN 1958, p. 103.

[91] John D. Vautier, Diary, p. 165. USAMHI, Mss. Dept., Carlisle Barracks, PA.

Chapter Two

[1] Robertson, p. 156.
[2] Von Borcke, I, p. 229.
[3] *Ibid.*, p. 330.
[4] Robertson, p. 156.
[5] James Longstreet, *From Manassas to Appomattox*, Indiana University Press, Bloomington, 1960, p. 241.
[6] Stickley, CV, XXII, p. 66.
[7] Worsham, p. 85-86.
[8] Green, p. 111.
Robert T. Hubard, Notebook 1860-1866, p. 143-144, "Damnation of Vancouver" and "Turvey" Manuscripts, 10522, Manuscript Department, University of Virginia Library, Charlottesville, VA.
Richard H. Watkins, Letter to wife, 9/18/62, Richard Henry Watkins Papers, VA Historical Society, Richmond, VA.
Ezra Carman Mss., Chapter 15, p. 71, David A. Lilley Memorial Collection, Western Maryland Room, Washington County Free Library, Hagerstown, MD.
[9] Poague, p. 45.
[10] Moore, p. 151.
[11] Cope, Map 1.
[12] Krick, *Parker's*, p. 51.
[13] Bruce Catton, *Mr. Lincoln's Army*, Doubleday and Co., Inc., Garden City, 1965, p. 267.
[14] Nolan, p. 134.
[15] *Ibid.*, p. 130.
[16] *Ibid.*, p. 133.
[17] *Ibid.*, p. 129.
[18] *Ibid.*, p. 137.
[19] John Gibbon, *Personal Recollection of the Civil War*, Morningside Bookshop, Dayton, OH, 1978, p. 81.
[20] Nolan, p. 137.
Rufus R. Dawes, *Service With the Sixth Wisconsin Volunteers*, Morningside Bookshop, Dayton, OH, 1984, p. 87.
[21] Gibbon, p. 81.
Dawes, p. 87.
[22] Nolan, p. 131.
[23] *Ibid.*

[24] *Ibid.*, p. 138.
Dawes, p. 88 and 92.
[25] Catton, p. 272.
[26] Nolan, p. 138.
Dawes, p. 88.
[27] *Ibid.*
[28] *Ibid.*
[29] Nolan, p. 132.
[30] *Ibid.*
[31] Cope, Map 2.
[32] Krick, *Parker's*, p. 316.
[33] *Ibid.*, p. 55
[34] *Ibid.*
[35] *Ibid.*, p. 54.
[36] *Ibid.*, p. 312.
[37] *Ibid.*, p. 54.
[38] *Ibid.*
[39] *Ibid.*
[40] Cope, Map 2.
[41] Moore, p. 151.
[42] *Ibid.*
[43] *Ibid.*, p. 150.
[44] Robertson, p. 157.
[45] *Ibid.*, p. 44.
[46] Stickley, CV, XXII, p. 66.
[47] Alfred Kelly, Letter to brother, Williamson Kelly, 10/3/62, in the Williamson Kelly Papers, 1852-1882, Manuscript Department, Duke University Library, Durham, NC.
[48] Nisbet, p. 102.
[49] *Ibid.*, p. 103.
[50] Robertson, p, 158.
Dawes, p. 89.
[51] Nolan, p. 139.
Dawes, p. 89.
[52] Gibbon, p. 81.
Dawes, p. 89.
[53] Nolan, p. 139.
[54] Otis, p. 261 and 263.
[55] Commager, p. 213.
[56] B. R. Marynisk, "The Famous Long Ago," Buffalo CWRT, July, 1986, p. 27.
Nolan, p. 137.
[57] Patrick, p. 147.
[58] Commager, p. 213.
[59] Frank H. Schell, "A Great Raging Battlefield Is Hell", *CIVIL WAR TIMES ILLUSTRATED*, VOL. VIII, #3, June 1969, Harrisburg, PA, p. 15.
[60] James M. Merrill, (ed.), *Uncommon Valor*, Rand McNally and Company, NY, 1964, p. 201.
[61] Schell, p. 15.
[62] Merrill, p. 201.
[63] Moore, p. 151.

[64] Poague, p. 46.

[65] Moore, p. 151.

[66] Robertson, p. 157.

[67] *Ibid.*, p. 158.

[68] Marynisk, p. 26.

[69] Patrick, p. 147.

Chapter Three

[1] Schell, p. 15.

[2] Gibbon, p. 83.

[3] Commager, p. 213.

[4] Dawes, p. 95.

[5] Cope, Map 3.
C. A. Stevens, *Berdan's United States Sharpshooters in the Army of the Potomac, 1861-1865*, Morningside Bookshop, Dayton, OH, 1984, p. 202-203.

[6] Commager, p. 213.

[7] Frassanito, p. 119.

[8] Commager, p. 213.

[9] Schell, p. 15.

[10] Commager, p. 213.

[11] Cope, Map 3.

[12] Nisbet, p. 103-104.

[13] *Ibid.*, p. 104.

[14] Cope, Map 3.

[15] Ronald H. Bailey and the Editors of Time-Life Books, *"The Bloodiest Day, The Battle of Antietam"*, THE CIVIL WAR, Time-Life Books, Alexandria, VA, 1904, p. 71.
Wilshin, p. 6.

[16] John W. Schildt, *Drums Along the Antietam*, McClain Printing Co., Parsons WVA, 1972, p. 185.

[17] Cope, Map 3

[18] Frassanito, p. 119.

[19] *Ibid.*, p. 124.

[20] Cope, Map 3.
Private Prince A. Dunton, 13th MA, Letter, 9/24/62, Antietam National Battlefield.

[21] Stearns, p. 126-127.

[22] Cook, p. 72.

[23] Stearns, p. 127.

[24] Cook, p. 72.

[25] I. G. Bradwell, "Bravery and Cowardice in Battle", *CONFEDERATE VETERAN*, XXXII, 1924, p. 133.

[26] Commager, p. 213.

[27] Moore, p. 152.

[28] Worsham, p. 87.

[29] *Ibid.*, p. 149.

[30] Cope, Map 3.

[31] Thomas M. Rankin, *23rd Virginia Infantry*, 1st ed., H. E. Howard Inc., Lynchburg, VA, 1987, p. 50-51.

[32] J. M. Polk, *Memories of the Lost Cause*, Austin, TX, 1905, p. 7.

[33] Beyer and Keydel, Vol. 1, p. 75.
Nolan, p. 137.

[34] *Ibid.*, p. 137

[35] Marynisk, p. 27.
Nolan, p. 139.

[36] Beyer and Keydel, Vol. 1, p. 75.

[37] Cope, Map 3.

[38] Commager, p. 306.

[39] *Ibid.*, p. 306-307.

[40] Cook, p. 68.

[41] *Ibid.*, p. 72-73.
Joseph E. Blake, 12th MA, Letter to brother, Stephen, 10/21/62, CW Misc. Coll., USAMHI Mss. Dept., Carlisle Barracks, PA.

[42] Stearns, p. 127-128.

[43] Commager, p. 213-214.
C. A. Stevens, p. 203.

[44] Cope, Map 3.

[45] Polley, p. 121-122.

[46] *Ibid.*, p. 123.

[47] *Ibid.*, p. 124.

[48] *Ibid.*, p. 120.

[49] *Ibid.*, p. 121.

[50] *Ibid.*, p. 120.
Elliott Stephen Welch, Letter to Parents from Winchester, VA, 9/22/62, in the Elliott Stephen Welch Papers, 1862-1865, Manuscript Department, Duke University Library, Durham, NC.

[51] A. Buell, p. 35.

[52] Nisbet, p. 104.

[53] Stearns, p. 128-129.

[54] Cope, Map 4.

[55] Krick, *Parker's*, p. 317 and 54.
Edward S. Duffey, Diary, 9/17/62, p. 53, Edward S. Duffey Diary, VA Historical Society, Richmond, VA.

[56] *Ibid.*, p. 54.

Chapter Four

[1] Catton, p. 269.

[2] *Ibid.*, p. 267.
Frank H. Taylor, *Philadelphia in the Civil War*, published by the city, 1913, p. 1-9.

[3] U.S. Department of the Army Public Information Division, *The Medal of Honor of the United States of*

America, U.S. Government Printing Office, Washington, D.C., 1948, p. 117.
Bailey, p. 71-72.

[4] Dept. of Army, *Medal of Honor*, p. 118.
John D. Vautier, Diary, p. 167, USAMHI, Mss. Dept., Carlisle Barracks, PA.

[5] Cook, p. 73.

[6] Murfin, p. 217.
Blake, Letter, 10/21/62. CW Misc. Coll., USAMHI, Mss. Dept., Carlisle Barracks, PA.

[7] Polley, p. 200-201.

[8] *Ibid.*, p. 121.
Elliott Stephen Welch, Letter to Parents from Winchester, VA, 9/22/62, in the Elliott Stephen Welch Papers, 1862-1865, Manuscript Department, Duke University Library, Durham, NC.

[9] *Ibid.*

[10] Polley, p. 121.

[11] *Ibid.*, p. 200-201.

[12] *Ibid.*, p. 124-125.

[13] Cope, Map 4.

[14] Commager, p. 214.

[15] Gibbon, p. 83.
John Gibbon definitely identified the gun in the road as belonging to Sergeant Mitchell.

[16] Cope, Map 4.

[17] Polley, p. 124-125.

[18] A. Buell, p. 34.

[19] Gibbon, p. 85.

[20] Beyer and Keydel, Vol. 1, p. 115.

[21] Gibbon, p. 83.

[22] *Ibid.*, p. 85.

[23] Beyer and Keydel, Vol. 1, p. 75.

[24] Willard A. Heaps. *The Bravest Teenage Yanks*, Buell, Sloan, and Pearce, New York, 1963, p. 61.

[25] *Ibid.*, p. 59.

[26] Beyer and Keydel, Vol. 1, p. 75.
Nolan, p. 144.

[27] Gibbon, p. 83.
In his memoirs, Gibbon states that Sergeant Mitchell was injured after the general had assisted with the aiming of the gun in the road. Klinefelter, the gunner, however, who was assisted by the general, made no mention of the sergeant's injury. Mitchell, apparently, was hurt prior to the general's arrival.

[28] Beyer and Keydel, Vol. 1, p. 76.
Nolan, p. 141.
Otis, p. 261-262.

[29] A. Buell, p. 39.

[30] Gibbon, p. 83.

[31] Commager, p. 215.

[32] Gibbon, p. 83.

[33] A. Buell, p. 39.
Gibbon, fn p. 83-84.

[34] Commager, p. 214.

[35] Heaps, p. 61-62.

[36] Heaps, p. 61-62.
Nolan, p. 141.

[37] Commager, p. 215.

[38] *Ibid.*

[39] Pennsylvania at Gettysburg Battlefield Commission, *Pennsylvania at Gettyburg*, Vol, I, E.K. Meyers, State Printer, Harrisburg, PA, 1893, p. 247.

[40] Cope, Map 4.

[41] Marynisk, p. 27.

[42] *PA. at Gettysburg*, Vol. I, p. 232.

[43] James S. Johnston, Jr., Letter, 9/24/62.

[44] Cope, Map 4.

[45] Commager, p. 306-307.
Allan D. Thompson, "Notes 1 and 2 on John and Leo Faller, A Co., 36th PA (7th Res.)", May, 1956, HCWRT Coll, USAMHI, Mss. Dept., Carlisle Barracks, PA.

[46] Commager, p. 306.

[47] *Ibid.*, p. 306.
Catton, 271.
Both Frank Holsinger and Mr. Catton insisted the 6th Georgia struck the 8th Pennsylvania Reserves. The 6th Georgia was not committed to combat yet. The regiment was the 6th North Carolina.

[48] Commager, p. 306.

[49] O. T. Hanks, *History of Captain B. F. Benton's Company, Hood's Texas Brigade, 1861-1865*, Morrison Books, Austin, 1984, p. 16-17.

[50] Polley, p. 126-127.

[51] Lt. F. Halsey Wigfall, Letter, 10/4/62, Trezevant Wigfall Collection, Manuscript Division, Library of Congress.

[52] Elliott Stephen Welch, Letter to Parents from Winchester, VA, 9/22/62, in the Elliott Stephen Welch Papers, 1862-1865, Duke University Library, Durham, NC.

[53] Polley, p. 121.

[54] *Ibid.* p. 120.

[55] *Ibid.*, p. 122.

[56] *Ibid.*, p. 131.

[57] Polk, p. 7-8.

[58] *Ibid.*

[59] Polley, p. 122.

[60] James S. Johnston, Jr., Letter, 9/24/62.

[61] Marynisk, p. 27.

[62] Commager, p. 306.

[63] Cope, Map 4.

[64] Polley, p. 132.

[65] *PA at Gettysburg*, Vol. I, p. 232.
John D. McQuaide, C Co., 38th PA Letter 9/22/62, CWTI Coll, USAMHI, Mss. Dept., Carlisle Barracks, PA.
Mahaffey was buried on Saturday, 9/20/62.

[66] A. Buell, p. 35
Kept only for the quote.
Beyer and Keydel, I, p. 115.
Gibbon, p. 85.

[67] Cook, p. 73.

[68] Polley, p. 128.
Lieutenant Gaston was identified as the standard bearer of the 1st Texas.

[69] Stickley, CV, XXII, p. 66.

Chapter Five

[1] Alonzo H. Quint, *The Record of the Second Massachusetts Infantry 1861-65*, James P. Walker, Boston, 1867, p. 135.
Brown, p. 238-239.

[2] Cope, Map 5.
Brown, Map, p. 244.
John Mead Gould, *History of the First—Tenth—Twenty-Ninth Maine Regiment*, Stephen Berry, Portland, 1871, p. 233.

[3] Francis Winthrop Palfrey, *The Antietam and Fredericksburg*, Charles Scribner's Sons, NY, 1002, p. 70, fn.

[4] Quint, *2nd MA*, p. 135.

[5] *Ibid.*
Brown, p. 243.

[6] Cope, Map 5.

[7] Quint, *2nd MA*, p. 135.

[8] Cope, Map 5.

[9] The Regimental Committee, *History of the One Hundred Twenty-fifth Regiment Pennsylvania Volunteers 1862-1863*, 2nd ed., J.B. Lippincott Co., Philadelphia, 1907, p. 94.

[10] Palfrey, p. 78, fn.

[11] Frassanito, p. 148.

[12] *Ibid.*, p. 152.

[13] F. H. Taylor, p. 71.
The 4th Pennsylvania Reserves suffered 75 casualties.

[14] Frassanito, p. 152.

[15] Cope, Map 5.

[16] Gould, p. 235-237.
Alonzo H. Quint, *The Potomac and the Rapidan*, Crosby and Nichols, Boston, 1864, p. 220.

Cook, p. 69.

[17] Cope, Map 5.

[18] Polley, p. 123.

[19] Nisbet, p. 104-105.

[20] *Ibid.*, p. 105.

[21] *Ibid.*

[22] Gould, p. 237-240.

[23] Cope, Map 5.

[24] *125th PA*, p. 94.

[25] Bosbyshell, p. 150.

[26] Catton, p. 276.
Brown, p. 243.

[27] Cope, Map 5.

[28] *B & L*, II, pt. 2, p. 641.

[29] Nisbet, p. 105.

[30] Gould, p. 240.

[31] *B & L*, Vol, II, pt. 2, p. 641.

[32] Bosbyshell, p. 135.
Nisbet, p. 105.
After the war, Gould told *CENTURY MAGAZINE* that he and two sergeants took the dying general down the Smoketown Road where they commandeered a Black cook from the I Corps to help them lift the portly Mansfield into an ambulance. In a letter to Nisbet, Gould stated that he left Mansfield by a branch (stream ?) where the general died.
In *CENTURY MAGAZINE*, the 125th Pennsylvania claimed that some men from their outfit carried Mansfield off the field in a blanket.
The regimental historian in Pennsylvania at Antietam insisted that Mansfield rode up to the 125th Pennsylvania as related in this book.
In all likelihood, the historian of the 125th is more accurate. It seems highly unlikely that a regiment under fire, such as the 10th Maine, would have allowed three file closers to leave the ranks to care for anyone. Gould also wrote two very contradictory accounts of Mansfield's wounding and death, whereas the historian of the 125th Pennsylvania was more succinct and less melodramatic.

[33] Cope, Map 5.

[34] Nolan, p. 141.
Patrick, p. 148.

[35] Patrick, p. 148.

[36] Jubal Anderson Early, *War Memoirs*, James I. Robertson, Jr., (ed.), Indiana University Press, Kraus Reprint Co., NY, 1969, p. 143.

[37] Marynisk, p. 28.

[38] Frassanito, p. 139.

[39] *Ibid.*, p. 142.

[40] Ashbury Hull Jackson, Letter to Mother from

Martinsburg, VA, 9/23/62, in the Edward Hardin Papers, Manuscript Department, Duke University Library, Durham, NC.
[41] Schildt, Drums, p. 185.
[42] Henry Kyd Douglas, *I Rode With Stonewall*, Chapel Hill, University of North Carolina, 1940, p. 170.
[43] Catton, p. 279.
[44] Cope, Map 6.
[45] Krick, Parker's, p. 342.
[46] *Ibid.*, p. 55
[47] *Ibid.*
[48] A. Buell, p. 35.
[49] *Ibid.*, p. 36.
[50] Patrick, p. 148-149.

Chapter Six

[1] *CONFEDERATE VETERAN*, Vol, IX, 1901, p. 265.
[2] Cope, Map 6.
[3] Calvin Leach, Diary, 9/17/62, p. 14-15, Calvin Leach Diary, in the Southern Historical Collection, University of North Carolina, Chapel Hill, NC.
[4] *Ibid.*, p. 15.
CONFEDERATE VETERAN, Vol. VI, 1898, p. 217.
[5] Bosbyshell, p. 150.
[6] Cope, Map 6.
[7] Gould, p. 239-242.
[8] Polley, p. 123.
Hanson, p. 42.
[9] Cope, Map 6.
Hanson, p. 42.
[10] Poague, p. 46.
[11] Gibbon, p. 83.
[12] Bosbyshell, p. 150.
[13] *CONFEDERATE VETERAN*, Vol. IX, 1901, p. 265.
R. H. Daniels, "The Battle of Sharpsburg or Antietam", CV, IX, 1901, p. 217.
[14] Cope, Map 7.
[15] Frassanito, p. 152.
[16] Green, p. 121.
[17] *Ibid.*, p. 120-121.
[18] *Ibid.*, p. 130.
[19] *Ibid.*, p. 121.
[20] *Ibid.*, p. 111.
[21] Cope, Map 7.
[22] D. Cunningham and W.W. Miller, (comp.) *Antietam*, Report of the Ohio Antietam Battlefield Commission, Springfield Publishing Co, State Printers, Springfield, OH, 1904, p. 33.
[23] Cope, Map 7.
[24] Cunningham and Miller, p. 45-46.

Gould, p. 237.
[25] Quint, *2nd MA*, p. 136.
[26] Catton, p. 277.
Brown, p. 246-247.
[27] Catton, p. 280.
Brown p. 249-250.
[28] Catton, p. 280.
Brown, p. 249.
[29] *3rd PA Cav.*, p. 126.
[30] Brown, p. 239.
[31] Quint, *2nd MA*, p. 136.
[32] Cunningham and Miller, p. 46.
3rd PA Cav., p. 126-127.
Julian Wisner Hinkley, *A Narrative of Service With the Third Wisconsin Infantry*, Wisconsin History Commission, September, 1912, p. 57.
[33] Quint, *2nd MA*, p. 137.
Brown, p. 247.
[34] Wendell D. Croom, *The War History of Company "C" (Beauregard Volunteers) Sixth Georgia Regiment*, Fort Valley, "Advertiser Office", 1879, p. 15.
[35] Stephen W. Sears, *Landscape Turned Red. The Battle of Antietam*, Ticknor & Fields, New Haven, 1983, p. 211.
[36] Ezra A. Carman "The Maryland Campaign of September 1862," Chapter 16, p. 154, David A. Lilley Memorial Collection, Western Maryland Room, Washington County Free Library, Hagerstown, MD.
[37] *Medal of Honor*, p. 117.
Cunningham and Miller, p. 34.
Hinkley, p. 57.
[38] *Ibid*, p. 111.
[39] Green, p. 129.
[40] *Ibid*, p. 11
[41] Frassanito, p. 152-153.
[42] Green, p. 121.
[43] Polley, p. 128.
Berry stated that he was escorted to a cavalry regiment which was stationed along a public road. The 12th Pennsylvania Cavalry was the only cavalry regiment in the immediate vicinity.
[44] *Ibid.*
Mr. Catton is in error when he stated that the colonel of the 2nd Massachusetts captured the colors of the 1st Texas. No mention of such a capture is made in the regimental history. No colonel in his right mind would have surrendered such a trophy to an enlisted man either.
[45] *Ibid.*, p. 128-129.
[46] *Ibid.*, p. 123.
[47] Bailey, p. 81.

[48] Nisbet, p. 106.
[49] Ibid.
[50] Huyette, p. 49.
[51] Ibid., p. 35-36.
[52] Ibid., p. 49.
[53] Ibid., p. 36.
[54] 125th PA, p. 69.
[55] Frassanito, p. 124.
[56] Huyette, p. 37.
[57] B & L, Vol. II, pt. 2, p. 641.
[58] Fox, vol. II, p. 762.
[59] Stearns, p. 129-130.
[60] Marynisk, p. 29.
[61] Worsham p. 87.
[62] Bosbyshell, p. 122.
[63] Fox, Vol. II, p. 762.
[64] Cunningham and Miller, p. 46.
[65] Huyette, p. 36.
[66] Bosbyshell, p. 137.

Chapter Seven

[1] Gibbon, p. 86-87.
[2] Schell, p. 17.
[3] Ibid., p 17-18
[4] Andrew E. Ford, The Story of the Fifteenth Regiment Massachusetts Volunteer Infantry in the Civil War. 1861-1864, Press of W.J. Coulter, Courant Office, 1898, p. 193.
[5] Blackford. p. 151.
[6] Von Borcke, p. 231.
[7] Memoirs of Samuel D. Buck, p. 47-48, in the Samuel D. Buck Papers, Manuscript Department, Duke University Library, Durham, NC.
[8] James Dinkins, 1861-1865, By an Old Johnnie Personal Recollections and Experiences in the Confederate Army, Morningside Bookshop, Dayton, OH, 1976, p. 58.
[9] Ibid., p. 57.
[10] Ibid., p. 57-58.
[11] Ibid., p. 56.
[12] Early, p. 142.
[13] Ibid.
[14] Schell, p. 17.
[15] Ford, p. 194.
[16] Ernst Linden Waitt, (comp.), History of the Nineteenth Regiment Massachusetts Volunteer Infantry. 1861-1865, Salem Press, Co., Salem, MA, 1906, p. 134.
[17] Schell, p. 17-18.
[18] Ford, p. 193.
[19] Schell, p. 17-18.
C.V. Tevis and D.R. Marquis, (comp.), The History of the Fighting Fourteenth, Brooklyn Eagle Press, 1911 (?), p. 45 and 48.
[20] Gibbon, p. 86.
3rd PA Cav., p. 127.
[21] Cope, Map 7.
[22] Huyette, p. 38.
[23] Ibid.
[24] Ibid., p. 36.
[25] Ibid., p. 36-37.
Huyette was, apparently, mistaken about Hooker being shot in the right instep.
[26] 3rd PA Cav., p. 103.
[27] Ibid., p. 127.
[28] Bosbyshell, p. 137.
Cope, Map 7.
[29] Blackford, p. 150-151.
[30] Edwin P. Alexander, Military Memoirs of a Confederate, Charles Scribner's Sons, NY, 1907, p. 256.
[31] 125th PA, p. 69-70.
[32] Huyette, p. 38.
[33] 125th PA, p. 69.
Carman 18, p. 188.
Jacob Higgins, "At Antietam", THE NATIONAL TRIBUNE, June 3, 1886, p 1
Soldiers and Sailors Historical Society of Rhode Island "Battery D, First Rhode Island Light Artillery at the Battle of Antietam," PERSONAL NARRATIVES, 3rd Series, #16, 1885-1887, J. Albert Monroe, Providence, RI, 1886, p. 44.
[34] Bosbyshell, p. 137.
[35] Huyette, p. 49.
[36] 125th PA, p. 71.
Poague, p. 46.
[37] Poague, p. 46.
[38] Huyette, p. 40.
125th PA, p. 71.
[39] 125th PA, p. 71.
[40] Ibid.
Higgins, 6/3/86, NATIONAL TRIBUNE, p. 1.
[41] Poague, p. 46.
[42] Early, p. 142-143.
[43] Poague, p. 47.
[44] Ibid.
[45] 125th PA, p. 71.
[46] Bosbyshell, p. 138.
125th PA, p. 71-72.
[47] Huyette, p. 38-39.
[48] 125th PA, p. 72-73.
Huyette, p. 50.
[49] Andrews, CV, XVI, 1908, p. 579.
[50] 125th PA, p. 71.

[51] Huyette p. 39.
[52] D. Augustus Dickert, *History of Kershaw's Brigade With Complete Roll of Companies, Biographical Sketches, Incidents, Anecdotes, Etc.*, Morningside Bookshop, Dayton, OH, 1976, p. 155.
[53] Bosbyshell, p. 137.
[54] Huyette, p. 39.
[55] *125th PA*, p. 202.
[56] *Ibid.*, p. 201.
[57] *Ibid.*, p. 203.
[58] Huyette, p. 39.
[59] *Ibid.*, p. 49.
    125th PA, p. 71.
    Higgins, 6/3/86, *NATIONAL TRIBUNE*, p. 1.
[60] Poague, p. 47.
[61] Patrick, p. 149.
[62] Cope, Map 8.
[63] Waitt, p. 134.
    Hinkley, p. 58.
    Hinkley, who observed the advance from some distance, insisted that all of the officers but Sumner dismounted. I doubt this.
[64] Gibbon, p. 87.
[65] Waitt, p. 135.
[66] *Ibid.*
    Ford, p. 194.
    Robert Goldwaite Carter, *Four Brothers in Blue*, University of Texas Press, Austin, 1978, p. 114.
[67] Carter, p. 113-114.
    C.V. Stevens, p. 205-206.
[68] Waitt, p. 135.
[69] *Ibid.*, p. 134.
[70] Bosbyshell, p. 138.
    125th PA, p. 50.
[71] Huyette, p. 50.
[72] *125th PA*, p. 142.
    Higgins, 6/3/86, *NATIONAL TRIBUNE*, p. 1.
[73] Bosbyshell, p. 138.
[74] *Ibid.*, p. 72.
[75] *Ibid.*, p. 72-73.
[76] Huyette, p. 39.
[77] *125th PA*, p. 72.

Chapter Eight

[1] Krick, *Parker's*, p. 55.
[2] *Ibid.*, p. 57.
[3] *Ibid.*, p. 59.
[4] Cope, Map 8.
[5] Calvin L. Collier, *"They'll Do to Tie To"*, *The Story of the Third Regiment. Arkansas Infantry, C.S.A.*, Major James D. Warren, 1959, p. 94.
[6] Dickert, p. 155.
[7] Dinkins, p. 59.
[8] Early, p.145.
    Cope, Map 8.
[9] Early, p. 145.
[10] Cope, Map 8.
[11] Early, p. 146-147.
[12] Cope, Map 8.
[13] Cunningham and Miller, p. 45.
[14] *Ibid.*, p. 46.
[15] Frassanito, p. 171.
[16] Cope, Map 8.
[17] Frassanito, p. 188-189.
[18] Waitt, p. 137.
[19] *Ibid.*, p. 136.
[20] Ford, p. 195.
[21] Cope, Map 8.
    Memoirs of Samuel D. Buck, p. 48, in the Samuel D. Buck Papers, Manuscript Department, Duke University Library, Durham, NC.
[22] Moore, p. 152-153.
[23] *Ibid.*, p. 153-154.
[24] Waitt, p. 136.
[25] Moore, p. 154.
[26] Waitt, p. 136.
[27] Schildt, *Drums*, p. 190-191.
[28] Carter, p. 114.
[29] Waitt, p. 136.
[30] Ford, p. 191, map.
[31] Waitt, p. 137.
[32] Ford, p. 196.
    Murfin, p. 240.
[33] Moore, p. 155.
[34] Poague, p. 47.
[35] Moore, p. 155.
[36] Poague, p. 47.
[37] Moore, p. 155-156.
[38] Blackford, p. 150.
    Collier, p. 101.
    B & L, Vol. II, pt. 2, p. 224.
[39] Cope, Map 8.
[40] Dinkins, p. 59.
    Hodijah Lincoln Meade, Letter to Mother from Sharpsburg, 9/18/62, Meade Family Papers, Sec. 1, VA Historical Society, Richmond, VA.
[41] Andrews, CV, Vol. XVI, p. 579.
[42] John T. Parham, "The 32nd Virginia at Sharpsburg", *SOUTHERN HISTORICAL SOCIETY PAPERS*, Vol. 34, Kraus Reprint Co., Millwood, NY, 1979, p. 252.
[43] Edward M. Morrison, "One of the Gamest of Modern Fights", *SOUTHERN HISTORICAL SOCIETY PAPERS*, Vol. 33, Kraus Reprint Co., Millwood, NY, 1979, p. 102.

[44] Cope, Map 8.

[45] This is based on the location of the 15th Massachusetts' monument and the Bowlby map which is sold at Antietam. The road, which is now the Sharpsburg Pike, was Confederate Avenue. During the war it was a country lane.

[46] Based upon personal observation of the terrain.

[47] Quint, *2nd MA*, p. 137.

[48] Patrick, p. 149.

[49] Cope, Map 8.

[50] Patrick, p. 149.

[51] Dinkins, p. 60 and 62.

[52] *125th PA*, p. 73 and 75.

[53] Huyette, p. 50.
Higgins, 6/3/86, *NATIONAL TRIBUNE*, p. 2.

[54] *Ibid.*, p. 1.
Huyette, p. 50.

[55] *125th PA*, p. 203.

[56] Huyette, p. 39.

[57] *125th PA*, p. 207.

[58] Bosbyshell, p. 144.

[59] *125th PA*, p. 74, 207, and 208.

[60] *Ibid.*, p. 201.

[61] Gibbon, p. 88.
Cope, Map 8.

[62] *125th PA*, p. 202-203.
Strickler mistakenly thought the battery was McCowan's.

[63] Huyette, p. 39-40.
Higgins, 6/3/86, *NATIONAL TRIBUNE*, p. 1.

[64] *125th PA*, p. 74 and 208.
Catherine S. Crary, (ed.), *Dear Belle*, Wesleyan University Press, Middletown, CN, 1965, p. 152.

[65] Huyette, p. 40.
125th PA, p. 200.

[66] Cunningham and Miller, p. 47-48.

[67] Huyette, p. 40.

[68] Robert N. Scott, (comp.), *The War of the Rebellion, A Compilation of the Official Records of the Union and Confederate Armies*, Government Printing Office, Washington, D.C., 1887, Vol. XIX, pt. 1, p. 866.

[69] Huyette, p. 40.

[70] *125th PA*, p. 203.
Thomas M. Aldrich, *A History of Battery A First Regiment Rhode Island Light Artillery in the War to Preserve the Union*, Snow and Farnham Printers, Providence, 1904, p. 143.
Aldrich in researching his work mistakenly identified the units around him as Weber's and Kimball's troops. Despite this, he does substantiate that an infantryman scooped up the colors of a Confederate regiment ten feet in front

of his battery. Tomkin's Battery engaged Kershaw's Brigade at the location described by Aldrich. The colors had to be those which Jacob Orth won the Medal of Honor for.

[71] *OR, XIX*, pt. 1, p. 510 fn and p. 866.

[72] *Medal of Honor*, p. 117.

[73] *125th PA*, p. 205.

[74] Mrs. B. A. C. Emerson, "How a Boy Won His Spurs At Antietam", *CONFEDERATE VETERAN*, Vol. XXI, 1913, p. 121.
Soldiers and Sailors Historical Society of Rhode Island, *PERSONAL NARRATIVES*, 3rd Series, #16, 1885-1887, "Battery D, First Rhode Island Light Artillery at the Battle of Antietam," J. Albert Monroe, Providence, RI, 1886, p. 24-31.

[75] Dickert, p. 155.
Murfin, p. 238.

[76] George W. Skinner, *Pennsylvania at Chickamauga and Chattanooga*, William Stanley Ray, State Printer of PA, 1901, p. 275.

[77] F.H. Taylor, p. 58.

[78] Bosbyshell, p. 143-144.

[79] Cunningham and Miller, p. 49.
This is a rough estimate.

[80] This is a very rough estimate, intended to relay a general impression of the severity of the fighting.

[81] Gibbon, p. 88.

[82] Quint, *2nd MA*, p. 137-138.
George L. Andrews, Letter to Wife, 9/23/62, George L. Andrews Collection, USAMHI, Carlisle Barracks, PA.

[83] Samuel J. Fletcher, 2Lt. H Co., 15th MA, Recollections, p. 1, Antietam National Battlefield.

[84] Ford, p. 192.

[85] Morrison, p. 102.

[86] *Ibid.*, p. 98.

[87] Parham, p. 252.

[88] *Ibid.*, p. 253.

[89] Crary, p. 153.

[90] Parham, p. 253.

[91] "The Haw Boys in the War Between the States", *CONFEDERATE VETERAN*, Vol. XXXIII, 1925, p. 256.

[92] Parham, p. 253.

[93] Morrison, p. 107.

[94] Andrews, CV, XVI, p. 579.

[95] Sam Bloomer, "A Wounded Federal Color Bearer," *CONFEDERATE VETERAN*, Vol. XVII, 1909, p. 169.

[96] Catherine Drinker Bowen, *Yankee From Olympus, Justice Holmes and His Family*, Monthly Press, Little, Brown, and Co., Boston, 1944, p. 155 and 168.

[97] Waitt, p. 137.
Ford, p. 196.
Oliver O. Howard, "General O. O. Howard's Personal Reminiscences of the War of the Rebellion," 4/3/84, THE NATIONAL TRIBUNE, p. 1.
[98] Murfin, p. 240.
[99] Frassanito, p. 189-190.
[100] Waitt, p. 137.
[101] Catton, p. 287.
[102] Ibid.
[103] Ford, p. 197.
[104] Patrick, p. 149-150.
[105] Hildebrand, p. 53.
[106] Andrews, CV, XVI, p. 579.
[107] Hildebrand, p. 53.
[108] Bloomer, CV. XVII, p. 169.
[109] Hildebrand, p. 53.
[110] Schildt, Drums, p. 180.
[111] Oliver Wendell Holmes, Jr., Touched With Fire, Mark DeWolfe Howe, (ed.), Harvard University Press, Cambridge, MA, 1947, p. 64.
[112] Ford, p. 197.
Charles H. Eagar, 15th MA, Letter, 9/19/62, Book 15, Lewis Leigh Coll., USAMHI, Mss. Dept., Carlisle Barracks, PA.
[113] Waitt, p. 138.
[114] Morrison, p. 107.
[115] Waitt, p. 138.
[116] Nathan Bartlett Jordan, H Co., 19th MA, monograph, p. 4, Antietam National Battlefield.
[117] Poague, p. 47.
[118] Memoirs of Samuel D. Buck, p. 48, in the Samuel D. Buck Papers, Manuscript Department, Duke University Library, Durham, NC.
[119] Waitt, p. 138-141.
[120] Memoirs of Samuel D. Buck, p. 48, in the Samuel D. Buck Papers, Manuscript Department, Duke University Library, Durham, NC.
[121] Waitt, p. 138-141.
[122] Frassanito, p. 190.
[123] Ibid.
[124] Frederick W. Oesterle, 7th MI, E Co., "1861-1865 Incidents Connected With the Civil War as recorded by one of the veterans, fifty years after," F. W. O., 1911, Pontiac, MI, p. 5, CWTI Coll., USAMHI, Carlisle Barracks, PA.
[125] Monroe, p. 31.

Chapter Nine

[1] Schell, p. 18.
[2] Ibid.
[3] B & L, Vol. II, pt. 2, p. 680.
[4] Schell, p. 18.
[5] Ibid.
[6] Ibid.
[7] R.C. Miller, The Battlefield of Antietam, Oliver T. Reilly Publisher, 1906, Reprint, Hagerstown Bookbinding and Printing Co., Hagerstown, MD, p. 26.
[8] Bosbyshell, p. 190.
[9] Schell, p. 18.
[10] Cope, Map 8.
[11] John Calvin Gorman, "Memoirs of a Rebel", George Gorman, (ed.), MILITARY IMAGES, Nov.-Dec., 1981, p. 6.
[12] Ibid.
[13] James W. Shinn, Orderly Sergeant, B Company, 4th NC, Diary, September 17, 1862, Antietam National Battlefield.
[14] Gorman, p. 6.
Benjamin M. Collins, "Reminiscences,", p. 13, Benjamin Mosely Collins, in the Southern Historical Collection, University of North Carolina, Chapel Hill, NC.
[15] John B. Gordon, Reminiscences of the Civil War, Charles Scribner's Sons, NY. 1905, p. 84.
[16] Gorman, p. 6.
[17] R.C. Miller, p. 10, photograph.
[18] Frederick Tilberg, Antietam, National Park Service Historical Handbook Series, #31, Washington, D.C., 1960, p. 35.
[19] Gorman, p. 6.
[20] Gordon, p. 84 and 88.
[21] Gorman, p. 6.
[22] Cope, Map 8.
[23] Gorman, p. 6.
[24] Schell, p. 18.
[25] Cope, Map 8.
H. S. Stevens, Souvenir of Excursion to Battlefields by the Society of the Fourteenth Connecticut Regiment and Reunion at Antietam September 1891, Gibson Bros., Printers & Bookbinders, Washington, D. C., p. 49-50. Page, p. 35-36.
[26] Schell, p. 18.
[27] Gorman, p. 6.
[28] Ibid.
Gorman's watch, according to the Federal watches, was about one hour slow. He recorded the time as 8:00 A.M.
[29] Bosbyshell, p. 156.
[30] Ibid. p. 150.
Schell, p. 19.

[31] Gorman, p. 6.

[32] Cope, Map 8.
Page, p. 36-37.

[33] Edward W. Spangler, *My Little War Experience*, York Daily Publishing, York, PA, 1904, p. 32-33.

[34] Bosbyshell, p. 161-162.

[35] Schell, p. 19.

[36] Bosbyshell, p. 161.

[37] Hemminger, E Co., 130th PA, Diary, 9/17/62, Michael Winey Coll., USAMHI, Mss. Dept., Carlisle Barracks, PA.

[38] Bosbyshell, p. 161.

[39] R.C. Miller, p. 26.

[40] Gorman, p. 6.

[41] Galwey, p. 39.

[42] *Ibid.*

[43] Cope, Map 8.

[44] Frederick L. Hitchcock, *War From the Inside*, J. B. Lippincott Co., Phila., 1904, p. 56-57.

[45] Gordon, p. 84.
He mentions the Federals were four ranks deep.

[46] Gorman, p. 6.
Captain Gorman states the Yankees were about fifty yards from Colonel Tew.

[47] Cope, Map 8

[48] *Ibid.*

[49] Gordon, p. 85
The 1st Delaware was to his immediate front, therefore, the unhorsed officer most likely was Colonel John W. Andrews.

[50] *Ibid.*, p. 87.

[51] *Ibid.*

[52] Gorman, p. 6.

[53] RHSP, p. 153.

[54] Gordon, p. 87.

[55] B & L, Vol. II, pt. 2, p. 598.

[56] *Medal of Honor*, p. 117.

[57] Frassanito, p. 198.

[58] Schell, p. 19-20.

[59] Bosbyshell, p. 161.

[60] Galwey, p. 40.
William P. Seville, *History of the First Regiment Delaware Volunteers*, The Historical Society of Delaware, Wilmington, 1884, p. 48.

[61] Gordon, p. 87.

[62] *Ibid.*
Gorman, p. 6.
Hitchcock, p. 59.

[63] Galwey, p. 39.
H. S. Stevens, p. 55.
Page, p. 39, 49, and 51.

[64] Seville, p. 48-49.

[65] *Medal of Honor*, p. 117.

Beyer and Keydel, p. 83-84.

[66] Murfin, p. 256-257.

[67] Page, p. 41 and 49.
H. S. Stevens, p. 55.

[68] Spangler, p. 35.

[69] Galwey, p. 40.

[70] Bosbyshell, p. 191.

[71] Gordon, p. 87.

Chapter Ten

[1] Schildt, *Drums*, p. 180.

[2] Mark DeWolfe Howe, *Justice Oliver Wendell Holmes. The Shaping Years, 1841-1870*, The Belknap Press of Harvard University Press, Cambridge, MA, 1957, p. 127.

[3] Holmes, p. 65.

[4] Howe, p. 127.

[5] Holmes, p. 64.

[6] Howe, p. 126.

[7] Murfin, p. 240.

[8] Carter, p. 114-115.

[9] Moore, p. 156.

[10] Merrill, p. 201-202.

[11] Howe, p. 128.

[12] Bowen, p. 169.

[13] Holmes, p. 64-65.

[14] Cope, Map 9.

[15] Howe, p. 128.

[16] Holmes, p. 64-65.

[17] *Ibid.*, p. 65.

[18] Nathan Jordan, H Co., 19th MA, p. 5.

[19] Gibbon, p. 88-89.

[20] Holmes, p. 65.

[21] C. C. Cummings, "Sharpsburg — Antietam", *CONFEDERATE VETERAN*, XXIII, 1915, p. 199.

[22] Robert K. Krick, *30th Virginia Infantry*, H.E. Howard Inc., Lynchburg, 1st ed., 1983, p. 25-26.
Journal of Samuel H. Walkup, p. 17, in the Samuel Hoey Walkup Journal, Manuscript Department, Duke University Library, Durham, NC.

[23] Cope, Map 9.

[24] Krick, *30th VA*, p. 26-27.

[25] *Ibid.*
B & L, Vol. II, pt. 2, p. 678.
Gilmer W. Crutchfield, Diary, 9/17/62, Aug. 1 - Dec. 31, 8773b, Manuscript Department, University of Virginia Library, Charlottesville, VA.

[28] *Ibid.*
Journal of Samuel H. Walkup, p. 17, in the

Samuel Hoey Walkup Journal, Manuscript Department, Duke University Library, Durham, NC.

[27] Cope, Map 9.
The map is in error. It does not show the 13th NJ on the right flank of the brigade.

[28] Cunningham and Miller, p. 48.
Eugene Powell, "Lee's First Invasion," 6/27/1901, THE NATIONAL TRIBUNE, p. 2.

[29] Journal of Samuel H. Walkup, p. 17, in the Samuel Hoey Walkup Journal, Manuscript Department, Duke University Library, Durham, NC.

[30] Cope, Map 9.

[31] Commager, p. 216.

[32] Collier, p. 95.

[33] Commager, p. 216.
Bart Johnson, Letter to Editor of CONFEDERATE VETERAN, 3/17/95, p. 3, David A. Lilley Memorial Collection, Western Maryland Room, Washington County Free Library, Hagerstown, MD.

[34] Collier, p. 96-97.
Commager, p. 216.

[35] Collier, p. 97.

[36] Sears, p. 248-249.

[37] Cope, Map 9.

[38] Journal of Samuel H. Walkup, p. 17, in the Samuel Walkup Journal, Manuscript Department, Duke University Library, Durham, NC.

[39] Cope, Map 9.
Hitchcock, p. 58.

[40] Galwey, p. 40.

[41] Gorman, p. 6.

[42] Galwey, p. 42.

[43] Ibid., p. 40-41.
Jack Shepherd was this fellow's alias. His real name was Victor Aaron. He apparently used the alias to disguise his religious creed.

[44] Gorman, p. 6.

[45] Galwey, p. 42.
Cope, Map 9.
Hanson, p. 41-42.

[46] Galwey, p. 41.

[47] B & L, Vol. II, pt. 2, p. 602.
Shinn, Diary, 9/17/62, Antietam National Battlefield, files.
William W. Chamberlaine, Memoirs of the Civil War, Byron S. Adams, Washington, DC, 1912, p. 32.

[48] Galwey, p. 42-43.

[49] Hitchcock, p. 66.

[50] Ibid., p. 61.

[51] Ibid., p. 59.

[52] Ibid., p. 62.

[53] John D. Hemminger, E Co., 130th PA, Diary, 9/17/62, Michael Winey Coll., USAMHI, Mss. Dept., Carlisle Barracks, PA.

[54] Paul Jones, The Irish Brigade, Robert B. Luke, Inc., Washington, D.C., 1967, p. 141.

[55] Fox, Vol. II, p. 512.

[56] Ibid.

[57] Ibid., p. 499.

[58] Catton, p. 296.

[59] Jones, p. 141.

[60] Fox, Vol. II, p. 499.

[61] R.C. Miller, p. 26.

[62] Medal of Honor, p. 117.
Beyer and Keydel, p. 80.

[63] Fox, Vol. II, p. 513.
Beyer and Keydel, p. 80.

[64] R.C. Medal, p. 26.

[65] Jones, p. 141.

[66] Catton, p. 295.

[67] Jones p. 142.

[68] Cope, Map 9.
Sears, p. 244.

[69] John F. McCormack, Jr., "The Irish Brigade", CIVIL WAR TIMES ILLUSTRATED, Vol. VIII, #1, April, 1969, p. 39.

[70] Catton, p. 296.

[71] McCormack, p. 41.

[72] Gorman, p. 6.

[73] B & L, Vol. II, pt. 2. p. 684.

[74] Gorman, p. 6.
Gordon, p. 87.

[75] Gorman, p. 6.

[76] Gordon, p. 87.

[77] Gorman, p. 6.

[78] Cope, Map 9.

[79] Charles A. Fuller, Personal Recollections of the War of 1861, News Job Publishing House, Shirburne, NY, 1906, p. 58.

[80] Fox, Vol, II, p. 412.

[81] Benjamin Franklin Clarkson, "Vivid in My Memory", John M. Priest, (ed.), CIVIL WAR TIMES ILLUSTRATED, Vol. XXIV, #8, Dec. 1986, p. 21-22.

[82] David Nicol, Battery E, PA Light Artillery, letter, 9/21/62, HCWRT Coll., USAMHI, Mss. Dept., Carlisle Barracks, PA.
He noted the time as 10:00 A.M.
Monroe, p. 32-33.

[83] Cope, Map 9.

Chapter Eleven

[1] *OR*, Vol. XIX, pt. 1, p. 402-403.
[2] Clarkson, p. 22.
[3] Thomas W. Hyde, *Following the Creek Cross or Memories of the Sixth Army Corps*, Boston, 1895, p. 94.
[4] Clarkson, p. 22.
[5] James P. Stewart, Battery E, PA Light Artillery, letter, 9/21/62, CWTI Coll., USAMHI, Mss. Dept., Carlisle Barracks, PA.
[6] Cope, Map 10.
[7] Catton, p. 299.
[8] Green, p. 129-130.
Cope, Map 9.
[9] Schell, p. 19-20.
[10] *B & L*, Vol. II, pt. 2, p. 680.
[11] Schell, p. 21.
[12] *OR*, Vol. XIX, pt. 1, p. 412.
[13] *Ibid.*, p. 402-403.
[14] Clarkson, p. 22.
[15] Gordon, p. 88.
[16] *OR*, Vol. XIX, pt. 1, p. 332.
Bosbyshell, p. 162.
[17] Spangler, p. 35-36.
[18] *OR*, Vol. XIX, pt. 1, p. 332.
Galwey, p. 43.
[19] Gordon, p. 88-90.
J. M. Thompson, p. 18, 30, and 32.
[20] Spangler, p. 36.
[21] Gordon, p. 88-90.
[22] Galwey, p. 43.
[23] *OR*, Vol. XIX, pt. 1, p. 332.
[24] Galwey, p. 43.
This is by implication. Galwey never mentioned seeing any other Confederate run from the fighting.
[25] Spangler, p. 36.
[26] Galwey, p. 43.
[27] Bosbyshell, p. 163.
[28] Bailey, p. 97.
Hitchcock, p. 60-61.
[29] RHSP, p. 154.
[30] Bosbyshell, p. 164.
[31] Commager, p. 164.
[32] Green, p. 130-131.
OR, Vol. XIX, pt. 1, p. 402-403.
[33] Clarkson, p. 22-24.
[34] *Ibid.*, p. 24.
[35] Merrill, p. 202.
[36] Emerson, CV, XXI, 1913, p. 121.
[37] Moore, p. 156.
Poague, p. 48.
[38] Poague, p. 48.
[39] Moore, p. 157.
[40] Moore, p. 157.
Poague, p. 48.
According to Moore the conversation ran, "General, are you going to send us in again?" "Yes, my son, you all must do what you can to drive these people back."
[41] Moore, p. 158.
[42] Calvin Leach, Diary, 9/17/62, p. 15, Calvin Leach Diary, in the Southern Historical Collection, University of North Carolina Library, Chapel Hill, NC.

Chapter Twelve

[1] Cunningham and Miller, p. 34.
[2] Sears, p. 249.
[3] Cope, Map 10.
Samuel Toombs, *Reminiscences of the War*, The Journal Office, Orange, NJ, 1878, p. 21. "D" Society, *13th Regiment, New Jersey Vols.*, D. H. G. Gildersleeve & Co., Publishers and Printers, Newark, N J, 1875, p. 17-18.
[4] James P. Stewart, Battery E, PA Light, Letter, 9/21/62, CWTI Coll., USAMHI, Mss. Dept., Carlisle Barracks, PA.
[5] Hanson, p. 49.
David Nichol, Battery E, Pa Light, Letter, 9/21/62, HCWRT Coll., USAMHI, Mss. Dept., Carlisle Barracks, PA.
[6] Commager, p. 216.
"D" Society, p. 18.
[7] Cope, Map 10.
[8] Commager, p. 216.
[9] *B & L*, Vol. II, pt. 1, p. 644.
[10] Cope, Map 10.
[11] Commager, p. 216.
David Nichol, Battery E, PA Light, Letter, 9/21/62, HCWRT Coll., USAMHI, Mss. Dept., Carlisle Barracks, PA.
Cunningham and Miller, p. 34.
[12] Collier, p. 98.
[13] Cope, Map 10.
[14] Bailey, p. 103 1n3 104.
Commager, p. 212 and 216.
[15] Collier, p. 98.
Cope, Map 10.
[16] Fuller, p. 58.
[17] McCormack, p. 41.
Fox, Vol. II, p. 513.
Page, p. 40.

[18] Commager, p. 219.
[19] Fox, Vol. II, p. 513.
[20] Ibid.
[21] Commager, p. 222.
Fox, Vol. II, p. 466.
OR, Vol. XIX, pt. 1, p. 291.
Fuller, p. 58-59.
[22] Cope, Map 10.
[23] Commager, p. 219.
[24] Alexander D. Betts, Experiences of a Confederate Chaplain 1862-1865, William Alexander Betts, (ed.), Privately printed, p. 17.
[25] Commager, p. 219.
[26] Clarkson, p. 24.
[27] Sears, p. 250.
Commager, p. 216.
Cope, Map 10.
[28] Collier, p. 98.
Commager, p. 216.
[29] Collier, p. 98.
[30] Commager, p. 216.
[31] Clarkson, p. 24.
[32] Mrs. B. A. C. Emerson, "How a Boy Won His Spurs at Antietam", CONFEDERATE VETERAN, XXI, 1913, p. 121.
[33] R.C. Miller, p. 26.
Murfin, p. 244.
Emerson, CV, XXI, 1913, p. 121.
[34] C. A. Richardson, "General Lee at Sharpsburg", CONFEDERATE VETERAN, XV, 1907, p. 411.
[35] Beyer and Keydel, p. 84-85.
Cope, Map 10.
[36] Fuller, p. 61-63.
[37] Diary, James W. Shinn 9/17/62, Antietam National Battlefield.
Gorman, p. 6.
Catton, p. 297.
[38] William W. Chamberlaine, Memoirs of the Civil War, Byron S. Adams, DC, 1912, p. 33.
[39] OR, Vol. XIX, pt. 1, p. 1036-1037.
[40] Bosbyshell, p. 197.
[41] Fox, Vol. II, p. 466.
[42] Fuller, p. 59.
[43] Beall, CV, I, 1893, p. 246.
S. A. Ashe, "North Carolina in the War Between the States", CONFEDERATE VETERAN, XXXVII, 1929, p. 173.
[44] Murfin, p. 253.
[45] Beall, CV, I, 1893, p. 246.
William Alexander Smith, The Anson Guards Company C Fourteenth North Carolina Volunteers, 1861-1865, Stone Publishing Co., Charlotte, NC.,p 1914, p. 159.

[46] Bosbyshell, p. 197.
[47] Hitchcock, p. 62.
[48] Bailey, p. 103.
[49] Murfin, p. 253.
[50] Medal of Honor, p. 116.
Fox, Vol. II, p. 466.
Beyer and Keydel, Vol. I, p. 87.
Lieutenant Greig mistakenly thought he took the flag of the 4th Alabama, a regiment which was not there.
[51] Commager, p. 220 and 22.
The "massacre" was inferred by the author based upon the paucity of prisoners taken in Posey's Brigade and other sources which imply that it happened.
[52] Diary, James W. Shinn, 9/17/62.
Gorman, p. 6.
[53] R. L. Lagemann, "Summary of the Artillery Batteries in positions to support the Infantry during the action at 'Bloody Lane', with a Map showing their locations", March, 1962.
[54] Chamberlaine, p. 33-34, 36.
Westwood A. Todd, "Reminiscences of the War Between the States, April 1861 – July 1865", Part 1, p. 65, Westwood A. Todd Reminiscences, in the Southern Historical Collection, University of North Carolina Library, Chapel Hill, NC.
[55] Beall, CV, I, 1893, p. 246.
[56] Ibid.
[57] A Story of the War, p. 138-139.
[58] Galwey, p. 44.
[59] Cope, Map 10.
[60] Commager, p. 216.
Bart Johnson, Letter, 3/17/95, p. 3-4.
[61] Ibid., p. 216-217.
Murfin, p. 257.
[62] Commager, p. 217.
[63] Ibid.
[64] Cope, Map 10.
[65] Murfin, p. 253.
[66] Galwey, p. 4.
[67] Hyde, p. 104.
[68] OR, Vol. XIX, pt. 1, p. 412.
[69] Hyde, p. 94.
[70] Ibid., p. 96.
[71] George T. Stevens, Three Years in the Sixth Corps, S.R. Gray Publisher, Albany, NY, 1866, p. 148.
[72] George A. Townsend, Rustics in Rebellion, p. 166.
Hyde, p. 94.
[73] OR, Vol. XIX, pt. 1, p. 415.
[74] Hyde, p. 94.
[75] Ibid., p. 95.
[76] Ibid., p. 94-95.

[77] Commager, p. 217.

[78] Stevens, p. 148.
Bart Johnson, Letter, 3/17/95, p. 4.

[79] Hyde, p. 95.

[80] Frederick David Bidwell, (comp.), *A History of the Forty-Ninth New York Volunteers*, J.B. Lyons Co., Buffalo, 1917, p. 20.

[81] *Medal of Honor*, p. 116.

[82] OR, Vol. XIX, pt. 1, p. 414.

[83] Stevens, p. 149.
OR, Vol. XIX, pt. 1, p. 415.

[84] Hyde, p. 96-97.
Bart Johnson, Letter, 3/17/95, p. 4-5.

[85] OR, Vol. XIX, pot. 1, p. 415.
Medal of Honor, p. 116.

[86] Chamberlaine, p. 35.

[87] OR, Vol. XIX, pt. 1, p. 414-415.
Stevens, p. 149.

[88] OR, Vol. XIX, pt. 1, p. 195.
Stevens, p. 149.

[89] OR, Vol. XIX, pt. 1, p. 415.

[90] Beall, CV, I, 1893, p. 246.
Weymouth T. Jordan Jr., (ed.), *North Carolina Troops 1861-1865, A Roster*, Vol. V, Division of Archives and History, Raleigh, NC, 1975, p. 454.

[91] Hyde, p. 96.

[92] *Ibid.*, p. 96.

[93] Stevens, p. 149.

[94] Hyde, p. 97.

[95] Cope, Map 10.

[96] Commager, p. 220.
Fox, Vol. II, p. 466.

[97] Longstreet, p. 251.
Fox, Vol. I, p. 412.

[98] Henry Gerrish, 7th NY, "Memoirs", p. 28, CWTI Coll., USAMHI, Mss. Dept., Carlisle Barracks, PA.

[99] Bartlett, p. 138-139.

[100] Longstreet, p. 250-251.

[101] Chamberlaine, p. 35-36.

[102] Fox, Vol. II, p. 466.

[103] Fox, Vol. I, p. 413.

[104] Gerrish, p. 28, CWTI Coll., USAMHI, Mss. Dept., Carlisle Barracks, PA.

[105] Fuller, p. 60.

[106] Fox, III, p. 1355.

[107] R.C. Miller, p. 20.

[108] Chamberlaine, p. 36.

[109] Fuller, p. 62.

[110] Commanger, p. 220-222.

[111] Hitchcock, p. 64-65.

[112] Fox, Vol. II, p. 513.
Hyde, p. 96.

[113] Catton, p. 297.

[114] Hyde, p. 96.
Page, p. 43-44.

[115] Fuller, p. 60.

[116] The officers were: 61st/64th NY—Colonel Francis Barlow: 63rd NY—Lieutenant Colonel Henry Fowler and Major Richard C. Bentley; 69th NY—Lieutenant Colonel James Kelly; 57th NY—Lieutenant Colonel Philip J. Parisen; 132nd PA—Colonel Richard A. Oakford; 1st DE—Lieutenant Colonel Oliver Hopkinson; 5th MD—Major Leopold Blumenberg

[117] H. S. Stevens, p. 59.

[118] Clarkson, p. 25.
B & L, Vol, II, pt. 2, p. 644.
A Committee of the Regimental Association, *History of the Thirty-fifth Regiment Massachusetts Volunteers, 1862-1865*, Mills, Knight and Co., Printers, Boston, 1884, p. 38-39.

[119] Schell, p. 21-22.

[120] Galwey, p. 44.

[121] Monument to the 8th Ohio at Antietam.

[122] Monument to the 14th Indiana at Antietam.
Bosbyshell, p. 197.

[123] Galwey, p. 45-46.

[124] Merrill, p. 203.

[125] Anne Barineau Collection, not paginated, CW Misc. Coll., USAMHI, Mss. Dept., Carlisle Barracks, PA.

[126] Moore, p. 158.

[127] Gibbon, p. 90-91.

Chapter Thirteen

[1] OR, Vol. XIX, pt. 1, p. 356-357.

[2] Thomas Evans, "The enemy sullenly held on to the city", *CIVIL WAR TIMES ILLUSTRATED, VOl VII, #1, April, 1968*, p. 34-35.

[3] William Renwick Smedberg, 14th U.S. Letter, 10/6/62, CW Misc. Coll., USAMHI, Mss. Dept., Carlisle Barracks, PA.

[4] *B & L*, Vol. II, pt. 2, p. 656.

[5] Evans, p. 34-36.

[6] Cope, Map 8.

[7] Evans, p. 36.

[8] *Ibid*.

[9] Nathaniel Wood, *Reminiscences of Big I*, McCowat-Mercer Press, Inc., Jackson, TN, 1956, p. 37-38.

[10] Cope, Map 8.
Wood, p. 38.

[11] Wood, p. 39.

[12] Cope, Map 8.

[13] This estimate is based upon Dooley's and

Hunter's statements that the men were deployed in extended order, and upon the distance covered by the brigade.

[14] John Dooley *John Dooley, Confederate Soldier*, Joseph T. Durkin, (ed.), Washington, D.C., 1945, p. 45.
Alexander Hunter, "A High Private's Sketch of Sharpsburg", Paper #2, *SOUTHERN HISTORICAL SOCIETY PAPERS*, Vol, XI, Kraus Reprint Co., Millwood, NY, 1977, p. 16.

[15] Dooley, p. 45.
Hunter, p. 14.

[16] Hunter, p. 14 and 17.

[17] Dooley, p. 45.

[18] *Ibid.*
Cope, Map 9.
Hunter, p. 17.
Hunter said the battery had four guns. Dooley's diary, being the more contemporary account, recorded that a section (two guns) were in the spot described by Hunter. Murfin's map shows Bachman's Battery in the vicinity.

[19] Cope, Map 8.

[20] John Williams Hudson, Letter, 10/16/62. Typed, unpublished manuscript, p. 2.

[21] Murfin, p. 274.

[22] Hudson, Letter, 10/16/62, p. 2.

[23] Carter, p. 104 and 105, 109-111.

[24] *Ibid.*, p. 112.

[25] *B & L*, Vol. II, pt. 2, p. 671.

[26] *Ibid.*
Longstreet, p. 255 and 257.
Sorrel, p. 104-105.

[27] Cope, Map 8.

[28] Cunningham and Miller, p. 54.
35th MA, p. 38

[29] *35th MA*, p. 38.

[30] Cope, Map 8.

[31] Edward O. Lord, *History of the Ninth Regiment New Hampshire Volunteers, in the War of the Rebellion*, Republican Press Association, Concord, NH, 1895, p. 126.

[32] *35th MA*, p. 38.

[33] *Ibid.*

[34] Frassanito, p. 230.
He says the action lasted ten minutes.

[35] Diary, 9/17/62, Captain James Wren, B Co., 48th PA, Typed, unpublished manuscript.

[36] H.L. Benning, "Notes by General H.L. Benning on Battle of Sharpsburg", *SOUTHERN HISTORICAL SOCIETY PAPERS*, Vol, XVI, Jan. - Dec., 1888, Kraus Reprint Co., Millwood, NJ, 1977, p. 393.

[37] Cope, Map 9.

[38] *Ibid.*
Rossiter Johnson, *Campfires and Battlefields, A Pictorial Narrative of the Civil War*, 5th ed., The Civil War Press, NY, 1967, p. 80.
Benning, p. 393.
William Y. Thompson, "Robert Toombs, Confederate General", *CIVIL WAR HISTORY*, Dec. 1961, p. 417.

[39] Benning, p. 393.
Thompson, p. 417.

[40] *Ibid.*

[41] Cope, Map 8.

[42] Frassanito, p. 226 and 230.

[43] *Ibid.*, p. 230.
Longstreet, p. 259.

[44] Longstreet, p. 418.

[45] Thompson, p. 418.

[46] Hudson, Letter, 10/16/62, p. 3.

[47] *Ibid.*, p. 4.
Cope, Map 8.
Hudson account.

[48] Lord, p. 131.

[49] *Ibid.*

[50] Cope, Map 9.
Hudson, Letter, 10/16/62, p. 4.
Longstreet, p. 259.

[51] Cope, Map 9.
Used to establish the order of march only. Actual formations are inaccurate on the map.
Dimon, p. 140.

[52] Dimon, p. 140.

[53] Cope, Map 9.

[54] Dimon, p. 141.

[55] Hudson, Letter, 10/16/62, p. 5.

[56] Dimon, p. 141-142.

[57] Longstreet, p. 259.

[58] Lord, p. 125.

[59] *Ibid.*, p. 122-123.

[60] *Ibid.*, p. 110.

[61] Hudson, Letter, 10/16/62, p. 5.
35th MA, p. 40.

[62] Lord, p. 110.

[63] *Ibid.*, p. 110 and 122.

[64] *Ibid.*, p. 120.

[65] *Ibid.*, p. 105 and 110.

[66] *Ibid.*, p. 123.

[67] *Ibid.*, p. 110.

[68] Hudson, Letter, 10/16/62, p. 4-6.

[69] Dimon, p. 141-142.

[70] Hudson, Letter, 10/16/62, p. 4-6.

[71] Lord, p. 105.

[72] *Ibid.*, p. 111.

[73] *35th MA*, p. 39.

[74] *Ibid.*, p. 39-40.
[75] Thomas H. Parker, *History of the 51st Regiment of P. V. and V. V.*, King & Baird Printers, Phila., 1869, p. 230-231.
[76] Hudson, Letter, 10/16/62, p. 6.
[77] *Ibid.*, p. 12.
35th MA, p. 39.
[78] Hudson, Letter, 10/16/62, p. 12.
[79] Parker, p. 231-232.
[80] Hudson, Letter, 10/16/62, p. 7.
35th MA, p. 40.
[81] Hudson, Letter, 10/16/62, p. 7.
[82] *Ibid.*
[83] *35th MA*, p. 39-40.

Chapter Fourteen

[1] William Miller Owen, *In Camp and Battle with the Washington Artillery of New Orleans*, Ticknor and Co., Boston, 1885, p. 150-151.
[2] Dimon, p. 144.
Hudson, Letter, 10/16/62, p. 7.
[3] Hudson, Letter, 10/16/62, p. 7-8.
[4] Bosbyshell, p. 64.
Wren, Diary, 9/17/62, p. 110.
[5] Parker, p. 235.
[6] Wren, Diary, 9/17/62, p. 111.
[7] *Ibid.*, p. 114-115.
[8] Cope, Map 10.
[9] Murfin, p. 275.
[10] Hudson, Letter, 10/16/62, p. 8.
Murfin, p. 275.
35th MA, p. 40.
[11] Hudson, Letter, 10/16/62, p. 8.
35th MA, p. 40.
[12] Hudson, Letter, 10/16/62, p. 8.
[13] Lord, p. 105.
[14] Hudson, Letter, 10/16/62, p. 8.
[15] *Ibid.*, p. 8-9.
35th MA, p. 41.
[16] Dimon, p. 144.
[17] Hudson, Letter, 10/16/62, p. 9.
[18] Benning, p. 393.
Thompson, p. 418.
[19] John H. DeVotie, Letters to Father from Gordonville, VA, 9/23 and 9/28/62, in the John H. DeVotie Papers, Manuscript Department, Duke University Library, Durham, NC.
[20] "The Burk Sharpshooters", *CONFEDERATE VETERAN*, XXXII, 1924, p. 464.
[21] Frassanito, p. 237.
Bailey, p. 126.

[22] Catton, p. 304.
[23] Murfin, p. 275.
35th MA, p. 41.
[24] Dimon, p. 144.
[25] "The Burk SS", CV, XXXII, 1924, p. 464.
[26] Wren, Diary, 9/17/62, p. 114.
[27] Hudson, Letter, 10/16/62, p. 9-10.
Murfin, p. 275.
[28] Catton, p. 304.
Dimon, p. 144, fn.
[29] Hudson, Letter, 10/16/62, p. 10.
[30] *35th MA*, p. 41.
[31] Hudson, Letter, 10/16/62, p. 9-10.
[32] *Ibid.*, p. 10.
[33] *35th MA*, p. 42.
[34] Graham, p. 288.
[35] Commager, p. 225.
[36] Graham, p. 288-289.
[37] *Ibid.*, p. 289.
[38] Commager, p. 225.
[39] Graham, p. 289.
Johnson, p. 80.
[40] Graham, p. 289-290.
Commager, p. 226.
[41] *Ibid.*, p. 226.
[42] Graham, p. 290-291.
Commager, p. 226.
[43] Cope, Map 11.
[44] Graham, p. 290-291.
[45] Murfin, p. 277.
[46] Benning, p. 393.
[47] Murfin, p. 276.
[48] Hudson, Letter, 10/16/62, p. 10.
[49] Parker, p. 236.
[50] *Ibid.*, p. 10-11.
35th MA, p. 41.
[51] *35th MA*, p. 41.
[52] *Ibid.*
Lord, p. 105.
[53] Dimon, p. 144.
[54] *35th MA*, p. 42.
[55] Lord, p. 129.
[56] *35th MA*, p. 42
[57] Benning, p. 393.
35th MA, p. 42.
Parker, p. 235.
[58] Benning, p. 393.
Murfin, p. 276.
[59] Hudson, Letter, 10/16/62, p. 11.
[60] *35th MA*, p. 42-43.
[61] *Ibid.*
Dimon, p. 146.
[62] *35th MA*, p. 42-43

Parker, p. 237.

63 Hudson, Letter, 10/16/62, p. 11-12.

64 Lord, p. 130.

65 Parker, p. 231.

66 Edwin Bennett, Sgt., D. Co., 51st PA, Letter,
9/28/62, Bell Papers, Chester County Historical
Society.

67 Hudson, Letter, 10/16/62, p. 11-12.

68 Wren, diary, 9/17/62, p. 111-112 and 114-115.

69 Dimon, p. 144.

70 Wren, Diary, 9/17/62, p. 115.

71 James Madison Stone, *Personal Recollections of the
Civil War*, by the author, Boston, 1918, p. 91.

72 Lord, p. 125.

73 *Ibid.*, p. 129-130.

74 Cope, Map 10.

75 Evans, p. 37.

76 Cope, Map 10.

77 Warren Pursley, Letter to Mary F. J. Pursley,
9/27/62, in the Mary Frances Jane Pursley Papers,
1854-1900, Manuscript Department, Duke
University Library, Durham, NC.

78 *OR*, Vol. XIX, pt. 1, p. 358.

79 *B & L*, Vol. II, pt. 2, p. 656.

80 Charles W. Squires, "The Last of Lee's Battle
Line", W. H. T. Squires, (ed.), written 1894,
p. 23, CWTI Coll., USAMHI, Mss. Dept., Carlisle
Barracks, PA.

81 Wren, Diary, 9/17/62, p. 112-114.

82 Cope, Map 10.

83 Wren, Diary, 9/17/62, p. 112.

84 Graham, p. 291-292.

85 Wren, Diary, 9/17/62, p. 112-113.

86 Bailey, p. 160.
Benning, p. 393.
Thompson, p. 417.

87 Cope, Map 11.
Johnson, p. 80.

88 Benning, p. 393-394.
Thompson, p. 418.
Abstract from H. L. Benning to E. P. Alexander,
not dated (post war), in the Robert Augustus
Toombs Papers 1846-1881, Manuscript Depart-
ment, Duke University Library, Durham, NC.
Ivey W. Duggan, Letter, 10/1/62, David A. Lilley
Memorial Collection, Western Maryland Room,
Washington County Free Library, Hagerstown,
MD.

Chapter Fifteen

1 Davis E. Johnston, "Concerning the Battle of
Sharpsburg, " *CONFEDERATE VETERAN*, VI,
1898, p. 28.

2 Hunter, p. 14-15.

3 Wren, Diary, 9/17/62, p. 113.

4 Cope, Map 12.

5 Hudson, Letter, 10/16/62, p. 13.

6 Graham, p. 292.
Cope, Map 12.

7 Graham, p. 393.

8 *Ibid.*

9 Hudson, Letter, 10/16/62, hand drawn map at end
of manuscript.

10 *35th MA*, p. 43.

11 *Ibid.*, p. 43.
Hudson, Letter, 10/16/62, p. 13.

12 *35th MA*, p. 44.

13 Hudson, Letter, 10/16/62, p. 13.

14 *35th MA*, p. 44.

15 Graham, p. 293.

16 Hunter, p. 15.

17 *Ibid.*

18 *Ibid.*, p. 16.

19 Dimon, p. 143-144, text and fn. 21, fn. 8, p. 137.

20 *35th MA*, p. 44.

21 Hudson, Letter, 10/16/62, p. 13-15.
Parker, p. 238.
Ferrero was not sitting on the bridge as Parker
reported. He also mistook the horse as a mule.

22 *Ibid.*, p. 14.

23 Cope, Map 12.
These positions are not "written in stone".
Fairchild's, Harland's and Nagle's positions at
3:00 P.M. are drawn from Graham (p. 393), *16th
CN*, p. 18). Lord (p. 106, 128-129.), and the *35th
MA* (p.45.).
Autobiography, Samuel W. Compton, p. 102, in
the Samuel Wilson Compton Papers, 1840-1925.
Manuscript Department, Duke University
Library, Durham, NC.

24 *35th MA*, p. 45.

25 Parker, p. 240-241.

26 Frassanito, p. 244.

27 Cope, Map 12.
Krick, *Parker*, p. 60.

28 Wood, p. 39.

29 Commager, p. 226.

30 Graham, p. 293-294.

31 Commager, p. 226.

32 Graham, p. 294.

33 Lord, p. 129.

34 Johnston, CV, VI, 1898, p. 28.

35 David E. Johnston, *The Story of a Confederate Boy*

in the Civil War, Commonwealth Press, Inc., Radford, VA, (1980, Leonard Parr), Reprint of 1914 ed. by D. E. Johnston, p. 150.
[36] Cope, Map 12.
16th CN, p. 18.
[37] Wood, p. 39.
[38] Dooley, p. 46.
[39] Hunter, p. 16-17.
Cope, Map 12.
[40] Hunter, p. 17.
[41] Dooley, p. 46.
[42] Lord, p. 129.
[43] Commager, p. 226.
[44] Graham, p. 295.
[45] Commager, p. 227.
[46] *Ibid.*
[47] Graham, p. 295.
[48] Commager, p. 226.
[49] Graham, p. 294.
[50] Dooley, p. 46.
[51] Hunter, p. 17.
[52] Hunter, p. 18.
[53] Dooley, p. 46.
[54] Hunter, p. 18.
[55] J. L. Napier, "McIntosh's Battery at Sharpsburg," *CONFEDERATE VETERAN,* XIX, 1911, p. 429.
[56] David G. McIntosh, "Collection of Civil War Papers", Vol. I, p. 27 and 28.
[57] Graham, p. 296.
[58] Commager, p. 227.
[59] Graham, p. 296.
Johnston, CV, VI, 1898, p. 28.
[60] Hunter, p. 18-19.
[61] Benning, p. 394.
[62] McIntosh, p. 28-29.
Napier, CV, XIX, 1911, p. 429.
[63] Dooley, p. 46.
[64] Graham, p. 296-297.
Medal of Honor, p. 117.
[65] *OR,* XIX, pt. 1, p. 363.
[66] Squires, p. 23-24. CWTI Coll., USAMHI, Mss. Dept., Carlisle Barracks, PA.
[67] Warren Pursley, Letter to sister, Mary F. J. Pursley, 9/27/62, in the Mary Frances Jane Pursley Papers, 1854-1900, Manuscript Department, Duke University Library, Durham, NC.
[68] Wood, p. 39.
Cope, Map 13.
Catton, p. 306.
[69] Hanson, p. 42
[70] Mixon, p. 32.
Coker, p. 111.

[71] *B & L,* Vol, II, pt. 2, p. 500.
[72] Bailey, p. 137.
[73] Frederick, Pettitt, C Co., 100th PA, Letters 9/16/62, 9/21/62, 9/23/62, CWTI Coll., USAMHI, Mss. Dept., Carlisle Barracks, PA.
[74] Benning, p. 394.
[75] *16th CN,* p. 19.
Graham, p. 326.
[76] *Ibid.*
[77] Cope, Map 13.
[78] *16th CN,* p. 19.
[79] Benning, p. 394.
[80] Commager, p. 227.
[81] Graham, p. 299.
[82] Hunter, p. 19.
[83] Murfin, p. 355.
[84] Hunter, p. 19.
[85] Cope, Map 13.
[86] Graham, p. 298.

Chapter Sixteen

[1] Caldwell, p. 45-46.
Felix Motlow, "Campaigns in Northern Virginia," *CONFEDERATE VETERAN,* II, 1894, p. 310.
[2] *Ibid.,* p. 45.
Benning, p. 394.
[3] *Ibid.*
[4] *Ibid.,* p. 298-299.
[5] Letter, Almon L. Reed, F Co., 89th NY, not dated. Charles F. Johnson, *The Long Roll,* The Roycrofters, East Aurora, NY, 1911, Mary S. Johnson, (Hagerstown Bookbinding and Printing, Inc., 1986, Reprint), p. 195.
[6] *16th CN,* p. 20.
[7] Reed, Letter.
[8] Benning, p. 394.
[9] Caldwell, p. 45-46.
[10] Benning, p. 394.
[11] Catton, p. 310.
[12] *16th CN,* p. 19-20.
OR, XIX, pt. 1, p. 197.
The Official Records do not report any MIA or CIA. The regimental history reported 26 CIA. 52 MIA. 47 KIA, and 173 WIA.
[13] McIntosh, p. 28.
[14] Benning, p. 394.
Abstract from H. L. Benning to E. P. Alexander, not dated (post war), in the Robert Augustus Toombs Papers 1846-1881, Manuscript Department, Duke University Library, Durham, NC.

[15] Motlow, CV, II, 1894, p. 310.

[16] Johnston, *Confederate Boy*, p. 150.

[17] Dooley, p. 47.

[18] *Ibid.*, p. 48.

[19] *Ibid*

Cope, Map 13.

OR, XIX, pt. 1, p. 850.

Osmun Latrobe, diary, 9/17/62, p. 10, 10a, 10b, VA Historical Society, Richmond, VA.

[20] Benning, p. 394.

[21] Hunter, p. 20.

[22] Cope, Map 13.

McIntosh, p. 28-29.

[23] Graham, p. 299.

Hudson, Letter, 10/19/62, p. 14.

35th MA, p. 46.

The regimental history states a section which had run out of ammunition left the field. I presume it was Clark's because it was the only battery in front of the 35th MA. Durrell's Battery was further to the left.

[24] Hudson, p. 14.

[25] *Ibid.*

Graham, p. 299.

[26] Graham, p. 299.

[27] Hudson, p. 14.

[28] *Ibid*

[29] *35th MA*, p. 46.

[30] Hudson, p. 15.

35th MA, p. 46.

[31] Hudson, p. 15.

[32] George H. Allen, *Forth-Six Months With the Fourth R. I. Volunteers in the War 1861 to 1865*. J. A. & R. A. Reed, Printers, Providence, RI, 1887, p. 146.

[33] Caldwell, p. 46.

[34] Berry Benson, "Reminiscences", Vol. 1. p. 118. Berry Greenwood Benson Papers and Books, in the Southern Historical Collection, University of North Carolina, Chapel Hill, NC.

[35] OR, XIX, pt. 1, p. 456.

Murfin, p. 284.

Allen, p. 146-147.

[36] Berry Benson, "Reminiscences", Vol. 1, p. 118-119, Berry Greenwood Benson Papers and Books, in the Southern Historical Collection, University of North Carolina, Chapel Hill, NC.

[37] Caldwell, p. 46.

Murfin, p. 284.

[38] Autobiography, Samuel W. Compton, p. 103, in the Samuel Wilson Compton Papers 1840-1925. Manuscript Department, Duke University Library, Durham, NC.

[39] Berry Benson, "Reminiscences", Vol. 1, p. 119-

120, Berry Greenwood Benson Papers and Books, in the Southern Historical Collection, University of North Carolina, Chapel Hill, NC.

[40] Autobiography, Samuel W. Compton, p. 103, in the Samuel Wilson Compton Papers, 1840-1925. Manuscript Department, Duke University Library, Durham, NC.

[41] Cope, Map 14.

Caldwell, p. 46.

The location of Gregg's Brigade on Murfin's map does not coincide with Caldwell's account.

[42] Edward E. Schweitzer, I Co., 30th OH, typed recollection, p. 15-16, CWTI Coll., USAMHI, Mss. Dept., Carlisle Barracks, PA.

[43] Berry Benson, "Reminiscences", Vol. 1, p. 121. Berry Greenwood Benson Papers and Books, in the Southern Historical Collection, University of North Carolina Library, Chapel Hill, NC.

[44] Edward E. Schweitzer, p. 15-16. CWTI Coll., USAMHI, Mss. Dept., Carlisle Barracks, PA.

Dooley, p. 46.

McBrien, p. 49.

Caldwell, p. 46.

[45] Berry Benson, "Reminiscences", Vol. 1, p. 121. Berry Greenwood Benson Books and Papers, in the Southern Historical Collection, University of North Carolina Library, Chapel Hill, NC.

[46] Commager, p. 227.

[47] Autobiography, Samuel W. Compton, p. 103-104, in the Samuel Wilson Compton Papers, 1840-1925. Manuscript Department, Duke University Library, Durham, NC.

[48] Bailey, p. 137.

[49] Commager, p. 227.

Caldwell, p. 46.

[50] Cope, Map 13.

[51] Bailey, p. 137-138.

[52] OR, XIX, pt. 1, p. 197.

Graham, p. 327.

[53] Hudson, p. 15.

[54] Cope, Map 14.

[55] Caldwell, p. 46-47.

[56] Motlow, CV, II, 1894, p. 310.

[57] *35th MA*, p. 46.

Joseph M. Hanson, p. 7 and 51. Murfin, Map, "Situation at 5:30 P.M."

[58] *35th MA*, p. 46 and 48.

Albert Augustus Pope, 2nd LT, I Co., 35th MA, "Journal of the Southern Campaign, War of the Rebellion, August 27, 1862 - June 9, 1865," p. 4, CWTI Coll., USAMHI, Mss. Dept., Carlisle Barracks, PA.

William N. Merserve, "Antietam", *MERSERVE*

CIVIL WAR RECORD, Richard Alden Huebner,
(ed.), 1st ed., RAH Publications, Oak Park, MI,
1987, p. 4.
[59] Hudson, p. 15-16.
[60] 35th MA, p. 47.
    Marcus A. Emmons, K Co., 21st MA, Letter,
    9/22/62, Lewis Leigh Coll., USAMHI, Mss. Dept.,
    Carlisle Barracks, PA.
    Stone, p. 92.
[61] Thompson, p. 419.
[62] Squires, p. 25, CWTI Coll., USAMHI, Mss Dept.,
    Carlisle Barracks, PA.
[63] Bailey, p. 137.
[64] Cope, Map 14.
    McBrien, p. 150.
    Benning, p. 395.
[65] Benning, p. 395.
    Bailey, p. 137.
    McBrien, p. 149-150.
    CV, II, 1894, p. 150.
[66] 35th MA, p. 46-50, and 53.
    The regimental line ran left to right C G K E H I F
    A D.
    Merserve, p. 5-6.
[67] McIntosh, p. 29.
[68] Ibid., p. 52.
[69] Hudson, p. 16.
[70] Krick, Parker, p. 61-62.
    Squires, p. 24.
[71] Mixon, p. 32-34.
    OR, XIX, pt. 1, p. 946.
    Coker, p. 112.
[72] Squires, p. 24, CWTI Coll., USAMHI, Mss. Dept.,
    Carlisle Barracks, PA.
[73] Krick, Parker, p. 61.
    Evans, CV, XXXVII, 1929, p. 216-217.
[74] Ibid.
    Krick, Parker, p. 62.
    OR, XIX, pt. 1, p. 362-363.
[75] B & L, Vol. II, pt. 2, p. 656.
[76] Fitz John Porter, Letter to Lafayette McLaws,
    6/16/86, in the Lafayette McLaws Papers, 1862-
    1895, Manuscript Department, Duke University
    Library, Durham, NC.
[77] Nisbet, p. 108.
[78] Ibid.
    OR, XIX, pt. 1, p. 813.
    Taylor, Walter, p. 71.
[79] Hildebrand, p. 54-55.
[80] Hyde, p. 99.
[81] OR, XIX, pt. 1, p. 195.
    Hyde, p. 99.
[82] Hyde, p. 98.

[83] Sorrel, p. 94.
    I interjected this anecdote here because Longstreet
    was present with this wing of the ANV and
    Fairfax's story coincides with Hyde's account.
[84] Dinkins, p. 60-62.
[85] Michael Shuler, Diary, 9/17/62, Vol. 1.
[86] Nathan Jordan, H Co., 19th MA, p. 5.
[87] Clarkson, p. 25.
[88] Peter A. Filbert, Cpt., B Co., 96th PA, Diary,
    9/17/62, HCWRT, USAMHI, Mss. Dept., Carlisle
    Barracks, PA.
    Jacob W. Haas, Cpt., G Co., 96th PA, Diary,
    9/17/62, HCWRT, USAMHI, Mss. Dept., Carlisle
    Barracks, PA.
[89] Hyde, p. 97-98.
[90] Ibid., p. 99.
    OR, XIX, pt. 1, p. 409-410.
    The time was estimated from Irwin's and Hyde's
    reports of the action.
[91] OR, XIX, pt. 1, p. 412-413. Hyde's report.
[92] Hyde, p. 100.
[93] OR, XIX, pt. 1, p. 409-410. Irwin's report.
[94] Ibid.
    Hyde, p. 100.
[95] Lyman F. Shorey, Lt., F Co., 7th ME, Biographical
    sketch in a published excerpt from History of
    Industry, "The Boys In Blue," p. 376. CW Misc.
    Coll., USAMHI, Mss. Dept., Carlisle Barracks, PA.
[96] Hyde, p. 100.
[97] Ibid., p. 101.
    OR, XIX, pt. 1, p. 412-413. Hyde's account.
[98] Hyde, p. 100-101.
[99] Shorey, p. 376.
[100] Westwood A. Todd, "Reminiscences of the War
    Between the States April 1861 - July 1865, Part 1,
    p. 66, Westwood A. Todd Reminiscences, in the
    Southern Historical Collection, University of
    North Carolina, Chapel Hill, NC.
[101] G. W. Edmontson, "Individualism in Battle,"
    CONFEDERATE VETERAN, XXVI, 1918, p. 239-
    240.
[102] OR, XIX, pt. 1, p. 412-413. Hyde's report.
[103] Shorey, p. 376-377, CW Misc. Coll., USAMHI,
    Mss. Dept., Carlisle Barracks, PA.
[104] Hyde, p. 101-104.
    Fox, William F., Regimental Losses in the American
    Civil War, 4th ed., Joseph McDonough, Albany,
    NY, 1898, p. 29.
[105] Hyde, p. 104.
[106] Sorrel, p. 105-107.
[107] Chamberlaine, p. 37-38.
[108] Hudson, p. 16.
    35th MA, p. 49.

[109] Pope, p. 5, CWTI Coll., USAMHI, Mss. Dept., Carlisle Barracks, PA.

[110] *35th MA*, p. 49-50.

[111] Pope, p. 5, CWTI Coll., USAMHI, Mss. Dept., Carlisle Barracks, PA.

Emmons, Letter, 9/22/62, Lewis Leigh Coll., USAMHI, Mss. Dept., Carlisle Barracks, PA.

Chapter Seventeen

[1] *35th MA*, p. 50-51.

Emmons, Letter, 9/22/62, Lewis Leigh Coll., USAMHI, Mss. Dept., Carlisle Barracks, PA.

[2] Hunter, p. 20-21.

[3] Schweitzer, p. 17, CWT Coll., USAMHI, Mss. Dept., Carlisle Barracks, PA.

[4] Reed, Letter.

[5] Commager, p. 227.

[6] Berry Benson, "Reminiscences", Vol. 1, p. 119, Berry Greenwood Benson Papers and Books, in the Southern Historical Collection, University of North Carolina Library, Chapel Hill, NC.

[7] Jennie Porter Arnold, "At Antietam, a True and Graphic Story of the 16th Connecticut," *THE NATIONAL TRIBUNE*, 10/18/88, p. 1.

[8] Pettitt, Letter, 9/19/62, CWTI Coll., USAMHI, Mss. Dept., Carlisle Barracks, PA.

[9] Beyer and Keydel, I, p. 88.

[10] Beyer and Keydel, I, P. 88-89.

Hudson, p. 17-18.

35th MA, p. 51.

[11] Wren, p. 116.

[12] Dimon, p. 146.

[13] Johnson, p. 197-198.

[14] *OR*, XIX, pt. 2, p. 356-360.

[15] Evans, p. 37.

[16] Nisbet, p. 107 and 111.

[17] Stickley, CV, XXII, 1914, p. 66-67.

[18] Sorrell, p. 83.

[19] Chamberlaine, p. 39.

[20] Elliott Stephen Welch, Letter to Parents from Winchester, VA, 9/22/62, in the Elliott Stephen Welch Papers, Manuscript Department, Duke University Library, Durham, NC.

[21] Carter, p. 115.

[22] *B & L*, Vol. II, p. 681.

[23] Bloomer, CV, XVII, 1909, p. 169.

[24] Clarkson, p. 25.

[25] Robert T. Bowie, "Left for Dead on the Field", *CONFEDERATE VETERAN*, XXX, 1922, p. 71.

[26] James S. Johnston, Jr., Letter, 9/27/62.

[27] Merrill, p. 204-205.

[28] Marynisk, p. 29.

[29] Squires, p. 25, CWTI Coll., USAMHI, Mss. Dept., Carlisle Barracks, PA.

[30] Owen, p. 158.

[31] *Ibid.*, p. 156-158.

[32] P. J. White, "The 5th Virginia Cavalry", *CONFEDERATE VETERAN*, XVII, 1909, p. 72.

[33] Bloomer, CV, XVII, 1909, p. 169.

[34] Autobiography, Samuel W. Compton, p. 105, in the Samuel Wilson Compton Papers 1840-1925, Manuscript Department, Duke University Library, Durham, NC.

[35] Stone, p. 93.

Emmons, Letter, 9/22/62, Lewis Leigh Coll., USAMHI, Mss. Dept., Carlisle Barracks, PA.

[36] Wren, p. 118-119.

Carter, p. 115.

[37] Dooley, p. 50.

[38] Reed, Letter.

Wren, p. 116-117.

[39] Mrs. Charles Wesley Andrews, Letter, 9/18/62, in the Charles Wesley Andrews Letters 1861-1865, Manuscript Department, Duke University Library, Durham, NC.

[40] Corn Exchange Association, *Antietam to Appomattox With the 118th Pennsylvania Volunteers, Corn Exchange Regiment*, J. L. Smith, Map Publishers, Phila., 1892, p. 47.

Carter, p. 115.

[41] *118th PA*, p. 48-50.

[42] *Ibid.*, p. 50.

[43] Pettitt, Letter, 9/19/62, CWTI Coll., USAMHI, Mss. Dept., Carlisle Barracks, PA.

Bosbyshell, p. 77.

[44] Hyde, p. 100 and 107.

[45] Gibbon, p. 90-91.

[46] Cleve Rowan, "False Flag of Truce at Antietam", *CONFEDERATE VETERAN*, IV, 1896, p. 324.

F. H. Venn, "That Flag of Truce at Antietam", *CONFEDERATE VETERAN*, IV, 1896, p. 389.

[47] Richard H. Watkins, Letter to Wife, 9/18/62. Richard Henry Watkins Papers, VA Historical Society, Richmond, VA.

[48] Journal of Samuel H. Walkup, p. 17-18, in the Samuel Hoey Walkup Journal, Manuscript Department, Duke University Library, Durham, NC.

Bart Johnson, Letter, 3/17/95, p. 5.

[49] Samuel S. Johnson, Diary, 9/19/62, Samuel S. Johnson Diary, 10 March 1862 - 29 August 1864, 8493, Manuscript Department, University of Virginia Library, Charlottesville, VA.

[50] Bloomer, CV, XVII, 1909, p. 169.

51 James S. Johnston, Jr., Letter, 9/22/62.

52 Calvin Leach, Diary, 9/17/62, p. 15, Calvin Leach Diary, in the Southern Historical Collection, University of North Carolina, Chapel Hill, NC.

53 Jacob W. Haas, G Co., 96th PA, Diary, 9/18/62, HCWRT, USAMHI, Mss. Dept., Carlisle Barracks, PA.

Henry Flick, E Co., *War of the Rebellion 1861-1864*, Jan. 1925, p. 10, HCWRT, USAMHI, Mss. Dept., Carlisle Barracks, PA.

Murfin, p. 295-297.

Carter, p. 115-116.

Charles Morey, 2nd VT, Diary, 9/18/62, USAMHI, Mss, Dept., Carlisle Barracks, PA.

54 Owen, p. 159-160.

55 Thompson, p. 419.

56 Carter, p. 116.

Ivey Duggan, Letter, 10/1/62.

57 E. T. Stetson, Letter to Brother, 9/21/62, in the E. T. Stetson Papers, Manuscript Department, Duke University Library, Durham, NC.

58 James M. Green, Letter to Miss Annie R. Shoemaker, 9/21/62. Manuscript Department, Duke University Library, Durham, NC.

59 George K. Harlow, Letter to Family, 6/3/63, The Harlow Family of Louisa County, VA Papers 1858-1869, Sec. 2, VA Historical Society, Richmond, VA.

Appendix

1 OR, XIX, 1, p. 862.

All regimental totals from OR cited.

The total given for the brigade is the total from all regiments as listed in the OR.

2 Dickert, p. 159.

3 Stegeman, p. 61.

4 OR, XIX, 1, p. 874.

5 *SOUTHERN HISTORICAL SOCIETY PAPERS*, XIII, p. 273.

6 SHSP, XXXIII, p. 97.

7 OR, XIX, 1, p. 874.

8 *Ibid.*, p. 862.

All regimental numbers from the OR cited.

9 *Ibid.*, p. 862.

10 Reports of Operations of the Army of Northern Virginia, II, R. M. Smith Public Printer, Richmond, 1864, p. 107.

11 OR, XIX, 1, p. 861.

12 Chamberlaine, p. 32.

He cites tremendous straggling the evening of 9/16/62. The brigade had 82 men present at the end of the fighting.

13 *Report of ANV*, II, p. 108.

14 *Ibid.*

15 Palfrey, p. 105, fn.

16 Trask, p. 19.

17 Chamberlaine, p. 32.

18 *Report of ANV*, II, p. 108.

19 *Ibid.*

20 Carman, 24, p. 3.

21 *Ibid*, 24, p. 4

22 *Ibid*, 24, p. 3.

23 SHSP, XVI, p. 393.

24 Abstract H. L. Benning to E. P. Alexander, in the Robert Augustus Toombs Papers, Manuscript Department, Duke University Library, Durham, NC.

25 *Ibid.*

26 SHSP, XVI, p. 393.

27 Johnson, *Campfires and Battlefields*, p. 180.

28 OR, XIX, 1, p. 898, 900, 901, 904.

This accounts for the 8th, 18th, 28th, and 56th VA.

29 Wood, p. 40.

30 Dooley, p. 45.

31 Riggs, p. 16.

32 Bell, p. 32.

33 SHSP, XIII, p. 273.

34 *B & L*, II, p. 530.

35 *Ibid.*, p. 577.

36 Andrews, CV, XVI, 1908, p. 578.

37 Carman, 24, p. 4.

38 Bailey, p. 104.

39 Commager, p. 217.

40 Sears, p. 232.

41 *Report of ANV*, II, p. 107.

42 *Ibid.*

43 Polly, p. 120-125.

Total based upon Halsey Wigfall's letter

44 F. Halsey Wigfall, Letter, 10/4/62.

45 F. Halsey Wigfall, Letter, 10/4/62.

He gives the size of the 4th Texas as 204.

Casualties are proportionately calculated with the losses of the brigade.

46 Carman, 20, p. 16.

47 *Ibid.*

48 OR, XIX, 1, p. 945-946.

49 OR, XIX, 1, p. 945-946.

50 Carman, 24, p. 5.

51 OR, XIX, 1, p. 846.

52 Carman, 24, p. 6.

53 Krick, *Parker*, p. 59.

54 Nichols, p. 53.

55 Carman, 16, p. 64.

I used Carman's figures because they were not beyond a reasonable variation from Taylor's.

56 Samuel D. Buck, Memoirs, in the Samuel D. Buck Papers, Manuscript Department, Duke University Library, Durham, NC.

57 D. R. Johnston, *Confederate Boy*, p. 156.

58 Caldwell, p. 48.

59 McBrien, p. 48.

60 Krick, *40th VA*, p. 18.

61 Carman, 24, p. 8.

62 *Ibid.*, estimate by Carman.

63 *Ibid.*

64 *Ibid.*, estimate by Carman.

65 This represents the balance between the Division's and the other brigades' strengths.

66 Carman, 15, p. 84.

67 Kittrell, J. Warren, History of the 11th Georgia Volunteers, Smith, Baily and Co., Printers, Richmond, VA, 1864, p. 52 fn.

68 Robertson, *Stonewall Brigade*, p. 160.

69 Alfred Kelly, Letter, 10/3/62, in the Williamson Kelly Papers, Manuscript Department, Duke University Library, Durham, NC.

70 Chapla, p. 27.

71 Carman, 15, p. 83.

72 *Ibid.*, 24, p. 11.

73 *Ibid.*

74 *Ibid.*

75 *Ibid.*

76 *Ibid.*

77 *Ibid.*

78 Taylor is in error. The total of all known troop strengths, exclusive of Carman's figures, indicates a force much larger than 3000.

79 Carman, 16, p. 152.

80 Calvin Leach Diary, 9/17/62, p. 15, Calvin Leach Papers, in the Southern Historical Collection, University of North Carolina Library, Chapel Hill, NC.

81 CV, VI, 1898, p. 217.

82 OR, XIX, 1, p. 1037-1038.

83 *Brief Historical Sketches of Military Organizations Raised in Alabama During the Civil War*, Alabama State Department of Archives and History, 1966, p. 596, 598, 608, and 631.

84 Carman, 16, p. 141.

85 Benjamin M. Collins, Recollections, Benjamin Mosely Collins, in the Southern Historical Collection, University of North Carolina, Chapel Hill, NC.

86 *Report of ANV*, II, p. 108.

87 *Ibid.*

88 *Ibid.*

89 This number represents the total of the regimental strengths.

90 Gorman, p. 4.

91 Shinn, Diary, 9/17/62.

92 W. A. Smith, p. 159.

93 Carman, 16, p. 154.

94 *Report of ANV*, II, p. 108.

95 Carman, 16, p. 155.

96 *Ibid.*, 16, p. 154.

97 *Report of ANV*, II, p. 108.

98 *Ibid.*

99 *Ibid.*

100 Carman, 16, p. 155.

101 *Ibid.*, 24 p. 9.

102 *Ibid.*

103 *Ibid.*

104 *Ibid.*

105 *Ibid.*, 24, p. 12.

106 *Ibid.*

107 *Ibid.*

108 *Ibid.*

109 *Ibid.*

110 *Ibid.*

111 *Ibid.*

112 *Ibid.*

113 OR, XIX, 1, p. 234.

114 Tevis, p. 45.

115 C. A. Stevens, p. 202.

116 OR, XIX, 1, p. 237-238

117 Carman, 15, p. 75.

118 Marynisk, p. 26.

119 Carman, 15, p. 82.

120 Total is from the regimental strengths.

121 *Indiana at Antietam*, p. 111.

122 Nolan, p. 142.

123 Commager, p. 215.

124 *Ibid.*, p. 145.

125 Carman, 15, p. 68.

126 OR, XIX, 1, p. 262.

127 Carman, 15, p. 68.

128 Blake, Letter, 10/21/62.

129 Carman, 15, p. 87.

130 OR, XIX, 1, p. 144.

131 Fuller, p. 57.

132 *Ibid.*, p. 58.

133 McCormack, p. 41.
Fox, *Regimental Losses*, p. 31.

134 McCormack, p. 41.
Fox, *Regimental Losses*, p. 31.

135 OR, XIX, 1, p. 298.

136 *Ibid.*, p. 301.

137 *Ibid.*, p. 302.

138 Eagar, Letter, 9/19/62.

[139] *OR*, XIX, 1, p. 315.
[140] Fox, p. 311.
[141] *Ibid.*
[142] C. A. Stevens, p. 205.
[143] Charles H. Banes, *History of the Philadelphia Brigade*, J. B. Lippincott Co., 1876, p. 118.
[144] Fox, p. 31.
[145] *Ibid.*
[146] *OR*, XIX, 1, p 329.
[147] Monument at Antietam.
[148] Hitchcock estimated the 132nd PA was twice the size of the 14th IN and the 8th OH.
[149] H. S. Stevens, p. 48.
[150] 1st LT W. F. Smith, D Co., 1st DE, Letter, 9/18/62, Lewis Leigh Coll., USAMHI, Mss. Dept., Carlisle Barracks, PA.
[151] *OR*, XIX, 1, p. 336.
[152] *Ibid.*, 2, p. 134.
[153] *Ibid.*
[154] Hyde, p. 95.
[155] *Ibid.*, p. 94.
[156] Personal Study of Roster.
[157] Personal Study of Roster.
[159] *OR*, XIX, 1, p. 415.
[160] Monument of Antietam.
[161] Stone, p. 92.
[162] *35th MA*, p. 48, 52, 53. Estimate. Merserve, intro.
[163] Carman, 21, p. 18, est.

[164] Graham, p. 327.
[165] Carman, 21, p. 52.
[166] Frassanito, p. 226.
[167] *Campfires and Battlefields*, p. 181. Regimental strength for 16th CN. Blakeslee, p. 22. Regimental losses for 16th CN.
[168] Carman, 16, p. 124. Estimate.
[169] *Ibid.*
[170] *Ibid.*, 16, p. 152.
[171] *Ibid.*, 16, p. 134-135. Estimate.
[172] Hinckley, p. 60.
[173] Carman, 16, p. 144.
[174] Cunningham and Miller, p. 34.
[175] *Ibid.*
[176] Palfrey, p. 78.
[177] Carman, 16, p. 144. Carman states that the 28th PA had 20 officers and 766 enlisted men present. I reduced this number by ten to accommodate the brigade total as stated by Carman.
[178] *Ibid.*
[179] Palfrey, p. 78.
[180] Carman, 16, p. 144.
[181] Palfrey, p. 78.
[182] Carman, 16, p. 143.
[183] *OR*, XIX, pt. 1, p. 511.
[184] *Ibid.*
[185] *Ibid.*
[186] *Ibid.*, p. 515.

Primary

Aldrich, Thomas M., *The History of Battery A. First Rhode Island Light Artillery in the War to Preserve the Union,* Snow and Farnham, Printers, Providence, RI.

Alexander, Edwin P., *Military Memoirs of a Confederate,* Charles Scribner's Sons, NY, 1907.

Allen, George H., *Forty-Six Months With the Fourth Rhode Island Volunteers in the War of 1861 to 1865,* J. A. & R. A. Reid, Printers, Providence, RI, 1887.

Banes, Charles H., *History of the Philadelphia Brigade, Sixty-ninth. Seventy-first, Seventy-second, and One Hundred Sixth Pennsylvania Volunteers,* J. B. Lippincott & Co., 1876.

Bartlett, Napier, *A Story of the War, Including the Marches and Battles of the Washington Artillery,* New Orleans, Clark and ?, 1874.

Bates, Samuel P., *History of Pennsylvania Volunteers 1861-5,* 3 vols., B. Singerly, State Printers, Harrisburg, 1869.

Betts, Alexander D., *Experiences of a Confederate Chaplain 1861-1865,* William Alexander Betts, (ed.), Privately.

Bidwell, Frederick David, (comp), *A History of the Forty-Ninth New York Volunteers,* J. B. Lyons, Co., Buffalo, NY, 1917.

Blackford, William Willis, *War Years With Jeb Stuart,* Charles Scribner's Sons, NY, 1945.

Bosbyshell, Oliver C., (comp), *Pennsylvania at Antietam,* Harrisburg Publishing Co., State Printer, Harrisburg, PA 1906.

Brown, Edmund R., *The Twenty-Seventh Indiana in the War of the Rebellion 1861-1865,* Butternut Press, Gaithersburg, MD (Reprint).

Buell, Augustus, *The Cannoneer,* The National Tribune, Washington, DC, 1890.

Caldwell, J. F. J., *The History of a Brigade of South Carolinians Known as "Gregg's" and Subsequently as McGowan's Brigade,* King & Baird Printers, Philadelphia, 1866, (Reprint, Continental Book Co., Marietta, GA.

Carter, Robert Goldwaite, *Four Brothers in Blue,* University of Texas Press, 1978.

Chamberlaine, William W., *Memoirs of the Civil War,* Byron S. Adams, Washington,

DC, 1912.

Child, William, *A History of the Fifth Regiment New Hampshire Volunteers in the American Civil War, 1861-1865,* R. W. Musgrove, Printer, Bristol, NH, 1893.

Coker, James L., *History of Company G Ninth S. C. Regiment, Infantry, S. C. Army and of Company E, Sixth S. C. Regiment, Infantry, C. S. Army,* The Attic Press Inc., Greenwood, SC.

Commager, Henry Steele, (ed.), *The Blue and the Gray,* The Bobbs-Merrill Co., Inc., Indianapolis, IN, 1950.

Committee of the Regimental Association, *History of the 35th Regiment Massachusetts Volunteers, 1862-1865,* Mills, Knight & Co., Printers, Boston, 1884.

Cook, Benjamin F., *History of the Twelfth Massachusetts Volunteers (Webster Regiment),* Twelfth (Webster) Regimental Association, Boston, 1882.

Corn Exchange Association, *Antietam to Appomattox With the 118th Pennsylvania Vols.,* Corn Exchange Regiment, J. L. Smith Map Publisher, Philadelphia, 1892.

Cunnigham, D. and W. W. Miller, *Report of the Ohio Antietam Battlefield Commission,* 1904.

"D" Society, *Historical Sketch of Co. "D" 13th Regiment, N. J. Vols.,* D. H. Gildersleeve & Co., Publishers and Printers, NY, 1875.

Dawes, Rufus R., *Service With the Sixth Wisconsin Volunteers,* Morningside Bookshop, Dayton, OH, 1984.

Dinkins, James, *1861-1865 By an Old Johnny, Personal Recollections and Experiences in the Confederate Army,* Morningside Bookshop, Dayton, OH, 1976.

Dooley, John, *Confederate Soldier,* Joseph T. Durkin, (ed.), Washington, DC, 1945.

Douglas, Henry Kyd, *I Rode With Stonewall,* University of North Carolina, Chapel Hill, 1940.

Early, Jubal Anderson, *War Memoirs,* James I. Robertson, (ed.), Indiana University Press, Kraus Reprint Co., NY, 1969.

Ford, Andrew E., *The Story of the Fifteenth Regiment Massachusetts Volunteer Infantry in the Civil War 1861-1864,* Press of W. J. Coulter, Courant Office, 1898.

Fox, William F., *New York at Gettysburg,* 3 Vols., J. B. Lyon Co., Printers, Albany,

1900.

Fuller, Charles A., *Personal Recollections of the War of 1861*, News Job Publishing House, Shirburne, NY, 1906.

Galwey, Thomas Francis, *The Valiant Hours*, The Stackpole Co., Harrisburg, PA, 1961.

Gibbon, John, *Personal Recollections of the Civil War*, Morningside Bookshop, Dayton, OH, 1978.

Gordon, John B., *Reminiscences of the Civil War*, Charles Scribner's Sons, NY, 1905.

Gould, John Mead, *History of the First - Tenth - Twenty-Ninth Maine Regiment*, Stephen Berry, Portland, ME.

Graham, Matthew J., *The Ninth Regiment New York Volunteers (Hawkins' Zouaves) Being History of the Regiment and Veteran Association from 1860 to 1900*, E. P. Coby & Co., Printers, NY, 1900.

Green, Robert M., (comp), *History of the 124th Regiment Pennsylvania Volunteers*, Philadelphia, 1907.

Hanks, O. T., *History of Captain B. F. Benton's Company, Hood's Texas Brigade, 1861-1865*, Morrison Books, Austin, TX, 1984.

Hilderbrand, Virginia Mumma, *Antietam Remembered*, Book Craftsmen Association, Inc., NY, 1959.

Hinkley, Julian Wisner, *A Narration of Service With the Third Wisconsin Infantry*, Wisconsin History Commission Democrat Printing Co., State Printer, September 1912.

Hitchock, Frederick L., *War From the Inside*, J. B. Lipppincott, Co., Philadelphia, 1904.

Holmes, Jr., Oliver W., *Touched With Fire*, Mark DeWolfe Howe, (ed.), Harvard University Press, Cambridge, MA, 1947.

Huyette, Miles C., *The Maryland Campaign and the Battle of Antietam*, Hammond Press, Buffalo, NY, 1915.

Hyde, Thomas W., *Following the Greek Cross or Memories of the Sixth Army Corps*, Boston, 1895.

Indiana at Antietam, *Report of the Indiana Antietam Monument Commission and Ceremonies at the Dedication of the Monument*, Indianapolis, IN, 1911.

Johnson, Charles F., *The Long Roll*, The Roycrofters, East Aurora, NY, 1911, Mary S. Johnston (Reprint, Hagerstown Bookbinding and Printing, Inc., 1986.)

Johnson, Robert Underwood, and Clarence Clough Buel, (ed.), *Battles and Leaders of the Civil War*, II, Part 2, Grant — Lee Edition, The Century Company, NY, 1888.

Johnson, Rossiter, *Campfires and Battlefields*, a Pictorial Narrative of the Civil War, 5th Ed., The Civil War Press, NY, 1967.

Johnston, David E., *The Story of a Confederate Boy in the Civil War*, Commonwealth Press, Inc., Radford, VA, (1980, Leonard A. Parr).

Longstreet, James, *From Manassas to Appomattox*, Indiana University Press, Bloomington, IN, 1960.

Lord, Edward O., *History of the Ninth Regiment New Hampshire Volunteers in the war of the Rebellion*, Republican Press Association, Concord, NH, 1985.

Merrill, James M., (ed.), *Uncommon Valor*, Rand McNally and Co., NY, 1964.

Merserve, William N., "Antietam," *Merserve Civil War Record*, Richard Alden Huebner, (ed.), 1st ed., RAH Publications, Oak Park, MI, 1987.

Mixon, Frank M., *Reminiscences of a Private*, The State Co., Columbia, SC, 1910.

Moore, Edward A., *The Story of a Cannoneer Under Stonewall Jackson*, J. P. Bell, Inc., Lynchburg, VA, 1910.

Nichols, G. W., *A Soldier's Story of His Regiment*, Continental Book Co., Kennesaw, GA, 1961.

Nisbet, James Cooper, *4 Years on the Firing Line*, Bell I. Wiley, (ed.), McCowat — Mercer Press Inc., Jackson TN, 1963.

Otis, George H., *The Second Wisconsin Infantry*, Alan D. Gaff, (ed.), Morningside Bookshop, Dayton, OH. 1984.

Owen, William Miller, *In Camp and Battle with the Washington Artillery of New Orleans*, Ticknor & Co., Boston, 1885.

Page, Charles D., *History of the Fourteenth Regiment Connecticut Volunteer Infantry*, The Horton Printing Co., Meriden, CN, 1906.

Palfrey, Francis Winthrop, *The Antietam and Fredericksburg*, Charles Scribner's Sons, NY, 1882.

Parker, Thomas H., *History of the 51st Regiment of P. V. and V. V.*, King and Baird Printers, Philadelphia, 1869.

Patrick, Marsena R., *Inside Lincoln's Army*,

David S. Sparks, (ed.), Thomas Yoseloff, NY, 1964.

Pennsylvania Gettysburg Battlefield Commission, *Pennsylvania at Gettysburg,* I, E. K. Meyers, State Printer, Harrisburg, PA, 1893.

Poague, William Thomas, *Gunner With Stonewall,* Monroe F. Cockrell, (ed.), McCowat — Mercer Press, Jackson, TN, 1957.

Polk, J. M., *Memories of the Lost Cause,* Austin, TX, 1905.

Polley, Joseph B., *Hood's Texas Brigade,* Morningside Bookshop, Dayton, OH, 1976.

Quint, Alonzo H., *The Potomac and the Rapidan,* Crosby and Nichols, Boston, 1864.

Quint, Alonzo H., *The Record of the Second Massachusetts Infantry, 1861-65,* James P. Walker, Boston, 1867.

Regimental Committee, *History of the One Hundred and Twenty-fifth Regiment Pennsylvania Volunteers 1862-1863,* J. B. Lippincott Co., Philadelphia, 1907.

Regimental History Committee, *History of the Third Pennsylvania Cavalry, Sixtieth Regiment Pennsylvania Volunteers in the American Civil War 1861-1865,* Franklin Printing Co., Philadelphia, 1905.

Scott, Robert N., (comp.), *The Official Records of the War of the Rebellion,* XIX, pt. 1, pt. 2, and XLI, Government Printing Office, Washington, DC, 1887.

Seville, William P., *History of the First Regiment Delaware Volunteers,* The Historical Society of Delaware, Wilmington, 1885.

Sixteenth Regiment Connecticut Volunteers, *Excursion and Reunion at Antietam Battlefield, September 17, 1889,* Case, Lockwood & Brainard Co., Hartford, CN, 1889.

Skinner, George W., (comp.), *Pennsylvania at Chickamauga and Chattanooga,* William Sranley Ray, State Printer, 1901.

Smith, W. A., *The Anson Guards, Company C, Fourteenth North Carolina Volunteers 1861-1865,* Stone Publishing Co., Charlotte, NC, 1914.

Soldiers and Sailors Historical Society of Rhode Island, *Personal Narratives,* 3rd Series, #16, 1885-1887, "Battery D First Rhode Island Light Artillery at the Battle of Antietam, September 17, 1862," J. Albert Monroe, Providence, 1886.

Sorrel G. Moxley, *Recollections of a Confederate Staff Officer,* Bell I. Wiley, (ed.), McCowat — Mercer Press Inc., Jackson, TN, 1958.

Spangler, Edward W., *My Little War Experience,* York Daily Publishing Co., York, PA, 1904.

Stearns, Austin C., *Three Years With Company K,* Arthur A. Kent, (ed.), Farleigh Dickinson University Press, Rutherford, 1976.

Stegeman, John F., *These Men She Gave,* University of Georgia Press, Athens.

Stevens, C. A., *Berdan's United States Sharpshooters in the Army of the Potomac, 1861-1865,* Morningside Bookshop, Dayton, OH, 1984.

Stevens, George T., *Three Years in the Sixth Corps,* S. R. Gray, Publisher, Albany, 1866.

Stevens, Henry S., *Souvenir of Excursions to Battlefields by The Society of the Fourteenth Connecticut Regiment and Reunion at Antietam, September, 1891,* Gibson Brothers, Printers and Bookbinders, Washington, DC, 1893.

Stone, James Madison, *Personal Recollections of the Civil War,* Boston, by the Author, 1918.

Taylor, Walter H., *Four Years With General Lee,* James I. Robertson, Jr., (ed.), Indiana University Press, Bloomington, IN, 1962.

Thompson, James Monroe, *Reminiscences of the Autauga Rifles, (Co. G. Sixth Alabama Volunteer Regiment, C. S. A.),* William Stanley Hoole, (ed.), Prattville, AL, 1879.

Todd, William, *The Seventy Ninth Highlanders,* New York Volunteers in the War of the Rebellion 1861-1865, Press of Brandow, Barton and Co., 1886.

Toombs, Samuel, *Reminiscences of the War,* Journal Office, Orange, NJ, 1878.

Von Borcke, Heros, *Memoirs of the Confederate War for Independence,* I, Peter Smith, NY, 1938.

Wainwright, Charles S., *A Diary of Battle,* Allan Nevins, (ed.), Harcourt, Brace and World, Inc., NY, 1962.

Waitt, Ernst Linden, (comp.), *History of the Nineteenth Regiment Massachusetts*

Volunteer Infantry, 1861-1865, Salem Press, Salem, MA, 1906.

Walcott, Charles F., *History of the 21st Regiment Massachusetts Volunteers in the War for the Preservation of the Union. 1861-1865,* Boston, 1882.

Warren, Kittrell J., *History of the Eleventh Georgia Volunteers,* Smith, Baily and Co., Printers, Richmond, VA, 1863.

Washburn, George H., *A Complete Military History and Record, of the 108th Regiment New York Volunteers From 1862-1894,* Rochester, NY (Press of E. R. Andrews, 1894.)

Worsham, John H., *One of Jackson's Foot Cavalry,* James O. Robertson, Jr., (ed.), McCowat — Mercer Press Jackson, TN, 1964.

Wood, Nathaniel, *Reminiscences of Big I,* McCowat — Mercer Press, Jackson, TN, 1956.

Manuscripts

David A. Lilley Memorial Collection, Western Maryland Room, Washington County Free Library, Hagerstown, MD.
Carman, Ezra, "The Maryland Campaign of 1862."
Duggan, Ivey W., K Co., 15th GA, Letter, October 1, 1862.
Johnson, Bart, 3rd AR, Letter, March 17, 1895 to S. A. Editor of the *CONFEDERATE VETERAN.*
Vertical File, Western Maryland Room, Washington County Free Library, Hagerstown, MD.
Hudson, John Williams, D Co., 35th MA, Letter to Sophy, October 16, 1862.
Reed, Almon Luce, F Co., 89th NY, Undated Letter.
The Virginia Historical Society, Richmond, VA.
Duffey, Edward S., Parker's Virginia Battery, Diary, September 17, 1862, Edward S. Duffey Diary.
Harlow, George K., D Co., 23rd VA. Letter, June 21, 1863, Letter to Family, The Harlow Family of Louisa Co., VA, Papers, 1858-1869.
Latrobe, Osmun, Longstreet's staff, Diary, September 15-20, 1862, Osmun Latrobe Diary.
Lee, Robert E., Letter, September 25, 1866,

to Mrs. T. J. Jackson, Letterbook of Robert E. Lee, 1865 April 2 - 1866 November 27.
Meade, Hodijah Lincoln, McCarthy's Battery, Letter, September 18, 1862, to Mother, Meade Family Papers, Sec. 1.
War Record 1861-65 of Dr. James McClure, 10th VA CAV., Sarah Travers Lewis Anderson.
Watkins, Richard Henry, K Co., 3rd VA CAV., Letters, September 18 and 22, 1862, to Wife, Richard Henry Watkins Papers, Sec. 1.
Chester County Historical Society.
Bennett, Edwin, Sgt., D. Co., 51st PA. Letter to Parents, September 28, 1862. Bell Papers.
Manuscript Department, University of Virginia Library, Charlottesville, VA.
Crutchfield, Gilmber W., F Co., 30th VA, Diary, September 17, 1862, Gilmer W. Crutchfield Collection, 8773 b, c, d.
Hubard, Robert Thurston, G Co., 3rd VA CAV., Notebook, "Damnation of Vancouver" and "Turvey" Manuscripts, 10522.
Johnson, Samuel S., 1st MA Light Artillery, Diary, September 19 and 21, 1862, Samuel S. Johnson Collection, 8493.
Levering, John, 14th IN, Recollections, John Levering Papers, 10113c.
Painter, James Barney, 28th VA, Letter October 5, 1862, to Brother, James Barney Painter Collection, 10661.
Manuscript Department, United States Army Military History Institute, Carlisle Barracks, PA.
Andrews, George L., 2nd MA, Letter, September 23, 1862, to Wife, George L. Andrews Collection.
Ann Barineau Collection, 8th FL, Civil War Miscellaneous.
Blake, Joseph E., 12th MA, Letter, October 21, 1862, Civil War Miscellaneous Collection.
Eagar, Charles H., 15th MA, Letter, September 19, 1862, Book 15, Lewis Leigh Collection.
Emmons, Marcus A., K Co., 21st MA, Letter, September 22, 1862, Book 5, 16-18, Lewis Leigh Collection.
Faller, John and Leo, A Co., 36th PA, 7th Res., Notes by Mr. Allan D. Thompson,

Harrisburg Civil War Round Table Collection.

Filbert, Peter Augustus, B Co., 96th PA, Diary, September 17 and 18, 1862, Harrisburg Civil War Round Table.

Flick, Henry, E Co., 30th PA, 1st Res., War of the Rebellion 1861-1864, Jan. 1925, Harrisburg Civil War Round Table Collection.

Gerrish, Henry, 7th NY, Memoirs, Civil War Times Illustrated Collection.

Haas, Jacob W., G Co., 96th PA, Diary, September 17, 1862, James F. Haas, (ed.), Harrisburg Civil War Round Table Collection.

Hemminger, John D., E Co., 130th PA, Diary September 16 and 17, 1862, Michael Winey Collection.

McIntosh, David G., 1st SC Vols., Pee Dee Battery, "Collection of Civil War Papers," I, Civil War Miscellaneous Collection.

McQuaide, John D., C Co., 38th PA, 9th Res., Letter, September 22, 1862, Civil War Times Illustrated Collection.

Morey, Charles C., 2nd VT, Charles C. Morey Coll.

Nichol, David, Battery E, PA Light Artillery, Letter, September 21, 1862, Harrisburg Civil War Round Table Collection.

Oesterle, Frederick W., E Co., 7th MI, "Incidents Connected With the War As recorded by one of the veterans fifty years after," Pontiac, MI, F. W. O., 1911, Civil War Times Illustrated Collection.

Pettitt, Frederick, C Co., 100th PA, Letters, September 19, 21, and 23, 1862, Civil War Times Illustrated Collection.

Plumb, Isaac, C Co., 61st PA, Memoirs of the War, Civil War Miscellaneous Collection.

Pope, Albert Augustus, I Co., 35th MA, "Journal of the Southern Campaign, War of the Rebellion, August 27, 1862 - June 9, 1865," Civil War Times Illustrated Collection.

Schweitzer, Edward E., Memoir, I Co., 30th OH, Civil War Times Illustrated Collection.

Shorey, Lyman F., F Co., 7th ME, Biographical Sketch, in an excerpt from "The Boys in Blue," History of Industry, Civil War Miscellaneous Collection.

Smedberg, William Renwick, 14th US Inf.,

Letter, October 6, 1862, Civil War Miscellaneous Collection.

Smith, William F., D Co., 1st DE, Letters, September 18 and October 3, 1862, Lewis Leigh Collection.

Squires, Charles W., Squires' Battery, "The Last of Lee's Battle Line," W. H. T. Squires, (ed.), 1894, Civil War Times Illustrated Collection.

Stewart, James P., Battery E, PA Light Artillery, Letter, September 21, 1862, Civil War Times Illustrated Collection.

Vautier, John D., D Co., 88th PA, John D. Vautier Collection.

Manuscript Department, University of North Carolina Library, Southern Historical Collection, University of North Carolina, Chapel Hill, NC.

Benson, Berry G., 1st SC, Reminiscences, I, Berry Greenwood Benson Papers and Books.

Collins, Benjamin M., 12th NC, Recollections, Benjamin Mosely Collins.

Leach, Calvin, B Co., 1st NC, Diary, September 17, 18, and 19, 1862, Calvin Leach Diary.

Todd, Westwood A., A Co., 12th VA, "Reminiscences of the War Between the States," I, Westwood A. Todd Reminiscences.

Manuscript Department, Duke University Library, Duke University, Durham, NC.

Abstract H. L. Benning to E. P. Alexander, Robert Augustus Toombs Papers, (15th, 17th GA, 11th GA Bttn.)

Andrews, Mrs. Charles Wesley, Letter, September 18, 1862, Charles Wesley Andrews Papers.

Buck, Samuel D., H Co., 13th VA, Memoirs Samuel D. Buck Papers.

Compton, Samuel, F Co., 12th OH, Autobiography, Samuel Compton Papers.

DeVotie, James H., Letters, September 23 and 28, 1862, James H. DeVotie Correspondence.

Greene, James Mercer, 17th MS, Letter to Annie R. Shoemaker, September 21, 1862, Annie R. Shoemaker Papers.

Jackson, Ashbury Hull, C Co., 44th GA, Letter, September 23, 1862, Edward Harden Papers.

Kelly, Alfred, 21st VA, Letter, October 3, 1862, Williamson Kelly Papers.

Porter, Fitz John, V Corps, Letter, June 6, 1886, Lafayette McLaws Papers.

Pursley, J. Warren, G Co., 18th SC, Letter, September 27, 1862, Mary Frances Jane Pursley Papers.

Stetson, Ephraim T., G Co., 1st ME Cav., Letter, September 21, 1862, E. T. Stetson Letters.

Walkup, Samuel H., 48th NC, Journal, Samuel Hoey Walkup Journal.

Welch, Elliott Stephen, Hampton's Legion, Letter, September 22, 1862, Elliott Stephen Welch Papers.

Manuscript Division, Library of Congress, Washington, DC.

Johnston, Jr., James Steptoe, 11th MS, Letter, September 22, 1862, Mercer Green Johnston Collection.

Shuler, Michael, H Co., 33rd VA, Diary, September 16 and 17, 1862, M. Shuler Collection.

Wigfall, F. Halsey, 1st TX, Letter, October 4, 1862, Louis Trezevant Wigfall Collection.

Antietam National Battlefield

Dunton, Prince A., 13th MA, Letter, September 24, 1862, Vertical File.

Fletcher, Samuel J., H Co., 15th MA, Memoirs, Vertical File.

Jordan, Nathan Bartlett, H Co., 19th MA, Monograph, Vertical File.

Shinn, James W., B Co., 4th NC, Diary, Photocopy, Vertical File.

Wren, James, B Co., 48th PA, Diary, Library.

Periodicals

THE NATIONAL TRIBUNE

Arnold, Jennie Porter, "At Antetam, A True and Graphic Story of the 16th Connecticut," October 18, 1888, p. 1: 6-7.

Higgins, Jacob, "At Antietam," June 3, 1886, p. 1: 6-7, p. 2: 1-2.

Howard, Oliver O., "General O. O. Howard's Personal Reminiscences of the War of the Rebellion," April 3, 1884, p. 1: 1-2.

Powell, Eugene, "Lee's First Invasion," June 27, 1901, p. 2: 1-4.

THE CONFEDERATE VETERAN

Andrews, W. H., "Tige Anderson's Brigade at

Sharpsburg," XVI, 1908, p. 578-580.

Ashe, S. A., "North Carolina in the War Between the States," XXXVII, 1929, p. 173.

Beall, T. D., "In the Bloody Lane," I, 1893, p. 246.

Bloomer, Sam, "A Wounded Federal Color Bearer," XVII, 1909, p. 169.

Bowie, Robert T., "Left for Dead on the Field," XXX, 1922, p. 71.

Bradwell, I. G., "Bravery and Cowardice," XXXII, 1924, p. 133.

Cummings, C. C., "Sharpsburg—Antietam," XXIII, 1915, p. 199.

Daniels, R. H. "The Battle of Sharpsburg or Antietam," IX, 1901, p. 217.

Edmontson, G. W., "Individualism in Battle," XXVI, 1918, p. 239-240.

Emerson, Mrs. B. A. C., "How a Boy Won His Spurs at Antietam," XXI, 1913, p. 121.

Evans, William McK., "A Night to be Remembered," XXXVII, 1929, p. 216-217.

"Gen. and Gov. William Smith," VIII, 1900, p. 162-163.

Hamby, W. R. "Hood's Texas Brigade at Sharpsburg," XVI, 1908, p. 19.

Johnston, David E., "Concerning the Battle of Sharpsburg," VI, 1898, p. 28.

Motlow, Felix, "Campaigns in Northern Virginia," II, 1894, p. 310.

Napier, J. L., "McIntosh's Battery at Sharpsburg," XIX, 1911, p. 429.

Richardson, C. A., "General Lee at Sharpsburg," XV, 1907, p. 411.

Rowan, Cleve, "False Flag of Truce at Antietam," IV, 1896, p. 324.

Stickley, E. E., "Battle of Sharpsburg," XXII, 1914, p. 66.

"The Haw Boys in the War Between the States," XXXIII, 1925, p. 256.

"The Sharpsburg Memorial," XXVI, 1918, p. 73. (6th VA).

The True Citizen, "The Burke Sharpshooters," XXXII, 1924, p. 464.

Venn, F. H., "That Flag of Truce at Antietam," IV, 1896, p. 389.

White, P. J., "The 5th Virginia Cavalry," XVII, 1909, p. 72.

Untitled Articles, THE CONFEDERATE VETERAN

I, 1893, p. 235.

II, 1894, p. 150.

VI, 1898, p. 217.

IX, 1901, p. 265.

XV, 1907, p. 40.

THE SOUTHERN HISTORICAL SOCIETY PAPERS

Benning, H. L., "Notes by General H. L. Benning on Battle of Sharpsburg," XVI, p. 393+.

Hunter, Alexander, "A High Private's Sketch of Sharpsburg," Paper #2, XI, p. 11+.

Morrison, E. M., "One of the Gamest of Modern Fights," XXXVI, p. 97+.

Parham, John T., "The 32nd Virginia Infantry at Sharpsburg," XXXIV, p. 252+.

CIVIL WAR TIMES ILLUSTRATED

Clarkson, Benjamin Franklin, "Vivid in My Memory," John M. Priest, (ed.), XXIV, #8, December, 1985, p. 20+.

Evans, Thomas E., "The Enemy Sullenly Held on to the City," VII, #1, April, 1968, p. 32-40.

Schell, Frank H., "A Greet Raging Battlefield Is Hell," VIII, #3, June, 1969, p. 14+.

Miscellaneous Periodicals

"Civil War Letters of Francis Edwin Pierce of the 108th New York Volunteer Infantry," *ROCHESTER IN THE CIVIL WAR,* The New York Historical Society Publications, XXII, Rochester, NY, 1944, p. 150-156.

Dimon, Theodore, "A Federal Surgeon at Sharpsburg," James I. Robertson, Jr., (ed.), *CIVIL WAR HISTORY,* VI, #2, June 1960, p. 134+.

Gorman, John Calvin, "Memoirs of a Rebel," George Gorman, (ed.), *MILITARY IMAGES,* Nov./Dec. 1981, p. 4-6.

Marynisk, B. R., "The Famous Long Ago," Buffalo Civil War Round Table, July, 1986, p. 26-29.

Wagstaff, H. M., (ed.), "The James A. Graham Papers, 1861-1884," *THE JAMES SPRUNT HISTORICAL STUDIES,* XX, #2, University of North Carolina, Chapel Hill, 1928.

Reference

Beyer, W. F. and O. F. Keydel, (ed.), *Deeds of Valor,* I, Perrin—Keydel Co., Detroit, MI, 1907.

Clark, Walter, (ed.), *Histories of Several Regiments and Battalions From North Carolina in the Great War, 1861-65,* 5 vols., Releigh and Greensborough, NC, 1901.

Fox, William F., *Regimental Losses in the American Civil War, 1861-1865,* 4th ed., Joseph McDonough, Albany, NY, 1898.

Hardee, William J., *Rifle and Light Infantry Tactics for Light Infantry or Riflemen,* 2 vols., Greenwood Press Publishers, Inc., Westport, CN, 1971. (Reprint from 1855.)

Jordan, Jr., Weymouth T., (ed.), *North Carolina Troops 1861-1865, A Roster,* 6 vols., Division of Archives and History, Raleigh, NC, 1975.

Massachusetts Soldiers, Sailors, and Marines in the Civil War, Norwood Press, Norwood, MA, 1931.

U. S. Department of the Army, Public Information Division, *The Medal of Honor of the United States of America,* U. S. Government printing Office, Washington, D.C., 1948.

Regimental Histories

Bell, Robert, T., *11th Virginia Infantry,* H. E. Howard, Inc., Lynchburg, VA, 1985.

Chapla, John D., *42nd Virginia Infantry,* 1st Ed., H. E. Howard Inc., Lynchburg, VA, 1983.

Collier, Calvin L., *"They'll Do to Tie To," The Story of the Third Regiment,* Arkansas Infantry, C. S. A., Major James D. Warren, 1959.

Driver, Jr., Robert J., *52nd Virginia Infantry,* H. E. Howard Inc., Lynchburg, VA, 1986.

Glover, Edwin A., *Bucktailed Wildcats, A Regiment of Civil War Volunteers,* Thomas Yoseloff, NY, 1960.

Henderson, William D., *41st Virginia Infantry,* H. Howard Inc., Lynchburg, VA, 1986.

Jones, Paul, *The Irish Brigade,* Robert B. Luke, Inc., Washington, D. C., 1967.

Krick, Robert K., *Parker's Virginia Battery, C. S. A.,* Virginia Book Company, Berryville, VA, 1975.

Krick, Robert K., *30th Virginia Infantry,* 1st Ed., H. E. Howard Inc., Lynchburg, VA, 1983.

McBrien, Joe Bennett, *The Tennessee Brigade,*

Hudson Printing and Lithographing Co.,
Chattanooga, TN, 1977.

Murray, Alton J., *South Georgia Rebels*, Alton J.
Murray, St. Mary's Georgia, 1976.

Nolan, Alan T., *The Iron Brigade*, MacMillan
Co., NY, 1961.

Rankin, Thomas M., *23rd Virginia Infantry*,
H. E. Howard Inc., Lynchburg, VA,
1985.

Riggs, David F., *7th Virginia Infantry*, H. E.
Howard Inc., Lynchburg, VA, 1982.

Robertson, Jr., James I., *4th Virginia Infantry*,
1st Ed., H. E. Howard Inc., Lynchburg,
VA, 1982.

Robertson, Jr., James I., *The Stonewall Brigade*,
Louisiana State University Press, Baton
Rouge, LA, 1962.

Taylor, Frank H., *Philadelphia in the Civil War*,
Published by the City, 1913.

Tevis, C. V. and D. R. Marquis, (comp.), *The
History of the Fighting Fourteenth*, Eagle
Press, Brooklyn, 1911.

Trask, Benjamin H., *9th Virginia Infantry*, H.
E. Howard Inc., Lynchburg, VA, 1984.

Antietam National Park Studies

Hanson, Joseph Mills, "A Report on the
Employment of the Artillery at the Battle
of Antietam, MD," U.S. Department of
the Interior, National Park Service, May
27, 1940.

Lagemann, R. L., "Summary of the Artillery
Batteries in positions to support the
Infantry during the action at 'Bloody
Lane', with a Map showing their
locations," March, 1962.

Lammers, Pat and Dave Smith, "Artillery at
Antietam," Antietam National Battlefield,
U. S. National Park Service, May 1981.

Tilberg, Frederick, *Antietam*, National Park
Service Historical Handbook Series, #31,
Washington, D. C., 1960.

Wilshin, Francis F., "Antietam Historic
Structures," National Park Service, U. S.
Department of the Interior, August 28,
1968.

Antietam Books and Pamphlets

Bailey, Ronald H., and the Editors of Time-
Life Books, "*The Bloodiest Day, The Battle
of Antietam*," THE CIVIL WAR, Time-Life
Books, Alexandria, VA, 1984.

Catton, Bruce, *Mr. Lincoln's Army*, Doubleday
and Co., Garden City, NY, 1965.

Frassanito, William A., *Antietam*, The
Photographic Legacy of America's
Bloodiest Day, Charles Scribner's Sons,
NY, 1978.

Miller, R. C., *The Battlefield of Antietam*, Oliver
T. Reilly Publisher, 1906. (Reprint,
Hagerstown Bookbinding and Printing
Co., Hagerstown, MD.)

Murfin, James V., *The Gleam of Bayonets*,
Bonanza Books, NY, 1965.

Schildt, John W., *Drums Along the Antietam*,
McClain Printing Co., Parsons, WV,
1972.

Schildt, John W., *September Echoes*, The Valley
Register Publishers and Printers,
Middletown, MD, 1960.

Sears, Stephen W., *Landscape Turned Red, The
Battle of Antietam*, Ticknor and Fields,
New Haven, 1983.

Miscellaneous Books and Periodicals

Ankrum, Freeman, *Sidelights of Brethren
History*, The Brethren Press, Elgin, IL,
1962.

Bowen, Catherine Drinker, *Yankee From
Olympus, Justice Holmes And His Family*,
Atlantic Monthly Press, Little, Brown and
Co., Boston, 1944.

Crary, Catherine S., ed., *Dear Belle*, Wesleyan
University Press, Middletown, CN, 1965.

Heaps, Willard A., *The Bravest Teenage Yanks*,
Duell, Sloan and Pearce, NY, 1963.

Howe, Mark De Wolfe, *Justice Oliver Wendell
Holmes, The Shaping Years, 1841-1870*,
The Belknap Press of Harvard University
Press, Cambridge, MA, 1957.

McCormack, John F., "The Irish Brigade,"
CIVIL WAR TIMES ILLUSTRATED, VIII,
#1, April 1969, p. 36+.

Thompson, William Y., "Robert Toombs,
Confederate General," *CIVIL WAR
HISTORY*, Dec. 1961, p. 406+.

INDEX

A

Abbott, Robert A. (Cpt., G Co., 132nd PA) — 157
Adams (Cpt., A. P. Hill's staff) — 262
Aiken, D. W. (Col., 7th SC) — 124
Aiken, Stephen (Pvt., D Co., 125th PA) — 107
Alabama: Infantry
    3rd — 136
    4th — 15, 55, 73, 74, 76, 83
    5th — 136, 190
    6th — 136-137, 144, 146, 156, 162, 169-170, 190
    8th — 204
    12th — 136
    13th — 69, 83, 88
    14th — 157
    15th — 2
    26th — 136
    44th — 157
    47th — 49
    48th — 49
Aldrich, Harry (Pvt., K Co., 21st MA) — 247
Aldrich, Thomas M. (Pvt., Btty. A, 1st RI) — 123
Alexandria, VA — 103
Allebaugh, William (Cpt., C Co., 51st PA) — 239
Allen, Thomas S. (LTC, 2nd WI) — 40
Alston (Maj, 1st SC) — 279
Anderson, George B. - CSA - (BG) — 139, 157, 207
    (Brigade of) — 136
Anderson, George "Tige" - CSA - (Col.) — 9, 118
    (Brigade of) — 7, 9, 113, 117, 128, 129, 203, 218, 292
Anderson, Richard H. - CSA - (BG) — 189, 193, 207
Anderson, Robert (LTC, Brigade of) — 20
Anderson, Thomas M. (Cpt., 2nd Bttn., 12th US) — 290
Anderson, William H. (Pvt., Btty. E, PA Light) — 179
Andrews, Mrs. Charles Wesley — 310
Andrews' Company of MA Sharpshooters — 106-107, 148
Andrews, George L. (Col., 2nd MA) — 86, 125
Andrews, John W. (Col., 1st DE) — 142
Andrews, Stephen H. (Cpt., A Co., 35th MA) — 285
Andrews, William H. (1st Sgt., M Co., 1st GA Reg.) — 7, 9, 10, 118, 128, 129, 130, 292
Angell, Manton C. (Cpt., E Co., 61st NY) — 162
Antietam Creek — 5, 11, 25, 35, 37, 41, 98, 114, 115, 140, 141, 159, 177, 212, 215, 216, 234, 256-257, 273, 279, 284, 300, 305, 311
Appich (Pvt., E Co., 17th VA) — 259
Appleman, Hiram (LTC, 8th CT) — 268
Archer, James J. - CSA - (BG)
    (Brigade of) — 271, 273, 280
Arkansas: Infantry

3rd — 148, 152, 154, 180, 186, 187, 194, 196, 197, 299, 313
Army of Northern Virginia — 3, 5, 11, 23, 93, 111, 288, 290, 300, 305, 316
Army of the Potomac — 35, 94, 117, 166
Ashby, Philip S. (Cpt., C. O., 7th VA) — 259

B

Babbitt, John W. (Cpt., I Co., 9th NH) — 247
Bachelder, George W. (Cpt., 19th MA) — 133
Bachman, Alois O. (LTC, 19th IN) — 76
Bachman, W. K. (Cpt., Charleston German Btty. SC) — 214, 218
Baldwin, James (Lt., D Co., 35th MA) — 245, 246, 256, 287, 304
Ball's Bluff, VA — 147
Barksdale, William - CSA - (BG) — 111, 306
    (Brigade of) — 97, 110, 117, 119, 125, 127, 150
Barlow, Francis (Col., 61st/64th NY) — 162, 180, 182, 204
Barnes, Dixon (Col., 12th SC) — 273
Barnes, James (Col., Brigade of) — 216, 311
Barry, John (Pvt., C Co., 19th MA) — 133
Barry, William E. (Lt., G Co., 4th TX) — 89
Bartlett, Napier (Pvt., M. B. Miller's Btty., CSA) — 6, 203
Barton, Clara — 148-149, 175, 210, 307, 310
Bass, F. S. (Cpt., E Co., 1st TX) — 66
Battle, Henry (Cpt., C Co., 21st GA) — 305
Beach, Francis (Col., 16th CT) — 273
Beal, George L. (Col., 10th ME) — 73, 74
Beall, Thomas B. (Cpt., I Co., 14th NC) — 190, 193, 200
Beckham (officer, Kemper's staff) — 259
Bell, Alexander T. (Assistant Surgeon, 3rd VA CAV) — 30
Bell, Thomas (LTC, 51st PA) — 243, 245, 246, 257
Bennett, Edwin (Sgt., D Co., 51st PA) — 245
Bennett, Risden Tyler (Col., 14th NC) — 190, 198, 200
Benning, Henry L. - CSA - (Col.) — 239, 250-251, 271-272, 277
    (Brigade of) — 218, 220, 253, 271, 273, 275
Benson (Sgt., 7th ME) — 297
Benson, Berry G. (1st SC) — 279-281, 302
Beyer, Hillary (Lt., H Co., 90th PA) — 59
Bisbane, George W. (Cpt., I Co., 51st PA) — 257
Black (Surgeon, Grigsby's Brigade, CSA) — 305
Blake, Joseph (Pvt., B Co., 12th MA) — 54
Blackford, William (Cpt., JEB Stuart's staff, CSA) — 23, 29, 97, 100
Blevins, Jr., James Wesley (Lt., H Co., 21st GA) — 57

379

Y

Z